UNITED STATES FOREIGN POLICY

AN INTRODUCTION WITH CASES

UNITED STATES FOREIGN POLICY

AN INTRODUCTION WITH CASES

SHELDON APPLETON
Oakland University

 Little, Brown and Company   BOSTON

LIBRARY OF CONGRESS CATALOG CARD NO. 68-17864

FIRST PRINTING

Published simultaneously in Canada
by Little, Brown & Company (Canada) Limited

PRINTED IN THE UNITED STATES OF AMERICA

To Betty
and
to the memory of
Ben Miller

PREFACE

Ours is a time of protest. Today's young people seem less willing than yesterday's to accept uncritically the maxims and rationalizations presented to them by many of their elders.

Ours is a generation oriented toward action — a useful emphasis in a society in which pious words have often been used as a substitute for effective deeds, where men often preach the sermon on the mount even while they act ruthlessly to serve their own self-interest — and perceive no inconsistency in doing so.

But mindless action is no better than actionless piety, and unthinking rebellion against yesterday's ideas is no better than unthinking acceptance of them. To deserve to be taken seriously we must ourselves take seriously both the issues which concern us and the consequences of our own political actions.

This book is addressed to those who believe in both thought and action, in that order; to those who care enough about the great foreign policy issues of our day to take the trouble to formulate intelligent opinions about them. I have tried to make these issues intelligible by placing them within a meaningful frame of reference, by considering them in relation to questions such as these: How is United States foreign policy made? How much influence do or should presidents, congressmen, diplomats, soldiers, intelligence agents, and private citizens have in making it? What are the fundamental forces in the world which our policies must cope with? What instruments and methods are available to us in dealing with these forces? Why do we — and others — spend so much of our resources on weapons of destruction and so little on alleviating the suffering of our fellow men? What are the causes of violence in our world — and in our own cities? And what are the conditions which must be met if we are to live together in peace?

Though this book is primarily about United States foreign policy, I have included case studies dealing with middle-class apathy and with riots in

vii

our black ghettos at home as well as with civil wars and diplomatic crises abroad. I have done so because I believe that in certain respects the outbreaks of violence in our own cities and in foreign lands have common causes; that in some ways keeping the peace in our own communities and keeping the peace in the world at large are but two faces of one problem.

To learn to do his own thinking about issues like these, the student must not only be acquainted with theory, but must be given an opportunity to put that theory into practice. I have tried to provide that opportunity by integrating one or more case studies into every chapter of this book, cases illustrating and illuminating many of the analytical concepts and recent research findings introduced in the text of the chapter. These cases are designed to stimulate thoughtful discussion by involving the student in "live" issues of human interest and historic significance, and to challenge outstanding students to attempt some inductive "theory building" of their own.

Each case is preceded by pointed questions calling upon the reader to make his value judgments explicit, to consider alternatives, to calculate consequences — in short, to apply in specific instances the general principles he has studied. There are no correct answers to many of these questions. The field of foreign affairs is vast and our knowledge of it imperfect. It is better that we learn to ask ourselves the right questions than that we commit to memory somebody else's right answers.

*   *   *   *   *

The textbook writer's debts are many. Some of my intellectual debts are acknowledged in footnotes in the pages that follow. Donald R. Hammonds, John H. Andrews, and David W. Lynch of Little, Brown have been the kind of editors every author should have — personally cordial, professionally critical and challenging, at each step in the preparation of the manuscript.

Bernard Cohen and Robert Holt read all or most of the first draft of the manuscript and made useful suggestions for its revision, many of which were adopted. Thomas Casstevens, Melvin Cherno, David Lowy, Fred Pearson, and Edward Starr commented on particular chapters or helped with specific points. Waldo Chamberlin, Charles O. Hucker, Werner Levi, Herbert McClosky, A. W. Salomone, John Turner, and the late James O. Wettereau have exercised formative influences, over the years, on my thinking about foreign affairs and on my approaches to teaching it.

Students in my classes in International Politics and United States Foreign Policy at Oakland University for the past six years have contributed by reacting in class to a majority of the case materials and accompanying questions included in this volume. Gloria Goldman, Janet Hufford, and Phyllis Wilson did the major portion of the typing with unfailing patience and good will. Oakland University granted a sabbatical leave which enabled me to finish the manuscript.

Finally, Betty Appleton has reviewed — and often collaborated on — the manuscript as spokesman for the general reader. I hope, most of all, that I have not failed her, or the readers for whom she spoke, too often.

SHELDON APPLETON

TABLE OF CONTENTS

xi

UNITED STATES FOREIGN POLICY

AN INTRODUCTION WITH CASES

Chapter One

WORLD POLITICS:
THE SEARCH FOR PEACE

The United States of America is one of the more than one hundred "sovereign" national states which comprise the international system today. Through its claim to sovereignty, each of these states declines to recognize any legal authority superior to its own. It does not feel bound to accept any decisions arrived at without its concurrence and reserves the right to oppose by force, if it chooses, any attempt to impose such decisions upon it. This key and inherent characteristic of the international system may be simple — but its implications are far-reaching.

Living together in interdependence in the modern world, nations, like men, are bound to have differences of interest and differences of opinion. Within a well-ordered national community, differences among men can usually (though not always) be worked out peacefully, since most of the people who live in such communities *do* recognize that there is a superior legal authority — usually the national government — and are willing to accept its decisions. The relatively few residents of such communities who are unwilling to accept the government's authority can generally be *made* to do so because effective governments usually wield preponderant force in the territories under their jurisdiction. Thus, within a well-ordered community, outbreaks of large-scale violence can be eliminated, and conflicts of interest between individuals are resolved peacefully either by the government or by the parties themselves under legal and institutional rules endorsed by the government.

In an age of nuclear weapons, similarly, sane men prefer to resolve these differences peacefully. But it is the very essence of a sovereign state system that its members should reject any attempt by an external authority to resolve these differences without their consent — or even to prescribe the

1

means by which they may be resolved. Thus nations, if they are to resolve their differences peacefully, must find mutually agreed, rather than externally imposed, means for doing so. There are a number of ways in which this can be, and has been, attempted.

NEGOTIATION AND BALANCE OF POWER

The most obvious of these methods is *diplomatic negotiation,* which involves an attempt by representatives of the nations concerned to discuss their disagreements in trying to find a mutually acceptable settlement. Competent negotiators, working in an atmosphere of good will, can exploit effectively any possibilities for agreement they can uncover. Even when good will is lacking, a resourceful disinterested *mediator* may be able to offer suggestions which will lead to a settlement.[1]

But what if there is no arrangement even minimally acceptable to all of the nations concerned? In a sovereign state system none of the parties to a dispute can be legally bound without its consent. The alternatives to a negotiated settlement, therefore, are either deadlock or the use of force. And even deadlock involves an implicit agreement that the indefinite continuation of the status quo is minimally acceptable to all concerned.

Precisely what a given nation may find "minimally acceptable" in any particular case generally will depend more on the power context surrounding the negotiations than on the course of the negotiations themselves. With resort to arms always in the background as an alternative in case negotiations fail, the militarily weaker party to a dispute is apt to be more modest in its definition of what is "minimally acceptable" to it than is the militarily stronger party. Thus, even if the outbreak of war can be prevented, might rather than right is likely to be the decisive arbiter of disputes in such a system.

If the ability of nations to secure what they believe to be justice in matters of the utmost importance to them depends on their ability to marshal military potential behind their diplomacy, the leaders of these nations will make it their business to maximize this potential. Not only will they arm, but they will seek allies whose strength, at critical moments, can be added to their own. The most useful ally, of course, is one ready to back you — to the point of war, if need be — whatever his own view of the matter. And, normally, the only way to win such an ally is to *be* one. To gain reliable allies, then, a nation must be prepared to surrender much of its freedom of action in matters not necessarily of direct importance to itself. If we use the

---

1 Mediation is a purely voluntary third-party procedure. Its success depends primarily on the prestige of the mediator(s) and on his skill in sensing the needs and moods of the parties to a dispute and framing acceptable compromises. *Arbitration,* in contrast, requires the parties to agree in advance to abide by the decision of a third party designated as arbitrator. The nature and techniques of negotiation, when used as an instrument of policy, will be discussed in a later chapter.

expression "vital interest" to refer to each state's leaders' own definition of what is vital to that state (that is, worth fighting over, if necessary), we can say that reliable allies must be willing to fight for each other's vital interests, as well as for their own.[2] To the extent that this is true, then, the more alliances there are, the greater will be the chance that *one* nation's rigidity in defining "minimally acceptable" terms of settlement may touch off a large-scale war.

A classic example is the outbreak of World War I in Europe in 1914. In a foreign policy speech at the University of Maine a month before his assassination, President John F. Kennedy recalled that soon after the start of that war, "Prince Bülow, the former German Chancellor, said to the then Chancellor, Bethmann-Hollweg: 'How did it all happen?' and Bethmann-Hollweg replied: 'Ah, if only one knew.' "

Greatly oversimplified, here is what happened: during a visit to the capital of Serbia in 1914, Archduke Francis Ferdinand of Austria was assassinated by a Serbian ultranationalist fanatic. Since there was a long history of conflict and ill feeling between these two countries, this incident provoked an open dispute. Austria, knowing that it was more powerful, made extravagant demands. Serbia, counting on the support of its allies, Russia and France, refused to yield. Russia had for some time identified herself with the aspirations of her fellow Slavs, the Serbs. Moreover, in previous and somewhat similar disputes, she had yielded to Austrian pressures. Now fearing that another retreat would encourage Austria to continue to increase its power at her expense, thereby altering unfavorably the ratio of power between them, Russia prepared to fight. Germany then felt compelled to aid its ally, Austria, France to aid its ally, Russia, and England to aid its ally, France. Soon all of Europe was at war.

Most of these nations did not want a war. The German government, for example, was not even convinced that its Austrian ally was appropriately reasonable in its demands on Serbia. But if Austria would not yield, Germany — its leaders felt — could not stand by while its ally was defeated in war. The leaders of other nations reasoned similarly.[3]

The process by which nations seek to improve their own power position relative to that of potential rivals, by alliance or otherwise, is often referred to as the *balance of power*. The usefulness of this term is limited, however, by the widespread tendency to use it to describe a number of different

---

[2] We can then use the term *national interest* to refer to each state's leaders' own definition of what is in the interest of their nation. Some national interests will be considered "vital," and thus worth fighting over, and others will not. (The distinction between national, subnational, and supranational interests is discussed in Chapter Eight.)

[3] The literature on the origins of World War I is voluminous. For the results of a recent content analysis of relevant documentary materials, and a short bibliography, see Ole R. Holsti and Robert C. North, "The History of Human Conflict," Elton B. McNeil (ed.), *The Nature of Human Conflict* (Englewood Cliffs, N.J.: Prentice-Hall, 1965), pp. 155–170.

things. Thus, the "balance of power" may refer to a worldwide or regional international system in which power is divided fairly evenly between rival groupings (that is, balanced power or equilibrium) — or to a policy which aims to bring about such an equilibrium (a "balance of power policy"). Or it may refer to an international system in which one group of nations possesses greater power than its rivals (that is, "holds the balance of power," as the United States does, for example, in the American hemisphere) — or to a policy which aims to bring this about. It may refer to certain supposed rules by which states do or should determine how to align themselves in international affairs. Or, finally, it may simply refer to any power configuration which exists in any international system at any given time — in which case "balance of power politics" becomes, by definition, a description of whatever political maneuverings may actually take place in such a system.

In some of the senses in which the words "balance of power" have been used, it has been claimed that one of the virtues of the system (or policy) is its ability to prevent the outbreak of war. A number of scholarly analyses have demonstrated, however, the fallacies involved in such claims; [4] and, more important, the periodic outbreak of devastating wars in international systems presumably managed by the "balance of power" have made it clear that those who seek a guarantee of perpetual peace must look elsewhere for the means of accomplishing it.

COLLECTIVE SECURITY

One of the most widely known theories promising peace for mankind is *collective security*. Collective security proposes to outlaw aggressive war by marshaling a preponderance of power against any would-be aggressor. Under collective security, all members of the system agree to join in opposing *any* aggression by *any* state against *any* other. Confronted with the certainty that aggression would achieve nothing but humiliation at the hands of a united international opposition, a state which might otherwise contemplate aggressive action normally will be restrained. Actual military measures in behalf of collective security, therefore, will need to be undertaken only on very rare occasions.

In theory, collective security works admirably. In practice, however, it assumes a number of conditions which experience suggests cannot safely be assumed in the international system as we know it. It assumes, first, that

---

[4] On the balance of power, see Hans J. Morgenthau, *Politics Among Nations* (3rd ed.; New York: Knopf, 1960); Inis Claude, Jr., *Power and International Relations* (New York: Random House, 1962); and Ernst B. Haas, "The Balance of Power as a Guide to Policymaking," *The Journal of Politics* (August, 1953), 370–398.

Though it has often failed to keep the peace, the "balance of power" system *has* provided some advantages to the states involved, including, usually, the maintenance of their independence and national identity.

power in the international arena is sufficiently diffused so that preponderant power can, in fact, be arrayed against any aggressor. If any state were so strong that the combined strength of all the others might still be insufficient to insure its defeat, that state might not be deterred from aggression.

Second, the theory of collective security assumes that all states — or at least all major powers — will be members of the collective security system. If they were not, some might support the aggressor, rather than the victim, nullifying the deterrent effect desired.

Third, it is assumed that all members of the system will agree about what constitutes aggression. If they do not, or even if they may not, the certainty of massing preponderant force against the aggressor — and the deterrent effect of this certainty — is lost.

Finally, members of the system must be willing as well as able to undertake armed action in support of collective security *whenever* it is called for, no matter who the aggressor may be, no matter who the victim may be, no matter how unimportant the area in which the aggression took place may seem, and no matter what the consequences for their own power position. If it seems likely that important members of the system may fail to join against the aggressor, again the deterrent value of certain defeat is lost and the temptation to risk aggression is increased.

Even a cursory look at the world of our generation suggests clearly the inapplicability of these assumptions. Power in today's world is not widely diffused but is largely concentrated in the hands of two "superpowers," the United States and the Soviet Union. Even if the whole rest of the world were arrayed against one of these giants, the result would be not a small police action, but a world nuclear holocaust — a prospect as likely to deter the potential peacekeepers as the potential warmakers.

Even within the strictly limited collective security system of the United Nations, not all of the world's major powers have been included. Such important states as West Germany and Communist China remain outside the system. Moreover, almost never have all members of the Security Council agreed as to what constituted an act of aggression. In a world of subversion, economic and propaganda pressures, limited international intervention in civil wars, and paramilitary operations, it is difficult enough for an objective observer to decide what is and what is not aggression, let alone for a group of nations with opposed ideologies, viewpoints, and national interests to do so.[5] Was the Communist coup d'état in Czechoslovakia in 1948 aggression? The landing of Cuban exiles at the Bay of Pigs in 1961 managed and financed by the United States? Communist Chinese suppression of Tibetan resistance in 1960 and after? The Indian takeover of

[5] In 1952, the United Nations General Assembly appointed a fifteen-man committee to attempt to define aggression. The committee has met frequently in the years since without succeeding in reaching agreement on the meaning of this term, even in principle. This has not prevented member nations from continuing to use the term to suit their own purposes.

Portuguese Goa in 1961? United States and North Vietnamese intervention in South Vietnam in the 1960's?

Finally, in a world divided ideologically as well as politically, is it realistic to expect nations to follow the dictates of *collective* security — even at the risk of *national* security — in all instances? When the United Nations undertook collective security action in Korea, for example, many of its members did not behave as an effective collective security system would have required. The Soviet Union and its fellow Communist states, far from contributing to the defeat of the aggressor, actually aided North Korea against the victim. Many other states stood on the sidelines or offered only token aid. Only sixteen nations provided military forces of any kind, and one of these, the United States, clearly bore the main burden of carrying on the war. As a result of this lack of collective action, and of the fact that a non-member of the system, Communist China, joined forces with the United Nations designated aggressor, the United Nations had to content itself, after three years of fighting and talking, with a military stalemate and a negotiated truce.

If Great Britain, say, or Canada, committed aggression against the Soviet Union or Communist China, is it conceivable that the United States would conscientiously follow the prescriptions of collective security and assist the latter to defeat the former? If Britain and France had refused to back down in the Suez crisis of 1956, after the Security Council had called upon them to withdraw from Egypt, would the United States really have been willing to join with the Soviet Union in raining missiles upon them until they relented? Yet these are precisely the actions which a strictly conceived collective security system might call for in these embarrassing circumstances. Collective security does not distinguish between friends and rivals — only between aggressors and victims.[6]

ARMS LIMITATION AND DISARMAMENT

Another idea of great appeal to those searching for a way to "save succeeding generations from the scourge of war" is *disarmament* or, more accurately, arms limitation. After all, it may be argued, nations cannot very well fight if they have nothing to fight with. And reduction of armaments would diminish mutual fear and distrust while minimizing the possibility of accidental war, freeing large sums of money for more constructive uses, and lessening the influence of militarists on national policy. The very simplicity of this idea in a world filled with harsh complexities has so added to its popularity that the Soviet Union as well as the United States

6 On collective security, see Claude's *Power and International Relations* and chap. 12 in the same author's *Swords into Plowshares* (New York: Random House, 1959). Many of the insights presented in the present chapter were drawn from these two works. They are recommended to the reader as the best starting point for gaining further understanding of most of the concepts introduced in this chapter.

feels called upon to pay lip service periodically to the desirability of "general and complete disarmament."

As mentioned earlier, however, nations, like men, living together in interdependence in the modern world, are bound to have differences of interest and differences of opinion. If these differences are not to be resolved by force, some other method of dealing with them must be provided. Advocates of peace by disarmament do not *demonstrate* but merely *assume* that once nations are disarmed some peaceful means of dealing with their differences will be found.

Men were not born in possession of armaments. They have been known in the past to fight over their differences with stones, knives, slingshots, bows and arrows, shotguns, axes, and fists, when these were the only weapons available. Why should they not do so in the future when their efforts to resolve differences peacefully fail? Moreover, short of performing brain surgery on all scientists familiar with nuclear weaponry, biological warfare, chemical warfare, etc., disarmament cannot deprive modern nations of the capacity to rearm themselves with these terrible weapons once they have become involved in an international conflict.

Though advocates of peace by disarmament are sometimes inclined to say that "the way to disarm is to disarm," the problem has proved much more difficult in the real world. Nations arm to seek "security" (however they may define that highly elusive term), and they do not feel secure when they are disarmed and their potential opponents are armed. Nor is the mere act of unilateral disarmament necessarily likely to disarm one's opponents. To illustrate, let us not ask how the Soviet Union and Communist China might react to clear evidence that the United States had disarmed unilaterally. Let us ask, rather, how *we* would react to the news that *they* had disarmed. Can we honestly say of ourselves and our fellow countrymen that there would be few who would suspect a trick? That there would be none arguing that, trick or no, the Communists might change their minds next week or next month and that the golden moment for "liberating the enslaved peoples" of China and Eastern Europe was here and now? Can we honestly feel confident that advocates of these points of view would have no chance of winning public office on this basis? If we cannot be sure of our own attitudes, how sure can we be that the Russians and Chinese would react less suspiciously to the announcement that *we* had disarmed?

Besides, disarmament cannot really be total. Every nation requires a police force, at least, to maintain internal order. And some nations — big ones, or dictatorships depending on repression of the opposition — may need larger police forces than others. How will it be decided exactly what level of armaments each nation needs for its internal security or is entitled to? Is the present ratio of power between major nations to be preserved? (Would this be acceptable to a nation like Communist China, which hopes to industrialize and change its power position in the years to come?) If so, in calculating the power to be allotted each state, how will it be decided what weights are to be assigned to the different elements of national power? These are usually thought to include not only armed forces and weapons of war, but also geographic position, natural resources, industrial capacity, population, and such immeasurables as national character and the quality of national leadership.[7]

How many divisions is Russia's geographic position, spanning the Eurasian land mass, worth? How many additional missiles should the Soviet Union be allowed to offset the United States' superior productive capacity? How many Chinese Communist men under arms are equivalent to one nuclear submarine? A group of impartial military experts would have its hands full deciding questions like these. What then could be expected of a group of diplomats arguing from the perspectives of their individual national interests?

And once the arms ratio was agreed upon, how would adherence to it be guaranteed? How could the United States be reassured, for instance, that an unreported stockpile of nuclear weapons was not hidden away in an underground cache in the wastes of Siberia? If violations were discovered, how could adherence to the original agreement be enforced — except by reversion to a helter-skelter arms race, with the advantage going to the violator? The first violation might break down the whole elaborate system.

This does not mean that any attempt to limit or reduce armaments is bound to be undesirable and impractical. On the contrary, some arms limitation agreements are highly desirable and could make very important contributions to the maintenance of international peace. Means have been devised to cope with some of the problems of verification and inspection mentioned here. Aerial surveillance, inspection of limited areas chosen at random, and other technical and statistical procedures can at least keep the need for inspection of national territories to a minimum.[8] Some sorts of arms limitation agreements, in fact, are already in force — the limited nuclear test-ban treaty, for example, and treaties barring the militarization of Antarctica and of space. An agreement to prevent the widespread acquisition of nuclear weapons may be possible and would be of enormous value.

But the more sweeping the extent of the arms reductions contemplated,

---

[7] See Morgenthau, *op. cit.*

[8] Some of these devices are outlined in Ernest Lefever (ed.), *Arms and Arms Control* (New York: Praeger, 1962). This volume contains a detailed annotated bibliography of the literature in this field. A more recent study, sponsored by the United States Government's Arms Control and Disarmament Agency, and conducted by the Washington Center for Foreign Policy Research — an affiliate of Johns Hopkins University — is Arnold Wolfers, *et al., The United States in a Disarmed World* (Baltimore: Johns Hopkins University Press, 1966). This study warns that rather than leading automatically to the establishment of an enduring peace, general and complete disarmament could both jeopardize United States' national interests and destabilize world politics.

the more difficult these problems of inspection and verification become, and the greater the risks which participating nations are called upon to incur. In the extreme case of general and complete disarmament, effective verification and enforcement could be carried out only by an authority with access to the territory of every nation and with an international military force sufficient to keep potential violators in line — in other words, only by a limited world government.

WORLD GOVERNMENT

Unlike negotiation, the balance of power, collective security, and disarmament, the establishment of a *world government* would fundamentally alter the sovereign state system rather than try to work within it. Under world government, peace would be kept in the international realm much as it is within national realms. There would be a single, supreme legal authority with the power to make laws governing the behavior of men and nations, and with the military strength to enforce them. Yet, in accordance with the federal principle, the national governments composing this new world union would retain a good measure of control over their populations. The world federal government need be ceded only that minimum of sovereignty essential to enable it to enforce world peace through world law. The establishment of such a world order would require most of all the giving up of the rigid emotionalism which has led men to glorify the concept of national sovereignty. Faced with the threat of nuclear extinction, men must, can, and will realize that the alternatives for tomorrow are one world or none.

This hopeful vision of a federally governed brave new world, however, ignores the problems underlying the current world crisis, rather than solving them. Suppose that the leaders of all the world's nations suddenly did discard all narrow conceptions of national interest and agreed to join together in a world federal government. How would the central government be organized? To have it organized along communistic lines would certainly be unsatisfactory to us. (We can have *that* kind of a world government any time we want to.) Should the Communist nations be expected to accept a government patterned on American or British democracy?

Even if agreement on a democratic constitutional framework could be reached, how would the policymaking organs be constituted? Would *governments* choose and instruct *delegates,* as they now do in the United Nations? Or would *representatives* be elected by the *people?* If there were elections, who would certify that they were genuinely free and fair? How could there be genuinely free and fair elections in societies where freedom of speech is restricted and all media of communication are government controlled? To permit free discussion of issues and equal access to communications media for opposing candidates and parties would change the very nature of the social and political system in nations like the Soviet Union, Communist China, Spain, Portugal, the Union of South Africa, and others. Can we really expect the leaders of these nations to join in a governmental scheme which would undermine the sources of their own power, fundamentally alter their nation's way of life, and deny the validity of the ideologies to which they are committed.

In the new federally governed world, remember, overwhelming military force will be turned over to the supranational government. How, then, will unpopular governments keep themselves in power in case of popular revolt? Is the world central government supposed to stand by while "freedom fighters" are mowed down in the streets with weapons allotted the constituent national units for domestic "police" purposes? If it intervenes, whom should it help, the national government or the revolutionists? If the revolutionists set up a competing government, which should the world government recognize and seat in its policymaking bodies? If it is free to make decisions of this kind, will not the world central government ultimately be deciding the forms of government which may be used by its constituent *national* units? If it should decide to aid Communist-led rebellions or "national liberation wars" against democratic governments, would this be acceptable to us? Should we expect the Communists to accept interventions in support of anticommunist "freedom fighters"? If so, are we not asking them to risk signing their own death warrants when they affix their signatures to a world constitution including provisions of this sort?

On what basis will the citizens and nations comprising the new world government be represented? The "one man, one vote" principle would leave the masses of Asia solidly in command. Would Americans be willing to accept having about one-third as many votes as India and one-fourth as many as Communist China? Would the Russians? Would England, France, and Germany be willing to accept less representation in the central government — and therefore less control over its presumed nuclear monopoly — than Pakistan, Indonesia, or Brazil? Would not the problems of the world's "population explosion" be magnified by a system in which national power to influence world government decisions depended primarily on the size of a nation's population? Would the representatives of the world's poorest nations be content to utilize their overwhelming parliamentary majority solely in support of a world order in which their peoples come off so shabbily? Would the wealthier nations be willing to accept major transfers of wealth to rectify this situation?

The "one nation, one vote" principle does not promise any happier results. Is it satisfactory for Togo, Luxembourg, Upper Volta, Jamaica, Kuwait, and Albania to have votes equal to those of the United States and the other great powers? Can we expect decisions voted by nations possessing say 10 per cent of the world's population, and less of its wealth and power, to be accepted by citizens or governments of more powerful and populous nations? There is already grumbling in the United States about the allegedly irresponsible actions of the United Nations General Assembly where the "one nation, one vote" principle is followed. Yet the Assembly has only the power to recommend actions, not the power to make decisions binding on member states, nor the power to command the world's most imposing military force — as a world government must.

Formulas for "weighted" voting could no doubt be devised, but considering the stakes involved it might well prove difficult to secure agreement on any one of them. Surely the national representatives engaged in drawing up the world constitution may be forgiven if, before giving their assent, they calculate the effects which any particular arrangement would be likely to have on their nations' goals and aspirations.

And what would be the geographic boundaries of the constituent nations of the world federal union? In several cases these are in dispute. Will there be one Germany, or two? If two, who will control Berlin and who will reconcile the German people to living with this situation indefinitely? If one, will it be governed democratically or communistically? Will there be one China, or two? If one, who will control it, the Communists or the Nationalists? If the Communists, what will happen to Taiwan (Formosa) and the offshore islands? What of the two Koreas and the two Vietnams? Is Cuba to stay in Communist hands indefinitely? Eastern Europe?

Of course it may be argued that these problems could best be coped with by the new world government itself, after it had been set up. But at least tentative decisions would have to be made immediately. Who would represent China, Germany, Korea, and Vietnam in the world government? The representatives of these rival national governments thus far have often proved unwilling to coparticipate even in humanitarian specialized agencies or in Olympic sports competitions! What will now make them coparticipate in a world government with power to dispose over their competitive claims? If the world could reach a *modus vivendi* on all of *these* issues, the prospects for peace would brighten considerably even without a world government!

Most basically, how will enforcement measures be taken? Will American soldiers under world government command be willing to participate in military action against their homeland in case of action taken by the world government against the United States? After all, the United States of America dissolved into civil war some eighty years after its constituent states had committed themselves to live together under a single federal government. If this could happen in a federally governed nation of people with a common language, a common religious and ethical heritage, and a common political tradition, why should it not happen in a federally governed world without these bonds. If Robert E. Lee could choose to lead the defense of his state against the Government of the United States, why should not some future Eisenhower, De Gaulle, MacArthur, Montgomery, Zhukov, or Lin Piao choose to defend his nation against a world government?

FOUNDATIONS OF WORLD COMMUNITY

What kind of a *world community*, then, must be built in order to minimize the risk that the inevitable differences among nations will lead to war? Many scholars have studied the political processes by which differences are resolved within nations or regional groupings of nations. Others have investigated the process by which smaller-scale political units have grown into nations, or into "security-communities" in which differences are resolved peacefully over long periods of time. On the basis of these studies, we can make some tentative observations as to the kind of world in which the settlement of disputes by peaceful means would be most likely.[9]

In a genuine world community, the world's peoples would share many of the same goals and values and feel loyalties to at least some common symbols. Membership in the world community would be seen as highly advantageous by almost all the groups and persons within it. At least the intellectual elite of the community, including the leaders of most major groups, would hold basically similar views as to what constituted "acceptable" or "legitimate" means of pursuing individual and group goals. Political and economic interest groups and personal friendship groups would frequently cut across national lines rather than be confined within them, and there would be considerable overlap in the membership of many of these groups. Men — and perhaps also messages and goods — would be able to move reasonably freely across international boundaries. Real efforts would be made to meet the needs of the impoverished and distressed, affording them some valid ground for trust in their fellow men. Able individuals everywhere would have a reasonable chance to better their positions in life without revolutionizing the established order. Finally, there would be some institutional arrangements for resolving disputes among men and groups, and a history of success in adjusting differences peacefully.

To illustrate and clarify a number of these points, let us contrast conditions in international society today with conditions within the United States — a society in which we feel fairly confident that internal differences can be resolved without large-scale violence.

[9] Among the studies upon which the following discussion is based are Karl Deutsch, Sidney Burrell, Robert Kann, Maurice Lee, Martin Lichterman, Raymond Lindgren, Francis Loewenheim, and Richard Van Wagenen, *Political Community and the North Atlantic Area* (Princeton, N.J.: Princeton University Press, 1957) ; Karl Deutsch, *Political Community at the International Level* (Garden City, N.Y.: Doubleday, 1954); Philip E. Jacob and James V. Toscano (eds.), *The Integration of Political Communities* (Philadelphia: Lippincott, 1964); Gabriel Almond and Sidney Verba, *The Civic Culture* (Boston: Little, Brown, 1965, originally published by Princeton University Press in 1963); and Bruce Russett, *Trends in World Politics* (New York: Macmillan, 1965).

Reared in a common (Judaeo-Christian) religious tradition and in a common (liberal democratic) political tradition, the values and goals of the overwhelming majority of Americans are remarkably similar. Educated in schools with roughly similar curricula, they identify with the American flag, "The Star-Spangled Banner," the American eagle, the presidency, and the cartoon image of Uncle Sam, and respond with respect and pride to such names as George Washington, Thomas Jefferson, and Benjamin Franklin. Most Americans derive considerable psychological satisfaction from identifying themselves as Americans and would strongly resist any suggestion that they surrender their citizenship privileges voluntarily.

In the world as a whole, on the other hand, no political or religious creed can be said to be predominant — Christianity, Islam, Buddhism, Confucianism, and Hinduism all claim hundreds of millions of adherents. As many people live under dictatorial or Communist rule as under liberal democracy. There is a United Nations flag, a Secretary General, a martyred hero in Dag Hammarskjöld. But nowhere do these evoke the feelings and loyalties which their nationalistic counterparts can summon. There is little feeling yet that we are "citizens of the world" and that loss of this status would entail a significant personal loss.

In the United States, for the most part, political, economic, social and friendship groups — even family groups — tend to cut across state and even regional lines, and group memberships overlap considerably. The AFL-CIO, the National Association of Manufacturers, the American Legion, the Rotary, Kiwanis, and Lions Clubs, the American Medical Association, the League of Women Voters, and the Democratic and Republican parties are nationwide organizations with chapters or members in all sections of the country. Lions Club members often belong also to the Legion and to one of the political parties. The local PTA or Legion post is likely to have within it both Democrats and Republicans, Catholics and Protestants, businessmen and union workers, teachers, doctors, and engineers. These people will get to know one another. They will become acquainted with, if not necessarily converted to, one another's viewpoints. They will form meaningful friendships and working business relationships which they will not sacrifice lightly. On any issue of public policy, they are apt to have some personal friends or business associates or organizational connections on more than one side of the question. The personal cost to them of any attempt to settle questions of public policy by force — with all the bitterness this implies — rather than by consent, would therefore be very high. The incentive to moderation is correspondingly great. The workings of this process among millions of individuals at all levels of a society add up to the essence of real community.[10]

10 Almond and Verba, in their study of five nations, found the incidence of group memberships, of multiple memberships by the same individuals, and of active participation in such groups all related to the development of the citizen attitudes and competences essential to the maintenance of democratic stability. *Op. cit.*, pp. 244–265.

Conversely, in the world at large most groups are organized along national or regional lines, rather than on a worldwide basis, and the overlap among group memberships is minimal. Most of the world's Communist party members, for instance, are located within the Communist bloc; Western Communist party members are rarely also bona fide members of their local Rotary Club, Episcopal Church, or American Legion chapter. Argentine gauchos, Russian collective farm managers, American farmers, and Indian peasants are not often alumni of the same schools or members of the same professional associations or social groups. They do not even speak the same language. Only infrequently do they get to know one another personally, form friendships, or even establish meaningful business relationships. The ideas and way of life of each seem to the others odd, alien, worthy of suspicion. The Legion, the Rotary Club, the AFL–CIO local, the Congregational Church, the Democratic party, and the local bowling club are all likely to be unanimous in feeling that democracy is a better form of government than communism, that Cuba would be better off without Castro, or that Russian troops had better stay out of West Berlin. Similarly, the Soviet worker's "trade union" organization, his neighborhood recreation association, the Young Communists League, and other organizations to which he may belong are likely to be united too on these issues — but on precisely the opposite side. In such a situation, a moderate attitude can become a real social liability: continued contact with exponents of the same viewpoint reinforces the notion that all good and right-thinking men agree on the issue and that compromise is tantamount to disloyalty to the group.

Thus Almond and Verba found that citizens' attribution of favorable qualities to the political parties they opposed, and their willingness to see adherents of these opposition parties marry into their families, were both positively related to political stability.[11] Few Democrats mind if their daughters marry a Republican. But, from a world political point of view, how many Americans would accept with equanimity the announcement that their daughter was marrying a Communist?

Within the United States, the one major national issue which could not be resolved without resort to large-scale violence involved an attempt to leave the federal union by the most socially and culturally isolated region within it — a region which was in 1861 more rural, Protestant, and "native stock" than most of the rest of the nation. (Nor is it a coincidence that the most dissident group in the predominantly English-Protestant society of our Canadian neighbors are the French-Canadian Catholics of Quebec, where a separatist-terrorist movement has recently sprung up.) That the important and emotion-laden differences between North and South are today being resolved without the large-scale violence of a century ago — though still with

11 *Ibid.*, pp. 85–116 and 356–360.

considerable difficulty — is a result of the binding together of the United States by the often intangible personal and organizational bonds which create a sense of genuine community among Americans everywhere.

Technical and political barriers to the movement of persons within the United States are minimal. The far corners of the American nation are connected by one of the most extensive and intensive transportation and communications networks ever known to man. It is practical to keep in touch with relatives or friends living a considerable distance away, to exchange visits with them on holidays, to move from job to job or from assignment to assignment in a single job quickly, with a minimum of political obstacles, and at moderate expense.

The spread of modern transportation and communications facilities is also rapidly reducing the technical barriers to world travel. But even when technical obstacles are overcome, political barriers sometimes spring up to take their place. Immigration into many nations, including the United States, is severely restricted; emigration from others, like East Germany and Communist China, is tightly controlled. Even the temporary exchange of visitors and journalists is barred between such nations as the United States and Communist China. And despite the post-Stalin thaw, the interchange of persons between the United States and the Soviet Union is in no way comparable to the interchange among American states or European nations.[12]

Though there remain sizable inequalities of income and all too many impoverished and distressed individuals and families in the United States, our governments — federal, state, and local — accept to a considerable extent the obligations of feeding the hungry, providing hospital care for the aged and infirm, making available decent educational opportunities for the nation's children, and aiding the unemployed. Karl Deutsch has noted that the ratio between government revenue collections and the total income of a society is a good general indicator of the degree of community (or "integration") that exists within it. For national societies, the ratio between government revenues at all levels and Gross National Product (GNP) ranges from about 10 per cent for India to over 36 per cent for West Germany.[13] For the United States, in 1960, this ratio was about 28 per cent.

World inequalities in income and educational opportunity are far greater than those in the United States. GNP averages close to $3,000 per person in the United States, and close to $100 per person in nations like China and India. And this gap is not narrowing but widening. Between 95 and 100

---

[12] Deutsch and his collaborators found the free mobility of persons to be a much more important factor in the establishment of "security-communities" than the free movement of money or goods. Deutsch, *et al.*, *Political Community and the North Atlantic Area.* Nevertheless, the differences in the freedom of movement of money and goods within the United States, as compared with the world at large, would be as striking as any of those outlined here.

[13] Karl Deutsch, "The Price of Integration" in Jacob and Toscano (eds.), *The Integration of Political Communities*, pp. 147–148.

per cent of the adult population is literate in Europe and the United States; less than 25 per cent of the adult population is literate in India, Egypt, Nigeria, Pakistan, or Indonesia. Almost 90 per cent of American children aged 5 to 14 are in school; but three-quarters of the Indian children in this age group are not. Yet the funds collected by the United Nations, its specialized agencies, and all other international organizations combined, come to only about one-twentieth of 1 per cent of the total world GNP. And no major nation spends as much as 2½ per cent of its GNP aiding nations poorer than itself. (The United States spends less than 1 per cent.)

Those who are not cared for by their society return the favor. Since their society has not identified with them, they do not identify with it, or its leaders and institutions. They cannot be brought into a community with those who feel no community of interest with them. Their experiences are likely to be reflected in a generalized distrust of people and a feeling that nobody cares what happens to them. A high incidence of such feelings of distrust and alienation, Almond and Verba conclude, bodes ill for the maintenance of political stability and democracy.[14] Karl Deutsch has warned: "Studies have demonstrated that evenness of income distribution and high average wealth are positively correlated with each other and with a high degree of political stability. . . . The price of 'community' clearly indicates acceptance of governmental redistribution policies for the welfare of the entire nation." [15]

In American society the Horatio Alger legends symbolize the widespread belief that any able and industrious young man can make his way up in the world. Though in reality this may not be as common as folk myths suggest, it clearly is possible for many of the young and talented to raise their social and economic status by working within the existing economic and political system. The myths reinforce this reality.

In many other parts of the world today, however, a young man — no matter how bright — may feel held down by stark poverty, by the need to work on the land from an early age, by illiteracy, by lack of educational opportunity, by caste or class status, by the holding of unacceptable political views, by discrimination on the part of a foreign elite in his own nation. Even if educated at one of the great universities of the world, his future may be limited in the preindustrial economy of his own nation, by the lack of jobs suitable for qualified engineers, chemists, or nuclear physicists. Deprived of real opportunities for self-fulfillment under the existing system, in some cases spending much of their time in enforced leisure, these individuals may be forgiven if their thoughts turn to ways and means of changing the system which oppresses them — by force if necessary. In this frame of mind they may seize upon whatever revolutionary dogma promises

14 Almond and Verba, pp. 212–214 and 356 ff.
15 Deutsch, "The Price of Integration," pp. 146–147 and 177.

them the shibboleths, rationale, and financial and organizational support they think they need to make the brave new world they seek a reality.[16]

The Constitution of the United States provides well-conceived institutional arrangements for the peaceful resolution of conflicts between individuals or groups within the nation. Under these arrangements, the issues which divide men may be resolved by executive decision, by legislative deliberation and voting, by court action, or through electoral processes. The arrangements are such that, while these issues are being considered, advocates of one or another "solution" to them may work to forward their proposals in a number of nonviolent ways — by voting, writing letters to Congressmen and public officials, initiating legal action, contributing money or effort to the political campaigns of preferred candidates, etc. The institutional machinery is such that even a relatively small minority of the population — if it is sufficiently concerned — may find it possible to block majority action on a given issue.

Decisions are made by a constantly shifting succession of coalitions of minorities, and it is a rare minority which is not a member of the winning coalition at least some of the time. Regardless of decisions on specific issues, then, almost everybody has some stake in maintaining the existing order — apart from the values of order itself. Decisions, moreover, are almost never final, and losers may console themselves with the thought that the system virtually guarantees them the right to try again another day; there will soon be another election, a new legislature, a new president, a change of heart by the Supreme Court, or a constitutional amendment.

American elections, moreover, are not single issue affairs. Even in a given election, most voters concerned with issues will have had to compromise on a number of matters in casting a vote for either major party candidate. Even an extraordinarily sweeping victory for the candidates of one or another of these parties is likely to mean to the average supporter merely the temporary victory of the candidates who stand closer to his own beliefs on a few more, rather than a few less, of the important issues of the day.

The leaders of the losing party, above all, are normally committed to the existing order as a matter both of conscience and of personal interest. With rare exception, they have won their leadership through their political skill. Even in defeat, they often retain important governmental positions — governor, senator, etc. Thus they are committed to leading their followers to accept defeat gracefully rather than to rallying them to contest electoral decisions on the field of battle. The nation's long history of settling political issues without military conflict (with one great exception) further leads its dissentient citizens to think of pressing their claims and grievances through political rather than revolutionary channels.

Again, the contrast with the world society is striking. The international

16 See Eric Hoffer, The True Believer (New York: New American Library, 1950).

system, too, possesses a quasi-constitutional document (the United Nations Charter) setting forth institutional arrangements by which international issues may be resolved peacefully. But, as we have noted, these arrangements call for the settlement of disputes by mutual agreement. They do not provide adequately for situations in which such agreement cannot be obtained. The United Nations General Assembly is not an international legislature, and does not have the power to reach decisions binding on its members. (In certain circumstances the Security Council *may* make binding decisions — but only with the consent of the five great powers.) [17] This means, in effect, that the major issues dividing the great powers of the world — the issues most dangerous to the maintenance of world peace — cannot be resolved by legislative action in the Security Council either.

There is an International Court of Justice, but member states may bring their disputes to it or not as they see fit. Only by prior agreement of all parties to a dispute may judicial process be made binding; and even then there are no established procedures for enforcement action against a nation failing to abide by a decision of the International Court.

The most important disputes between nations, moreover, are not *legal* at all, but *political*. The question at issue, therefore, is not what the law *is* and whether or not it has been broken, but what it *ought* to be. By law, for instance, there is no question that Portugal controls and exercises sovereignty over the African colony of Angola. But African Angolans and the representatives of the former colonial nations are understandably not satisfied with this situation — any more than the American colonists would have been satisfied in 1776 to abide by the British government's legal right of sovereignty in the thirteen colonies. Revolutions are always illegal.

The important point is that in international society — unlike the United States — there is no way (other than by negotiation in hope of winning the agreement of one's opponents) that unjust laws or unjust situations may be set right peacefully. *International law* is generally the result of agreements among nations or of long-standing international custom.[18] Agreements entered into under duress — as after defeat in war — are recognized as legiti-

---

[17] The General Assembly may make recommendations by simple majority vote though on "important" questions a two-thirds majority is required. In doubtful cases a simple majority may decide whether a question at issue is "important." Nine affirmative votes are required for action on "procedural" matters by the fifteen member Security Council. (Until 1965, the Council had 11 members and 7 affirmative votes were needed for action.) On "substantive" matters, according to the United Nations Charter, these 9 affirmative votes must include those of the five permanent members of the Council — the United States, Britain, France, the Soviet Union, and (Nationalist) China. In practice, however, abstentions by these powers are not construed as "vetoes." In doubtful cases the decision as to whether a question is "substantive" or "procedural" is normally treated as substantive, and thus vetoable.

[18] For a discussion of some of the important contributions which international law *can* make to the peaceful resolution of international conflicts, see Richard A. Falk, "World Law and Human Conflict," Elton McNeil (ed.), *The Nature of Human Conflict*, pp. 227–249.

mate. There is no legislature to make and change laws or to register changes in the balance of political strength within the world community. There are no worldwide elections in which changes in public policy may be advocated, struggled for peacefully, and eventually implemented. Even negotiated agreements effecting changes are normally reached with the explicit or implicit threat of force in the background.

In most nations, in fact, a key role in foreign policymaking is played by men who owe their positions of leadership to their mastery of the military arts. Often, moreover, these military leaders have a "vested interest" in maximizing the size and importance of their nations' military establishments. In addition, since international problems have usually been resolved in a context involving the actual or potential use of force, national leaders are bound to conceive of the use of force as at least one possible alternative in dealing with international disputes.

India's armed occupation in 1961 of the Portuguese controlled territory of Goa, a small enclave on the Indian subcontinent, provides a useful illustration of the inadequacy of international procedures for the peaceful adjustment of disputes. India was much criticized for resorting to force in this instance, the more so since in the preceding decade its leaders had constantly exhorted others to avoid international violence in settling their disputes. Without attempting to pass judgment on this Indian action, it is worth looking at the situation from India's point of view. From this perspective, the sole alternative to force apparently available to India at the time was to permit the indefinite continuance of what it considered to be a moral and political wrong — the continued subjection of an Indian people to European colonial dominance. Portugal considered Goa a province of Portugal itself and refused even to negotiate the matter. The United States was prevailed upon to try to influence Portugal to acquiesce in the peaceful decolonization of Goa, but its efforts were without visible success. General Assembly resolutions urging the desirability of liquidating colonial possessions were passed — but were not binding upon Portugal. An appeal to the International Court of Justice would most likely have produced not justice but merely the finding that Portugal was the rightful legal authority in Goa. For fourteen years attempts to resolve the question peacefully were frustrated. That the Indian government, impelled by rising popular passions, should ultimately have resorted to a remarkably easy forcible takeover of the territory, then, may not meet with our moral approval, but certainly should not provoke our astonishment.

We have already noted that the differences separating nations such as the Soviet Union or Communist China and the United States tend to be cumulative in their impact, and that international issues tend to be settled in a context involving at least the implicit threat of force. Thus whenever a nation gets the worst of a settlement on one issue, the inference may well be drawn by other national leaders that this is a reflection of its power weakness relative to that of its rivals. To the extent that this conclusion is drawn, that nation's chances of winning its way on other issues may be correspondingly reduced. In addition, international settlements are usually final since there is no institutionalized provision for peaceful change without the consent of one's rivals and no institutionalized assurance that a loser will have the opportunity to reverse the decision by peaceful means another day. Thus, the cost of losing a decision in the world arena is much higher than within a national political system, and the incentive to acquiesce in an apparently unsatisfactory solution is correspondingly less.

In illustrating the meaning of community by comparing the United States with the international system, however, we have overstated our case. Important groups have been "left out" of the American community to a substantial extent — migratory workers, residents of Appalachia, and, most notably, American Negroes. In the mid-1960's, for instance, the average white family in the United States earned nearly twice the income of the average nonwhite family. Unemployment among nonwhites was double that among whites, and the average nonwhite had three years less education and seven years lower life expectancy at birth than the average white. Close to 90 per cent of Negro children attended all-Negro schools. Almost five times as many nonwhites as whites were illiterate. And a special study sponsored by the United States Government in 1964–65 showed that 67.5 per cent of the 18-year-old Negroes who took the armed forces qualification tests failed them on mental grounds, as compared to 18.8 per cent of the non-Negro 18-year-olds.[19] (In the world as a whole, too, racial differences coincide dangerously with economic and social inequities and reinforce them.)

Yet the United States is one of the most highly integrated national communities in the world today. Fortunately, there is no reason to assume that the world as a whole must achieve the degree of community which exists in the United States in order to become a "security-community." Nor is it necessary — or even clearly advisable — to have a world government in order to preserve world peace over a period of time. Deutsch and his colleagues found that "security-communities" which did not "amalgamate" into a single governmental unit were both easier to attain and less likely to disintegrate than "amalgamated security-communities" governed from a single center. The advantage of the latter, in the cases studied in the North Atlantic area, lay in their greater ability "to act quickly and effectively for positive goals," rather than in their ability to keep the peace. The non-

19. These figures were taken by the writer from the *1965 Statistical Abstract of the United States*, issued by the Bureau of the Census of the U.S. Department of Commerce, sold as *The U.S. Book of Facts, Statistics and Information* (New York: Pocket Books, 1965). The results of the armed forces qualification test study were reported in *The New York Times*, Oct. 2, 1966, p. 1.

amalgamated form, which imposed less burdens on member units and peoples, actually proved more often effective in avoiding the outbreak of large-scale violence — especially where highly disparate populations were involved. Thus there has been far less armed conflict between the United States and Mexico since 1850, than within either the United States or Mexico over the same period.[20] And, relative to population, there have been more deaths by armed mass violence since the end of World War II in such national states as China, Indonesia, and Cuba, than in the world at large.

All of this suggests that a certain degree of community is needed if the world is to manage its conflicts peacefully over a long period of time; but that we do not know precisely how *much* community will be enough to attain this goal. It suggests, also, that for all its weaknesses, the United Nations may provide the institutional framework that should be most useful in helping the embryonic world community, at its present stage of development, to grow stronger.

THE UNITED NATIONS

Plainly, the United Nations cannot be expected to perform on the international level all, or even most, of the functions the American federal government performs on the national scene. It cannot pass laws resolving international disputes peacefully, and it cannot enforce the peace on matters involving the vital interests of the great powers. Even a Charter amendment removing the requirement for great power unanimity in the Security Council would not enable it to do this for the veto power is a reflection, rather than a cause, of the United Nations' inability to coerce the great powers. Would elimination of the right of veto enable the United Nations to order Soviet military forces to support United Nations enforcement action in Korea or Hungary or the Congo if the Soviet Government did not want them to?

It is significant that the United Nations' one large-scale collective security action to date — the defense of South Korea — was based on a *recommendation* rather than an *order* by the Security Council, even though the absence of the Soviet delegates at the time would have made it possible to secure an order if this had been desired. The General Assembly could have mobilized collective security action on the basis of a similar recommendation in the Hungarian revolt of 1956, *if* its noncommunist members had been willing to supply the necessary forces and bear the military and political risks involved.

A clear example of the limited utility of legal authority unsupported by power was the financial crisis occasioned by great power opposition to the United Nations' Congo operation. When United Nations representatives in the Congo went further than the Soviet Union and France wanted them to,

20 *Political Community and the North Atlantic Area, op. cit., passim.*

these nations (among others) simply refused to pay their share of the costs of this operation. The United Nations Charter required that they be deprived of their votes in the General Assembly if they did not make some payments toward meeting these costs within two years, and the United States pressed the matter. But, faced with the prospect of driving the Soviet Union out of the United Nations, a majority of the members backed away from enforcing the Charter. Instead, for a full session of the Assembly, it was arranged that no substantive votes be taken, to avoid a direct United States-Soviet confrontation on this issue! By the start of the next session (1965), the United States, too, had decided to acquiesce in a new *de facto* understanding that key members cannot be compelled to provide financial support for undertakings they oppose, the Charter notwithstanding.[21]

It must be emphasized, however, that the United Nations *can* make important contributions to the keeping of the peace. The United Nations can and does provide an additional instrument of diplomacy and an additional channel of communication between nations in a world where failures of communication can be dangerous. (The lack of contact between the United States and Communist China in the early stages of the Korean War is a good illustration. See Chapters Five and Eleven.) It can provide skilled mediators to aid in devising means for settling disputes peacefully and can offer arbitral and judicial procedures for nations willing to make use of them.

These United Nations procedures can sometimes offer nations the possibility of acquiescing in somewhat unfavorable settlements of international issues without necessarily giving the impression that their acquiescence is a sign of weakness. By offering face-saving devices to national leaders, it may reduce the cost to them of accepting a compromise settlement or even a strategic retreat. Soviet Premier Khrushchev's backdown in the 1962 Cuban missile crisis, for instance, may have been facilitated by the opportunity offered him by United Nations Secretary General U Thant and others to characterize his actions as stemming from a deep concern for peace rather than from military weakness. (See Chapter Eleven.)

The United Nations can also be useful in supporting and implementing national policies, as it was for the United States in Korea and, in part, in the Congo. It can bring pressure to bear upon member nations to avoid offending the opinions of other world leaders and peoples by belligerent or unreasonable actions. In the case of disputes in which the United States and the Soviet Union are either agreed or not directly involved, it may even be able to insist on peaceful settlements. Palestine (1948), Suez (1956), Cyprus (1964), and to some extent Kashmir (1965), are examples. When the United States and the Soviet Union are opposed, the United Nations Emergency Force, composed of units of military forces from less powerful nations, can

---

[21] Congressional reaction to the discovery that a small portion of the United Nations' technical assistance funds were scheduled to be used in Cuba indicates that the United States might well feel constrained to act as France and Soviet Russia did if the shoe were on the other foot.

be brought into action as a means of avoiding the dangerous direct confrontation of American and Soviet troops in a chaotic international situation — such as that in the former Belgian Congo in 1960.

The United Nations can serve, too, as a sounding board for national
complaints. In so doing, it can sometimes help national leaders to make
their peoples feel that something is being done about national grievances
which might otherwise provoke moods of popular belligerence and willingness to use force. The sight of their leaders dealing with the heads of great
nations on a basis of equality offers a sorely needed source of national satisfaction to the citizens of impoverished new nations whose postindepend-
ence triumphs are exasperatingly few. The disproportionate influence, relative to their power, which these and other small nations exercise in the
General Assembly gives them also a stake in strengthening the United Nations and in building the kind of world in which the United Nations can
be most influential. This may prove to be one of the United Nations' most
important by-products. For some of the preindustrial states which it is helping to commit to the cause of international order today will become more
powerful and significant in international affairs tomorrow.

Nor should the United Nations' trusteeship program, and its major contribution to the amazingly rapid and peaceful decolonization of Africa and
Asia be overlooked. When the United Nations was born, a generation ago,
only a very optimistic observer would have dared to predict that the great
European empires would be largely decolonized in so short a time and
with so relatively little violence.

Finally, the United Nations is contributing directly, if slowly, to building
the kind of genuine world community we have been discussing through its
economic, social, and technical assistance programs, its Secretariat, and its
parliamentary diplomacy. Such United Nations specialized agencies as the
Food and Agriculture Organization and the World Health Organization
are working to serve humanitarian goals and to narrow, however modestly,
the dangerous gap in living standards between the "have" and the "have-
not" nations. Others, such as the Universal Postal Union and the International Telecommunications Union are helping to improve international communications. The Secretariat and the specialized agencies are affording men
from different nations the opportunity to work together to solve economic
and social problems which cut across national boundaries — a collaborative
effort which in itself helps to foster a worldwide outlook on the part of the
men concerned and the governments they may come to influence.

The political organs of the United Nations, particularly the informal
"United Nations community" which has emerged at United Nations headquarters in New York, generate similar incidental benefits. Gary Best's
interviews in 1960 with randomly selected members of the United Nations
delegations of 78 member states showed the majority asserting that at
United Nations headquarters — as compared with diplomatic assignments

to national capitals — they had more contact with diplomats from other countries in general and with representatives of unfriendly nations in particular; and that they were more likely to communicate with these colleagues informally, across diplomatic ranks and "off-the-record."[22] In addition, the United Nations itself has the potential to become a symbol toward which men's affections, and eventually loyalties, may come to be directed.

In relation to the whole problem of building a world community, these are undoubtedly very small steps. But they are steps in the right direction. As Inis Claude has pointed out:

> . . . It is less significant that international organization is not a federal world government than that it is engaged in the effort to do the sort of thing that must be done, by the sort of method that can be used, to produce the sort of community that can, with proper management, sustain a peaceful existence. In this sense, the experiment of governing the world is now in operation, and the task of making the world governable is already being undertaken.[23]

In the international system as it is, then, the future of the human race depends not only on the United Nations but even more upon the good judgment, good will, and sense of perspective of those who make national policies. In particular, it depends on the constancy, wisdom, and forebearance of the world's great powers. How well, then, is the United States prepared — by its historical experience, by its traditions, by its governmental system, and by the values and character of its people — to meet the challenge of leadership in such a world? The chapters which follow deal with this critical question.

❦CASE
STUDY   *THE WATTS RIOTS*

It is not only on the international scene that conflicts may lead to violence. One of the largest and costliest riots in recent American history broke out in the summer of 1965 in the Watts district of southeastern

---

[22] Gary Best, "Diplomacy in the United Nations" (unpublished doctoral dissertation, Northwestern University, 1960), cited by Chadwick F. Alger, "Personal Contact in Intergovernmental Organizations," Herbert Kelman (ed.), *International Behavior* (New York: Holt, 1965), pp. 523–547.

Alger cites some social-psychological studies suggesting that these characteristics of the United Nations system may produce benefits of value to the building of a world community. See also Chadwick F. Alger, "United Nations Participation as a Learning Experience," *Public Opinion Quarterly*, Fall, 1963, 411–426.

[23] Claude, *Swords into Plowshares, op. cit.,* p. 445.

Los Angeles. There, within five days, thirty-four persons were killed, over 1,000 injured, and more than 3,400 arrested. Property damage exceeded $40 million, and more than 15,000 national guardsmen and police officers were employed in an effort to keep looting and violence under control.

Racial resentments were clearly a major factor. Of the 80,000 persons who live in the 25 square block Watts district, 98 per cent are Negroes, and 30 per cent are unemployed. "Two-thirds of its adults have less than a high school education, an eighth is illiterate; 30 per cent of the children are from broken homes." [24] The California Bureau of Criminal Identification and Investigation later reported that the "average" convicted rioter "was a Negro male who had lived in Los Angeles for more than five years . . . was a high school dropout . . . employed as either a domestic or unskilled laborer, earning from $200 to $400 a month . . . and had an arrest record." [25]

Soon after the riots, Governor Edmund G. Brown appointed an eight-man Commission on the Los Angeles Riots, headed by John McCone, former Director of the Central Intelligence Agency. After an intensive investigation and interrogation of witnesses, the commission issued a report of eighty-six pages (plus appendices). This report was criticized by some observers as, in effect, a whitewash of the status quo. (One of the members of the commission, in fact, dissented on some points.) Nevertheless, the report's description of the riots themselves, and of some of the factors underlying them, will serve our purposes quite adequately.

1. What were the immediate and underlying causes of the Watts riots?

2. How do you account for the general lack of respect for the law and those who enforce it evidenced in the prolonged looting and violence?

3. To what extent have the people of Watts been included in, and to what extent excluded from, the Los Angeles community?

4. Seven months after the riots described here, another outburst claimed two more lives. Do you think there will be further rioting in Watts in the years to come? Why or why not? Are there any changes in institutional arrangements or public policy which would help to prevent future outbreaks?

5. In what ways do conditions in the Los Angeles area seem to you to be essentially analogous to those in the contemporary world as a whole? In what ways do conditions on the international scene seem to be fundamentally different?

6. All things considered, do you think the prospects for peace in the world are better or worse than the prospects for peace in Watts? Defend your position.

[24] *The New York Times*, August 22, 1965, Sec. 4, p. 1.
[25] Quoted in *The New York Times*, Sept. 4, 1966, p. 52.

7. On the basis of this case study, what basic United States foreign policy orientations do you believe would contribute to making large-scale international violence less likely?

GOVERNOR'S COMMISSION ON THE LOS ANGELES RIOTS

. . . In the summer of 1964, Negro communities in seven eastern cities were stricken by riots.* Although in each situation there were unique contributing circumstances not existing elsewhere, the fundamental causes were largely the same:

> — Not enough jobs to go around, and within this scarcity not enough by a wide margin of a character which the untrained Negro could fill.
> — Not enough schooling designed to meet the special needs of the disadvantaged Negro child, whose environment from infancy onward places him under a serious handicap.
> — A resentment, even hatred, of the police, as the symbol of authority.

These riots were each a symptom of a sickness in the center of our cities. In almost every major city, Negroes pressing ever more densely into the central city and occupying areas from which Caucasians have moved in their flight to the suburbs have developed an isolated existence with a feeling of separation from the community as a whole. Many have moved to the city only in the last generation and are totally unprepared to meet the conditions of modern city life. At the core of the cities where they cluster, law and order have only tenuous hold; the conditions of life itself are often marginal; idleness leads to despair and finally, mass violence supplies a momentary relief from the malaise. . . .

When the rioting came to Los Angeles, it was not a race riot in the usual sense. What happened was an explosion — a formless, quite senseless, all but hopeless violent protest — engaged in by a few but bringing great distress to all. . . .

This case study has been excerpted (with the order of paragraphs occasionally rearranged) from *Violence in the City — An End or a Beginning? A Report by the Governor's Commission on the Los Angeles Riots,* submitted to Governor Brown on December 2, 1965.

*   SUMMARY OF 1964 RIOTS

City	Date	Killed	Injured	Arrests	Stores damaged
New York City	July 18–23	1	144	519	541
Rochester	July 24–25	4	350	976	204
Jersey City	August 2–4	0	46	52	71
Paterson	August 11–13	0	8	65	20
Elizabeth	August 11–13	0	6	18	17
Chicago (Dixmoor)	August 16–17	0	57	80	2
Philadelphia	August 28–30	0	341	774	225

144 HOURS IN AUGUST 1965

On August 11, 1965, California Highway Patrolman Lee W. Minikus, a Caucasian, was riding his motorcycle along 122nd Street, just south of the Los Angeles City boundary, when a passing Negro motorist told him he had just seen a car that was being driven recklessly. Minikus gave chase and pulled the car over at 116th and Avalon, in a predominantly Negro neighborhood, near but not in Watts. It was 7:00 P.M.

The driver was Marquette Frye, a 21-year-old Negro, and his older brother, Ronald, 22, was a passenger. Minikus asked Marquette to get out and take the standard Highway Patrol sobriety test. Frye failed the test, and at 7:05 P.M., Minikus told him he was under arrest. He radioed for his motorcycle partner, for a car to take Marquette to jail, and a tow truck to take the car away.

They were two blocks from the Frye home, in an area of two-story apartment buildings and numerous small family residences. Because it was a very warm evening, many of the residents were outside.

Ronald Frye, having been told he could not take the car when Marquette was taken to jail, went to get their mother so that she could claim the car. They returned to the scene about 7:15 P.M. as the second motorcycle patrolman, the patrol car, and tow truck arrived. The original group of 25 to 50 curious spectators had grown to 250 to 300 persons.

Mrs. Frye approached Marquette and scolded him for drinking. Marquette, who until then had been peaceful and cooperative, pushed her away and moved toward the crowd, cursing and shouting at the officers that they would have to kill him to take him to jail. The patrolmen pursued Marquette and he resisted.

The watching crowd became hostile, and one of the patrolmen radioed for more help. Within minutes, three more highway patrolmen arrived. Minikus and his partner were now struggling with both Frye brothers. Mrs. Frye, now belligerent, jumped on the back of one of the officers and ripped his shirt. In an attempt to subdue Marquette, one officer swung at his shoulder with a night stick, missed, and struck him on the forehead, inflicting a minor cut. By 7:23 P.M., all three of the Fryes were under arrest, and other California Highway Patrolmen and, for the first time, Los Angeles police officers had arrived in response to the call for help.

Officers on the scene said there were now more than 1,000 persons in the crowd. About 7:25 P.M., the patrol car with the prisoners, and the tow truck pulling the Frye car, left the scene. At 7:31 P.M., the Fryes arrived at a nearby sheriff's substation.

Undoubtedly the situation at the scene of the arrest was tense. Belligerence and resistance to arrest called for forceful action by the officers. This brought on hostility from Mrs. Frye and some of the bystanders, which, in turn, caused increased actions by the police. Anger at the scene escalated and, as in all such situations, bitter recriminations from both sides followed. . . .

As the officers were leaving the scene, someone in the crowd spat on one of them. They stopped withdrawing and two highway patrolmen went into the crowd and arrested a young Negro woman and a man who was said to have been inciting the crowd to violence when the officers were arresting her. . . .

Following these arrests, all officers withdrew at 7:40 P.M. As the last police car left the scene, it was stoned by the now irate mob.

As has happened so frequently in riots in other cities, inflated and distorted rumors concerning the arrests spread quickly to adjacent areas. The young woman arrested for spitting was wearing a barber's smock, and the false rumor spread throughout the area that she was pregnant and had been abused by police. Erroneous reports were also circulated concerning the treatment of the Fryes at the arrest scene.

The crowd did not disperse, but ranged in small groups up and down the street, although never more than a few blocks from the arrest scene. Between 8:15 P.M. and midnight, the mob stoned automobiles, pulled Caucasian motorists out of their cars and beat them, and menaced a police field command post which had been set up in the area. By 1:00 A.M., the outbreak seemed to be under control but, until early morning hours, there were sporadic reports of unruly mobs, vandalism, and rock throwing. Twenty-nine persons were arrested.

On Thursday morning, there was an uneasy calm, but it was obvious that tensions were still high. . . . Between 6:45 and 7:15 P.M., crowds at the scene of the trouble of the night before had grown to more than 1,000. Firemen who came into the area to fight fires in three overturned automobiles were shot at and bombarded with rocks. The first fire in a commercial establishment was set only one block from the location of the Frye arrests, and police had to hold back rioters as firemen fought the blaze.

Shortly before midnight, rock-throwing and looting crowds for the first time ranged outside the perimeter. Five hundred police officers, deputy sheriffs and highway patrolmen used various techniques, including fender-to-fender sweeps by police cars, in seeking to disperse the mob. By 4:00 A.M. Friday, the police department felt that the situation was at least for the moment under control. . . .

. . . Around 8:00 A.M., crowds formed again in the vicinity of the Frye arrests and in the adjacent Watts business area, and looting resumed. . . . By mid-morning, a crowd of 3,000 had gathered in the commercial section of Watts and there was general looting in that district as well as in adjacent business areas. . . .

Early Friday afternoon, rioters jammed the streets, began systematically to burn two blocks of 103rd Street in Watts, and drove off firemen by sniper fire and by throwing missiles. By late afternoon, gang activity began to spread the disturbance as far as fifty and sixty blocks to the north. . . .

The first death occurred between 6:00 and 7:00 P.M. Friday, when a Negro bystander, trapped on the street between police and rioters, was shot and killed during an exchange of gunfire.

Friday was the worst night. The riot moved out of the Watts area and burning and looting spread over wide areas of Southeast Los Angeles several miles apart. . . . Police officers made sweeps on foot, moving en masse along streets to control activity and enable firemen to fight fires. By midnight, Friday, another 1,000 National Guard troops were marching shoulder to shoulder clearing the streets. By 3:00 A.M. Saturday, 3,356 guardsmen were on the streets, and the number continued to increase until the full commitment of 13,900 guardsmen was reached by midnight on Saturday. The maximum commitment of the Los Angeles Police Department during the riot period was 934 officers; the maximum for the Sheriff's Office was 719 officers.

. . . On throughout the morning hours of Saturday and during the long day, the crowds of looters and patterns of burning spread out and increased still further until it became necessary to impose a curfew on the 46.5 square-mile area on Saturday. . . . When the curfew started at 8:00 P.M., police and guardsmen were able to deal with the riot area as a whole. Compared with the holocaust of Friday evening, the streets were relatively quiet. . . .

During the day Sunday, the curfew area was relatively quiet. Because many markets had been destroyed, food distribution was started by churches, community groups, and government agencies. Governor Brown, who had returned Saturday night, personally toured the area, talking to residents. Major fires were under control but there were new fires and some rekindling of old ones. By Tuesday, Governor Brown was able to lift the curfew and by the following Sunday, only 252 guardsmen remained. . . .

As the word of the South Los Angeles violence was flashed almost continuously by all news media, the unrest spread. Although outbreaks in other areas were minor by comparison with those in South Central Los Angeles, each one held dangerous potential. San Diego, 102 miles away, had three days of rioting and 81 people were arrested. On Friday night, there was rioting in Pasadena, 12 miles from the curfew zone. There, liquor and gun stores were looted and Molotov cocktails and fire bombs were thrown at police cars. Only prompt and skillful handling by the police prevented this situation from getting out of control.

Pacoima, 20 miles north, had scattered rioting, looting, and burning. There was burning in Monrovia, 25 miles east. On Sunday night, after the curfew area was quiet, there was an incident in Long Beach, 12 miles south. About 200 guardsmen and Los Angeles police assisted Long Beach police in containing a dangerous situation which exploded when a policeman was shot when another officer's gun discharged as he was being attacked by rioters. Several fires were set Sunday night in the San Pedro-Wilmington area, 12 miles south.

After a thorough examination, the Commission has concluded that there is no reliable evidence of outside leadership or pre-established plans for the rioting. . . .

This is not to say that there was *no* agitation or promotion of the rioting by local groups or gangs which exist in pockets throughout the south central area. The sudden appearance of Molotov cocktails in quantity and the unexplained movement of men in cars through the areas of great destruction support the conclusion that there was organization and planning after the riots commenced. In addition, on that tense Thursday, inflammatory handbills suddenly appeared in Watts. But this cannot be identified as a master plan by one group; rather it appears to have been the work of several gangs, with membership of young men ranging in age from 14 to 35 years. All of these activities intensified the rioting and caused it to spread with increased violence from one district to another in the curfew area.

The final statistics are staggering. There were 34 persons killed and 1,032 reported injuries, including 90 Los Angeles police officers, 136 firemen, 10 national guardsmen, 23 persons from other governmental agencies, and 773 civilians. 118 of the injuries resulted from gunshot wounds. Of the 34 killed, one was a fireman, one was a deputy sheriff, and one a Long Beach policeman. . . .

It has been estimated that the loss of property attributable to the riots was over $40 million. More than 600 buildings were damaged by burning and looting. Of this number, more than 200 were totally destroyed by fire. The rioters concentrated primarily on food markets, liquor stores, furniture stores, clothing stores, department stores, and pawn shops. . . . Between 2,000 and 3,000 fire alarms were recorded during the riot, 1,000 of these between 7:00 A.M. on Friday and 7:00 A.M. on Saturday. We note with interest that no residences were deliberately burned, that damage to schools, libraries, churches and public buildings was minimal, and that certain types of business establishments, notably service stations and automobile dealers, were for the most part unharmed. . . .

The conduct of law enforcement agencies, most particularly the Los Angeles Police Department, has been subject to severe criticism by many Negroes who have appeared before the Commission as witnesses. The bitter criticism we have heard evidences a deep and long-standing schism between a substantial portion of the Negro community and the Police Department. "Police brutality" has been the recurring charge. One witness after another has recounted instances in which, in their opinion, the police have used excessive force or have been disrespectful and abusive in their language or manner. . . .

EMPLOYMENT — KEY TO INDEPENDENCE

The most serious immediate problem that faces the Negro in our community is employment — securing and holding a job that provides him an opportunity for livelihood, a chance to earn the means to support himself and his family, a dignity, and a reason to feel that he is a member of our community in a true and a very real sense. Unemployment and the consequent idleness are at the root of many of the problems we discuss in this report. Many witnesses have described to us, dramatically and we believe honestly, the overwhelming hopelessness that comes when a man's efforts to find a job come to naught. Inevitably, there is despair and a deep resentment of a society which he feels has turned its back upon him. Welfare does not change this. It provides the necessities of life, but adds nothing to a man's stature, nor relieves the frustrations that grow. In short, the price for public assistance is loss of human dignity.

The welfare program that provides for his children is administered so that it injures his position as the head of his household, because aid is supplied with less restraint to a family headed by a woman, married or unmarried. Thus, the unemployed male often finds it to his family's advantage to drift away and leave the family to fend for itself. Once he goes, the family unit is broken and is seldom restored. Changes in welfare administration designed to hold together rather than break apart the family have not been wholly successful.

From unemployment, other problems develop. In a discouraged frame of mind, the unemployed is driven toward anti-social behavior. Even if he remains at home, he neither serves as a worthy example to his children nor does he actively motivate them to go to school and study. Thus, a chain reaction takes place. The despair and disillusionment of the unemployed parent is passed down to the children. The example of failure is vividly present and the parent's frustrations and habits become the children's. ("Go to school for what?" one youngster said to us.) . . .

Education — Our Fundamental Resource. Are the students in the disadvantaged areas able to read and write? Achievement test scores of students in the study areas provide a distressing answer. Average achievement test scores for students in disadvantaged areas were shockingly lower than city-wide and advantaged area averages in *all* subjects and at *all* grade levels. . . .

On the basis of these scores, it appears that the average student in the fifth grade in schools in the disadvantaged areas is unable to read and understand his textbook materials, to read and understand a daily newspaper, or to make use of reading and writing for ordinary purposes in his daily life. This degree of illiteracy seriously impairs his ability to profit from further schooling. . . .

. . . the relative achievement of eighth grade students in the disadvantaged areas is even lower than in the fifth grade. . . . Currently, in the Los Angeles City School District, about 30 per cent of children entering the ninth grade drop out before completing high school. . . . Essentially, the reading and writing level of students in the disadvantaged areas is far too low for them either to advance in school or to function effectively in society. . . .

Environmental Factors. There is increasing evidence to indicate that children who live in disadvantaged areas begin school with a deficiency in environmental experiences which are essential for learning. Several factors outside the school itself appear to relate to low achievement in school, such as the level of education of adults in disadvantaged area communities, mobility, and disciplinary and law enforcement problems.

The educational level of any community and of parents substantially influences the achievement of children in school. There is a serious educational deficit in the adult population in disadvantaged areas. According to the 1960 census, about two-thirds of the adults in the disadvantaged areas had failed to graduate from high school. In addition, a high percentage (almost 14 per cent) of the adults living in the four study areas were classified as functional illiterates (defined as completing less than five years of school). Adding to the problem of education has been the tremendous inmigration of Negroes from the South where educational opportunities are limited.

Rapidly increasing school enrollment and high population mobility also characterize the disadvantaged areas. The lack of stability in these communities is reflected in extremely high student transiency, that can impair both the learning ability of students and the effectiveness of teachers. In addition, many schools in the disadvantaged areas are faced with serious disciplinary problems and with disturbing conditions in the neighborhood that can also affect the educational achievement of students. These conditions include loiterers and distracting and unsavory elements near school sites. The personal security of both teachers and students is often threatened. We believe that adequate school personnel should be provided to deal with disciplinary problems in schools and adequate law enforcement personnel should be provided at or near schools where necessary.

Children in disadvantaged areas are often deprived in their pre-school years of the necessary foundations for learning. They have not had the full range of experiences so necessary to the development of language in the pre-school years, and hence they are poorly prepared to learn when they enter school. Their behavior, their vocabulary, their verbal abilities, their experience with ideas, their view of adults, of society, of books, of learning, of schools, and of teachers are such as to have a negative impact on their school experience. Thus, the disadvantaged child enters school with a serious educational handicap, and because he gets a poor start in school, he drops further behind as he continues through the grades. His course toward academic failure is already set before he enters school; it is rooted in his earliest childhood experiences. The Commission concludes that this is the basic reason for low achievement in the disadvantaged areas.

The schools in the disadvantaged areas do not provide a program that meets the unique educational needs of culturally disadvantaged children. Although special remedial programs are offered in an attempt to compensate for deficiencies in learning, the *basic* organization and orientation of schools is the same in advantaged and disadvantaged areas. The same educational program for children of unequal background does not provide an equal opportunity for children to learn. . . .

The Consumer and the Commuter. . . . There are serious problems for the consumer in this disadvantaged area, just as there are wherever there is poverty. One is the costly and inadequate transportation from within the south central area to other parts of Los Angeles which tends to restrict residents of that area to the nearby stores, and which we discuss in more detail later in this section. Another problem is "easy credit" which can become harsh indeed if the disadvantaged person defaults on his installment obligations. The debtor may experience the loss of his property through repossession, or the loss of his job through repeated garnishments of his wages. While it is easy to say that the improvident debtor brought this state upon himself, we deplore the tactics of some merchants and lenders who help induce low-income persons to become heavily debt-burdened. Still another problem for the Negro consumer is the lack of an adequate remedy when he feels he has been unfairly treated. Public and private agencies exist to help the consumer in such a situation, but while manned by able and conscientious professionals, these agencies are generally understaffed, underfinanced, and overburdened. Often the consumer does not even know of the agency's existence. . . .

. . . the inadequate and costly public transportation currently existing throughout the Los Angeles area seriously restricts the residents of the disadvantaged areas such as south central Los Angeles. This lack of adequate transportation handicaps them in seeking and holding jobs, attending schools, shopping, and in fulfilling other needs. It has had a major influence in creating a sense of isolation, with its resultant frustrations, among the residents of south central Los Angeles, particularly the Watts area. . . .

WELFARE AND HEALTH

Public Welfare. The public welfare program in Los Angeles County involves an annual expenditure of over $400 million.* Administered by the County Bureau of Public Assistance, the program is funded by contribu-

* [The regular United Nations budget for 1965 was approximately $90 million. Total expenditures by the United Nations, its specialized agencies, peacekeeping forces and assorted special programs in the same year were under $500 million.]

tions from the federal government (42 per cent), the state government (39 per cent), and the county (19 per cent). The magnitude of this program can be somewhat better grasped by comparing it with the expenditures under the federal War on Poverty which will amount to roughly $30 million in the Los Angeles area in 1965. In August 1965, approximately 344,000 persons or 5 per cent of the county's population received some form of welfare aid. In the same month 94,000 persons or 14 per cent of the total population of the curfew area as a whole received public assistance. In the Watts area, approximately 24 per cent of the population received such assistance.

Six major welfare programs exist in Los Angeles, five financed by the federal, state and county governments (Old Age Security, Aid to the Disabled, Aid to the Blind, Medical Assistance to the Aged, and Aid to Families with Dependent Children), and one financed by the county alone — General Relief. The costliest of these programs are Old Age Security ($125 million per year in 1965) and Aid to Families with Dependent Children (about $95 million per year in 1965). . . .

Health Problems. Statistics indicate that health conditions of the residents of south central Los Angeles are relatively poor and facilities to provide medical care are insufficient. Infant mortality, for example, is about one and one-half times greater than the city-wide average. Life expectancies are considerably shorter. A far lower percentage of the children are immunized against diphtheria, whooping cough, tetanus, smallpox, and poliomyelitis than in the rest of the county. . . .

The Dull Devastating Spiral of Failure. In examining the sickness in the center of our city, what has depressed and stunned us most is the dull, devastating spiral of failure that awaits the average disadvantaged child in the urban core. His home life all too often fails to give him the incentive and the elementary experience with words and ideas which prepares most children for school. Unprepared and unready, he may not learn to read or write at all; and because he shares his problem with 30 or more in the same classroom, even the efforts of the most dedicated teachers are unavailing. Age, not achievement, passes him on to higher grades, but in most cases he is unable to cope with courses in the upper grades because they demand basic skills which he does not possess. ("Try," a teacher said to us, "to teach history to a child who cannot read.")

Frustrated and disillusioned, the child becomes a discipline problem. Often he leaves school, sometimes before the end of junior high school. (About two-thirds of those who enter the three high schools in the center of the curfew area do not graduate.) He slips into the ranks of the permanent jobless, illiterate and untrained, unemployed and unemployable. All the talk about the millions which the government is spending to aid him raise his expectations but the benefits seldom reach him.

Reflecting this spiral of failure, unemployment in the disadvantaged areas runs two to three times the county average, and the employment available is too often intermittent. A family whose breadwinner is chronically out of work is almost invariably a disintegrating family. Crime rates soar and welfare rolls increase, even faster than the population.

This spiral of failure has a most damaging side effect. Because of the low standard of achievement in the schools in the urban core and adjacent areas, parents of the better students from advantaged backgrounds remove them from these schools, either by changing the location of the family home or by sending the children to private school. In turn, the average achievement level of the schools in the disadvantaged area sinks lower and lower. . . .

The road to the improvement of the condition of the disadvantaged Negro which lies through education and employment is hard and long, but there is no shorter route. The avenue of violence and lawlessness leads to a dead end. To travel the long and difficult road will require courageous leadership and determined participation by all parts of our community, but no task in our times is more important. Of what shall it avail our nation if we can place a man on the moon but cannot cure the sickness in our cities?

Chapter Two

THE AMERICAN
NATIONAL STYLE

Observation and common sense tell us that people from different countries, with different histories and cultures, behave differently in certain situations. In given circumstances — say, when a decision is called for — a group of Americans might interact and decide differently from a group of Chinese, Germans, or Russians. It would be foolish for us to ignore those differences in trying to understand national foreign policies.

Yet when we try to discuss these differences in national behavior, we find ourselves on treacherous ground. In the first place, the nature of the discussion itself virtually forces us to generalize about vast, diversified aggregates as though they were individual, unified wholes. Take this simple statement: "Americans are a very individualistic people." Before accepting such an observation, a careful scientist would probably insist on something like the following procedure. First, "individualism" would have to be clearly defined. Some objective test would have to be devised to measure this trait with high reliability — that is, most of those classified by this test as highly "individualistic" would have to be perceived in fact as highly individualistic by most trained observers. Then this validated test would have to be administered to large random samples of individuals in all — or many — nations. The results would have to be tabulated and tested for statistical significance. Then and only then, if the results sustained it, might the careful scientist accept, with some modifications for greater precision, the claim that "Americans are a very individualistic people." [1] (Actually, we have

---

[1] For a review of literature and a discussion of methodological problems, see Alex Inkeles and Daniel J. Levinson, "National Character: The Study of Modal Personality and Sociocultural Systems," *Handbook of Social Psychology*, Gardner Lindzey (ed.) (Reading, Mass.: Addison-Wesley, 1954), II, 977–1020. The authors suggest that " 'national character'

oversimplified. Many additional control procedures normally would be insisted upon before such a hypothesis could be considered even tentatively established.)

If there were no supporting evidence of this kind, the scientist would consider the suggestion of an observer that "Americans are very individualistic" as limited in value in several respects. It would be limited first by the clarity and concreteness of the observer's conception of individualism; second by the extent and randomness of his observations both in the United States and elsewhere; and finally by his own ability to free himself from nationalistic bias.

Unfortunately, both makers and students of foreign policy often find it necessary to make use of untested assertions of just this kind, despite all these limitations. For the example we have been using, prohibitively high costs and political difficulties would make it nearly impossible to establish with high validity how individualistic Americans are, compared with others. There are, however, some useful general statements about American attitudes toward foreign affairs which *can* be supported by a growing body of survey research data. Some of these will be summarized in Chapter Seven.

This chapter will be devoted to precisely the type of broad untested generalizations we have been warning against. It will deal with what W. W. Rostow has called "the American national style" — the distinctive patterns of response to its internal and international environment which our nation has evolved during its historical experience:

> The concept of the national style is a way of describing how the United States has typically gone about solving its problems. The ultimate motivating forces of nations — like those of the human beings who make them up — are complex and elusive. The recurrent pattern of a nation's performance, however, is more accessible to study and to description. Once the main elements in a national style are established one can consider how, out of the interplay of men and their environment, a national style slowly changes.[2]

American attitudes and ways of doing things have changed, in important respects, over the years — most particularly since World War II. Since a large quantity of survey data relevant to these changes is available, they will be discussed in Chapter Seven.

---

refers to *relatively enduring personality characteristics and patterns that are modal among the adult members of the society*" (p. 983). They indicate that there may well be more than one modal personality in a given society, particularly in a modern industrial nation, but emphasize that the existence of modal national personality types remains to be proven or disproven by empirical research.

2 W. W. Rostow, *The United States in the World Arena* (New York: Harper, 1960), p. xix. See also the Spring, 1958 issue of *Daedalus*, devoted to "The American National Style." The Rostow volume is the most discerning discussion of United States foreign policy between 1941 and 1958 known to the writer.

Nevertheless, key aspects of our national style appear to have crystallized long before even the most rudimentary opinion polling or attitude testing techniques had been developed. What we say here, then, will be based not on the fruits of scientific inquiry, but on the insights recorded by keen native and foreign observers of the American scene from revolutionary times to the present; and on historical study of the ways in which the United States government has in fact acted in foreign affairs. There is no assurance — or even any expectation — that traits here suggested as characteristically American are shared by all Americans or even by a majority of Americans. Often, large groups of Americans react to foreign affairs in diametrically opposed ways. Sometimes the very existence of one distinctive set of responses may give rise to the reactive development of its opposite. In such cases, an appreciation of both these tendencies is important to an understanding of the American approach to foreign affairs. Which of these antithetical tendencies may be characteristic of a majority or plurality of Americans at any given time may not be critical; strong minority tendencies are as likely to prevail as those of the nominal majority.

In America, as elsewhere, foreign policy is made by elites rather than by the populace, and elite values are likely to differ from those of the masses. But American political institutions and traditions ordinarily ensure that the nation's political leaders will share the fundamental value orientations of their followers, at least in part. In addition, the electoral power of the populace is sufficient to set important basic limitations on the freedom of those who make United States foreign policy. Thus, even though some of the attitudes and approaches described here may be characteristic of masses in general rather than particularly American masses, their impact on foreign policy may be greater in the United States than they would be in a nation with less democratic political institutions or more elitist traditions.

Finally, the relative youth of the United States — as compared with European nations — as a participant in the international political community may be an important influence both on the popular attitudes discussed here and on United States foreign policy in general, especially prior to World War II. Some elements of family resemblance between early American foreign policy and the international behavior of the new nations of today will be noted in Chapter Nine.

In sum, the insights put forward in this chapter are certainly challengeable. They are advanced here as meriting the attention of the serious student of foreign policy — at least as a starting point for further inquiry and thoughtful meditation. The reader should be aware of their limitations. But he should remember, too, that in our daily lives we are accustomed to making important decisions — especially in our dealings with other people — on a base no firmer than that. The decisionmaker or statesman cannot afford to wait, as the scientist often can, until all the facts are in. He must do the best he can with the facts he has. So must we. In the last analysis, all that we cherish depends today as it has always in human history on the imperfect judgment of informed individuals doing the best they can in the circumstances.

THE AMERICAN IDENTITY —
INDEPENDENCE FROM EUROPE

The very founding of the new American nation was an assertion of an American identity separate and independent from that of Britain and Europe. Inevitably, then, the major goal of the young republic's foreign policy would be guarding that newly won independence for which the founding fathers had so recently pledged "our lives, our fortunes and our sacred honor."

Even before independence was won, the hazards of entanglement in the "power politics" and diplomatic intrigues engaged in by the ruling houses of Europe were forcefully impressed on the settlers in the New World. "However much they may have desired to carve out their own destiny without let or hindrance," Thomas A. Bailey has noted, "they were repeatedly embroiled in wars of Europe's making. Between 1689 and 1815, England and France fought seven times — nearly sixty years of warfare in one hundred and twenty-six years. . . . And the American people were involved in every one of them, whether they wanted to be or not." [3]

The political doctrines upon which the new nation was based represented a sharp break with the prevailing traditions of the Old World. Europe was monarchical; America republican. Europe was aristocratic and socially hierarchical; America was to be democratic and socially equalitarian. By and large, the colonists who migrated to the New World did so because of their dissatisfaction with the state of affairs under the old order in Europe. Their roots were not in the aristocracy, but in the multitude. If they felt sensitive about the fact that — as foreign observers frequently remarked — America was culturally less refined and "civilized" than Europe, they compensated for this latent suspicion of their inferiority by scorning the pretentious, the "highfalutin," the intellectual attitudes, and manners which they associated with the European aristocracies. Intelligence and ingenuity were much prized. But the suggestion that a man's cultural attainments made him better than his fellows ran against the grain of the American democratic experiment — and the man whose manners appeared to make this suggestion was looked on as not merely snobbish and despicable, but as "un-American." To this day, America remains a land in which the intellectual pretends to speak the language of the commoner more often than vice versa.

[3] *A Diplomatic History of the American People* (4th ed.; New York: Appleton-Century-Crofts, 1950), pp. 5–6.

In America, then, unlike Europe, each man was as good as the next. And from the belief that all men were created equal and had an equal right to their own opinions, it was for many but a small step to the corollary that all opinions, too, were of equal value. Wrote Lord Bryce, one of the shrewdest of foreign commentators on the American scene, in 1888:

> Since every question that arises in the conduct of government is either a question of ends or a question of means, errors may be committed by the ruling power either in fixing on wrong ends or in choosing wrong means to secure those ends. It is now . . . at last agreed that as the masses are better judges of what will conduce to their own happiness than are the classes placed above them, they must be allowed to determine ends . . . but assuming the end to be given, who is best qualified to select the means for its accomplishment? To do so needs in many cases a knowledge of the facts, a skill in interpreting them, a power of forecasting the results of measures, unattainable by the mass of mankind. . . .[4]

Insistence on positive independence and a distinctly *national* identity provided the psychological foundations for what has come to be called — not altogether accurately — the tradition of isolation. The object of "isolationism" was not to cut the United States off from the outside world, but to avoid "entangling alliances" which would allow European nations to help define America's national interests. The same note has been sounded by some of the newly independent nations of our own day, discomfiting many Americans unaware or forgetful of their nation's early history. ". . . It does not matter what war takes place; we will not take part in it unless we have to defend ourselves. If I join any of these big groups I lose my identity; I have no identity left. . . . Are we going to continue to be dragged and tie ourselves to Europe's troubles, Europe's hatred and Europe's conflicts? I hope not. . . ." These words were uttered not by George Washington in 1796 (though they well might have been), but by Prime Minister Nehru of India in 1955.[5]

THE LAND OF OPPORTUNITY

The American character was shaped, above all, by the American continent. In Europe land was scarce but on the American frontier it was abundant; and there were few vested interests to keep a good man down. This abundance made it possible for Americans to compete with nature, rather than with each other. In an economy of scarcity what one man gains, another must lose; and the same stroke of fortune which reinforces one man's self-confidence and optimism stimulates in another resignation and

---

4 *The American Commonwealth* (New York: Macmillan, 1893), II, pp. 582–583.
5 Quoted in McLellan, Olson, and Sondermann, *Theory and Practice of International Relations* (Englewood Cliffs, N.J.: Prentice-Hall, 1960), p. 323.

pessimism. But in America, ingenuity and industry generally yielded their promised rewards, and the American's optimism — his faith in man's capacity to forge his own destiny — became a central part of the American character.[6]

The environment and doctrines of the new nation converged, moreover, to make "nothing succeed like success." In aristocratic Europe money could not buy social status. In America, material success conferred almost automatically the only kind of social status available. If virtue brought success, then success must be an indication of virtue. Did not the laissez faire economic doctrine demonstrate that earnings were payment for productive economic contributions to the society, and that he served his country's interests best who best served his own? What more compelling evidence, then, than wealth that a man was contributing to the growth of his country and merited the respect of his countrymen? Did not the Calvinist ethic suggest that those whom the Lord had chosen might be known by their earthly success in their "calling" and by the dignified way of life which that success made possible? Truly, he who succeeded in America was thrice-blessed.

But if there was no success quite like American success, there was, correspondingly, no failure quite equal to an American failure. The European aristocrat who suffered financial reverses still had his social status and his good name to fall back on. And should the European commoner fail to better his lot in life, he could always console himself with the knowledge that this was in the nature of things and was the system's fault rather than his own. The luckless American enjoyed no such solace. In his own eyes as well as those of his fellows, his failure was his own. It is no accident that to this day equalitarian America spends a lower percentage of its national income on social welfare for its "failures," than does any major state of less equalitarian Europe.

Continental abundance, therefore, made America "the land of perfectionism," as Henry Steele Commager has commented:

> The American knew that nothing was impossible, in his brave new world, and history confirmed his intuition. Progress was not, to him, a mere philosophical ideal but a commonplace of experience, and he could not understand why foreigners should see vulgar realities where he saw visions. He was outraged at any failure, at any imperfection even, could not tolerate a depression or a military defeat, could not acquiesce in any inadequacy of culture, or, as Roussy de Sales pointed out, even of marital infelicity.[7]

A former member of the State Department's Policy Planning Staff sug-

[6] See David M. Potter, *People of Plenty: Economic Abundance and the American Character* (Chicago: University of Chicago Press, 1954).

[7] H. S. Commager (ed.), *America in Perspective* (New York: Mentor, 1948), p. xiv.

gested in 1952 something of the restrictions which this American characteristic imposes on our policymakers:

> . . . Power is the capacity to achieve intended results. It is always
> limited. Not all the elements bearing on a nation's destiny can ever be
> brought completely within the nation's control.
>
> Yet some of my friends, and many persons in this country, some of
> whom write editorials or sit in seats of authority, persist in believing the
> desirable and achievable situation for the State to be in is one of perfect
> efficacy in its world relations. When perfect efficacy is not obtained, these
> people feel dismay and sense betrayal. . . .
>
> This is consequential. As an accountable Government, our Govern-
> ment must stay within the limits permitted by public opinion. To the
> degree that unrealistic notions about what is feasible are factors in pub-
> lic opinion, unnecessary limits are imposed on the scope of action in
> foreign affairs, and rigidities harmful to our true interests result. This is
> borne constantly upon the mind of anyone having responsibilities in
> the making of foreign policy.[8]

Short time perspectives, moreover, are built into the American political
system. If a President's policies do not bear fruit within less than four
years, he will usually not be in office to reap the harvest. A successor may
reverse — and thereby undo — them. Within eight years, at the most, a new
administration will be on the scene and foreign policy planning will be in
the hands of a new group of officials. The electoral perspectives of members
of the House of Representatives from competitive districts must be even
shorter. Up for re-election every other year, they will not be helped much by
the ability to claim that they have supported measures which may bring
results in another decade or so, if all goes well. Here we observe another
legacy of the American frontier: the emphasis on the visible and concrete
as against the abstract and intangible. The American wants to see results;
not listen to theoretical analyses. When he watches a sports event — as he
frequently does — he wants to know first of all who is winning and who is
losing. And he wants to "know the score" in plain numbers that can be
toted up on a board. He finds installment buying plans which permit him
to get something tangible *now* in return for something less visible, to be
paid later, well-nigh irresistible.[9] But effective foreign policy measures require a long-range orientation. And usually they must be paid for now in
the hope that something barely perceptible (though vital) will be gained in

8 Charles Burton Marshall, "The Nature of Foreign Policy," *Department of State Bulletin,* Vol. XXVI, no. 664 (March 17, 1952), 415–420.

9 The spread of installment buying in Europe and Japan suggests that susceptibility to
"buy now, pay later" appeals may be characteristic of the masses in high mass consumption,
private enterprise economies in general, rather than of Americans alone. Nevertheless,
American business and American advertising have been pioneers in the use of this device.
And, as noted previously, the effect of mass attitudes on foreign policy may be much
greater in the United States than in nations with more elitist political institutions and
traditions.

return at some unspecifiable future date. Thus, much to the nation's detriment, those who advocate the kind of foreign policies most likely to prove effective in the long run are often at a critical disadvantage in the political marketplace.

The effect of the American experience and the American dream upon popular attitudes toward foreign affairs has been pervasive and significant. First, until the frontier disappeared near the beginning of the twentieth century, it turned American energies inward toward exploiting a continent rather than outward toward international affairs. Throughout most of the nation's history, foreign affairs have been of secondary importance to the American people. In Europe, aristocrats whose fortune and status were secure could afford to devote themselves to diplomacy. The able American, however, was normally — and understandably — engaged in the effort to win his own status and fortune. Occasionally, to be sure, foreign affairs intruded unavoidably into American life and distracted Americans from their more enduring concerns. But these unpleasant intrusions were to be ignored whenever possible. And if the system of European power politics was such that it forced Americans to participate in Europe's quarrels against our will, then the object of our participation must be to alter that system itself. Why could not Europeans learn from our example to keep the peace on their continent as we had on ours?

The consequent sporadic quality of American involvement in foreign affairs has caused George F. Kennan, one of the nation's most distinguished contemporary diplomats, to

> . . . sometimes wonder whether in this respect a democracy is not uncomfortably similar to one of those prehistoric monsters with a body as long as this room and a brain the size of a pin; he lies there in his comfortable primeval mud and pays little attention to his environment; he is slow to wrath — in fact, you practically have to whack his tail off to make him aware that his interests are being disturbed; but, once he grasps this, he lays about him with such blind determination that he not only destroys his adversary but largely wrecks his native habitat. You wonder whether it would not have been wiser for him to have taken a little more interest in what was going on at an earlier date and to have seen whether he could not have prevented some of these situations from arising instead of proceeding from an undiscriminating indifference to a holy wrath equally undiscriminating.[10]

One important effect of the normal indifference of the many to foreign affairs has been to increase the influence of the few. Relatively small groups of Americans with an interest to defend or an axe to grind have been able

[10] *American Diplomacy, 1900–1950* (Chicago: University of Chicago Press, 1951), p. 66. Copyright 1951 by the University of Chicago. Reprinted by permission. See also Gabriel Almond, *The American People and Foreign Policy* (New York: Praeger, 1960), chaps. 3–6. Originally published in 1950 by Harcourt, Brace and Company.

— particularly when organized — to exercise an influence on foreign policy all out of proportion to their number. The ability of special interests to secure tariff protection even when the President considers it is not in the national interest is one example. And the American tradition of single-minded pursuit of private interests — even perhaps to the neglect of community-wide concerns — offers some ideological sanction for such actions.

A NATION OF IMMIGRANTS

Another major force in the molding of the American national style has been the diversity of the national and cultural origins of the American people. The most obvious result has been the influence of ethnic minorities on American politics. Urban political machines in key swing states with a large number of electoral votes have often been built up with the support of recent immigrants. It has been an important political maxim, therefore, that ethnic group support must not be alienated by the espousal of foreign policies offensive to their lands of birth. Since large numbers of "hyphenated-Americans" represented all the major powers of Western Europe, this maxim tended to add to the political virtues of the policy of isolation. By not taking sides in Europe's quarrels, American leaders could avoid giving offense to any of the major ethnic groups whose support they were wooing, and, at the same time, could avoid posing political issues which would divide the citizenry of the young nation. When in the early twentieth century the Wilson administration felt obliged to pursue a course which led to war with Germany, ethnically rooted political divisions were created which continue to play a significant role in American politics half a century later.[11]

But there is a price to be paid for the forging of unity out of diversity. Other nations built their unity upon a long history, a common culture and language, the symbols and trappings of monarchy, and often a state religion as well. The American nation has had to find other unifying symbols and forces.

One of the most important of these has been the American commitment to democracy. Many foreign observers have noted the unusual and almost unique citizen attachment to political ideals and institutions in the United States.[12] The principles underlying the American Revolution and the

[11] See Samuel Lubell, *The Future of American Politics* (3rd ed., rev.; New York: Harper, 1965), chap. 7.

[12] A major study based on a cross-national survey confirms this observation. Of about 1,000 citizens questioned in each of five countries — the United States, Britain, Germany, Italy, and Mexico — 85 per cent of the Americans volunteered that their government or political institutions were among the things about their country they were most proud of. The comparable percentage for British respondents was 46, for Germans, 7, for Italians, 3, for Mexicans, 30. Gabriel Almond and Sidney Verba, *The Civic Culture* (Boston: Little, Brown, 1965), p. 64. Originally published by Princeton University Press in 1963. This study also found Americans much more likely than those in the other countries studied to feel satisfaction when going to the polls, to enjoy election campaigns, to think that the ordinary

American experiment have been viewed as universally valid. All peoples must echo them, even if their rulers did not. American sympathy has gone out to oppressed fellow human beings, and it became part of the American mission to provide aid — short of war — to democratic nations and subjugated peoples whenever possible. When America did go to war, it was never a war against the common people of our adversary. Inevitably, they had to be, in their hearts, on our side, and, freed to express their inner longings by the defeat of their aristocratic (or, later, totalitarian) oppressors, they would hail us as their liberators.[13] It followed also that since whatever actions America took were actions in the service of democracy and freedom, it was entirely appropriate to judge by different sets of standards the foreign policies of the United States, on the one hand, and the policies of states devoted to dynastic aggrandizement, on the other. When European nations extended their rule to new territories, this was imperialism or aggression. When the United States extended its domain to new territories, peacefully or by force of arms, this was an advance for democracy. It was not aggression, but "manifest destiny" — the destiny of the United States to lead the world to a new birth of freedom and a better way of life.

Recent research has demonstrated that although virtually all Americans respond with reverence and approval to the terms democracy and freedom, they frequently disagree considerably as to the precise meanings of these terms.[14] This is not really surprising, since one of the primary functions of such terms was the creation of at least an apparent consensus by submerging differences and emphasizing values which were widely shared. The vaguer the term, the greater the number of regionally and ethnically diverse Americans who could respond to it emotionally and rally beneath its banner. Thus, northern Negro and southern white alike could dedicate themselves to an all-out effort in the name of democracy. If it were to be insisted, however, that the exact meaning of that word be spelled out in advance instead of allowing each to interpret it as he saw fit, it might have proved more difficult to enlist the energies of both in behalf of a common cause. However, once immediate goals have been achieved, the piper must be paid. Someone is bound to feel disillusioned, even betrayed, by the disparity between the concrete results of his labors and his own interpretation of the ideal toward which he thought himself striving.

---

man should be active in his local community, to feel they can do something about an unjust national law or regulation, and to trust other people generally. *Ibid.*, pp. 108, 127, 142, and 213.

[13] Ironically, communist ideology makes the same distinction between peoples and their governments — on grounds of Marxist class analysis. See Chapter Ten.

[14] See James W. Prothro and C. W. Grigg, "Fundamental Principles of Democracy: Bases of Agreement and Disagreement," *Journal of Politics* (Spring, 1960), 276–294; and Herbert McClosky, "Consensus and Ideology in American Politics," *The American Political Science Review*, LVIII, no. 2 (June, 1964), 361–382.

This need for idealistic slogans as a source of unity seems also to have contributed to the American tendency to dichotomize, to view the world as one of competing moralistic essences. Influenced further, in some cases, by the legacy of the stark metaphysics of fundamentalist Protestantism, many Americans have tended to view the international scene as a struggle between the forces of Good and the forces of Evil, between Freedom and Democracy and Peace represented by the United States, and Tyranny and Oppression and Aggression represented by its adversaries. (America's allies belong to the Free World even when — like Salazar's Portugal, Ngo Dinh Diem's Vietnam, or Batista's Cuba — they happen to be dictatorships.) In such a struggle it goes without saying that compromise is immoral and that the only acceptable outcome must be the complete triumph of Virtue over Vice. To suggest that Virtue cannot conquer Vice is to suggest that American material and moral power is inadequate to fulfill America's destiny: a suggestion which seems to contradict the whole burden of the American experience in taming a continent. To suggest that Virtue can but *should* not conquer Vice is to flinch contemptibly from the nation's responsibility as bearer of the American Idea, to appease the forces of Evil and allow them to corrupt and corrode the moral fiber of American life.

The American emphasis on the art of salesmanship has also helped to encourage this penchant for dichotomy. To make the potential customer's decision easier, it is standard operating procedure to exaggerate both the virtues of the product to be sold and the dire consequences of failing to purchase it. The pervasive voices of American advertising not only promise that the buyer of the right cake of soap will be young, lovely, and engaged, they warn that failure to use same may leave one a social outcast. Devotees of political panaceas often try to "sell" their programs in the same way. And mass media, interested in the sales produced by the spectacular and the dramatic, tend to emphasize the most extreme arguments advanced by each side. Advocates of the seating of Communist China in the United Nations, for example, contend that this would be a major step toward reducing East-West tensions. Opponents insist that it would totally destroy the United Nations. What might best be viewed as a tactical problem, to be handled in accordance with the requirements of overall American strategy in world affairs, may thus come to be seen as a fundamental moral issue to be dealt with in terms of eternal moral principles. Thus another increment of executive flexibility in foreign affairs may be lost.[15]

It is not only the different views of different Americans at the same time which put a premium on vague abstractions, but the different views of the same Americans at different times. America has been a nation of immigrants and a nation of rapid social and economic change. As the children of im-

15 See Sheldon Appleton, *The Eternal Triangle? Communist China, The United States and The United Nations* (East Lansing, Mich.: Michigan State University Press, 1961).

migrants attended American public schools and became assimilated into
American life; as the farmer moved to the city where advances in technology
had increased opportunities for employment; as the industrialist's son, born
to wealth, searched for new arenas in which to prove his manhood and
worth — as these Americans changed their styles of life, they changed their
values. And value terms which were not too precise in their content made it
possible to do this by maintaining allegiance to the same symbols while altering their content — a process much more psychologically satisfactory
than the outright rejection of the values inculcated by one's parents. The
trenchant Tocqueville saw this before the Civil War:

> . . . Democratic nations have a taste, and sometimes a passion, for
> general ideas . . . as their situation in life is forever changing, they are
> never held fast to any of their opinions by the certain tenure of their
> fortunes. Men living in democratic countries are, then, apt to entertain
> unsettled ideas, and they require loose expressions to convey them. As
> they never know whether the idea they express today will be appropriate
> to the new position they may occupy tomorrow, they naturally acquire a
> liking for abstract terms. An abstract term is like a box with a false bot-
> tom: you may put in it what ideas you please, and take them out again
> without being observed. . . .[16]

The conflict between parental and peer group values characteristic of
immigrant America has been reflected in value conflicts *within* as well as
among individuals. Schooled in the virtues of Christian humility and unselfishness, the ambitious American nevertheless is pressured to pursue self-
oriented goals by aggressive means. If he does not, he must suffer the
penalties of failure in a highly competitive society. This value conflict has
imposed considerable psychological stress on many Americans — particularly men. Often this stress has been dealt with by *compartmentalization*,
that is, by following an idealistic ethic in one's personal life, and an expedient in one's business affairs. Thus the "Sunday Christian" — scrupulous, generous, and compassionate in personal relationships, but ruthless
and willing to bend both law and morals to immediate needs in his business dealings.

The confusion that these conflicting sets of standards may create is well
illustrated by the events culminating in the Hungarian "freedom fighters"
revolt of November, 1965. For several years, responsible United States officials and Voice of America broadcasters had spoken repeatedly of the United
States' unwillingness to accept the permanent enslavement of the peoples of
Eastern Europe. Their liberation was declared to be an important goal of
United States foreign policy. Precisely *how* liberation might be accomplished
or what its costs might be, however, was not discussed with any precision. It

[16] *Democracy in America*, trans. *Henry Reeve* (New York: Oxford University Press,
1947; London: 1959), pp. 339–340.

would be surprising if this idealistic verbal policy did not help in at least some small way to encourage discontented Hungarian students and others to expect that American aid might be forthcoming if they should make an all-out attempt to "liberate" their own people. When revolt came, however, the policy that prevailed was based on expediential calculations of American national interest. The liberation of Hungary was devoutly to be wished, to be sure. But the entry of Soviet tanks into Budapest suggested that the price of this liberation might be war between the Soviet Union and the United States, a prospect apparently less pleasing to both policymakers and the public than the prospect of continued Hungarian "enslavement." By not posing the issue before November, 1956 as a conflict between ideal and expediential values, our policymakers had spared many Americans the unpleasant necessity of coming to terms with reality. It may be that some Hungarian "freedom fighters" paid for this favor with their lives. As Abraham Kaplan has put it, "What is needed . . . is not more idealism, but more realistic ideals, . . ." [17] (The problem of finding a more integrated ethic upon which foreign policy decisions may be based will be explored in Chapter Eight.

It is difficult to predict in advance whether politically aware Americans will tend to view a given foreign policy problem in an idealistic or pragmatic context. Most often, some will see the question from one of these standpoints, and some from the other. To maximize public support for his foreign policy, therefore, an American political leader is likely to try to rationalize policy decisions on *both* idealistic and pragmatic grounds, whatever the actual considerations underlying the policy may be. When moral and pragmatic values in fact conflict, such rationalizations may require considerable distortion. This, in turn, may produce rigidity as well as confusion in the long run. Rigidity because it will be found difficult to alter on grounds of expediency a position justified on the grounds of moral principle. Confusion because both our adversaries and our friends may fail to perceive clearly our real purposes.

At a given moment, for example, American policymakers may think it prudent to announce their willingness to defend the islands of Quemoy and Matsu, just off the China coast, against possible Communist attack. Underlying this decision may be the expediential calculation that the loss of these islands would lower the morale of our ally, the Chinese Nationalist government on Taiwan (Formosa), while at the same time Chinese Communist naval and air strength is not great enough to pose a threat to the islands, given a minimum of American material support. But the official announcement of this policy would be likely to declare it to be based primarily on the principle of defending freedom against Communist aggression. Suppose that, some years later, conditions should happen to change so that the loss of

17 "American Ethics and Public Policy," *Daedalus* (Spring, 1958), p. 48.

Matsu and Quemoy would not seriously impair the morale of the residents of Taiwan. Suppose further that Chinese Communist air and naval forces had grown by this time to the point where only large-scale United States bombing of mainland China would suffice to defeat a Communist attempt to take over the offshore islands. An American leader seeking to alter United States policy on the defense of these islands because of these changed conditions would undoubtedly be criticized as having abandoned freedom to Communist aggression — even if careful provision were made to evacuate all of the relatively small number of inhabitants of the islands who chose to leave.

The instability and compartmentalization of values which we have been discussing also help to explain the tendency to extreme swings of mood commented upon earlier. Unable to look to the values of his (often immigrant) parents as a practical guide to everyday conduct, the American — particularly the urban American — has usually looked to his peer group instead. It is the opinions of his schoolmates, his co-workers, his friends which mold his own opinions. The American is eager to be liked. As the nation has become increasingly characterized by the growth of large organizations, likability — the ability to get along rather than merely to produce — has become crucial to the American's economic success. And one essential in getting along is to keep your opinions from moving too far out of line with those of the groups to which you belong. With so many people striving to keep their opinions in line with those of their fellows, it is not surprising that ideas and policies sometimes come to or fall out of fashion, like women's hats, and that movements of opinion concerning foreign affairs — opinions often only superficially held — can be very rapid.[18]

The ethnic, religious, and political diversity of America has helped to produce still another important trait which warrants mention. Since Americans frequently disagreed, at least latently, on substantive political goals, much of the American political consensus seems to have been built around agreement as to the *procedures* by which these substantive disagreements could be settled. In a land of diversity, agreement upon constitutional procedures was an indispensable condition of national unity. Thus Americans, whose frontier tradition permits them to wink at the law or take it into their own hands in some situations, view their constitutional order with a respect bordering on reverence. By and large, they consider the political order which the laws represent and guard a good order. The laws themselves have been sanctioned as expressions of the people's will, rather than being viewed — as they often have been elsewhere — as the arbitrary impositions of despots. Needed reforms could be made in good time by following established procedures. Though prohibition is but the most conspicuous of many failures to reform American morals by legislation, such failures have generally

18 See Almond, *op. cit.*, esp. chap. 4.

been seen as the exceptions which proved the rule that when something went wrong, "there oughta be a law" to set it right.[19] In conducting sit-ins and protest demonstrations against particular laws they condemn, Americans affirm their respect for the concept of the law in general — their conviction that laws are important and ought to accord with justice. The supreme act of disrespect for law is not dramatic defiance in an effort to make it right, but a cynical lack of concern either for its rightness or — in the absence of a policeman — for its observance.

It has often been said that Americans tend to project their view of the association between law and morality onto the international scene. George F. Kennan has written:

> . . . I see the most serious fault of our past policy formulation to lie in something that I might call the legalistic-moralistic approach to international problems. . . .
>
> . . . This belief undoubtedly represents in part an attempt to transpose the Anglo-Saxon concept of individual law into the international field and to make it applicable to governments as it is applicable here at home to individuals. It must also stem in part from the memory of the origin of our own political system — from the recollection that we were able, through acceptance of a common institutional and juridical framework, to reduce to harmless dimensions the conflicts of interest and aspiration among the original thirteen colonies and to bring them all into an order and peaceful relationship with one another. Remembering this, people are unable to understand that what might have been possible for the thirteen colonies in a given set of circumstances might not be possible in the wider international field.
>
> . . . We tend to underestimate the violence of national maladjustments and discontents elsewhere in the world if we think that they would always appear to other people as less important than the preservation of the juridical tidiness of international life. . . .[20]

AMERICAN ATTITUDES TOWARD PEACE AND WAR

In keeping with the bent toward dichotomy previously noted, Americans have thought of peace and war as mutually exclusive and antithetical states of affairs. Normally, Americans go about their business of building a better America at peace. This is the way things should be. At times, the aggressive policies of some evil or misguided nation may force the United States,

---

[19] Almond and Verba's findings, cited above, that Americans are more likely than others to believe they can do something about an unjust national law, and to take pride in their political institutions, are relevant here also. In addition, American and British respondents were more likely than those in Germany, Italy, and Mexico to expect to receive equal treatment at the hands of government bureaucrats and the police. *Op cit.*, p. 70.

[20] *Op. cit.*, pp. 95–97. Copyright 1951 by the University of Chicago. Reprinted by permission.

reluctantly, to go to war. In this case, the nation's goal must be to restore the peace and to punish the aggressors so they will learn not to disturb our tranquility again. Then the United States will be free to return to "normalcy" once more.

This attitude is reflected in the way Americans approach both the waging of war and the enjoyment of peace. When Americans fight, they fight not to achieve specific political objectives, but simply to win — that is, to destroy the enemy's will or capacity to resist. Thus, in World War II, Winston Churchill's suggestions that military operations be conducted with an eye toward the situation that would exist years after the conclusion of the war itself were not received sympathetically by American leaders. Nor was there much disposition to worry about what might be the postwar costs of Soviet entry into the war against Japan. Immediate military objectives were predominant.[21]

When the war ended, the fighting was obviously over. The "boys" were brought home, and the nation rejoiced. Within less than three years, however, it became clear that all the nation's wartime sacrifices had somehow failed once again to make the world safe for democracy and secure for the American nation. The war had begun with Nazi aggression in Eastern Europe. Now joint allied pledges that free elections would be held in the countries of this region were dishonored and, step by step, Poland, Hungary, Rumania, Bulgaria, Albania, and Yugoslavia were brought under the control of the Soviet Union. America's great ally during the war against fascism was soon revealed to be the political and ideological pivot of a messianic international movement seeking the destruction of the American way of life. In 1948, the Communist seizure of power in Czechoslovakia by subversion stirred memories of Hitler's 1938 maneuvers at Munich. The blockade of West Berlin followed, to be countered by a dramatic airlift to supply the besieged Berliners.

These events forced Americans to realize that there was a threat of war once again, and the United States began to organize the North Atlantic Treaty Organization (NATO) to fight such a war if necessary. But the war Americans were preparing to fight was the war they had always fought: a total war culminating in total victory. Not only the American people, but many political and military leaders seem to have been caught off balance by the limited Communist initiative in Korea. Had the United States anticipated that hostilities might begin with this sort of move, diplomatic warnings and policy statements might have sufficed to avert this aggression. But when the North Korean attack came, Gallup polls showed that most Americans actually believed that World War III had begun. That there could be any other kind of war seems to have been a new idea to most Americans. Surveys of American opinion concerning United States involvement in Viet-

21 See Rostow, *op. cit.*, pp. 45 ff.

nam in the mid-1960's suggest that although some Americans came to accept the notion of limited war as a result of our experience in Korea, a large segment of the electorate continued to cling to the traditional view. (See the case study dealing with American opinion and the war in Vietnam in Chapter Seven.)

The grave and totally unexpected developments of the years immediately following World War II were highly distressing to the American people. Had the great efforts and sorrows of the war years won only the substitution of international Communism for international Fascism as a threat to world peace and freedom? Most Americans began slowly to adjust to the hard new facts of international life, all the more embittered and resentful because the dreams and promises which had sustained them during the war had proven so insubstantial. America some said, more in bewilderment than in reproach, always wins the war and loses the peace.

Some went further. Unable to live with the notion that they had been betrayed by their own hopes and conceptions of political reality, they sought to trace the betrayal to others. If they could prove the fault lay outside themselves they need not undertake the series of painful reassessments involved in altering their own ideas and images of the world. Those, especially, who had always seen Franklin Roosevelt as a dangerous subverter of traditional American institutions found a satisfying explanation of the nation's postwar predicament ready at hand. The fruits of American victory had been consumed by Roosevelt and his New Dealers — by their woolly headed approach to communism, or even, perhaps, by their treason.

This extreme view was never espoused by a majority of the American people in the postwar years, but it has played an important role in recent American politics. It helped to nourish support for McCarthyism during the 1950's and for the John Birch society during the 1960's. And in a more subtle form it has undoubtedly influenced the opinions on public issues of many American moderates.

Compartmentalized conceptions of war and peace can be a serious national liability in an age of "cold war" — a new expression coined by Americans to describe a new experience. For national ends today are pursued by a wide variety of means which are neither 100 per cent peaceful nor 100 per cent warlike. Today, the instruments of national policy utilized by major nations include: cultural exchanges; propaganda pronouncements; trade and other economic transactions; technical, economic, and military aid; agitation by local Communist parties; espionage; guerrilla warfare — with varying degrees of open or undercover outside support; limited conventional war; and at least the threat of limited and all-out nuclear war.[22]

In the face of some of these tactics, Americans find it difficult to get their bearings. Is Communist subversion in Czechoslovakia an act of war or of

[22] The gradations are infinite. See Chapter Eleven.

peace? What about a blockade of Berlin? The employment of Chinese Communist "volunteers" in Korea? The guerrilla war carried on in South Vietnam by Vietnamese forces, armed and supported in part by Communist China and the Soviet Union? Though a large number of Americans today seem prepared to support limited United States responses to limited Communist initiatives, the policymaker who calls for such limited responses must expect to be criticized — by some because he has acted too weakly in a situation in which the nation is clearly at war; by others because he has acted too belligerently in peacetime.

Even more dangerous in the missile age is the tendency to think of "war" and "peace" as though they have clear and specific meanings, apparent to everyone. As words, "war" and "peace" can be made the subjects or objects of sentences just as words like "book," "pencil," or "automobile" can. It is tempting to think of them as having concrete referents in the real world which can be pointed to, like books, pencils, and cars. But "war" and "peace" are more like such words as "good," "beautiful," and "love." Ask thirty people to write exactly what such words mean to them and you will get thirty different definitions, some of them mutually contradictory. (Thus the tribulations of the bemused teenager seeking to discover what love "really is," and whether he or she is really in it.)

This fallacy is related to another: thinking of peace and war as ends in themselves. Every sane American and every sane Russian is of course "for" peace. Nobody wants to see his country devastated in a nuclear holocaust. Soviet leaders declare that peace is their most cherished goal. They mean it. So do American policymakers when they extol the blessings of peace. It is easy to rush from these assumptions to the conclusion that, if only the truth were known, Soviet goals and our own are really the same, and that the real problem is to break down the ideological rigidities which obscure this.

This is a happy conclusion, but not an accurate one. The correct conclusion is rather that the soviet leaders do not mean by "peace" the same thing that most Americans do. Neither of us means by "peace" merely the absence of "war." If this were all we wanted, either of us could have it simply by submitting to the other. What Americans really mean is that we want to be left in peace to enjoy our high standard of living and our free political institutions. What the Soviet leaders mean, following Marxist–Leninist doctrine, is that the virtues of the Communist system inevitably will enable it to prevail all over the world through economic and political competition. Though they are willing to fight for this end if necessary — as we are willing to fight for our goals — they prefer to achieve it by peaceful *means*, without a mutually destructive war. At least some of our goals, therefore, are different and opposed.

Thinking of war as an end in itself is just as illusory and hazardous, because it stops us from thinking beyond the war into the future. Thinking in this way therefore persuades us that victory in war can achieve whatever we want it to — even to the point that "victory" itself becomes our actual objective. This, in turn, may keep us from facing the unpleasant fact that there are some goals which cannot be achieved — even by the United States of America — either by peaceful means or by waging war. A Communist-dominated Eastern European country, for example, cannot be made "free" by fighting a nuclear war over its territory, any more than some of our allies in Latin America, South Vietnam, and South Korea can be made democratic by the application of diplomatic pressure and the distribution of American aid dollars. Perhaps American hopes in World War II were betrayed precisely because many failed to understand what the economic dislocations, disintegration of colonial empires, and shifts in the world balance of power brought about by the war would mean for the future. All that our victory achieved — and it was no small achievement — was to prevent Hitler and the Axis from taking over the world and running it their way. It made the world safe *from* Nazi fascism, but it did not — and could not — make it safe *for* democracy. Only the attainment of decent world living standards, the gradual evolution of democratic traditions, and the slow growth of genuine world community could do that. We won an unconditional surrender, but a very limited victory.

Today, a nuclear war with the Soviet Union and China, even if won, would leave a war-torn America in custody of a devastated and impoverished world. Would the survivors — many of them with memories of mothers, sons, husbands, and homes destroyed by our hydrogen bombs — be grateful to us for "liberating" them? Who would feed them? Would such a world be safer for democracy than the one brought into being by our unconditional victory in 1945?

THE HERITAGE OF HISTORY

The geographic situation, historic origins, and domestic experience of a nation incline it to deal with outsiders in certain accustomed ways. These dealings evolve into a national style through continuous testing and tempering in the crucible of international reality. Deeply ingrained approaches may be abandoned if they are clearly and repeatedly perceived as unsuccessful in achieving national goals. Other approaches to international affairs, adopted almost accidentally at first, may in time win popular acceptance as policies of unchallengeable wisdom and virtue, if they have the appearance of success. Here again, it may seem that nothing succeeds like apparent success; for traditional policies themselves may become useful foci of national unity. Their names may be used by leaders seeking support for policies only tenuously related to the traditional one. And, of course, any successes which seem to be won in the name of the traditional policy will add to its aura and to the regard in which it is held by a proud and grateful people.

"No Entangling Alliances." [23] One of the earliest and most famous of American approaches to foreign affairs was that enunciated by George Washington in his Farewell Address to the American People (September 19, 1796):

> Europe has a set of primary interests, which to us have none, or a very remote relation. Hence she must be engaged in frequent controversies, the cause of which are essentially foreign to our concerns. Hence, therefore, it must be unwise in us to implicate ourselves, by artificial ties, in the ordinary vicissitudes of her politics, or the ordinary combinations and collisions of her friendships and enmities.
>
> Our detached and distant situation invites and enables us to pursue a different course. . . .
>
> Why forego the advantages of so peculiar a situation? Why quit our own to stand upon foreign ground? Why, by interweaving our destiny with that of any part of Europe, entangle our peace and prosperity in the toils of European ambition, rivalship, interest, humor, or caprice?
>
> 'Tis our true policy to steer clear of permanent alliances with any portion of the foreign world. . . .
>
> Taking care always to keep ourselves, by suitable establishments, in a respectable defensive posture, we may safely trust to temporary alliances for extraordinary emergencies. . . .

We have already noted the colonists' resentment of being involved as pawns in European conflicts and their disdain for the diplomatic intrigues of European aristocrats. These factors, combined with the spirit of independence and separation from Europe which animated the Revolution and the young nation's preoccupation with the exploitation of the American continent, made noninvolvement in the affairs of Europe a highly attractive policy to Americans. Yet the firm — even rigid — attachment to this policy evidenced by future generations of Americans was as much the result of the perceived historical successes of this policy as of its origins.

It is true that the United States did not entirely manage to stay out of Europe's quarrels in the century that followed. Less than two decades after Washington's warning, the United States became involved in the final phase of the Napoleonic wars — and on the French dictator's side. The defense of America's trading rights as a neutral, and the maddening British practice of impressing American seamen into His Majesty's navy were the official — and to some extent also the actual — bases for American involvement. Another important factor was the militant leadership of young Henry Clay and the congressional "War Hawks," who yearned for an occasion to add Canada and perhaps Florida (the colony of Britain's ally, Spain) to the territory of the United States. The fighting was limited to North America and the high seas. American privateers acquitted themselves nobly, but Canada proved more difficult to overrun than the War Hawks had anticipated, and in 1814 British troops invaded the United States, captured Washington, and

---

[23] The phrase is not Washington's, but Jefferson's.

burned the Capitol and the White House. The peace treaty signed soon afterward was a peace of mutual exhaustion, which simply restored the prewar territorial status quo and made no promises whatever as to future respect for American neutrality. Nevertheless, Andrew Jackson's victory at New Orleans — weeks after the treaty had been signed, but before the news of its signing had crossed the Atlantic — led many Americans to think of the war as a victory.

The United States was not to be involved in another European war for more than a century. Throughout that period, therefore, the policy of nonintervention was a conspicuous success. The fundamental reason was that there were no general European wars in the century following the Congress of Vienna in 1815. Only Britain had the naval power to challenge the United States in North America during this century; and Britain had neither the desire nor the respite from involvement in European power politics to attempt to regain her American colonies. In this century more lives were lost in combat in the United States than in Europe, and one of the great triumphs of American diplomacy in this period was not keeping the United States out of Europe's internal strife, but keeping Britain and Europe out of our own civil war. Over the whole of this century, Europe's internal distresses, the breadth of the Atlantic, and Britain's occasional enlightened beneficence made it possible for successive generations of Americans to enjoy unprecedented international peace and domestic prosperity. This was attributed — in part correctly — to our adherence to the sage counsel of the Father of the Republic.

In the American hemisphere, these same considerations again proved to be the essential ingredients in the American recipe for almost continuous national success. The purchase of Louisiana in 1803 doubled the land area of the United States. The Floridas were purchased from 1810 to 1819. Annexation of the Lone Star Republic of Texas in 1845 soon brought war with Mexico, which also claimed the territory. The peace treaty of 1848 ceded to the United States not only Texas, but most of the American Southwest.

All these territorial gains, incidentally, were accomplished by means which ignored the strict observance of legal and moral niceties. The United States contracted to purchase Louisiana from Napoleon, for instance, even though our government knew that the French dictator had acquired this territory on the condition that he might not resell it. And it was President James Polk, rather than the Mexicans, who ordered the provocative military actions which were the immediate cause of the Mexican War. Americans who worried about such things, however, were comforted by the knowledge that, by whatever means, the domain of Democracy was being expanded and the nation's manifest destiny fulfilled.

Evolution of the Monroe Doctrine. When Spain's New World colonies began their struggles for independence in the early years of the nineteenth century, Americans saw in these struggles an extension of our own revolution, another battle for freedom and republicanism against European monarchic oppression. And obviously, both American trade and security interests made it desirable that European colonial power in the Americas be minimized. To Britain, too, the independence movements in the New World were an important windfall. As long as Spain controlled these lands she could encourage her own trade with them at the expense of outsiders. Independence would throw their markets open to free competition, in which British industrial efficiency and naval supremacy were likely to win first place.

British Foreign Minister Canning therefore invited the United States to join in opposing European intervention in Spanish America. The American Secretary of State, John Quincy Adams, preferred, however, to seize this opportunity for a bold stroke of unilateral American diplomacy rather than "to come in as a cock-boat in the wake of the British man-of-war." He correctly calculated that there was little actual danger of European intervention, and that if intervention should take place, Britain's interests would lead that nation to oppose it in any case.

The result was the now hallowed Monroe Doctrine: not a treaty having any status in international law; not an act of Congress; but part of a presidential message to Congress on December 2, 1823. Monroe's message was based both on the realities of national interest and on the notion that the American system of government was different from — and inherently superior to — the political systems of Europe:

> . . . The American continents, by the free and independent condition which they have assumed and maintain, are henceforth not to be considered as subjects for future colonization by any European powers. . . .
>
> In the wars of the European powers in matters relating to themselves we have never taken any part, nor does it comport with our policy to do so. It is only when our rights are invaded or seriously menaced that we resent injuries or make preparation for our defense. With the movements in this hemisphere we are, of necessity, more immediately connected, and by causes which must be obvious to all enlightened and impartial observers. The political system of the allied powers is essentially different in this respect from that of America. This difference proceeds from that which exists in their respective Governments. We owe it, therefore, to candor, and to the amicable relations existing between the United States and those powers, to declare that we should consider any attempt on their part to extend their system to any portion of this hemisphere as dangerous to our peace and safety. With the existing colonies or dependencies of any European power we have not interfered and shall not interfere. But with the governments who have declared their independence and maintained it, and whose independence we have, on great consideration and on just principles,

acknowledged, we could not view any interposition for the purpose of oppressing them, or controlling in any other manner their destiny, by any European power, in any other light than as the manifestation of an unfriendly disposition toward the United States. . . .

. . . Our policy with regard to Europe, which was adopted at an early stage of the wars which have so long agitated that quarter of the globe, nevertheless remains the same, which is, not to interfere in the internal concerns of any of its powers; to consider the government *de facto* as the legitimate government for us; to cultivate friendly relations with it, and to preserve those relations by a frank, firm, and manly policy, meeting, in all instances, the just claims of every power, submitting to injuries from none. But in regard to these continents, circumstances are eminently and conspicuously different. It is impossible that the allied powers should extend their political system to any portion of either continent without endangering our peace and happiness; nor can anyone believe that our southern brethren, if left to themselves, would adopt it of their own accord. It is equally impossible, therefore, that we should behold such interposition, in any form, with indifference. . . .

Initially, the United States had no intention of supporting these policies by force of arms. Though requested to do so, it declined to enter into alliances with the new Latin American Republics. But as the nation's power grew, the Monroe Doctrine became the cornerstone of the United States policy of domination in the Americas. By 1895, when Great Britain refused to submit to arbitration all of the territories involved in a boundary dispute with Venezuela, President Cleveland and a unanimous Congress went to the extent of appointing an arbitral commission to set a boundary, and announcing their readiness to defend the commission's ruling by force, if necessary. Just prior to this action, Secretary of State Olney had dispatched a note to the British Government invoking both the Monroe Doctrine and the Farewell Address, and declaring:

. . . Today the United States is practically sovereign on this [that is, the North *and* South American] continent, and its fiat is law upon the subjects to which it confines its interposition. Why? It is not because of the pure friendship or good will felt for it. It is not simply by reason of its high character as a civilized state, nor because wisdom and justice and equity are the invariable characteristics of the dealings of the United States. It is because, in addition to all other grounds, its infinite resources combined with its isolated position render it master of the situation and practically invulnerable as against any or all other powers. . . .

Britain's navy was still far greater than that of the United States. But the British people had no desire to fight with the United States over a few bits of jungle in the wilds of Venezuela. The Boer War and the rise of German power in Europe left Her Majesty's government with more important matters to worry about. Britain's conciliatory response in the face of the United States action led to the acceptance of American arbitration — but on terms close to those Britain had offered to the Venezuelans all along.[24] The decision of the arbitrators was not handed down until almost four years after the "war scare," long after agitation over the question had died down. The Monroe Doctrine and "rough and ready" diplomacy had scored another victory, at least in the public mind.

Theodore Roosevelt's presidency saw United States interpretation of the Doctrine further extended. When the Colombian Senate refused to ratify a treaty allowing the United States to build an interoceanic canal through its territory of Panama, Roosevelt encouraged Panamanian nationalists to launch a revolt. Then, under a strained interpretation of an 1846 treaty with Colombia, he blocked the entry of Colombian troops to put down the revolt, and extended diplomatic recognition to the new Panamanian Republic within hours of receiving news of the uprising's success. Less than two weeks later a treaty between the United States and the new Government of Panama was signed, giving the United States the right to build a canal on highly favorable terms.

Roosevelt also enunciated a corollary to the Monroe Doctrine claiming the right of the United States to intervene in Latin America in cases involving debt disputes between the American republics and European powers:

> . . . On the one hand, this country would certainly decline to go to war to prevent a foreign government from collecting a just debt; on the other hand, it is very inadvisable to permit any foreign power to take possession, even temporarily, of the customhouses of an American Republic in order to enforce the payment of its obligations; for such temporary occupation might turn into a permanent occupation. The only escape from these alternatives may at any time be that we must ourselves undertake to bring about some arrangement by which so much as possible of a just obligation shall be paid. . . .

Later the United States intervened in the Dominican Republic, Haiti, and Nicaragua under the Roosevelt corollary, and these Caribbean republics were reduced, for considerable periods of time, to the status of virtual protectorates of the "colossus of the North." Within the United States, meanwhile, the popularity of the Monroe Doctrine reached such heights as to generate anecdotes like that repeated by D. W. Brogan of "the badly frightened citizen who, rescued from a lynching bee, protested: 'I didn't say I was against the Monroe Doctrine: I love the Monroe Doctrine, I would die for the Monroe Doctrine. I merely said I didn't know what it was.' "[25]

[24] British restraint in this instance was of great value in laying the groundwork for an Anglo-American relationship in the twentieth century when twice Britain's former colony came to her aid in general wars against German-led coalitions.

[25] *The American Nation* (New York: Vintage, 1956), p. 156.

Under Presidents Hoover and Franklin Roosevelt, however, the United States came to exercise its power in the Americas with more tact and discretion. The principle of nonintervention was endorsed; and eventually the Monroe Doctrine was made multilateral — that is, it was agreed that acts of aggression by or against any American state would be met with combined inter-American force only by a vote of two-thirds of the Organization of American States (OAS), composed of the American republics themselves.[26]

Nevertheless, since World War II, the Central Intelligence Agency has organized covert attempts to overthrow by force "leftist" governments in Guatemala (successfully, in 1954) and Cuba (unsuccessfully, in 1961). During the Cuban missile crisis of 1962, President Kennedy announced that the United States would "quarantine" (blockade) Cuba before formal OAS approval was obtained.[27] And the Johnson administration's intervention in the Dominican Republic in 1965 was undertaken without OAS approval — though the OAS was later brought into efforts to stabilize the situation and lay the groundwork for free elections. These recent interventions suggest that the United States has not relinquished in fact as it has in form the policy of taking unilaterally whatever steps it deems necessary to keep potentially hostile powers from gaining a foothold in the American hemisphere.

The Open Door. If the traditional goals of United States policy toward Europe and the Americas can be oversimplified as "noninvolvement" and "predominance," respectively, the young nation's policy in the Orient can be similarly characterized as aiming primarily at an "Open Door." Protection of commercial interests was everywhere an important part of American policy; in Asia this goal was not so diluted by strictly political considerations as elsewhere. Though American trade with China had never amounted to more than about 3 per cent of our total international trade, important American business groups were always aware of the enormous potential of the China market. Thus, although the United States did not participate in the forcible extortion of unequal treaties from China in the latter half of the nineteenth century, it showed no compunctions about sharing the spoils of this extortion through the device of the "most favored nation" clause.

In 1854, by judicious application of a combination of threat and tact, Commodore Perry had induced an isolationist Japan to open itself to trade with the West. Though Japan was to become and, for the most part, remain a better customer of the United States than China, Perry had envisioned it primarily as a potential naval base and coaling station en route to the vaunted China market. Half a century later, Japan's remarkable drive toward rapid modernization had progressed to the point where Japan was

26 Canada is not a member of the OAS, and Cuba was expelled from membership in 1962.
27 Nearly unanimous OAS approval was secured after this announcement, but before the "quarantine" was legally put into force.

able to defeat China in the Sino-Japanese War of 1894–95. The full extent of the once great Middle Kingdom's weakness was now revealed to the West, and a race began for leaseholds on Chinese territory and for the staking out of spheres of influence. If China should be divided into spheres of influence, the dominant powers in these areas could be expected to favor their own commerce over those of other nations. This would be detrimental to China; to Great Britain, which held, as usual, the lion's share of the China trade in *all* regions; and to the United States, whose domestic preoccupations and foreign policy traditions would hamper its participation in a race for spheres of influence.

Nevertheless, initial British overtures for a joint Anglo-American statement in support of what was later to become known as the Open Door in China were not taken up by the McKinley administration. The British proceeded to protect themselves by staking out leaseholds and spheres of influence of their own. Meanwhile, John Hay became Secretary of State, and American business and missionary interests, seeking some protection for American interests in China began to apply pressures. Hay consulted his friend W. W. Rockhill, a diplomat with considerable experience in the Orient and a high regard for Chinese culture. Rockhill recommended that the United States seek assurance from the powers concerned that the commerce of all nations would receive equal treatment in the spheres of influence of any nation in China. Such a policy, he noted, would reduce the incentive for establishing spheres of influence, and thus would benefit China as well as the United States.

Following this advice, Hay, on September 6, 1899, addressed a circular letter to Japan and to the European powers with interests in China. It asked for assurance that each of these powers:

> *First.* Will in no way interfere with any treaty port or any vested interest within any so-called "sphere of interest" or leased territory it may have in China.
>
> *Second.* That the Chinese treaty tariff of the time being shall apply to all merchandise within said "sphere of interest" (unless they be "free ports"), no matter to what nationality it may belong, and that duties so leviable shall be collected by the Chinese Government.
>
> *Third.* That it will levy no higher harbor dues on vessels of another nationality frequenting any port in such "sphere" than shall be levied on vessels of its own nationality, and no higher railroad charges over lines built, controlled, or operated within its "sphere" on merchandise belonging to citizens or subjects of other nationalities transported through such "sphere" than shall be levied on similar merchandise belonging to its own nations transported over equal distances. . . .

China's territorial integrity was not mentioned, nor was the term "Open Door" used. The replies of the nations addressed were evasive, and each

conditioned a qualified acceptance of the principles involved on the willingness of all the other nations to accept them too. Nevertheless, Secretary Hay
announced that the assurances received were "final and definitive."

The following year, a Chinese secret society known as "the Boxers" attacked the foreign legations in Peking in a paroxysm of protest against the
frustrations and humiliations which foreigners had imposed upon the
proud Chinese Empire. The United States, the European powers, and
Japan dispatched troops abroad to rescue the besieged legations. This incident, and the demands against China for reparations which followed, renewed the danger that the Middle Kingdom might be partitioned. Secretary
Hay responded with the second of the Open Door notes, a circular letter to
the powers concerned, dated July 3, 1900. This time the American goal of
equal opportunity for trade was declared to extend to all of China rather
than to the foreign spheres of interest alone. And this aim was now related
to the preservation of China's territorial integrity:

> In this critical posture of affairs in China . . . the policy of the
> government of the United States is to seek a solution which may bring
> about permanent safety and peace to China, preserve Chinese terri-
> torial and administrative entity, protect all rights guaranteed to friendly
> powers by treaty and international law, and safeguard for the world the
> principle of equal and impartial trade with all parts of the Chinese
> Empire. . . .

The effect these notes had on future imperial rivalry in China is debatable. American influence toward moderation in the negotiations over the
Boxer indemnity may well have helped to reduce the size of the penalty imposed; and the subsequent American action of remitting almost two-thirds
of the United States' share of this indemnity certainly produced considerable good will toward the United States in China. Yet it was clear from the
beginning that American devotion to the principle of the Open Door did
not extend to willingness to use force to support it. Hay himself told the
Japanese this within seven months after the issuance of the second of the
Open Door notes. Nor was American dedication to this moral imperative
so great as to restrain the United States either from applying a closed door
principle in its own colony of the Philippines, or from seeking before the
end of 1900 (via instructions issued by John Hay) to acquire for itself a
coaling station in Fukien province on the China coast.

Plainly, a policy which the United States would not and did not back
with even the threat of force could not suffice to protect China against a
power which *was* willing to back its policy with force. Thus, Japan was
permitted to encroach gradually upon China's territorial integrity in the
decades which followed. By 1931, the Chinese territory of Manchuria had
been converted into the Japanese puppet state of Manchukuo, and plans
were being laid for incorporating all of China into a "Greater East Asia

Co-Prosperity Sphere" under Japanese leadership. America's *declaratory* policy — beginning with the Open Door notes and continuing through the 1932 Stimson Doctrine of nonrecognition of territorial gains achieved by force of arms — led the nation to consider immoral, and to refuse to accept, the real changes in the status quo which were taking place in the Orient. Our *operational* policy, at the same time, did nothing to prevent Japan from continuing to bring about these changes. Ultimately, the widening divergence between these two sets of policies opened a gap between American and Japanese conceptions of the status quo in East Asia which was closed only as an aftermath of the violence which began at Pearl Harbor and ended at Hiroshima and Nagasaki.

These tragic developments, of course, could not be foretold at the turn of the century, and American opinion hailed the Open Door notes as a great victory for American unselfishness and morality over European power politics and imperialism. The appeal of a policy which appeared to serve both American business and the American conscience while requiring no more international involvement than the example of American moral excellence — and occasional lectures to less enlightened nations — was well nigh irresistible. In time, the Open Door achieved a place close to the Monroe Doctrine in American hearts, as another eternal verity against which might be measured the morality of foreign nations and the wisdom of policies pursued by the United States of America.

Manifest Destiny Abroad. It was during this period of American exuberance at the turn of the century that the nation embarked upon its first major effort to extend the blessings of manifest destiny beyond the shores of the North American continent. The "splendid little war" (John Hay's phrase) which ended with the United States cruelly "pacifying" reluctant little brown brothers in the Pacific, began with a rush of American sympathy for the plight of oppressed little brown brothers in the Caribbean.

Early in 1895 a group of discontented Cuban insurgents launched a major rebellion against Spanish rule. American properties of considerable value were destroyed. The struggle was savagely fought on both sides. In particular, pressed by the peculiar frustrations of an unpopular counterinsurgency operation, the Spaniards used a program of reconcentrating civilians similar to the rural pacification program which the United States was to utilize in the 1960's in South Vietnam. The Hearst and Pulitzer newspapers in New York, and sensationalist journals throughout the country, headlined the situation in the most lurid and irresponsible manner imaginable. Glossing over the offenses of the insurgents, they emphasized the atrocities of the Spaniards and called for American action in the name of humanity. American sympathies were aroused, and a tide of opinion surged forward in favor of American intervention in support of Cuban independence.

Both President Cleveland and President McKinley attempted to handle the matter by diplomacy. When riots broke out in Havana in 1898 and American lives and property seemed endangered, the battleship "Maine" was sent to Havana to show the flag. On February 15, 1898, a tremendous explosion sank the American vessel and took over 250 lives. Subsequent inquiries failed to establish clearly the cause of the sinking, but American opinion blamed it on the hated Spaniard. War fever rose higher, and even Spain's willingness to revoke the reconcentration policy and to grant the insurgents an indefinite armistice — though not the outright independence desired for them by the United States — failed to break it. At last, the reluctant McKinley turned the matter over to a Congress which had long demanded war. The final resolution for war included the so-called Teller Amendment which disclaimed any American intention to annex Cuba. America would fight not for selfish ends, but for humanity. (As it turned out, Cuba was not annexed but its sovereignty was restricted substantially, and it remained virtually a protectorate of the United States until 1934.)

The war was an unequal one. Hostilities in the Caribbean ended in less than four months — ptomaine poisoning, malaria, and yellow fever killed more American soldiers than did the enemy. Before the actual outbreak of war, Admiral George Dewey had been ordered to proceed to the Spanish colony in the Philippines, in case of hostilities, with the aim of destroying the Spanish fleet there. Within a week after the declaration of war he had accomplished his mission. America's imagination was excited by this unexpected victory. An expeditionary force was sent to support Dewey, and an exiled Filipino rebel leader was encouraged by local American officials — without authorization from Washington — to lead an anti-Spanish resistance movement in the expectation that the United States would grant independence to the Philippines after victory was won. Soon this rebel leader, Emilio Aguinaldo, had won control of most of the island of Luzon and had staked out a claim to Philippine independence.

The United States was confronted with a significant and unanticipated choice. Dewey's victory had undermined Spanish authority in the Philippines. If the United States did not fill this power vacuum, Germany or Japan might be tempted to do so. Should the champion of anti-imperialism itself then become an imperialist power? This question was debated heatedly both in the Senate and in the nation. By the treaty of peace, Spain ceded the Philippines (for which the United States paid $20 million), Puerto Rico, and Guam to the United States, and renounced all claims to Cuba. The settlement barely passed the senate. At one point, only the tie-breaking vote of the Vice President prevented the passage of a resolution promising the Philippines independence as soon as a stable government had been established. The treaty was finally approved by a margin of only 2 votes more than the two-thirds required by the Constitution — and might not have passed, according to some historians, had not anti-imperialist

Democrats, led by William Jennings Bryan, preferred to conclude peace first and then campaign in 1900 against American imperialism in the Philippines. Thus it became our unhappy task to suppress ruthlessly the Filipino independence movement — still led by Aguinaldo — which our agents abroad had recently encouraged.

It was in January, 1900, almost a year after the Senate had ratified the peace treaty, that Senator Albert J. Beveridge delivered one of the most frequently quoted orations in American history. Beveridge, a distinguished progressive, was urging passage of a resolution which would declare the Philippines to be a territory of the United States and proclaim the nation's intention to retain them as such. His remarks cannot be claimed to be representative of the feelings of the American people as a whole, or even of all of those who continued to support the annexation of the Philippines in spite of a bloody revolt by the Filipino forces under Aguinaldo. Nevertheless, Beveridge unquestionably reflected the mixture of selfish and idealistic sentiments that held sway over many of his fellow legislators and countrymen at the time:

> Mr. President, the times call for candor. The Philippines are ours forever, "territory belonging to the United States," as the Constitution calls them. And just beyond the Philippines are China's illimitable markets. We will not retreat from either. . . .
>
> . . . To hold it [the Philippines] will be no mistake. Our largest trade henceforth must be with Asia. . . . Where shall we turn for consumers of our surplus? Geography answers the question. China is our natural customer. . . . The Philippines gives us a base at the door of all the East. . . .
>
> But if they did not command China, India, the Orient, the whole Pacific for purposes of offense, defense, and trade, the Philippines are so valuable in themselves that we should hold them. I have cruised more than 2,000 miles through the archipelago, every moment a surprise at its loveliness and wealth. I have ridden hundreds of miles on the islands, every foot of the way a revelation of vegetables and mineral riches. . . .
>
> Mr. President, this question is deeper than any question of party politics; deeper than any question of the isolated policy of our country even; deeper even than any question of constitutional power. It is elemental. It is racial. God has not been preparing the English-speaking and Teutonic peoples for a thousand years for nothing but vain and idle self-contemplation and self-admiration. No! He has made us the master organizers of the world to establish system where chaos reigns. He has given us the spirit of progress to overwhelm the forces of reaction throughout the earth. He has made us adept in government that we may administer government among savage and senile peoples. Were it not for such a force as this the world would relapse into barbarism and night. And of all our race He has marked the American people as His chosen nation to finally lead in the regeneration of the world. This is the

> divine mission of America, and it holds for us all the profit, all the glory, all the happiness possible to man. We are trustees of the world's progress, guardians of its righteous peace. The judgment of the Master is upon us: "Ye have been faithful over a few things; I will make you ruler over many things."
>
> . . . And so, Senators, with reverent hearts, where dwells the fear of God, the American people move forward to the future of their hope and the doing of His work. . . .

President McKinley himself later described to a visiting Methodist missionary group how his thinking had progressed on the Philippine annexation question. Though its strict accuracy as a statement of historical fact can be neither affirmed nor denied, his account is unquestionably intriguing:

> The truth is I didn't want the Philippines and when they came to us as a gift from the gods, I did not know what to do about them. . . . I sought counsel from all sides — Democrats as well as Republicans — but got little help. I thought first we would take only Manila; then Luzon; then other islands, perhaps, also. I walked the floor of the White House night after night until midnight; and I am not ashamed to tell you, gentlemen, that I went down on my knees and prayed Almighty God for light and guidance more than one night.
>
> And one night late it came to me this way — I don't know how it was, but it came: (1) that we could not give them back to Spain — that would be cowardly and dishonorable; (2) that we could not turn them over to France or Germany — our commercial rivals in the Orient — that would be bad business and discreditable; (3) that we could not leave them to themselves — they were unfit for self-government — and they would soon have anarchy and misrule over there worse than Spain's was; and (4) that there was nothing left for us to do but to take them all, and to educate the Filipinos, and uplift and civilize and Christianize them, and by God's grace do the very best we could by them, as our fellow-men for whom Christ also died. And then I went to bed, and went to sleep and slept soundly.[28]

The benefits of the conquest of the Philippines did not turn out to be as great as the advocates of annexation had expected. The disadvantages of having to protect these remote outposts in the Pacific soon seemed to outweigh such military advantages as their possession may have conferred. Before long, American distaste for imperialism, the sugar industry's distaste for the importation of duty-free Philippine sugar, and the American worker's distaste for the cheap labor of Filipino immigrants, led the Congress to adopt a policy of granting self-government and independence to the Filipinos as soon as feasible. Commonwealth status was granted in 1934, and on July 4, 1946, the Republic of the Philippines became an independent

[28] *Christian Advocate* (New York), Jan. 22, 1903. Quoted in Bailey, *op. cit.*, 7th ed., pp. 473-474.

nation. As to the "Christianization" of the islands, the Filipinos were preponderantly Catholic when the Americans left in 1946 — as they had been when the Spaniards left half a century earlier.

The decade and a half following the pacification of the Filipinos saw Americans return to their normal preoccupation with domestic affairs. This period was to be labelled "the Progressive era," a time when Americans directed their attention to "trustbusting," "muckraking," and reform; to perfecting the American way of life rather than to spreading it. In 1913, Woodrow Wilson became President of the United States, and one of the most comprehensive reform programs in American political history was rapidly enacted into law. The Federal Reserve Act, the Clayton Anti-Trust Act, the Federal Trade Commission Act, and the Federal Farm Loan Act were passed. The sixteenth and seventeenth amendments to the Constitution, providing for the levying of a federal income tax and the direct election of United States Senators, respectively, were adopted.

In the midst of this wave of reform, on June 28, 1914, a Serbian nationalist assassinated Archduke Francis Ferdinand, the heir to the Austro-Hungarian throne. A month later, Europe was faced with its first general war since the defeat of Napoleon at Waterloo a century before; and the United States was faced with an increasingly difficult problem of neutrality.

CASE
STUDY *AMERICA GOES TO WAR — 1917*

The case study which follows reviews in some detail the Wilson administration's efforts to keep America out of war. After a little less than three years of precarious neutrality, the United States was drawn in — as it has been into every general European conflict before and since. It was the first time an American expeditionary force had engaged in large-scale military action across the seas, and the experience became a formative influence upon the thought of a whole generation of Americans, particularly in regard to foreign affairs.

1. How much did the European origins of some segments of the electorate influence popular attitudes toward the war in Europe? How did these attitudes effect United States government policy?

2. What role did American attitudes toward law play in precipitating United States involvement? Why did international law fail to provide an adequate basis for resolving peacefully the questions at issue between Germany and the United States?

3. What do you believe were the real causes of our ultimate entry into the war?

4. Was President Wilson really "neutral"? Could he have avoided American participation in the war, without sacrificing vital national interests, by following some more judicious policy? If so, how?

5. Were Wilson's policies consonant with the traditional American attitudes outlined in this chapter? Was Senator Borah's view?

6. In what ways could the President's announcement that the goal of United States participation was to make "the world safe for democracy" be expected to affect American opinion during the war? After the war ended?

ALEXANDER DECONDE

On June 28, 1914, . . . a Serbian nationalist, at Sarajevo in the province of Bosnia (now a part of Yugoslavia), assassinated Archduke Franz Ferdinand, heir to the throne of Austria-Hungary. Few Americans realized that the revolver shots in that distant Balkan province would lead to a world war. Since Austria was determined to crush Serbian nationalism, she served an ultimatum on Serbia that started the war. By August 6 the major *Entente* powers, France, Great Britain, and Russia, later joined by Japan and Italy, were at war with the principal Central Powers, Germany and Austria-Hungary, joined later by Bulgaria and Turkey.

SYMPATHY FOR THE ALLIES

The actual outbreak of war stunned most Americans. Numbed by previous European crises, they could hardly believe that war had truly come. They were, however, grateful that the fighting was remote and apparently not vital to their interests. The United States, they believed, could remain aloof. It was, Wilson said, "a war with which we have nothing to do, whose causes cannot touch us. . . ." He promptly issued formal declarations of neutrality and also offered to mediate the conflict, but the belligerents refused. Two weeks later he appealed to Americans not to take sides. "We must," he said, "be impartial in thought as well as in action. . . ."

Although most Americans did not want to become involved in the fighting, they and their government soon found it impossible to be impartial. As Britain and Germany, the major wartime belligerents, fought desperately to destroy each other, the United States saw that any action it took against one of them in defense of its rights would benefit the other. If it acquiesced in the maritime restrictions of one belligerent, it would injure the other. As the war went on, it became clear that whatever the United States did or

Reprinted with the permission of Charles Scribner's Sons from *A History of American Foreign Policy,* pages 440–459, by Alexander DeConde. Copyright © 1963 Charles Scribner's Sons.

perhaps did not do, because of its power and resources, could mean the difference between victory or defeat for either side. American neutrality, therefore, had a deep significance not only for the American people but also for the peoples of the world.

The United States hoped to trade with all the warring powers, subject to the usual rules of war, and relied on traditional international law to safeguard its rights. It generally observed its technical obligations as a neutral but encountered trouble in enforcing its neutral rights as it understood them.

One reason for American difficulties was that not since the Declaration of Paris of 1856 had the powers recodified international maritime law. In 1914, therefore, maritime law contained rules of conduct that were outmoded. Its rules defining contraband of war and blockade, for example, were based on a relationship between neutrals and belligerents that had prevailed before the industrial era. Powerful sovereign states, recognizing no authority higher than their own and fighting for survival, refused to be bound by those old rules when they ran contrary to their own interests. Neutrality ceased to have the same meaning as in the past.

At the expense of traditional neutral rights, belligerents expanded their own rights in technical violations of international law of the nineteenth century. Fighting in an era when a nation needed to mobilize its total resources to survive, they destroyed the old idea that war could be limited to combatants. Ironically, the United States found itself forced to rely on traditional neutral rights precisely when they were undergoing radical change.

Another reason why the United States found neutrality a burden was the attitude of the American people toward the belligerents. Americans were never impartial; most of them favored the Allied powers. Ties of blood, language, and culture bound many of them to England, and England's careful cultivation of American friendship since the end of the nineteenth century had made the bond stronger than ever. Sentimental ties of friendship dating back to the Revolutionary War drew many Americans to France.

. . . Although Americans of Irish and German ancestry generally favored the Central Powers, Germany had been unpopular with Americans since the 1880's. They distrusted the German government, considering it unprincipled and militaristic. . . . Later, Germany's crushing of Belgian neutrality, her deportation of Belgian civilians for labor in Germany, and her other violations of traditionally accepted standards of international conduct, all added to popular resentment against the Central Powers and hence increased American sympathy for their enemies.

Since immigrants in the United States and first generation descendants of immigrant parents still had close ties with friends and relatives in the belligerent countries, the war divided their loyalties. Yet, the pattern of opinion toward the belligerents among these "new" Americans was about the same as among the older elements of the population. According to the census figures of 1910, the "new" Americans accounted for about 35 per cent of the total population, or approximately 32 million out of a total population of 92 million. Only 9 per cent of them were German and only 3 per cent were Austrian. Few others, except some of the Irish, sympathized with the Central Powers. Sentiment for the Allies among the foreign-born, however, did not preponderate until after Italy joined the Allies in 1915. Like those of English ancestry, those Americans of continental European ancestry felt the pull of blood and culture but were unable to influence policy directly because they had meager political power.

Those who made and influenced foreign policy within the Wilson administration reflected the popular support for the Allies, except that they were generally more strongly pro-Ally and anti-German in their sentiments than were other Americans. Wilson's cabinet, except for Secretary of State Bryan, favored the Allies. Robert Lansing, the Counselor for the Department of State, and Colonel Edward M. House, Wilson's personal adviser, were pro-British, as were most of the ambassadors at important posts. Walter Hines Page, the Ambassador to England, believed so intensely that nothing was as important as friendship with England, that the President in time had to discount his dispatches as being little more than British propaganda.

Wilson himself favored the British, but struggled within himself to think and act impartially. Although there is no evidence to support the view that Wilson's personal sympathy for the British controlled the development of his foreign policy, Sir Cecil Spring-Rice, the British Ambassador in the United States, could write that "all the State Department are on our side except Bryan who is incapable of forming a settled judgment on anything outside party politics. The President will be with us by birth and upbringing. . . ."

Neither the President nor the American people were so devoted to the Allied cause that they were willing to fight by the side of the Allies. Most Americans wanted a policy of neutrality that would keep their country at peace.

NEUTRAL RIGHTS

Controversies with the belligerents over neutral rights, mainly those of trade and travel by sea, began shortly after the war started. Britain and Germany tried to throttle all maritime trade with their enemies. Each violated international law and American rights, but each, until 1917, tried to keep her violations from injuring the United States so seriously that it would intervene.

Almost all of the early troubles over neutral rights were with the British.

Although the Germans had entered the war better prepared, hoping for a quick victory, Britain had the advantage in the maritime war. Her superior navy gave her control of the seas and access to the strategic materials of the world outside of Europe. . . .

Although the British effort to strangle trade with Germany has generally been called a blockade, the Allies never formally declared a blockade, but beginning in March, 1915, they tried openly to stop all trade with Germany whether or not it was in contraband. By applying what was a blockade in all but name to neutral ports as well as to Germany, the British enlarged the concepts of blockade and continuous voyage beyond existing legal standards. They forced neutral states bordering Germany — Denmark, Holland, and Sweden — who imported supplies by sea, to agree that they would not re-export the goods to Germany and would not substitute similar goods of their own for export to Germany. The British gradually compelled American shippers, who traded with the neutrals of western Europe, to do so through special corporations they organized.

The British maritime system, by the summer of 1915, choked off virtually all American trade with the Central Powers and the neutral states of Europe. The United States protested. "This Government," Secretary Bryan wrote, "cannot but regard the detention of cargoes of non-contraband goods as without legal justification. . . ." Sometimes the British heeded American complaints. Fearing the wrath of the American cotton interests, for example, they did not immediately put cotton on the list of absolute contraband even though it was an ingredient of gunpowder. Occasionally they paid for cargoes they held, sometimes they ignored American complaints, and at other times they evaded or delayed replies to American protests.

In answering some protests, Sir Edward Grey pointed out that in her blockade Britain was following the practice of the United States in the Civil War. He also argued that new methods of trade called for modifications of international law. . . .

The United States never accepted the British arguments as valid, yet it never went beyond protests in attempting to enforce its interpretation of neutral rights. One reason for the American attitude was that the British followed the policy of placing as much restraint on neutral rights as was compatible with retaining American friendship. "Blockade of Germany was essential to the victory of the Allies, but the ill-will of the United States meant their certain defeat," Grey wrote. "The object of diplomacy, therefore, was to secure the maximum of blockade that could be enforced without a rupture with the United States."

While the Allies were strangling American trade with the Central Powers, they were also strengthening their own economic ties to the United States. When the war broke out, the United States was suffering from a business depression. Within six months, Allied purchases of munitions and other supplies transformed the depression into a modest war boom. Germany lamented bitterly that the sale of munitions was making the United States an arsenal of the Allies. For, as the German Ambassador in Washington, Count Johann H. Bernstorff, pointed out, American industry was "actually delivering goods only to the enemies of Germany."

Technically, the one-sided munitions trade did not grow out of American partiality for the Allies. It was, under international law, a legal trade for a neutral. The United States made its goods available exclusively to the Allies primarily because Britain controlled the seas.

At first the Allies paid cash for American goods, but France, as soon as the war began, tried to obtain a loan from the New York banking firm of J. P. Morgan & Company. Early in August, 1914, the bank asked the Secretary of State what the attitude of the government would be toward private loans to certain belligerents. With the support of Wilson, Bryan replied that loans, although legal, were "inconsistent with the true spirit of neutrality." Five days earlier he had written that "money is the worst of contrabands because it commands all other things." The bankers did not make the loan.

This policy of opposing loans to belligerents worked to the disadvantage of the Allies and hence lasted barely two months. In the middle of October the Department of State, backed by Wilson, changed its position. One spokesman explained that there was a distinction between loans made by the government of the United States to belligerent governments and loans made by individual citizens. Loans by individuals were legal; loans by neutral governments violated neutrality. Before the month was over New York bankers began extending short-term commercial credits to Allied governments. Even Bryan reversed himself. He announced that the government still disapproved of loans but had no objection to "credit arrangements." There was virtually no difference between credit arrangements and loans.

As the Allies increased their purchases in the United States and depleted their gold balances, they found that they needed more credits and even large outright loans to continue buying. In September, 1915, Secretary of State Lansing, who had replaced Bryan, and the Secretary of the Treasury persuaded the President to allow the Allies to float large loans on the American market. The Secretaries argued that without such loans the Allies could not continue to buy American goods and without Allied purchases the United States would slip into another depression.

The House of Morgan, acting as the purchasing agent for the Allied governments, then assisted in floating an issue of a half-billion dollars in Allied war bonds in the United States. Although the loans linked American prosperity to the Allied cause and operated to the disadvantage of Germany, there is no evidence that Wilson himself showed an unneutral preference for the Allies for economic reasons.

GERMANY AND THE SUBMARINE

While not cordial, American relations with the Central Powers during the first six months of the war, unlike those with the Allies, were relatively tranquil. German leaders had counted on a lightning victory by land, so they had avoided direct controversy with the United States. By the end of 1914, Germany's attempt to deliver a knockout blow had failed, and both sides settled down to monotonous trench warfare.

Now that the war had become one of attrition, the Germans lost their initial advantage of better preparation. Unless they could regain access to raw materials overseas, their war machine might break down. Since their navy could not destroy England's surface fleet, German military commanders decided to retaliate against the Allied blockade with the only weapon at their disposal — the untried submarine.

"England wants to starve us!" the head of the German admiralty announced in a public interview. "We can play the same game. We can bottle her up and torpedo every English or Allied ship which nears any harbor in Great Britain thereby cutting off large food supplies."

Ordinarily, belligerent warships had the right to stop and search merchantmen on the high seas and to sink those who resisted search, but international law also required the warship to provide for the safety of the passengers and crew. Small, cramped, thin-shelled, and lightly armed for surface warfare, the submarine could not comply with these rules of traditional cruiser warfare. If it surfaced to search a merchantman, it ran the risk of destruction by ramming or by deck guns, since many merchant vessels were armed. Therefore, the submarine usually had to deliver its torpedo without warning, sink its prey, and flee. This would lead to the indiscriminate destruction of neutral passengers and property, a particular concern of Americans because they traveled and shipped goods on Allied ships.

At the beginning of 1915, Germany had only about seven submarines able to operate in Allied waters. She could not strike decisively without more, so she adopted a policy of cutting the flow of American goods to the Allies without provoking war with the United States. In effect, she adjusted her early sea warfare to the demands of the United States and to the capabilities of her limited submarine fleet.

Germany launched her submarine policy on February 4 by proclaiming a war zone around the British Isles. After the eighteenth of the month, she said, her submarines would destroy enemy ships within the zone on sight. Since the British were disguising their ships with neutral flags, she warned neutrals that they entered the area at their own peril. Germany justified her new policy as a reprisal against British violations of international law, particularly the food blockade, and argued that new weapons and conditions of war called for a revision of traditional international law.

The submarine policy abruptly changed the character of Germany's relations with the United States. Although Wilson had not protested Britain's illegal blockade of the North Sea, he immediately sent a stern warning to Germany. The United States, he said, would hold the German government to a "strict accountability" for attacks on American ships and lives. It would, moreover, take any steps necessary "to secure to American citizens the full enjoyment of their acknowledged rights on the high seas."

Less than a week later, the United States tried to effect a compromise between the blockade policies of the belligerents. It asked Germany to restrict her use of mines and employ submarines only for visit and search, and Britain to relax her food blockade and abandon the use of neutral flags. Both belligerents opposed the plan. Germany demanded access to raw materials as well as food.

Soon, Germany's submarines began taking a heavy toll of Allied shipping. Without allowing sufficient time for the passengers and crew to escape, a U-boat on March 28, 1915, torpedoed the British liner *Falaba* off the Irish sea and took one American life. The sinking shocked the American people. It also stimulated a debate within the Department of State on national policy.

Headed by Secretary Bryan, one group argued that if Americans traveled on belligerent ships they should do so at their own risk. True neutrality, it held, required the United States to condone the German violations of international law as it had done the British violations. Speaking for the other group, Counselor Lansing insisted that the government must defend the right of Americans to travel on Allied ships. He denounced the sinking of the *Falaba* as a "flagrant violation of international law and international morality," and so inhumane that the United States in defense of its honor must protest strongly.

Even though Lansing had not been entirely accurate in his interpretation of the rights of neutrals on belligerent ships, the President in theory sided with him, but was finally so moved by Bryan's pleas that he decided to make no protest. According to international law, those who traveled on belligerent ships, since a ship was a part of a nation's territory for jurisdictional purposes, could properly look to the belligerent government for protection. Yet, the United States came to adopt the policy that its citizens had the lawful right to travel in safety on British ships and could turn to their own government for protection of that right.

While the President was considering the implications of the *Falaba* case, he received news that on May 1 an American oil tanker, the *Gulflight*, suffered several casualties when hit by a torpedo in a fight between a British naval patrol and a submarine. The German attacks were violent, dramatic, and ruthless. The average American who could not understand the grievances against the Allies rooted in the intricacies of international law could feel the resentment the submarine sinkings aroused. Contemporary opinion held Germany responsible for a barbaric innovation in warfare.

THE *LUSITANIA* CRISIS

Aware of American resentment, German officials in the United States, on the very day of the *Gulflight* incident, placed in some fifty newspapers an unusual advertisement which warned Americans not to take passage on British ships carrying munitions. That afternoon almost two hundred Americans left for Europe on the British Cunard liner *Lusitania*. Besides her passengers and other cargo, the *Lusitania* carried 4200 cases of rifle cartridges. Off the Irish coast, in a chance encounter on May 7, 1915, a U-boat torpedoed the great ship. The liner sank in eighteen minutes, with the loss of 1198 lives, 128 of them American, including women and children.

Americans were horrified by what they construed to be mass murder by order of the German government. Some of them screamed for war. "The nation which remembered the sailors of the *Maine* will not forget the civilians of the *Lusitania!*" the New York *Tribune* announced with some truth. The British were able to take advantage of the heated anti-German feelings through publication, six days later, of the Bryce *Report* on German atrocities in Belgium. In view of the ruthless submarine campaign, the *Report*'s thesis, based on dubious evidence, that the German army had used cruelty as a deliberate policy in Belgium, seemed plausible to many Americans. "Proof," *The New York Times* explained, "now comes to hand."

Despite the uproar, the majority of Americans did not want war. The President immediately placed himself at the head of the moderate forces. "There is such a thing as a man being too proud to fight," he told a Philadelphia audience three days after the *Lusitania* tragedy. "There is such a thing as a nation being so right that it does not need to convince others by force that it is right."

Wilson now put his policy of strict accountability to its first real test. In a stiff protest he demanded that Germany disavow the sinking. There was, the Baltimore *Sun* said, "all the red blood in the message that a red-blooded nation can ask." Germany answered two weeks later, but regarding the reply as unsatisfactory, Wilson drafted a second *Lusitania* note that was so vigorous that Bryan objected. He believed it might lead to war. The only way to keep peace, he insisted, was to curtail American travel on belligerent ships.

Unable to persuade the President to accept his reasoning, Bryan resigned rather than sign the second note. Sent on June 9, under the signature of Robert Lansing, Bryan's successor, that note again demanded that the German government disavow the sinking of the *Lusitania,* pay a reparation for injuries, and abandon its campaign against passenger liners. The United States, Wilson said, was concerned with more than rights of property; it was "contending for nothing less high and sacred than the rights of humanity."

Already inflamed against the United States for its sale of munitions to the Allies, the German public now believed that Wilson was trying to force its government to sheath its most potent naval weapon without compelling the British to adhere to international law. The German government itself was unwilling to surrender publicly on the issue of the *Lusitania,* but it also did not want to risk a break with the United States. While the diplomats argued, therefore, it had already issued secret orders to submarine commanders to spare large passenger liners. The new instructions failed to prevent a U-boat from sinking the British liner *Arabic* on August 19 with a loss of two American lives.

Under pressure from Wilson, who considered breaking off relations with Germany, Count von Bernstorff expressed regret for the sinking of the *Arabic* and offered an indemnity. In a note of September 1, sometimes known as the *Arabic* pledge, he went beyond his instructions and promised that German submarines would not attack unarmed passenger ships without warning unless the ships resisted or tried to escape.

Even though Wilson had won a significant diplomatic victory and tension with Germany eased, the sinkings did not stop. When a German submarine flying Austrian colors sank the Italian liner *Ancona* on November 7 with loss to American life, Wilson sent Austria a virtual ultimatum. Austria-Hungary disavowed the sinking and promised indemnity payments. Finally, on February 4, 1916, Germany apologized for the destruction of the *Lusitania* and offered an indemnity, but would not admit that the sinking was illegal. "I cannot," the German Chancellor Theobald von Bethmann-Hollweg said, "concede a humiliation of Germany and the German people, or the wrenching of the submarine weapon from our hands."

THE *SUSSEX* CRISIS

A week later Germany again expanded her submarine warfare by announcing that after March 1 her U-boats would sink armed merchant ships without warning. Although it made some Americans indignant, the new policy tended to confirm the views of others that the President's insistence on upholding the rights of his people to travel as they pleased would lead to war. Sentiment in Congress then crystallized behind two resolutions, introduced by Representative Jeff McLemore of Texas and Senator Thomas P. Gore of Oklahoma, warning Americans against travel on armed belligerent ships. Congress appeared ready to approve the Gore-McLemore resolutions with large majorities.

Wilson met this threat to his control of foreign policy from members of his own party with an open letter to the chairman of the Senate Foreign Relations Committee. He could not, the President said, "consent to any abridgement of the rights of American citizens in any respect." After he conferred with congressional leaders on the following morning, Congress shelved the resolutions.

Americans continued to take passage on belligerent ships without restraint, and on March 24 several of them were injured in the torpedoing of the French passenger steamer *Sussex* in the English channel. At the time, the sinking appeared to be a deliberate violation of the *Arabic* pledge and hence touched off one of the most serious crises yet with Germany.

Secretary Lansing urged breaking off relations. Wilson proceeded slowly but finally acted on the views of his advisers. In a virtual ultimatum he warned that "unless the Imperial Government should now immediately declare and effect an abandonment of its present methods of submarine warfare against passenger and freight-carrying vessels, the Government of the United States can have no choice but to sever diplomatic relations with the German Empire altogether."

Faced with the possibility of war with the United States, Germany's military and civilian leaders debated whether or not to leash the submarine. Over the protests of the military, who wanted unrestricted submarine warfare, the civilians yielded to American pressure for the last time. On May 4 the German government promised that its submarines would not sink merchant ships without warning and without saving lives. This so-called *Sussex* pledge also contained the contingency that the United States must compel England to stop her illegal practices, particularly the food blockade. Wilson accepted the promise, but not the reservation.

During the *Sussex* crisis, and even before, the British took certain actions that provoked American antagonism against them. In January, 1916, in seeking another solution to the submarine question, Secretary Lansing had asked the Allies to disarm their merchant ships and the Germans to observe the usual rules of visit and search. The British answered that the proposals would so handicap their side that if the United States persisted, Allied ships would no longer visit American ports and prosperity would suffer. Germany's renewal of submarine warfare against merchantmen kept the issue from arousing bitter controversy with Britain.

In April, when British authorities in Ireland ruthlessly crushed the Easter Rebellion there and later executed its leaders, even American Anglophiles were shocked. "The Dublin executions have done more to drive America back to isolation than any other event since the war began," the *New Republic* declared. Americans also resented and protested the seizure and examination of their mail, but what angered them most was Britain's publication in July of a "blacklist" for the United States. The Allies forbade their subjects to trade with eighty-five American firms and individuals on the list.

Although the Allies had the legal right to boycott those suspected of trading with their enemies, the blacklist infuriated Wilson. "I am, I must admit," he wrote, "about at the end of my patience with Great Britain and the Allies. This blacklist business is the last straw." After he had protested and the British refused to withdraw their blacklist, the President asked

Congress for retaliatory powers. Before adjourning in September, Congress voted him the authority he requested, but Wilson never used it since the British eased their boycott of American firms. . . .

In defying international law the British violated only property rights whereas the German use of the submarine destroyed lives as well and hence aroused greater resentment. Wilson made the distinction clear in one of his speeches. When American rights were violated, he said, "this was our guiding principle: that property rights can be vindicated by claims for damages when the war is over, and no modern nation can decline to arbitrate such claims; but the fundamental rights of humanity cannot be. The loss of life is irreparable. . . ."

Agitation for preparedness had begun in October, 1914, with a small but articulate group headed by Theodore Roosevelt. Fearing and distrusting Germany, the men in this group, Elihu Root, Henry Cabot Lodge, and others, believed that the United States should intervene in the war on the side of the Allies. "I am entirely convinced," one of the preparedness advocates explained, "that the German cause is unholy and, moreover, a menace to the principles of democracy." Since public opinion overwhelmingly favored neutrality, the interventionists cloaked their objectives with patriotic pleas for enlarging the armed forces.

At first the preparedness propaganda had little effect, for many Americans saw no danger to their country from the European war and hence little justification for building up a powerful navy and army. Opponents of the preparedness movement saw in it the seeds of war. The President apparently spoke for most Americans when he announced that "no one who speaks counsel based on fact or drawn from a just and candid interpretation of realities can say that there is reason to fear that from any quarters our independence or the integrity of our territory is threatened."

Since the early preparedness movement had an anti-administration bias and most of its leaders were Republicans, Wilson opposed it, but the German submarine campaign in 1915 changed his mind. On the day he sent the third *Lusitania* note, July 21, 1915, he instructed his Secretaries of War and Navy to make plans for a wise and adequate national defense. In November, he presented his preparedness program to the country, calling for naval expansion and an increase of the Army.

Pacifists, progressives, and peace groups immediately began a nation-wide campaign opposing Wilson's program, which, they said, was merely disguised militarism and imperialism. Since nothing threatened American security, they pointed out, the United States should not prepare for war but should try to bring peace to the world. The opposition, particularly in Congress, was so strong that Wilson decided to take the issue to the people.

In January, 1916, the President began a speaking tour of the East and Middle West to sell the voters military preparedness. At St. Louis he said the United States should have "incomparably the most adequate navy in the world." He also gave the impression that he opposed militarism and would do all in his power to keep the nation out of war. Wilson apparently made few converts to preparedness and gained little support from the interventionists, who denounced him for not arming directly against the Germans.

While involved in the preparedness controversy, Wilson made one of his major efforts to end the war. At the end of January, 1915, he had sent Colonel House to London, Paris, and Berlin to explore the possibilities of mediation. After months of negotiation, nothing came of House's efforts. "Everybody seems to want peace," he wrote, "but nobody is willing to concede enough to get it." House returned to the United States in June believing his country would be drawn into the war.

Convinced that the only sure way of keeping the United States out of the war was to end it, Wilson sent the Colonel on another peace mission to Europe in January, 1916. The President had already come to believe that intervention was preferable to a German victory, but at this time he considered the war a stalemate. Hence the military situation provided the United States with an opportunity to promote a peace without a crushing victory for either side. Wilson was prepared, if necessary, to use American power to bring the reluctant side into line.

House talked with British, French, and German leaders. He assured the French that the United States would intervene before allowing Germany to defeat them. In London he and Sir Edward Grey signed an agreement on February 22 known as the House-Grey Memorandum, saying that whenever England and France considered the time "opportune," Wilson would call a peace conference. If the Allies accepted the invitation and Germany refused it, the United States would probably enter the war against Germany. If the Germans accepted, Wilson would help the Allies secure a favorable peace. If the Germans refused reasonable terms at the conference, the United States would join the war on the Allied side.

Before accepting the agreement, the President inserted the word "probably" before the second clause promising American intervention. He did not change the essential meaning of the commitment. Since only Congress could declare war, he merely made the memorandum conform to his constitutional power.

As the Allied military position improved in the spring and summer of 1916 and Grey doubted that the President could bring the United States into the war if the projected conference failed, nothing came of the memorandum. Both sides, moreover, at this time were opposed to mediation because each was still confident of ultimate victory.

After the failure of his peace plan, Wilson devoted himself to his re-election campaign which began during the controversy over preparedness. His leadership of this cause virtually killed it as a campaign issue. To strengthen the Army, Congress passed the National Defense Act on June 3, followed by a huge Naval Appropriations Bill of August 15 that prompted a congressional leader of the anti-preparedness forces to exclaim that "the United States today becomes the most militaristic naval nation on earth." Despite angry opposition, the President signed the bill.

Yet neither preparedness nor the horror excited by German sabotage and submarine warfare had aroused a broad sentiment for war. At the presidential nominating conventions politicians of both major parties realized that the voters passionately desired peace. The Democrats renominated Wilson, this time by acclamation, and endorsed his foreign policy. The Republicans passed over Theodore Roosevelt and other interventionists and nominated Charles Evans Hughes, an associate justice of the Supreme Court.

From the outset the Democrats advertised Wilson as the champion of peace, covering the country with the cry, "he kept us out of war." At times the President felt the slogan raised false hopes. "I can't keep the country out of war," he confided to a cabinet member. "They talk of me as though I were a god. Any little German lieutenant can put us into the war at any time by some calculated outrage." Yet he could also say that "I am not expecting this country to get into war."

On the eve of the election some of Wilson's supporters summed up the issue in an advertisement that read in part:

> You are Working — *Not Fighting!*
> Alive and Happy; — *Not Cannon Fodder!*
> Wilson and Peace with Honor?
> or
> Hughes with Roosevelt and War?

Republican politicians tried to convince the electorate that Hughes opposed intervention more than Wilson did. "A vote for me is not a vote for war," Hughes declared. "It is a vote for lasting peace." He could not, however, control Roosevelt's fiery demands for intervention. Since he accepted Roosevelt's support and stood behind his bellicose speeches, many voters gained the impression that the Republican party stood for war. The German Ambassador was probably close to the truth when he reported that "if Hughes is defeated he has Roosevelt to thank for it."

Other issues perhaps were equally important, but the distribution of votes indicated that where the peace issue was decisive, Wilson led. He had, in effect, fused the peace issue with the ideals of progressivism. Wilson narrowly won the election, but his party did not do as well as he, retaining only a precarious control in Congress.

During the election campaign, in September and October, the Germans indicated that they were anxious to make peace. They told Wilson they would be receptive if he were to offer his good offices, hinting that otherwise they might resume unrestricted submarine warfare. Even though he feared that American involvement might become inevitable unless the war ended, Wilson would not move until after the election. As soon as he had won, he decided to try to bring the belligerents together in a peace conference, hoping that it would result in a compromise settlement and an international organization to keep the peace.

When November passed and Wilson did not act, the Germans grew impatient. Before the President could reveal his plan, they took the initiative. Anxious to exploit a military situation that had turned in their favor on both western and eastern fronts, they announced on December 12 that they were willing to discuss peace with their enemies.

That announcement forced Wilson to modify his own plan but not to abandon it. Six days later he sent identical notes to the belligerents asking them simply to state their war objectives. Publicly, the Allies said they would consider neither the German nor the American proposal, but privately the British told the President they were willing to talk peace if the Germans would do so on reasonable terms. The Germans informed Wilson they preferred the direct negotiations they had suggested. Actually, neither side was willing to discuss peace on Wilson's terms. Their objectives were so sweeping that only a victor's peace could justify them.

Wilson, meanwhile, had decided to explain his concept of what kind of a peace there should be to the peoples of the world. For months he had considered the idea of trying to ensure peace at the end of the war with a league of nations. In January, 1917, he went before the Senate and outlined the kind of peace he thought the United States would support. There must be, he said, "a peace without victory" since a conqueror's peace would not last. It must be a peace based on the equality of all nations, upon freedom of the seas, upon a general reduction of armaments, and other general principles, "a peace made secure by the organized major force of mankind."

The president's unprecedented offer to use the power of the United States for world peace brought no results. Three days earlier, Ambassador Bernstorff had received word that his government would resume unrestricted submarine warfare beginning February 1. Germany's decision, made firm at a memorable "Crown Council" at Pless on January 9, constituted a victory for the military authorities and a defeat for the civilian government.

The civilian leaders believed that the submarine campaign would fail and would assure Germany's defeat by bringing the United States into the war. The military leaders knew that unrestricted submarine warfare would push the United States into the war but calculated that it would make no difference. The German generals had decided that the army could not break the stalemate on land and that only the submarine could bring victory. They counted on the underwater fleet, now enlarged to more than a hun-

dred U-boats, to knock out the Allies before the military power and resources of the United States could become effective. "We are counting on
the possibility of war with the United States," one of them explained, "and
have made all preparations to meet it. Things can not be worse than they
are now."

Bernstorff tried to persuade his superiors to reconsider, but was unsuccessful. On January 31, at the same time he delivered Germany's answer to
Wilson's request for peace terms, he announced the decision to resume unrestricted submarine warfare. Three days later Wilson broke off diplomatic
relations. Still hoping to avoid war, he told a joint session of Congress that
only "actual overt acts" would make him believe that Germany would carry
out her threat.

Germany had not been bluffing; her submarines began their campaign of
terror on schedule. Frightened by the undersea warfare, many American
shippers kept their ships and cargoes in port. Wilson's advisers and others
demanded armament and protection for American ships. The President at
first refused to ask Congress for authority to arm merchant vessels, but the
Zimmermann Telegram, received in the State Department on the evening
of February 24, convinced him of Germany's hostile intentions and
changed his mind.

Sent originally by the German Foreign Minister, Alfred Zimmermann, to
Bernstorff for relay to the German Minister in Mexico, the telegram had
been intercepted and decoded by British naval intelligence and turned
over to the Department of State. If the United States went to war against
Germany, it said, the German Minister in Mexico should ask Mexico to
join an alliance with Germany and Japan, Britain's ally. Mexico's reward,
if Germany won, would be her "lost territory" of Arizona, New Mexico, and
Texas.

Two days later Wilson asked a joint session of Congress for authority to
arm merchant ships and to "employ any other instrumentalities and methods" to protect American ships and lives. What he wanted, he explained,
was an "armed Neutrality" that need not lead to war. On the following day,
black newspaper headlines shouted that a German submarine sank the
Cunard passenger liner *Laconia*. Two American women and an American
seaman lost their lives in the icy waters of the Atlantic. Many Americans
considered this the "overt act" the President awaited.

Three days later the government published the Zimmermann Telegram.
Americans were stunned; here was another overt act of German hostility.
Strong anti-German feeling swelled up throughout the country, particularly
in the Southwest where it previously had been mild. Even though Germany
had an undeniable right to seek allies against a possible enemy, the Zimmermann proposal was a blunder, compounded when Zimmermann admitted
its authenticity. As an ally to Germany, Mexico was virtually useless. Her

nuisance value hardly justified the risk of precipitating more American anger against Germany. The Washington *Post* called the proposal "sheer lunacy" and the *Literary Digest* aptly described it as "elephantine diplomacy."

Publication of the Zimmermann Telegram prompted the House to give quick approval to Wilson's request to arm merchant ships, but a dozen senators under the leadership of Robert La Follette and George W. Norris filibustered it to death. The President denounced them as "a little group of willful men, representing no opinion but their own," and then armed the ships on his own authority. American merchantmen, with guns ready to shoot, were moving through the war zones before the end of March. More Americans lost their lives on March 18 when three American ships went down in torpedo attacks. "Now Germany has committed an indisputable overt act," the Chicago *Daily Tribune* pointed out. "If the United States is going to make good its word, it must go to war."

In the face of the German attacks on American lives and property, neutrality seemed no longer possible. Germany's several overt acts, Wilson believed, left no alternative but war. The policy of strict accountability had run its course. The decision for war tormented the President. "Once lead this people into war," he told a newspaper friend, "and they'll forget there ever was such a thing as tolerance. To fight you must be brutal and ruthless, and the spirit of ruthless brutality will enter into the very fibre of our national life. . . ." On the following evening, April 2, 1917, Wilson read his war message to the Congress he had called into joint session.

Since a March revolution in Russia held promise of a democratic regime in place of the autocratic tsars, Wilson could say in his message that the major Allied governments were democratic. "The world must be made safe for democracy. Its peace must be planted upon the tested foundations of political liberty," he declared. He also denounced the submarine as waging "a warfare against mankind" and "against all nations."

Four days later Congress passed a formal declaration of war. In the House the vote was 373 to 50 and in the Senate, 82 to 6.

Since the President had consistently condemned the unbridled use of the submarine and only retreat or war seemed possible when Germany persisted in using it, war came over the immediate issue of the submarine. Wilson and his advisers, however, also believed that the welfare of their country would be served better with a victory for the Allies than for Germany. In addition, Wilson apparently feared that Germany, if victorious, would destroy the balance of power necessary for the new order based on democracy and international law he wanted to see in the postwar world.

Most Americans, on the other hand, apparently went to war with reluctance or indifference, envisaging nothing beyond the defeat of Germany. Senator William E. Borah of Idaho spoke for others besides himself when he said, "I join no crusade; I seek or accept no alliances; I obligate this Government to no other power. I make war alone for my countrymen and their rights, for my country and its honor." This fundamental difference between the President's objectives and those of some of his own people was to influence the peace.

WOODROW WILSON

We have no quarrel with the German people. We have no feeling towards them but one of sympathy and friendship. It was not upon their impulse that their government acted in entering this war. It was not with their previous knowledge and approval. It was a war determined upon as wars used to be determined upon in the old, unhappy days when peoples were nowhere consulted by their rulers and wars were provoked and waged in the interest of dynasties or of little groups of ambitious men who were accustomed to use their fellow men as pawns and tools. . . .

We are accepting this challenge of hostile purpose because we know that in such a Government, following such methods, we can never have a friend; and that in the presence of its organized power, always lying in wait to accomplish we know not what purpose, there can be no assured security for the democratic Governments of the world. We are now about to accept gauge of battle with this natural foe to liberty and shall, if necessary, spend the whole force of the nation to check and nullify its pretensions and its power. We are glad, now that we see the facts with no veil of false pretense about them, to fight thus for the ultimate peace of the world and for the liberation of its peoples, the German peoples included: for the rights of nations great and small and the privilege of men everywhere to choose their way of life and of obedience. The world must be made safe for democracy. Its peace must be planted upon the tested foundations of political liberty. We have no selfish ends to serve. We desire no conquest, no dominion. We seek no indemnities for ourselves, no material compensation for the sacrifices we shall freely make. We are but one of the champions of the rights of mankind. We shall be satisfied when those rights have been made as secure as the faith and the freedom of nations can make them.

Excerpts from President Wilson's Message to Congress, April 2, 1917.

Chapter Three

THE PRESIDENT
AND CONGRESS

Very few human beings bear such awesome responsibilities or wield such extensive powers in the nuclear age as the President of the United States. Yet the crucial thing to be comprehended in attempting to understand how United States foreign policy is made is that control over foreign policy is *fragmented*. The President's powers, great as they are, are not adequate to meet his foreign policy responsibilities without cooperation from others — most notably the Congress — who share responsibility for foreign policy-making.

From this sharing of power, the problem of coordination arises. Over the years, moreover, a number of customs and practices which often complicate this problem have become woven into our political system. Those who benefit from them, or think they do, will not allow them to be changed easily. These customs and practices, together with the relevant provisions of the Constitution itself, form the institutional framework within which American foreign policy is made.

THE PRESIDENT'S POWERS

Article II of the Constitution grants the following powers to the President:

> The executive power shall be vested in a **President of the United States of America** . . . he may require the opinion, in writing, of the principal officer in each of the executive departments, upon any subject relating to the duties of their respective offices. . . .
>
> The President shall be the **commander in chief of the army and navy.** . . .
>
> He shall have the power, by and with the advice and consent of the Senate, to make treaties, provided two thirds of the senators present

concur; and he shall nominate, and by and with the advice and consent
of the senate, shall appoint ambassadors, other public ministers and consuls, judges of the Supreme Court, and all other officers of the United
States, whose appointments are not otherwise herein provided for. . . .

He shall receive ambassadors and other public ministers; he shall
take care that the laws be faithfully executed, and shall commission all
the officers of the United States.

In practice, the President today has primary responsibility in conducting
the nation's foreign policy. He alone is entitled to receive official communications from foreign governments; he alone can officially declare and
communicate to foreign governments the policies of the United States. He
determines which foreign states and governments the nation will recognize
and deal with. He is at liberty to withdraw recognition, or sever diplomatic
relations, at his discretion. It has also been established that American delegates to international organizations, such as the United Nations, are appointed by, removed by, and responsible to, the President, who is therefore
able to decide how the nation shall vote and act in such bodies.

With the consent of the Senate, the President may conclude treaties with
other nations; and even without Senate consent he may enter into executive
agreements not clearly distinguishable from treaties in their effects under
both national and international law. Moreover, should the Senate, in consenting to a treaty, make revisions he finds unacceptable, the President is
not obliged to proclaim it in force. The Congress, to be sure, is not legally
bound to pass legislation needed to implement an executive agreement. But
many of these agreements do not require implementing legislation, and
when congressional action is needed, the moral or political pressure on the
legislature to comply may be considerable.

The President's control over our enormous civilian and military bureaucracy is another major source of his power. Through the gathering and
analysis of military, political, and economic intelligence the President has
at his disposal a quantity of information available to no other unit of government. The small professional staffs available to Congress for the study of
foreign affairs cannot hope to match the executive bureaucracy in generating
the basic information necessary for the formulation of sound, independent foreign policy alternatives. (Thus there have been relatively few successful congressional foreign policy initiatives in recent years.) [1] For this reason
too, the President is bound to have certain advantages in a foreign policy

---

[1] A conspicuous exception was the Monroney Resolution of 1958, which led to the
establishment of an International Development Association to make loans on relatively
easy terms to developing nations. In this connection, it should be recalled that the President is at liberty to veto congressional initiatives of which he may disapprove — subject to
being overridden by repassage by two-thirds votes in each house. More important, he may
simply decline to act in ways which may be necessary to the implementation of the initiative in question.

debate with Congress or with critics outside the government. And, of course, the President is also authorized to decide what portion of the information collected by the executive branch is to be made public, and when.

Nor can congressional power to ratify his appointments keep the chief executive from making use of executive agents — not subject to Senate confirmation — to negotiate on his behalf with enemies and allies and to handle other critical foreign policy assignments. Presidents Wilson and Franklin D. Roosevelt, for example, made extensive use of such personal agents (Colonel Edward M. House and Harry Hopkins), for just such purposes.

As commander-in-chief, finally, the President controls the movements of the national military establishment. Though only the Congress can actually declare war, he may issue orders which will put the nation at war in fact whether Congress declares so formally or not. In the event of war or national emergency, legislative delegations of power, his role as commander-in-chief, and his responsibility to "take care that the laws be faithfully executed" combine to give the President nearly dictatorial power over the nation. In an era of pushbutton war, it is the President who decides, ultimately, if and when the buttons will be pushed.

THE POWERS OF CONGRESS

The imperatives of the missile age and the rapid expansion of the powers of the presidency have created some concern, in the Congress and in the nation, that one man holds in his hands the power of life and death over us all, whatever the elected representatives of the people in Congress may think or say. When the President, as commander-in-chief, commits American soldiers to military action, can the Congress really refuse to provide them with arms and supplies, whatever its view of the President's policies? This concern has become a painful dilemma to those who oppose President Johnson's policy in Vietnam. We cannot afford to have foreign policy made by the 535 men who make up the Congress. But should we be satisfied to have it made essentially by one man instead?

Actually, it is somewhat of an oversimplification to pose the question in this way. Power to commit the nation to war *does* and *must* lie with the President in situations where speed and secrecy are necessary for national survival. The Congress could probably find ways to limit the American commitment in Vietnam *if* it were unified in opposing the President's policies there, but it cannot pursue a foreign policy of its own opposed to the President's. Deadlocks due to legislative-executive differences on domestic policy are bad enough. In foreign policy, they could be fatal. Decisions must be made. In a parliamentary system, such a deadlock might be resolved by replacing the prime minister with a successor responsive to the views of the legislature. In a presidential system, like our own, it is the chief executive who normally has the final say.

Nevertheless, the Congress of the United States remains the most power-ful legislative body in any of the major states of the world today. The Con-stitution (in Article I) assigns the Congress, too, important responsibilities relating to foreign affairs:

> All legislative powers herein granted shall be vested in a Congress of the United States, which shall consist of a Senate and a House of Representatives.
>
> The House of Representatives . . . shall have the sole power of im-peachment . . . The Senate shall have the sole power to try all im-peachments. . . .
>
> The Congress shall have the power
>
> To lay and collect taxes, duties, imposts, and excises, to pay the debts and provide for the common defense and general welfare of the United States; . . .
>
> To regulate commerce with foreign nations. . . .
>
> To establish a uniform rule of naturalization. . . .
>
> To define and punish piracies and felonies committed on the high seas, and offenses against the law of nations;
>
> To declare war. . . .
>
> To raise and support armies, but no appropriation of money to that use shall be for a longer term than two years;
>
> To provide and maintain a navy;
>
> To make rules for the government and regulation of the land and naval forces;
>
> To provide for calling forth the militia to execute the laws of the Union, suppress insurrections and repel invasions;
>
> To provide for organizing, arming, and disciplining the militia, and for governing such part of them as may be employed in the service of the United States. . . .
>
> To make all laws which shall be necessary and proper for carrying into execution the foregoing powers. . . .
>
> The immigration or importation of such persons as any of the states now existing shall think proper to admit, shall not be prohibited by the Congress prior to the year one thousand eight hundred and eight. . . .
>
> No money shall be drawn from the Treasury, but in consequence of appropriations made by law.

In addition, of course, are the provisions previously quoted requiring Sen-ate approval of treaties, by two-thirds vote, and of executive appointments.

Most important among these powers today is the "power of the purse." The President is totally dependent upon Congress for the funds needed to support a military establishment adequate to defend the nation and to afford it a position of strength in negotiations with foreign governments. Only the Congress can provide the funds for the foreign aid programs which have become a principal instrument of American foreign policy since World War II; for the upkeep of such executive agencies as the Department of State, the Foreign Service, the United States Information Agency, and the Central Intelligence Agency; or for carrying out a space program which the President may consider vital to our international prestige. In deciding, say, to appropriate more funds for the Air Force and less for the Army, or more for aid to Vietnam and less for India, the Congress is making decisions of grave import to national security.

In addition to regulating the quantity of funds for foreign policy purposes, Congress may impose restrictions on their use. Thus, nations engaging in strategic trade with Cuba, trading at all with Communist China, providing military aid to any Communist nation, or expropriating American-owned property without "just compensation" have been barred from receiving United States aid on various occasions.

Similarly, the Senate is in a position to amend or attach reservations to treaties as a condition of consenting to them. Considerable controversy has centered around the exercise of this power in the course of American history. Actually, the Senate has rarely rejected major treaties outright. But on many occasions the President has been induced to withdraw or revise treaties which were not well received in the Senate. More important still, the requirement of Senate approval — and particularly the two-thirds rule — must always be in the minds of American diplomats while negotiations are in progress. Since the Versailles Treaty disaster, important treaties have generally been submitted to Congress only after extensive consultation with leaders of both parties in the Senate, and often in the House as well.

The congressional prerogative to declare war is of minimal importance today. At Pearl Harbor and in Korea and Vietnam, American military forces were engaged in fighting an enemy before Congress could begin to discuss, let alone decide, whether war should be formally declared. In the Korean case, no declaration of war was ever requested or issued; yet American troops fought on that Asian peninsula for over three years and suffered many more casualties than in all our previous foreign wars combined, save the two world wars. In Vietnam, again, no declaration of war has been requested. Though some congressional leaders were displeased in both cases by the President's failure to consult them, the appropriations needed for prosecution of the conflicts were quickly approved. It is hard to imagine that, in the future, any large-scale military action will begin in such a way that a congressional resolution will determine whether or not America goes to war.

The power of Congress to regulate our foreign trade, on the other hand, has grown increasingly important in this era of "competitive coexistence." Economists and political scientists have established beyond question the close relationship between trade and political ties among nations. The current prohibitions on strategic trade with the Communist bloc, and on *any* trade with Cuba and Communist China are illustrations of the use of trade as a political weapon by the United States today. Less obvious, but perhaps more significant, is the effect of United States tariff and trade policies on our relationships with our NATO allies, Japan, and the Latin American republics. Since the Reciprocal Trade Act of 1934, Congress has delegated substantial discretionary authority over trade policy to the President. But these delegations of power have been temporary, and the President's need to seek their renewal periodically has left Congress in possession of a useful bargaining counter.

Congressional immigration policies, too, may contribute to the improvement or deterioration of our relations with other nations. Perhaps the classic illustration is the National Origins Act of 1924 which excluded Japanese immigrants entirely, in violation of the "Gentlemen's Agreement" reached by the United States and Japanese governments in 1907. President Coolidge opposed the Japanese exclusion provisions; and less than 250 Japanese would have been able to enter the country annually if the quota formula applied to most nations had been followed in Japan's case also. But neither of these facts was able to dissuade the Congress from action which gave grave offense to the government and people of Japan. In 1943, in contrast, congressional action to end the Chinese exclusion policy and to renounce American extraterritorial privileges in China, provided a helpful gesture of sympathy toward a wartime ally. (The national origins criterion was finally abandoned in 1965.)

The houses of Congress may also express their foreign policy opinions to the executive and to the world singly by passing simple resolutions or jointly by passing concurrent resolutions. Neither subject to veto nor legally binding upon the President, these resolutions compel at least the thoughtful attention of both the President and the nation. They may strengthen the President's hand at a critical moment — as did the 1948 "Vandenberg Resolution" which paved the way for American participation in the North Atlantic Treaty Organization. Or, they may tend to restrict the President's freedom of action — as in the case of repeated nearly unanimous congressional resolutions expressing opposition to the seating of Communist China in the United Nations.

Finally, members of Congress may express and try to rally support for their opinions on foreign policy questions in debate on the floor of the Senate or House, during committee hearings or investigations, at political meetings and rallies, in statements to the press, or on trips abroad.

Congressional committees enjoy wide discretion in conducting and structuring hearings and investigations. Thus the real purposes and effects of these proceedings may vary widely. Some hearings may be intended to build support for the President's policies; others — like those held in 1966 by both the Senate Foreign Relations and the House Foreign Affairs Committees — to provoke public debate concerning the wisdom of these policies. Some investigations may be designed primarily to inform the Congress; others — like the Senate Internal Security Subcommittee investigations conducted in the early 1950's under the guidance of Senators Patrick McCarran and Joseph McCarthy — may become primarily a means of embarrassing administration foreign policy officials and even career Foreign Service Officers.

The activities of individual legislators may also provide either aid or substantial discomfort to the administration. On the one hand, Democratic Speaker Sam Rayburn and Senate Foreign Relations Committee Chairman Walter F. George saved the day for President Eisenhower's foreign policy proposals on more than one occasion. On the other, southern Democratic Senator Allen Ellender's scathing public criticisms of the domestic policies of the African nations he visited in 1963 embarrassed the Kennedy administration considerably. How, after all, were his unlettered listeners supposed to know that the segregationist views of this important United States official were not shared by the President and other responsible policymakers?

In addition to its specific powers relating to foreign affairs, Congress retains important residual powers simply by virtue of its general legislative authority in all matters foreign and domestic. The line between foreign and domestic legislation has become highly blurred under the pressure of the total war and total diplomacy of modern times. In the long run, congressional willingness to support policies which will build up the nation's economic strength in generations to come may prove more significant for America's position in the world than the passage of an adequate reciprocal trade bill here and now. And appropriations to accelerate national progress in the "space race" may have less impact on American prestige than the effectiveness with which the Congress deals with the civil rights proposals before it.

If worst came to worst, Congress' power to impeach the President and other executive officials, and to initiate constitutional amendments, might prove potent weapons in an all-out struggle for control of foreign policy. The Constitution restricts grounds for impeachment to "treason, bribery, or other high crimes or misdemeanors" and requires a two-thirds vote by the Senate for conviction. No American President has ever been removed from office in this manner. One, Andrew Johnson, was impeached but not convicted. Yet cries of "impeach the President" have been legion in American history, and probably the mere spectacle of Congress giving serious consideration to such a proposal would be a substantial embarrassment to any chief executive.

The possible effect on foreign affairs of the power to initiate constitutional amendments was illustrated not long ago when the George resolution

— a watered-down version of the Bricker amendment — failed by only one vote to secure the two-thirds needed for Senate approval. This proposed amendment, introduced by Senator John Bricker, would have restricted severely the President's power to negotiate treaties and executive agreements with other nations by, in some cases, requiring ratification by each of the (then) forty-eight state legislatures in addition to approval by two-thirds of the Senate and a majority of the House of Representatives!

An all-out struggle between Congress and the executive would be disastrous. For while it takes the cooperation of *both* the President *and* the Congress to formulate and carry out an effective foreign policy, extreme or irresponsible action on the part of either *one* is sufficient to make an effective foreign policy impossible. Either congressional failure to appropriate funds for national defense, or presidential refusal to make use of such funds, for example, would leave the nation completely defenseless.

The respective spheres of jurisdiction of Congress and the President should therefore not be taken too literally. Nominally, for instance, the power to recognize foreign governments belongs wholly to the President. But if the President should recognize a government — say that of Cuba or Communist China — against the strong feelings of congressional leaders, his ability to secure the passage of adequate foreign aid appropriations or reciprocal trade legislation might well be impaired. As a result, he must take careful account of the views of the Congress even in formulating policies which, constitutionally, are clearly within his own sphere of jurisdiction.

THE PROBLEM OF COORDINATION

Thus, the problem faced by our foreign policymakers is not how to wrest control from the upstarts in "the other branch" of the government. It is rather how the many formidable barriers to the achievement of a unified and effective foreign policy can be overcome within the framework of shared powers laid down by the Constitution. This problem of how to secure executive-legislative cooperation in making foreign policy is not an easy one to solve; for many political — as well as constitutional — obstacles to cooperation are built into the system.

In the first place, neither the executive nor the legislative branch is united within itself on foreign policy questions. The Secretary of State may favor a particular nuclear test ban agreement, whereas the Secretary of Defense opposes it. Within these departments, similarly, the same treaty may be favored strongly by the Assistant Secretary of State for International Organization Affairs — thinking, perhaps, of the good will the conclusion of such a treaty might create among delegates of the large group of uncommitted nations in the United Nations General Assembly; it may be opposed with equal vigor by the Assistant Secretary for Congressional Relations, who feels it may antagonize the Senate minority leader and thereby jeopardize support for other important administration policy measures. Within the Department of

Defense, in turn, the Secretary of the Army may favor the treaty on the ground that it portends greater emphasis on conventional weapons and ground forces in the future; the Secretary of the Air Force may oppose it for precisely the same reason.

In the executive branch there is, at least, an authoritative point of decision at which these differing policy views may be reconciled and coordinated. That point of decision is, of course, the presidency — a state of affairs reflected in President Truman's desk placard: "The Buck Stops Here."

In the legislative branch, in contrast, there is no authoritative point at which "the buck stops." And this is true *within* each of the houses of Congress as well as between them. A search for the centers of foreign policy influence within the Congress therefore requires a brief discussion of the formal and informal organization for foreign policy decisionmaking in each house.

FOREIGN POLICYMAKING IN THE SENATE

Because of its smaller size and greater freedom of debate, as well as because of its special constitutional prerogatives in ratifying treaties and executive appointments, the Senate has traditionally been the senior congressional partner in the making of foreign policy.

Within the Senate, the most significant center of influence on foreign policy legislation is unquestionably the Foreign Relations Committee. Its size has varied between thirteen and nineteen since the Legislative Reorganization Act of 1946. Studies of its role in the decade following showed that its recommendations were approved by the Senate almost 90 per cent of the time; that its members introduced nearly half of the foreign policy bills considered by the Senate; and that it is probably the most prestigious committee in the upper house. Its members are more likely than most of their colleagues to be interested in foreign affairs, and, after some service on the committee, are certainly better informed in this field than most Senators. They are also more likely than members of other Senate committees to have had previous experience in law or college teaching rather than in business, before entering politics; and, in general, to support "internationalist" measures and presidential foreign policy initiatives.

Indications are, in fact, that service on the committee in itself tends to influence new committee members toward increased willingness to support foreign aid and other internationalist foreign policy proposals. In addition, the committee's legislative effectiveness — and its bargaining position with the executive branch — have been increased in the postwar years by its high degree of unity on the measures it has considered.

The Foreign Relations Committee divides into seven subcommittees, with each member of the full committee serving on two. In order to facilitate liaison with the Department of State, the areas of jurisdiction of these subcommittees have been designed to correspond, for the most part, with those of the key geographic and functional administrative subdivisions of the Department.

The chairmanship of the Foreign Relations Committee — as of all other Senate and House committees — is determined by the seniority rule. Thus the member of the majority party with the longest term of service on the committee receives this coveted post. Ability or willingness to support the President, or even his own party's Senate leadership, is not required. So long as the voters in his state continue to re-elect him, he will not be removed from his position until control of the Senate passes to the opposition party.[2] At this point, the chairmanship will pass into the hands of a similarly chosen Senator of the new majority party, and the previous chairman will become ranking minority member of the committee and often the leading foreign policy spokesman for his party in the Senate.

Despite its great influence, however, the Foreign Relations Committee is not the only Senate committee which acts on legislation affecting foreign policy. Such major foreign policy measures as military and foreign aid appropriations fall within the jurisdiction of the Appropriations Committee. Selective service, military strategy and tactics, and the size and organization of the armed forces are reviewed by the Armed Services Committee. And most of the Senate's fifteen committees act at least occasionally on bills which affect foreign affairs. Members of these committees are frequently less sympathetic to administration foreign policy requests than their colleagues on the Foreign Relations Committee. Holbert Carroll notes:

> The attitude of many members of Congress regarding . . . [State Department] appropriations . . . may be illustrated by an incident that occurred in 1953. The Bureau of the Budget, for reasons of economy, had failed to include an appropriation in the annual budget for Oahe Dam in South Dakota. Following negotiations between Senator Karl E. Mundt (R., S. Dak.) and the director of the Budget Bureau, the sum of $8,250,000 was restored to the budget for the dam. In a report to his constituents, Senator Mundt explained what happened: "With budget approval, it now appears we'll get our eight and a quarter million, and last week I fulfilled my part of the promise. On motions made by me in the Senate Appropriations Committee, $8,000,000 was cut from the funds approved for State Department personnel." Before the Senator had performed his part of the bargain, the House had reduced appropriations for salaries and expenses for the State Department by 30 per cent.[3]

2 A partial exception to this rule occurred in 1959 when the aged chairman of the committee, Theodore F. Green of Rhode Island, was persuaded to resign his chairmanship in favor of J. W. Fulbright of Arkansas.

3 *The House of Representatives and Foreign Affairs* (University of Pittsburgh Press, 1958; rev. ed.; Boston: Little, Brown, 1966), pp. 183–184.

Much of the preceding paragraphs is drawn from David N. Farnsworth, *The Senate Committee on Foreign Relations* (Urbana, Ill.: University of Illinois Press, 1961), and from

FOREIGN POLICYMAKING
IN THE HOUSE

In a number of respects, the procedures for dealing with foreign policy legislation in the House are similar to those in the Senate. Most basic decisions are made in committee rather than on the floor of the House. Chairmanships and, to a considerable extent, committee assignments and transfers as well, are determined by the seniority system. And members of the Foreign Affairs Committee have generally treated the President's foreign policy requests more sympathetically than their colleagues on other key house committees — though the appointment of five conservative Republicans to vacancies on this committee in 1963, while five liberal Democrats were being appointed to the Appropriations Committee has begun to alter this tendency.

But there are important differences as well. The House played a relatively minor role in foreign policy matters until World War II. As a result, the prestige of its Committee on Foreign Affairs was low. More recently, the growing importance of the appropriations power has greatly augmented the influence of the lower house in foreign policy, and assignment to the Foreign Affairs Committee has become a much sought after prize. Nevertheless, this committee's prestige does not yet match that of its Senate counterpart, and may actually have declined since the 1950's.[4] At times, in fact, the Foreign Affairs Committee seems to be overwhelmed by the influence of the other powerful House committees with which it must share jurisdiction over foreign policy questions. These include not only the Appropriations and Armed Services Committees, as in the Senate, but that bulwark of congressional conservatism, the Rules Committee.[5] Consequently, coordination of foreign policy measures in the House is even more difficult than in the Senate.

The power of the Appropriations Committee is especially formidable.

U.S. Senate, Committee on Foreign Relations, *Background Information on the Committee on Foreign Relations*, 89th Cong., 2nd sess., Committee Print, January, 1966.

On the role of Congress in making foreign policy, see also Robert A. Dahl, *Congress and Foreign Policy* (New York: Harcourt, Brace, 1950); James A. Robinson, *Congress and Foreign Policy-Making* (Homewood, Ill.: Dorsey Press, 1962); David B. Truman (ed.), *The Congress and America's Future* (Englewood Cliffs, N.J.: Prentice-Hall, 1965); Nelson W. Polsby, *Congress and the Presidency* (Englewood Cliffs, N.J.: Prentice-Hall, 1964); and Richard F. Fenno, Jr., *The Power of the Purse* (Boston: Little, Brown, 1966).

4 See Carroll, *op. cit.*, p. 354.

5 The Rules Committee's ability to block legislation, though still formidable, has been curbed by recent reforms. In 1961, its membership was increased from twelve to fifteen, and two liberal Democrats were appointed to it. In 1965, a rule was adopted permitting the Speaker to recognize any member of the substantive committee concerned to introduce a bill directly onto the House floor if the Rules Committee failed to report it within twenty-one days. And in 1966, Howard W. Smith of Virginia, long the chairman and dominant member of the Rules Committee, was defeated in a primary election in his reapportioned district.

Its decisions are rarely overruled on foreign or domestic matters — no Congressman is eager to court the disfavor of a committee which may control the level of federal expenditures in his own district. Its power, moreover, is divided among about a dozen subcommittees which are practically sovereign in their assigned domains. Their decisions almost invariably become the decisions of the full committee and consequently of the whole House. Unlike their Senate counterparts, they do not permit members of the substantive committees directly concerned to attend their deliberations.

Perhaps the most important of these subcommittees, for foreign policy purposes, is the Foreign Operations Subcommittee, into whose jurisdiction foreign aid bills fall. And "fall" is the right word; for the subcommittee's chairman for much of the past decade has been Otto Passman who openly opposes the whole concept of foreign aid and uses his influence accordingly.[6] As a result, House cuts in presidential foreign aid requests have been so steep that the administration has often depended on "appeal" to the Senate, and subsequent conference committee compromise, to restore the final figure to an amount consistent with national security needs, as the President sees them.[7]

AN AID BILL RUNS
THE CONGRESSIONAL GAUNTLET

Thus, Congressional legislative procedure subjects foreign policy proposals to much more than merely *double* jeopardy. Richard Fenno, Jr. has written:

> Since House decision is a composite of several formal (and countless informal) decisions, and since at each stage in decision-making a different cluster of House leaders may prevail, supporters of a given bill must build a series of majorities — in the substantive committee, in the Rules Committee, on the floor, and in conference — if they are to be successful. Opponents of a bill, however, need to build but a single majority — at any one stage in the process — to achieve their ends.[8]

When, for example, the President requests that a certain amount of economic aid be provided to an ally of the United States, a bill to *authorize* this expenditure must be considered first by the House Foreign Affairs Com-

[6] Some exchanges between Representative Passman and administration officials testifying before his subcommittee are included as part of a case study in the chapter on the developing nations.

[7] Carroll, *op. cit.*, chap. 9. Support for administration foreign policy proposals in the Senate has dwindled in recent years due to differences between President Johnson and key members of the Foreign Relations Committee over United States policy in Vietnam. Thus administration appeals to the Senate to restore House foreign aid cuts will probably not be fruitful at least during the remainder of President Johnson's term in office. For an explanation of the Senate's greater "liberalism," based on a comparative analysis of Senate and House constituencies, see Louis A. Froman, Jr., *Congressmen and Their Constituencies* (Chicago: Rand-McNally, 1963).

[8] Truman (ed.), *op. cit.*, p. 60.

mittee. Then, if approved, it is forwarded to the Rules Committee to be cleared for floor debate by the House as a whole. In the Senate, a similar bill must be reported out of the Senate Foreign Relations Committee before being scheduled by the Senate leadership for debate on the floor.[9]

Almost certainly, the bill will not pass both houses in identical form; so a conference committee must be convened to iron out differences. Nominally, conference committees are appointed by the presiding officers of the two houses, the Vice President and Speaker, respectively. In practice, the chairman and ranking minority members of the committees which considered the bill usually make the selections. Once a compromise has been agreed upon, the bill is brought once more to the floor of each house and voted upon again. At this point, the presidential request, appropriately modified — and probably considerably reduced — has been "authorized," but no funds have been made available. Before the amount authorized actually can be spent, the bill must run the *appropriations* gauntlet.

The process starts in Representative Passman's Foreign Operations subcommittee, then on to the full Appropriations Committee, then to the House itself (through the Rules Committee). Similarly in the Senate, the Appropriations Committee and the whole Senate have their say. Then the bill goes to a conference committee once again for compromise of remaining differences. (The Senate has cut a step from the process by eliminating appropriations subcommittees' consideration of foreign aid bills.) Finally the conference committee's version is voted upon in the House and in the Senate and sent to the President for signature or veto.

Merely listing the stages involved in the passage of a single foreign policy bill suggests something of the burden of initiative borne by an executive charged with responsibility for securing legislative action. In addition, the need for top administration officials to testify at committee hearings, and to consult with legislators informally, draws heavily upon the time and energy of men who are often overworked already. Former Secretary of State Dean Acheson estimated that approximately one-sixth of his time in office was spent in committee hearings and legislative liaison.

This diffusion of legislative authority leaves no individual or small group in a position to commit the Congress to a course of action previously decided upon in consultation with the President. In 1951, for example, President Truman requested authority to send United States surplus wheat to India to relieve a serious famine. The bill authorizing this request was endorsed by former Republican President Herbert Hoover and other leaders of both parties, but it was pigeonholed in the House Rules Committee for seven weeks before being released for floor debate and House approval. In the

[9] A relatively small number of Senators, if they are determined, can forestall a vote on any measure before the Senate indefinitely by *filibustering* — that is by talking continuously until the bill is shelved or *cloture* is invoked, by a two-thirds vote. Filibusters on foreign affairs legislation have been infrequent, however.

interim, the Soviet Union took the initiative in supplying some of the foods needed to relieve the famine.

If American political parties were disciplined, centralized organizations, the executive might be able to bring about effective coordination simply by consulting regularly with the leaders of both parties in the two Houses. But American parties are decentralized; and congressional party leaders need the support of leading committee chairmen more than the latter need them. After all, the chairman, since his position depends on his seniority, will not be overturned for incurring the displeasure of his party leader; but the latter may be removed as party leader by a simple majority vote of his party's Congressional delegation.[10] And congressional tradition opposes "interference" with legislation by the party leadership until the critical stage of committee consideration is over and the bill has come to the floor. (Nevertheless, party affiliation remains the most important influence on congressional voting.)

The situation outlined above has at times thwarted presidential programs (foreign and domestic) supported by a large majority of the American people. In response, many students of politics have suggested that one of the principal needs of the American republic today is for a tightening of party discipline under the leadership of the President and the elected party officials in each house. But minor revisions in legislative and party procedure can only mitigate, not remove, the basic problem. And, if history is any guide, major changes, desirable or not, are nearly impossible to bring about — basically because the American political system provides no dependable machinery for resolving executive-legislative deadlocks.

PRESIDENTIAL AND CONGRESSIONAL CONSTITUENCIES

Let us suppose that a President tired of having his legislative programs defeated in Congress by individuals representing only a minority of the American people decides to do something about it. His party controls both houses of Congress. He decides that he will not support members of his party who vote regularly against his program. He announces this dramatically to the people, travels to the districts of some of the worst offenders and campaigns against them. Assuming that he is right — that a majority of the people support *his* program — these offenders will be defeated; replacements more favorably disposed toward his program will be elected; and the other members of his party in Congress will be forewarned that consistent opposition to the President's legislative proposals will jeopardize their own seats.

[10] George Goodwin, Jr. has studied voting records of the 80th to 85th Congresses (1947–1959) and found that, within the President's party, committee chairmen and ranking minority members were slightly less likely to support presidential legislative proposals than the average member of their party. "The Seniority System in Congress," *The American Political Science Review* (June, 1959), 428–429.

In 1938, one of the most popular Presidents in American history, Franklin D. Roosevelt, attempted precisely this. His famous "purge" attempt became one of the signal failures of his political career.

The national electorate of the United States undoubtedly supported Roosevelt's program. But there was no constitutional way to put the question to *them*. Roosevelt had to go to Georgia, for instance, to ask the voters of *that* constituency to retire Senator Walter George, who opposed him, from office. In this kind of contest, the President's position was bound to be very weak. There was only one effective political party in the state of Georgia. Senator George was a part of it. Roosevelt was not. Since 1938 was an off-year election, the President's name was not even on the ballot.

The President and the Congress are elected by different constituencies. The electoral laws which determine the President's constituency put a premium on successful appeal to urban and ethnic minority groups in key, "swing" states with large numbers of electoral votes. Congressional districts, on the other hand, are drawn up by state legislatures usually to maximize the power of rural and conservative interests. In many states, this overrepresentation of rural constituents has resulted from legislative failures to keep pace with the rapid urbanization of the population in this century by redistricting. State legislators have been understandably reluctant to reapportion themselves out of office. In *Baker v. Carr* (1962) and in *Wesberry v. Sanders* and other decisions in 1964, the Supreme Court laid the groundwork for far-reaching changes in legislative apportionment by requiring congressional districts within each state to be substantially equal in population. Close to half the states have been redistricted since, either in whole or in part. The legislative impact of these changes is hard to assess at this time, however, since they coincided with the Democratic landslide in the elections of 1964. One important result, in any event, was the defeat in the 1966 Democratic primary in a reapportioned Virginia district of "Judge" Howard W. Smith, then chairman of the House Rules Committee.

Even in two-party states, Congressmen are likely to try to use their political influence to have their party colleagues in the state legislatures draw up relatively safe districts for them. About three-fourths of the incumbents in Congress, therefore, are generally assured of repeated re-election. The more often a man is re-elected, the more he will accumulate influence and prerogatives under the seniority system, and, correspondingly, the greater will be his ability to service his district's needs. Such men usually retain control of the Congress — at least enough to block action they oppose — regardless of nation-wide electoral trends. They need the President's electoral support less than he needs their legislative and electoral cooperation. Nothing is more likely to antagonize the senior members than an attack on the seniority system, which is the key source of their power. For most of the last two decades, moreover, the seniority system has tended to favor southern Democrats and midwestern Republicans, whom the record shows to be more reluctant than most members of their parties to support presidential foreign policy recommendations. (But there is some evidence to suggest that liberal northern Democrats may be among the chief beneficiaries of the seniority system in the years to come.) [11]

A presidential attempt to "buck" this system would be made more difficult by the fact that local elections are generally fought out on local issues. The restraints imposed on the President by his national constituency do not allow him to rival the appeal which local candidates can make on issues of special interest to their home districts. Can the President afford to take as strong a stand against integration as a senator from Mississippi? As strong a stand in favor of farm price supports as a senator from Iowa? As strong a stand for federal aid to parochial schools as a Congressman from a heavily Catholic district in Boston or New York? Yet these issues are more likely to decide the elections in these districts than the candidates' stands on foreign aid or American intervention in Vietnam. And, half the time, all Congressmen, even those who strongly support the President's program, must win elections when the President himself is not on the ballot. In such elections local issues receive even more emphasis, but many of those attracted to the polls by the glamour and fanfare of a Presidential campaign stay at home. "Riding the President's coattails" becomes extremely difficult under these circumstances.

Professor James MacGregor Burns acknowledges all these points and suggests that the hope of the future may lie in an energetic long-term effort by the Presidential wings of both major parties to build new grassroots party organizations capable of supporting national programs and a more disciplined party system.[12] Perhaps some great political leaders will prove equal to this challenge in the years to come. During the years of struggle, however, this task would probably absorb all the energy, influence, and political capital at their command, leaving little of these precious commodities for use in ensuring that American foreign policy remained adequate to the demands of a world in crisis. This fact alone should be enough to make any President contemplating major revision of the American political *status quo* pause and ponder.

If a major overhaul of our national policy machinery costs too much politically to be worthwhile, we will simply have to try to improvise minor adjustments which will keep it moving as smoothly as possible under the circumstances. A number of techniques developed for this purpose in years past are likely to continue to bear much of the burden of legislative-execu-

[11] See Raymond E. Wolfinger and Joan Haifetz, "Safe Seats, Seniority and Power in Congress," *The American Political Science Review* (June, 1965), 346–348. Among the factors leading to this change are population movements, reapportionment, and the growth of party competition in some parts of the south.

[12] *The Deadlock of Democracy* (Englewood Cliffs, N.J.: Prentice-Hall, 1963), p. 339.

tive coordination in the years ahead. Foremost among these are "bipartisanship," what we might call "education by participation," and plain old presidential and legislative leadership.

BIPARTISANSHIP

No precise definition as to what constitutes "bipartisanship" or "nonpartisanship" in foreign affairs is commonly agreed on. But the word certainly connotes, at the least, (1) a measure of agreement between the President and opposition party leaders on the basic orientation of American foreign policy; (2) legislative support by a substantial segment of the opposition party for key items in the President's foreign policy programs; and (3) the soft-pedalling in presidential campaigns of fundamental foreign policy issues. In return for this measure of support and restraint, the President must consult with opposition congressional leaders before important foreign policy decisions are made — or at least before they are announced publicly. Also, he must refrain from claiming partisan credit for foreign policy successes.

Yet even if both the President and the congressional leaders involved are willing to meet these conditions, they may not be able to do so. If bipartisanship is to succeed, there must be congressional leaders capable of committing the opposition party or at least a substantial part of it. Such leaders are not always available. During the post-World War II period, bipartisanship has proved most fruitful when the chairman of the Senate Foreign Relations Committee has been a man of commanding stature and influence in his party generally — when, in other words, the influence of the man and the position have reinforced one another. The most notable instances were Senator Arthur Vandenberg's collaboration with President Truman in the Republican-controlled Eightieth Congress (1947–1949), and Senator Walter George's with President Eisenhower in the Democratic-controlled Eighty-fourth Congress (1955–1957). But strong congressional leadership may lead to conflict with the chief executive, as well as to cooperation, as it did in 1919–1920, when Woodrow Wilson was President and Henry Cabot Lodge was Senate majority leader as well as chairman of the Foreign Relations Committee. (See the first case study in this chapter.)

Since World War II, interestingly, it has proved easier to secure bipartisan cooperation between a Republican President and a Democratic Congress, than between a Democratic President and a Republican Congress. Democratic Presidents, during this period, have tended to be more liberal and internationalist than Republican Presidents and presidential candidates. Southern Democratic congressional leaders have therefore tended to be closer in their overall foreign policy orientation to the latter than to the former. Republican congressional leaders, on the other hand, have generally been less liberal-internationalist than the President and presidential candidates of their own party, and thus have stood further still in their fundamental foreign policy orientation from Democratic Presidents. Notice, for instance, the striking contrast between the embittered Republican criticisms of Secretary of State Acheson and President Truman during the Korean War, and the relatively cordial relations between President Eisenhower and the Democratic majorities which controlled Congress for six of his eight years in office. Our one postwar Republican President, in contrast, found his most difficult opponents in the congressional wing of his own party. Thus President Eisenhower's "chief of staff," Sherman Adams, has written that ". . . when it became apparent to him [Eisenhower] that many of the Democrats were more willing to accept his foreign programs than his own leaders [in Congress] were . . ." he wondered whether the time had come for party realignment.[13]

Lyndon Johnson, however, partly by using some of the techniques discussed here, has contrived to maintain the support of Senate minority leader Everett McKinley Dirksen and other influential congressional Republicans for his Vietnam policies. His severest critics have come instead from the liberal-internationalist wing of his own party, led by Senators J. W. Fulbright, George McGovern, and Wayne Morse. Their differences with the President are not centered on the issues that dominated executive-legislative relations in the first postwar generation — foreign aid, and the American commitments to the United Nations and the defense of Europe; rather they deplore what they see as sterile emphases on blatant anticommunism and on the use of force as an instrument of policy. In frustration at their inability to prevent an increasing American commitment in Vietnam, some have reacted by seeking to restrict the President's discretion in the use of foreign aid, hoping in this way to forestall similar American commitments elsewhere. It is possible that these differences foreshadow the emergence of new issues over which Presidents and Congresses will contend in the decade to come, with the Congress now representing the "liberal" view and the President the "conservative" one. The possibility of so dramatic a turnabout should forewarn those who would advocate basic structural reforms in our political system in order to forward their present policy goals that today's advantage may be tomorrow's hindrance.

When executive and legislative good will and leadership combine to make it work, bipartisanship can enable presidential foreign policy requests to win legislative approval despite defections within the President's own party. No less important, it provides a continuity which reassures our allies that the pattern of American commitments abroad will not be changed suddenly and basically when the voters decide to "throw the rascals out."

But even at its best, bipartisanship is an intricate feat, warranting the label "Fragile — Handle with Care." For example, it requires cooperation between the President and the actual foreign policy leaders of the opposition

[13] *First-Hand Report* (New York: Harper, 1960), p. 28.

party. Yet the continued willingness of these leaders to advocate presidential policies may cause their colleagues to come to look upon them as the President's men, rather than as their own. If their position is not to be undermined, they will have to take issue with the President and express an independent congressional point of view on some issues, at least. If their co-operation is not to be jeopardized, then, the President will have to make concessions to their views on these issues. Further, the President must take care to buttress the prestige of these leaders whenever the opportunity presents itself — as Roosevelt and Truman were so careful to do with Senator Vandenberg — so that they may continue to command widespread support within their own party on foreign policy matters.

Though they may be time-consuming on both sides, continuous consultation and liaison are essential to bipartisanship. This means frequent presidential meetings with congressional foreign policy leaders, appearances of executive officials before legislative committees, regular meetings and consultation between congressional subcommittees and their opposite numbers in the executive branch, and effective liaison by presidential assistants and by the Assistant Secretary of State for Congressional Relations. These liaison officers must be placed high enough to keep Congress informed accurately as to the direction of administration thinking on particular issues. And they must have an opportunity to participate in policy formulation at an early enough stage to gain top-level executive consideration for congressional views *before* major decisions have become crystallized.

Who is to be included in these bipartisan consultations? The ranking minority members of the foreign affairs committees, certainly, and most likely the elected party congressional leaders as well. But how about members from the appropriations and armed services committees? Or members of other committees, or even subcommittees or special committees, which may at the moment be dealing with foreign policy bills? Should House leaders be consulted on treaties or nominations which are clearly within the constitutional purview of the Senate alone? These can be touchy questions to answer in a Congress where jurisdictional jealousies are so strong.

Another difficulty involves drawing the line between foreign policy, where bipartisanship is presumably desirable, and domestic policy, where presumably it is not. How, for example, is a tariff bill to be categorized from this standpoint? An immigration bill? A selective service bill? A space program?

Just how much is the President — who, after all, supposedly represents a majority of the nation, and is constitutionally charged with primary responsibility for the conduct of foreign affairs — justified in deferring to the views of opposition party leaders in order to secure their cooperation?

Finally, are those who enter into bipartisan collaboration with the President thereby obligated not to voice any public criticism of the administration's foreign policy failures? How can any degree of democratic participation in foreign policymaking be preserved under such limitations? If a certain degree of criticism is compatible with bipartisanship, how much, and of what kind? And who decides when such criticism passes the vague boundary between responsible debate and irresponsible demagogy?

Plainly, these are all questions which must be dealt with "by ear" according to the circumstances and personalities involved. With diligence and goodwill on both sides, nevertheless, the record shows that bipartisanship can be made to prevail on a number of issues vital to the survival of the republic. However, given the high tension under which it must run, it should not be too surprising if the machinery of bipartisanship breaks down at embarrassing times.

Nor can it be said that bipartisanship is always a good thing. Those who oppose the bipartisan policies being followed are likely to complain, with some justice, that they are being deprived of their ability to express their dissent from these policies effectively. Bipartisanship is an instrument which can be used to advance a multitude of ends. Like other instruments used by men, it can be either helpful or dangerous depending on the men who use it. The most useful alternative open to those who oppose a policy which enjoys bipartisan support is to find a leading figure in one of the major parties who will espouse their point of view. If there is sufficient sympathy for this dissenting viewpoint in the national electorate, such a man should not prove too difficult to find.

"EDUCATION BY PARTICIPATION"

One of the main benefits of bipartisanship is the extent to which it involves what we may call "education by participation." As any athletic coach knows, it is much easier to second-guess decisions which have turned out badly than to suggest alternatives which will turn out well. One of the best ways to head off uninformed criticism, when time and secrecy requirements permit, is to bring potential critics into the decisionmaking process. As participants, Senator X and Representative Y will be exposed to the circumstances influencing executive branch policymakers. They may also help these officials acquire a better understanding of the pressures and limitations which Congressmen must face.

Equally important, once these legislators have taken part in reaching a decision by consensus, they may feel identified with that decision and with the men who made it. They may even communicate some of this sense of identification to congressional colleagues who did not participate. The building of such a consensus and sense of identification is, in fact, one of the primary benefits of group deliberation on any problem. If all that is wanted is decisive action, with or without broad agreement, an individual can usually do this better than a committee. We have already noted, in this connection, that in time new members of the Senate Foreign Relations Committee tend to become more responsive to executive foreign policy requests. And, of course, members of the Foreign Relations and Foreign Affairs Committees of the two houses are more sympathetic to presidential foreign policy proposals than Congressmen serving on committees which participate less frequently or less directly in foreign policymaking.

This strategy of promoting education by participation has been used in executive-legislative relations since the early days of the republic, and never more extensively than in the years since World War II.

The peace treaty ending the Spanish-American War in 1899 would almost certainly have failed to secure the necessary two-thirds Senate majority had it not been for the support provided by the three senior Senate Foreign Relations Committee members appointed by President McKinley to the commission to negotiate the peace.

Republicans Henry Stimson and Frank Knox served as Secretary of War and of the Navy, respectively, in the wartime unity cabinets of Presidents Roosevelt and Truman.[14] Bipartisan cooperation on the United Nations Charter was the fruit of consultations which began on a formal basis, within six months after Pearl Harbor, in the form of an Advisory Committee on Postwar Policy which included many influential Senators and Representatives from both parties. The chairmen and ranking minority members of the Foreign Relations and Foreign Affairs Committees were appointed as delegates to the San Francisco Conference at which the Charter was drawn up. And ever since then, several Congressmen have been appointed each year to serve on the American delegation to the United Nations General Assembly.

Bipartisan support for the Marshall Plan was facilitated by the European travels of special House committees headed by Representatives William Colmer (D., Miss.) and Christian Herter (R., Mass.), and by the appointment, at Senator Vandenberg's suggestion, of Republican Paul Hoffman as first Administrator of the European Recovery Program. The Truman administration also entrusted Republican John Foster Dulles, a special consultant to the State Department, with the negotiation of the Japanese Peace Treaty. President Eisenhower found special advisory positions, upon their retirement from Congress, for Senator Walter George and Representative James Richards, former Democratic chairmen of the Foreign Relations and Foreign Affairs committees, respectively.

President Kennedy made extensive use of Republicans in foreign policy positions, among them McGeorge Bundy as Assistant to the President for National Security Affairs; Robert McNamara (a nominal Republican) as Secretary of Defense; John McCone as Director of the Central Intelligence Agency; the late Christian Herter, former Republican Governor, Congressman, and Secretary of State, as the President's Special Foreign Trade As-

14 Stimson had been Governor of New York and Secretary of State under Herbert Hoover. Knox was the 1936 Republican vice presidential nominee.

sistant; and Henry Cabot Lodge, Jr., former Senator, Ambassador to the United Nations, and 1960 vice presidential candidate, as Ambassador to South Vietnam. Most of these men continued to serve under President Johnson also, at least for a time. Lodge resigned to seek the Republican presidential nomination in 1964, but was subsequently reappointed Ambassador to Vietnam — a good indication of his value in helping to minimize Republican opposition to United States policy in Vietnam. Even after the end of his second tour of duty as Ambassador to Vietnam, Lodge continued to serve the Johnson Administration as ambassador-at-large.

Of course, education by participation is not a cure-all. Those sufficiently opposed to a specific policy, out-of-sympathy with the President generally, or simply desirous of maintaining full freedom of criticism, may decline to accept an invitation to participate. Once an opposition party member has been appointed moreover — and especially if he commands a substantial popular or congressional following — he is in a position to hamper the President's program by resigning unless his recommendations, and possibly those of other leaders of his party, are taken into account to an extent satisfactory to him.

SUGGESTED REFORMS

Various other devices have been suggested to help bridge the gap between the legislature and the executive. Authority to veto individual items within appropriations and other bills, for instance, would undoubtedly strengthen the President's hand immensely. As it is now, he may be forgiven if he chooses to sign, rather than reject completely, a bill which includes both some distasteful provisions and essential defense or foreign aid appropriations. Election of the House of Representatives every fourth (presidential) year, instead of biennially, would also add to the President's legislative influence by increasing the value of his political support in congressional elections — in which he would always head the party ticket. President Johnson proposed a four-year term for House members in his 1965 State of the Union Message. But both this electoral revision and the item veto would require constitutional amendments, and the requisite majorities for such amendments could not be marshalled readily. In the case of the four-year term, a principal obstacle is the Senate. For if Representatives were elected for four years they could run against incumbent Senators in off-year elections without giving up their seats in the House. Understandably, many Senators are reluctant to encourage this.

Other suggestions have been advanced which would require only legislative, rather than constitutional, action. Either authorizations or appropriations, or both, on foreign affairs matters, might be made for longer than one year at a time, thus facilitating longer-range planning and reducing the burden of legislative leadership on the executive. In effect, this would involve asking the Congress, and especially several of its committees, to surrender voluntarily an important part of their negotiating position vis-à-vis the executive branch. The appropriations committees, in particular, are reluctant to do this. Making authorizations, but not appropriations, available for a longer period would tend to weaken the relative influence of the committees most in tune with the executive — the foreign affairs committees; nor would it guarantee that the amounts authorized would be appropriated. Soon after taking office, President Kennedy "won" a hard fight to secure a five-year authorization for development loans abroad, on the basis of expert advice concerning the critical need for long-range planning by the countries concerned. But the limited value of this "victory" was revealed the following year, when Congressman Passman's appropriations subcommittee slashed the sum requested — and authorized — by more than 20 per cent. This jeopardized not only American contributions to the development programs of the nations involved, but also the contributions of other Western nations which had been made contingent upon the availability of the "authorized" American commitments.

To attain greater coordination within the Congress itself, it has been suggested that foreign policy questions be dealt with by joint or special congressional committees, either in place of or in addition to current procedures. For example, a national security committee, drawing together key party and committee leaders concerned with foreign affairs legislation, might become a focal point of congressional coordination on foreign policy. But there is no indication that the existing committees would allow themselves to be by-passed by such a device. And adding a new committee to those already active in the foreign policy field might complicate the legislative process even further, and would certainly add to the pressures on the time of top congressional leaders.

Other types of special and joint committees have been utilized on occasion in the past, with varying success. The Colmer and Herter committees mentioned above in connection with the achievement of bipartisanship on the Marshall Plan, the Special Senate Committee to study the Foreign Aid Program (in 1956–57), and the Joint Committee on Atomic Energy are examples. But these devices seem to work only in certain circumstances. Normally, Senate standing committees hesitate to work jointly with House committees for fear of being overwhelmed by the latter's larger membership and confined by the stricter rules of debate which must govern a larger body.

Both special and joint committees, furthermore, are thought of as encroaching on the jurisdiction of established standing committees and their chairmen. Even so successful a special committee as the Herter committee was not immune to criticism on this score. The effectiveness of the Joint Committee on Atomic Energy, similarly, may be traced to the peculiarities of its area of jurisdiction. When this committee was formed, atomic energy was a new field, largely outside the realms of established committees with vested interests; and the secrecy in which it was cloaked put a premium on minimizing the number of individuals and groups which would deal with it.

Certainly there will be times in the future, as in the past, when the appointment of special or joint committees will contribute to the evolution and acceptance of worthwhile foreign policy measures. At the least, willingness by the House appropriations subcommittees to follow the lead of their Senate counterparts in inviting a few members of the substantive committees to their deliberations would be a welcome advance toward foreign policy coordination in the House.

Finally, some steps could be taken within the present framework of congressional organization and custom which might help to improve the capacity of Congress to participate effectively in foreign policymaking: the professional staffs of committees and of important leaders dealing with foreign affairs could be augmented; the number of foreign affairs specialists in the Legislative Reference Service, which provides Congress with information to aid its deliberations, could be increased; and Congress could commission independent studies by experts outside the government, as has the Foreign Relations Committee in recent years, under Senator Fulbright's direction.

Though the adoption of at least some of these suggested reforms would probably prove beneficial, it would be a mistake to think that the fundamental limitations imposed by our constitutional and political system can be overcome by organizational devices alone. Even with favorable adjustments in the organizational machinery, and even with the best of intentions on both sides of the congressional aisle and on both sides of Capitol Hill, the American system requires effective leadership if it is to produce effective policy. And the principal responsibility for providing this leadership falls on the President.

"Leadership" is a vague and slippery concept, easy to talk about but difficult to define. One of the case studies in this chapter includes some illuminating comments about the nature of presidential leadership and power. For now let us say that it involves conscious and consistent use of all of the formal — and, even more, the informal — powers at the President's command. The chief executive's control of patronage, his influence as party leader, his unique ability to command the attention of the mass media and the people may be more useful instruments of leadership than the powers granted him by the Constitution. For the key to presidential leadership must be *persuasion*. There are occasions, of course, when the President can accomplish what he wants to by giving orders. But those occasions are few, and their cost is high. Influential individuals, even the Congress as a whole, sometimes may be compelled to acquiesce in a given policy without being persuaded the need to do so, but the cost is likely to be more determined opposition to other policies, at other times, when presidential commands cannot get the job done. Thus President Johnson has been able to pursue the policy he prefers in Vietnam despite the opposition of the chairman of the Foreign Relations Committee and other Senators and Representatives. As noted above, however, many of these dissenters have responded by imposing restrictions on United States aid programs in other parts of the world.

❦ CASE
STUDY   *THE TREATY OF VERSAILLES*

Now let us turn to the classic instance in twentieth-century American history when a President, revered for his fine qualities of leadership, *failed* to persuade — with disastrous consequences.

1. To what extent was the rejection of the treaty due to the constitutional framework within which United States foreign policy must be made? To what extent did congressional custom and seniority rule enter into the picture? What role was played by partisan politics and personal feelings?

2. Was Wilson's legislative strategy at fault? If so, what steps might he have taken which would have improved his chances of winning his goals? Which of the presidential powers available to him did Wilson rely upon most heavily? Were there any powers available to him which he failed to use, but which might have helped the treaty to pass? Why did his plan to make the election of 1920 a referendum on the treaty fail?

3. What congressional prerogatives did Senator Lodge rely on? What powers and tactics did the small minority of "Irreconcilables" make use of in their successful efforts to defeat the treaty? What lessons does the case suggest for the conduct of American foreign policy today?

OSCAR T. BARCK, JR. AND NELSON M. BLAKE

The first Armistice Day was one of delirious rejoicing. Wilson's own happiness was reflected in an exultant statement he gave out to the newspapers:

> Everything for which America fought has been accomplished. It will now be our fortunate duty to assist by example, by sober friendly counsel

Reprinted with permission of The Macmillan Company from Oscar T. Barck, Jr. and Nelson M. Blake, *Since 1900* (rev. ed.; © Copyright The Macmillan Company, 1965), pp. 243–263. Omissions are indicated by ellipses.

and by material aid in the establishment of a just democracy throughout the world.

It is no wonder that the President used such phrases. The triumph of his
principles appeared to be as complete as the victory of the Allied arms. Not
only had the Fourteen Points been accepted as the basis of peace by friend
and foe alike, but German military autocracy seemed utterly vanquished.
The peace-hungry German people, convinced that the Kaiser's continued
presence on the throne was a barrier to the granting of an armistice, had
risen in revolt. On November 9 the government was turned over to the
Socialists, who proclaimed a German Republic, and the emperor fled across
the border into Holland. It was another great victory for the American
statesman who had called for "the destruction of every arbitrary power."

Actually, however, Wilson's position was less impregnable than these
diplomatic victories would indicate. Not only in Europe but in America
powerful elements resented his leadership and were waiting for the first
opportunity to make their opposition felt.

The most influential Republican was still Theodore Roosevelt, and his
hatred for Wilson had become more intense with the passing of the years.
Thoroughly loyal and patriotic, Roosevelt supported the war in vigorous
public speeches, but at the same time he maintained a constant barrage of
criticism of the Wilson administration. He was particularly contemptuous
of the President's peace program, although as early as 1910 he himself had
expressed the idea that world peace must be backed up by force. Even after
the war had begun, Roosevelt said that if the idea of an international police
power was utopian, then we must choose between "Utopia or Hell." Yet by
1918 his dislike for Wilson had taken him so far that he tried to sabotage
Wilson's October negotiations with Germany by calling upon the Senate
to repudiate the Fourteen Points. "Let us dictate peace by the hammering
guns," he declared, "and not chat about peace to the accompaniment of
clicking typewriters. . . ."

Equally hostile was Senator Henry Cabot Lodge of Massachusetts. He
and Roosevelt were close friends, and for years in their private correspondence they had heaped scorn upon the professor in the White House. Like
Roosevelt, Lodge thought that an association of nations to enforce future
world peace was an excellent idea. . . . But following Wilson's fervent plea
for a league in his "Peace without Victory" speech of January, 1917, the
Massachusetts Senator reversed himself completely, warning the Senate that
such an international organization might force Oriental immigration upon
the United States or "might plunge us into war at any moment at the bid-
ding of other nations."

The Republican leaders were naturally eager to return to power in the
national government. They believed that the country was normally Republican and that the Democrats had enjoyed their brief hour of glory only

because of animosities within the ranks of the dominant party. With the congressional election of November, 1918, approaching, strenuous efforts were made to patch up the old quarrel. A new and energetic national chairman, Will H. Hays of Indiana, was appointed, while Roosevelt, Taft, and Root appeared together on public platforms as a visible demonstration that the schism of 1912 was ended. Wilson was accused of desiring a negotiated peace with the Kaiser rather than unconditional surrender, and the third of the Fourteen Points was depicted as a threat to the protective-tariff system. Democratic Congressmen, worried by the aggressiveness of the opposition, beseeched the President for help. Somewhat reluctantly, he issued an appeal to the voters through the newspapers on October 24. Among other things, he said:

> If you have approved of my leadership and wish me to continue to be your unembarrassed spokesman in affairs at home and abroad, I earnestly beg that you will express yourselves unmistakably to that effect by returning a Democratic majority to both the Senate and the House of Representatives. . . . The leaders of the minority in the present Congress have unquestionably been pro-war, but they have been anti-administration. At almost every turn since we entered the war they have sought to take the choice of policy and the conduct of the war out of my hands and put it under the control of the instrumentalities of their own choosing. . . . The return of a Republican majority to either house of the Congress would . . . be interpreted on the other side of the water as a repudiation of my leadership.

Wilson's appeal proved to be a blunder. It offered the Republicans the excuse for casting off the restraint that they might have felt over attacking the President during wartime. Chairman Hays denounced Wilson's words as "ungracious . . . wanton . . . mendacious." The President, it was charged, had cast a slur upon Republican patriotism.

When the votes were counted on November 5, it was learned that the new House of Representatives would have 237 Republicans, 191 Democrats, and 7 Independents, while in the Senate there would be 49 Republicans and 47 Democrats. It was a defeat for the President's party and also for the President himself since, in his own words, Wilson had defined confidence in his leadership as one of the issues of the campaign. The exultant victors asserted that the President had been decisively repudiated. In reality, it was by no means certain that this was so. The war was nearly over, and many voters expressed with their ballots their impatience with wartime restrictions or their sentiments on local issues rather than their opinion of Wilson. Republican victory under the circumstances was probably inevitable, but it was made more damaging to the President than it needed to have been by the role he had assumed during the campaign.

WILSON GOES TO EUROPE

Before November was over, the names of the American peace commissioners were announced. Wilson had long before decided to attend the peace conference in person: to go with him he now named Secretary of State Robert Lansing, Colonel Edward House, General Tasker H. Bliss, and Henry White. It was a competent group. Next to the President himself, Lansing and House were obviously the two best informed men in the country on recent diplomatic developments. Bliss was not only a military expert, but a scholar with an excellent grasp of European economic and political problems, and White had had an unusually distinguished diplomatic career, having held important posts in London, Paris, and Rome.

The President's opponents, however, criticized the appointments severely. Natural though it might seem that the President should wish to go to Paris himself, he was breaking a precedent. Earlier chief executives had left to other men the actual work of negotiating treaties of peace. Wilson's decision to head his own delegation was attributed to his vanity or to his "Messiah complex." The commission was further criticized as giving inadequate recognition to the Republicans. True, White was a Republican, but not an active partisan. Why had the President ignored such distinguished leaders as Charles Evans Hughes, William Howard Taft, and Elihu Root? Finally, the absence of Senators on the delegation was resented as a slight to the body that must give its consent to the ratification of any peace treaty. Although much of the criticism was mere partisanship, it does appear that Wilson's failure to take with him to Paris at least one prominent Senator from each party was a serious mistake — a mistake that played directly into the hands of his enemies.*

On December 4, 1918, the liner *George Washington* left New York, bearing the peace commission and scores of advisers and experts on various problems. Key men from the war administration were aboard, as well as numerous college professors and other specialists in history, geography, and economics. These experts had been assembled by Colonel House over the course of the past year. Known as "The Inquiry," they had been gathering facts and figures at their headquarters in New York City for many months. Even this evidence of earnest preparation for the serious tasks ahead was ridiculed by unfriendly newspapers, which sneered at "Colonel House's troupe of performing professors."

The *George Washington* docked at Brest on December 13, but not for another month did the peace conference begin its work. During this period of waiting, President Wilson visited Paris, London, and Rome, where he

---

* Thomas A. Bailey, *Woodrow Wilson and the Lost Peace* (New York: Macmillan, 1944), pp. 87–105, gives the best account of the selection of the members of the peace commission and the arguments pro and con as to why Wilson took no member of the Senate and no prominent Republican.

received a most extraordinary welcome. The enthusiasm of the crowds lining the streets surpassed anything that men could remember. With pathetic trust, common people in all countries were counting on the American President to achieve an impossible goal — a perfect peace settlement.

LIONS IN THE PATH

At the very moment when Wilson was enjoying his greatest triumphs, the dangers that confronted him were clearly evident. Behind him in America his opponents were ceaseless in their activity. Even before the President sailed, Theodore Roosevelt had warned in a statement to the press:

> Our allies and our enemies and Mr. Wilson himself should all understand that Mr. Wilson has no authority whatever to speak for the American people at this time. His leadership has been emphatically repudiated by them. . . . Mr. Wilson and his fourteen points and his four supplementary points and his five complementary points and all his utterances every which way have ceased to have any shadow of right to be accepted as expressive of the will of the American people. . . .

This bitter document was one of Roosevelt's last contributions to American public discussions. The former President was a desperately sick man, fighting a losing struggle with a tropical ailment he had contracted during a trip to the Amazon in 1913. On January 6, 1919, he died.

But Henry Cabot Lodge remained very much alive. On December 21, 1918, he addressed the Senate at length, stating his belief that the Allies should be permitted to make any territorial settlement they desired without Wilson's interference, and that the League of Nations should not be included as a part of the peace treaties. The Senate, he said, could, and often had, refused to ratify treaties; many other agreements — and these were significant words — had been "virtually amended." Without waiting to see what kind of league of nations would be proposed, Lodge was already laying careful plans to oppose it. He even went to the extreme of suggesting to Henry White that the latter should communicate these ideas to leading Allied statesmen in order to encourage them to oppose the President, but White honorably refrained from acting upon the suggestion. . . .

What President Wilson regarded as "the heart of the Covenant" was Article 10, which read:

> The Members of the League undertake to respect and preserve as against external aggression the territorial integrity and existing political independence of all Members of the League. In case of any threat or danger of such aggression the Council shall advise upon the means by which this obligation shall be fulfilled.

The day after this draft of the Covenant was presented, Wilson embarked on the *George Washington* for America. Congress was about to adjourn and the President had to be available to sign bills and attend to various affairs that had accumulated during his absence.

At Colonel House's suggestion, Wilson entertained the members of the Senate Foreign Relations Committee at a White House dinner on the evening of February 26. Until nearly midnight the President explained the Covenant to the Senators and answered their questions. The Democratic members of the committee were much impressed, the Republicans were not. . . .

The President's failure to win over the skeptics was made all too clear less than a week later. On March 4, the last day of the session, Senator Lodge requested unanimous consent for consideration of a resolution, asserting that "the constitution of the League of Nations in the form now proposed to the peace conference should not be accepted by the United States" and that the whole proposal should be postponed until after peace was made with Germany. Immediate objection was registered by a Democratic member — just as Lodge had hoped. This gave him his opportunity to read into the *Congressional Record* the names of thirty-nine Republican Senators, or Senators-elect, who would have voted for the resolution had they been given the opportunity. This challenge to the President, henceforth known as the "Round Robin," had been the idea of Senator Brandegee; its support by thirty-nine Senators was of serious import, since only thirty-three votes were required to block the ratification of a treaty.

The President was entirely unwilling to yield to the Round Robin threat insofar as that maneuver sought to compel him to separate the League Covenant from the peace treaty. If this were done, he feared that the world's best opportunity to secure a league would be lost and the project would be subjected to indefinite delay. On the evening of the same March 4, Wilson and Taft addressed a huge and enthusiastic audience in the Metropolitan Opera House in New York City. In a fighting speech, the President accepted the gauge of battle flung down by his opponents. When the treaty was completed, he said, not only would the Covenant be in it, but so many threads of the treaty would be tied to the Covenant that the Covenant could not be dissected from the treaty without destroying the whole vital structure. That the treaty itself might be rejected, the President apparently had no fear.

On the other hand, Wilson was not hostile to really constructive criticism. Following his return to Paris, a careful study was made of all the suggestions that had been offered by prominent Republicans like A. Lawrence Lowell, Hughes, and Root, and by Democrats like William Jennings Bryan and Senator Gilbert Hitchcock of Nebraska. Lodge also had been urged to make specific recommendations, but had refused to do so. Although the President believed that the plan as already drafted adequately safeguarded American rights, he decided to ask for a number of amendments in order to satisfy hesitant Senators. The League of Nations Commission was reconvened, and numerous concessions to the United States were written into the Covenant. The right of a member state to withdraw from the League was recognized, as was the right to refuse a mandate. Domestic questions such as immigration control and tariffs were specifically exempted from League jurisdiction, and provision was made that, for all important questions, the Council and the Assembly would have to agree unanimously upon any course of action. Finally, and most important, it was stated that nothing in the Covenant should be deemed "to affect the validity . . . of regional understandings like the Monroe Doctrine. . . ." The formal recognition of this historic American policy represented a striking diplomatic victory.

Wilson thus fought for and won safeguards that had been demanded by American opinion, but in order to do so he found it necessary to moderate his opposition to certain things that the other powers were seeking. . . .

DELAY ON THE TREATY

The President's confidence that the concessions he had obtained during his second stay at Paris would disarm his opponents proved to be entirely unwarranted. Lodge announced to the country that the League in its revised form was worse than before and went ahead with his plans to attack the whole Wilsonian settlement.

The Republican leader was a master strategist. His first achievement was to secure the organization of the newly elected Senate in a way certain to create difficulties for the President. Through a well-planned filibuster the Republicans had held up the passage of necessary appropriation bills before the old legislature adjourned on March 4, 1919. This action made it necessary for Wilson to call the new Congress into special session in May. Thus the opposition was given ample opportunity to form its battle lines before the President returned to America with the completed treaty. Not only was Lodge chairman of the powerful Senate Foreign Relations Committee, but the latter was packed with anti-League Republicans.

On July 10, the day after his return, the President appeared before the Senate to submit the treaty and to make a personal appeal for its approval. His position still seemed strong. Even his most bitter opponents were of the opinion that if the treaty came to an immediate vote it would probably be accepted without change. Therefore their strategy had to be one of delay. The Foreign Relations Committee began a leisurely consideration of the document that held it up for the next two months. . . .

The committee then requested the President to place all his records of the Paris negotiations at its disposal. This Wilson refused to do — a refusal that gave credence to the charge that he was concealing something. Instead, he invited the committee to confer with him at the White House on August 19. There, after reading a prepared statement in which he tried to answer the various arguments that had been offered against the treaty, he permitted himself to be questioned for more than three hours during which he was asked about every controversial issue. Article 10 of the League Covenant, already under bitter attack, was carefully considered. Of this undertaking "to respect and preserve as against external aggression the territorial integrity and political independence of all Members of the League," Wilson pointed out that the League Council could only "advise upon" the means by which the obligation should be carried out in any particular case. Unless the United States were already involved in the controversy, no advice at all could be given without the assent of the American representative. Moreover, the vote of the Council was only advice, which each government would be free to reject if it pleased. Article 10 created "a moral, not a legal obligation." It left Congress absolutely free to put its own interpretation upon the commitment in all cases that called for action. Notwithstanding this fact, Article 10 seemed to Wilson "to constitute the very backbone of the whole Covenant. Without it the League would be hardly more than an influential debating society."

Concerning reservations to the treaty, he could see no objection to the Senate's passing resolutions interpreting the sense in which the United States accepted the obligations of the Covenant, provided they were not made part of the formal ratification itself. He did, however, strongly oppose reservations that would have to be accepted by other signatories. Not only would they indefinitely delay final ratification, but they would cause other governments to follow the American example so that "the meaning and operative force of the treaty would presently be clouded from one end of its clauses to the other."

But the President made no converts. As in the February conference, the Democrats went away convinced that Wilson had met every reasonable objection, while Lodge and his followers persisted in their contention that the treaty should be ratified only with important reservations, if at all.

Both supporters and opponents of the League counted upon the creation of a vast tide of popular sentiment that would overwhelm the opposing faction. At first the pro-League forces seemed to have the better of it. Out of 1,377 newspaper editors polled by the *Literary Digest* in April, 1919, 718 unconditionally favored the League, 478 favored it conditionally, and only 181 opposed it. Thirty-two state legislatures passed resolutions favoring the entrance of the United States into some form of international organization, thirty-three governors were similarly on record, while pro-League sentiment was also very strong among Protestant clergymen. The League to Enforce Peace, at the height of its power and influence, staged meetings throughout the country to urge ratification of the treaty without reservations. Prominent in this movement was Taft, who sharply denounced the partisan maneuvers of his fellow Republicans.

But the anti-Leaguers were also active: A self-constituted general staff held frequent meetings. . . . Two Pennsylvania multimillionaires, Henry Clay Frick and Andrew W. Mellon, provided the group with ample funds. The Hearst press was already engaged in violent denunciation of the League; its efforts were now supplemented by a great mass of literature warning against the perils of foreign entanglements. A League for the Preservation of American Independence held protest meetings against "the evil thing with a holy name." . . .

Alarmed by the success of his opponents in delaying action and beclouding the issues, Wilson set out in September on a speaking trip to carry his cause directly to the people. He visited the states of the Midwest, of the Pacific coast, and of the Rocky Mountains. During the space of 22 days he traveled more than 8,000 miles and delivered 37 speeches averaging an hour in length. For a frail man of 63, already overtaxed by his labors, this was too much. After his speech at Pueblo, Colorado, on September 25, Wilson suffered a serious breakdown. All thought of further activity had to be abandoned, and the President's special train speeded back to Washington. Stricken with partial paralysis the day after his return, Wilson was never again a well man. During the crucial rounds of the battle over the treaty, he was desperately sick, confined to his bedroom where he received little news from the outside world except through his wife and his doctor. Observers disagreed as to whether or not the heroic effort that had cost the President his health strengthened his cause. He had been greeted by large and enthusiastic crowds, many of his speeches were remarkably eloquent, thousands of listeners were impressed by his impassioned earnestness, but he gained no additional support in the one place where he most needed it — in the Senate — and big crowds also applauded the anti-League speeches of Borah, Johnson, and McCormick who pressed hard on the President's heels during the tour.

THE DEFEAT OF THE TREATY

The Senate Foreign Relations Committee finally made its recommendations on September 10, 1919. The majority report, concurred in by nine of the ten Republican members, advocated no less than forty-five amendments and four reservations to the treaty. On the other hand, six of the seven Democrats signed a minority report calling for ratification without change. The stage was now set for a long debate on the floor of the Senate.

For purposes of clarity and convenience, the members of the Upper House may be divided into four major groups. All but about seven Democrats were willing to vote for the treaty without change — either out of devotion to the League idea itself or out of loyalty to Wilson as a party leader. The Republicans, on the other hand, were divided into three factions, roughly equal in size. Some fourteen were staunch isolationists — the so-called irreconcilables, determined to vote against the treaty as long as it incorporated the League in any form. A second faction, headed by Lodge, consisted of strong reservationists; some of them believed basically in an association of nations, but felt that the Wilson version must be drastically amended to safeguard American interests; others were probably against any league, but believed that it was more strategic to emasculate the treaty with amendments than to attempt to obtain its outright rejection. The remainder were mild reservationists, at heart pro-League, yet believing that Wilson's work needed some clarification.

The initial advantage appeared to lie with the friends of the treaty. All of the amendments originally recommended in the majority report of the Foreign Relations Committee were voted down by an alliance of the Democrats with the mild reservationists. But Lodge made an extraordinary recovery from this setback. He now presented a battery of fourteen reservations and, by adroit political generalship, won a majority of the Senate to their support. The strong reservationists favored the Lodge proposals as minimum safeguards if the United States were to accept the suspect treaty; the irreconcilables voted for them because they wanted to weaken the treaty in any way possible even if they could not kill it outright; the mild reservationists accepted Lodge's leadership because they wanted to get the treaty ratified and believed that the reservations would serve that end. The Democrats made their worst tactical error in not developing a rival program that would hold the support of these pro-League Republicans.

Senators were impelled to support the reservations for a variety of motives. Staunch Republicans were reluctant to let Wilson's treaty go through without change lest the Democratic party get too much credit with the voters. Sticklers for Congressional prerogatives feared that League membership might weaken Congress' sole authority to declare war. The bogy that Article 10 constituted an entangling alliance impressed isolationists generally and particularly the Irish, who argued that the United States might become involved in helping suppress the Irish Republic. Much was made of the contention that the British Empire had six votes in the League Assembly to one for the United States (although English influence over the votes of South Africa or Canada was in reality not likely to be as great as that of the United States over the votes of Panama or a dozen small neighboring republics). Wilson was accused of insulting the Senate in the choice of his peace commission, of thwarting the aspirations of the Italians and the Chinese, and of lying in his denial that he had known about the secret treaties before he went to Paris.

In the end, the Lodge reservations were approved by a majority of the Senate. All but one of the Republicans voted for them; most but not all of the Democrats voted against them. The most important of the reservations was the one practically nullifying Article 10 of the Covenant: the United

States would assume no obligation under it unless Congress decided to act in a particular case. Other reservations claimed for the United States complete freedom to declare any issue a domestic one and as such excluded from the jurisdiction of the League; the sole right to interpret the Monroe Doctrine; refusal to agree to the Shantung settlement; and refusal of the United States to be bound by any League decision in which member states of the British Commonwealth cast in the aggregate more than one vote.

Lodge's motives in pushing through these reservations are still a matter of controversy. Those who believe in the Senator's sincerity contend that he really wanted an association of nations such as he had championed in earlier years and that he was seeking only to protect vital American interests that Wilson's project had jeopardized. Those who doubt Lodge's sincerity regard him as a bitter partisan determined to kill Wilson's project by maneuvering its Senate approval in such mutilated form that Wilson would not attempt to obtain its ratification by other powers. They point out that Lodge had taken a leading part in killing arbitration treaties in 1903 and 1911 by just this device.

The question now was: would the treaty with the Lodge reservations obtain the two-thirds vote essential for final Senate approval? Wilson's position on the issue was made clear in a letter to Senator Hitchcock of Nebraska, the Democratic leader. The President expressed hope that the friends and supporters of the treaty would vote against this proposal because it provided not for ratification, but "rather for nullification of the treaty."

On November 19, when the important roll call was finally taken, only 39 Senators voted to approve the treaty with the Lodge reservations, while 55 opposed it. The nays were cast by 42 Democrats, most of them guided by the advice from the White House, and 13 Republican irreconcilables, who were opposed to a League whatever the safeguards. The sentiment of the Senate on ratification without reservation was then tested, but only 38 Senators, all but one of them Democrats, would support the treaty in unadulterated form, while 55 opposed it, both groups of reservationists joining forces with the irreconcilables.

It seemed fantastic that, although there were only 17 Senators who were completely opposed to the treaty, ratification could not be obtained. Moderates from both parties sought to discover an escape from the impasse through a bipartisan conference in January, 1920. The Democrats offered to accept several reservations, including one to Article 10 that had been drafted by Taft. The conference made such apparent progress that the irreconcilables became alarmed and threatened to bolt the party if Lodge gave ground. In the end, the Massachusetts Senator refused all terms except complete Democratic acquiescence in the Lodge reservations, and the attempt to compromise failed.

On March 19, 1920, the Senate took the final vote on the treaty. The

fourteen Lodge reservations had been strengthened rather than weakened
and a fifteenth reservation of Democratic parentage had been adopted, stating that in the judgment of the United States Senate the Irish people were
entitled to a government of their own choice. The treaty with its fifteen
reservations came within seven of the two-thirds vote necessary for ratification; now 49 Senators voted for it and 35 against it. Half of the Democrats
who had voted against the treaty with reservations the previous November
now voted for it, convinced that approval in this form was better than no
ratification at all. But the other half voted against it, following the advice
of Wilson. Once again it was their votes, added to those of the irreconcilables, that killed the treaty.

An interesting speculation is whether the result would have been different if Wilson had retained his health. Perhaps pro-League public opinion
would have been more effectively rallied. Perhaps the President, more conscious of the realities of the situation, might have seen the need for Republican votes and, by timely compromise, have won the support of the more
reasonable reservationists. Such an outcome of the struggle should have
been possible if the good offices of Taft and other pro-League Republicans
had been employed. But to compromise was impossible for the Wilson of
1920; many critics considered this to be his fatal weakness, although his
admirers have insisted that compromise would have been equivalent to
surrender. . . .

President Wilson never lost faith that American opinion would eventually rally to the League in such volume as to override the obstructionists.
He looked forward to the 1920 election as "a solemn referendum" on the
issue. But as will be shown later, the election proved to be meaningless as
such a referendum. What the American people really thought of the
League is difficult to determine. Undoubtedly time worked to the advantage
of the anti-Leaguers. Over the course of the months, the combined efforts of
the irreconcilable Senators, the nationalist press, the Irish, and other groups
succeeded in convincing millions of Americans that the League was a sinister
plot against American independence. Millions of others did not lose their
faith in the ideal, but they became hopelessly divided in opinion as to how
to realize it. Taft and other leaders of the League to Enforce Peace shifted
their ground, giving up their fight to obtain the treaty without change and
urging ratification with the Lodge reservations, even though they considered
some of them "harmful." On the other hand, many believed that the President was right and that the Lodge reservations were impossible to accept
because they nullified the treaty.* Baffled and confused, more and more
Americans became tired of the whole debate and more than willing to forget
the war and the League. Sadly commenting on this, Wilson declared: "They

* Whether other signatories of the treaty would have accepted the reservations is uncertain, although there is some evidence that they were willing to do so.

will have to learn now by bitter experience just what they have lost. . . . We had a chance to gain the leadership of the world. We have lost it, and soon we shall be witnessing the tragedy of it all."

JAMES MACGREGOR BURNS

Like the disruption of the union sixty years before, the failure of the United States to join the League of Nations still stands as one of the historic misadventures of American politics. . . .

How could such a cause be lost, and lost so irretrievably? Many reasons have been advanced: Wilson's and Lodge's hate for each other; the stubbornness of both the President and the Republican leadership in the Senate; the two-thirds requirement for Senate ratification; the post-war slump in missionary idealism and the upsurge of nationalism; Republican control of both Senate and House; failure of party leaders to follow a bipartisan policy in foreign policy. Doubtless all these factors played a part. Yet all of them could have been overcome, as similar difficulties had in earlier times. Democrats and Republicans, for example, had often disagreed about treaties and still managed to compromise. What was so insuperable about the cleavage of 1920?

The answer is the same for 1919–1920 as it was for 1850–60. The struggle was not simply between parties or between leaders or between different branches of government; it was rooted in the electoral system, in group and party interests, in governmental machinery, in such a way that majority opinion could never be brought to bear on the issue. This is not to say that the system was at fault and not the leaders; the leaders are part of the system. It is to say that the protagonists had little leeway for conciliation because the political context in which they operated fortified their intransigence and hence inexorably forced them toward a fatal deadlock. It was not simply a series of blunders and misunderstandings that kept the United States out of the League; the outcome was inherent in the situation; and only rare statesmanship and good luck could have brought adherence. This time Americans had neither. . . .

Whether deep down in his heart Lodge really wanted a League is still an open question: probably he preferred a Rooseveltian policy of the big stick, international conferences, and the balance of power. In any event, the League was of secondary importance to the gentleman from Massachusetts; what he most certainly wanted was to block Wilson from getting his League

From "Wilson v. Lodge: No Advice, No Consent," in the book *Deadlock of Democracy* by James MacGregor Burns. © 1963 by James MacGregor Burns. Published by Prentice-Hall, Inc., Englewood Cliffs, N.J. and reprinted with their permission.

and then using it as a vote-getting issue in the 1920 campaigns. His main interest, in short, was the Republican party — or at least his wing of it — not the League. Lodge's situation in the Senate was a ticklish one. Of the 49 Republicans, about a dozen were "mild reservationists" who would accept the treaty without major changes. These Republicans were close to the more moderate, international wing of the party headed by men like Taft, Hughes, and Root. On Lodge's right flank were about fourteen "irreconcilables" who stood bitterly and vocally opposed to the treaty in any form. Lodge's own troops consisted of about twenty "strong reservationists" who reflected Lodge's willingness to take a league but only on his own terms.

Washington politicians watched, fascinated, as these two veteran politicians, the crusading President and the shrewd old Senator, worked out their battle plans. Wilson calculated that if the Senate turned down his League, he could establish a dramatic issue on which the Democratic party could win the election of 1920. The President was probably ready to run for a third term if necessary to turn the 1920 election into a "solemn referendum." And he had made the League and the treaty essentially a party issue by appointing to the peace conference a delegation that included only one Republican, a diplomat who had little standing with the congressional wing of the party. And he scorned the mild reservationists who could have supplied enough votes to win majorities for Wilson on reservations and amendments (only final ratification of the treaty required a two-thirds vote). To keep the issue unentangled, focused, headlined, the President planned also to make a "swing around the circle."

Lodge's tactic was just the opposite — to delay, obfuscate, and finally to suffocate Wilson's League. This tactic called for room to maneuver, since it meant veering back and forth, working first with one Republican faction and then another, conciliating his followers, stiffening them, yielding to them, as the situation demanded. And here Lodge took a step that raises doubt as to whether he really wanted any kind of meaningful league. As majority leader and as chairman of the Foreign Relations Committee the Senator could select new Republican appointees to this high-prestige committee. He chose two strong reservationists (one of them Warren G. Harding of Ohio) and two irreconcilables (one of them Hiram Johnson of California). He offered a post to a mild reservationist, Frank B. Kellogg of Minnesota (later Secretary of State under Coolidge) but only on the understanding that he support Lodge on the League. Kellogg demurred; Lodge renewed his conditional offer, using the amiable Harding as an intermediary. Kellogg declined. Lodge wanted only those moderates who would go along with him, but at the same time he accepted — evidently without conditions — two bitter-enders who later helped put pressure on him to stand firm against the League.

Still, the gentleman from Massachusetts was operating within bounds set by the Republican party in the Senate, and he had to adjust to the compulsions of the system. So did Wilson. For after all, he too had "stacked his committee" — the delegation to Paris — and he was just as willing as Lodge to deadlock the treaty in the Senate if this would give him a clear case on which to appeal to the people. Each man in his own medium operated like a virtuoso. Lodge dulled and confused public discussion of the issue by endless delays. He read aloud to his bored committee the entire text of the 268-page treaty; held six weeks of public hearings; helped trigger outcries from minority groups, especially the Anglophobe Irish; and demanded from the President executive documents he knew Wilson would never surrender. As Lodge proved master of the Senate, Wilson prepared to go to *his* constituency, the American people.

Wilson's appeal to the people in September, 1919, has become one of the nation's imperishable memories: the hopeful departure of the presidential train packed with reporters, clerks, secret service men, and the President's wife and his personal retinue; the mixed receptions to his speeches in the isolationist Midwest; the huge crowds, sometimes fervent, sometimes just friendly, but always reverent; the train puffing through the Rockies with a stop at Coeur d'Alene, in Borahland; the never-ending bustle and strain within the hot, crowded trains; the milling crowds in the far West, aroused to fever pitch by Wilson's eloquence, the pounding headaches that racked the President as he hunched over his portable typewriter; the climactic address in Pueblo where an exhausted President almost broke into tears as he described the burial places of American soldiers in France and asserted that this tragedy should not be enacted again; more racking headaches that night, now amid nausea; the anguished decision to cancel the rest of the tour; the return of the presidential special to Washington, with curtains drawn; then the thrombosis, the collapse, the semi-paralysis, and the long imprisonment in the White House.

Yet the fact seems to be that Wilson's appeal to the people, though made with brilliance and boldness and capped by tragedy, did not change a single Senator's vote. The President might almost as well have been campaigning in another country. The wise old Senators knew their political world just as the President knew his. They knew that the people were fickle, that their passions would ebb as the issue of the League was obscured and devitalized during the year that would elapse before the election. Indeed, only one-third of the Senators would have to face the voters in 1920. But beyond all this, most of Wilson's foes in the upper chamber were confident of their strength back home. The crowds in Idaho and California might cheer the Commander-in-Chief, but Borah and Johnson and the others had their own support, built up by years of mulish independence nationally, combined with steady obeisance to local interests and attitudes.

So the Senate was unmoved, and the treaty and the League headed inexorably to defeat. Wilson still would not compromise or confer with Lodge, he still preferred to keep his treaty intact and turn 1920 into a great and solemn referendum. Lodge was stuck fast too; when he seemed at one point on the verge of making concessions to the moderates, the bitter-enders called a council of war, summoned Lodge, and threatened to oust him as majority leader. (Borah said later that he had never seen a man look so scared.) On March 19, 1920, the Senate took the final vote on the resolution of ratification, which incorporated the Lodge reservations. The vote was 49 to 35 in favor — a majority, but fifteen votes short of the necessary two-thirds. About half the Democrats went over to Lodge in order to support some kind of League, but the other half — all Southerners — stuck with the President. Combined with the irreconcilables, they killed the League. Once again, as in 1860, the moderate elements in the middle had shrunk, the extremists had carried the day. And the League, like the Union, was dead.

But dead for how long? Now Wilson, still ailing, looked toward the fall elections for a popular mandate for his party and his cause. It was not to be. Although the President seemed to make himself available for renomination on the eve of the convention, this was out of the question; and the Democrats chose an Ohio governor identified neither with the Administration nor with the cause. While James M. Cox and his young running mate, Franklin Roosevelt, endorsed the League in general, they ran on a Democratic platform that itself fuzzed over the crucial questions of reservations.

Perhaps Wilson's plan for a referendum would have worked if the Republicans had nominated the leader and symbol of Senate opposition, Senator Lodge. But Lodge, whatever his failings, knew himself; he knew that he was a senatorial, not a presidential, type. Nor did he want such a clear-cut posing of the issue as his candidacy would afford. He and his colleagues simply made sure that they would dominate Republican strategy. The convention was "government of the Senate, by the Senate, and for the Senate," said *The New York Times*. Lodge was both keynoter and permanent chairman of the Republican convention, appropriately held in isolationist Chicago. His men dominated the platform committee, and it was essentially Lodge's clique in the Senate, after the leading candidates for the nomination had deadlocked, that gathered in Room 404 of the Blackstone Hotel to choose a fellow Senator whose slovenly intellect and wabbling ways could be depended on to drown the League issue in a flood of double-talk and verbiage.

Where were the moderate Republicans in all this — where were Hughes and Taft and Herbert Hoover? During the Senate proceedings they had tried to moderate Lodge's position, but their pressure on the Massachusetts Senator had not overcome the opposing pressure from the irreconcilables. During the convention the moderates had lacked a clear-cut contender of their own; Root and Stimson were not popular enough; Hughes, grieving over the loss of his eldest daughter, would not run. Herbert Hoover was tainted by his service under Wilson. So, the moderates had to go along with Harding. During the campaign they tried to win middle-of-the-road support and to push the wavering Harding toward a more pro-League stand by issuing a public appeal stating that the issue was between an extreme Wilson League and a modified Harding League. This was the intellect and conscience of the Republican party speaking out, and it served only to muddy the waters further.

Harding and the Republican party duly swept to victory in November, 1920; they carried the electoral college 404 to 127, won 64 per cent of the two-party popular vote, and gained topheavy majorities in Congress. But no one to this day has determined whether the campaign turned more on the League or a host of other issues and personalities and popular moods. Wilson's scheme had failed; the great and solemn referendum of 1920, as Bailey says, had turned into a great and solemn muddlement.

❦ CASE
STUDY   *WINNING APPROVAL FOR*
THE MARSHALL PLAN

The second case study in this chapter stands in sharp contrast to the first. It is the story of a success rather than of a failure.

In retrospect, the Marshall Plan stands out as perhaps the most creative and successful United States foreign policy initiative of the postwar period. Without firing a shot, it helped the nations of Europe to avoid economic disaster and possible Communist takeover — at a dollar cost far lower than the United States was soon to pay to keep South Korea out of Communist hands by military means. It aided the European nations to "find themselves" once again and to become strong and independent partners of the United States in the decades ahead. Finally, it marked a pioneering step in the constructive use of American economic power to achieve American political objectives. In time, foreign aid was to prove so useful a tool of foreign policy that the Soviet Union and Communist China would pay its originators the compliment of embarking upon aid programs of their own.

    1. What formal and informal presidential powers did Truman make use of in securing approval for the Marshall Plan?

    2. What aspects of the power structure within Congress at the time aided the President's efforts?

    3. What had Truman himself done to nourish such advantages as

were now available to him? How was bipartisan cooperation maintained?

4. From what persons and agencies within the United States government might opposition to the Marshall Plan have been expected to come? How was this opposition averted or overcome in this case?

5. What sources of support within the U.S. Government was the President able to draw upon? How did each help him? How did he "pay for" their help?

6. In view of the President's critical contributions, why wasn't the European Recovery Program called the "Truman Plan"?

RICHARD NEUSTADT

The constitutional convention of 1787 is supposed to have created a government of "separated powers." It did nothing of the sort. Rather, it created a government of separated institutions *sharing* powers. . . .

. . . When one man shares authority with another, but does not gain or lose his job upon the other's whim, his willingness to act upon the urging of the other turns on whether he conceives the action right for him. The essence of a President's persuasive task is to convince such men that what the White House wants of them is what they ought to do for their sake and on their authority. . . .

A President's authority and status give him great advantages in dealing with the men he would persuade. Each "power" is a vantage point for him in the degree that other men have use for his authority. From the veto to appointments, from publicity to budgeting, and so down a long list, the White House now controls the most encompassing array of vantage points in the American political system. With hardly an exception, the men who share in governing this country are aware that at some time, in some degree, the doing of *their* jobs, the furthering of *their* ambitions, may depend upon the President of the United States. Their need for presidential action, or their fear of it, is bound to be recurrent if not actually continuous. Their need or fear is his advantage.

A President's advantages are greater than mere listing of his "powers" might suggest. The men with whom he deals must deal with him until the last day of his term. Because they have continuing relationships with him, his future, while it lasts, supports his present influence. Even though there is no need or fear of him today, what he could do tomorrow may supply today's advantage. Continuing relationships may convert any "power," any

From Richard Neustadt, *Presidential Power* (New York: Wiley, 1960), pp. 33–57. Omissions are indicated by ellipses. Most footnotes have been omitted. Reprinted by permission of John Wiley and Sons, Inc.

aspect of his status, into vantage points in almost any case. When he induces other men to do what he wants done, a President can trade on their dependence now *and* later.

The President's advantages are checked by the advantages of others. Continuing relationships will pull in both directions. These are relationships of mutual dependence. A President depends upon the men he would persuade; he has to reckon with his need or fear of them. They too will possess status, or authority, or both, else they would be of little use to him. Their vantage points confront his own; their power tempers his. . . .

. . . Command has limited utility; persuasion becomes give-and-take. It is well that the White House holds the vantage points it does. In such a business any President may need them all — and more. . . .

Like our governmental structure as a whole, the executive establishment consists of separated institutions sharing powers. The President heads one of these; Cabinet officers, agency administrators, and military commanders head others. Below the departmental level, virtually independent bureau chiefs head many more. Under mid-century conditions, Federal operations spill across dividing lines on organization charts; almost every policy entangles many agencies; almost every program calls for interagency collaboration. Everything somehow involves the President. But operating agencies owe their existence least of all to one another — and only in some part to him. Each has a separate statutory base; each has its statutes to administer; each deals with a different set of subcommittees at the Capitol. Each has its own peculiar set of clients, friends, and enemies outside the formal government. Each has a different set of specialized careerists inside its own bailiwick. Our Constitution gives the President the "take-care" clause and the appointive power. Our statutes give him central budgeting and a degree of personnel control. All agency administrators are responsible to him. But they *also* are responsible to Congress, to their clients, to their staffs, and to themselves. In short, they have five masters. Only after all of those do they owe any loyalty to each other.

"The members of the Cabinet," Charles G. Dawes used to remark, "are a President's natural enemies." Dawes had been Harding's Budget Director, Coolidge's Vice-President, and Hoover's Ambassador to London; he also had been General Pershing's chief assistant for supply in the First World War. The words are highly colored, but Dawes knew whereof he spoke. The men who have to serve so many masters cannot help but be somewhat the "enemy" of any one of them. By the same token, any master wanting service is in some degree the "enemy" of such a servant. A President is likely to want loyal support but not to relish trouble on his doorstep. Yet the more his Cabinet members cleave to him, the more they may need help from him in fending off the wrath of rival masters. Help, though, is synonymous with trouble. Many a Cabinet officer, with loyalty ill-rewarded by his lights and help withheld, has come to view the White House as innately hostile to department heads. Dawes's dictum can be turned around.

A senior presidential aide remarked to me in Eisenhower's time: "If some of these Cabinet members would just take time out to stop and ask themselves 'What would I want if I were President?', they wouldn't give him all the trouble he's been having." But even if they asked themselves the question, such officials often could not act upon the answer. Their personal attachment to the President is all too often overwhelmed by duty to their other masters.

Executive officials are not equally advantaged in their dealings with a President. Nor are the same officials equally advantaged all the time. . . .

The more an officeholder's status and his "powers" stem from sources independent of the President, the stronger will be his potential pressure *on* the President. Department heads in general have more bargaining power than do most members of the White House staff; but bureau chiefs may have still more, and specialists at upper levels of established career services may have almost unlimited reserves of the enormous power which consists of sitting still. . . .

. . . Most men who share in governing have interests of their own beyond the realm of policy *objectives*. The sponsorship of policy, the form it takes, the conduct of it, and the credit for it separate their interest from the President's despite agreement on the end in view. In political government, the means can matter quite as much as ends; they often matter more. And there are always differences of interest in the means. . . .

. . . The European Recovery Program of 1948, the so-called Marshall Plan . . . [was] perhaps the greatest exercise in policy *agreement* since the cold war began. . . . What makes this policy most notable for present purposes, however, is that it became effective upon action by the 80th Congress, at the behest of Harry Truman, in the election year of 1948.

Eight months before [Secretary of State George C.] Marshall spoke at Harvard [in June, 1947], the Democrats had lost control of both Houses of Congress for the first time in fourteen years. Truman, whom the Secretary represented, had just finished his second troubled year as President-by-succession. Truman was regarded with so little warmth in his own party that in 1946 he had been urged *not* to participate in the congressional campaign. At the opening of Congress in January, 1947, Senator Robert A. Taft, "Mr. Republican," had somewhat the attitude of a President-elect. This was a vision widely shared in Washington, with Truman relegated, thereby, to the role of caretaker-on-term. Moreover, within just two weeks of Marshall's commencement address, Truman was to veto two prized accomplishments of Taft's congressional majority: the Taft-Hartley Act and tax reduction. Yet scarcely ten months later the Marshall Plan was under way on terms to satisfy its sponsors, its authorization completed, its first-year funds in sight, its administering agency in being: all managed by as thorough a display of executive-congressional cooperation as any we have seen since the Second World War. For any President at any time this would have been a great accomplishment. In years before mid-century it would have been enough to make the future reputation of his term. And for a Truman, at this time, enactment of the Marshall Plan appears almost miraculous.

How was the miracle accomplished? How did a President so situated bring it off? In answer, the first thing to note is that he did not do it by himself. Truman had help of a sort no less extraordinary than the outcome. Although each stands for something more complex, the names of Marshall, Vandenberg, Patterson, Bevin, Stalin, tell the story of that help.

In 1947, two years after V-J Day, General Marshall was something more than Secretary of State. He was a man venerated by the President as "the greatest living American," literally an embodiment of Truman's ideals. He was honored at the Pentagon as an architect of victory. He was thoroughly respected by the Secretary of the Navy, James V. Forrestal, who that year became the first Secretary of Defense. On Capitol Hill Marshall had an enormous fund of respect stemming from his war record as Army Chief of Staff, and in the country generally no officer had come out of the war with a higher reputation for judgment, intellect, and probity. Besides, as Secretary of State, he had behind him the first generation of matured foreign service officers produced by the reforms of the 1920's, and mingled with them, in the departmental service, were some of the ablest of the men drawn by the war from private life to Washington. In terms both of staff talent and staff's use, Marshall's years began a State Department "golden age" which lasted until the era of McCarthy. Moreover, as his Under Secretary, Marshall had, successively, Dean Acheson and Robert Lovett, men who commanded the respect of the professionals and the regard of congressmen. (Acheson had been brilliantly successful at congressional relations as Assistant Secretary in the war and postwar years.) Finally, as a special undersecretary Marshall had Will Clayton, a man highly regarded, for good reason, at both ends of Pennsylvania Avenue.

Taken together, these are exceptional resources for a Secretary of State. In the circumstances, they were quite as necessary as they obviously are relevant. The Marshall Plan was launched by a "lame duck" Administration "scheduled" to leave office in eighteen months. Marshall's program faced a congressional leadership traditionally isolationist and currently intent upon economy. European aid was viewed with envy by a Pentagon distressed and virtually disarmed through budget cuts, and by domestic agencies intent on enlarged welfare programs. It was not viewed with liking by a Treasury intent on budget surpluses. The plan had need of every asset that could be extracted from the personal position of its nominal author and from the skills of his assistants.

Without the equally remarkable position of the senior Senator from Michigan, Arthur H. Vandenberg, it is hard to see how Marshall's assets could have been enough. Vandenberg was chairman of the Senate Foreign Relations Committee. Actually, he was much more than that. Twenty years a senator, he was the senior member of his party in the Chamber. Assiduously cultivated by F.D.R. and Truman, he was a chief Republican proponent of "bipartisanship" in foreign policy, and consciously conceived himself its living symbol to his party, to the country, and abroad. Moreover, by informal but entirely operative agreement with his colleague Taft, Vandenberg held the acknowledged lead among Senate Republicans in the whole field of international affairs. This acknowledgement meant more in 1947 than it might have meant at any other time. With confidence in the advent of a Republican administration two years hence, most of the gentlemen were in a mood to be responsive and responsible. The war was over, Roosevelt dead, Truman a caretaker, theirs the trust. That the Senator from Michigan saw matters in this light, his diaries make clear. And this was not the outlook from the Senate side alone; the attitudes of House Republicans associated with the Herter Committee and its tours abroad suggest the same mood of responsibility. Vandenberg was not the only source of help on Capitol Hill. But relatively speaking, his position there was as exceptional as Marshall's was downtown.

Help of another sort was furnished by a group of dedicated private citizens who organized one of the most effective instruments for public information seen since the Second World War: the Committee for the Marshall Plan, headed by the eminent Republicans whom F.D.R., in 1940, had brought to the Department of War: Henry L. Stimson as honorary chairman and Robert P. Patterson as active spokesman. The remarkable array of bankers, lawyers, trade unionists, and editors, who had drawn together in defense of "internationalism" before Pearl Harbor and had joined their talents in the war itself, combined again to spark the work of this committee. Their efforts generated a great deal of vocal public support to buttress Marshall's arguments, and Vandenberg's, in Congress.

But before public support could be rallied, there had to be a purpose tangible enough, concrete enough, to provide a rallying ground. At Harvard, Marshall had voiced an idea in general terms. That this was turned into a hard program susceptible of presentation and support is due, in major part, to Ernest Bevin, the British Foreign Secretary. He well deserves the credit he has sometimes been assigned as, in effect, co-author of the Marshall Plan. For Bevin seized on Marshall's Harvard speech and organized a European response with promptness and concreteness beyond the State Department's expectations. What had been virtually a trial balloon to test reactions on both sides of the Atlantic was hailed in London as an invitation to the Europeans to send Washington a bill of particulars. This they promptly organized to do, and the American Administration then organized in turn for its reception without further argument internally about the pros and cons of issuing the "invitation" in the first place. But for Bevin there might have been trouble from the Secretary of the Treasury and others besides.

If Bevin's help was useful at that early stage, Stalin's was vital from first to last. In a mood of self-deprecation Truman once remarked that without Moscow's "crazy" moves "we never would have had our foreign policy . . . we never could have got a thing from Congress." George Kennan, among others, has deplored the anti-Soviet overtone of the case made for the Marshall Plan in Congress and the country, but there is no doubt that this clinched the argument for many segments of American opinion. There also is no doubt that Moscow made the crucial contributions to the case.

By 1947 events, far more than governmental prescience or open action, had given a variety of publics an impression of inimical Soviet intentions (and of Europe's weakness), and a growing urge to "do something about it." Three months before Marshall spoke at Harvard, Greek-Turkish aid and promulgation of the Truman Doctrine had seemed rather to crystallize than to create a public mood and a congressional response. The Marshall planners, be it said, were poorly placed to capitalize on that mood, nor had the Secretary wished to do so. Their object, indeed, was to cut across it, striking at the cause of European weakness rather than at Soviet aggressiveness, per se. A strong economy in Western Europe called, ideally, for restorative measures of continental scope. American assistance proffered in an anti-Soviet context would have been contradictory in theory and unacceptable in fact to several of the governments that Washington was anxious to assist. As Marshall, himself, saw it, the logic of his purpose forbade him to play his strongest congressional card. The Russians then proceeded to play it for him. When the Europeans met in Paris, Molotov walked out. After the Czechs had shown continued interest in American aid, a communist coup overthrew their government while Soviet forces stood along their borders within easy reach of Prague. Molotov transformed the Marshall Plan's initial presentation; Czechoslovakia assured its final passage, which followed by a month the take-over in Prague.

Such was the help accorded Truman in obtaining action on the Marshall Plan. Considering his politically straitened circumstances he scarcely could have done with less. Conceivably, some part of Moscow's contribution might have been dispensable, but not Marshall's, or Vandenberg's, or Bevin's, or Patterson's, or that of the great many other men whose work is represented by their names in my account. Their aid was not extended to the President for his own sake. He was not favored in this fashion just because they liked him personally, or were spellbound by his intellect or charm. They might have been as helpful had all held him in disdain, which some of them certainly did. The Londoners who seized the ball, Vandenberg and Taft and the congressional majority, Marshall and his planners, the officials of other agencies who actively supported them or "went along," the host of influential private citizens who rallied to the cause — all these played the parts they did because they thought they had to, in their interest, given their responsibilities, not Truman's. Yet they hardly would have found it in their interest to collaborate with one another, or with him, had he not furnished them precisely what *they* needed from the White House. Truman could not do without their help, but he could not have had it without unremitting effort on his part.

The crucial thing to note about this case is that despite compatibility of views on public policy, Truman got no help he did not pay for (except Stalin's). Bevin scarcely could have seized on Marshall's words had Marshall not been plainly backed by Truman. Marshall's interest would not have comported with the exploitation of his prestige by a President who undercut him openly, or subtly, or even inadvertently, at any point. Vandenberg, presumably, could not have backed proposals by a White House which begrudged him deference and access gratifying to his fellow-partisans (and satisfying to himself). Prominent Republicans in private life would not have found it easy to promote a cause identified with Truman's claims on 1948 — and neither would the prominent New Dealers then engaged in searching for a substitute.

Truman paid the price required for their services. So far as the record shows, the White House did not falter once in firm support for Marshall and the Marshall Plan. Truman backed his Secretary's gamble on an invitation to all Europe. He made the plan his own in a well-timed address to the Canadians. He lost no opportunity to widen the involvements of his own official family in the cause. Averell Harriman the Secretary of Commerce, Julius Krug the Secretary of the Interior, Edwin Nourse the Economic Council Chairman, James Webb the Director of the Budget — all were made responsible for studies and reports contributing directly to the legislative presentation. Thus these men were committed in advance. Besides, the President, continually emphasized to everyone in reach that he did not have doubts, did not desire complications and would foreclose all he could. Reportedly, his emphasis was felt at the Treasury, with good effect. And Truman was at special pains to smooth the way for Vandenberg. The Senator insisted on "no politics" from the Administration side; there was none. He thought a survey of American resources and capacity essential; he got it in the Krug and Harriman reports. Vandenberg expected advance consultation; he received it, step by step, in frequent meetings with the President and weekly conferences with Marshall. He asked for an effective liaison between Congress and agencies concerned; Lovett and others gave him what he wanted. When the Senator decided on the need to change financing and administrative features of the legislation, Truman disregarded Budget Bureau grumbling and acquiesced with grace. When, finally, Vandenberg desired a Republican to head the new administering agency, his candidate, Paul Hoffman, was appointed despite the President's own preference for another. In all of these ways Truman employed the sparse advantages his "powers" and his status then accorded him to gain the sort of help he had to have.

Truman helped himself in still another way. Traditionally and practically no one was placed as well as he to call public attention to the task of *Congress* (and its Republican leadership). Throughout the fall and winter of 1947 and on into the spring of 1948, he made repeated use of presidential "powers" to remind the country that congressional action was required. Messages, speeches, and an extra session were employed to make the point. Here, too, he drew advantage from his place. However, in his circumstances, Truman's public advocacy might have hurt, not helped, had his words seemed directed toward the forthcoming election. Truman gained advantage for his program only as his own endorsement of it stayed on the right side of that fine line between the "caretaker" in office and the would-be candidate. In public statements dealing with the Marshall Plan he seems to have risked blurring this distinction only once, when he called Congress into session in November 1947 asking both for interim aid to Europe *and* for peacetime price controls. The second request linked the then inflation with the current Congress (and with Taft), becoming a first step toward one of Truman's major themes in 1948. By calling for both measures at the extra session he could have been accused — and was — of mixing home-front politics with foreign aid. In the event, no harm was done the European program (or his politics). But in advance a number of his own advisers feared that such a double call would jeopardize the Marshall Plan. Their fears are testimony to the narrowness of his advantage in employing his own "powers" for its benefit.

It is symptomatic of Truman's situation that "bipartisan" accommodation by the White House then was thought to mean congressional consultation and conciliation on a scale unmatched in Eisenhower's time. Yet Eisenhower did about as well with opposition Congresses as Truman did, in terms of requests granted for defense and foreign aid. It may be said that Truman asked for more extraordinary measures. But it also may be said that Eisenhower never lacked for the prestige his predecessor had to borrow. It often was remarked, in Truman's time, that he seemed a "split-personality," so sharply did his conduct differentiate domestic politics from national security. But personality aside, how else could *he,* in his first term, gain ground for an evolving foreign policy? The plain fact is that Truman had to play bipartisanship as he did or lose the game.

Had Truman lacked the personal advantages his "powers" and his status gave him, or if he had been maladroit in using them, there probably would not have been a massive European aid program in 1948. Something of the sort, perhaps quite different in its emphasis, would almost certainly have come to pass before the end of 1949. *Some* American response to European weakness and to Soviet expansion was as certain as such things can be. But in 1948 temptations to await a Taft Plan or a Dewey Plan might well have caused at least a year's postponement of response had the "outgoing" Administration bungled its congressional, or public, or allied, or executive relations. Quite aside from the specific virtues of their plan, Truman and his helpers gained that year, at least, in timing the American response. As European time was measured then, this was a precious gain. The President's own share in this accomplishment was vital. He made his contribution by exploiting his advantages. Truman, in effect, lent Marshall and the rest the perquisites and status of his office. In return they lent him their prestige and their own influence. The transfer multiplied *his* influence despite his limited authority in form and lack of strength politically. Without the wherewithal to make this bargain, Truman could not have contributed to European aid.

Bargaining advantages convey no guarantees. Influence remains a two-way street. In the fortunate instance of the Marshall Plan, what Truman needed was actually in the hands of men who were prepared to "trade" with him. He personally could deliver what they wanted in return. Marshall, Vandenberg, Harriman, *et al.*, possessed the prestige, energy, associations, staffs, essential to the legislative effort. Truman himself had a sufficient hold on presidential messages and speeches, on budget policy, on high-level appointments, and on his own time and temper to carry through all aspects of his necessary part. But it takes two to make a bargain. It takes those who have prestige to lend it on whatever terms. Suppose that Marshall had declined the Secretaryship of State in January 1947; Truman might not have found a substitute so well-equipped to furnish what he needed in the months ahead. Or suppose that Vandenberg had fallen victim to a cancer two years before he actually did; Senator [Alexander] Wiley of Wisconsin would not have seemed to Taft a man with whom the world need be divided. Or suppose that the Secretary of the Treasury had been possessed of stature, force, and charm commensurate with that of his successor in Eisenhower's time, the redoubtable George M. Humphrey. And what if Truman then had seemed to the Republicans what he turned out to be in 1948, a formidable candidate for President? It is unlikely that a single one of these "supposes" would have changed the final outcome; two or three, however, might have altered it entirely. Truman was not guaranteed more power than his "powers" just because he had continuing relationships with Cabinet secretaries and with senior senators. Here, as everywhere, the outcome was conditional on who they were and what he was and how each viewed events, and on their actual performance in response.

Granting that persuasion has no guarantee attached, how can a President reduce the risks of failing to persuade? How can he maximize his prospects for effectiveness by minimizing chances that his power will elude him? The Marshall Plan suggests an answer: he guards his power prospects in the course of making choices. Marshall himself, and Forrestal, and Harriman, and others of the sort held office on the President's appointment. Vandenberg had vast symbolic value partly because F.D.R. and Truman had done everything they could, since 1944, to build him up. The Treasury Department and the Budget Bureau — which together must have jeopardized the plans these others made — were headed by officials whose prestige depended wholly on their jobs. What Truman needed for those "givers" he received, in part, because of his past choice of men and measures. What they received in turn were actions taken or withheld by him, himself. The things they needed from him mostly involved his own conduct where his current choices ruled. The President's own actions in the past had cleared the way for current bargaining. His actions in the present were his trading stock. Behind each action lay a personal choice, and these together comprised *his* control over the give-and-take that gained him what he wanted. . . .

. . . A President's own choices are the only means *in his own hands* of guarding his own prospects for effective influence. He can draw power from continuing relationships in the degree that he can capitalize upon the needs of others for the Presidency's status and authority. He helps himself to do so, though, by nothing save ability to recognize the pre-conditions and the chance advantages and to proceed accordingly in the course of the choice-making that comes his way.

Chapter Four

THE DEPARTMENT OF STATE
AND THE MANAGEMENT
OF FOREIGN POLICY

On April 30, 1965, United States marines intervened directly in the affairs of a Latin American state for the first time in more than thirty years. A few days later, President Lyndon B. Johnson addressed the American people on radio and television to explain why he had ordered this controversial military action. On the afternoon the decision was made, he noted, he had been reviewing the world situation with his three principal advisers on foreign affairs: Secretary of State Dean Rusk, Secretary of Defense Robert McNamara, and McGeorge Bundy, the President's Special Assistant for National Security Affairs. President Johnson continued:

> At shortly after 3 o'clock I received a cable from our Ambassador [to the Dominican Republic], and he said that things were in danger. He had been informed that the chief of police and the governmental authorities could no longer protect us. We immediately started the necessary conference calls to be prepared.
>
> At 5:14, almost two hours later, we received a cable that was labeled "critic," a word that is reserved for only the most urgent and immediate matters of national security. The cable reported that Dominican law enforcement and military officials had informed our embassy that the situation was completely out of control, and that the police and the government could no longer give any guarantee concerning the safety of Americans or of any foreign nationals.
>
> Ambassador Bennett, who is one of our most experienced foreign service officers, went on in that cable to say that only an immediate landing of American forces could safeguard and protect the lives of thousands of Americans and thousands of other citizens of some 30 other countries. . . .

> The matter was before the OAS [Organization of American States] peace committee on Tuesday at our suggestion. . . . But when that cable arrived, when our entire country team in the Dominican Republic, made up of nine men, one from the Army, Navy and Air Force, our Ambassador, our aid man and others, said to your President unanimously, "Mr. President, if you do not send forces immediately men and women, Americans and those of other lands, will die in the streets."
>
> Well, I knew there was no time to talk, to consult or to delay. . . .[1]

President Johnson's remarks on this occasion included an unusually explicit statement of the pivotal role played by American representatives abroad in making a historic foreign policy decision. In less extraordinary foreign policy decisions their role is, of necessity, even greater.

This chapter and the two that follow deal with the executive agencies principally concerned with making and conducting American foreign policy. This chapter deals with the Department of State and the Foreign Service, the Peace Corps, the United States Information Agency (USIA), and the Agency for International Development (AID). In the next two chapters we shall take up the activities and role of the military agencies, and the intelligence community, respectively.

FUNCTIONS AND ORGANIZATION
OF THE DEPARTMENT OF STATE

The Department of State is charged with primary responsibility for representing the United States abroad and for advising the President on foreign affairs. In performing these functions, it employs 25,000 people in Washington and in the main capitals and remote corners of the world. Some 10,000 of these are foreign nationals serving American missions abroad. The remainder are Americans, nearly equally divided between the Department in Washington and some three-hundred posts in well over one-hundred foreign nations. On an average working day, well over 5,000 cables, reports, and messages are exchanged between the Department and its posts abroad.

An official Department of State publication lists the following principal Departmental functions, in addition to reporting on political and economic developments abroad:

> . . . The Department
>
> represents the United States in over 100 countries;
> speaks for the United States in the United Nations and other international organizations;

[1] Whether the desire to save American lives was the principal motivation behind the President's decision to intervene in the Dominican Republic has been the subject of considerable debate. It has been contended that the desire to avert a possible takeover by forces supposedly sympathetic to communism was actually the main factor. See Theodore Draper, "The Dominican Crisis," *Commentary* (December, 1965), 33–68. But it is generally agreed that Ambassador W. Tapley Bennett's actions and advice played a key role in the making of this decision.

> negotiates treaties and agreements with foreign nations;
>
> promotes the interests of U.S. airlines and shipping overseas;
>
> helps to establish and expand foreign markets for the products of U.S. industry and agriculture;
>
> protects American property abroad and assists Americans living or traveling abroad who find themselves in difficulties;
>
> issues passports to U.S. citizens and visas to foreign nationals for visits to this country;
>
> arranges to bring foreign students, teachers, leaders, and specialists to visit this country, and arranges to send their American counterparts on exchange visits to further understanding around the world of our country, our way of life, and our national purposes; and
>
> helps to inform the U.S. public about our foreign relations.[2]

The organization of the Department reflects its functions. Most working-level foreign policy problems are first brought to the Department's attention by its representatives in the field. United States embassies, legations, consulates general and consulates are depended upon to keep the Secretary of State — and the President — informed about happenings abroad which may affect American security, American interests, or American citizens. Chart A, illustrating the organization of a typical diplomatic mission should make more explicit the basic tasks the mission is expected to perform.

The need to service and instruct these missions provides the basis for the organization of the Department in Washington as well — as Chart B, showing the organization of the Bureau of African Affairs (as of December, 1963), suggests. The country "desks" are the backbone of State Department operations. The desk officer receives copies of virtually all field reports from the country of his responsibility. When one of these reports requests, or seems to require, action by the Department, the desk officer is normally the initiator. He drafts the telegram or policy paper required, phones or hand carries it to other officials concerned — both within the Department and in other agencies — to secure their advice and concurrence ("clearance"), and then submits it to his chief, the "officer-in-charge." The Algerian desk officer, for instance, reports to the officer in charge of North African Affairs. (See Chart B.) The latter, in turn, must decide whether to approve the action on his own responsibility or to bring it to *his* chief, the Assistant Secretary for African Affairs. The few most important matters, of course, will be taken still further up the chain of command.

But the geographic subdivisions are no longer today, as they once were, virtually the Department's only organizational units. An organization chart for the Department as a whole (Chart C) shows, in addition, a number of functional bureaus and offices — for economic affairs, educational and cul-

2 *The U.S. Department of State: What It Is . . . What It Does . . .* (Washington, D.C.: U.S. Department of State, 1963), p. 3.

CHART A – BASIC ORGANIZATION OF A DIPLOMATIC MISSION

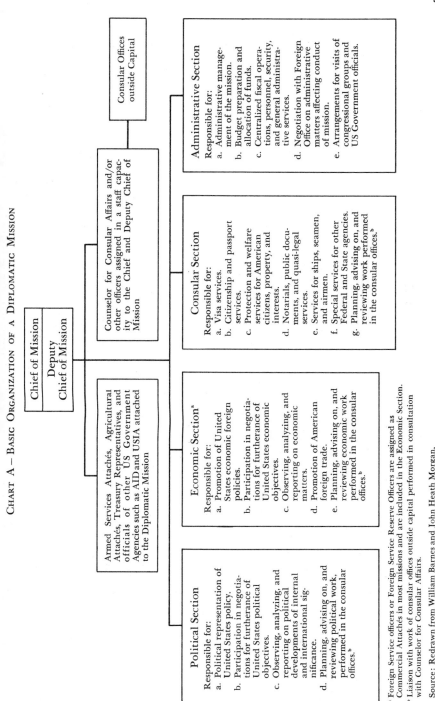

Chief of Mission

Deputy Chief of Mission

Counselor for Consular Affairs and/or other officers assigned in a staff capacity to the Chief and Deputy Chief of Mission

Consular Offices outside Capital

Armed Services Attachés, Agricultural Attachés, Treasury Representatives, and officials of other US Government Agencies such as AID and USIA attached to the Diplomatic Mission

Political Section

Responsible for:

a. Political representation of United States policy.

b. Participation in negotiations for furtherance of United States political objectives.

c. Observing, analyzing, and reporting on political developments of internal and international significance.

d. Planning, advising on, and reviewing political work, performed in the consular offices.[b]

Economic Section[a]

Responsible for:

a. Promotion of United States economic foreign policies.

b. Participation in negotiations for furtherance of United States economic objectives.

c. Observing, analyzing, and reporting on economic matters.

d. Promotion of American foreign trade.

e. Planning, advising on, and reviewing economic work performed in the consular offices.[b]

Consular Section

Responsible for:

a. Visa services.

b. Citizenship and passport services.

c. Protection and welfare services for American citizens, property, and interests.

d. Notarials, public documents, and quasi-legal services.

e. Services for ships, seamen, and airmen.

f. Special services for other Federal and State agencies.

g. Planning, advising on, and reviewing work performed in the consular offices.[b]

Administrative Section

Responsible for:

a. Administrative management of the mission.

b. Budget preparation and allocation of funds.

c. Centralized fiscal operations, personnel, security, and general administrative services.

d. Negotiation with Foreign Office on administrative matters affecting conduct of mission.

e. Arrangements for visits of congressional groups and US Government officials.

[a] Foreign Service officers or Foreign Service Reserve Officers are assigned as Commercial Attachés in most missions and are included in the Economic Section.

[b] Liaison with work of consular offices outside capital performed in consultation with Counselor for Consular Affairs.

Source: Redrawn from William Barnes and John Heath Morgan, *The Foreign Service of the United States: Origins, Development and Functions* (Washington, D.C.: Historical Office, Bureau of Public Affairs, U.S. Department of State, 1961), p. 303.

CHART B — BUREAU OF AFRICAN AFFAIRS, 1963

	Assistant Secretary		
	Offices		Offices

Inter-African Affairs

Offices: North African Affairs | East and South African Affairs | Central African Affairs | West African Affairs

North African Affairs
Country Desks:
- Algeria
- Ethiopia
- Somali Rep.
- Sudan
- Libya
- Morocco
- Tunisia

East and South African Affairs
- Rhodesia and Nyasaland
- Kenya and Seychelles
- Uganda
- Tanganyika and Zanzibar
- Rep. of South Africa
- Southwest Africa and High Commission Territories

Central African Affairs
- Congo (L)
- Congo (B) Rwanda and Burundi
- Angola, Mozambique Malagasy, Port. Guinea and Mauritius
- Chad, Gabon, Cent. African Rep. Cameroon and Spanish Guinea

West African Affairs
- Ghana
- Guinea and Mali
- Liberia and Sierra Leone
- Nigeria
- Gambia Mauritania and Senegal
- Dahomey, Ivory Coast, Niger, Upper Volta and Togo

Source: United States Senate, Committee on Government Operations, Subcommittee on National Security Staffing and Operations (Jackson Subcommittee), Pt. 6, p. 443.

CHART C.—ORGANIZATION OF THE DEPARTMENT OF STATE

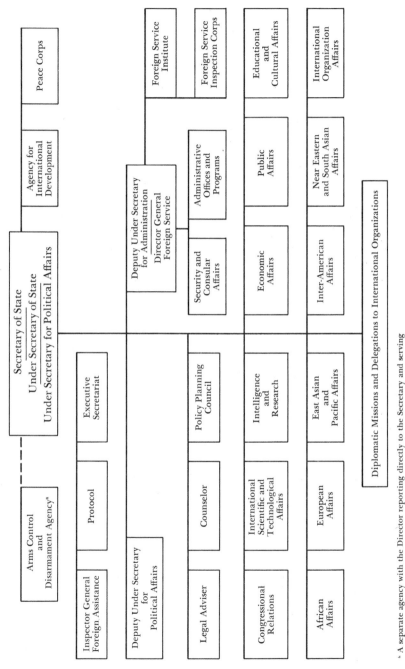

Secretary of State
Under Secretary of State
Under Secretary for Political Affairs

Arms Control and Disarmament Agency[a]

Peace Corps

Agency for International Development

Inspector General Foreign Assistance

Protocol

Executive Secretariat

Deputy Under Secretary for Political Affairs

Deputy Under Secretary for Administration
Director General Foreign Service

Foreign Service Institute

Foreign Service Inspection Corps

Legal Adviser

Counselor

Policy Planning Council

Security and Consular Affairs

Administrative Offices and Programs

Congressional Relations

International Scientific and Technological Affairs

Intelligence and Research

Economic Affairs

Public Affairs

Educational and Cultural Affairs

African Affairs

European Affairs

East Asian and Pacific Affairs

Inter-American Affairs

Near Eastern and South Asian Affairs

International Organization Affairs

Diplomatic Missions and Delegations to International Organizations

[a] A separate agency with the Director reporting directly to the Secretary and serving
as principal adviser to the Secretary and the President on arms control and disarmament.

Source: Department of State, November 1, 1966.

tural affairs, consular affairs, intelligence and research, and scientific affairs; and a number of bureaus which provide special services or advice to the Department and/or the Secretary of State — the Legal Adviser, the Executive Secretariat, the Protocol office, the Office of Congressional Relations, the Bureau of Public Affairs, the Bureau of Administration, the Foreign Service Institute, the Inspection Corps, and the Policy Planning Council.

The activities of most of these units are suggested by their titles. Among those whose titles are least descriptive, are: the Executive Secretariat which serves the top executives in the Department, arranging their schedules, providing briefings and summaries of incoming reports, and deciding what people and what papers get to these executives at what times. The Bureau of Educational and Cultural Affairs plans and administers programs for exchange of persons, grants to foreign educational institutions, and overseas cultural performances. The Foreign Service Institute provides in-service training for the Foreign Service Officers and others who man the Department and our posts abroad. Its courses include general orientation for incoming officers, language and area specialization training, short-term intensive language training prior to assignment to the field, and wide-ranging substantive courses for mid-career and senior officers. The Inspection Corps periodically reviews conditions and personnel performances in Washington and abroad, providing a check on the efficiency of post operation and on the fairness of the efficiency ratings given each Foreign Service Officer by his administrative superior in each assignment. The Policy Planning Council is charged with recommending long-range plans by which the goals of United States policy can be brought closer to realization.

Most of these functional bureaus and offices are on a level equal to that of the comparable geographic subdivisions. This means that differences between, say, the Congolese desk officer and an official in the News Division of the Office of Public Affairs about the wording of a press release dealing with a local uprising in the Congo normally can be resolved only by "negotiation" between them or by referring their differences to a higher level for resolution. In the case used as an illustration, the lowest official with authority to resolve such a difference by fiat would be the Deputy Under Secretary for Political Affairs. It is unlikely that the dispute would go this high, however, unless it involved a substantive policy issue of considerable importance. The most likely resolution would be for the drafting officer to rephrase the point in dispute so as to gloss over the difference; or for one or the other lower level official — more likely the News Division officer — to concede the point in the interest of maintaining a continuing working relationship.

Describing the structure of the Department, however, will take us just so far in understanding the way policy is made. To supplement such a description, we need a picture of how this machinery works in motion. Then we can go on to discuss some of the factors which keep it from working better.

When the Brookings Institution, some years ago, was commissioned by the Senate Foreign Relations Committee to undertake a study of *The Formulation and Administration of United States Foreign Policy,* it included as an appendix to its report a descriptive illustration of the Department of State's response to a hypothetical foreign policy problem. This appendix is reproduced in full here.[3]

> The Department of State is an organism that is constantly responding to a vast assortment of stimuli. A new Soviet threat to Berlin, a forthcoming conference of Foreign Ministers of the Organization of American States, a request from Poland for credit, a solicitation for support of a candidacy for the Presidency of the United Nations General Assembly, a plea from an ambassador that the head of the government to which he is accredited be invited to visit the United States officially, a refusal by another government to permit the duty-free importation of some official supplies for a U.S. consulate, a request from the White House for comment on the foreign affairs section of a major presidential address, an earthquake in the Aegean creating hardships which it appears the U.S. Navy might be able to alleviate, a request for a speaker from a foreign policy association in California, a transmittal slip from a Member of Congress asking for information with which to reply to a letter from a constituent protesting discriminatory actions against his business by a foreign government, letters from citizens both supporting and deploring the policy of nonrecognition of Communist China, a continuing inquiry by a press correspondent who has got wind of a top secret telegram from Embassy Bonn on the subject of German rearmament and is determined to find out what is in it, a demand by a Protestant church group that the Department take steps to prevent harassment of their coreligionists in a foreign country, a request by a delegation of a federation of women's clubs for a briefing on southeast Asia and suggestions as to how its members might be useful in their planned tour of the area, a request from Consulate General Brazzaville for a revision of cost-of-living allowances, a visit by a commission of inquiry into the operations of U.S. foreign aid programs, a notification from the staff of the National Security Council that a revision of the National Security Council paper on dependent areas is due, a telegram from a U.S. embassy in the Near East declaring that last night's flareups make a visit by the Assistant Secretary for Near Eastern and South Asian Affairs, now in mid-Atlantic, inopportune at the moment, a warning by a European Foreign Minister of the consequences should the United States fail to support his nation's position in the Security Council, and a counterwarning by an African representative at the United

[3] Reprinted from Charlton Ogburn, Jr., "The Flow of Policymaking in the Department of State," in *The Formulation and Administration of United States Foreign Policy,* Study No. 9 in United States Foreign Policy, prepared by the Brookings Institution at the request of the Committee on Foreign Relations, United States Senate, 86th Congress, 2nd Session, U.S. Government Printing Office, Washington, D.C., 1960, Appendix C, pp. 172–77.

Nations of the consequences should the United States do so — this is a sample of the requirements made of the Department of State in a typical day. Of course it does not include the oceans of informational reports that come into the Department by telegram and air pouch or the countless periodicals from all parts of the world that arrive by sea.

What is required to begin with is that the flow be routed into the right channels. This does not apply to press correspondents and foreign embassy officials; they usually know where to go without being directed. For the rest, almost every piece of business — every requirement or opportunity for action — comes within the Department's ken first as a piece of paper. These pieces of paper — telegrams, dispatches (or "despatches," as the Department prefers to call them), letters — must be gotten as speedily as possible into the hands of the officers who will have to do something about them or whose jobs require that they know about them.

The telegram and mail branches of the Division of Communication Services, a part of the Bureau of Administration, receive the incoming material and, after decoding and reproducing the telegrams, indicate on each communication the distribution it should receive among the bureaus or equivalent components of the Department. If, in the case of a letter or a dispatch, there are not enough copies to go around, the recipients are listed one after another and receive it consecutively, the original going first to the bureau responsible for taking whatever action the document requires. With telegrams, the deliveries are simultaneous. Several score copies of a telegram may be run off. A yellow copy, called the action copy, like the original of a dispatch or letter, goes to the bureau responsible for taking any necessary action; white copies go to all others interested.

A telegram (No. 1029, let us say) from a major U.S. embassy in Western Europe reports the warning of the foreign minister of X country that a grave strain would be imposed on relations between X and the United States should the latter fail to vote with X on a sensitive colonial issue in the United Nations General Assembly. Such a telegram would have a wide distribution. The action copy would go to the Bureau of European Affairs. The action copy of a telegram to the same purpose from the U.S. delegation to the United Nations in New York, quoting the X delegation, would go to the Bureau of International Organization Affairs. This is a matter of convention.

Information copies of a telegram of such importance would go to all officers in the higher echelons — the Secretary of State (via the executive secretariat), the Under Secretaries, the Deputy Under Secretaries, the counselor. They would also go to the Policy Planning Staff, to the Bureau of African Affairs because of the involvement of certain territories within its jurisdiction, to the Bureau of Far Eastern Affairs and the Bureau of Near Eastern and South Asian Affairs because the telegram concerns the incendiary question of European peoples' ruling non-European peoples, and of course to the Bureau of Intelligence and Research.* Other copies would go to the Department of Defense and the Central Intelligence Agency. The executive secretariat would doubtless make certain that the Secretary would see the telegram. In addition, its staff would include a condensation in the secret daily summary, a slim compendium distributed in the Department on a need-to-know basis. If classified top secret, it would be included in the top secret daily staff summary, or black book, which goes only to Assistant Secretary-level officials and higher.

In the bureaus, incoming material is received by the message centers. There a further and more refined distribution would be made of telegram 1029. Copies would go to the Office of the Assistant Secretary (the so-called front office), to the United Nations adviser, to the public affairs adviser (since the United States is going to be in for trouble with public opinion in either one part of the world or the other), and to whatever geographic office or offices may seem to have the major interest. In the Bureau of International Organization Affairs, this would be the Office of United Nations Political and Security Affairs. Another copy, however, might go to the Office of Dependent Area Affairs.

In the Bureau of European Affairs, the yellow action copy of the telegram goes to the Office of Western European Affairs and thence to the X country desk, where it is the first thing to greet the desk officer's eye in the morning. As it happens, the desk officer was out the evening before at an official function where he discussed at length with the first secretary of the X embassy the desirability of avoiding any extremes of action in the United Nations over the territory in question. In the front office of the Bureau, the staff assistant has entered in his records the salient details of the problem the Bureau is charged with and has passed the telegram on to the Assistant Secretary.

The following scenes are now enacted:

The X country desk officer crosses the hall to the office of his superior, the officer-in-charge, and the two together repair to the office of the Director of the Office of Western European Affairs. The three officers put in a call to the Assistant Secretary for European Affairs and tell his secretary that they would like as early an appointment as possible.

The Director of the Office of United Nations Political and Security Affairs (UNP) telephones the Director of the Office of Western European Affairs (WE). He says he assumes WE will be drafting an instruction to the U.S. embassy in X to try to dissuade the Foreign Office from its course, and that UNP would like to be in on it. He adds that they had thought of getting the U.S. delegation to the United Nations (US Del) to present this view to the X mission in New York but that there seemed to be no point in doing so since the latter would already be advising its government to take account of world opinion.

* [The Bureau of Far Eastern Affairs is now called the Bureau of East Asian and Pacific Affairs; and the Policy Planning Staff has been renamed the Policy Planning Council.]

After the Secretary's morning staff conference, where the matter is discussed briefly, a conference is held in the Office of the Assistant Secretary for European Affairs to decide on a line to take with the X government. The X desk officer is designated to prepare the first draft of a telegram embodying it. The draft is reviewed and modified by his officer-in-charge and the Office Director for Western European Affairs.

The telegram instructs the U.S. embassy in X to make clear to the X government our fear that its projected course of action "will only play into hands extremists and dishearten and undermine position elements friendly to West" and suggests that the X government emphasize its policy to take account of the legitimate aspirations of the indigenous population of the territory in order to improve the atmosphere for consideration of the problem by the General Assembly. The Assistant Secretary, after scrutinizing and approving the telegram, finds it necessary only to add the Bureau of Near Eastern and South Asian Affairs to the clearances. Those already listed for clearance are the Deputy Under Secretary for Political Affairs, the Bureau of International Organization Affairs, and the Bureau of African Affairs. He says it can be left to the Deputy Under Secretary for Political Affairs to sign the telegram; he does not see that the telegram need go higher.

It remains for the drafting officer to circulate the telegram for approval by those marked for clearance. In the Bureau of African Affairs the telegram is termed extremely gentle to the X government but is initialed as it stands. The Office of United Nations Political and Security Affairs (UNP) wishes to remind X that the United States, setting an example of its adherence to the principle of affording the widest latitude to the General Assembly, had even accepted on occasion the inscription of an item on the agenda accusing the United States of aggression. The X desk officer states, however, that WE would not favor such an addition, which might only further antagonize the X government. Thereupon, UNP, yielding on this point, requests deletion of a phrase in the telegram seeming to place the United States behind the X contention that the question is not appropriate for discussion in the United Nations. The drafter of the telegram telephones the Director of the Office of Western European Affairs who authorizes the deletion, having decided that he can do so on his own without referring the question to his superior, the Assistant Secretary.

With that, the Director of the Office of United Nations Political and Security Affairs initials the telegram for his Bureau, and the X desk officer "hand carries" the telegram (in the departmental phrase), with telegram 1029 attached, to the Office of the Deputy Under Secretary for Political Affairs and leaves it with his secretary. At 6 o'clock he is informed by telephone that the Deputy Under Secretary has signed the telegram (that is, signed the Secretary's name with his own initials beneath) without comment. The desk officer goes to the fifth floor, retrieves it, and takes it to the correspondence review staff of the executive secretariat, where the telegram is examined for intelligibility, completion of clearances, conformity with departmental practices, etc., before being sped to the Telegram Branch for enciphering and transmission.

The next morning, all offices of the Department participating in the framing of the telegram receive copies of it hectographed on pink outgoing telegram forms. The telegram, bearing the transmission time of 8:16 P.M., has entered history as the Department's No. 736 to the embassy in X. The X desk officer writes "telegram sent," with the date, in the space indicated by a rubber stamp on the yellow copy of the original telegram 1029, and the staff assistant in the front office makes an equivalent notation in his records. The yellow copy is then sent on to the central files, whence in time it will probably be consigned to the National Archives. Only the white copies may be kept in the Bureau's files.

In this case, however, no one is under any illusion that the matter has been disposed of. Scarcely 24 hours later comes a new telegram 1035 from the embassy in X reporting that, while the X government may possibly make some concessions, it will certainly wage an all-out fight against inscription of the item and will expect the United States to exert itself to marshal all the negative votes possible. The question is, what position will the United States in fact take and how much effort will it make to win adherents for its position? No one supposes for a moment that this explosive question can be decided on the bureau level. Only the Secretary can do so — as the Secretary himself unhappily realizes.

At the end of a staff meeting on Berlin, the Secretary turns to the Assistant Secretary for Policy Planning and asks him to give some thought within the next few days to the alternatives open on the question. The official addressed sets the wheels in motion at once. A meeting is called for the next morning. Attending are: the Assistant Secretary for Policy Planning himself and several members of his staff (including the European and African specialists), the Director of the Office of United Nations Political and Security Affairs, the Western European officer-in-charge, the X desk officer, a member of the policy guidance and coordination staff of the Bureau of Public Affairs, and two intelligence specialists, namely, the Director of the Office of Research and Analysis for Western Europe and the Director of the Office of Research and Analysis for the Near East, South Asia, and Africa.

The discussion explores all ramifications of the issues involved and is generally detached and dispassionate. The object of the meeting is to help clarify the issues so that the Policy Planning Staff may be sure all relevant considerations are taken into account in the staff paper it will prepare for the Secretary.

The Secretary is in a difficult position. The President's views on what course of action to take are somewhat different from his. The Congress is also of divided view, with some Members impressed by the irresistible force of nationalism among dependent peoples, others by the essential role of X in NATO and European defense. The ambassadors of some countries pull him one way, others another. One of the Nation's leading newspapers editorially counsels "restraint, understanding and vision." At the staff meeting he calls to arrive at a decision, the Secretary perceives that his subordinates are as deeply divided as he feared. He takes counsel with each — the Assistant Secretaries for Policy Planning, European Affairs, African Affairs, and Near Eastern and South Asian Affairs. At the end he sums up and announces his decision. Thereupon the following things happen:

The Assistant Secretaries take the news back to their bureaus.

An urgent telegram is sent to the U.S. Embassy in X reporting the decision.

Telegrams are sent to embassies in important capitals around the world instructing the ambassador to go to the Foreign Office and present the U.S. case in persuasive terms.

A similar telegram is sent to the U.S. delegation in New York for its use in talks with the delegations of other United Nations members.

Conferences attended by representatives of the geographic bureaus concerned, of the Bureau of Public Affairs and of the U.S. Information Agency, are held. Afterward, the representatives of the U.S. Information Agency return to their headquarters to draft guidances to the U.S. Information Service establishments all over the world. Such guidances tell how news of the U.S. decision is to be played when it breaks.

The more important the problem, the more the upper levels of the Department become involved. In a crisis — one brought about, say, by the overthrow of A, a Western-oriented government in the Middle East — the Secretary himself will take over. However, the bulk of the Department's business is carried on, of necessity, by the lower ranking officers. Even when a crisis receives the Secretary's personal day-to-day direction, the desk officer and the officer-in-charge are always at hand to provide the detailed information only specialists possess, while in the intelligence bureau, country analysts and branch chiefs will be putting in 10-hour days and 6- or 7-day weeks. Generally, moreover, the crisis will have been preceded by a good deal of work on the part of lower level officials.

In the case suggested, it was apparent for some time that all was not well in A. The U.S. Embassy in A was aware of growing discontent with the regime through its indirect contacts with opposition political elements, from information from Cairo, from evidences of tension, from clandestine publications. Additional straws in the wind were supplied by the public affairs officer in A both to the embassy and to the U.S. Information Agency because of his special contacts among professional groups. On the strength of these reports and of dispatches from American foreign correspondents in the area, and equipped with analyses from the Bureau of Intelligence and Research, all pointing in the same direction, the desk officer at a staff meeting of the Office of Near Eastern Affairs imparts his disquiet. He is directed to prepare a memorandum which, if convincing in its presentation, the Office Director undertakes to put before the Assistant Secretary.

What the desk officer has in mind will require national action, so what he drafts takes the form of a memorandum to the Secretary. It embodies a statement of the problem, the actions recommended, a review of the facts bearing upon the problem, and a conclusion. At the end are listed the symbols of the offices of the Department from which concurrences must be sought. Backing up the memorandum will be supporting documents, especially telegrams from the embassy, each identified by a tab. The mass fills a third of an in-box.

The problem is defined as that of strengthening the present pro-Western regime of A. By way of recommendation, the desk officer is especially sensitive to the problems and needs of the country for which he is responsible. He calls for more detachment of the United States from A's rival, B, expediting U.S. arms deliveries to A and the supply of certain recoilless rifles and jet fighter planes the A government has been requesting, support for A's membership in various United Nations agencies, a Presidential invitation to the Prime Minister of A to visit the United States. Much of what the memorandum recommends has to be fought out in the Bureau and even in the Office since it conflicts with the claims of countries (and the desk officers responsible for them) in the same jurisdiction. While neither the Office Director nor the Assistant Secretary doubts that support of B is a handicap in the region, they consider that a proposal for a radical departure would simply doom the memorandum by preventing anyone from taking it seriously.

As it finally leaves the Bureau with the Assistant Secretary's signature, the memorandum is considerably revised, and further change awaits it. The Department of Defense cannot provide the desired recoilless rifles and jet fighters. The Bureau of International Organization Affairs cannot offer any undertakings at this stage with respect to the question of membership in United Nations agencies. The Deputy Under Secretary for Political Affairs rules out a request of the President to invite the A Prime Minister for an official visit because the number of those invited is already too large.

Among recommendations in memorandums to the Secretary, as among salmon battling their way upstream to the spawning grounds, mortality is heavy. Almost everywhere in the world, things are far from satisfactory, but the United States cannot be doing everything everywhere at the same time. And A, far from seeming to cry out for attention, looks like the one Middle Eastern country about which it is not necessary to worry.

Then the uprising occurs in A. Early in the morning, the officer-in-charge of A and one other country is awakened by the ringing of the telephone. In a flash, before his feet have touched the floor, he has visualized every conceivable disaster that could have befallen his area and has picked the overthrow of the monarchy in C as the most likely. Or did the security people find a top secret document under his desk?

On the telephone, the watch officer at the Department tells him that a "Niact" (a night action telegram, which means "Get this one read immediately even if you have to rout someone out of bed") is coming off the machine and it looks serious — he had better come down. En route, the officer-in-charge turns on his car radio and picks up a news broadcast, but nothing is said about A. Uncle Sam has beaten the press agencies.

At the Department, he finds the telegram wholly decoded and reads the hectograph master. There is revolution in A. The top leadership has been either murdered or banished. The officer-in-charge could legitimately awaken the Assistant Secretary, but for the moment it seems there is nothing that can be done, so he decides to hold off until 6 A.M. and then call the Office Director and put it up to him. He does, however, call the A desk officer and tell him to get on his way. To share his vigil beside the watch officer's window there is a representative of the executive secretariat, who will have the telegram ready for the Secretary to read immediately on his arrival. In the Bureau of Intelligence and Research — it being now after 4 o'clock — the morning briefers have arrived to go over the night's take and write up items of importance, with analyses, for the Director's use in briefing the Secretary's morning staff conference. The briefer for the Office of Research and Analysis for the Near East, South Asia and Africa — a GS-11 specialist on India — takes one look at the Niact on A and gets on the telephone to the A analyst.

By the time the Secretary has stepped from his black limousine and headed for the private elevator a good deal has happened. In the Bureau of Near Eastern and South Asian Affairs, everyone concerned with A from the Assistant Secretary down, and including the officer-in-charge of Baghdad Pact and Southeast Asia Treaty Organization affairs and the special assistant who serves as a policy and planning adviser, has been in conference for an hour laying out the tasks requiring immediate attention. Two more Niacts have come in from A, one reporting that so far no Americans are known to have been injured but offering little assurance with respect to the future. The Assistant Secretary has already put in a call to the Director of Intelligence Research to ask that all possible information on the new leader of A and his connections be marshaled and that the Central Intelligence Agency be informed of the need. For the rest, the following represent the Assistant Secretary's conception of what should be done first:

1. The Department of Defense must be apprised of the Department of State's anxiety and be requested to have transport planes in readiness at nearby fields for the evacuation of Americans if necessary in accordance with prearranged plans. There must be consultation on what instruments are available if American lives have to be protected by force.

2. The U.S. embassy in C, a friendly neighbor of A's to which the Niacts have been repeated, will be heard from at any moment, and the Special Assistant for Mutual Security Coordination in the Office of the Under Secretary for Economic Affairs and, also, the Office of International Security Affairs in the Department of Defense will have to be alerted to the possibility of emergency military assistance for C.

3. Anything in the pipeline for A should be held up. The Special Assistant for Mutual Security Coordination must be advised of this.

4. The possibility of a demonstration by the U.S. Sixth Fleet in support of C's independence and integrity will have to be discussed with the Department of Defense.

5. A crash national intelligence estimate will be requested of the Central Intelligence Agency, provided the Agency does not consider the situation too fluid for a formal estimate to be useful.

6. The public affairs adviser will get in touch with the Bureau of Public Affairs, the departmental spokesman and the U.S. Information Agency to agree on the kind of face the United States will put on the affair.

7. The B Ambassador will probably have to be called in and apprised of the critical need for his government's acquiescence in overflights of B for the purpose of getting supplies to C. The B and C desk officers had better get busy immediately on a draft telegram to embassy B (repeat to C) setting forth the case the ambassador should make urgently to the B Foreign Office.

At 9:12, anticipating that he will be called to accompany the Secretary to the White House, the Assistant Secretary instructs his secretary to cancel all his appointments for the day, including one with the dentist but excepting his appointment with the C ambassador. ("Mr. Ambassador, you may assure His Majesty that my Government remains fully determined to support the sovereignty and territorial integrity of his nation.")

At 9:14, one minute before the scheduled commencement of the staff meeting, the Assistant Secretary joins his colleagues in the Secretary's anteroom, prepared to hear the estimate of the Director of Intelligence and Research and to give his own appraisal and submit his plan of action.

SOME ORGANIZATIONAL DILEMMAS

A careful reading of Ogburn's account reveals or hints at several of the problems which hamper the effective operation of the Department. One point that emerges clearly is that a great many individuals are normally involved in arriving at a policy decision even on matters of secondary importance. A second is that most of these people spend more time discussing, reviewing, and clearing policy than they do thinking about it or initiating it. Thus Parkinson's admonition that, in a bureaucracy, the quantity of work to be done expands to fill the amount of time available to be devoted to it, appears to be confirmed. A great deal of effort, energy, and taxpayers' dollars appear to be wasted, and the reaction time of the government is slowed enormously in the process.

The obvious answer to the problem, viewed from this angle, is to reduce drastically the number of officials involved in making such decisions, and to reduce accordingly the number of officials working in the Department in general. That would certainly save energy, tax dollars, and time, but, if pursued too far, it might also have serious undesirable consequences.

Secretary of State John Foster Dulles at one time offended the Government of India, and troubled many other Asian and African governments as well, by agreeing to a communiqué which referred to the enclave of Goa, on the Indian subcontinent, as Portuguese territory. (Legally, it was.) This may or may not have been due to a failure to consult the officials on the India desk or in the bureaus dealing with Asian and African affairs: information on this point is not publicly available. Nevertheless, this is an excellent example of the *kind* of error that can be caused by inadequate consultation.

The communiqué was issued after a meeting between representatives of the Portuguese and American governments. Clearly, "action" responsibility for initiating or advising the Secretary on this communiqué did not belong to the Office of Near Eastern and South Asian Affairs.[4] The man probably charged with primary responsibility — the Portuguese desk officer, (Office of Western European Affairs, Bureau of European Affairs) — could not be expected to be as well informed about the likely reaction of the Indian and other Asian and African governments to this statement as those who specialize in these areas. The Indian desk officer and his colleagues in the Bureau of Near Eastern and South Asian Affairs spend a good part of each working day reading reports on political trends in India and the rest of South Asia, and have probably spent several years, at least, at American posts there. Consulting with them would make an underestimation of Indian and Asian reactions to the statement much less likely. A decision which unnecessarily damaged American interests might thereby be avoided.

Ordinarily, the various clients and interests which the State Department must look after are taken into account through the participation in the policymaking process of those who are professionally concerned with them. For public officials normally absorb some of the outlook of the people they deal with every day — their opposite numbers who represent foreign governments or other interests to the United States. By and large, the man in the Department of State most likely to speak up for Indian interests is the India desk officer, the man most likely to speak up for the people's right to know is the press officer; the man most likely to insist that congressional views be taken into account is the legislative liaison; the man most responsive to the demands of international law is likely to be a legal adviser.

[4] At the time of the incident referred to this was the Bureau of Near Eastern, South Asian *and African* Affairs (italics added).

Within the Department, a form of balance of influence and counter influence is likely to emerge among these various spokesmen, corresponding — to a greater or lesser degree — to the comparative demands made by their respective "constituencies." So long as the actual importance of external pressures and the influence within the Department of those who represent them are roughly equivalent, misjudgments in day-to-day policymaking will be minimized. But a lack of correspondence between these parallel internal and external forces could lead to trouble.

From this standpoint, it can readily be seen how changes in organization may affect policy. In the mid 1950's, for example, the Bureau of Near Eastern, South Asian, and African Affairs was split into two bureaus, one dealing with Near Eastern and South Asian Affairs, the other with African Affairs, each headed by an Assistant Secretary. This was a reflection, of course, of the growing number of independent nations in Africa. Its effect within the Department was likely to increase the stature, and consequently the influence, of those who spoke for African interests within the Department. Again, if the Bureau of Economic Affairs were to be disbanded — to take a hypothetical example — and its officers reassigned as economic advisers within the regional bureaus, one probable result would be a marginal tendency to subordinate worldwide economic considerations to regional political and economic demands.

Not only current responsibilities, but also past assignments can color the outlook of policy officials. A present assignment as Portuguese desk officer is not going to erase the effects of, say, a four-year assignment to India in the mind of a Foreign Service official. A variety of geographic and functional assignments may minimize specialized expertise, but it is one of the best means known of promoting the breadth of view which is so essential to effective diplomacy. The man best qualified to weigh political, military, economic, and propaganda priorities against one another when a complex decision must be made is usually the man with some working experience in each of these fields.

But the nature of past assignment patterns impose biases as well as boons. Because of the historic importance of Europe to the United States and the generally greater size of American embassies in Europe compared with those in other parts of the world, most middle- and high-level officials in the Department have had more personal experience in Western Europe than elsewhere.[5] This, in turn, may influence the balance of forces within the

[5] As recently as 1962, nearly 40 per cent of United States Foreign Service Officers abroad were stationed in Europe, more than in any two other areas combined, John E. Harr, *The Anatomy of the Foreign Service — A Statistical Profile* (New York: Carnegie Endowment for International Peace, 1965), p. 22. Arthur Schlesinger, Jr., refers repeatedly to the pro-European orientation of the State Department in his account of his service as an adviser to President Kennedy, *A Thousand Days* (Boston: Houghton Mifflin, 1965), as does William Attwood (Ambassador to Guinea under President Kennedy and to Kenya under President Johnson), in *The Reds and the Blacks* (New York: Harper and Row, 1967).

Department. The policies the Department recommends will almost unavoidably, in these circumstances, reflect better understanding of Europe and its concerns than of, say, the new African nations and *their* concerns. Thus, in seeking to increase the language competence of Foreign Service Officers, by providing that all new Officers should receive three months' intensive training in a "world" language prior to their first assignments abroad, it was possible for the Department — in the late 1950's — to designate as "world" languages French, German, and Spanish, but not Russian, Chinese, or Arabic.[6]

This suggests that the prolonged absence of diplomatic relations between the United States and such a major power as China may have a significant and fairly long-term impact within the State Department as well as upon the world outside. There are no Foreign Service Officers staffing American posts in Communist China today — though there are many who specialize in Chinese Communist affairs from Hong Kong, Washington, and elsewhere. In time, this will probably result in less genuine understanding of the Chinese and their government than is desirable for at least a generation *after* relations between the two states are resumed. Only recently have we begun to shake off the effects of our lack of diplomatic relations until 1933 with the Soviet Union.[7]

None of these comments should be taken to suggest that no reduction in State Department staff or clearance procedures is called for.[8] They are

[6] By 1962, the strongest foreign language for over 85 per cent of Foreign Service Officers with a "useful" command of a foreign tongue was a European language. More of these officers reported Italian, for instance, as their strongest foreign language than reported all Asian and African languages combined! Harr, *op. cit.*, p. 26.

[7] Figures assembled by Robert W. Thiele from official government sources throw some light on these staffing patterns. Of a representative sample of Foreign Service Officers of Class 5 and above — that is, with about 6–8 or more years of service behind them — 83.5 per cent had served at one time or another in "Free" Europe, as compared with 15.5 per cent who had served in Eastern Europe (including the Soviet Union), 13.2 per cent in South Asia, and 8.2 per cent in China. James L. McCamy, *Conduct of the New Diplomacy* (New York: Harper and Row, 1964), pp. 220–221.

[8] To the contrary, a major reduction in staff would probably increase efficiency — and receptivity to new ideas — considerably. The existence of overstaffing in the State Department has been lamented by a number of recent observers, including President Kennedy and such career officers as George F. Kennan. (See Schlesinger, *op. cit.*, chap. 16, and Attwood, *op. cit.*) Deputy Undersecretary of State for Administration William J. Crockett explained to a subcommittee of the Senate Foreign Relations Committee recently one of the principal reasons why the Foreign Service has grown as large as it has:

> When you look just at the basic needs of the Service, you would say a hundred ambassadors, a hundred DCM's [Deputy Chiefs of Mission], a hundred political counselors, a hundred economic counselors, and not to mention the State Department, not to mention all of the consulates — this is 500 people right there. And to get 500 people at the top you have to start with a broader base. You don't start at 500 at the bottom. It is a continuous sifting.

Establishment of a Single Personnel System and Nominations of USIA Officers as Foreign Service Officers, Hearings Before a Special Subcommittee of the Committee on Foreign Relations, United States Senate, 89th Cong., 2nd sess., 1966, p. 27.

rather intended to indicate, in a very preliminary fashion, a few of the ways in which particular staff or procedural changes might affect policy. Only with these considerations in mind can specific proposals for organizational reform be evaluated properly. That an insider, fully aware of the implications of proposals for change, may still argue forcefully for organizational reform was illustrated by the testimony of several high officials before the Senate Subcommittee on National Security Staffing and Operations (Jackson Subcommittee) in 1963. Secretary of State Dean Rusk, for example, made the following suggestion:

> . . . This is a personal view that may or may not be shared by all of my colleagues, that inside of the Department our principal problem is layering.
>
> For example, when I read a telegram coming in the morning, it poses a very specific question, and the moment I read it I know myself what the answer must be. But that telegram goes on its appointed course into the Bureau, and through the office and down to the desk. If it doesn't go down there, somebody feels that he is being deprived of his participation in a matter of his responsibility.
>
> Then it goes from the action officer back up through the Department to me a week or 10 days later, and if it isn't the answer that I knew had to be the answer, then I change it at that point, having taken into account the advice that came from below. But usually it is the answer that everybody would know has to be the answer.
>
> I think we need to do something about layering, and one of the ways to do this is to upgrade the desk officer level. . . .
>
> It may be possible to eliminate the office level and have the desk officer not only report directly to the Assistant Secretary, but also to have the Assistant Secretary staffed to provide that desk officer with a good deal of the specialized advice that he needs and which we can't afford country by country. There would be an economics man, a labor man, and so forth; and these specialists should be grouped around the Assistant Secretary to help the deskmen on the special aspects of their problems. . . .[9]

But those who do not turn out to be leadership material are not readily dismissed after, say, ten to twenty years of faithful — if undistinguished — service. The Foreign Service, unlike the Civil Service, does have "selection out" procedures which separate from the service those ranked repeatedly in the lowest 5 to 10 per cent of officers at their grade. The number eliminated by these procedures, however, averages only about 2 per cent of the Foreign Service corps annually. (*Ibid.*, pp. 188–189.) A substantial increase in the percentage of officers "selected out" each year might increase the efficiency of the service, but it also might discourage promising young people from embarking on so hazardous a career. In addition, in some cases it would undoubtedly intensify the pressure on officers to avoid disagreeing too often with their superiors for fear of being penalized with a low rating.

[9] United States Senate, Committee on Government Operations, Subcommittee on National Security Staffing and Operations (Jackson Subcommittee), *Hearings.* 88th Cong., 1st sess., Dec. 11, 1963. Part 6, pp. 398–400. Hereafter: Jackson Subcommittee *Hearings.* Many

(The reader will find it useful to trace out, in the Ogburn account and in the preceding organization charts, the effects which the adoption of Secretary Rusk's proposal might have — both in reducing red tape and in losing potential sources of useful advice. On the basis of this review, a preliminary evaluation of the utility of this proposal might be attempted.)

The Secretary of State's Dual Role. To the uninitiated, it may seem odd that the Secretary of State should be casually advancing this sort of proposal. Why doesn't he simply carry it out himself? Isn't he the operating head of the Department?

Yes, he is. But he is at least as dependent upon his subordinates as they are on him. The Department is not staffed with names on organization charts, but with very human career officers who will still be at their desks when the Secretary is gone. Changes can be made over their opposition. But changes in formal organization can still be evaded on an informal level. And changes which lower the career officers' morale, which cause personal hardships to many among them, are not likely to improve the efficiency with which the Department does its job and helps the Secretary do his.

Besides, the Secretary is not *only* the operating head of the Department, he is also the President's principal adviser on foreign affairs. *This* job takes so much of his time and energy in this age of continuous crisis, that it is a rare Secretary who has enough of these scarce resources left to undertake a major reorganization of the Department.

Nor can the dual demands of the Secretary's role be relieved simply by divorcing the function of administering the Department from that of advising the President. For this step would also divorce the President from the Department. What is the use of improving the quality of the Department's work, if the results of this improved work do not get to the man with primary responsibility for directing American policy? And if the Secretary of State does not bring the benefits of his Department's expertise to the President, and tailor its operations to fit the President's needs, who will?

How closely the Secretary's relationship to the President, on the one hand, and to the State Department, on the other, approximates the ideal set forward here depends largely on the personalities and working styles of the principals involved. Cordell Hull had the confidence of his Department, for the most part, but not of President Roosevelt. John Foster Dulles, in contrast, was certainly President Eisenhower's principal foreign policy adviser; but he is reputed to have relied on the Department's career officers less fully than he might have. Perhaps the closest approximation to the preferred administrative model came during Dean Acheson's tenure as Secretary under President Truman. To outward appearances, Dean Rusk's rela-

of this Subcommittee's staff papers, and excerpts from the testimony of several witnesses, are assembled in Senator Henry M. Jackson (ed.), *The Secretary of State and the Ambassador* (New York: Praeger, 1964).

tionship to his department and to President Johnson seems almost equal to Acheson's under Truman. But the documents and memoirs of this Administration are not yet in. And Arthur Schlesinger, Jr.'s memoir of the Kennedy administration, at least, suggests that Rusk did not enjoy the confidence of the President who appointed him as he has that of the President who inherited him.[10]

Richard Neustadt testified before the Jackson Subcommittee on this point:

> Consider for a moment the responsibility of any modern Secretary of State. Always in form, usually in fact, the man becomes a very senior personal adviser to the President, a source of brainpower and judgment for him both as one man to another and at working sessions of his chosen inner circle — currently the executive committee of the National Security Council. Perhaps this was not Mr. Bryan's role — to reach far back — or Mr. Hull's, but certainly it was the role of Messrs. Marshall, Acheson, and Dulles, among others. Under conditions of cold war, this role is sharpened, rendered more intense by emergence of the Secretary of Defense, an officer with roughly equal claim but necessarily different focus, as a source of judgment in the foreign relations sphere. Balance of advice becomes important on each issue every day.
>
> The Secretary of State is much more than a personal adviser. He also is our ranking diplomat at large for sensitive negotiations just short of the summit. Furthermore, he serves as an administration voice to Congress, to the country, and abroad whose public word is weighty in proportion to his rank. At the same time he is actively in charge of a complex administrative entity. He is "Mr. State Department" and "Mr. Foreign Service," leader of officials, spokesman for their causes, guardian of their interests, judge of their disputes, superintendent of their work, master of their careers.
>
> The Secretary of State has a dilemma all his own. These roles are mutually reinforcing: his advice gains weight because he represents the whole Department, his public statements and internal orders gain in potency because he is so often at the White House. But these roles are also mutually antagonistic: fronting for officials strains his credit as an adviser, advising keeps his mind off management, negotiating preempts energy and time. No modern Secretary has performed the miracle of playing all these roles at once so skillfully and carefully that he obtains the benefits of all and pays no penalties. Presumably there is no way to do it.
>
> A Secretary cannot wriggle out of this dilemma by ditching his department and retreating to the White House, although at least one Secretary may have wished he could. His job cannot be done from there, nor is he needed there. Another man can serve, and does, as White House aide for national security affairs; like others of his kind the aide

---

[10] *A Thousand Days, op. cit.,* pp. 432–437.

stays close at hand to deal with action issues on the President's agenda when and how the President's own mind, interests, and work habits require as he meets his own time pressures and priorities. No doubt this personal assistantship includes a role as personal adviser. The Secretary also is a personal adviser. But this coincidence does not make them the same, nor would it help the President to have two such assistants and no Secretary.

The Secretary's usefulness as an adviser lies precisely in the fact that he is more than just another aide whose work is tied entirely to the President's. The Secretary has work of his own, resources of his own, vistas of his own. He is in business under his own name and in his name powers are exercised, decisions taken. Therefore he can press his personal authority, his own opinion, his adviser's role, wherever he sees fit across the whole contemporary reach of foreign relations, never mind the organization charts. He cannot hope to win all arguments in such a sphere, nor is he in position to contest them indiscriminately. But his status and the tasks of his Department give him every right to raise his voice where, when and as he chooses. To abandon his Department in an effort to escape its burdens and distractions is to cloud his title as adviser.

Yet to concentrate on running his Department — combating weaknesses, asserting jurisdictions, adjudicating feuds — is no better solution for a Secretary's problem. With the President absorbed, as Presidents must be, in foreign operations, in diplomacy, defense, no Secretary worth his salt would spend much time on management while others drafted cables in the Cabinet room. And if he did he would not long remain effective as a personal adviser.[11]

The Policy Planning Council. A similar dilemma confronts the members of the Department's Policy Planning Council. Their function is to view foreign policy in long-range terms. This requires a degree of freedom from concern with the day-to-day operations of the Department. If they spend too much time viewing the various trees, it will be hard for them to see the forest whole. Yet if the policy planners isolate themselves entirely from operations, their comprehension of the real nature of the problems faced by officials on the spot will become limited. If they fail to respond to departmental calls to assist in the formulation of short-range policies, their long-range plans will probably remain unimplemented pieces of paper. If they themselves will not exercise their own influence to see to it that their ideas get translated into practical operational measures, who can be depended upon to do it for them? Thus, in Ogburn's account, the participation of the Policy Planning Council (formerly the Policy Planning Staff) in the formu-

[11] Jackson Subcommittee *Hearings, op. cit.,* Part 1, pp. 82–83. For more detailed discussion of the Secretary's role, see Don K. Price (ed.), *The Secretary of State* (Englewood Cliffs, N.J.: Prentice-Hall, 1960); and The Jackson Subcommittee staff study, *The Secretary of State,* Committee Print, 88th Cong., 2nd sess., 1964.

lation of an immediate response to Country X's request for United States support in the General Assembly.

THE NEW DIPLOMACY: NEED FOR COORDINATION

Only about 14 per cent of the 120,000 civilian employees of the federal government stationed abroad as of mid-1965 were employed by the State Department. The other 86 per cent — including more than three-fourths of the American citizens involved — were working for other agencies.

In the years since World War II, diplomatic activity, strictly speaking, has come to comprise only a fraction of the foreign affairs activities of the United States government. Secretary Rusk told the Jackson Subcommittee that forty-four United States government agencies were represented at our embassy in London. The agencies concerned with United States foreign policy in one way or another range from cabinet level departments and the Bureau of the Budget to the Atomic Energy Commission and the Federal Aviation Agency. Obviously, there is no space here to review the functions, performances, and problems of most of them, but we will discuss a few of the administrative problems of the principal civilian agencies concerned. (The substantive aspects of their performances — except as these relate to administration — are taken up in other chapters.) [12]

If the agencies which formulate and execute United States foreign policy work at cross-purposes, the effectiveness of that policy will obviously decline sharply. Yet men from different agencies, with different contacts and constituencies, are liable to view policy issues in different ways. For example, an AID agricultural adviser, who deals mostly with the people and the local officials in a rural village, might favor channeling United States aid funds to these local officials directly. He might fear that if these funds were funneled through the central government excessive red tape and corruption would dissipate their potential impact. A Foreign Service Officer who lives in the capital, on the other hand, might put a higher priority on keeping the United States in the good graces of the central government, even at the cost of a little less efficiency in the use of American aid dollars.

[12] Historically, AID and USIA were given autonomous status by the Congress either because their programs were conceived of as temporary (as in the case of AID), and/or because of general congressional distrust of the State Department and desire to keep "operations" separate from policymaking. AID began as the Economic Cooperation Administration, formed to administer the Marshall Plan. Since then it has been renamed and reorganized so often that none of its organizational arrangements was allowed to prove itself in practice, until the present one, begun in 1961. USIA was established by the Eisenhower Administration in August, 1953 as an independent agency charged with explaining and interpreting American goals and policies to the world at large. It was composed for the most part of information programs and services handled by the Office of War Information during World War II and by the State Department thereafter. At this writing, AID is located administratively within the State Department while USIA remains an independent agency, subject to "policy guidance" from the Secretary of State.

The country desk officer in each agency in Washington might be inclined to sympathize with his own man in the field. And each of these men must look to his superiors in his own agency for future promotions and preferred assignments. How, then, do we decide which of these views to follow and how to secure full support for the policy adopted from officials in both agencies.

A number of approaches are employed. The Kennedy administration, for instance, introduced a device known as the Comprehensive Country Programming System. This calls for the preparation of national policy papers analyzing in depth the social, economic, and political forces at work in a given country. These papers then formulate United States goals in that country and advance an integrated plan — covering political, military, information, aid, and other projected activities — designed to realize the objectives stated. Interagency consultations in the course of preparing this national policy paper are relied on to lay the groundwork for well-coordinated implementation of the plan agreed upon. The expression of differences during these consultations is encouraged so that latent disagreements will be brought to the attention of top-level officials. Once these issues have been thrashed out and a comprehensive and integrated country plan has been produced, it is hoped that some of the differences which arise in carrying it out can be resolved by reference to the basic policy document.

Among the more traditional approaches to coordination in the field is the interagency committee, a group consisting of representatives from the principal agencies concerned with a given policy or program. Interagency committees schedule regular meetings to review and iron out disagreements. They are likely to prove most effective when the chairman — usually the State Department representative — is authorized to resolve day-to-day differences on his own responsibility after full consultation with his fellow committee members. Otherwise, differences must be compromised by negotiation or referred to a higher administrative level.

One device used to achieve coordination at the higher levels abroad calls for having one man serve concurrently as head of the Economic Section of the Embassy and of the AID mission (or, in another case, as Embassy Public Affairs Officer and head of the USIA mission). In some countries with small aid programs, the ambassador himself has functioned concurrently as director of the AID mission. Or conflicts can be discussed at meetings of the Ambassador with his "country team" — his chief deputies and the heads of other agencies' missions in that country.[13]

If the President usually backs the Secretary of State when interagency

13 See the Jackson Subcommittee's staff study, *The Ambassador and the Problem of Coordination.* 88th Cong., 1st sess., Document No. 36, 1963. (This study was written by the Historical Studies Division of the State Department's Bureau of Public Affairs); and Vincent M. Barnett, Jr. (ed.), *The Representation of the United States Abroad* (rev. ed. New York: Praeger, 1965).

disputes arise, and if the Secretary supports his deputies, officials on the spot at every level will soon learn that their best alternative is to work out differences under the general direction of the State Department representative concerned, except in the most extraordinary cases. In this way, the scarce time of top-level officials, both in Washington and in the field, can be conserved. If it is not expected that the ambassador's or the Secretary of State's view will most often prevail in controversies of this kind, no possible redrawing of organization charts will keep dissident officials from appealing Embassy decisions back to the chiefs of their particular agencies in Washington — whose influence on the President is presumably comparable to that of the Secretary of State.

It was to avoid such action that President Kennedy, in 1961, issued a circular letter specifically authorizing United States Ambassadors abroad to supervise the activities of *all* civilian representatives of the United States government in their country of assignment. In extreme cases, the ambassador was empowered to remove uncooperative personnel from any agency from their posts. In principle, then, the ambassador's coordinative authority is now perfectly clear. And in practice, too, President Kennedy's directive seems to have strengthened the ambassador's position.

On the basis of a special study conducted at the President's request by General Maxwell Taylor, the Johnson administration went one step further. In March, 1966, President Johnson ordered the Secretary of State "to assume responsibility to the full extent permitted by law for the overall direction, coordination, and supervision of interdepartmental [civilian *and* military] activities of the U.S. Government overseas." To support the Secretary in performing these functions, a Senior Interdepartmental Group responsible to him was established.

The Undersecretary of State was to act as "executive chairman" of this group, with authority to resolve differences arising within it on his own responsibility. The Assistant to the President for National Security Affairs, the Deputy Secretary of Defense, the AID Administrator, and the Directors of USIA and the Central Intelligence Agency were named as the other members of this group. At lower levels, a series of Interdepartmental Regional Groups were set up, headed in each case by the Assistant Secretary of State primarily concerned. (That is, the Interdepartmental Regional Group for European Affairs, and so on.)

Nevertheless, the problem of coordination cannot be solved by directives alone, however high their source or forceful their tone. The trick is to get interagency cooperation on the lesser issues without shielding the President from differences among his subordinates on the most important policy questions. For if most of the great issues the nation faces are decided, in effect, by the Secretary of State before they have even reached the President, the Secretary will be exercising in fact the responsibility for the conduct of foreign affairs which the Constitution reserves to the President. Keeping the desired balance between these extremes requires a special relationship of trust and intimacy between the President and the Secretary of State which organization charts can never ensure. At the heart of such a personal relationship must lie a mutual recognition of the proper administrative relationship between the offices themselves. Former Secretary of State Acheson has pointed out that Secretaries who were convinced that *they* should have been President have usually failed to maintain a satisfactory relationship with the men under whom they served:

> . . . It is highly desirable that from first to last both parties to the relationship understand which is the President. . . . It is enough here to mention two mutual obligations. One, of course, is the Secretary's duty to see that the President is kept fully and timely informed so that he may perform his constitutional duty of conducting the nation's foreign relations with all the freedom of decision which each situation permits. . . . The other . . . is recognizing who is Secretary of State. A President may, and will, listen to whom he wishes. But his relationship with the Secretary of State will not prosper if the latter is not accepted as his principal adviser and executive agent in foreign affairs, and the trusted confidant of all his thoughts and plans relating to them.[14]

The difficulties involved in interagency coordination have led some students of the administration of foreign affairs to suggest the appointment of a super-cabinet official charged with the overall direction of the civilian *and military* agencies concerned with the making of foreign policy, and reporting directly to the President. The comments of the Jackson Subcommittee staff on these proposals call attention to some of the hazards they may entail:

> Giving a man the title of "First Secretary" does not thereby give him power. Under this proposal, the Secretaries of State and Defense and other Cabinet officers would retain their present statutory functions and authority. These officials would continue to be accountable to the Congress for the proper performance of their statutory duties. They would equally continue to be responsible to the President. . . .
>
> The historical record shows that Presidential assistants draw effective power from their demonstrated intimacy with the President. . . .
>
> Yet the proposed First Secretary would be in a very poor position to sustain that intimate relationship even if he had it at the outset. His statutory position, his formal status in the Government, his supervision of assorted staffs, his chairmanship of manifold committees, his attraction for the press, and his accountability to the Senate which confirmed him — all would mitigate against the maintenance of his close, confidential, personal relationship with the President.

14 "The President and the Secretary of State," in Price, *op. cit.,* pp. 33–34.

It is most unlikely that a President would in fact give a First Secretary the consistent backing and support he would require to maintain his primacy over other Cabinet members. To do so would run the risk that the First Secretary would become an independent force, politically capable of rivaling the President himself. It would run the further risk of rousing combined opposition from departmental and congressional sources and from affected interest groups. . . .

Congressional committees long associated with particular governmental agencies could be expected to side with those agencies in their efforts to assert independence of the First Secretary. He would enjoy no counterpart of the solicitude which congressional committees often show to the heads of departments and agencies within their jurisdiction.

It is essential that a President have full, frank, and frequent discussions with his departmental and agency chiefs. To fully understand the meaning and consequences of alternative courses of action, he must expose himself directly to the clash of argument and counterargument between advocates of different policy courses. Papers, no matter how carefully staffed, can never convey the full meaning of the issues in question. To the degree a First Secretary insulated the President from day-to-day contact with key Cabinet officers, he would leave his chief less knowledgeable than ever about matters he alone had to decide.

Even if the President were to give the First Secretary substantial backing, this official would still be unable to do the job expected of him. For the critical budgetary decisions on the allocation of resources between national security needs and other national needs would still be outside his jurisdiction.

Only the President's responsibility is as wide as the Nation's affairs. Only he can balance domestic, economic, and defense needs — and if anyone else were to be given the job the President would become a kind of constitutional figurehead.

In summary: Our governmental system has no place for a First Secretary.[15]

THE NATIONAL SECURITY COUNCIL

It was in part to fill the need for top-level foreign policy coordination that the National Security Act of 1947 created the National Security Council (NSC). The Council is "to advise the President with respect to the integration of domestic, foreign and military policies relating to national security. . . ." Under the act, as amended in 1949, the President acts as Chairman of the Council; the Vice President, the Secretaries of State and Defense, and the Director of the Office of Emergency Planning [16] are statutory members; and the Director of Central Intelligence and the Chairman of the Joint Chiefs

[15] Jackson Subcommittee *Hearings, op. cit.,* Part 1, pp. 121–123.

[16] The Office of Emergency Planning is the successor to the Office of Defense Mobilization, and is responsible for planning to meet the nation's production, procurement, transportation, manpower, and similar needs in case of war or national emergency.

of Staff are statutory advisers. In addition, the President, with the consent of the Senate, may appoint other officials to participate as members in the Council's deliberations, either regularly or when matters of special concern to them are discussed. The Secretary of the Treasury, for example, has usually participated as a regular member, and the Director of the Bureau of the Budget, the Attorney General, the Chairman of the Atomic Energy Commission, and many other officials have participated from time to time at the President's request. A number of presidential Assistants, staff officers, and agency heads also attend regularly as observers. The Council reports directly to the President, as part of the Executive Office of the President, and is responsible for direction of the Central Intelligence Agency.

The NSC's deliberations are of course secret, and its recommendations to the President are purely advisory. Thus the President is free to make as much or as little use of the Council as he chooses, or to use some variation of it if he prefers — as President Kennedy did in setting up a so-called Executive Committee of the NSC to deal with the Cuban Missile crisis in 1962.[17]

Before an issue affecting national security is taken up by the Council, a series of papers is prepared reviewing the background of the issue, and summarizing the conclusions and recommendations of each of the departments and agencies concerned on the question. It is expected that differences of opinion within or among agencies, as well as areas of agreement, will be searched out so that they can be put before the Council when it begins its deliberations. When a decision is arrived at, it is written up, and an effort is made to see to it that each of the agencies concerned is carrying out its agreed tasks in the manner intended.

Until the Kennedy administration, the papers presented to the Council were drafted and cleared by a Planning Board, chaired by the Special Assistant to the President for National Security Affairs, and including officials at the assistant secretarial level from the agencies concerned. An Operations Coordinating Board, chaired by the same official and consisting of agency representatives at the undersecretarial level, took charge of assuring appro-

---

[17] The core of this group consisted of Secretary of State Rusk; Undersecretary of State George Ball; Assistant Secretary of State for Inter-American Affairs Edwin Martin; Deputy Undersecretary of State for Political Affairs U. Alexis Johnson; Llewellyn Thompson, a career Foreign Service Officer and Soviet specialist; Secretary of Defense Robert McNamara; Deputy Secretary of Defense Roswell Gilpatric; Assistant Secretary of Defense for International Security Affairs Paul Nitze; Chairman of the Joint Chiefs of Staff Maxwell Taylor; CIA Director John McCone; Attorney General Robert Kennedy; Secretary of the Treasury Douglas Dillon; and Presidential Assistants McGeorge Bundy and Theodore Sorenson. A handful of others, including Vice President Lyndon Johnson, sat in on the Executive Committee's deliberations from time to time. Sorenson, *Kennedy* (Bantam edition; New York: Harper, 1965), p. 760. As Sorenson points out, "these men had little in common except the President's desire for their judgment."

priate follow-through. Under President Kennedy, the Planning Board and the Operations Coordinating Board were eliminated, and the functions they performed were handled on a less formal level by the Special Assistant to the President for National Security Affairs — McGeorge Bundy — and his staff.

In 1966, when Bundy was succeeded by W. W. Rostow, the functions once performed by the Operations Coordinating Board were assigned to the Secretary of State, in an effort to strengthen his position. The Secretary, in turn, was to exercise this added authority through a Senior Interdepartmental Group chaired by his undersecretary. The NSC was no longer responsible for day-to-day coordination of foreign affairs, but would continue to advise the President on broad policy matters involving the integration of foreign, military, and domestic policies. (These measures had the effect of transferring to Secretary Rusk some of the authority formerly wielded by Bundy.)

There has been some controversy as to the effectiveness of the Council and its procedures. Critics have balked at the idea of entrusting such crucial responsibilities to a committee instead of an individual. They have warned that in the infighting among member agencies policy disagreements may be compromised rather than brought forward as conflicting alternatives; that lines of responsibility may be blurred in the process of reaching a consensus; and that differences of opinion may be "papered over" by vague phrases in recording NSC decisions, leaving each of the agencies concerned free to interpret the wording as it pleases, and therefore making the coordination achieved more apparent than real.

Some of these faults are undoubtedly inherent, to greater or lesser degree, in the National Security Council mechanism. Perhaps some alternative form of organization could avoid these faults without generating equally serious defects in their place. Some who have worked closely with existing procedures can be found in the camps of both the critics and the supporters of the National Security Council as it is presently constituted.[18] Without access to concrete information as to the workings of this mechanism in a number of specific instances, however, proposals for reform are extremely difficult to evaluate.

In any event, each President is likely to adjust the organizational arrangements for securing top-level advice on matters of national security to suit his own needs and his own working style. This is as it should be. The awesome responsibility for making final United States policy decisions affecting the future of the nation and of mankind rests with the President alone.

[18] See the following Jackson Subcommittee staff studies: *Organizing for National Security: Selected Materials*. Committee Print, 86th Cong., 2nd sess., 1960; and *Administration of National Security: Selected Papers*. Committee Report, 87th Cong., 2nd sess., 1962.

Surely he should not be denied the right to select the men whose advice he deems most useful, and the institutional arrangements he finds most helpful, in making these fateful choices.

FOREIGN AFFAIRS CAREERS
IN THE EXECUTIVE BRANCH

However efficiently the executive agencies involved in foreign affairs may be organized, the quality of United States foreign policy can scarcely be expected to exceed the quality of the men who make it. The United States government faces a special problem in this regard. In many nations government service is among the most prestigeful and remunerative of professions. In the United States, in contrast, careers in private business and in such professions as medicine, law, or the sciences have usually been regarded as more attractive than careers in government or diplomacy. Successful men in these private fields are likely to earn many times what they could earn in the public service. Even at the very top levels of the federal government, salaries rarely exceed $30,000 annually. Top business executives can earn up to ten times that amount — and have much more liberal expense accounts. Obviously, then, the foreign affairs agencies of the government must offer substantial compensations beyond money and status to compete for the always limited supply of people who are really first-rate.

One of the unique incentives which civilian or military government service can offer is the opportunity to serve one's country. Many of those who serve in the executive foreign affairs establishment were undoubtedly attracted, at least in part, by this opportunity — more, probably, than would admit to so unfashionable a motive.

The chance to travel widely and to combine periodic changes of job and locale with the continuity of a career service also appeals to many able people.

At their best, careers in foreign affairs also offer an opportunity to do interesting and meaningful work — a critical incentive in attracting good people. The State Department has run into some trouble here, because the needs of the Foreign Service and the interests of the officers who enter it often do not jibe. A large proportion of young Foreign Service Officers (FSO's) are primarily interested in political affairs. But less than a fifth of the positions to be filled are in this field. About a fifth of these positions are administrative, and a slightly smaller proportion are in economic and in consular affairs. The remaining positions are scattered among program direction, intelligence research, commercial affairs, and miscellaneous other categories. In the officer's first half dozen years in the service, moreover, the percentage of political and economic affairs assignments available to him is still lower.[19]

[19] Less than 10 per cent of assigned FSO's of grades 7 and 8 were involved in political affairs work in 1962. A majority were doing consular work, and economic and administra-

Many of the assignments which go to young officers — particularly those stationed in Washington or in big embassies abroad — also involve a good deal of routine work. And this problem was aggravated in 1954 by the integration of departmental Civil Service positions, many of them narrowly specialized, into the Foreign Service system.[20]

Another barrier to recruiting some needed personnel has been the traditional Foreign Service preference for the generalist as opposed to the specialist. In the past, the business of conducting foreign policy was far less concerned than it is at present with economic and cultural affairs, or with the special problems of little-known countries in what we now call the developing areas.[21] With the increasing complexity and breadth of "the new diplomacy," and with the integration of departmental specialists' positions into the Foreign Service, the need for competent specialists has increased. But highly trained specialists cannot be brought into the Foreign Service and kept there unless they have some assurance that they will be able to practice their specialties in the service, and be rewarded for doing so.

The traditional tendency of Foreign Service personnel panels to put the needs of the service above individual career needs, and of promotion panels to favor generalists and political officers, failed to provide this assurance. In 1956, however, a career management program was established within the Department. Now career management officers sit on personnel assignment panels to represent the individual Foreign Service Officer's long-range career development needs (not always the same as his personal preferences). Promotion panels are directed to consider mid-career officers by functional specialty, and to recommend a certain number in each specialty for promotion.[22] (At the top grades, those who advanced by way of different functional groupings must compete against one another again for promotion, and in the process of "selecting out" officers who seem unqualified for high-level responsibilities.) Assignments to language and area specialization

tive assignments were more common than political ones for these officers. These figures and, unless otherwise noted, all others given in this section, are taken or computed from Harr, *op. cit.,* and based on State Department personnel records as of 1962. Approximately 35 per cent of all FSO's were serving in the field of their first functional preference at that time.

20 This program is sometimes referred to as "Wristonization" since it was recommended by a committee headed by Henry M. Wriston, President Emeritus of Brown University.

21 Less than 6 per cent of FSO's, grades 6 and above, qualify as area specialists in areas other than Western Europe and Latin America, if an area specialist is defined as an officer with more than 5 years' experience in one of these areas and a professionally useful knowledge of at least one relevant foreign language. But one third of the posts in the service are either in, or primarily concerned with, these areas.

22 In the Foreign Service, unlike the Civil Service, each officer holds a *personal* rank (class 8, 7, 6, etc. through Career Ambassador) instead of being ranked solely on the basis of the job he performs. This system, similar to that used in the armed forces, affords personnel officers much greater flexibility in assigning men where they are needed. There is much less need, in the Foreign Service system, to match the grade of the officer under consideration with that of the position to be filled.

training and to graduate study at leading universities are also much more
common now than they were in the first postwar decade.

Yet an outside observer may still wonder to what extent these highly
desirable reforms have had the effect intended. The Herter Committee
(whose report is discussed in detail below) found that:

> . . . The opinion is widespread that the best way to get ahead in the
> Foreign Service is in political work. The evidence from the recommenda-
> tions of recent selection boards (which recommend promotion) is either
> that this opinion is in fact true or that the better officers gravitate to
> political work, or, very probably, some of both. For example, in the
> 1960 rankings of selection boards, about five times as many officers with
> both a political and geographic specialization appeared in the highest
> 10 per cent as in the lowest. In contrast, almost twice as many special-
> ized administrative officers and intelligence research officers appeared in
> the lowest tenth as in the highest.[23]

One of the special studies conducted by the Herter Committee's staff
elaborated further:

> . . . Three major groupings . . . are distinctive enough for the FSO
> system to be considered a three-career system. . . .
>
> The first group — Group A — is composed of officers who entered by
> the basic examination process and who have moved through the various
> functions to attain the favored economic and political fields, thus re-
> garding themselves as generalists. They have reached relatively high
> grades at younger ages than the total Service and very clearly form a
> high status, powerful group within the FSO corps. The second group —
> Group B — is composed of officers who entered the corps laterally and
> are found in every functional field but are tending strongly toward the
> political, economic, and program direction fields. These officers have
> usually come from the Civil Service; their educational background is
> comparable to or better than that of their typical examination entry
> colleague. They come close to the average in the age-by-grade index, and
> their status goes up as they take on the characteristics of Group A. The
> last group — Group C — is also composed of lateral entrants, but in
> contrast to Group B, these are officers who populate to an extraordinary
> degree both the consular field at the senior grades and the smaller
> specialized fields and are thus regarded as specialists. They probably
> have entered from the [Foreign Service] Staff corps. Their educational
> backgrounds are much less extensive than members of the other two
> groups; they lag behind in the age-by-grade index; and they have
> relatively low status. . . .
>
> Actually, the facts strongly suggest that the manner in which lateral
> entry has been used maintains the predominant position within the

23 The Committee on Foreign Affairs Personnel, *Personnel for the New Diplomacy*
(New York: Carnegie Endowment for International Peace, 1962), pp. 89–90. Hereafter
cited as *Herter Committee Report.*

Service of the examination entry officers and also keeps the main tradition of the corps intact. Lateral entry has made it unnecessary to change drastically the basic FSO recruitment process because it has provided a means of staffing the low status functions — administrative and consular work and the smaller specialized fields. . . .

The pattern outlined here does not yield easily to reform attempts, and it has its dysfunctional aspects. As long as the low status fields remain low in status and lateral entry is used primarily to staff these fields, one can expect that the quality of lateral entrants will drop; many of the more highly qualified lateral entrants already in the service will continue to press in the direction of the high status fields or will resign. In the long run, this will raise questions about the overall quality of the Service, the supply of executive talent, the capacity of the FSO corps to maintain a professional character in keeping with the times, and the ability of the State Department to fulfill its appointed role of leadership in foreign affairs.[24]

Old traditions persist — especially in the memories of officers brought up under the previous system and now commanding the top positions in the service. Even if the reforms noted are implemented 100 per cent as written, there is bound to be a time lag before the men whose careers are involved are satisfied that things have changed — and will stay changed. Nevertheless, the trend toward creating a number of rewarding career channels is certainly a step in the right direction.

The examinations for entry into the Foreign Service now de-emphasize current political knowledge and encourage some functional specialization. The service might conceivably put an even heavier emphasis on recruiting more individuals interested in consular and administrative work, economic affairs, and similar specialties. This would help to bring the interests of its officers closer into line with the needs of the service — but at the cost of turning away capable and knowledgeable young men interested in political affairs in favor of less capable candidates with more suitable interests.

The entrance examination utilized by the State Department and the USIA for beginning officers consists of one and a quarter- to one and three-quarter-hour tests in (1) general ability — to read, analyze, and interpret tabular data; (2) English expression; (3) general background; and (4) a choice of tests in administration, economics, commerce or (grouped together) history, government, the social sciences, and public affairs. (Candidates for USIA must take the last of these options.) The variety of options offered is a relatively new development made in response to the problem we have been discussing. An oral examination is given to those who pass the written exams.

24 Harr, *op. cit.*, pp. 79–81. Reprinted by permission of the Carnegie Endowment for International Peace.

Good men are hard to find. Figures released by the Board of Examiners for the Foreign Service show that, during the 1950's, only about one-fifth of those who took the written exam passed it. Between 60 per cent and 85 per cent of this select group failed the orals. In the end, well under 10 per cent of those who had taken the written exam were appointed as Foreign Service Officers by the President, with the consent of the Senate.[25]

Chart D, from an official State Department publication, illustrates the career of a presumably able young officer, following his admission to the service. A fuller portrait of the men who serve our foreign affairs agencies can be gleaned from a number of sources. For his book, *Conduct of the New Diplomacy,* James L. McCamy had Robert W. Thiele analyze the backgrounds of a sample of the foreign affairs officials listed in the State Department's *Biographic Register.* He found that the northeastern and western United States were slightly overrepresented in this sample, while the south and the midwest were correspondingly underrepresented. The median age of these officials was in the forties. Four-fifths had college degrees, almost two-thirds had some graduate work and almost two-fifths had one or more graduate or professional degrees. A third had received degrees from one or more of the following twelve universities (listed in order of the number of degrees granted to officials in the sample): Harvard, Columbia, California, Yale, Georgetown, George Washington, Wisconsin, Chicago, Minnesota, Princeton, Michigan, and Cornell. A majority of these officials had worked in more than one government agency and had at least some professional experience outside the government — in a wide variety of fields. Two-thirds had more than five years' experience in foreign affairs work, and almost two-fifths had more than ten years of such experience.[26]

The Foreign Service Officer corps — forming only a part of the group sampled by McCamy — was studied in detail by members of the Herter Committee staff in 1962. Over 85 per cent had at least one college degree, and a third had graduate degrees. About 60 per cent had majored in one of four broad fields: history, political science, international relations, and economics. The median age was forty-one, and about 55 per cent had entered the corps by the examination route. Almost 70 per cent could speak at least one foreign language at a professionally useful level.[27]

25 A booklet of sample questions from these examinations can be had for the asking by writing to the Department of State, Washington, D.C. 20201. In general, information about employment opportunities in any of the agencies mentioned here can be obtained by writing to the Employment Division of that agency, Washington, D.C. 20201. In order to be certified for appointment, applicants for the Foreign Service Entrance Examination must be between 21 and 31 years of age (at the time of examination), United States citizens of ten years' standing, and in good health. The figures cited in this section are based on William Barnes and John Heath Morgan, *The Foreign Service of the United States: Origins, Development and Functions* (Washington, D.C.: Historical Office, Bureau of Public Affairs, U.S. Dept. of State, 1961). The career chart presented is from this book.

26 *Ibid.,* pp. 202–225.

27 Harr, *op. cit.,* pp. 10, 12, 14, and 24.

CHART D—SAMPLE CAREER OF A FOREIGN SERVICE OFFICER

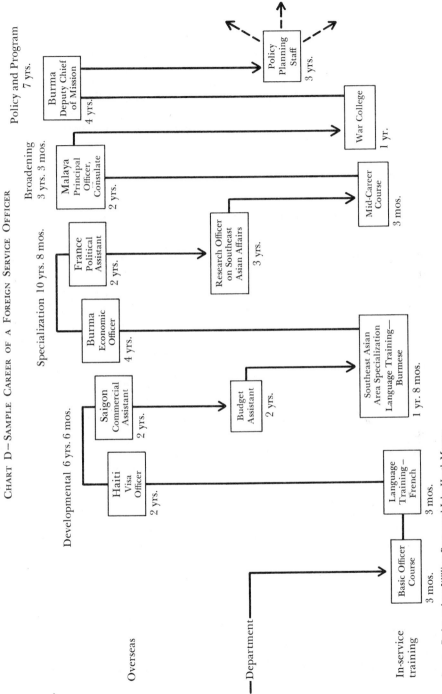

Source: Redrawn from William Barnes and John Heath Morgan, *The Foreign Service of the United States: Origins, Development and Functions* (Washington, D.C.: Historical Office, Bureau of Public Affairs, U.S. Department of State, 1961), p. 320

A sample survey of their orientations and behavioral styles indicated that:

> Compared with other occupational groups, the FSOs report that they like the kind of work that includes interpretation of data and the influencing of other people. Their style for analyzing information tends to be impressionistic and intuitive rather than formal, methodical, and statistical. Their preferred style for working with a formal organization is to do the work themselves rather than to work through a hierarchy. They greatly value personal intellectual achievement and place a moderate value on formal status, social service, and the approval of others. . . .
>
> . . . The officer given a superior rating . . . is both optimistic and self-confident, is interested in both data and people, sees himself as imaginative and ingenious, likes activity and excitement, and wants to be recognized as a success. . . . Approval from others and social service are less important to him than resourceful accomplishment and formal status.[28]

Chart E summarizes the results of this survey, comparing FSO's with other occupational groups on twenty-two attitudinal and behavioral dimensions. Many observers have expressed the view that Foreign Service Officers are made cautious and bureaucratic over the years by the need to avoid offending the immediate superiors who write the "efficiency reports" which determine the course of their careers. A careful inspection of the relative places of junior and senior FSO's on these scales seems to confirm this impression. Note that senior officers score higher than junior officers on the "hierarchical," "group identification" and "formal status" scales, and considerably lower on "autonomy." The evidence is not conclusive, however, since it is based on questionnaires administered to different groups of officers at the same time rather than to the same group of officers at different times. A changed recruitment pattern in recent years or a number of other factors could account for these results as well as the "caution and conservatism" theory does. (The study cited should be consulted for precise definitions of the dimensions listed, but the names assigned them give a reasonable notion of their meaning.)

The Herter Committee's Report. In 1961, a committee of distinguished Americans headed by former Secretary of State Christian Herter, Jr., was requested by Secretary of State Dean Rusk to examine the personnel problems of our foreign affairs agencies. This committee was sponsored by the Carnegie Endowment for International Peace and had the full cooperation

---

28 Regis Walther, *Orientations and Behavioral Styles of Foreign Service Officers* (New York: Carnegie Endowment for International Peace, 1965), p. 43. The accompanying chart is reproduced by permission from p. 9 of this study. The Peace Corps Volunteer group referred to in the chart was taken from a single Peace Corps project, and may not be a representative sample of the Corps as a whole. These findings are based on the results of a self-administered questionnaire.

Chart E — Comparison of Examination FSO's with Other Occupational Groups

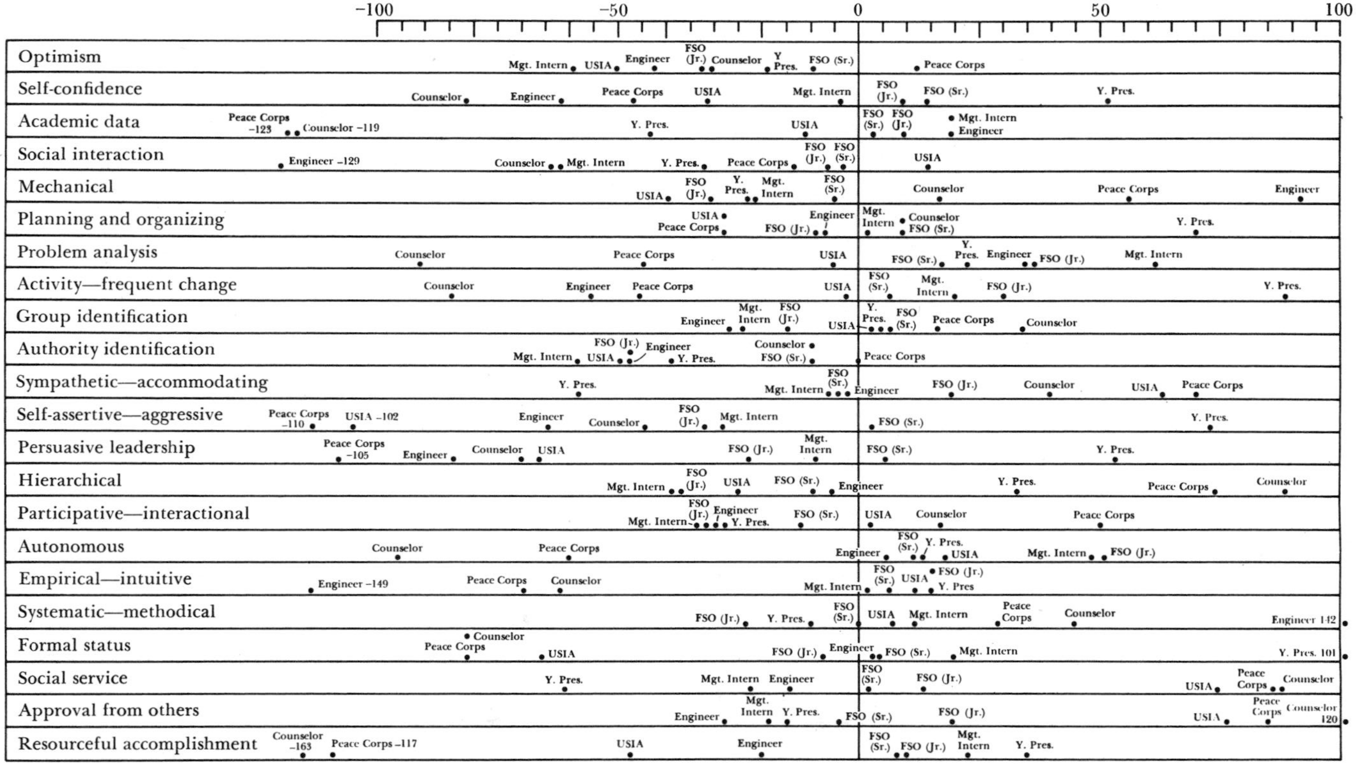
-100
-50
0
50
100
Optimism
Self-confidence
Academic data
Social interaction
Mechanical
Planning and organizing
Problem analysis
Activity—frequent change
Group identification
Authority identification
Sympathetic—accommodating
Self-assertive—aggressive
Persuasive leadership
Hierarchical
Participative—interactional
Autonomous
Empirical—intuitive
Systematic—methodical
Formal status
Social service
Approval from others
Resourceful accomplishment

KEY:
FSO (Jr.): Junior FSO
FSO (Sr.): Senior FSO
Mgt. Intern: Management Intern
Peace Corps: Peace Corps Volunteer
USIA: Junior USIA Officer
Y. Pres: Young President
Engineer: Research Engineer
Counselor: High School Counselor

NOTE: The mean scores for each of the occupational groups have been converted to standard scores based upon the average of the 296 superior performers from all the job categories. The mean for this group has been designated as zero; one standard deviation above the mean has been designated as 100; and one standard deviation below the mean has been designated as — 100.

Source: Regis Walther, *Orientations and Behavioral Styles of Foreign Service Officers* (New York: Carnegie Endowment for International Peace, 1965), p. 9.

of the government agencies concerned. At the end of its study and deliberations, it issued a report containing forty-three specific recommendations. The most important of these were proposals to (1) replace the present chaotic foreign affairs personnel system with "a family of compatible systems reflecting substantial uniformity in personnel policies and coordinated personnel operations"; (2) establish "a National Foreign Affairs College which would provide in-service training at an advanced level for professional personnel"; and (3) create a new post of Executive Undersecretary of State to manage the Department and see to it that policies are translated into action programs.[29]

The wisdom of administering United States aid and information programs through independent agencies instead of through the State Department directly has often been questioned. A number of proposals have been made, therefore, for the merger of USIA, AID, and the State Department into a single foreign affairs agency, staffed by a single Foreign Service. The Herter Committee's recommendation on this subject strikes a deft balance between these proposals and the status quo.

There is no wholly satisfactory solution to the problem. The differing needs of the agencies concerned prohibit the assignment of aid, information, and diplomatic personnel interchangeably. Yet if separate career tracks were maintained in the new amalgamated Foreign Service, the old problem of favoritism toward the "old line" officers would probably arise again in even more aggravated form. If so, the morale of officers in the more specialized career tracks would suffer, and the possibilities of attracting good men in these specialties would decline accordingly.

Numerous temporary dislocations would also result. It appears to be easier to advance in the career hierarchies of the aid and information agencies than in the Department of State itself. If relatively high-ranking aid and information officials were brought into the Foreign Service at ranks commensurate to their present ones, the morale of the younger career Foreign Service Officers might be lowered by seeing outsiders, who came up the "easy" way, taking over the upper-level positions *they* have been working toward. As it is, barely one quarter of the executive positions in the Department of State, in Washington, and abroad, are held by Foreign Service Officers who entered via the examination route.[30] Yet the aid and information officers may have joined their agencies partly because they did offer greater opportunity for rapid advancement. Why should they now be brought into the Foreign Service at reduced ranks, give up their hard-won advancement, and serve under men who see themselves as some sort of "elite corps"?

Thus the Herter Committee elected to recommend the formation of a

29 *Herter Committee Report, passim.*

30 *Ibid.*, pp. 52–53. This is due in part to the integration of departmental civil service employees into the Foreign Service under the "Wristonization" program of 1954.

career Foreign Information Service for USIA employees, and a career Foreign Development Service for the core professional personnel only of AID. (This career service would exclude about three-fourths of AID's present specialized and technical personnel who would continue to be employed on a temporary basis to fill particular assignments.) These career services and the Foreign Service would then be organized into a family of compatible services, with:

(a) substantial uniformity in personnel policies and equality in conditions of service;

(b) joint conduct of personnel operations wherever desirable;

(c) systematic interchange of personnel and provision for lateral transfer; and

(d) consideration of senior personnel of all three services in filling top executive posts in foreign affairs.[31]

Members of all three services would be paid on a single salary schedule, but each agency would continue to control personnel actions involving its own employees.

In 1964, the Johnson administration acted to implement this recommendation, at least in part. A career specialization for Foreign Information (USIA) officers was established within the Foreign Service, and a limited merger of personnel was effected, by administrative agreement between the State Department and USIA. The following year, the establishment of a single unified foreign affairs personnel system was proposed to the Congress. Under this proposal, which goes a step beyond the Herter Committee's recommendations, almost all USIA and AID personnel would eventually be brought into the Foreign Service personnel system. Civil Service officials in the three agencies, who are not subject to assignment overseas, would be transferred into a new "Foreign Affairs officer" category. Most professional USIA and core AID personnel would be integrated eventually into the FSO corps. They would continue to be responsible to the agencies employing them in carrying on their day-to-day work; and separate career tracks for aid and information officers would be maintained by the Foreign Service at all but the very top levels. But all Foreign Service personnel would be subject to common pay scales, retirement benefits, promotion, assignment, and "selection-out" procedures, and exchanges of personnel between the agencies and the State Department would presumably be much more frequent than at present.

Even before this bill was submitted to Congress, a list of more than seven

31 *Ibid.*, p. 28. In addition, the Committee recommended a positive program for recruiting able men in various professions into these services at the middle and higher levels. Pp. 75 ff. Such a program would help to broaden the perspectives of these services without diluting their quality, for all of these so-called "lateral entrants" — in fact, all persons entering any of these three career services at any rank, would first be required to pass a vigorous competitive examination.

hundred USIA officers, proposed for appointment as Foreign Service Officers, had been presented to the Senate for confirmation. In support of these nominations, Deputy Undersecretary of State for Administration William J. Crockett told a special subcommittee of the Foreign Relations Committee:

> The attitudes of people in private life, and the influences which play upon their opinions, have an important effect on our relations with foreign countries and on the positions they take on international issues of vital concern to the United States. . . .
> We want to be certain that every one of the officers of the Department of State gives due attention to the element of public affairs in his own work. We want to be certain that USIA officers whose advice plays a part in our policy decisions are as competent to advise as our own officers and have a concept of duty as broad as our own officers do. We will have these assurances if a substantial cadre of USIA officers is admitted to the Foreign Service Officer Corps. That will bring information and cultural relations within the normal scope of the training, experience and professional concerns of career officials in the Foreign Service of the United States.[32]

The most thoughtful of the objections to these new proposals raised at the subcommittee's hearings was voiced by Senator Claiborne Pell, himself a former FSO:

> . . . I wonder from the struggle to label USIA officers Foreign Service officers, [whether] we have not tended to forget that we are seeking specialists trained in propaganda. . . .
> In connection with this, I wonder how USIA can prevent its best officers from seeking State Department duty as being more prestigious and more reliable to promotion than USIA work.
> For instance, a USIA officer gets to the top in his early forties. Well, he knows the way to move ahead and be an Ambassador is to get into that political section, as a rule. . . .
> . . . Can the agency maintain an esprit de corps of its own when eventually the really successful men in it will tend to become chiefs of mission or consuls general or DSM's?[33]

A "National Foreign Affairs College"? The National Foreign Affairs College recommended by the Herter Committee was envisaged as a semiautonomous institution, governed by a board of trustees appointed directly by the President of the United States. Staffed by a small permanent core faculty and by temporary faculty from the government and the academic world, it would

---

[32] *Establishment of a Single Foreign Affairs Personnel System and Nominations of USIA Officers as Foreign Service Officers, op. cit.,* p. 12.

[33] *Ibid.,* pp. 207–208. "DSM's" is probably a misprint for "DCM's," that is, Deputy Chiefs of Mission. This proposal, and the accompanying nominations, were tabled by the 89th Congress in 1966.

provide advanced professional training "embracing the totality of foreign affairs work" to employees of all United States government agencies with foreign affairs responsibilities.[34]

Legislation to create a National Academy for Foreign Affairs, along lines similar to those suggested by the Herter Committee, was introduced into the Congress in 1963, but not enacted. Among those opposing this legislation was former Secretary of State Dean Acheson. Acheson's position was that experience was more effective than contemplative study in training men to deal with high-level foreign affairs responsibilities. He felt, moreover, that under the circumstances certain limits on the academic freedom of the faculty were bound to make themselves felt. He concluded:

> There are existing academic institutions, state and private, many of which offer excellent facilities for advanced international studies and research work. If funds were made available for the tuition of officer-students and outright grants to the universities for increased overhead and faculty expense for, say, a period of 10 years, both instruction and research under conditions of true academic freedom could be made available.[35]

An "Executive Undersecretary of State"? The Herter Committee's recommendation to create the post of Executive Undersecretary of State was in large part a response to two problems discussed earlier in this chapter: coordination and the inability of the Secretary to give much time to the management of the Department. At present, management of the Department is lodged in a Deputy Undersecretary of State for Administration. The Herter Committee's proposal would have the effect of upgrading this function by entrusting it to a man ranking third in the Department, after the Secretary and Undersecretary, who presumably would have ready access to these officials. His high rank would also help to make it possible for him to exercise supervisory authority over the personnel of other agencies in a way that the Secretary and Undersecretary normally would not have the time to do. By filling this post, generally, with a career officer, a degree of continuity in personnel management might also be provided even through changes in presidential administrations.

The Executive Undersecretary, the committee asserted,

> . . . should bring to bear the resources of the several departments and agencies of the Government concerned with Foreign Affairs in order to achieve the objectives of our foreign policy. He should play a central role in the orderly programming of the operations of the foreign affairs agencies and their translation into personnel and budgetary terms. . . .

[34] *Herter Committee Report*, pp. 103–109.
[35] Jackson Subcommittee *Hearings*, Part 5, pp. 378–383. The comments were made in the form of a letter to the Chairman of the Senate Foreign Relations Committee, dated July 29, 1963.

> [His] primary responsibility should be to make sure that the resources of the Department of State and the other principal foreign affairs agencies are giving maximum support to the Secretary of State in his role of leader and coordinator, under the President, of the foreign relations of the United States.[36]

The Herter Committee recognized the special problems faced by AID in recruiting technicians for overseas service. Government can rarely match the salaries paid highly skilled technicians in private industry. In addition, since the skills called for in aid programs vary widely from country to country, most AID personnel cannot readily be assigned to a new post when they have completed an assignment. As a result, most AID positions are contracted on a temporary basis, and the Agency's inability to offer career status to technicians often handicaps its recruiting efforts further. (Sometimes, however, these difficulties can be surmounted through contracts between AID and private firms and universities.) The Committee suggested that AID seek to overcome these disadvantages by encouraging the professional groups concerned to build the field of development into their professions. Thus "development education" and "development agriculture," for instance, might be established as important subspecialties within the fields of education and agriculture. This should be followed up by "an aggressive and continuing recruiting program" and an adequate orientation program for new AID personnel prior to sending them to their posts abroad.[37]

Political Appointments. One more issue deserves consideration here. Historically, high American Foreign Service positions have frequently been awarded as political plums — often in return for sizable election campaign contributions — with little concern for the effect of such appointments on the quality of our representation abroad. This is primarily a residue from the days when Americans felt they had little at stake in international affairs. For instance, it was not until the passage of the Rogers Act in 1924 that the merit principle was established in the Foreign Service. This act amalgamated the diplomatic and consular services, introduced the principle of a personal rank carried by an individual to whatever position he was assigned, provided a retirement and disability system for Foreign Service Officers, and raised Foreign Service salaries enough to make it possible for the first time to recruit men without independent incomes for diplomatic posts.

Nevertheless, some key ambassadorial positions continued to be awarded on political grounds. As recently as the Eisenhower administration, a good deal of justified indignation was aroused by the appointment of a business

[36] *Herter Committee Report,* pp. 11–15. In the legislation submitted to the Congress in 1965, and reviewed above, primary responsibility for administering the unified foreign affairs personnel system would be lodged in the Director General of the Foreign Service (a top-ranking career officer), and the Board of the Foreign Service.

[37] *Ibid.,* pp. 113–121. The legislation submitted to Congress in 1965 would enable AID to offer career status and benefits to an increased percentage of its employees.

executive without foreign affairs experience as ambassador to a small country in Asia. Questioned by the Senate Foreign Relations Committee prior to his confirmation, he proved unable to name the Prime Minister of his country of assignment; but he admitted that he had donated between $20,000 and $30,000 to his party's election campaign chest during the previous year.

Until 1961, the representation allowances provided by Congress for the main embassies in Western Europe were so hopelessly inadequate that only independently wealthy men could afford to meet the social obligations of serving as ambassadors there. At the outset of his administration, however, President Kennedy sought and secured the cooperation of Congress in adjusting representation allowances to these posts sufficiently to enable him — and his successors — to choose men to fill them on the basis of ability, without regard to their financial status.

Actually, most of our ambassadors today *are* career men. The percentage of chiefs of United States missions who are career Foreign Service Officers has varied from 56 per cent to 69 per cent since World War II. Nor is there anything wrong with the appointment of noncareer ambassadors — despite the occasionally farcical political appointment. Of the 35 noncareer ambassadors serving the United States abroad in November, 1963, for example, 13 came from careers in government or public service, 7 from the legal profession, 5 from the academic world, 4 from journalism, 4 from business and 1 each from a foundation and a labor union. Few had made large campaign contributions. One of this noncareer group was Lincoln Gordon, Ambassador to Brazil. Rhodes Scholar, Oxford D./Phil., Harvard professor, Ambassador Gordon had also served about a dozen years in various federal foreign affairs agencies prior to his appointment. (Later he left the government to become President of Johns Hopkins University.) Gordon commented to the Jackson Subcommittee on this matter:

> . . . I believe in a strong career service. Such a service can attract and hold good men only if they have a legitimate expectation of coming to serve as chiefs of mission or Assistant Secretaries of State. With over 100 posts abroad, I would normally expect well over half of them to be headed by career officers.
>
> I am not persuaded, however, that the interests of the United States would be served by reserving all of these posts to career officers. The exigencies of our oversea operations in today's world — and for the foreseeable future — sometimes require experience and qualifications which occur only rarely among career officers. I have noted the distinction made by some of your witnesses between purely political appointments, based merely on contribution to political party finances, and semiprofessional appointments of men or women with broad experience in public service as well as in civilian life. Like the other witnesses, I am opposed to the former type of appointment, but see great merit in the latter. Taking at random the names of a baker's dozen of men out

of personal acquaintance among present or recent Ambassadors I would offer for your consideration Ambassadors John Badeau, Chester Bowles, David Bruce, Ellsworth Bunker, Charles Cole, James Conant, John Ferguson, Kenneth Galbraith, Averell Harriman, Walter Howe, Henry Labouisse, George McGhee, and Edwin Reischauer as examples of this semiprofessional category. To these male names I would add those of Mrs. [Eugenie] Anderson and Mrs. [Claire Booth] Luce. All of them have served with distinction, and very much to the positive interest of the U.S. Government. . . .

The basic guiding rule for the selection of Ambassadors, I believe, should be to find the most competent people for the jobs. As the quality of recruitment and career management in the Foreign Service are improved, career officers should in increasing proportion come to be the best qualified. In cases of close choice, I would give preference to the career man. I should be surprised, however, if 20 to 30 per cent of the ambassadorial posts did not continue to be filled, under this criterion, by semiprofessional candidates. . . .

From the viewpoint of the noncareer Ambassador himself, there is the advantage of the greater sense of independence he feels through not having a vested interest in his own future within the career. If he carries this to the extreme of developing a policy of his own, at variance with the Government's policy, this independence can become counter-productive. But if he exercises it constructively to contribute to the formulation of policy jointly with his superiors in Washington, it may prove a real asset in the management of our foreign relations.[38]

Each society, by the compensations and status it accords to those of its citizens in various lines of work, helps to determine the quality of the people who will be attracted into its public service. Our system, and we ourselves, have arranged things so that a movie actress can earn more making one Hollywood spectacular than the President of the United States and the heads of all of the foreign affairs agencies mentioned in this book, combined, earn in one year.

Popular suspicion of the "cookie pushers" in the State Department makes it possible for Congress to appropriate tens of billions of dollars in military expenditures with minimal debate, while subjecting State Department, USIA, and AID requests for a small fraction of that amount to minute critical scrutiny. Public willingness to believe the worst about our diplomats also encouraged Senator Joseph McCarthy and others to make irresponsible and unproven slurs against the reputations of a number of State Department officials in the early 1950's. As a result, a generation of Foreign Service Offi-

---

38 Jackson Subcommittee *Hearings*, Part 5, pp. 373–374. Figures in this paragraph are from *ibid.*, Part 4, p. 336. Harr found political appointees to high State Department positions better educated, on the average, than career officials in similar jobs. Three-fourths of these appointees had at least a Master's degree, as of 1962, and more than a fifth held the Ph.D. *Op. cit.*, pp. 75–76.

cers — and young people considering Foreign Service careers — were made aware that mistaken, or even merely unpopular, political reporting might result in the ruination of their careers in the government. Though the worst excesses of the McCarthy era have not been repeated, congressional mistrust of our diplomatic establishment continued into the 1960's.

In view of these societal attitudes and priorities, it is not surprising that it is hard to find enough first-class foreign affairs officials to meet our nation's needs. The wonder is that we get as many good men as we do.

THE PEACE CORPS

An innovation of the New Frontiersmen of the Kennedy administration, the Peace Corps is designed to make modest contributions to at least three very immodest objectives: (1) to help the people of the emerging nations develop the skills and attitudes required to enable their countries to industrialize; (2) to improve America's image abroad; and (3) to add to our own nation's understanding of foreign peoples. If it achieves these goals, the Peace Corps will be aiding in the gradual building of a world community, as discussed in Chapter One.

The Peace Corps sends American Peace Corps Volunteers — predominantly, but not exclusively, young people — abroad for two-year assignments to developing nations which have requested them. These Volunteers work not with governments, but directly with the people, and are paid only enough to live approximately as well as those they serve. (An additional $75 monthly is credited to them at home and presented to them when they complete their tour of duty.) Many of the Volunteers have special training in teaching, nursing, agriculture, or industrial skills. Others are given brief, intensive training in language and technical skills after entering the Corps. All are expected to communicate by example initiative and the "can do" approach so vital to both economic and political development.

The Peace Corps is more interested in the character of those it sends overseas than in their technical training or intellectual attainments — although both are desirable factors. A college education is not required for consideration. Peace Corps examinations are administered monthly in most major cities and are used more for determining applicants' skills than for testing their educational achievements. The Peace Corps needs highly motivated and resourceful young people who are willing to live less comfortably than they could at home in return for a chance to help others, to serve their country, and to add breadth and a unique experience to their personal development.

The Peace Corps encountered some difficulty, initially, in filling its staff positions, especially in the field, with men experienced in the culture and environment of the countries whose programs they were supervising. In many cases, the Volunteers in the field soon developed more familiarity with these conditions than the men directing them — an unfortunate state of affairs. As numbers of Volunteers return and assume — as many have — Peace Corps staff positions, these problems should diminish.

The Peace Corps has taken extraordinary measures to avoid becoming bureaucratized. It has had written into its enabling legislation a limitation on the number of years (five) that its professional staff members will be permitted to serve the agency. This legislation will also ensure the availability of staff positions to top-rated Volunteers on their return. Robert Textor has commented, "As far as is known, this is the first time in the history of the American republic that a federal agency has deliberately moved to limit the tenure of its own personnel for the specific purpose of avoiding bureaucratic arteriosclerosis." [39]

More than 85 per cent of the 12,000 plus Volunteers serving in 46 countries, or in training, by mid-1965 were engaged in educational or in "community development" (or "community action") programs.[40] Community development programs aim at changing traditional inertia and passivity rather than at material change alone. When successful they can help people learn how to help themselves in addition to affording them some experience in village democracy and economic enterprise.

Tom Carter, a 22-year-old Volunteer, described his experience in a community action program in Peru in these words:

> I get a lot of letters from people saying "how exciting your work must be" or "how picturesque," or "how much you must enjoy it." They imagine Volunteers hiking along in the Tanganyikan sunset, or teaching to eager, bright-eyed students . . . glory and rewards heaped upon Volunteers by loving, thankful natives, topped by a naive conclusion that what the world really needs is less "stuffy old politicians" and more "real folks."
>
> Volunteers call this the Albert Schweitzer complex. These dreams would not be harmful were it not for what happens to the Volunteer overseas and to his co-workers when he joins for these reasons.
>
> I live in a picturesque bamboo mat house I built myself. I buy my water from a picturesque boy with a burro loaded down with water

39 *Cultural Frontiers of the Peace Corps* (Cambridge, Mass.: Massachusetts Institute of Technology Press, 1966), p. 323.

40 These figures are from the *Fourth Annual Peace Corps Report* (Washington, D.C.: Government Printing Office, 1965), pp. 5–12.

By mid-1966 "a profile of the typical Volunteer began to emerge: he (60% are male) is college educated (. . . 90% have at least a B.A. degree); a liberal arts major (85%). . . . 24.1 years of age." Fifteen per cent are married. Of the more than 15,000 Volunteers serving in mid-1966, 35 per cent were in Latin America, 30 per cent in Africa, 20 per cent in North Africa, the Near East, and South Asia, and 15 per cent in East Asia and the Pacific. *Peace Corps Fifth Annual Report* (Washington, D.C.: Government Printing Office, 1966), pp. 58–59.

cans. I read and write under a kerosene lantern, sleep on a cot, and cook on a camp stove. There comes a day when all this suddenly becomes no longer picturesque, no longer quaint, but furiously frustrating and you want like crazy to just get out of there, to go home. This is called "culture shock." It happens to one and all, usually about the third or fourth month. How hard it hits you and for how long depends largely on this problem of false motives.

Let me tell you about what I do down here. I'm involved in a program of "Urban Community Development." I live in a giant slum or *barriada* on the edge of Chimbote, a city of 120,000 people. My neighbors have come down from the mountains, attracted by the money and in hope of a better life. Because of a lack of marketable skills — for generations they have known only farming and grazing — they find it hard to get a job and end up in unbelievable slums, with diseases and starvation rampant. Largely illiterate, and sometimes speaking Spanish only as a second language after their Indian tongue, they get almost no public service, and many of their rights aren't protected . . .

My job is to get these people, my neighbors, organized, to make them better able to compete in the city for their rights, and to try and get them to raise their standard of living. I teach in the local school during the days and I teach carpentry to adults at night. Both are important jobs, but I consider them only a beginning.

For example, our school has no roof. It would be a ten-dollar project and about one day's labor for two or three Peace Corpsmen to build that roof. Yet we don't do it. If we gave my school a roof it would always be that, a gift, the Gringo's roof. When it needed fixing, no one would fix it. If it takes me a year to talk my neighbors into putting on that roof it will be worth it. Because it will then be *their* roof on *their* school. It would be a small start, but in the right direction. Maybe then we'll take on a little harder project, and step by step build up a powerful organization that is interested in progress and strong enough to do something about it. It has to be an organization that doesn't need me, however; otherwise, it would collapse when I leave.

In another barriada in my town, there are two schools. One is a several thousand dollar complex with classrooms, meeting halls, and a medical clinic. It was built by Peace Corps Volunteers: Architects labored with social workers pouring cement, laying concrete blocks, putting in lights and plumbing. It is now completed and in partial use. Peruvians call it the "gringo school."

Next door to this complex stands a two-room school, built out of grass mats, without windows or lights, and a dirt floor. It was built because the barriada grew and because classroom space was needed. The teacher, a Peace Corps Volunteer, talked the parents of the students into building those two rooms. Though the school was put up in a day and Volunteers only gave limited aid in construction, I consider the grass-school a success, and ten times more valuable to the community than the big complex it sits next to. I think it will remain a symbol to the barriada people of what they can do — working together.

A Volunteer has to be careful and not become too much of a leader. As I have said, if I stir up all the action, what will happen when I leave? I hint at things and let my neighbors come up with the ideas and I let them lead the action. A really good Peace Corps program receives little credit. Keep that in mind when you read Peace Corps success stories. This, then, in short, is what I try to do in Barrio San Pedro. I have a lot of failures, few tangible successes, and a great deal of frustration. (I was a dreamer once, too, and my fall was hard.) Now, all things considered, I think I'm doing something worthwhile. I don't think I'll sign up for another stretch but you can't drag me away from this one.[41]

Much criticism has been directed at the way of life of American diplomats, servicemen, and other Americans overseas.[42] Some of this criticism has been exaggerated and unfair, and much is based on the presence of the few "lemons" to be found in any sizable group of people. Nevertheless, there is truth in some of these charges.

On the average, American officials probably do live more graciously overseas than they could afford to live "stateside." Few, for instance, could afford full-time servants at home. But the services which machines provide for Americans at home can usually be provided abroad only by hiring several human servants. American diplomats, moreover, spend most of their time entertaining or dealing with host government officials, VIP's or other diplomats, all of whom live much better than the masses in their own countries. American officials who lived in mud huts and walked around in rags to impress the common people would be thought insane, rather than dedicated, by their diplomatic counterparts from other nations.

Certainly, Americans living in low income countries abroad in a style comparable to that enjoyed by successful Americans at home are conspicuous, and it is natural that at times this should lead to popular resentment. But few Americans will embark voluntarily on careers which involve taking their families abroad to live at subsistence levels, when they could live so much more comfortably at home. The "ugliness" this situation produces reflects the disparity between Western and non-Western standards of living, not the unique ugliness of a particular group of Americans. For overseas Americans in general care more about the peoples they live with than do their fellow Americans back home.

By living in the villages or cities with the people they serve — and by

41 *Third Annual Peace Corps Report* (Washington, D.C.: Government Printing Office, 1964), pp. 17–20.
42 The most widely read critique of American government employees' behavior abroad is William Lederer and Eugene Burdick, *The Ugly American* (New York: Norton, 1958). A long-run best seller, its title became part of the language. Ultimately it was made into a motion picture starring Marlon Brando.

living without their families, except when both husband and wife are Volunteers [43] — Peace Corps Volunteers are in a unique position to help counter the "ugly American" effect.

In time, several generations of American young people will return home from Peace Corps service to resume their careers. (It has been estimated that there will be about 50,000 returned Peace Corps Volunteers by 1970, 200,000 by 1980.) [44] Some will eventually achieve public office. Many more will come to serve as opinion leaders on foreign affairs questions, exercising a subtle but useful maturing influence on American attitudes toward foreign peoples. So, at least, goes the theory which underlies the Peace Corps experiment.

Results are hard to measure. The Peace Corps has proved quite successful in winning public support both in the United States and among the peoples it has served. Opinion surveys show that a large majority of Americans support the Peace Corps idea. And requests from governments abroad for additional Volunteers have multiplied many times in the relatively short period since the first group of 120 Volunteers began operations in 1961 in only three countries. By mid-1965, 150,000 Americans had volunteered for Peace Corps service, and 15,000 had actually served. In the interim, thirty other nations in Europe, Latin America, Asia, and Africa had established national or international voluntary service agencies modeled on the Peace Corps; and the first group of exchange volunteers (five Indian college graduates experienced in community development work in their own country) had arrived in the United States to help train Peace Corps Volunteers for service in India and then to take VISTA (Volunteers in Service to America) assignments in the "war on poverty" program in the United States.[45]

One evaluative study of Peace Corps programs in thirteen countries concluded that "the Peace Corps Volunteers have succeeded to a remarkable degree in projecting a new and better image of Americans," and have impressed favorably the national elites in nearly all these countries. Their contribution to these nations' development was found much harder to assess, but certainly had "in most important respects been smaller than originally envisaged by many of the early senior staff members of Peace Corps/Washington." However, the advantages of providing training and experience of this sort for substantial numbers of young Americans was seen as extraordinarily valuable to the United States and the individuals concerned:

> [In 1957, none of] the 852 Americans listed as working for the U.S. government in Thailand [could] . . . speak the local language [well enough to carry on their work in that language]. Now, just eight years later, the Peace Corps has given us some hundreds of Volunteer "alumni," most of whom are more or less capable of functioning effec-

[43] Couples with young children are not accepted into the Peace Corps.
[44] Textor, *op. cit.*, p. 4.
[45] *Fourth Annual Peace Corps Report*, pp. 5, 16, and 28–29.

tively in the Thai language and culture. Most of these Americans are still young, with their careers still ahead of them. They represent — or soon will, after further university training — a wide variety of useful technical skills and professional specialties. In a few short years, then, the Peace Corps has made it possible for the United States, for the first time in history, to choose technicians, teachers, advisers and diplomats for service in Thailand who possess *both* the necessary professional expertise *and* the necessary linguistic and cultural proficiency. The implications of this are truly revolutionary.[46]

Perhaps the most disquieting aspect of the Peace Corps is the trouble some Volunteers have had in making the transition back to their more prosaic, less demanding jobs and lives in the United States. But difficulties in readjustment are not a new thing for Americans returning from service overseas. And it is just possible that these Peace Corps Volunteers' disappointments are due as much to real weaknesses in American society as to unrealistic expectations on their part.

A survey of 3,800 of the first 4,500 Peace Corps Volunteers to return from overseas service showed that 39 per cent of them were continuing their education — almost two-thirds of these in graduate school; 15 per cent were employed in the government — almost half in Peace Corps staff positions; 15 per cent were teaching — and many more planned teaching careers after completing their education; the rest were scattered among business, agricultural, social service, military, and other pursuits.[47] Long-term career information on returned Peace Corps Volunteers will not be available, of course, for at least a generation.

All in all, the Peace Corps' record in its first five years of operation seems encouraging in a society just recently inclined to label its youth a "beat generation."

[46] Textor, *op. cit.* The quotations are from pp. 300, 311, and xiv, respectively. This volume was written by fifteen trained social scientists, each with some previous official connection with the Peace Corps. Three were themselves returned Volunteers. The others had served in administrative positions, or, most often, had assisted in training Volunteers prior to their service overseas. None was employed by the Peace Corps at the time of writing.

The acceptance won by Peace Corps Volunteers among the common people they served appeared in one well-publicized incident during the United States intervention in the Dominican Republic in May, 1965. Dominican rebels notified United States military forces that they would release six United States Marines they had captured if a Peace Corps representative would serve as an intermediary. But the activities of some Volunteers in providing food to the hungry and first aid to the injured on *both* sides of the battle line drew criticism as well as praise within the United States. The Richmond, Virginia *Newsleader* complained that the Volunteers were "giving aid and comfort to the enemy at the same time the enemy's troops are still shooting at American soldiers in the streets of Santo Domingo." The Peace Corps' comment: "Before the outbreak of fighting, the Volunteers had been advised to avoid political partisanship, and this was still the operative rule for their behavior during the civil strife. An injured man was an injured man, and food went to those who were hungry." *Fourth Annual Peace Corps Report*, p. 70.

[47] The figures are from the *Fourth Annual Peace Corps Report, op. cit.*, pp. 41-45.

♥ CASE
STUDY *EXPERIENCES OF A CAREER*
FOREIGN SERVICE OFFICER

Robert Murphy began his career in the State Department in 1917 as a
code clerk. Three years later, he passed the Foreign Service examinations and was assigned to serve as a consular officer in Switzerland. In
the course of his almost forty years of service, he rose through the ranks
to become President Roosevelt's personal representative in French
Africa during World War II, Ambassador to Belgium, and to Japan,
Assistant Secretary of State for United Nations Affairs, and Undersecretary of State for Political Affairs — the top ranking career post in
the Department of State.

The selections below deal with his service in Munich from 1921
through 1925, at the beginning of his career, and with his assignment in
1953 as Assistant Secretary for United Nations Affairs.

1. What functions did Murphy perform for his government and its
citizens in the course of the assignments described in these selections? Do
you believe his abilities and those of his colleagues were utilized effectively in these assignments? If not, in what ways could they have been
utilized more effectively?

2. In what respects did Murphy's early assignment to Munich help to
prepare him for subsequent service to his country?

3. Do you think it was wise or unwise for the State Department to
leave Murphy in charge of his post in Munich for three years? To what
extent might United States policy have been advantaged or disadvantaged by the assignment of a senior officer to this post instead?

4. What do you believe to be the best way to handle problems such
as those Murphy encountered in his dealings with Ambassador Lodge?
Would it be best to avoid naming prominent political figures to head
the United States mission to the United Nations, despite the fact that
this would mean foregoing also the opportunity to utilize their personal
prestige on behalf of United States policy there? Should the head of
our United Nations mission be denied cabinet rank, regardless of his
personal political standing?

ROBERT MURPHY

CRAM COURSE IN HITLER'S MUNICH (1921–25)

Six months after I became a consular officer, I was given by rare good fortune
one of the most enlightening assignments of my diplomatic career. In Novem-

From *Diplomat Among Warriors* by Robert Murphy. Copyright © 1964 by Robert
Murphy. Reprinted by permission of Doubleday & Company, Inc.

ber 1921 I was sent to Munich, Germany, and remained there almost four years. Only now, as I look back, can I fully appreciate how valuable the Munich years were to me. Nowhere else in Europe in the 1920's was the past, present, and future of that turbulent continent more dramatically revealed. What I learned in Munich about the behavior of victors and vanquished after the First World War enabled me to anticipate much of the behavior of victors and vanquished after the Second World War. These recollections became my greatest asset when I was appointed advisor on German affairs to General Eisenhower in September 1944 and later, during the first four postwar years, chief representative in Germany for the State Department.

When I arrived in Munich in 1921 a man whose name meant nothing to me then, Adolph Hitler, had just begun to make that city the spawning ground for his National Socialist movement. I met Hitler and other members of the Nazi high command while they were still obscure agitators. I also met Hitler's only famous collaborator of that time, the bitter and frustrated General Erich Ludendorff, who had been commander in chief on the western front when Germany surrendered in 1918. I attended several of the earliest Nazi meetings to make official reports to Washington. Like almost all foreign observers in Munich then, I found it impossible to believe that the demagogue Hitler, so unconvincing to me, would ever amount to much.

But at the same time I was learning what a dangerous situation the First World War had created in Europe. That war undermined the European system built up through many generations, before any acceptable new system had been devised to replace it. From what I saw, I developed great doubts about the wisdom of Woodrow Wilson in brashly forcing the issue of self-determination. His sweeping ideas and superficial knowledge of the practical aspects of European life helped promote European disintegration. Every other person I met in Munich seemed to be involved in some kind of intrigue, because the whole of Europe was in a state of flux. The German and Austro-Hungarian empires had been replaced by shaky republics in which most citizens had little confidence and which were viciously hated by fanatical minorities. The chaotic condition of society was such that there was genuine reason to fear that Bolshevism might take the same advantage of confusion in Germany and Austria which it had taken in Russia after the collapse of the Czarist empire. Above all, while I was in Munich I watched the wildest runaway inflation in modern history wipe out the savings of generations of Germany's and Austria's most decent, substantial people, leaving millions of them in dazed despair. That inflation, in my opinion, did more than any other single factor to make Hitlerism possible. Fortunately, the lessons it taught were skillfully utilized to prevent repetition of inflation after World War II. . . .

I was sent to Munich in 1921 with three other Consular Service officers to reopen our consulate general, which had been closed in 1917 by the war. An experienced officer, William Dawson, was in charge of our trio of very junior vice consuls, and he was as fine a teacher as any budding diplomat could have. Dawson had the reputation, which I can testify was thoroughly deserved, of a severe taskmaster. I offered to resign at least three times during the eight months I served under him, but he calmly ignored my offers and did not abate in the slightest his determination that his three vice counsuls should not only do their work well, but also get into the habit of self-education. He prided himself upon his own linguistic ability and insisted that learning languages is largely a matter of application, not some God-given talent like being an artistic virtuoso. He was equally fluent in German, French and Spanish, and made it a rule that his vice consuls should never use English in talking with him in his office. I had to discuss everything with him in German, one of my colleagues in Spanish, the third in French. In that way, Dawson kept perfecting his own languages and obliged us to do the same.

But after only eight months in Munich, Dawson was promoted and transferred, and since I was slightly senior to the other two vice consuls, I was instructed to take charge until a successor to Dawson arrived. Probably I would have had a severe case of stage fright if I had been told that, except for a brief interval, no successor would appear for three years, during which time I would remain in Bavaria as chief representative of the United States. Fortunately for my peace of mind, I never knew from one day to another when I would be relieved. I would like to flatter myself that I was left so long in this post because of rare ability, but the evidence suggests that our Government did not think it mattered much who represented it in Munich. It was an exhilarating experience for me, as a young man, to be left so completely on my own. Before long I began to think of the diplomatic service as my permanent career rather than as a temporary adventure.

How eagerly we worked then, my fellow vice consuls and I; without their unstinted assistance I never could have held down that assignment. From the moment the consulate general reopened we were overwhelmed with work, usually spending twelve hours or more a day in the offices. . . . the people poured in; it seemed to us that the whole of Bavaria wanted to emigrate to the United States. Immigration was almost unrestricted then and despite our limited facilities we soon were granting an average of four hundred visas per day. Our offices became frantically busy with such matters as approving thousands of visas for emigrants, issuing a large volume of American passports, making out consular invoices, and preparing economic reports which we had to type ourselves because the State Department could not afford to provide us with sufficient clerical help. I remember that this routine called for several hundred signatures daily. It was lucky for me that I had gone to business college, since I had to type all my own reports and correspondence.

It was a welcome relief from these chores to transform ourselves into political reporters for the benefit of the State Department, which was listed in routine regulations as one of our duties. I am rather vain about some of the political reports I made describing Hitler's earliest raucous efforts; when I looked them up recently in the National Archives in Washington, they seemed reasonably perceptive. But while we were sending in our reports so earnestly, we never knew whether or not anybody in Washington read them. They were accepted in total silence. Americans never have been more isolationist than they were in the 1920s. During my Munich years I saw nothing to indicate that the American Government or people were mildly interested in the political developments which seemed so ominous and significant to us on the spot. The only real American interest in Germany at that time was concerned with money; a few Americans made fortunes out of the German inflation; American promoters high-pressured unrealistic loans upon German communities and corporations, loans which were defaulted later at the expense of American bondholders. Not once did our State Department ask my opinion about any political event, nor express concern over the developing Nazi movement. No comment came from Washington when I sent an eyewitness report of the Hitler group's attempt to overthrow the government of Bavaria in 1923, as a first step toward the national dictatorship which they eventually achieved. Our able ambassador to Germany, Alanson B. Houghton, periodically summoned me to Berlin for conferences of regional representatives, and listened thoughtfully to our reports of various local situations, but that was the only attention our political investigations received. Yet we were dealing with the origins of World War II.

This vast tide of emigration from Europe after World War I was a symptom of the prevailing chaos. American critics of our immigration policy complained then that we were getting the riffraff of Europe, but that certainly was not true of Munich. Moreover, I do not believe it was generally true. Unemployment was widespread and the war had been bitterly disillusioning, particularly for young people. At least 80 per cent of our applicants were Bavarians, mostly young and from solid middle-class or working-class families. Many of them were craftsmen and most had some skills. They saw no future in Germany or Europe, inflation was wiping out any savings they had made or could make, and they fully intended to become permanent and serious American citizens. I am sure that the great majority of them did so. Probably it was true that our immigration laws were too lax and that some undesirable persons slipped through. Our Munich applicants were required to make out their own application forms and we did not have the facilities to check them carefully. But I am confident that, on balance, the great flood of immigrants from Europe after World War I greatly benefited the United States. Later in the 1920s, Congress swung to intensive restrictions, until today the United States has the most complicated system of immigration laws in the world.   . . .

After Dawson left Munich, I found myself in a peculiar position. I represented one of the richest and most powerful countries on earth in a place which European governments considered important enough to deserve high-ranking diplomats. I carried locally the impressive title of Acting Consul General, but actually I still was only a junior vice consul, drawing a vice consul's pay of $2750 a year, with almost none of the perquisites which provided my colleagues in the consular corps with ample entertainment and other allowances. If we managed to repay a few social obligations in Munich's active diplomatic society, it was thanks only to the inflation which was ruinous to Germans but temporarily helpful to those of us paid in dollars. . . .

However, we were getting experiences in Munich upon which one cannot set a price. Thanks to my official position, I had a wide and diverse acquaintance in that cultured community. Everybody in Bavaria, from highest to lowest, was accessible to the official representatives of the United States, and American visitors to Munich usually called at the consulate general. One American who slipped into town so unostentatiously that we did not know of his presence for several days was Thomas R. Marshall, former Vice President of the United States. . . .

We also had a number of friends among the group of Americans who established their homes in Munich after the war. One of these was James Loeb, of the great New York banking firm of Kuhn, Loeb & Company, who after an illness retired to a country estate near Munich. He came to see me one day at the consulate, where we had a pleasant chat, and as he was leaving, he said, "If there is anything I can do to help you, don't hesitate to call on me." Not long after that, an American who was penniless came to our consulate for help. Our government provided no funds for needy citizens, and not infrequently our consular and diplomatic officers advanced their own money — which many of them could ill afford to spare — to wandering Americans in distress. This time I remembered Loeb's offer, so I telephoned to him and described the case. Loeb responded, "Of course I will give the man enough to return home," which he did. After that, Loeb made gifts and loans to a number of indigent Americans whom I referred to him, and his intelligent generosity was a great help, not only to our citizens who found themselves alone and in trouble in an alien land, but also to our consulate.

My colleagues in the Munich consular corps were exceptional men in one way or another, and all were friendly and helpful to me. They must have been astonished that the United States Government was content to leave so junior a diplomat in the Munich post, but they never treated me with anything but the kindest consideration. Today even our youngest diplomats are better equipped than I was in the 1920s, for they are given substantial preliminary training in essential matters before being sent abroad.

The titular head of the Munich consular corps was the Papal Nuncio,

Monsignor Eugenio Pacelli, who later became Pope Pius XII. The Vatican always had maintained close relations with Bavaria, which remained Catholic throughout the Reformation while many other German communities were becoming Lutheran. Monsignor Pacelli, through his intimate knowledge of international politics, was one of the first to recognize that the future of Europe depended largely upon what happened in Germany. I had many enlightening conversations with him in Munich, and two decades later I was to renew my association with him after he became Pope, when I entered Rome with American troops in 1944 as President Roosevelt's personal representative. . . .

Another Munich colleague was William Seeds, the British consul general, an Irishman of charm and quick intelligence. He was especially helpful in showing me how to write effective political reports, something which my own government never taught me. He permitted me to read some of his reports and analyses, which combined wit with wisdom. Haniel von Haimhausen, the brilliant if cynical Minister to Bavaria from the State of Prussia, provided some of my first intimate glimpses into central European politics. . . .

One man who was more helpful to me than any of my diplomatic colleagues was a German employee of the American consulate general, Paul Drey. When we reopened our Munich office in 1921 he was working for the Spanish mission which had handled our affairs during the war, and Dawson persuaded him to come to work for us. He was in his late thirties then, a member of a distinguished Jewish family which had lived in Bavaria four hundred years. He was respected among Bavarians and could quickly arrange for me any interviews I desired. His knowledge of local politics and personalities was encyclopedic, he was in every sense a cultured gentleman, and he soon became my close friend. But Paul Drey unwittingly misled me about one man and his group: Adolph Hitler. I recall the first Hitler meeting I attended with Paul; as we went out, he exclaimed: "How does this Austrian upstart dare to tell us Germans what to do?" Paul and I later attended many more Nazi rallies in order to report this violent political phenomenon to the State Department. But when I asked Paul, "Do you think these agitators will ever get far?" he answered firmly, "Of course not! The German people are too intelligent to be taken in by such scamps!". . .

Paul Drey paid dearly for his faith in the German people, among whom he firmly numbered himself until the end. In 1938, thirteen years after I left Munich, I read one morning in Paris that the Nazis had burned down a synagogue in Munich, and I immediately arranged to fly to that city to persuade my friend Paul to leave Germany, assuring him of employment with the State Department in a safer place. He thanked me, but shook his head, saying, "No, this is a temporary madness. Self-respecting Germans will not tolerate these louts much longer." Paul's faith was greater than mine, and I could not dissuade him.

I was one of the first American civilians to enter Munich after its capture in 1945, and immediately made inquiries about Paul Drey. A leading Munich banker, August Bauch, told me that he had last seen Paul in a work gang shoveling snow on a Munich street, and later heard that he had been sent to the Dachau death camp. When I visited Dachau shortly afterward and confirmed Paul's death there, I was more stricken by the fate of my friend than by the certified deaths in that horror chamber of 283,000 other victims.

Paul Drey runs all through my memories of Munich. I was with him on the memorable morning of November 9, 1923, when Hitler staged his first rebellion against the republic in the mistaken belief that Bavarian monarchists would support a break away from Berlin at that time. Paul and I arrived in the central square of Munich, the Odeonsplatz, just in time to see Hitler's storm troopers marching into the square toward a contingent of the Bavarian police. Hitler's famous collaborator, General Ludendorff, had foolishly decided to join this premature rebellion and was marching with Hitler at the head of the armed rebels. That scene has been described in many books, and the disparities in details show that reporting is not an exact science. Most reports say that when the police opened fire, Hitler lost his nerve and in order to save himself dropped to the ground with such force that he broke a shoulder, while Ludendorff marched fearlessly on. Paul and I were right there when the firing started, and we recognized Hitler and Ludendorff, whom we had seen many times. Of course it does not matter now, but for the record I can testify that both Ludendorff and Hitler behaved in an identical manner, like the battle-hardened soldiers they were. Both fell flat to escape the hail of bullets. Ludendorff's body servant, marching at his side, was killed, as were several of Hitler's cronies.

Paul and I had stayed up all the previous night reporting the rapidly moving developments. The Nazi guerrillas had seized the Bavarian Government offices, the banks, the City Hall, and of course the telephone and telegraph offices. I was refused permission to send a telegram in code to Washington, and indignantly demanded an interview with Hitler himself. After hours of argument, I finally did get in to see him at 3 A.M., only to be told rather mildly that I could not send my telegram. My protest was only a formality by that time, since I already had sent my colleague, Halstead, in a car to file the telegram from Stuttgart. And later I learned that I had demanded from Hitler rights which I did not possess.

Four months later I covered the trial of the conspirators, which I reported to the State Department under date of March 10, 1924. As is well known, Hitler was sentenced to five years in Landsberg Fortress, a sentence which was suspended after he served eight months, during which time he wrote *Mein Kampf*. Ludendorff was acquitted, and I cited as an example of the "insolent bravado" of the defendants during the trial that Ludendorff denounced his acquittal as an outrage since his comrades had been found guilty, and shouted that the decision was an insult to the uniforms worn by the judges in the court-martial. My conclusion was not too bad: "While the putsch in November 1923 was a farcical failure, the nationalist movement behind it is by no means extinguished in Bavaria. It has simply been delayed. . . . It is contemplated that upon completion of his term Hitler, who is not a citizen, will be expelled from the country. Further nationalist activity on his part, for the present at least, appears to be excluded." My disposal of Hitler was not quite so cavalier as that of the British ambassador to Germany, Lord D'Abernon. His memoirs, *An Ambassador of Peace,* did not consider Hitler worth more than a footnote, which remarked that after Hitler's release from prison he "vanished into oblivion" — which illustrates why wise diplomats think it prudent to hedge in their judgment of men and events.

I did have one interview with Hitler early in 1923 in which, according to my official report, his attitude was "cordial." I had read somewhere that the elder Henry Ford, who allegedly was financing an anti-Semitic publication in Detroit, had also contributed money to Hitler's Nazis, and I decided to ask Hitler whether the report was true. He received me amiably — the only occasion when he did so — and explained that "unfortunately Mr. Ford's organization has so far made no money contributions to our party." He added that the party's funds were coming principally from "patriotic Germans living abroad," and I believe that in those days Hitler did have more financial supporters abroad than in Germany.

Also about that time I had my first break in intelligence work, one of the principal functions of a diplomat. This experience taught me, early in my career, that it is not necessary always to become a "secret agent" in order to gather important military secrets. Our naval attaché in Berlin wrote me that it was rumored that Bavarian factories were turning out diesel engines especially designed for Japanese submarines, in violation of the terms of the Versailles Treaty. A short time before, Paul Drey had introduced me to a young man named Diesel who said he was planning to emigrate to the United States. I remembered him well because it had not occurred to me that Diesel was the name of a family as well as an engine; this young man's father was the inventor. I was told that he was an official in the Munich-Augsburg Machine Company which made diesel engines, and I decided to ask him frankly about the report. He said it was quite true, and that he did not like this kind of operation and would provide me with full details. Soon he brought me copies of ledgers showing the quantities and types of submarine engines being shipped to Japan labeled "agricultural machinery." So I was congratulated for my "undercover skill," and young Diesel went to the United States where he prospered.

Americans abroad call upon their consular officers to help them in many surprising ways, but Munich is the only place where I felt bound to serve as a second in a duel. One day a young American student came into my office with a problem. He said someone had stepped on someone's foot in a trolley car, and a German major who felt he had been insulted had challenged the American student to a duel. The officer had formally presented his card, saying he would have his second call upon the American's second to arrange details. The young man sought my advice and we agreed that this matter should be treated unofficially. I could remember nothing in the regulations of the State Department forbidding consuls to act as seconds in duels, but I preferred not to submit the question to higher authority. The student explained that he knew nothing about dueling, was not a good shot, and had never even handled a sword. So we studied his situation. I told him that under German dueling rules he had the choice of weapons, as the challenged party, and I asked if there was any kind of weapon he did know how to use. To my delight, he replied that he was an expert archer. Now I began to see daylight ahead and I agreed to act as his second — in a strictly unofficial capacity.

The next day, at my invitation, the major's second called on me. I informed him that we would be quite happy to have the duel occur at a time and place of their choosing, but of course my principal would assert his privilege of selecting the weapons. The major's second solemnly agreed, and asked what the weapons would be. "Bows and arrows," I replied blandly. My German visitor turned purple with indignation, protesting that nobody ever fought a duel with bows and arrows, weapons used only by savages and barbarians. I replied imperturbably that apparently he was unfamiliar with American dueling practices, since bows and arrows were standard weapons in my country, having been used by the inhabitants of the North American continent for centuries. The type of German who challenges to duels usually is deficient in a sense of humor, especially in matters regarding duels, so it required several days of discussions before I had an opportunity to meet the challenger himself. When the major finally called on me, he already had come to the conclusion that I had devised an ingenious way to save his honor and my principal's skin. I invited all concerned to the Hofbrau Haus where we engaged in a beer duel which hurt nobody, and the German officer and the American student became friends.

Possibly I have given Hitler a disproportionate amount of attention in this chapter because he became such an evil genius later. Actually, in my Munich days he and his movement were considered much less important than the one thing which affected every man, woman, and child — inflation. German money, the mark, was losing its value, gradually during my first year, then more swiftly, then in a rush which destroyed its value altogether. Americans of the Confederacy experienced similar runaway inflation after they lost the Civil War, when their money became worthless. Their inflation had some of the same psychological effects upon the people of our southern states as the 1919–24 inflation had upon the Germans, and some of the demoralizing effects still linger in both places.

Lord D'Abernon, the British Ambassador to Germany from 1920–26, was a financial expert and his description of German inflation is the best I know. Day after day for years he wrote in his diary that the German Government, by permitting its printing presses to turn out paper money without limit, was heading straight for disaster. He warned Germans, he warned Frenchmen, he warned Britons and Americans, with little result. The French and Belgian governments were interested only in collecting the reparations due them, and did not care how much paper money the Germans printed. Some Germans, headed by the multimillionaire steel king, Hugo Stinnes, favored inflation as a means of avoiding payment of reparations. Other Germans discovered that they could get rich from inflation, so long as it was held within limits. . . .

The prewar value of the German mark was twenty-five cents. When I first went to Munich at the end of 1921, I already could get about a hundred marks for a dollar. A year later I was getting about sixty-five hundred marks for the dollar. Then, in January 1923, French armies marched into Germany's richest industrial region, the Ruhr, and the German government decided to finance passive resistance to such foreign military occupation. This was heartily approved by the Ruhr's mine owners and mine workers. The government undertook to pay wages to the resisting miners and subsidies to the resisting owners, and for this purpose printed enormous additional amounts of paper money. A month after the occupation of the Ruhr, I was getting more than forty thousand marks for a dollar, and the bottom of the money market began to drop out completely. By August a dollar was buying millions, in September billions, in October trillions of marks. A sad cartoon appeared in a Munich paper showing a little girl sitting beside two huge bundles of paper money, crying pitifully. A passerby was saying: "Why are you crying, little girl?" She answered: "Someone stole the leather straps off my money!" I occasionally played a dollar limit poker game for German marks. When we began that game, the limit was one hundred marks; in October 1923, one trillion marks. It was quite a thrill to raise a trillion.

Finally, that month, the German Government virtually repudiated its enormous public debt by introducing a new unit of value called the rentenmark. The State redeemed at one million-millionth of the prewar value all outstanding currency, all treasury bonds and notes, and all saving deposits and mortgages. You could figure out the value of what had been the most conservative securities in the country by knocking off twelve zeros. This meant that every German who had sacrificed and saved to provide for his old age and for his family was ruined. Our sixty-five-year-old cook, Louisa, who for years as cook for Mark Twain's daughter had thriftily accumulated German marks equivalent to twenty thousand dollars, invested in State savings bank deposits. She ended up penniless.

As Lord D'Abernon pointed out, the only gainer was the State, which was relieved of debts estimated at $50,000,000,000. Once the full circle had been completed, all classes of private creditors were wiped out. By ironic justice, the heaviest losses were suffered by individuals who had most favored inflation in earlier stages; they had piled up huge paper profits which, in the final crash, all vanished. . . .

DIFFICULTIES AT THE UNITED NATIONS

When I flew into Washington in response to the urgent summons from Secretary Dulles, I was surprised to see that I was to be in charge of about one hundred and forty men and women. The new office for UN Affairs had been in existence less than a decade, but already it had as many employees as the State Department's entire Washington staff in earlier days. Furthermore, my assistants were all busy, often frantically so, in an around-the-clock operation which went on every day of the year. It was the duty of the staff to keep in touch with everything affecting the relations of the United States with the UN, which comprised some sixty countries at that time. Of course, there has been rapid expansion of UN membership ever since, until now the flags of more than one hundred nations hang at UN headquarters in New York. The UN may be required at any moment to consider almost any military, political, economic, or social problem anywhere on earth, under the seas, or in outer space. So the UN office of the State Department is supposed to examine, at least superficially, all the incredible deluge of documents, resolutions, surveys, complaints, reports which pour in from the member-governments and all branches of the UN organizations — the Secretary-General's Office, the General Assembly, the Security Council, the Trusteeship Council, the Economic and Social Council, and numerous special agencies. Obviously a lot of people are needed merely to extract from this flood of paper essential information for the President and his chief foreign policy adviser, the Secretary of State.

It took no time at all for me to become aware that the morale of my staff was low, and I was not surprised. For three years a Senate subcommittee headed by Senator Joseph R. McCarthy had been investigating alleged penetration of the State Department by Communists and fellow travelers, and attention had been concentrated particularly upon people assigned to the office of UN Affairs. Those Senate hearings had aroused interest even in faraway Japan, because McCarthy was endeavoring to show that American officials sympathetic to Communism were partly responsible for Communist victories in China. Japanese newspapers published reports of the McCarthy inquisition and I was distressed, while Ambassador to Japan, to observe how newspaper readers there were getting the impression that the State Department was riddled with disloyal employees. But even that publicity in Japan did not prepare me for the attitude of Americans at home. Having lived abroad for years, I was startled when an old friend greeted me in Milwaukee with the question: "Bob, how can you bring yourself to work in that nest of

Commies and homosexuals in the State Department?" I thought perhaps he was making a poor joke but found he was entirely in earnest. As this friend had never been near the State Department, I asked where he was getting his information and he told me he read about it in the Chicago *Tribune.*

Several government agencies were investigating my office when I took over direction of UN Affairs. A few doubtful staff members already had been dismissed, and I examined in detail the records of individuals who still were considered suspect. It seemed to me that all these men were loyal and competent, and I sympathized with their resentment at having been made victims of clumsy security measures which had opened the way for unjustifiable congressional and press attacks. I decided that one reason why this situation had developed was because a fundamental rule of the Foreign Service had been ignored in the new office. This rule was that Foreign Service officers should be rotated regularly. Sometimes a most capable officer, if left too long at the same post, may acquire a wrong attitude which can be rectified by transfer to a different environment. But ever since the establishment of UN Affairs, a number of officers had been left uninterruptedly in certain positions where their specialized knowledge was valuable. However, this was unfair to the men concerned, not only because it tied them to work which tended to become monotonous, but more importantly because it left them open to charges of being "internationalists" — a word which conveyed lack of patriotism to a good many Americans. There was a feeling that some members of the staff had become so imbued with UN ideas that they had lost their American viewpoint. Rightly or wrongly, the dog had acquired a doubtful name.

While the office of UN Affairs at the State Department in Washington was thus being half-smothered under a cloud of innuendo, the American delegation at UN headquarters in New York was flourishing. Aware of Roosevelt's high hopes for the world organization, Truman decided in 1945 to enhance the status of the American Ambassador to the UN by informally ranking that official practically as a member of the President's cabinet, and he appointed to that post Warren R. Austin, a statesman of great dignity and charm who had been senator from Vermont for fourteen years. This selection by the Democratic President of a Republican Ambassador was indicative of the intention to lift United States policy at the UN indisputably above domestic politics.

Later, however, when the Ambassador to the UN was ranked formally as a member of the cabinet, the Presidents who followed Truman selected only members of their own party. Eisenhower named Henry Cabot Lodge, Jr., former Republican senator from Massachusetts, as his choice for Ambassador of [to] the UN and Kennedy named Adlai Stevenson, the twice-defeated presidential candidate of the Democrats, as his appointee. Ambassador Austin was by nature a peacemaker; he disliked public controversy as much as he disliked personal publicity. In the UN debates, he rarely raised his voice or used a harsh word in response to strident Soviet propaganda against the United States, and his replies to Russian oratorical attacks were usually made only after careful preparation, thus enabling the Russians to gain the headlines unimpeded.

But Cabot Lodge was not the Austin type. When he became American Ambassador at the UN, he decided that every Russian attack should be countered sharply, and his method of immediately challenging Soviet misrepresentation had a salutary effect. His opponent at times was Andrei Vishinsky, my former traveling companion in Italy, who had become Soviet Foreign Minister and occasionally chief Russian delegate to the UN. When Lodge and Vishinsky exchanged verbal blows, both contestants seemed to enjoy the match, and so did American radio and television audiences. Knowing that he was cast by American viewers as the villain, Vishinsky played his role with relish. Taunting "capitalist" governments had been standard procedure with Bolshevik orators, and Vishinsky adapted this tactic to the UN forum with considerable effectiveness. All UN speakers know that whenever their views are broadcast, they are addressing an audience vastly greater than the delegates assembled at UN headquarters, and they plan their performances on the world stage as carefully as any actor. Offstage, Vishinsky's manner usually changed. No matter how bitter the official arguments had been, he would discuss the most controversial issue good-humoredly in the delegates' private lounge. . . .

I quickly learned that I would have to practice a form of diplomacy in my new post which I had not anticipated. During the Korean debates, a resolution was proposed on which the vote promised to be closely divided. There were discussions at the office of UN Affairs in Washington about how the United States should vote, and after due consideration we decided that the American vote should be "Yes." We submitted our conclusion to Secretary Dulles and he approved it, so instructions were sent to the United States mission in New York to vote "Yes." But the next morning I was dismayed to read in the newspapers that Lodge had voted "No." As soon as I could talk to him by long distance telephone I said, "Apparently our instructions failed to reach you." Lodge repeated, "Instructions? I am not bound by instructions from the State Department. I am a member of the President's cabinet and accept instructions only from him." I knew that personal and official relations between Lodge and the President were exceptionally close. Lodge had been one of the original group which launched the "Eisenhower for President" movement, and he had directed Eisenhower's contest for the Republican nomination in 1952 against Senator Robert A. Taft. But no one had warned me that Lodge regarded himself as independent of the State Department and I protested, "But you also are head of an embassy, and our ambassadors accept instructions from the Secretary of State." After a moment's pause, Lodge replied, "I take note of the Department's opinions." I was flabbergasted. As an Ambassador myself, I had acted under instructions for many years. "This is a new situation to me," I said, "and I'll have to discuss it with the Secretary." Lodge replied coolly, "Yes, do that. He will set you straight." When I did report to Dulles, he listened carefully without comment until I finished, and then said, "This is one of those awkward situations which require special consideration. If it happens again, just tell me and I'll take care of it."

My personal relations with Lodge were always agreeable. Once I understood that the Secretary of State did not choose to challenge the virtual autonomy which Lodge claimed for his embassy at the UN, I realized it was not appropriate for me to do so. A word from President Eisenhower or a call from the Secretary of State personally were accepted by Lodge in good grace, but there were explosions from time to time if instructions, or even strong suggestions, were sent by the State Department to the American mission at UN headquarters. Lodge would tolerate no poaching on what he considered his own preserve. He was as anxious as anybody to promote a consistent American foreign policy, but he interpreted his functions as much broader than those of an ordinary ambassador. He believed that his position in New York entitled him to help formulate policy as well as execute it, and of course the State Department made every effort to have him participate in policy making. . . .

The American mission's assertion of independence from the State Department continued through the eight years of the Eisenhower administration. The political influence and exceptional ability of Ambassador Lodge gradually transformed the American delegation at the UN until, as the years passed, our mission behaved less like an embassy than a second Foreign Office of the United States Government. The staff in New York grew at a tremendous rate — it numbered well over one hundred when I had dealings with it — and the range of its functions expanded accordingly. No other government maintains such an impressive bureaucracy to conduct its relations with the UN organization.

Chapter Five

THE ROLE OF
THE MILITARY

The possibility of the use of force in international relations is a critical constant in the contemporary world. As we have seen, who gets what as a result of even the most peaceable negotiations among nations is often determined by calculated estimates of the participants' war potential. In such a setting, the interplay between military strength and foreign policy is unavoidably intimate. Today's military choices limit the alternatives open to foreign policymakers tomorrow; and today's policy choices create the commitments which military men will be called upon tomorrow to defend with their lives.

Twice in a decade, for instance, Czechoslovakia — an important pro-Western industrialized nation — lost its independence partly because of the prior military choices of its actual or potential allies. In 1938, France and Britain failed to support Czechoslovakia against pressure from Nazi Germany, despite a treaty of alliance between Czechoslovakia and France. One factor which helped to persuade France not to aid its ally was the realization that such aid would have to take the form of an *offensive* against Germany, whereas France's military establishment and strategic plans were all geared to *defensive* warfare. In the end, Czechoslovakia was dismembered at the Munich conference.

In 1948, Czechoslovakia succumbed to Soviet Russian pressure and internal subversion. The United States decision during World War II not to try to liberate Prague, the Czech capital, before the Russians did, contributed to Czech vulnerability to Communist subversion after the war. American military leaders based this decision predominantly on military considerations. Three years later, in 1948, only strong United States support could have enabled Czechoslovakia to withstand mounting internal and external Communist pressure. But the American military force of World War II had already been demobilized, and United States military strategy relied heavily upon the West's temporary nuclear monopoly. The options open to the Truman administration were thus fewer and less pleasant than they might have been had different military choices been made in the past. The Czechs were advised not to depend on American support and fell under Communist domination soon afterward.[1]

MILITARY PARTICIPATION IN FOREIGN POLICYMAKING

The President may draw upon three main institutional sources for military advice on foreign policy: the Department of Defense, the Joint Chiefs of Staff (JCS), and the National Security Council (NSC), which was discussed in Chapter Four. From the Council's origin in 1947 until 1949, it included four representatives of the military — the Secretary of Defense and the three service secretaries (Army, Navy, Air Force). Since 1949, only the Secretary of Defense has represented the military as a full member of the Council, though the Chairman of the Joint Chiefs of Staff also participates regularly in its deliberations as an adviser.

The Department of Defense manages the United States military establishment, employing more than a million civilian employees and supervising the expenditure of some $70 billion annually. It was created by the National Security Act of 1947 as the National Military Establishment and renamed the Department of Defense in 1949. The National Security Act, in turn, was a compromise between advocates and opponents of completely unifying the nation's three military services.

The Department is headed by the Secretary of Defense, the principal military assistant to the President in all matters relating to this department. Both the Secretary and his deputy are required by law to be civilians. Initially, the Secretary of Defense was intended merely to serve as a coordinator in establishing general policies for the three independent executive departments of the Army, Navy, and Air Force. Successive amendments to the National Security Act and executive reorganizations, however, have added greatly to the Secretary's authority, subtracting from that of the service departments. Since 1949, the latter have lost their independent status and function as subordinate military departments within the Department of Defense. In addition, the staff assistance available to the Secretary of Defense has been expanded manifold. These statutory and organizational changes have gone a long way — without integrating the military services directly — toward enabling the Secretary of Defense to give the military establishment unified and effective direction.

[1] The case studies in Chapter Eleven provide excellent illustrations of the constant and unavoidable interplay between political and military considerations in the making of foreign policy decisions. These cases deal with the Cuban missile crisis of 1962, and with the future of NATO.

Nevertheless, controversy on the fundamental issue of whether the military establishment should be completely unified has not been stilled. Historically, of course, the Army and Navy were managed and represented separately by the War and Navy Departments. After World War II, the increased importance of air power led to separate status for the Air Force as well. But most military specialists agree that the ground-sea-air distinction is not the most functionally relevant in modern warfare. Thus, President Eisenhower, a former Army Chief of Staff, suggests in his memoirs that "modern combat forces (as contrasted with logistical support forces) can be classified as follows: (1) *Nuclear retaliatory or strike forces, . . . , (2) Forces deployed overseas* [to help defend allied countries] *. . . , (3) Forces to keep the sea lanes open in the event of emergency . . . , (4) Forces to protect the United States from air attack . . . ,* [and] *(5) Reserve forces."* [2] Other organizational schemes based on function have also been proposed.

Retention of the traditional military organization, therefore, involves important disadvantages. Full cooperation in unified functional commands is difficult to obtain since the career interests of key officers usually remain in the separate service hierarchies. Relatively few officers below the top levels in each service have the opportunity to accumulate the varied experience which best fits a man to assume a unified command. Interservice rivalry for programs involving new weapons systems becomes virtually unavoidable, and duplication of effort often results. During the 1950's, each service felt it had to propose a missile development program of its own if only to protect its share of influence and budgetary support. As Henry Kissinger has pointed out,

> Each service pushes weapons development in every category without much regard for the program of other services, and each service seeks to obtain control over as many weapons as possible as a form of insurance against drastic budgetary cuts in the future. Because to relinquish a weapons system may mean to relinquish the appropriations that go with it, each service has a powerful incentive to hold onto every weapon even after it has outlived its usefulness. A weapons system, no matter how obsolescent, represents a budgetary category [already approved].[3]

Presidents Truman and Eisenhower, General Marshall, and others recommended legislation designed to increase centralization and unification in the defense establishment. They were forced by opponents within the military and in Congress to accept watered-down compromises, however. Naval officers, especially, feared that a unified military establishment might be dominated by the Army. Key Congressmen, such as House Armed Services Committee Chairman Carl Vinson, were aware that centralizing power within the

2 Dwight D. Eisenhower, *Mandate for Change* (New York: Doubleday, 1963), pp. 538–539.

3 *Nuclear Weapons and Foreign Policy* (New York: Harper, 1957), p. 412.

executive branch would diminish congressional influence in military affairs. Even civilian *executive* leverage on the military would be reduced by a single unified organization directing and speaking for the military establishment. Integrating the services would also affect the morale of the officer corps. The individual officer's pride in and loyalty to his own service have great functional value for a society which demands so much of its top military personnel yet rewards them so meagerly.

The results of the compromise on unification as it evolved after World War II are illustrated in Chart A. The three services remain and retain the formal prerogative of direct access to Congress; however, commands over major concentrations of United States forces have been geographically and functionally unified. Since the reorganization of 1958, "full operational command" over these forces has been vested *not* in the individual services, but in the Joint Chiefs of Staff, the Secretary of Defense, and the President. Budget appropriations, too, are now assigned according to function.

Most academic writers on military affairs agree that although total integration of the military establishment is undesirable or unfeasible at present, increasing administration through functional units is advisable. Henry Kissinger advocates keeping the Army, Navy, and Air Force as administrative and training units, but dividing the military establishment for all other purposes into a Strategic Force capable of waging all-out war and a Tactical Force geared to limited war. Harry Howe Ransom urges reorganizing the unified commands functionally rather than geographically; "a speed-up of the integration of the technical forms and procedures," — including uniform systems of procurement, supplies, and paper work; and perhaps also the reorientation of military education toward a functional rather than an individual service approach.[4]

Samuel Huntington cautions that there are real advantages to retaining the traditional services while simultaneously strengthening functional units and programs:

> Overlapping memberships in interest groups moderate the conflicts among those groups. . . . Similarly, with the military . . . the emergence of the functional programs tended to moderate interservice rivalry. . . . "Unification" was more likely to come not from the reduction or elimination of intramilitary conflict but from its multiplication. . . .
>
> Diversification of function benefits not only the individual services but also the entire military establishment. The value of the services stems precisely from their incomplete commitment to any strategic doctrine. An organization such as the SAC [Strategic Air Command] or the Continental Defense Command, which exists for only one strategic

---

[4] For Kissinger's view, see *Nuclear Weapons and Foreign Policy, op. cit.,* pp. 418 ff. For Ransom's, see *Can American Democracy Survive Cold War?* (New York: Doubleday, 1964), pp. 83–84.

CHART A — DEPARTMENT OF DEFENSE

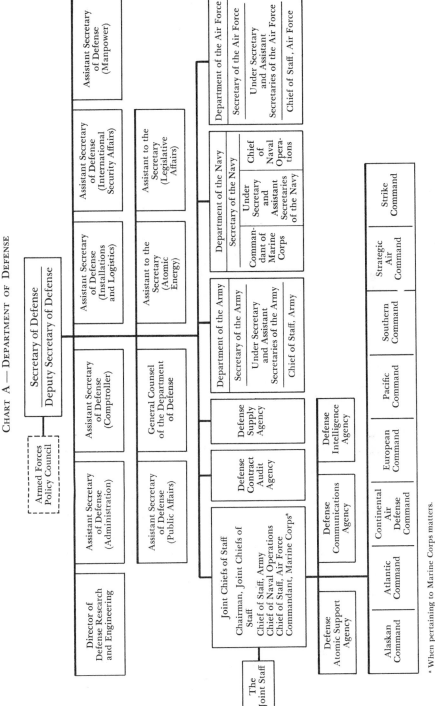

* When pertaining to Marine Corps matters.

Source: Department of Defense, April 1, 1965.

purpose, cannot be receptive to changes in its purpose or to the creation of new organizations embodying competing purposes. The functional commands of today are the vested interests of tomorrow. . . . Organizational permanence is the partner of strategic flexibility. Thus, the unified and specified commands may become the instruments of strategy, and yet the political castles of the services may also continue to stand, with their storied keeps of service loyalty and tradition . . . battered but untaken, long after the decisive battles — both political and military — have shifted to other fields.[5]

THE JOINT CHIEFS OF STAFF

The conflicting pressures of the "unification" controversy are reflected in the dual role of the Joint Chiefs of Staff (JCS). A careful look at Chart A will show that each member of the Joint Chiefs, except the chairman, appears twice on the chart, in two chains of command. Each is the operating head of his service, reporting to his service secretary and through him to the Secretary of Defense. A few boxes to the left, each appears again as a member of the JCS, reporting directly to the Secretary and sharing in the direction of the unified and specified commands.

Under the National Security Act of 1947, as amended, the JCS are the principal military advisers to the President and the National Security Council, as well as to the Secretary of Defense. They are charged with preparing strategic plans and providing for the strategic direction of the armed forces. In addition, they recommend to the Secretary of Defense the quantity and types of troops and supporting material needed to carry out these strategic plans. They are aided by a joint staff of not more than 400 officers, assigned to them from each of the three services, in about equal numbers. On matters of interest to the Marine Corps, its Commandant meets with the JCS as a full member. The Chairman of the JCS serves as presiding officer, provides an agenda for its meetings, manages the joint staff, and serves as a link between the JCS and the President, NSC, and Secretary of Defense.

Unfortunately, the requirements of the two roles which the Joint Chiefs fill in the chain of command sometimes conflict sharply. Ransom notes that:

> Each service chief annually certifies to his department Secretary and the Defense Secretary that the budget he submits represents the minimum required for his service to perform its mission. Shortly thereafter the Defense Secretary refers the budgets of all the armed services to the JCS for their recommendations. At this stage each service chief must judge his own budget in the context of all other service requirements and against an over-all dollar-target ceiling.[6]

[5] *The Common Defense: Strategic Programs in National Politics* (New York: Columbia University Press, 1961), pp. 422–425. Reprinted by permission. Coexistence of both the armed services and unified functional commands is also advocated by Lt. Gen. James M. Gavin, *War and Peace in the Space Age* (New York: Harper, 1958), pp. 253–285.

[6] Ransom, *op. cit.*, p. 82.

The members of the JCS, in other words, are required to serve as both advocates and judges in formulating the defense budget. In addition, their ability to think about overall strategic plans is limited by the voluminous administrative work they must handle as operational chiefs of the services.

The JCS' final budgetary estimates therefore are often based on interservice compromise and logrolling instead of being decided according to carefully thought out plans for meeting national policy requirements. Decision by compromise among the services and other interested groups within the executive branch may be unavoidable as long as there are independent services — or even independent functional units. After all, *there is no purely objective means of determining the value of competing military programs.* The men who make the final decisions are bound to be influenced by their cumulative career experiences. But the Joint Chiefs might be free to approach military programs from a more completely national standpoint if they were relieved of their responsibilities to act also as the chief representatives of the individual services.

Yet there is an understandable reluctance to divorce the strategic planning and operational command functions entirely, since this would leave those who will have to execute the plans with little or no voice in making them. There is no happy solution for this dilemma. In practice, the expedient adopted has been to strengthen the positions, vis à vis the service chiefs, of those whose roles *do* encourage an outlook transcending interservice rivalries — the Chairman of the Joint Chiefs and the Secretary of Defense.

But this "compromise," too, has its weaknesses. Added to the greatly expanded staff assistance provided to the Secretary of Defense by successive reorganizations of the military establishment since 1949, it increases civilian influence and diminishes that of military officers in top-level Defense Department decisionmaking. Military officials and others have complained that civilian amateurs are dabbling in the details of military management and "are making decisions without responsibility. That is, they safely and arrogantly propound various theories of strategy without having the responsibility of command." [7] Thus Secretary Robert McNamara's "tight ship" at the Pentagon has been dubbed by one noted military writer "the McNamara Monarchy." [8]

THE DEFENSE BUDGET

The defense budget is the principal "action-forcing paper" — to use Richard Neustadt's term — which compels the nation's chief policymakers to make strategic choices affecting national security. A decision is required, first, as to the share of national resources and government spending to be devoted to

[7] These are the views of former Air Force Chief of Staff Thomas D. White, as summarized by *The New York Times* correspondent Jack Raymond, *Power at the Pentagon* (New York: Harper, 1964), p. 289.

[8] Hanson Baldwin of *The New York Times,* quoted in *ibid.,* p. 280.

national defense. Second, within the limitations imposed by this decision, further choices must be made in apportioning these resources to a number of competing military programs. These choices, over the years, determine the state of the nation's defenses and its ability to pursue national goals which depend on military strength.

One possible approach to this series of decisions is to begin with a statement — presumably from the JCS — of what the nation's military requirements are. Even if the administration chooses, due to budgetary limitations, not to meet these requirements entirely, it would at least know precisely where and by how much it had fallen short.

Another approach is to determine first what the country can afford to spend on national defense — or, alternatively, how much defense spending the American people will support — and then to request that the JCS prepare strategic plans with these limitations in mind.

Each of these relatively simple and clear-cut approaches has appealed to some political leaders, civil servants, and commentators on military affairs since World War II. Unfortunately, both are unsound because both depend on key words which have no meaning or which mean different things to different people at different times.

The misleading words in the first approach are "military requirements." There is no such thing as a purely military requirement. Military capacity provides the *means* of achieving certain *ends*. Consequently, military requirements can be calculated only on the basis of explicit or implicit assumptions about national policy goals. Additional assumptions regarding the capability and probable intentions of other nations usually are involved also.

Certainly one national goal is avoiding a successful attack on United States territory. Since the military means for effective defense against such an attack do not exist, our estimates of the strength, intentions and attitudes of the strongest possible attacker (the Soviet Union) suggest that a large nuclear retaliatory force (a *deterrent* force) is the best military means of attaining this goal. But how great a retaliatory force will absolutely guarantee us against such an attack — that is, will fully meet our national defense requirements? Plainly, *no* retaliatory force, however great, could provide such a guarantee. We might fail to convince a potential opponent of our willingness to employ our power against him. Or he might refuse to believe our power was great enough to destroy him. Or he might simply be driven to irrational behavior under the stress of a seemingly intolerable political crisis.[9] Certainly Japan's attack on Pearl Harbor was not based on its leaders' conviction that their country was militarily capable of defeating the United States in an all-out struggle.

If absolute deterrence cannot be had — and if we do not wish to spend all our national resources beyond subsistence requirements for national defense — the question becomes not "how much must we spend to meet mili-

[9] Deterrence and related concepts are discussed in Chapter Eleven.

tary requirements?" but "how many alternative civilian and military goals are worth sacrificing in order to purchase successive increments of deterrence?"

One of the great debates on military policy in recent times has concerned the relative merits of the *massive retaliation* and *graduated deterrent* strategies. The latter requires that we be able to conduct several types of limited war in addition to all-out nuclear war. In this way, an opponent's initiative in any area could be met with the least violence necessary to prevent its success, leaving to our opponent the burden of deciding whether to *escalate* to a higher level of violence. Massive retaliation, on the other hand, calls for us to concentrate our resources on developing our nuclear retaliatory capacity. Then, we count on our threat that we might respond by using this devastating capacity to deter an opponent from making even limited or localized aggressive moves. (See Chapter Eleven.)

The advisability of adopting one or the other of these strategies cannot be determined on military grounds alone. If our only major *political* goal is defending American territory, the need for equipment with which to wage limited war is unlikely to warrant the expenditures required. If we have also the goal, however, of preventing native Communist parties from gaining power in countries far from our shores, being able to wreak nuclear destruction on the Soviet Union, or elsewhere, may not help us very much.

The misleading word in the second approach is "afford." In an all-out war, presumably we could "afford" to spend almost all of our national wealth — once the barest subsistence needs had been met — to escape subjugation or extinction. What we can "afford" obviously is predicated on how we evaluate the threat to ourselves and our nation. During both the Truman and Eisenhower administrations, military spending was strictly limited by assumptions as to what the nation could "afford." In fact, these spending limits represented a judgment, possibly implicit, that maintaining living standards should take precedence over increasing our nation's military power. There is nothing inherently wrong in such a calculation — *in fact, precisely such a calculation, explicit or implicit, must always be made at some point in preparing the national defense budget.* Where the line is drawn is the only point open to controversy.

What "the public will support" is little more concrete than what "the nation can afford." Samuel Huntington has shown that on a number of occasions since World War II public opinion polls have revealed a popular willingness to accept larger military expenditures than the government then was requesting. Yet administration officials were at the same time citing public opposition to military spending as a reason for reducing defense expenditures.[10] As we will see in a later chapter on public opinion, moreover, even a general public predisposition against arms spending might pos-

10 *The Common Defense, op. cit.,* pp. 234–251. Several of the main concepts discussed here are drawn from Huntington's book.

sibly be reversed by a President prepared to enlist his energies and prestige in an effort to do so.

If the size of the defense budget represents an explicit or implicit decision about the relative value to the nation of military uses of our resources, allocations *within* the defense budget similarly represent decisions about the relative contribution which competing military programs can make to achieving the nation's foreign policy goals. In this sense, the defense budget is not merely a fiscal document, but a basic strategy document. It fulfills its proper function when it makes these choices explicit rather than implicit — that is, when it clarifies the choices which must be made and their consequences.

The experience of our first Secretary of Defense, James V. Forrestal, offers a helpful illustration of how this can be done:

> From the start, Forrestal was faced with a presidential ceiling of $15 billion on the [1950] military budget. The President had established this on the advice of the Budget Bureau apparently without consulting either the JCS or the NSC. The uncoordinated original estimates of the three military services, on the other hand, totaled $30 billion. The task of the Secretary was to find the optimum balance of security and economy between these two extremes. . . . Forrestal constantly emphasized the relation between strategy and money. . . . A budget of $15 billion, . . . Forrestal eventually drew from the JCS, would only permit the United States to mount a strategic bombing offensive from Britain [in case of war]. Forrestal presented these alternatives to the President, but the latter appeared definite on the $15 billion ceiling. Nonetheless, Forrestal obtained tacit permission to go ahead along two lines: the $15 billion budget and another "intermediate" budget which would permit not only the air offensive from Britain, but which would also enable the United States to maintain control of the Mediterranean. The JCS estimated that this second strategy would require $16.9 billion. The alternatives in terms of dollars and policy were thus clear. When submitted to the President a few weeks before the budget was due to be presented to Congress, Truman again reaffirmed his decision in favor of the $15 billion, British air offensive choice. In one last effort, Forrestal then proposed that the President grant the military an additional $770 million so that they could add a half dozen more bomber groups. If the United States was to limit its capabilities to a strategic air offensive, he wanted to have sufficient air strength to insure success. The President still maintained a deaf ear, however, and in the end the Budget Bureau even reduced the budget somewhat below the $15 billion ceiling.
>
> The 1950 military budget was thus a case where a firm presidential ceiling was set and maintained. This did not, however, prevent Forrestal from functioning as a creative policy strategist. Both sides of the coin were constantly before him. An increase in the budget had to be justified in terms of its "functional" strategic gains. A decrease in the budget had

to be weighed in terms of its effect on American capabilities in the event of war. Every dollar had a strategic implication and justification.[11]

It is the job of the President and his top advisers to set the nation's foreign policy goals. But the authority to set goals is meaningless without the power to direct the nation's resources toward realizing these goals. It is less relevant to know how many tanks, planes, or ships the nation is purchasing than to know what *functional capabilities* our defense expenditures are creating. Thus, the information our policymakers need to make decisions about defense spending is not only how many missiles we can build or how many men we can keep under arms at a given price, but how great a capacity we can maintain — and at what cost — for, say, waging war in Vietnam under the conditions prevalent there in the 1960's.

Secretary of Defense Robert S. McNamara instituted an important advance in budgetary procedure in 1961 by replacing such traditional major budget categories as equipment procurement costs, operation and maintenance, and pay and allowances for military personnel, with new cross-service functional categories. The principal categories in the defense budget in the mid-1960's became: strategic retaliatory forces; continental air and missile defense forces; general purpose (limited war) forces; airlift/sealift forces; reserve and guard forces; research and development; general support (food, clothing, and shelter for the armed forces); retired pay; and military assistance. In addition, estimates in each of these categories, including dollar costs, are projected at least five years into the future to give the President, his advisers, and the Congress a clearer picture of the choices before them.

Thus, in the hands of McNamara and his Comptroller, Charles J. Hitch, budgeting procedures helped to avert decisions by compromise among rival armed service positions. Instead, the defense budget became a key policy instrument, opening the way for responsible civilian authorities to make rational choices among explicit alternative military strategies for achieving national goals.

CIVIL-MILITARY RELATIONS

The problem of civil-military relations involves much more than the relationship between policymakers in and out of uniform. It concerns as well the interplay between the political and military aspects of policy itself.

The limited nuclear test ban treaty of 1963 provides a *relatively* simple illustration. It commits the United States to refrain from conducting atmospheric nuclear weapons tests so long as the Soviet Union and other signatories do the same. (Underground tests are not covered by the treaty.) The Kennedy administration's willingness to undertake this commitment un-

11 Samuel P. Huntington, *The Soldier and the State* (New York: Vintage, 1964), pp. 445–446. Originally published by Harvard University Press in 1957 and reprinted by permission of Harvard University Press.

doubtedly rested in part on estimates of its military consequences. What would be the short-, middle-, and long-range results of foregoing further atmospheric nuclear testing on the relative development of the United States and Soviet nuclear arsenals? What military advantage would the Soviet Union gain if it should violate this treaty and thereby obtain more advanced scientific information than that possessed by the United States? Military and scientific estimates of this type would make it possible to reach a *military* judgment as to the net advantage or disadvantage to the United States of signing the test ban treaty.

But nonmilitary considerations were also significant. Might such a treaty mitigate Soviet-American hostility and contribute to the possibility that the two nations might reach further mutually advantageous agreements? Might American willingness to conclude such a treaty improve the image of the United States abroad? Would the slower development of nuclear weapons systems which might result save tax dollars for the United States; or, alternatively, might it cost more dollars to achieve continuing weapons development without atmospheric testing? How many lives might be saved and how much human suffering avoided by the reduction of nuclear fallout which the test ban would achieve? Would such a treaty help to slow the spread of nuclear weapons? Would it enhance or damage the President's domestic political prestige — and his freedom of action in foreign affairs?

These nonmilitary factors, in turn, are likely to have military implications — and vice versa. Thus, an improved United States image abroad might make it possible to establish a military base in a strategically located country which otherwise might not have allowed it. Or, if the Soviet Union were to gain a major military advantage over the United States by violating the treaty, nations particularly vulnerable to Soviet military power might defect from the Western alliance.

These calculations could be continued several "steps" further — by "translating" military into political consequences at one step, projecting the further military implications of these political developments at the next, and so on until our ability to project with reasonable accuracy gives out.

Now, if the traditional democratic principle of civilian supremacy is to be observed, the final step must be an assessment of the ultimate *political* consequences of the action being considered. In the end, military factors must be treated as instrumental, as having no intrinsic value apart from enabling us to achieve political goals set by democratically chosen civilian authorities.

When the decision as to whether the United States should participate in the test ban treaty was being considered, therefore, any military disadvantage the United States might incur by participating should have been weighed solely according to its political consequences. The ultimate criterion should be whether, in the long run, United States participation in the test ban treaty would or would not bring our nation closer to its political (societal) objectives (for example — national survival; world peace; individual self-realization; increasing material prosperity; cultural excellence, etc.).

Thus, to speak of "purely military considerations," divorced from explicit or implicit political goals, is to speak nonsense. Is it militarily essential that Communist control of West Berlin (Taiwan, the Dominican Republic, Vietnam, Quemoy, etc.) be avoided? This question has no meaning. To ask it of a military officer is to invite — even require — him to make at least implicit assumptions as to what our political objectives should be. Military power is an instrument for achieving political goals. Its adequacy therefore cannot be determined without referring to those goals, and to the relative priorities we assign to them. What we should ask, rather, is: How would Communist control of West Berlin affect our ability to achieve our societal goals? (Notice that formulating the question in this way compels us to take into account the direct non-military — as well as the military — consequences of losing West Berlin.)

These observations apply equally whether the nation is at war, at peace, or in some twilight zone between them, and conflict with the traditional American penchant, discussed in Chapter Two, for viewing war and peace as fundamentally different states, each with its own logic and goals.

The relationship between civilian and military *officials* is only a special case of this more general problem of the relationship between civilian and military *values and goals*. (In another sense, it is a special case, also, of the problem of relations between the specialist and the layman, discussed in Chapter Seven.) Civilian supremacy requires that decisions affecting national security be made by responsible civilian authorities aided by competent professional advice on military questions. Thus, the final power to set societal goals and weigh alternative means of attaining them should rest in civilian hands, and the influence of military advisers should be limited to matters in which they have special professional competence. If the Air Force Chief of Staff were to advise that the nation should adopt a massive retaliation strategy because the costs of maintaining a graduated deterrent would bring about economic collapse, for example, he would be violating the principle of civilian supremacy. (What special competence has an air force general for deciding under what conditions a depression is likely?)

The other side of the coin is that relying on civilian advice on tactical military questions is similarly inappropriate. It is the general rather than the Secretary of State who should prevail about, say, whether Quemoy could be held without bombing mainland China in case of an all-out Communist Chinese invasion attempt. This professional military advice might then lead directly to a decision to bomb the mainland if Quemoy is attacked, or to allow the Chinese Communists to take over the island. But *this* decision should be made by responsible *civilian* authorities, after they have considered fully its probable nonmilitary (as well as military) consequences.

The lack of an appropriate relationship between military and civilian officials in foreign policymaking is likely to prove severely detrimental to national security. If military officers fail to accept, without public dissent, the policy decisions made by civilian authorities, or if they fail to carry out these decisions to the best of their abilities, wasted effort and internal squabbling, at the least, will probably result. It may become very difficult to communicate American purposes accurately to adversaries, allies, and our own citizenry; and the costs of this failure in American lives and resources, and in our ability to achieve political goals, may be high.

More frequent than conflict due to direct clashes on policy is the simple failure to keep civilian and military advisers from overstepping the boundaries of their professional competence. Yet when nonmilitary choices are left to the generals, instead of to those who *do* have special competence in these fields, the advantages of professional expertise are lost. The converse, of course, is also true.

It has sometimes been suggested that military men are poorly equipped to make diplomatic and political choices precisely because of their military training and experience. War, so the argument goes, puts a premium on force, on neat and total solutions, on forms of social organization founded on hierarchic obedience and subordinating the individual to the group. The arts of democratic politics and diplomacy, on the contrary, demand avoidance of force, willingness to compromise and to live with partial solutions, and forms of social organization built on voluntary cooperation and personal autonomy. To the extent that this argument is true, there are few dangers greater than allowing essentially political choices to be made by military men.

Unfortunately, military leaders' attitudes toward foreign policy have not been studied sufficiently to substantiate or refute this appealingly plausible line of reasoning. Morris Janowitz, however, provides some useful clues.[12] He finds that compared with the United States white population as a whole, a disproportionate number of military leaders are native-born (and born of native parents and grandparents), from rural areas or small towns, Protestant (especially Episcopalian), of southern origin, and — except in the Air Force — of upper middle-class upbringing.[13] (These tendencies have been reduced

12 *The Professional Soldier* (Glencoe, Ill.: The Free Press, 1960). The findings cited in this paragraph are from chaps. 5 and 12. This study is based in part on: (1) analysis of biographical data on military officers; (2) responses of more than 500 officers to self-administered questionnaires; and (3) intensive interviews with 113 high-ranking officers selected on the basis of their potential for future promotion.

See also William H. Honon, "Meet the Generals (Yes, Sir!)," *The New York Times Magazine,* December 18, 1966, pp. 42–58.

13 The foreign policy approaches characteristic of these and other socio-economic groupings in the American population are reviewed in Chapter Seven. The backgrounds of West Point cadets in recent years, however, have been much more representative of the teen aged population of the United States as a whole. Negroes and Jews are still under-represented, but Catholics, urban residents, and Northerners are not. See John P. Lovell, "The Professional Socialization of the West Point Cadet," in Morris Janowitz (ed.), *The*

since World War II, but they have not been eliminated.) A strikingly large percentage — particularly considering their high educational level — regard themselves as conservatives in *domestic* politics.

Janowitz also comments that military educational institutions — the service academies and the specialized training and war colleges — overemphasize the utility of force and fail to give the officer a sound comprehension of "the realities of practical politics." He cites a small-scale preliminary study which gives some indication that, in risk situations, military men are more likely to "go for broke" — to select "high payoff, low probability solution[s] than comparable civilian groups." [14] Other studies, concerned with the attitudes of American college students, suggest that West Point cadets are more likely than students at most other colleges to accept traditional, ethnocentric, and authoritarian statements — but at the same time to reject all kinds of stereotypes, regardless of content.[15]

It is Janowitz's conviction that the thinking of American military officers is characterized in general by one of two military-political orientations:

> One school of thought, the "absolute," is a direct outgrowth of the frontier and punitive expedition tradition. Warfare — actual or threatened — is the most fundamental basis of international relations. Since the political objectives of war are gained by victory, the more complete the victory, the greater the possibility of achieving political goals. In short, there is no substitute for "total victory." Contrariwise, the other is the "pragmatic" school. Warfare is but one instrument of international relations, along with ideological and economic struggle. The political objectives of warfare are gained by adapting the use or threat of violence to the objectives achieved. To use too little or too much is self defeating.
>
> . . . The "absolutists" assume the end as given — total victory; the means must be adjusted in order to achieve it. The "pragmatists" are concerned not only with adapting military means to achieve desired political ends, but insist that the end must be conditioned by what military technology is capable of achieving. In short, some ends cannot be achieved.[16]

Among the officers interviewed for this study, "absolutists" were more likely than "pragmatists" to believe nuclear war inevitable. Nevertheless, almost two-thirds of those interviewed thought that nuclear war was *not* inevitable — although almost all these officers took the likelihood of limited

---

New Military (Science ed.; New York: Wiley, 1967), pp. 119–157. Originally published by the Russel Sage Foundation in 1964.

[14] *Ibid.*, pp. 226 and 429.

[15] George G. Stern, Morris I. Stein, and Benjamin S. Bloom, *Methods in Personality Assessment* (Glencoe, Ill.: The Free Press, 1956), chap. 10. Cited in Philip E. Jacob, *Changing Values in College* (New York: Harper, 1957), pp. 100–102.

[16] Janowitz, pp. 264–265.

wars for granted. Both groups, Janowitz believes, overemphasize military factors and the utility of force in international relations.[17]

Oddly enough, in addition to risking overemphasis upon forcible and clear-cut solutions, excessive military participation in foreign policymaking may result in a sacrifice of *military* as well as of civilian professional expertise. Samuel Huntington has argued persuasively that when military officers are asked to make political judgments, they are in effect being invited or required to abandon their role as spokesmen for military viewpoints in an effort to achieve a higher synthesis. But if those who represent the military fail to bring relevant military perspectives into the foreign policy process, who will? Perhaps civilian officials will — though most likely in a fashion reflecting their lack of expertise in military affairs. Or perhaps nobody will. If the nation's top military men are regularly called upon to make political assessments, moreover, we should not be surprised if men are selected for the highest military positions on the basis of their political skills — or even their political opinions — rather than their professional military competence. The resulting policy decisions in any case, are likely to be based at least in part on the military judgments of civilians and the political judgments of generals — scarcely an ideal system for promoting foreign policy decisions of high quality.[18]

Given the dangers of an inappropriate role for the military in foreign policymaking, the question that remains is how these unhappy consequences can best be avoided. This subject is too complex to be dealt with in detail here,[19] but a few general guidelines may be helpful.

1. *Clear statements of political goals and assumptions by civilian authorities minimize the temptation for military advisers to supply their own — often implicit — goals and assumptions.* Making such statements, however, requires a high order of political courage and leadership. For ours is a country accustomed to achieving consensus by keeping political goals and assumptions vague enough to mean different things to men of differing outlooks.

2. *The organizational framework within which foreign policy decisions are made can aid or hinder the achievement of a proper role for the military.* If the key policymaking units include no one competent to give professional military advice, relevant military considerations may be ignored. More likely, they will be taken into account in consultations with military advisers ex-

---

[17] *Ibid.*, pp. 266–267, 275, and 429. When the strategic perspectives of students at West Point and Dartmouth were surveyed, a much higher proportion of both freshman and senior West Point cadets gave "absolutistic" responses. Lovell, *op. cit.*, pp. 128–130.

[18] Huntington, *The Soldier and the State, op. cit.*, chaps. 3 and 13.

[19] This question is dealt with at length in Huntington, *The Soldier and the State* — especially chaps. 7, 13, 14, and 16; and in Burton M. Sapin and Richard C. Snyder, *The Role of the Military in American Foreign Policy* (Garden City, N.Y.: Doubleday, 1954). The analysis presented in the pages following owes much to these two works.

cluded from top-level discussions and therefore less than fully aware of political considerations.

A preponderance of military officials in the top policymaking units, on the other hand, may give undue weight to military points of view. Thus, during World War II, President Roosevelt's tendency to exclude Secretary of State Hull from top policy conferences, while including the nation's top military officers, may have resulted in (or reflected?) an overemphasis on military goals at the expense of political ones. Robert Murphy has written:

> Despite Eisenhower's conviction that military commanders should not usurp civilian functions, he and his staff were required during the final months of the war to make a number of political decisions which have had lasting international consequences. These decisions were imposed upon the Supreme Commander because the civilians responsible for American foreign policy — the President and the Secretary of State — did not choose to assert their authority. The most important example was the decision not to try to capture Berlin, a decision of such international significance that no Army chief should have been required to make it. . . . General Marshall, as Chief of Staff, and General Eisenhower as Theater Commander . . . accepted this responsibility without complaint . . . but it was inevitable that they would regard Berlin from the military point of view.[20]

After the war, military commanders were assigned important political responsibilities as the military governors of occupied nations and territories — including Japan and the United States zone of Germany. And including the three service secretaries, in addition to the Secretary of Defense, in the National Security Council from 1947 to 1949 seriously overrepresented the military establishment — but not the military *profession* — in that body. Since 1949, changes in the structure of the NSC and the Defense Department — discussed above and in Chapter Four — have corrected this imbalance and enabled the Secretary of Defense to exercise more effective civilian control over the military. (Some would say, in fact, that the Secretary's position has been strengthened too much.)

The dual role of the Joint Chiefs of Staff remains a weakness in the present structure, as noted previously. A President or a Secretary of State or of Defense who has no alternative but to accept the professional judgments of the service chiefs on faith is at a grave disadvantage. Access to independent sources of military expertise would enable them to ask more searching questions on strategic matters and help them to prod their military advisers to devise additional tactical alternatives capable of achieving civilian policy objectives at prescribed cost and risk.

And such access would work in two ways. It would also assure competent

[20] *Diplomat Among Warriors* (Pyramid edition; Garden City, N.Y.: Doubleday, 1964), *op. cit.*, p. 257.

military men, unrestricted by parochial attachments, of the opportunity to bring their professional opinions regularly to the attention of the Secretary of Defense and the President. It would be of great value, therefore, to establish a council of senior military advisers, without operating responsibilities, that would provide professional military advice to these officials directly, upon their request. This need not prevent the operating chiefs from retaining direct access to the Secretary and the President as well, or from providing advice that only an operating chief can give. In any event, men with experience as operating service chiefs normally would be logical candidates for such a council.[21]

Nevertheless, no structural arrangements, however sound, can guarantee satisfactory civil-military relations. Too much depends on the quality and attitudes of the human beings concerned for machinery alone to do the job.

3. *Broader educational emphases in both the service academies and the war colleges — with special attention to the nonmilitary aspects of international politics — would be helpful in developing within the military officer corps attitudes and outlooks conducive to appropriate civil-military relations.* Equally, a better acquaintance with military affairs on the part of civilian foreign policymaking officials would aid them in using military advice effectively and properly. Interchanging diplomatic and military officer personnel, where feasible, would help on both counts. So would expanded opportunities for diplomats to receive war college training and for military officers to receive advanced training at private and governmental civilian educational institutions.

4. *Maintaining a proper role for the military in foreign policymaking requires that military officers on active duty avoid political involvement.* This calls for restraint on the part of both military and political officials. The military officer must loyally carry out directives issued by his civilian commanders regardless of whether or not he agrees with the political goals they are designed to forward. When they call for what he believes to be unsound military strategy or tactics, he is entitled, and even obliged, to press his views through the appropriate channels until overruled. In the end, however, he must obey the orders issued to him. Nor is it enough that he carry out the letter of his orders while violating their spirit. He is not at liberty

---

21 General Gavin and General Maxwell Taylor, who served as Army Chief of Staff from 1955 to 1959 — and later as Chairman of the JCS under President Kennedy, have suggested reorganizations which would separate operational command from the function of providing top-level military advice to the Secretary of Defense and the President. Gavin proposes appointing the service chiefs, after their tours of duty, to a Senior Military Advisory Group charged with advising the Secretary of Defense. *Op. cit.*, pp. 261–262. Taylor suggests a single Defense Chief of Staff, aided by two deputy chiefs of staff from the services other than his own; and a Supreme Military Council, consisting of four-star generals from each service, either retired or on their last tour of duty, to provide staff advice to the President, the Secretary of Defense, and the Congress. *The Uncertain Trumpet* (New York: Harper, 1960), pp. 175–177.

to promote the political goals *he* believes in at the expense of those which responsible civilian authorities have set.

When he disagrees with the directives issued to him, or with any national policy, the military officer is entitled to have his say only privately, within the executive branch. If he cannot refrain from seeking to change established policy by applying political pressure against his civilian superiors, he should resign from active service. This applies to public speeches, "leaks" to the press, and representations to members of Congress. The latter restriction, however, is mitigated by his obligations to a co-equal branch of the government with important foreign affairs responsibilities of its own. *Upon its request,* Congress is entitled to the best professional advice on the *military* aspects of policy which he is capable of giving it — even when this advice conflicts with established administration positions.

It is not easy for the military officer to draw the fine line between fulfilling this obligation to Congress and maintaining his loyalty to his political chiefs. Executive officials oversensitive to criticism and congressional hunters after political issues can make his position close to untenable. As General Taylor has remarked:

> No sooner has he [a Chief of Staff] read his prepared statement supporting the position of the Department of Defense [to a congressional committee] than he must face a battery of interrogators bent upon bringing forth his original views and contrasting them with the ultimate position of the Secretary of Defense and of the President. Very shortly a Chief of Staff will find himself in the position either of appearing to oppose his civilian superiors or of withholding facts from the Congress. Personally, I have found no way of coping with the situation other than by replying frankly to questions and letting the chips fall where they may.[22]

Inevitably, the constitutional separation of powers sometimes raises the question of which of the two masters the officer owes his loyalty to.[23] Nevertheless, it is important to his country's security that he try to furnish the professional judgments asked of him without directly questioning the judgment of his civilian superiors in the executive branch. What others may infer from the expert military opinions he has provided cannot be helped. Still, the tone of his presentation may be more important than its literal content.

When his responsibilities as a military leader require him to arrange for the indoctrination of the men under his command, the officer must avoid the temptation to insert his own opinions or biases on nonmilitary — and especially partisan political — issues: again a basic principle of democracy is in-

[22] *Op. cit.,* pp. 112–113.
[23] See Huntington, *The Soldier and the State,* chaps. 7 and 15.

volved. Moreover, if troop indoctrination programs go beyond the needs of maintaining discipline and morale to encompass political — and even partisan — issues, it may be difficult for civilian political officials, in the long run, to resist the temptation to exercise their ultimate control of the military establishment to further their own political goals.

Our highest military leaders, in order to observe these restrictions, must subject themselves to a great deal of restraint and self-discipline. Yet the very sense of duty and loyalty which may enable them to meet this challenge may lead them astray in another direction. For military leaders can be involved in politics in *support* of administration policies as well as in opposition to them. And it will not be easy for them to resist pressures from the President and Secretary of Defense to speak out in support of administration foreign policy to Congress and the American people. Here it is the turn of our top political officials to exercise self-discipline and restraint to maintain proper civil-military relations.

These political prohibitions, though paid lip service, have been transgressed frequently since World War II. In 1967, President Johnson called General William Westmoreland home from his combat command in Vietnam to address the Congress and to help counter rising criticism of the United States involvement in Vietnam. The Truman administration used the prestige of military officers extensively to secure public and congressional support for its foreign policy proposals — including foreign aid requests and sending American troops to Europe. Some of these officers were appointed to high civilian positions, but others were engaged in this sort of political activity while still on active service. In fact, as one of the case studies in Chapter Three suggests, the prestige of men such as General Marshall seems to have been indispensable to some of the Truman administration's most impressive foreign policy achievements.

One result was that some military leaders became embroiled in political controversy. General Marshall became one of Senator Joseph McCarthy's favorite targets, and Senate Republican leader Robert A. Taft was moved to declare publicly in April, 1951, that he no longer respected the political neutrality of the JCS. If he were elected President, he added, he would replace General Omar Bradley as chairman. Later, the Eisenhower administration was to appoint an entirely new set of Joint Chiefs within months after it assumed office.

The risks generated by inappropriate civil-military relations are considerable, yet they are not the only dangers the nation may face. The Truman administration was confronted with the need to educate the American people to new responsibilities in world affairs. It had inherited the problems created by a great war; and Franklin Roosevelt's death had elevated to the Presidency a man without the prestige which war leadership often confers. The new administration chose — consciously or not — to bridge the gap by drawing upon the prestige which the war had conferred on outstanding military leaders. Whether the benefits of this action were great enough to warrant involving military officers in partisan controversy — and whether alternative actions might have served the same purpose at less cost — must be left for the historians of the future to debate.

❦ CASE
STUDY   *THE KOREAN WAR AND*
         GENERAL MACARTHUR'S DISMISSAL

When Soviet-armed North Korean troops swept across the thirty-eighth parallel — the boundary dividing North from South Korea — at 5:50 A.M. on June 25, 1950, many Americans believed that a third world war had begun. At the time, most informed Western observers viewed the invasion as a Communist probe of American willingness to tolerate aggression. In retrospect, however, it seems more likely that the Communists were attempting to unify Korea by force because they felt confident that there would be no effective Western response.

The United States was militarily unprepared and politically preoccupied with Europe when the attack came. Korea was a remote peninsula of minimal strategic importance which few Americans could have located on a map. In defining the American "defense perimeter" in the Pacific only six month earlier, Secretary of State Dean Acheson had omitted Korea; in case of attack, he had implied, its government would have to rely upon the United Nations for support.

But if the United States was unwilling to meet an invasion of South Korea with force, what could the United Nations do? Never yet had it undertaken collective military action against aggression. Had the Soviet Union expected it to do so in June, 1950, it might have ordered the return to the Security Council of its delegate, Jacob Malik, who had been boycotting the United Nations since its refusal to seat Communist China in January. Malik then could have vetoed any proposed military action and, at the least, forced the calling of a special session of the 59-nation General Assembly to debate and deal with the Korean problem. But, although specifically invited by United Nations Secretary General Trygve Lie to attend the Security Council's deliberations on Korea, Malik did not do so until a month later. The Kremlin had probably anticipated pious resolutions from the United Nations, but no effective military action in time to prevent the rapid takeover of all Korea by the vastly superior North Korean forces.

If this was how the Communist high command reasoned, it had miscalculated. The Government of the Republic of Korea, having been sponsored by the United States and elected under the supervision of the United Nations, had a special claim to the support of both. Communist forces had moved across a well-defined boundary. United Nations observers were on the spot, and their reports left no reasonable doubt what had happened. If South Korea fell, the United Nations' inability and the United States' unwillingness to protect small nations against communist attack would be all too clear. Moscow might be tempted to initiate other military probes in parts of the world less accessible to American air and naval forces than the Korean peninsula, bordering United States occupied Japan. Specters of Manchuria and Ethiopia and Munich haunted the minds of American policymakers.

On the positive side, Malik's fortuitous absence from the Security Council made it possible for United States action to be buttressed immediately by the moral and political support of the United Nations and most of the non-Communist world. (Eventually, fifteen other nations responded to the Security Council's recommendations with contributions of at least token military forces to the "U.N. Command" in Korea.) There was some risk of Soviet intervention, of course, but the Soviet Union had not associated itself openly with the North Korean invasion. If the United Nations moved with proper care, this risk could be minimized. It was thought at first, moreover, that United States naval and air support alone might enable South Korea to repulse the Communist assault. This support was provided, in Secretary Acheson's words, "solely for the purpose of restoring the Republic of Korea to its status prior to the invasion from the north. . . ." In addition, the Seventh Fleet was ordered to prevent a Communist takeover of Taiwan. Within the week the need for United States ground forces became clear, and these too were committed. The strength of the Communist offensive was greater than anticipated.

Pushed back to a small area around Pusan early in September, United Nations Command and South Korean forces under General Douglas MacArthur soon turned the tide with a brilliantly executed amphibious landing at Inchon on September 15. By the end of the month, Washington had to decide whether to halt at the thirty-eighth parallel, with its proclaimed goal achieved, or to attempt to unify Korea by carrying operations north of that line.

Thus far, the Korean War had proved a distinct political asset for the Truman administration. Gallup polls showed more than 80 per cent of the public approving the United States intervention there. Long-needed rearmament measures were speedily enacted by Congress. The economy was booming. Criticism of the administration for "softness toward communism" was blunted. The Soviet Union, like the United Nations, had carefully avoided widening the war.

But the policymakers were in some measure prisoners of their own success. South Korean President Syngman Rhee, General MacArthur, and influential congressional leaders were all forceful advocates of seizing what seemed a golden opportunity to accomplish the unification of Korea. Halting at the thirty-eighth parallel — not a sound military defense line in any event — would renew the administration's vulnerability to charges of "appeasement." And there was no assurance that the North Korean forces, once permitted to regroup, would refrain from recrossing the parallel in the future.

Premier Chou En-lai was threatening that Communist China would intervene if United States forces drove on into North Korea, but this might well be a brazen bluff. General MacArthur thought Chinese intervention unlikely. If it did come, he ventured, United Nations troops should be able to cope with it readily. The Central Intelligence Agency, according to Allen Dulles (then not yet its Director), estimated "that it was a tossup, but they leaned to the side that under certain circumstances the Chinese would probably not intervene." [24] The administration decided to change its objective. After allied support was lined up, MacArthur was authorized to advance across the parallel so long as no major Russian or Chinese force was sighted.

The next move was up to Mao Tse-tung and his cohorts in Peking. The completion of their victory in the Chinese civil war was being blocked by the United States Seventh Fleet's vigil in the Formosa Straits; now an American armed force was advancing along a traditional invasion route toward the frontier of Manchuria, the most industrialized region of China; in recent months, several American military and political leaders had made highly belligerent statements, some even calling for all-out preventive war against communism. Might these not be a more accurate indication of American intent than the bland reassurances from official quarters in Washington? In any event, the establishment of a militantly anti-Communist regime directly on China's border could not but impair the new Peking regime's prestige and jeopardize China's national security. Perhaps, too, Moscow was urging Chinese intervention. Whatever the reasons — and we can only guess at them — Chinese Communist troops began crossing the Yalu into Korea on October 15, 1950.[25] By the end of November the United Nations was engaged, in General MacArthur's words, in "an entirely new war."

On the battlefield, United Nations troops, deployed by MacArthur into two widely separated columns, were staggered by a massive new Communist offensive. Not until the following March were they able to fight their way back to the thirty-eighth parallel. Meanwhile, strong pressure from the United States induced the United Nations General Assembly to declare Communist China an aggressor. At home and at General MacArthur's headquarters in Tokyo, frustration mounted. MacArthur began to advocate openly a more militant policy than Washington was willing to pursue. To bring Peking to terms, he called for the

24 Allen W. Dulles, *The Craft of Intelligence* (Signet ed., New York: Harper and Row, 1963), p. 155.

25 On Peking's decision to intervene, see Allen S. Whiting, *China Crosses The Yalu* (New York: Macmillan, 1960).

bombing of Chinese bases in Manchuria,[26] a naval blockade and economic embargo of the China mainland, and the use of Chinese Nationalist forces both in Korea and in a direct invasion of South China by
Chiang K'ai-shek.

As the General later asserted in an address to the Congress (on April
19, 1951):

> I know war as few other men now living know it, and nothing to
> me is more revolting. I have long advocated its complete abolition as
> its very destructiveness on both friend and foe has rendered it useless
> as a means of settling international disputes. . . .
>
> But once war is forced upon us, there is no other alternative than
> to apply every available means to bring it to a swift end. War's very
> object is victory — not prolonged indecision. In war indeed, there
> can be no substitute for victory.
>
> There are some who for varying reasons would appease Red China.
> They are blind to history's clear lesson. For history teaches with un-
> mistakable emphasis that appeasement but begets new and bloodier
> war. It points to no single instance where the end has justified that
> means — where appeasement has led to more than a sham peace. Like
> blackmail, it lays the basis for new and successively greater alterna-
> tives. Why, my soldiers asked of me, surrender military advantages
> to an enemy in the field? I could not answer. Some may say to avoid
> spread of the conflict into an all-out war with China; others, to avoid
> Soviet intervention. Neither explanation seems valid. For China is
> already engaging with the maximum power it can commit and the
> Soviet will not necessarily mesh its actions with our moves. Like a
> cobra, any new enemy will more likely strike whenever it feels that the
> relativity in military or other potential is in its favor on a world-wide
> basis.

But the administration feared that following MacArthur's suggestions
might precipitate a third world war. At the least, it might lead our opponents to forego some of the limitations on *their* freedom of action
which they had tacitly accepted until now: they might stage all-out
bombing attacks on United States bases in South Korea or even launch
air attacks against United States bases in nearby Japan. In either event,
the United States would find itself involved, as General Omar Bradley
said, "in the wrong war, at the wrong time, in the wrong place, and with
the wrong enemy." The cost of again underestimating Chinese Communist determination to prevent the military defeat of North Korea
would be high.

Some months later, the assumptions underlying the respective out-

26 By the end of 1952, at least, MacArthur was advocating the use of
atomic bombs against North Korean military targets if our opponents would
not end the war on our terms. See Douglas MacArthur, *Reminiscences* (New
York: McGraw-Hill, 1964), p. 467.

looks of the General and his opponents were illuminated in an exchange between MacArthur and Senator J. William Fulbright:

> SENATOR FULBRIGHT. One of the things that seems to be very important to your case and one which has been alluded to but not developed, is why, in view of the difficulties the Japanese had over a period of 13 years in subduing the Chinese, just why you feel that we could with very few additional troops, and additional air power, subdue the Chinese? That is, subdue them to the extent at least that they would give up and come to terms.
>
> I am very interested as to why you think that could be done in view of the fact that the Japanese had a very fine military establishment. I believe it was much greater than the one we have; was it not?
>
> GENERAL MACARTHUR. The objective of the Japanese in China was to seize and exploit the entire country — a very large order. Our objective in the Korean campaign is a very limited one, indeed. It merely is to put sufficient pressure on the Chinese that they would withdraw their troops and cease their depredations in the area of North Korea. It is only a small fraction of what the Japanese Empire was attempting to do in China.
>
> SENATOR FULBRIGHT. Well, I can understand that, but the Chinese have proved themselves to be a very stubborn people. I would assume if you undertake such a project that you would have to do whatever it takes to accomplish it. You are not going to undertake the project and not go through with it. It would seem to me, as long as the whole country is not subdued, as long as there is a Communist group somewhere in China that is not subdued, they will still be able to furnish some opposition to you. However small it may be, they can still mount some kind of an offensive.
>
> That point bothers me more than any other one. Being such a large country and having been so difficult for a highly mechanized army to subdue, I do not see how we could do it. As I understand, the Japanese had airplanes, had good airplanes; they had complete freedom and domination of the air, and yet in approximately 13 years, maybe 15, they were not able to subdue it.
>
> I was wondering if the very primitive character of the Chinese is not in this case perhaps of great defensive value, to them. You cannot get at them to destroy them as you could if it was highly industrialized. Perhaps it is that while they have no offensive power beyond their immediate periphery, at the same time they are extremely difficult to destroy because their power is not concentrated.
>
> GENERAL MACARTHUR. You only have to destroy, Senator, their potentiality to maintain an army on foreign soil in North Korea. When you destroy their power to build the guns, the munitions, to supply the food for an aggressive army that way, they will have to cease utilizing that aggressive army. . . .

Now, the whole process of modern war depends upon the logistical potential of supplying your troops, feeding them, giving them the necessary munitions, all of the intricate paraphernalia that modern armies have to use on the battlefield. The capacity of China along those lines is very limited.

It is a country of poverty. The slightest dislocation in their normal processes of distribution causes the greatest convulsions in various sections of Chinese society.

If you, for instance, disturb or should disturb in the slightest degree the distributive systems of their food, you might well have 50,000,000 men, 50,000,000 people, starving at any one time.

They live only a couple of jumps ahead of starvation. In other materials, they are almost as bad. They have practically no indigenous products that they can manufacture; they have no great manufacturing centers whatsoever.

They are peculiarly vulnerable to the process of blockade, and the process of internal disruption by bombing.

The minute you apply those factors, it becomes logistically more difficult, probably impossible, for them to maintain a foreign army on the march.

It is different from the problem of Japan as day is from night. The problem of Japan was to occupy that enormous country of China, to administer it, to govern it; to do that, they have to put in a million normal administrative processes.

We do not contemplate anything of the sort. All I contemplate and hope for is to disrupt the capacity of that industrially weak nation to supply the sinews of war to their armies in Korea and, therefore, make them stop this savage slaughter of our troops.[27]

Whatever the relative merits of the courses of action favored by MacArthur and Truman, the latter had come to believe that MacArthur's public statements posed a challenge to the President's constitutional authority over his military field commanders which could no longer be ignored. On April 11, 1951, therefore, he dismissed General MacArthur from his commands.[28] A bitter — and often partisan — political controversy was launched.

Public response to MacArthur's dismissal was awesome. Both the flood of letters and telegrams to the President and the Congress, and the crowds arrayed to greet the General in a number of American cities, were wholly unprecedented. Overwhelmingly the public favored MacArthur. Public opinion polls showed majorities of better than two to one approving the General's recommendations for Korea and opposing

[27] United States Senate Committees on Armed Services and Foreign Relations, *Hearings into the Military Situation in the Far East.* 82nd Cong., 1st sess., 1951, pp. 135–137. Hereafter cited as *Hearings.*

[28] The United Nations had authorized President Truman to designate a Commander of all United Nations forces in Korea, early in the war. Truman had named MacArthur.

his dismissal. President Truman's popularity, as reflected in the polls, dropped to 24 per cent — very close to an all-time low for any chief executive in the age of the public opinion poll (that is, from Franklin Roosevelt through Lyndon Johnson). For the first time since Herbert Hoover's term of office, Opening Day crowds booed a President's traditional appearance at the ball park to throw out the first ball of the new baseball season.

Soon after a joint meeting of Congress had enthusiastically received MacArthur's nationally televised and broadcast address to it, comprehensive hearings were begun by the Senate Committees on Armed Services and Foreign Relations into the issues and circumstances surrounding his dismissal. These hearings extended through most of two months, producing in all more than 3,600 printed pages of testimony and documents.

While these hearings were still in progress, American willingness to accept a Korean settlement based on the restoration of the prewar boundary line was quietly made known. On June 23, 1951, Soviet United Nations delegate Jacob Malik suggested in a radio address that a ceasefire arrangement on this basis might be acceptable to the Communists also. Within a month, negotiations toward an armistice were initiated.

In October, the United Nations' insistence that the cease-fire line follow the actual battle line, rather than the thirty-eighth parallel itself, was accepted. By May, 1952, agreement had been reached on all major issues except the exchange of prisoners of war. Relatively early in the negotiations, the United Nations Command had taken a stand against the forcible repatriation of prisoners. Not until months later did a preliminary screening reveal — to the surprise of both sides — that well over a third of those held by the United Nations would resist repatriation. Acceptance of the "no forcible repatriation" principle would therefore have caused the Communists considerable embarrassment. Thus an impasse was created until, fifteen months later, an intricate "face-saving" compromise was reached, based essentially on the United Nations position.

Meanwhile, the hands on the reins of power had changed in both Moscow and Washington. Joseph Stalin's death was announced to the world on March 5, 1953, soon after Dwight D. Eisenhower assumed the Presidency of the United States. In May, the new Secretary of State, John Foster Dulles, told Prime Minister Nehru of India that, if a Korean truce was not arranged soon, Manchuria might be bombed and tactical atomic weapons used in Korea itself. This threat was undoubtedly communicated — as intended — to Moscow and Peking. Whether or not it influenced subsequent Communist actions significantly we do not know. Whatever the reasons, an armistice was finally signed on July 27, 1953, two years and seventeen days after the opening of negotiations.

Privately, Democratic Congressmen commented that the Truman

administration would have been charged with "appeasement" if it had concluded a truce on the same terms. As it was, Republican Senate leaders opposed the truce within White House councils. But the Eisenhower administration, with a fresh mandate from the voters, was not so vulnerable on this score as its predecessor, and its view prevailed. A trying chapter in American history had ended.

The dialogue which follows is taken from the *Hearings* of the Senate Armed Services and Foreign Relations Committees referred to above. The witnesses quoted are General George C. Marshall, then Secretary of Defense, and previously Army Chief of Staff and Secretary of State; and General MacArthur, himself a former Chief of Staff of the Army.

1. Do you believe General MacArthur's actions warranted his relief from command? Why or why not?

2. Do you agree with General Marshall's or with General MacArthur's view of an officer's responsibilities when faced with orders he believes detrimental to the safety of the nation he has sworn to defend? Why? What of the officer ordered — as some in Nazi Germany were — to act counter to international law and his own moral principles? Should "war crimes" tribunals such as those set up by the allies at Nuremberg generally accept pleas of "superior orders" as releasing military men from personal responsibility for their official actions?

3. What about the officer's responsibility, in a government of divided powers, to provide advice and information to Congress — do you believe General MacArthur's letter to Congressman Martin was a proper or improper exercise of this responsibility? On what criteria do you base this judgment?

4. Were MacArthur's differences with the administration grounded primarily in political or in military judgments?

5. How much did the *roles* of the key participants — as field commander, chief of staff, Secretary of Defense, President, etc. — seem to affect their views in this controversy? Do you think Marshall and MacArthur would have seen things differently had their positions been reversed? Why or why not?

6. What are your views of the substantive issues involved? Do you believe that the Korean War could have been shortened by adopting all or part of the program advocated by General MacArthur? If so, at what cost and risk? Do you believe that the course of action advised by MacArthur, or that adopted by the administration, was wiser? Why?

7. Assume that MacArthur was right and the administration wrong on the substantive issues and that these issues were critical to the future security of the United States (as MacArthur undoubtedly believed). Would this in any way change your view as to whether the President was right in relieving MacArthur of his commands? As to whether General MacArthur was right in acting as he did, even at the risk of being deprived of his commands? Why or why not? If you had been in

MacArthur's place, believing as he believed, how would you have acted? Why?

8. Would the United States benefit more as a nation from having most of its military officers act in such situations as MacArthur did, or as Marshall advocated? Defend your position.

SENATE ARMED SERVICES AND
FOREIGN RELATIONS COMMITTEES

SECRETARY OF DEFENSE GEORGE C. MARSHALL. From the very beginning of the Korean conflict, down to the present moment, there has been no dis-agreement between the President, the Secretary of Defense, and the Joint Chiefs of Staff that I am aware of.

There have been, however, and continue to be basic differences of judg-ment between General MacArthur, on the one hand, and the President, the Secretary of Defense, and the Joint Chiefs of Staff, on the other hand. . . .

Our objective in Korea continues to be the defeat of the aggression and the restoration of peace. We have persistently sought to confine the conflict to Korea and to prevent its spreading into a third World War. In this effort, we stand allied with the great majority of our fellow-members of the United Nations. Our efforts have succeeded in thwarting the aggressors, in Korea, and in stemming the tide of aggression in southeast Asia and else-where throughout the world. Our efforts in Korea have given us some sorely needed time and impetus to accelerate the building of our defenses and those of our allies against the threatened onslaught of Soviet imperialism.

General MacArthur, on the other hand, would have us, on our own initiative, carry the conflict beyond Korea against the mainland of Com-munist China, both from the sea and from the air. He would have us accept the risk involvement [sic] not only in an extension of the war with Red China, but in an all-out war with the Soviet Union. He would have us do this even at the expense of losing our allies and wrecking the coalition of free peoples throughout the world. He would have us do this even though the effect of such action might expose Western Europe to attack by the millions of Soviet troops poised in Middle and Eastern Europe.

This fundamental divergence is one of judgment as to the proper course

Hearings, pp. 27–28, 113–115, 282–285, 323–325, 341–345, 380–381, 388–391, 508–510, and 3542–3544. Omissions are indicated by ellipses. At the hearings, General MacArthur testified first, General Marshall second. For narrative purposes, that order has been reversed in the excerpts presented here. On the questions raised by this case study, see, in addition to the works cited previously, Harry S. Truman, *Years of Trial and Hope* (Garden City, N.Y.: Doubleday, 1956), Chapters 21–28; and Richard Rovere and Arthur Schlesinger, Jr., *The MacArthur Controversy* (New York: Farrar, Straus and Giroux, 1965). (Both available in paperback editions.)

of action to be followed by the United States. This divergence arises from the inherent difference between the position of a field commander, whose mission is limited to a particular area and a particular antagonist, and the position of the Joint Chiefs of Staff, the Secretary of Defense, and the President, who are responsible for the total security of the United States, and who, to achieve and maintain this security, must weigh our interests and objectives in one part of the globe with those in other areas of the world so as to attain the best over-all balance.

It is their responsibility to determine where the main threat to our security lies, where we must fight holding actions, and where and how we must gain time to grow stronger. On the other hand, the responsibilities and the courses of action assigned to a theater commander necessarily apply to his own immediate area of responsibility. It is completely understandable and, in fact, at times commendable that a theater commander should become so wholly wrapped up in his own aims and responsibilities that some of the directives received by him from higher authority are not those that he would have written for himself. There is nothing new about this sort of thing in our military history. What is new, and what has brought about the necessity for General MacArthur's removal, is the wholly unprecedented situation of a local theater commander publicly expressing his displeasure at and his disagreement with the foreign and military policy of the United States.

It became apparent that General MacArthur had grown so far out of sympathy with the established policies of the United States that there was grave doubt as to whether he could any longer be permitted to exercise the authority in making decisions that normal command functions would assign to a theater commander. In this situation, there was no other recourse but to relieve him. . . .

CHAIRMAN [RICHARD B.] RUSSELL [D., Ga.]. Now, Mr. Secretary, one of the issues here is as to whether or not General MacArthur directly or indirectly violated any orders or directives issued to him by you, as a representative of the Department of Defense or by the President of the United States?

I would like to have you discuss that.

SECRETARY MARSHALL. In relation to the conduct of the campaign, no, he has not, not that I can recall. In relation to public statements, he has.

CHAIRMAN RUSSELL. Now, do you know what instructions were given him with respect to public statements?

SECRETARY MARSHALL. A general instruction was issued to all Government activities, and specifically to all military commanders, that they would refrain from any public statements regarding foreign relations that were not formerly cleared. . . .

This directive had been preceded by a series of public statements and releases by General MacArthur concerning the failure of the offensive launched on November 24 and on November 30.

In reply to an inquiry from Mr. Arthur Krock of *The New York Times,* General MacArthur had stated that he had received no suggestions from any authoritative source that his command should stop at any line short of the international boundary, and that the strategic course of the campaign in Korea was not responsible to any degree for the massive attack of the Chinese Communists.

On December 1 in response to the inquires [*sic*] of the *United States News and World Report,* General MacArthur stated that the limits imposed on his pursuit of the Chinese forces and attacks on their bases constituted an enormous handicap without precedent in military history.

Also on December 1 General MacArthur sent a message to the president of the United Press in which he stated that his command was faced with an entirely new war resulting largely from expansion of military odds unprecedented in history. The statement went on to criticize the imposition of limitations on effective retaliation by his command against the Communist Chinese. . . .

CHAIRMAN RUSSELL. Well, was it considered by you or any of General MacArthur's supervisors that those statements were in violation of any order or regulation?

SECRETARY MARSHALL. Yes, sir.

CHAIRMAN RUSSELL. What specific regulation or order do you think they violated? . . .

SECRETARY MARSHALL. Comments in relation to matters that pertain to our foreign relations, our relations with our allies and the general Government decisions as to policy to be followed in the campaign.

CHAIRMAN RUSSELL. Well, had he been notified of that policy or was that a standing policy of the Defense Establishment? . . .

SECRETARY MARSHALL. He had received no specific instructions or any instructions so far as I know on that subject until this message of December 6.

CHAIRMAN RUSSELL. So he had not received up until that time any specific orders calling attention to what you regarded as either the inadvisability or inappropriateness of his issuing these statements to these representatives of the press?

SECRETARY MARSHALL. I think that is correct, sir. . . .

CHAIRMAN RUSSELL . . . Now what specific instances after the receipt of this directive, do you have where General MacArthur violated that directive? . . .

SECRETARY MARSHALL. Yes, sir; there was another occasion, which I will refer to in a moment, but his relief was not based solely on those factors.

During the early part of March, when it appeared likely that the forward movement of the United Nations' forces would soon bring them back to the vicinity of the thirty-eighth parallel, it was decided that consideration should be given to the preparation of a statement to be issued by the President as the executive agent of the United Nations, relating to the possibility of obtaining a negotiated settlement for the Korean conflict.

After a series of discussions between the Joint Chiefs of Staff and representatives of the Department of State, a draft of a proposed presidential declaration on the Korean situation was prepared by the State Department. . . .

On March 20 the Joint Chiefs of Staff dispatched the following message to General MacArthur:

> State planning a Presidential announcement shortly that with clearing of bulk of South Korea of aggressors, United Nations now prepared to discuss conditions of settlement in Korea. United Nations feeling exists that further diplomatic efforts toward settlement should be made before any advance with major forces north of the thirty-eighth parallel. Time will be required to determine diplomatic reactions and permit new negotiations that may develop.
>
> Recognizing that the parallel has no military significance, State has asked Joint Chiefs of Staff what authority you should have to permit sufficient freedom of action for next few weeks to provide security for United Nations forces and maintain contact with the enemy, Your recommendation desired.

In his reply on the 21st of March, General MacArthur stated that his present directive establishing security of command was adequate for his needs.

He also requested that no further limitations be imposed upon him.

On the 24th of March, General MacArthur issued a public statement with respect to the Korean conflict. . . .

[The statement read, in part:

> . . . Even under inhibitions which now restrict activity of the United Nations forces and the corresponding military advantages which accrue to Red China, it has been shown its complete inability to accomplish by force of arms the conquest of Korea.
>
> The enemy therefore must by now be painfully aware that a decision of the United Nations to depart from its tolerant effort to contain the war to the area of Korea through expansion of our military operations to his coastal areas and interior bases would doom Red China to the risk of imminent military collapse.
>
> These basic facts being established, there should be no insuperable difficulty arriving at decisions on the Korean problem if the issues are resolved on their own merits without being burdened by extraneous matters not directly related to Korea, such as Formosa and China's seat in the United Nations.

The Korean nation and people which have been so cruelly ravaged must not be sacrificed. That is the paramount concern. Apart from the military area of the problem where the issues are resolved in the course of combat, the fundamental questions continue to be political in nature and must find their answer in the diplomatic sphere.

Within the area of my authority as military commander, however, it should be needless to say I stand ready at any time to confer in the field with the commander in chief of the enemy forces in an earnest effort to find any military means whereby the realization of the political objectives of the United Nations in Korea, to which no nation may justly take exceptions, might be accomplished without further bloodshed.]

At the time the foregoing statement was issued, the clearance of the proposed Presidential declaration with the other 13 nations having forces in Korea had very nearly been completed. In view of the serious impact of General MacArthur's statement on the negotiations with these nations, it became necessary to abandon the effort, thus losing whatever chance there may have been at that time to negotiate a settlement of the Korean conflict. . . .

. . . As a result of this . . . the Joint Chiefs of Staff were directed by the President to call General MacArthur's attention to the President's order of December 6, 1950, which, in effect, required that all officials of the United States Government, military as well as civilian, should not release any speech, press, or other public statement concerning foreign policy without prior clearance by the Department of State, or if concerning military policy, with the Department of Defense. . . .

. . . Shortly after General MacArthur's statement of March 24, Congressman Joseph Martin of Massachusetts released for publication a letter addressed to him by General MacArthur, dated March 20, 1951. In this letter, which like the March 24 release had not been cleared in accordance with the President's directive of December 6, General MacArthur dealt further with the questions of whether to carry the war to China, whether to use the Nationalist Chinese forces on Formosa, and whether to apply our maximum strength in Asia or in Europe.

[The exchange of letters between Martin and MacArthur read, in part:

My Dear General: . . . Enclosed is a copy of an address I delivered in Brooklyn, N.Y., February 12 . . . suggesting that the forces of Generalissimo Chiang Kai-Shek on Formosa might be employed in the opening of a second Asiatic front to relieve the pressure on our forces in Korea.

I would deem it a great help if I could have your views on this point, either on a confidential basis or otherwise. Your admirers are legion, and the respect you command is enormous. . . .

Dear Congressman Martin: . . . My views and recommendations with respect to the situation created by Red China's entry into war against us in Korea have been submitted to Washington in most complete detail. Generally these views are well known and clearly understood, as they follow the conventional pattern of meeting force with maximum counterforce as we have never failed to do in the past. Your view with respect to the utilization of the Chinese forces on Formosa is in conflict with neither logic nor this tradition.

It seems strangely difficult for some to realize that here in Asia is where the Communist conspirators have elected to make their play for global conquest, and that we have joined the issue thus raised on the battlefield; that here we fight Europe's war with arms while the diplomats there still fight it with words; that if we lose the war to communism in Asia the fall of Europe is inevitable, win it and Europe most probably would avoid war and yet preserve freedom. As you pointed out, we must win. There is no substitute for victory. . . .]

This letter was brought to the attention of the President on April 5. Thereafter the President called a meeting of his special assistant, Mr. Averell Harriman, the Secretary of State, the Secretary of Defense, and General Bradley. No decision was taken at this meeting, but after full discussion the President requested that all records bearing on the subject be brought to his attention.

On the following day, Saturday, this same group again met with the President at 8:50 in the morning for a further discussion of the subject. It was suggested that the matter be considered individually over the week end. The President directed me as Secretary of Defense to secure the views of the Chiefs of Staffs from a purely military point of view. . . . Sunday, April 8. . . . the three Chiefs of Staff met with me and General Bradley and stated their recommendations in the matter based on purely military considerations. These recommendations were reported to the President by General Bradley at a meeting the next morning, Monday, April 9, which was also attended by Mr. Harriman, the Secretary of State, and myself. With the unanimous concurrence of all those present, the President at that time took his decision to relieve General MacArthur. . . .

SENATOR [STYLES] BRIDGES [R., N.H.]. General Marshall, you commented yesterday about General MacArthur answering the letter of Congressman Joseph Martin. Don't you believe that if a United States Senator or a Congressman of the United States writes a letter to a military-policymaking man in authority, whether it is here or in some area of the world, that he is entitled to get a frank reply?

GENERAL MARSHALL. No, sir; I don't think from the senior commander when he knows he is advocating something to the leader of the opposition party to the administration that he as the commander is in total disagreement with his own people. That sets up a chain of events in this tragic state that we have arrived at here, which is a most unfortunate thing for everybody concerned.

SENATOR BRIDGES. What is the rule so far as anybody in the Military Establishment answering a letter from a Senator or a Congressman?

SECRETARY MARSHALL. Well, I think he has to use considerable discretion. I have had to write a good many thousand, and it depends on the back and forth, but I don't think I would ever be involved myself in a criticism of the Commander in Chief to any Congressman of either party concerned.

I don't think — that goes contrary to my precepts and understanding as a soldier. I think on the other hand what we suffer from at times, rather critically at times, is the willingness of the individual to take issue on the confidential basis with his commander in chief. That is pretty hard to get people to do. There is where you state your case and put your own commission or command or position in peril, and there is where we lack and there is the place to state. . . .

You preach loyalty all the time. You are dealing with an organization where a man receives an order from even a captain which leads to his death or his wound, and he has to obey that order. He doesn't abate it, he obeys it, and that has to be instinctive. Now, if the example at the top is contrary to that, then you have got a very serious situation.

I am reminded now of a criticism that was brought to me regarding myself shortly after I became Chief of Staff, and the criticism was to this general effect: That I was giving my support to the then Secretary of War, Mr. [Harry] Woodring, and not giving it to others.

Now, my reply, I remember distinctly, was this. When the Chief of Staff of the Army sets an example to the whole Army by disloyalty to his Chief and superior, who is the Secretary of War, he has just about ruined the Army in my opinion. . . .

I recall General [John J.] Pershing telling me of his own experience. In the first place, he was suddenly ordered to conduct an operation into Mexico, and I think he went some 600 miles into Mexico in the effort to capture Villa.

In the first place, he was barred from using the railroad. We had no motortruck organizations in that day, and they just had to buy trucks and organize and do the best they could to carry tremendous supplies over these tremendous distances, in many cases there being no trails. He was barred from using the railroads. That was the most severe prohibition that could be placed on him. I don't think he ever made a public comment; he assured me he had not.

It went further than that. Just as he thought he was going to effect the capture of Villa, he received a communication to cease his efforts and retire, which meant he failed in his business. He told me he didn't mention that to any of his staff, and that he walked around his tent, and around the bivouac there most of the night, and gave the order the next morning for the beginning of the withdrawal without any explanation whatever to any-body concerned. That was his reaction from a military basis to Mr. [Wood-row] Wilson's prohibition and to Mr. Wilson's orders.

I think it was a very good model to follow in the Army.

SENATOR BRIDGES. Don't you think there is a little difference between issuing a public statement, General Marshall, and writing a letter to an official of the United States Government like a United States Senator or Congressman?

SECRETARY MARSHALL. Well, I don't know how to better explain it than I have gone into it, because you have to take the background preceding that letter into consideration — what had happened. . . .

SENATOR [BOURKE] HICKENLOOPER [R., Iowa]. There is a book called *The Armed Forces Officer* that is rolling on the press right now, issued by the Secretary of Defense, General Marshall. It took me considerable time to get hold of a copy of this book but I have it, and I would like on that very point to read passages which are put out for the official guidance of officers of the Army or of the Armed Forces.

I am reading from page 8, so that the record will be clear.

> The service officer is charged only to take a lively interest in all such discussions

— that is about public matters and affairs of the military —

> has no more right to condemn the service unfairly than has any other American. On the other hand, he is not expected to be an intellectual eunuch oblivious to all the faults in the institution to which he gives his loyalty; or to the contrary, that the nature of that loyalty requires that he will use his force toward righting of those things which reason convinces him are going wrong, though making certain that his actions will not do more damage than repair. His ultimate commanding loyalty at all times is to his country and not to his service or superior.

I thought perhaps that might be pertinent in connection with the obli-gations and responsibilities of officers at this point in your questioning, Senator Bridges. . . .

SENATOR BRIDGES. Well now, what is your idea, General Marshall — is an officer's first loyalty, as this order in this book reads, this directory reads, is his first loyalty to his country?

SECRETARY MARSHALL. Yes; it is to his country. . . .

SENATOR BRIDGES. Now, General, for a minute assuming in World War II, where you served with distinction as Chief of Staff of the United States Army, you had felt that a policy enunciated by the administration at that time was not in the best interests of the United States, you felt very strongly then about that, what would you have done?

SECRETARY MARSHALL. I would have done my best directed [*sic*] to the President to have it changed, and I might say I had some very difficult scenes with Mr. Roosevelt over certain phases of the matter, because naturally he had a great many irons in the fire and I only had one, which was the Army and the Air Corps; but I didn't make any public speeches.

I was frequently embarrassed here before the Congress and committees as to the questions, because I thought it was ruinous. I honestly thought it was ruinous for me to come out in opposition to my Commander in Chief.

I must find some other way to accomplish the end, and in most instances I was able to do so. In some I was not. Some, later, it seemed to me the President was right. Others I thought it was convincingly proved that I was right, but I had very difficult scenes in the early stages, particularly when we were building up our forces, but I had them with the President directly, and I was not a very cheerful visitor on many occasions. In the end, Mr. Roosevelt gave me his confidence, and we had no discussions and debates whatsoever. . . .

SENATOR BRIDGES. Now, my question to you General is:

Suppose the difference between you and the administration, the President, had become an absolute difference of opinion, where you thought the best interests of the country were not being served by the President or the administration?

What would you have done, then?

SECRETARY MARSHALL. I probably would have resigned as Chief of Staff.

SENATOR BRIDGES. And then, following your resignation, what would you have done?

SECRETARY MARSHALL. That would have depended on the effect of my resignation. That might be effective without any explanation; and, then again, I might have felt that the situation was so glaring that I must talk to the public. . . .

SENATOR HICKENLOOPER. Now, General, getting to the question of propriety of General MacArthur's statements, I want to read to you the policy as publicly announced by the Chief of Staff of the Army on or about the first part of February. It can be ascertained.

Page 160 of the hearings before the Foreign Relations Committee and the Armed Services Committee on Senate Concurrent Resolution 8, regarding the troops-to-Europe issue, this question was asked of General [J. Lawton] Collins [Army Chief of Staff] by Senator [Henry Cabot] Lodge, [Jr., R., Mass.] a member of this committee. Senator Lodge said as follows:

> I would like to ask you this question. There has been a good deal of talk about there being a gag on officers in the armed services insofar as expressing their opinions before committees of Congress is concerned. Can you tell me is there such a gag?
>
> GENERAL COLLINS. Definitely not.

SENATOR LODGE. In other words, an officer is free to respond to an invitation by any committee of Congress to come up and say what he thinks?

GENERAL COLLINS. Completely so. So far as the Army is concerned. I can say without any reservation whatever that here in essence are the instructions that we have complied with for years. An officer called before a committee of the Congress must present the considered view of the Department of the Army or the War Department. I think that is a logical thing because then, rather than getting mere individual opinions, the Congress has the benefit of something that has been carefully processed and evaluated by the staff and acted upon by the Secretary of the Army or the War Department itself. That rule still holds.

However, an officer is permitted in answer to queries complete and utterly unfettered personal views so long as he says, "This is my personal view."

. . . I can assure you that no Army officer is inhibited in any way from giving you his personal views so long as he makes it clear that they are his personal views.

SENATOR LODGE. And if an Army officer comes up here and says, "It is my personal view that we should have more armored divisions and less infantry divisions," he has a right to say it, and it will not be held against him later; is that right?

GENERAL COLLINS. Absolutely. He does say it right within our own Department. In other words, if the day comes when we could get unanimity of opinion among our officers, then I would think there was something the matter with us.

. . . there is a statement made publicly in an official capacity, I take it, by the Chief of Staff of the Army, who was General MacArthur's superior, and from whom General MacArthur received his orders and his directives. . . .

I will admit for the sake of the discussion which may follow that he says before a committee of Congress. But I submit that is only a technical distinction between a committee of Congress where an officer is testifying publicly and the officer expressing his personal views to a Member of Congress who is an official of this branch of the Government.

In the light of that apparent policy, where is the ground for the castigation or the recall of General MacArthur for expressing his personal views, for instance, in a private letter to Representative Martin? . . .

SECRETARY MARSHALL. That particular issue, of course, has been up many times. Without elaborating, I said virtually the same thing the other day. I have forgotten in connection with what it was.

Here I think, though, is quite a different situation. You say it is a technical point, that that is before a committee of the Congress. I think it is more than technical when you are considering releases to the press, to the whole world from the commander of the force putting himself before the whole world in various releases or statements in direct contradiction of the President of the United States, our Commander in Chief. That, I think, is quite a different situation, and I think you yourself would really have to agree with that.

Let me illustrate a little bit.

You are talking before a committee of Congress, and almost 9 times out of 10, or 19 out of 20, that is a member of the department here in Washington, the Navy Department, the Air Department, or the Army Department.

Now, we are turning to a supreme commander of an international force who, in one way or another, is bringing before the entire world and all our allies an issue of rather complete difference with his Commander in Chief, who is the executive agent of those allies of the United Nations and whose troops are in his armies.

Suppose, like was done during the Civil War, you call in the commander of an army which is engaged with the enemy . . . and he brings out his differences of opinion before the Congress with his own army commander, and to that extent really discredits him as to his judgment in the handling of that army, and that becomes a public property, that information?

Well, I think we all must admit that that would have a very destructive effect on the morale of the entire force. It would certainly have a very weakening effect on that commander concerned. . . .

SENATOR HICKENLOOPER. General, do you believe it is the duty of the Congress, which passes the laws of authorization, to inform itself, and the Members of the Congress to inform themselves? Or must the Congress just supinely take decisions that are built up in other departments of the Government, and follow them, without, in the long run being justified?

In other words, do not the Members of the Congress have the obligation to inform themselves as much as they can?

SECRETARY MARSHALL. Under the Constitution, the Congress does not command armies, and an army is a very special entity.

I feel that our greatest long-term security, in our procedure, our Government, and our military force, lies in the fact that our representatives in Congress are in the middle, as it were, of the general plot, and the people of this country are kept as fully informed as it seems safe to do so.

Now, it is a very difficult line to draw; but it is a very important one. . . .

What would you say, Senator, to this: Congress was not kept advised of our atomic developments. We couldn't. It would just defeat us entirely if we did that. We went a long time without any contact with Congress, and finally we did contact the top leadership but even then we didn't explain just what we were doing.

There are considerations of strategy. You could carry, I think, your argument into the field that the American people had a right to determine the strategy of a battle, or something of that kind. . . .

Certainly you would have profound confusion.

I think there are other methods, there are other means of the Congress to deal with such situations, but I don't think the example there is comparable to the real incident that we are considering. . . .

SENATOR BRIDGES. Have you ever, to your knowledge, refused to carry out a military order given you?

GENERAL MACARTHUR. Senator, I have been a soldier for 52 years. I have in that time, to the best of my ability, carried out every order that was ever given me. No more subordinate soldier has ever worn the American uniform.

I would repudiate any concept that I wouldn't carry out any order that was given me. If you mean to say that the orders I have carried out I was in agreement with, that is a different matter.

Many of the orders that I have received, I have disagreed with them, both their wisdom and their judgment; but that did not affect in the slightest degree my implementing them to the very best and maximum of my ability.

Any insinuation by anyone, however high his office, that I have ever in any way failed, to the level of my ability, to carry out my instructions, is completely unworthy and unwarranted. . . .

SENATOR [ESTES] KEFAUVER [D., Tenn.]. General MacArthur, I want to, if possible, get the record straight as to one thing. I do not believe you have been asked about it.

That is, that when you wrote the letter on March 20 to Congressman Martin, had you received the information from the State Department of the same day that any further statements by you must be coordinated as prescribed in the order of December 6, or do you remember?

GENERAL MACARTHUR. I had not.

SENATOR KEFAUVER. Do you know when you received the information given you the 20th of March 1951?

GENERAL MACARTHUR. I think it was the 25th, Senator.

SENATOR KEFAUVER. But you did not feel that the letter to Congressman Martin would have required coordinating his letter as required by the order of March 20? I mean you did not feel that the order of March 20 affected things like your letter to Congressman Martin?

GENERAL MACARTHUR. Not in the slightest.

SENATOR KEFAUVER. In any event —

GENERAL MACARTHUR. I see nothing in reviewing the case with all the information I had, how the letter to Congressman Martin was affected in any degree by any directive that I ever received.

SENATOR KEFAUVER. So even if the directive of the 20th of March had been received before you wrote the letter, you would have written it in any event?

GENERAL MACARTHUR. That I couldn't tell you. It might have had some influence to the extent that —

SENATOR KEFAUVER. Well, in any event the letter of Congressman Martin apparently was not given to the public until April 13, so that if you had thought the directive of March 20 should have required you not to have written the letter, you could have recalled it or asked him not to release it?

GENERAL MACARTHUR. Senator, as I said yesterday, my letter to Congressman Martin was merely a routine communication such as I turn out by the hundreds. It made so little impression upon me, as I said yesterday, that when I heard one of my staff officers saying there had been some criticism of what I had said to him, I had to go into the files. I didn't even recall what the circumstance was.

It was a casual letter in reply to a request from a distinguished Member of this body, and I would have honored it.

SENATOR KEFAUVER. But from his letter I took it that you knew that it would be released by him in the debate that was going on in this country.

GENERAL MACARTHUR. I didn't have the faintest idea of whether he would or whether he wouldn't release it. The concept never entered into my head.

SENATOR KEFAUVER. General MacArthur, he said in his letter that there was this discussion going on, he had been in debates on the subject, and in the last paragraph he says in part:

> I would deem it a great help if I could have your views on this point, either on a confidential basis or otherwise. Your admirers are legion, and the respect you command is enormous.

In your letter you didn't say anything about it being on a confidential basis, so I take it you must have assumed from his letter it would be made public because he discussed the debate and the argument that was going on.

GENERAL MACARTHUR. I never gave it the slightest thought, Senator. It was a matter for his discretion entirely.

SENATOR KEFAUVER. One clause in the letter that strikes me, General MacArthur, is:

> Here we fight Europe's war with arms while the diplomats fight it with words.

Was that intended to be a slap at the State Department or what did you mean by that?

GENERAL MACARTHUR. It wasn't intended to be anything except a statement of actual facts.

SENATOR KEFAUVER. General MacArthur, following up the question that Senator [Brian] McMahon [D., Conn.] asked, I agree fully, not knowing anything about military matters, however, that you were quite right in presenting your side of the controversy or any question to the Joint Chiefs of Staff and arguing it out; that a major general or a lieutenant general under you would be derelict in his duties if he did not present his point of view to you on some matters affecting the command in your theater, but do you think it proper or would you think it proper for a brigadier or major general under you to take issue with your general concept as the theater commander by writing a letter to a Member of the Congress when he knew that it would be used in the debate about the way your campaign was being carried on?

GENERAL MACARTHUR. I wouldn't have the slightest objection to any officer in my command stating his views on any subjects in any way he wished, just so he did it in a courteous, polite way following the normal code of a gentleman's conduct.

SENATOR KEFAUVER. You mean if in the reconquest of the Philippines some major general had a different view about how the whole campaign should have been carried on, had written me a letter, knowing that I was going to publish it and cause a debate about the general strategy of your Pacific Campaign, you would have sanctioned what he did?

GENERAL MACARTHUR. Senator, I think there is not a week goes by that things of that sort don't occur.

SENATOR KEFAUVER. I mean would you have sanctioned it?

GENERAL MACARTHUR. I would ask you to examine your own files to see if you haven't gotten a great many complaints in from juniors in the service of the seniors that are over them.

SENATOR KEFAUVER. Yes, but they always say, "Be sure and don't show this to anybody."

GENERAL MACARTHUR. Well, once more that is a matter of your discretion. Representative Martin exercised it. . . .

I can't tell you how many times my staff has disagreed with me not only privately but publicly. The only thing I ever required was complete honesty of their opinions.

SENATOR KEFAUVER. You do not think an opinion different from the immediate commander for public debate weakens you in the eyes of the enemy and shows a division in the ranks?

GENERAL MACARTHUR. I believe there is a certain degree of propriety in those things of course, Senator. . . .

SENATOR [WAYNE] MORSE [R., Ore.].* Is it your understanding that one of the reasons why you did not get authorization to broaden the Korean War was because it was felt that such action at this time might bring Russia into the war? . . .

GENERAL MACARTHUR. Senator, I do not know why I was recalled. The only statement that I have seen on it is the order for my recall. . . .

So far as I know, I have completely implemented, to the best of my ability, every directive, every policy that was given to me, but there is no possible charge that I have failed to carry out and implement or even take exception to any announced policy that the United States or the United Nations has made.

* [Senator Morse has since switched his partisan affiliation, and is now a Democrat.]

I can only interpret that order that the administration, knowing the views I held, was going to act in a very contrary way, and believed it was advisable not to place any strain upon my loyalty, if you might put it that way, and relieved me of the command. . . .

It might have been based upon what they had in mind for the future. It could not possibly have been based upon anything in the past.

I had made certain recommendations, most of which — in fact, practically all, as far as I know — were in complete accord with the military recommendations of the Joint Chiefs of Staff, and all other commanders. . . .

I have said before that the President is under no obligation to explain his actions. He acted within his complete authority, and his responsibility, and I don't challenge either, in any way, shape, or manner. . . .

SENATOR MORSE. . . . It is my understanding, from what I have read as to what is reported to have been statements that administration leaders have made about your recall, that it was considered that your statement to the Chinese military leaders, which I called "the notice" the other day, which others have called "an ultimatum," had the effect of extending the war in Korea from a war of limited operations to one of a broader operation in China; and that it was considered that that was in violation of known administration policies and served as a part of the basis for the recall. I am going to do what I can to find out whether or not that is their position.

GENERAL MACARTHUR. I don't believe there is the slightest validity in that comment. As I have explained, my statement was a cold military appraisal of the military situation that existed in Korea, and a suggestion to the enemy commander in chief that under such conditions it would be advisable to bring the matter to an end conclusively.

What I said seemed to me to be in complete support with everything that the administration was desirous of doing, with every directive outlining the missions that we had to consummate. . . .

Chapter Six

THE CIA AND THE
INTELLIGENCE COMMUNITY

ORGANIZATION

Foreign policy decisions cannot be much better than the information on which they are based. Within the executive branch at least a score of agencies, or units within agencies, take some part in collecting and analyzing intelligence relating to foreign affairs. Most important among these are army, naval, and air intelligence units within each of the armed services, and the Defense Intelligence Agency; [1] the State Department's Bureau of Intelligence and Research, the National Security Agency, [2] the Federal Bureau of Investigation, the Atomic Energy Commission, and the Central Intelligence Agency.

Under the National Security Act of 1947, the CIA was created to coordinate the activities of all of the executive agencies in this intelligence community, to perform intelligence services which can most efficiently be performed centrally, and to advise the National Security Council on intelligence matters.

The CIA is headed by the Director of Central Intelligence — the principal intelligence officer of the United States government — seconded by a

[1] The Defense Intelligence Agency was established in the Department of Defense in 1961 to combine and coordinate the intelligence agencies of each of the armed services. It is expected to assume increasing responsibility for meeting the intelligence needs of the Defense Department, the Joint Chiefs of Staff, and American military commanders in the field. Its growing operations may well raise the problem at some point of ensuring that it does not become a rival to the CIA.

[2] The National Security Agency is perhaps the least well known of the important intelligence units in the executive branch. Among its functions are making and breaking the codes which the United States and foreign governments use to send messages to their representatives in the field, intercepting such messages, when possible, and conducting electronic intelligence. It is administered as a unit of the Department of Defense.

deputy director. These officials are appointed by the President with the consent of the Senate. At least one of the two must be a civilian.

Below these officials in the CIA's hierarchy are four functional divisions: Intelligence; Science and Technology, which keeps up with the latest technological developments relevant to the agency's work and interprets high-altitude photos taken by reconnaissance planes and space satellites; Support, which procures needed supplies and handles codes and communications facilities; and Plans, which directs covert operations. All told, it has been estimated that the CIA employs some 15,000 persons — about 2,200 of them abroad — and spends close to half a billion dollars a year. (The cost of the operations of the intelligence community as a whole have been estimated at $3 billion. The National Security Agency spends twice as much as the CIA.) [3]

The Director of Central Intelligence also serves as chairman of the United States Intelligence Board, "the board of directors of the intelligence community," [4] composed of representatives of each of the nine agencies or units mentioned previously. (The Deputy Director of Central Intelligence represents the CIA, since the Director is considered the President's representative.) This Board coordinates the intelligence community's operations and oversees the preparation of National Intelligence Estimates (briefly discussed below) for presentation to the National Security Council.

FUNCTIONS: COLLECTING, ANALYZING, AND DISTRIBUTING INTELLIGENCE

It is the job of the CIA and the intelligence community to *gather, analyze,* and *distribute* information relating to the capabilities and intentions of foreign powers, and to carry out certain secret activities abroad — including counter-intelligence and undercover operations.

Most intelligence information is collected, not by secret agents in melodramatic espionage encounters, but by skilled specialists sitting at their desks or in libraries. Newspapers, magazines, scientific and technical journals, radio and television broadcasts, phone books and tourist maps, official government reports, encyclopedias, speeches and press releases, personal interviews — all these key sources of intelligence data ordinarily are open to anyone with the time to attend to them and the technical knowledge to

[3] These estimates are from a special survey of the CIA conducted by *The New York Times* in 1966, published in a series of five page-one articles on April 25, 26, 27, 28, and 29, 1966. The principal authors were Tom Wicker, John W. Finney, Max Frankel, and E. W. Kenworthy. For this survey, the *Times* conducted interviews with more than 50 present and former United States government officials, military officers, and Congressmen, and obtained reports from 20 foreign correspondents and editors with recent service in more than 35 foreign countries. The estimates cited here appeared on April 25, 1966, on p. 20. Other citations to *The New York Times* in this chapter also refer to this series of articles.

[4] The phrase quoted is from Harry Howe Ransom, *Can American Democracy Survive Cold War?* (New York: Doubleday, 1964), p. 137.

understand them. Another major source of intelligence is the regular and perfectly legal reporting of American government representatives in the field. Their reports are based on personal observation and on their conversations with officials, private citizens, and fellow diplomats.

In other societies like our own, it is much easier to collect useful intelligence data than in closed societies like the Soviet Union and Communist China. Privately published journals, government documents, congressional hearings, and newspaper reports divulge information about American capabilities and plans which are rarely found in the government-controlled media of the communist nations. Allen Dulles, Director of Central Intelligence from 1953 to 1961, writes that:

> The intelligence community has been well aware of this problem, and when he was Director of CIA Bedell Smith was so disturbed by the situation that he decided to make a test. In 1951 he enlisted the services of a group of able and qualified academicians from one of our large universities for some summer work. He furnished them publications, news articles, hearings of the Congress, government releases, monographs, speeches, all available to anyone for the asking. He then commissioned them to determine what kind of an estimate of U.S. military capabilities the Soviets could put together from these unclassified sources. Their conclusions indicated that in a few weeks of work by a task force on this open literature our opponents could acquire important insight into many questions of our national defense. In fact, when the findings of the university analysts were circulated to President Truman and to other policymakers at the highest level, they were deemed to be so accurate that the extra copies were ordered destroyed and the few copies that were retained were given a high [security] classification.[5]

These overt sources are supplemented by information obtained through secret and illegal activities abroad — activities engaged in by the United States and by the governments of every major power (and a good many of the minor ones, too). Dulles' book, among others, admits this readily.

Intelligence is not, of course, simply a matter of "just getting the facts." Huge compilations of facts are useless without the interpretation and analysis that give them meaning. The number of facts which can be collected about a foreign government in one day is infinite, but the political reporter or intelligence agent cannot even decide what facts are worth reporting without making some preliminary assessment as to meaning.

At a diplomatic reception in Moscow, the Prime Minister of the Soviet Union is seen drinking tea instead of his accustomed vodka. No doubt about it, this is a fact. But is it worth mentioning in a report to Washington? It may or may not be, depending on the context of other events and theories about events in which it occurred. Is there a reason to suspect that the Prime

5 *The Craft of Intelligence* (Signet ed.; New York: Harper, 1963), pp. 220–221. Copyright © 1963 by Allen W. Dulles. Reprinted by permission of Harper & Row, Publishers.

Minister's health is failing, and that this may lead to his partial retirement from political life in the near future? If so, his switch from vodka to tea might reflect a doctor's warning and presage important political events. At the least, it will be worth watching what he drinks at the next diplomatic reception he attends. If the Soviet Prime Minister is thought to be in excellent health, on the other hand, his switch to tea may be attributable merely to a personal whim or a slight cold. To report it — and "facts" of like significance — would be to burden the readers of intelligence estimates with mountains of trivia. The tough part of the intelligence community's job, then, is discerning meaning in the masses of "facts" already available.

The keys to the meaning of isolated facts are other facts and a frame of reference which will produce hypotheses as to their probable meaning. The Soviet Foreign Minister leaves a diplomatic reception unusually early one night, apparently with a cold. Has the Chinese ambassador in Moscow, or the Polish ambassador, or the Hungarian ambassador also canceled or cut short an engagement that evening, on whatever pretext? Is a crisis in Communist bloc relations known to be brewing over some emerging issue? Only these facts will make possible an accurate evaluation of the first item.

(Just two days before his announcement of the United States quarantine of Cuba in 1962, President Kennedy's press secretary told reporters that the President would have to cancel some scheduled political campaign speeches due to a bad cold. Actually, Kennedy was returning to Washington for the top-level deliberations which preceded the imposition of the quarantine. Intelligence information suggesting that the President did not really have a cold — or at least not one bad enough to force cancellation of his speaking engagements — might, *properly interpreted,* have proved of immense value to the Soviet Union at that time.)

The job of piecing together the various items of information available to intelligence officials sometimes can be aided by high-speed computers. Allen Dulles notes:

> The intelligence service needs a man who speaks Swahili and French, has a degree in chemical engineering, is unmarried and over thirty five but under five feet eight. You push a button and in less than forty seconds a machine — like those commonly used in personnel work — tells whether such a man is available, and if so, everything else there is on record about him. Similar machines are used in sorting and assembling the data of intelligence itself.[6]

For the most part, though, the intricate and puzzling task of evaluating the meaning of available information depends on the quality and effort of the all too human specialists who serve in our intelligence agencies.[7]

6 *The Craft of Intelligence, op. cit.,* p. 65.

7 About 50 per cent of the CIA's analysts are reported to hold graduate degrees; about 30 per cent hold doctorates. *The New York Times,* April 26, 1966, p. 30.

The CIA, of course, needs a very special type of person — one who can live with the

Humans must also see to it that the results of the intelligence community's labors are appropriately distributed. No matter how excellent intelligence estimates are, they cannot do much good unless they get to the right people at the right time. There may be a splendid and entirely accurate report on Communist influence and infiltration in the Dominican Republic, but does the President have it and know what it contains when he must decide on short notice whether to send American troops into Santo Domingo to avoid risking a Communist takeover there?

Equally important: Did the men who prepared the report know precisely what information the President and his advisers would consider most relevant in deciding whether or not to intervene, and if so, with how great a force? The intelligence community must understand the goals and working hypotheses of the policymakers it serves if it is to provide them with the information they need when important decisions have to be made.

There are of course standard forms in which intelligence is made available to policymakers. The CIA and other intelligence agencies distribute daily and weekly secret summaries of new developments to all high-level foreign policy officials. In addition, a Board of National Estimates within the CIA — in consultation with the other members of the United States Intelligence Board — drafts National Intelligence Estimates, reviewing and evaluating all the intelligence available on specified countries or problem situations. Any intelligence agency which disagrees with any of the major conclusions in these estimates may attach a dissent. National Intelligence Estimates can also be prepared on a "crash" basis, when necessary.

But these standardized summaries or estimates, like the special briefings or reports produced on request, can meet the policymaker's needs only if he has made those needs — and the thinking which underlies them — clear to the men who gather and evaluate intelligence.

SECRET OPERATIONS

Inevitably, the relatively quiet functions of intelligence collection and analysis have received less attention and stirred less public controversy than the CIA's secret political operations abroad. By now it is no secret that in the early 1950's the CIA organized and supplied Chinese Nationalist forces which had retreated into northeast Burma, and encouraged them, against the Burmese government's opposition, to make provocative raids into Chinese Communist territory; that it aided in overthrowing Premier Mohammed Mossadegh of Iran in 1953; that it financed and supported the forces

---

strains of secrecy and anonymity. Those with exceptional language competence, and/or with intensive training in the history, geography, politics, or economy of particular areas of the world are especially welcome. In search of such people, the CIA sends representatives to college campuses throughout the country to interview likely prospects.

of Colonel Castillo Armas, which drove the left-oriented regime of Jacobo Arbenz Guzman out of Guatemala in 1954; that it aided Indonesian rebel forces seeking to overthrow President Sukarno in 1956 (an American pilot on a bombing mission was shot down and captured during this episode); that it sent U-2 reconnaissance planes over Soviet territory from 1956 through 1960 to collect information about Soviet military capabilities and intentions; that U-2 and other reconnaissance flights have been conducted regularly over Cuba and Communist China during much of the 1960's — in cooperation with the Chinese Nationalist government, in the latter case; that the CIA stuffed ballot boxes on behalf of right-wing General Phoumi Nosavan in Laos in 1960; that it masterminded and financed the disastrous attempt to land a group of Cuban exiles at the Bay of Pigs in 1961 in an effort to overturn the Castro regime; and that it recruited veterans of this invasion to pilot bomber and fighter planes in supporting CIA protégé Joseph Mobutu in the Congo in 1964.[8] Many additional operations of this sort have been rumored; undoubtedly some of the rumors are true.

What does or should a government say when it is caught red-handed in an illegal espionage or paramilitary operation? The Soviet Union's capture of United States agent Francis Powers and his U-2 plane in an espionage mission over Soviet territory became at least the pretext for the failure of the Paris summit meetings of 1960. The Eisenhower administration was roundly criticized for its apparently inept handling of this episode; and presidential candidate John F. Kennedy was to be taunted for declaring at the time that President Eisenhower should simply have apologized to Soviet Premier Khrushchev for the incident.

Washington journalists David Wise and Thomas B. Ross discussed this intelligence dilemma in their best selling *The U-2 Affair:*

> The first [mistake] perhaps, was to issue any cover story at all. It might have been wiser to wait for the Russians to make the initial move and then to respond to each charge with the simple statement: "We are investigating."
>
> Instead, on May 5, when Khrushchev disclosed that the plane had been downed, the government issued an elaborately detailed lie. That was the point of no return. When Khrushchev exposed the lie two days later, on May 7, the United States was confronted with the choice of admitting it had lied or of trying to brazen it out.
>
> The government hedged by stating a half-truth — acknowledging the flight but insisting it had not been authorized by Washington.
>
> But when the President realized the full implication of the statement, he felt the necessity of asserting his full responsibility for the program. When he did so, a new and crucial element was added — the indication

[8] All of these are reported in *The New York Times*, April 25 and 26, 1966. Most are mentioned also in David Wise and Thomas B. Ross, *The Invisible Government* (New York; Random House, 1964).

that the flights were to continue. This was done despite the fact that Eisenhower knew, and said privately, that the flights were a blown instrument and would have to stop.

By lying, when it could have remained silent, by admitting it had lied, by disclaiming presidential responsibility, then admitting presidential responsibility, and finally by implying the flights would continue, the United States all but made it impossible for the summit meeting to take place.[9]

Allen Dulles, who was Director of Central Intelligence at the time of the U-2 incident, not unexpectedly sees the matter differently:

It is quite true that there is an old tradition, and one which was excellent in its day and age, that you never talk about any espionage operations and that if a spy is caught, he is supposed to say nothing.

It does not always work out that way in the twentieth century. The U-2 is a case in point. It is, of course, obvious that a large number of people had to know about the building of the plane, its real purposes, its accomplishments over the five years of its useful life and also the high authority under which the project had been initiated and carried forward. In view of the unique nature of the project, its cost and complexity, this proliferation of information was inevitable. It could not be handled merely like the dispatch of a secret agent across a frontier. Of course, all these people would have known that any denial by the executive was false. Sooner or later, certainly, this would have leaked out.

But even more serious than this is the question of the responsibility of government. For the executive to have taken the position that a subordinate had exercised authority on his own to mount and carry forward such an enterprise as the U-2 operation without higher sanction would have been tantamount to admission of irresponsibility in government and that the executive was not in control of actions by subordinates which could vitally affect our national policy. This would have been an intolerable position to take. Silence on the whole affair, which I do not believe could have been maintained, would have amounted to such an admission. The fact that both in the U-2 matter and in the Bay of Pigs affair the Chief Executive assumed responsibility for what had been planned as a covert operation, but had been uncovered, was, I believe, both the right decision to take and the only decision that in the circumstances could have been justified.[10]

These viewpoints are actually complementary rather than mutually exclusive. They suggest that the Eisenhower administration might best have responded with noncommittal statements until the situation had been clarified and then admitted its responsibility as gracefully as the circumstances allowed. The risk that the President of the United States might be caught in an obvious lie should have been avoided at all costs, but his general responsibility for the operation should not have been denied. This is easier to say after the event than it would have been to execute at the time.

The context in which a secret operation is uncovered is bound to vary widely; so it would not be wise to insist that the government should respond in the same way in all instances of this kind. Nevertheless, this brief consideration of the U-2 incident should suggest some guidelines that may prove useful in such instances in the future.

CRITICISMS

The failure at the Bay of Pigs, in particular, brought a great deal of criticism down on the CIA, and on the practice of having one agency engaged both in gathering intelligence and in secret paramilitary operations abroad. Admittedly, this practice increases the possibility that individuals committed to a paramilitary operation will, perhaps unintentionally, collect intelligence consistent with their commitment. Allen Dulles has written, in a different context:

> I feel that there are important reasons for placing the responsibility for the preparation and coordination of our intelligence analyses with a centralized agency of government which has no responsibility for policy or for choosing among the weapons systems which will be developed for our defense. Quite naturally policymakers tend to become wedded to the policy for which they are responsible, and State and Defense employees are no exception to this human tendency. They are likely to view with a jaundiced eye intelligence reports that might tend to challenge existing policy decisions or require a change in cherished estimates of the strength of the Soviets in any particular military field. The most serious occupational hazard we have in the intelligence field, the one that causes more mistakes than any foreign deception or intrigue, is prejudice. I grant that we are all creatures of prejudice, including CIA officials, but by entrusting intelligence coordination to our central intelligence service, which is excluded from policymaking and married to no particular military hardware, we can avoid, to the greatest possible extent, the bending of facts obtained through intelligence to suit a particular occupational viewpoint.[11]

Soon after the Bay of Pigs debacle, President Kennedy appointed a special committee to investigate it and to suggest any organizational reforms of the intelligence community they thought appropriate. The committee was headed by General Maxwell Taylor and included Attorney General

[11] *Ibid.*, pp. 52–53. Copyright © 1963 by Allen W. Dulles. Reprinted by permission of Harper & Row, Publishers.

Robert Kennedy, Allen Dulles, and former Chief of Naval Operations Admiral Arleigh Burke. Although a number of top-level personnel changes in the CIA soon followed — including the replacement of Allen Dulles by John McCone — the Taylor Committee apparently recommended against removing responsibility for conducting secret political operations from the CIA. It may have been influenced by the fact that it is difficult and expensive enough to recruit and maintain *one* overseas espionage network. Maintaining independent agencies for gathering intelligence and secret political operations would require much duplication of effort and additional expense. Possibly some changes have been made in the internal structure of the CIA to help offset the inherent dangers of combining intelligence and operations functions in one agency. If so, the change has not been announced publicly.

The secrecy with which the CIA must operate creates problems in an open society. It gives rise to persistent rumors which can never be positively disproved, even if they are utterly fantastic. The charge that the CIA was behind the assassination of President Kennedy is an example.[12] Secrecy also makes it extraordinarily difficult to evaluate the performance of the intelligence community. In the nature of things, failures attract more attention than successes, and the reputation of the CIA is bound to suffer.

The Bay of Pigs invasion was clearly a failure. The U-2 program unquestionably produced a great deal of valuable information for the United States until the plane piloted by Francis Powers was captured just prior to the abortive summit meetings of 1960. That incident, however, plainly embarrassed the Eisenhower administration. The CIA's procuring the text of Premier Khrushchev's secret de-Stalinization speech in 1956 proved of great moment in discrediting Communist claims to infallibility and in promoting discord within the Communist world. Its accurate warnings of imminent Chinese Communist nuclear tests enabled the United States government to lessen their shock value by predicting them. And the U-2's detection of Soviet missiles in Cuba in the fall of 1962 may be judged either a failure or a success, depending on your point of view. Those who feel that the missiles should have been sighted earlier deem the episode an intelligence blunder. Others believe that obtaining reliable evidence of their presence before they became operational was good enough, and all that could be expected.

The CIA has been criticized for failing to provide adequate warning of the North Korean invasion of South Korea in 1950, and later that year, of Communist China's readiness to intervene in the Korean conflict. Also, apparently, it gave no clear warning concerning the Communists' intention

12 Mrs. Marguerite Oswald, the mother of the President's alleged assassin, made this charge. See *Report of the Warren Commission on the Assassination of President Kennedy* (New York: Bantam Books, 1964), pp. 588–589. The Commission found no evidence to substantiate this charge.

to build the Berlin wall in 1961. In defense of the intelligence community, however, it has been argued that warnings of at least some of these events *were* provided, even if they were not acted upon by the political officials responsible for making policy. We know now that intelligence reports warned that North Korea could invade South Korea, *if* it chose to, and that Communist China was militarily capable of intervening in the Korean War *if* it was willing to pay the price this action might entail. Evidently, our top decisionmakers did not consider this information to be certain enough to justify major shifts in policy. Nevertheless, it seems a lot to ask of intelligence that it provide reliable advance information as to a potential enemy's *intentions* as well as its capabilities. The Soviet Union might not have allowed a North Korean invasion of South Korea in 1950 if its intelligence services had warned it how the United States and United Nations would respond to such a move. But how could Soviet intelligence have known how the United States would react, when the responsible American officials themselves did not know beforehand how they would respond? There can be no question that, at times, the American intelligence community faces similar handicaps in divining Soviet policymakers' intentions.

Most fundamentally, even those who accept the necessity for espionage and covert operations under contemporary conditions have questioned both the ethics and the wisdom of allowing the CIA to intervene in other countries' internal affairs so deeply as to overthrow governments, stuff ballot boxes, and provide financial support to candidates for political office in friendly (even allied) nations (as we did for Ramòn Magsaysay in the Philippines in 1953). We expect our young men to be willing to die to defend such principles as free elections and the inviolability of international frontiers. Should not our devotion to these principles also make us willing to forego, in their name, some of the advantages to be gained through the more extreme kinds of covert operations mentioned in this section?

Ethics aside, *The New York Times* survey cited above listed as one of its conclusions:

> . . . Regardless of the acts, the CIA's reputation in the world is so horrendous and its role in events so exaggerated that it is becoming a burden on American policy, rather than the secret weapon it was intended to be.[13]

In recent years, the CIA has been criticized also for its activities at home. It has been charged with compromising the objectivity of the American scholarly community by using university operated projects (like Michigan State University's advisory group in South Vietnam) as a "cover" for its agents; by subsidizing numerous academic institutions and publications (as in providing $300,000 in 1951 to help open the Center for International

13 *The New York Times*, April 25, 1966, p. 30.

Studies at the Massachusetts Institute of Technology); and by channeling CIA funds through a series of genuine and dummy foundations to such groups as the National Student Association, the Congress for Cultural Freedom, the Institute of International Education, and many other organizations, some of which take positions on domestic political issues.

When its connections with the National Student Association (NSA) came to light in 1967, the CIA defended itself by noting that it had begun to finance this organization in 1952. The political climate of the United States at that time, with Senator McCarthy at the height of his influence, made it impossible for a left-oriented organization such as the NSA — even though anti-Communist — to raise the funds needed to send its representatives to international student gatherings. The result was that these international meetings were regularly dominated by Communist students. It was to alter this embarrassing situation — and not in an effort to influence domestic politics — that the CIA made available some $3 million to NSA between 1952 and 1967.

Though questions might be raised about the methods used by the CIA in its dealings with this association, the desirability of making it possible for NSA to send students to represent the United States at international congresses may be conceded. It is most unfortunate that the uncritical "anti-Communism" which obsessed our society in the early 1950's prevented NSA from obtaining funds from private — or at least open — sources.

But it does not follow that the CIA was justified in circumventing constitutional procedures to fill the gap. The CIA, with the approval of four Presidents, believed that the decision implicitly arrived at through the workings of our nation's democratic processes — the "decision" not to finance organizations such as NSA — was the wrong one. This time they were probably right. But what if they are wrong next time? What if it should be decided that the re-election of Senator J. William Fulbright by the people of Arkansas — or of Senator James Eastland by the voters of Mississippi — would be counter to the interests of the United States? Fulbright, after all, has outspokenly criticized United States policy in Vietnam, and both President Johnson and General Westmoreland have asserted that such opposition aids the enemies of our country. And the words and actions of segregationist Eastland may well tarnish the reputation of the United States in Africa and Asia. The CIA has not shrunk from interfering with the democratic process in other nations. How can we be sure it will not happen here?

All this speculation may be far-fetched, but the fact remains that the precedent which has been set is a dangerous one — all the more so since the stakes in the NSA case were not high. The United States undoubtedly could have endured Communist domination of international student meetings quite satisfactorily. One fears to think what further expedients may be adopted when the stakes are higher.

Under the pressure of these public disclosures, the Johnson administration appointed a special committee and adopted its recommendation that "no Federal agency shall provide any covert financial assistance or support, direct or indirect, to any of the nation's educational or private organizations" unless "overriding national security interests," as determined by the Secretaries of State and Defense, require it. Instead, the committee urged, a public-private agency including government officials and distinguished private citizens should be established "to provide public funds openly for overseas activities of organizations which are adjudged deserving, in the national interest, of public support." [14] The adequacy of this formula will depend on how the words "overriding national security interests" are interpreted. Remembering things past, many Americans will not feel fully reassured.

CONTROLLING SECRET AGENCIES IN AN OPEN SOCIETY

Because the CIA operates in secret, there is considerable — and fully justified — concern over how it is to be controlled. Wholly secret power is unchecked power. By manipulating the information available to it, a secret intelligence agency could influence policy in an unauthorized and undesirable manner. Effective supervisory machinery is needed to guard against this danger.

Administratively, the Director of Central Intelligence and the CIA report to the National Security Council and through it to the President. Since 1954, the NSC has exercised its supervisory authority through the "54-12 group" (named after the date of its formation, December, 1954). Consisting of the Director of Central Intelligence, undersecretarial level officials of the State and Defense Departments and the President's assistant(s) for national security affairs, this group meets about once a week to examine in detail proposed CIA operations. This group's control over covert operations apparently was strengthened after the Bay of Pigs failure, and its approval is now said to be needed to authorize expenditures as small as $10,000.[15]

Within the executive branch, in addition, CIA's budget requests are reviewed by the Bureau of the Budget. And from time to time special committees have investigated and evaluated the intelligence community's performance: a Hoover Commission task force in 1948; a special committee headed by Allen Dulles in 1951; a special committee headed by General James Doolittle in 1954; another Hoover Commission task force, led by General Mark Clark, in 1955; and the Taylor committee in 1961. Finally, a nine-man Foreign Intelligence Advisory Board, constituted by President

14 *The New York Times*, April 2, 1967, Sec. 4, p. 1. See also *ibid.*, February 26, 1967, Sec. 4, p. 1. The special committee referred to consisted of Undersecretary of State (and former Attorney General) Nicholas Katzenbach (chairman), Director of Central Intelligence Richard Helms, and Secretary of Health, Education and Welfare John Gardner.

15 *The New York Times*, April 28, 1966, p. 28.

Eisenhower in 1956 and reactivated by President Kennedy in 1961, meets periodically to review our intelligence operations. In the Johnson administration this Board was headed by Clark Clifford, a man with the full confidence of the President, and included General Maxwell Taylor and career Foreign Service Officer Robert Murphy.

In contrast, the Congress as a whole is not informed of CIA activities nor given an opportunity to pass on CIA requests for funds. Most of the agency's budget is concealed within Defense Department requests. Congress is represented, for the overseeing of CIA activities, by subcommittees of the Appropriations and Armed Services Committees of each house. Members of these four subcommittees are informed of CIA expenditures and activities at their request. (A proposal by Senator Eugene McCarthy in 1966 to add senior representatives of the Foreign Relations Committee to one of the Senate subcommittees failed to win Senate approval, primarily because of the opposition of Armed Services Committee chairman Richard B. Russell.)

Critics have argued that a single joint congressional committee, composed of House and Senate leaders, would be able to oversee United States intelligence operations more vigorously. In 1956, Senator Mike Mansfield introduced into the Senate a concurrent resolution to establish such a committtee, which would be structurally similar to the Joint Committee on Atomic Energy. It was opposed by a number of highly influential Senators, however, including some with experience in foreign affairs positions in the executive branch, and was defeated.

One objection to this proposal was that it might increase the risk that classified information would be disclosed. Another was that the power of the unified committee it sought to create might encourage congressional interference in an area which ought to remain primarily within executive discretion. Advocates of a Joint Committee on Central Intelligence nevertheless have continued to assert that the power wielded in secrecy by the CIA is too great to be supervised adequately by a series of subcommittees. Only a high-powered joint committee, they contend, could command the authority, the prestige, and the staff resources needed to ensure that the intelligence community's secret power remains the servant and not the master of the political officials elected by the American people.

After interviewing a large number of present and former United States government officials on this point, *The New York Times* study team reported widespread consensus among those interviewed that a joint congressional committee:

> would probably provide little more real control than now exists and might both restrict the agency's effectiveness and actually shield it from those who desire more knowledge about its operations. . . .
>
> Controlling the C.I.A. is a job that rests squarely upon the President of the United States, the director of the agency and the officials appointed

by the President to check its work. And if these men are to insist that they do control the agency, then they are the ones who must be blamed if control fails. . . .

. . . It is not an invisible government but the real government of the United States upon which the responsibility must lie whenever the agency may be found "out of control." For if that responsibility is accepted, there can be no invisible government.[16]

❧ CASE STUDY *THE BAY OF PIGS*

Some 1,400 exiled Cuban students, professional men, fishermen, land-owners, peasants, and soldiers — organized, trained, and supplied by the CIA — attempted to establish a beachhead at the Bay of Pigs on April 17, 1961. In less than three days they were routed by the overwhelmingly stronger military force mounted by the Cuban government under Fidel Castro. More than 1,000 of the invaders were taken prisoner — to be freed finally on Christmas eve of 1962, in return for $53 million worth of drugs, baby food, medical equipment, etc., raised by Attorney General Robert Kennedy from private American sources. The remaining 200 to 300 men involved apparently were either killed or missing in action.

President Kennedy considered the Bay of Pigs debacle the greatest failure in his public life (even though his personal popularity, as measured by the Gallup poll, rose sharply following the disaster). After a "decent interval," he replaced Allen Dulles with John McCone as Director of CIA and inaugurated the investigation of United States intelligence operations mentioned previously in this chapter. He has even been quoted by Arthur Schlesinger, Jr., as musing, while the invasion was in progress: " 'I made a mistake by putting Bobby [Kennedy] in the Justice Department. He is wasted there . . . Bobby should be in CIA.' " [17]

1. Why did President Kennedy allow the Bay of Pigs invasion to proceed despite his own misgivings? The operation was opposed by the Chairman of the Senate Foreign Relations Committee (J. William Fulbright), the Undersecretary of State (Chester Bowles), the Director of USIA (Edward R. Murrow), and a presidential assistant specializing in

---

[16] *The New York Times*, April 25, 1966, p. 20 and April 29, 1966, p. 18.

[17] *A Thousand Days* (Boston: Houghton Mifflin, 1965), p. 276. In addition to the sources cited in this case study, see Theodore Sorenson, *Kennedy* (New York: Harper, 1965), chap. 11.

Latin American affairs (Schlesinger). Why were they not able to prevail despite the President's predisposition in the matter?

2. What sources of information on probable reactions to the invasion inside Cuba were available to President Kennedy? What sources of information were closed off due to the secrecy of the operation? How did this affect the President's decision?

3. What do you believe you might have done in President Kennedy's place? Canceled the invasion? (If so, how would you have handled "the disposal problem"?) Committed as much United States naval and air support as necessary to ensure the success of the operation? (If so, how long do you think it would have taken to defeat Castro's forces?) What if United States *ground* forces had been needed?

4. What kind of government would have been likely to emerge in Cuba if the invasion had been successful? All told — and keeping in mind the later Soviet attempt to make Cuba a missile base — do you think the operation would have been worth undertaking if it had been highly likely to succeed? Why or why not?

5. Why did the invasion fail?

6. If you had been President, what steps would you have taken to prevent similar failures in the future?

ARTHUR M. SCHLESINGER, JR.

The first CIA plan was to form small groups designed to slip into Cuba and establish active centers of resistance. Arms and supplies flown in from outside would enable these bands to enlarge their operations until, like Castro himself, they could enlist enough popular support to challenge the regime. In August President Eisenhower approved a budget of $13 million for this project. It was explicitly stated at this point that no United States military personnel were to take part in combat operations. But in the meantime the military conception was beginning to change. The CIA people began to doubt whether the guerrilla theory would work. It is true that several hundred guerrillas were presently hiding out in the Escambray Mountains and that Manuel Ray was reactivating his underground in the cities; but the CIA found it hard to make contact with the Cuban resistance. Efforts to parachute supplies into the Escambray were not very successful. The CIA people feared that the guerrilla bands had been penetrated by Castro's agents. Certainly Castro, who knew all the tricks himself, was a master at counterguerrilla action. Moreover, his army was being strengthened by Soviet equipment, and his control was tightening over the civilian population: all this made him a far more formidable opponent than the Batista of 1958. For these reasons, as the Escambray resistance began to fade out, CIA now reconsidered its original plan. . . .

It is sometimes essential for a state, even for a democratic state, to undertake clandestine operations, as I learned in OSS [Office of Strategic Services] during the Second World War. But, when such operations are undertaken, it is important never to forget that the relationship between an intelligence agency and its instruments tends to be a corrupting one. The agency has a natural desire to control its operations as completely as possible and therefore a natural preference for compliant people. If people are not compliant to begin with, they are made so. The very process of recruitment begins the process: [Manuel] Artime, for example, was subjected to hours of interrogation, to psychological testing, even to a lie detector. Exiles are typically friendless, moneyless, jobless in a strange land; often they do not even speak the language. They become increasingly dependent on the agent. They know that, if they refuse to take his orders, he can cut off their income and expel them from their organizations.

The relationship is degrading for them and demoralizing for the agent. CIA's main contact with the exile leaders was a ubiquitous operative who went under the name of Frank Bender. His real name was Droller; he was a German refugee who had come to the United States before the war, entered the Army and moved into intelligence. He knew little Spanish and even less about Latin America. . . . But he had money and authority, and he fell easily into habits of command. His power appears to have gone to his head; he liked to say that he was carrying the counterrevolution around in his checkbook. The older exiles disliked and feared him, but they felt they had no choice but to obey him.

Ray and his people proved different. When Bender told him to bring the MRP [Ray's political party] into the Frente,* he refused. His personality, his politics and his advocacy of the underground thesis posed a threat both to the status of the more conservative exiles and to the control of the CIA. Accordingly the older exiles and the Agency were ready to collaborate in an attempt to discredit him. His policy was denounced as *Fidelismo sin Fidel* — Castroism without Castro. His group was denied access to CIA's secret radio transmitter on Swan Island and other forms of support. The more reactionary exiles called Ray a communist. . . .

By November 1960 the CIA operation had taken on a life of its own. The agents in the field were shaping it to meet their own needs. In favoring the "reliable" exiles — those who would take orders — they were conceivably endangering the whole project; for the men most capable of rallying popular support within Cuba against the Castro regime were bound to be more

* [The *Frente Revolucionario Democrático (Democratic Revolutionary Front)*, organized by the CIA among exiled Cuban leaders early in 1960.]

independent, more principled and more radical than the manageable types whom the intelligence agency preferred for operational reasons. As for the nominal Cuban leadership in the Frente, it was growing uneasily aware that it lacked authority; that, as it accepted its instructions and its cash from Bender and his associates, it lacked dignity; that it did not even know what was going on. . . .

On November 20, 1960, twelve days after he had heard about the Cuban project, the President-elect received from Allen Dulles a detailed briefing on CIA's new military conception. Kennedy listened with attention, then told Dulles to carry the work forward. The response was sufficiently affirmative for Dulles to take it as an instruction to expedite the project.

Dulles understood, however, that interest did not mean commitment. All Kennedy wanted at this point was to have the option of an exile attack on the Castro regime. Let the preparation go on for the time being: there would be ample opportunity after the inauguration for review and reconsideration. In the meantime, there was a legislative program to develop and those 1,200 jobs to fill . . . Kennedy saw the Cuban project, in the patois of the bureaucracy, as a "contingency plan." He did not yet realize how contingency planning could generate its own momentum and create its own reality. . . .

The plan was taking definite shape. Its sponsors said little now about the old ideas of guerrilla infiltration or multiple landings except as diversionary tactics. Instead they envisaged 600 to 750 Cubans coming ashore in a body at a point still to be chosen along the southern coast of Cuba. Air strikes from Nicaragua in advance of the attack would knock out Castro's air force. These strikes, along with supply flights, would continue during the landing. The invaders would also have artillery. The mission would be to seize and hold an area sufficiently large to attract anti-Castro activists, induce defections in Castro's militia and set off a general uprising behind the lines. As for the Brigade itself, the lieutenant colonel assured the Special Group [the secret interdepartmental committee charged with supervising special operations] that his charges were men of unusual intelligence and "motivation" and that their morale was superb. They would have no trouble, he said, in taking care of much larger numbers of Cuban militia. . . .

In particular, the Special Group seems not to have confronted the dilemma created by the change in military plans — the dilemma of the United States role. So long as the guerrilla thesis prevailed, this had not been a problem. CIA then contemplated an orthodox clandestine operation — an undertaking, in other words, which the United States would be able, if necessary, to disown. This meant, as a "ground rule" for planning, that the operation had to look to the world like one which the Cuban exiles would be capable of organizing and carrying out on their own. If it failed, only Cubans would be held accountable. Nor was the Eisenhower administration, in observing the ground rule and forbidding United States participation in combat, imposing a restriction likely to handicap seriously what was, after all, no more than an exercise in guerrilla infiltration.

But the new plan raised new questions. It called for an expeditionary force of size, scope and visibility; and it proposed to pit that force in pitched battle against defending armies of vastly superior numbers. Could the United States convincingly deny complicity in an expedition well trained and equipped to conduct an amphibious invasion? And, if it could not escape accountability, could it afford to let such an expedition fail? In short, if the United States kept its role small enough to conceal its responsibility, the operation might not have a fair chance of success; while if it made its role large enough to give the operation a fair chance of success, the responsibility could not be plausibly disclaimed in case of failure. Washington might then face the choice between the political humiliation of defeat and the commitment of United States troops to insure victory. . . .

The hiatus in Washington gave the CIA operatives in the field a free hand. Since the force in Guatemala was still too small for the new plan, recruitment now had the urgent priority. The political criteria laid down by the CIA in Washington and demanded by most members of the Frente were abandoned in the rush. Bender gave particular authority to a dubious figure in Miami named Joaquin Sanjenis, and Sanjenis favored men of the Cuban right. If they had been in Batista's army, no matter: *Time* reported that, when one member of the Frente complained about the recruitment of *Batistianos,* a United States officer replied, "They're anticommunists, aren't they?" Unmarked planes picked up the refugees in the supposedly deserted Opa-Locka airport in Miami and deposited them a few hours later at the Guatemalan base.

The influx of new recruits created problems in the training camp. Men who had taken part in the revolution had a natural hatred of officers who had served Batista. The American advisers, on the other hand, were impatient of what they regarded as political quibbling. They preferred men who had professional military experience (like Pepe San Román, who had received training at Fort Belvoir and Fort Benning in the United States) and could be relied on to follow orders. It is true that most of the *Batistianos* were so called because they had once been in Batista's army, not because they now wanted to return Batista to power. But this did not make the Cubans selected by the United States advisers to command the Brigade any more popular with the rank and file. . . .

. . . discontent increased. In January it broke out into mutiny. Almost half of the now more than 500 Cubans in the camp resigned. . . . When they were promised a visit from the Frente, most agreed to rejoin the Brigade, but a few still held out. In one of the unhappier passages in this whole unhappy story, the CIA operatives arrested a dozen of the ringleaders and held them prisoner under stark conditions deep in the jungle of northern Guatemala. . . .

This episode had scant impact on Washington. If it was ever reported to the new President, it must have been greatly minimized. The impression given at the White House meetings in March was that life in the Brigade could not be happier.

In the meantime, the CIA planners in Washington had settled on the town of Trinidad as the point of invasion. Trinidad, they pointed out, had the advantages of a harbor, a defensible beachhead, remoteness from Castro's main army and easy access to the Escambray Mountains. They proposed a heavy and concentrated amphibious assault, to take place at dawn and to be supported by paratroop drops on the hills behind the town and by simultaneous (though not advance) strikes against the Cuban air force. Once the landing force had established itself on the beaches, it could expect to rally support from the townspeople and overpower the local militia.

As the expeditionary force enlarged its hold, the CIA men argued, now introducing a new idea, a provisional government could be flown in; and, if the invaders could sustain themselves for ten days or two weeks, this government could receive recognition as the government of Cuba. Once this was done, the new government could request United States aid, though this aid was carefully defined as "logistic" and therefore presumably excluded military intervention. The CIA planners envisaged a continuous build-up and enlargement of the perimeter around the beachhead over a long period, rather like Anzio in 1944. The scheme envisaged victory by attrition rather than by rebellion and no longer assigned a significant immediate role to the internal resistance. As the invaders strengthened their position, this, along with their command of the skies and the acceptance of the new government by other American republics, would produce a steady withdrawal of civil support from Castro and his eventual collapse. And, if by any chance the attack failed, Trinidad was near enough the Escambray for the invaders to disappear into the hills. . . .

The Joint Chiefs, after brooding over CIA's Trinidad plan for a week, pronounced favorably on the chances of initial military success. The JCS evaluation was, however, a peculiar and ambiguous document. At one point it said categorically, in what would seem an implicit rejection of the Anzio model, that ultimate success would depend on either a sizable uprising inside the island or sizable support from outside. Then later, without restating these alternative conditions for victory, the document concluded that the existing plan, if executed in time, stood a "fair" chance of ultimate success. Even if it did not immediately attain all its goals, the JCS remarked philosophically, it would still contribute to the eventual overthrow of the regime.

There was plainly a logical gap between the statement that the plan would work if one or another condition were fulfilled and the statement that the plan would work anyway. One cannot know whether this gap resulted from sloppiness in analysis or from a conviction, conscious or unconscious, that once the invasion were launched, either internal uprising or external support would follow, and, if not the first, then the second — that, in short, once the United States government embarked on this enterprise, it could not risk the disaster of failure. Certainly this conviction permeated the thinking of the exiles themselves as well as of the United States officers in Guatemala. Since some, at least, of the Joint Chiefs had always been skeptical of the CIA ground rule, that conviction may well have lurked in the back of their minds too.

Late in February the Chiefs sent an inspection team to the Guatemala base. In a new report in early March, they dropped the point about external support and hinged victory on the capacity of the assault to produce anti-Castro action behind the lines. From the viewpoint of the Joint Chiefs, then, the Cuban resistance was indispensable to success. They could see no other way — short of United States intervention — by which an invasion force of a thousand Cubans, no matter how well trained and equipped nor how stout their morale, could conceivably overcome the 200,000 men of Castro's army and militia.

The pace of events was quickening. Roberto Alejos, the Guatemalan planter whose *finca* had been sheltering the Brigade, arrived in Washington in early March with a letter from President Ydígoras to President Kennedy. Ydígoras wrote that the presence of the Cubans was a mounting embarrassment and that he must request assurances that they depart by the end of April. For its part, the CIA reported that the Cubans themselves were clamoring to move; the spirit of the Brigade had reached its peak, and further postponement would risk demoralization. Moreover, the rainy season was about to begin, the ground would turn into volcanic mud, and training would have to stop. And there was another potent reason for going ahead: Castro, the CIA said, was about to receive jet airplanes from the Soviet Union along with Cuban pilots trained in Czechoslovakia to fly them; once the MIGs arrived, an amphibious landing would turn into a slaughter. After June 1, it would take the United States Marines and Air Force to overthrow Castro. If a purely Cuban invasion were ever to take place, it had to take place in the next few weeks.

By mid-March the President was confronted, in effect, with a now-or-never choice.

On March 11, about a week after my return from Latin America, I was summoned to a meeting with the President in the Cabinet Room. An intimidating group sat around the table — the Secretary of State, the Secretary of Defense, the director of the Central Intelligence Agency, three Joint Chiefs resplendent in uniforms and decorations, the Assistant Secretary of State for Inter-American Affairs, the chairman of the Latin American Task

Force, and appropriate assistants and bottle-washers. I shrank into a chair at the far end of the table and listened in silence. . . .

It was apparent now . . . that matters were still very much in flux. No final decision had yet been taken on whether the invasion should go forward at all and, if so, whether Trinidad should be the landing point. It fell to Allen Dulles and Richard M. Bissell, Jr., as the originators of the project to make the main arguments for action.

I had known both men for more than fifteen years and held them both in high respect. As an OSS intelligence officer in London and Paris during the war, I had admired the coolness and proficiency of Dulles's work in Bern; and, meeting him from time to time in the years after the war, I had come greatly to enjoy his company. Years in the intelligence business had no doubt given him a capacity for ruthlessness; but he was urbane, courtly and honorable, almost wholly devoid of the intellectual rigidity and personal self-righteousness of his brother. During the McCarthy years, when John Foster Dulles regularly threw innocent State Department officials to the wolves, Allen Dulles just as regularly protected CIA officers unjustly denounced on the Hill.

Richard Bissell, whom I had known as an economist in the Marshall Plan before he turned to intelligence work and became CIA's deputy director for operations, was a man of high character and remarkable intellectual gifts. His mind was swift and penetrating, and he had an unsurpassed talent for lucid analysis and fluent exposition. A few years before he had conceived and fought through the plan of U-2 flights over the Soviet Union; and, though this led to trouble in 1960, it still remained perhaps the greatest intelligence coup since the war. He had committed himself for the past year to the Cuban project with equal intensity. Yet he recognized the strength of his commitment and, with characteristic honesty, warned us to discount his bias. Nonetheless, we all listened transfixed — in this meeting and other meetings which followed — fascinated by the workings of this superbly clear, organized and articulate intelligence, while Bissell, pointer in hand, would explain how the invasion would work or discourse on the relative merits of alternative landing sites.

Both Dulles and Bissell were at a disadvantage in having to persuade a skeptical new administration about the virtues of a proposal nurtured in the hospitable bosom of a previous government — a proposal on which they had personally worked for a long time and in which their organization had a heavy vested interest. This cast them in the role less of analysts than of advocates, and it led them to accept progressive modifications so long as the expedition in some form remained; perhaps they too unconsciously supposed that, once the operation began to unfold, it would not be permitted to fail.

The determination to keep the scheme alive sprang in part, I believe, from the embarrassments of calling it off. As Dulles said at the March 11 meeting, "Don't forget that we have a disposal problem. If we have to take these men out of Guatemala, we will have to transfer them to the United States, and we can't have them wandering around the country telling everyone what they have been doing." What could one do with "this asset" if not send it on to Cuba? If transfer to the United States was out, demobilization on the spot would create even greater difficulties. The Cubans themselves were determined to go back to their homeland, and they might well forcibly resist efforts to take away their arms and equipment. Moreover, even if the Brigade were successfully disbanded, its members would disperse, disappointed and resentful all over Latin America. They would tell where they had been and what they had been doing, thereby exposing CIA operations. And they would explain how the United States, having prepared an expedition against Castro, had then lost its nerve. This could only result, Dulles kept emphasizing, in discrediting Washington, disheartening Latin American opponents of Castro and encouraging the *Fidelistas* in their attack on democratic regimes, like that of Betancourt in Venezuela. Disbandment might thus produce pro-Castro revolutions all around the Caribbean. For all these reasons, CIA argued, instead of turning the Cubans loose, we must find some means for putting them back into Cuba "on their own."

The contingency had thus become a reality: having created the Brigade as an option, the CIA now presented its use against Cuba as a necessity. Nor did Dulles's arguments lack force. Confronted by them, Kennedy tentatively agreed that the simplest thing, after all, might be to let the Cubans go where they yearned to go — to Cuba. Then he tried to turn the meeting toward a consideration of how this could be done with the least political risk. The first step was to form a more liberal and representative exile organization, and this the President directed should be done as soon as possible.

Bissell then renewed the case for the Trinidad plan. Kennedy questioned it as "too spectacular." He did not want a big amphibious invasion in the manner of the Second World War; he wanted a "quiet" landing, preferably at night. And he insisted that the plans be drawn on the basis of *no United States military intervention* — a stipulation to which no one at the table made objection. [Assistant Secretary of State for Inter-American Affairs] Thomas Mann seconded these points, stressing the probability of anti-American reactions in Latin America and the United Nations if the American hand were not well concealed. He was especially worried that the air strikes would give the show away unless they could seem plausibly to come from bases on Cuban soil; and the Trinidad airstrip could not take B-26's. The President concluded the meeting by defining the issue with his usual crispness. The trouble with the operation, he said, was that the smaller the political risk, the greater the military risk, and vice versa. The problem was to see whether the two risks could be brought into reasonable balance.

For the next three days the CIA planners canvassed alternative landing sites, coming up with three new possibilities, of which the most likely was about 100 miles west of Trinidad in the Zapata area around Cochinos Bay — the Bay of Pigs. . . . The President . . . authorized CIA to continue on the assumption that the invasion would occur. But he repeated his decision against any form of United States military intervention and added carefully and categorically that he was reserving his final decision on the plan itself. The expedition, he said, must be laid on in a way which would make it possible for him to call it off as late as twenty-four hours before D-day.

. . . In the meantime, the CIA had been carrying out Kennedy's instruction to bring representatives of the new Cuba into the Frente. Bender, reversing his earlier position, told the Frente that it must come to an agreement with Manuel Ray and his MRP. But, though Bender changed his line, he did not change his manner, nor were the more conservative members of the Frente themselves eager to embrace *Fidelismo sin Fidel*. Representatives of the Frente and the MRP engaged in complex and acrimonious negotiations. After persistent CIA pressure persuaded the negotiators to return to their groups with a draft agreement, the Frente rejected the common program as too radical.

The CIA now decided on direct intervention. On March 18 at the Skyways Motel in Miami a CIA operative — not Bender, whom the CIA belatedly concluded was not the man for the job — told the Frente that the two groups must unite, that they must together choose a provisional president for Cuba, and that if these things were not done right away, the whole project would be called off. The Frente finally caved in and reluctantly submitted a list of six possibilities for the presidency. For its part, the MRP was no happier about this coerced alliance. Ray and his people liked neither the CIA control nor the idea of an invasion, but, supposing that United States backing guaranteed success, they wanted both to defend the interests of the Cuban underground and to assure their own part in a post-Castro future. Accepting the list, they chose Dr. Miró Cardona as provisional president.

Miró, a lawyer and professor at the University of Havana, had been a noted leader in the civil opposition to Batista. He had inspired many students to work for the revolution, and Castro made him the first prime minister of the revolutionary regime. Though Miró did not last long in the government, Castro as late as May 1960 designated him ambassador to the United States. But by July, as the process of communization advanced, Miró, who had not gone on to Washington, resigned his ambassadorship and sought refuge in the Argentine Embassy. He finally came to the United States as an exile in the winter of 1960–61. He was a man of dignity and force, who faithfully represented the liberal ideals of the Cuban Revolution.

On March 22 Varona for the Frente and Ray for the MRP signed an agreement conferring on Miró Cardona authority to organize the Cuban Revolutionary Council. The document also pledged the Council to give "maximum priority" to the resistance inside Cuba, declared that no one who "held an objectionably responsible position with the criminal dictatorship of Batista" was to be admitted into any armed forces organized outside Cuba and said hopefully that the military command of such forces must pledge "their full deference" to the Council's authority. Miró then held a press conference to announce the formation of the Council as the basis for a provisional government of Cuba once it had gained "a piece of Cuban soil." This was all very well, but the CIA regarded the agreement as no more than a placebo, and the CRC's charter meant very little next to Bender's checkbook. Bender now asked Miró to ratify the selection of Artime as commander of the Brigade. When he did so, Ray, Varona and Carrillo all protested; but Miró wearily explained that he had no alternative: this was what the Americans wanted, and the Americans would make the invasion a success. . . .

[Schlesinger was asked to prepare a White Paper on Cuba, and, on March 28, discussed a draft of this Paper with the President.]

As we finished, I said, "What do you think about this damned invasion?" He said wryly, "I think about it as little as possible." But it was clear, as we talked, that he had of course been thinking about it a good deal. In his judgment, the critical point — the weak part of the case for going ahead — lay in the theory that the landings would touch off a mass insurrection against the regime. How unpopular was Castro anyway? I mentioned a series written by Joseph Newman, who had just visited Cuba for the *New York Herald Tribune,* citing a piece which reported the strength of sentiment behind Castro. Kennedy said quickly, "That must have been the fourth piece — I missed it. Could you get it for me?" I sent it over that evening. In a short while he called back to ask that I talk to Newman and obtain, as hypothetically as possible, his estimate about Cuban responses to an invasion.

We all in the White House considered uprisings behind the lines essential to the success of the operation; so too did the Joint Chiefs of Staff; and so, we thought, did the CIA. It was only later that I learned about the Anzio concept; it certainly did not come across clearly in the White House meetings. And it was much later that Allen Dulles wrote: "Much of the American press assumed at the time that this action was predicated on a mistaken intelligence estimate to the effect that a landing would touch off a widespread and successful popular revolt in Cuba. . . . I know of no estimate that spontaneous uprising of the unarmed population of Cuba would be touched off by the landing." * This statement plainly reflected the CIA notion that the invasion would win by attrition rather than by re-

* Allen W. Dulles, *The Craft of Intelligence* (New York, 1963), 169.

bellion. It also, strictly construed, was accurate enough in itself — if due attention is paid to such key words as "spontaneous," "unarmed" and "landing." Obviously no one expected the invasion to galvanize the unarmed and unorganized into rising against Castro at the moment of disembarkation. But the invasion plan, as understood by the President and the Joint Chiefs, did assume that the successful *occupation* of an enlarged beachhead area would rather soon incite *organized* uprisings by *armed* members of the Cuban resistance.

Dulles and Bissell themselves reinforced this impression. When questioned early in April about the prospects of internal resistance, instead of discounting it, which seems to have been their view, they claimed that over 2,500 persons presently belonged to resistance organizations, that 20,000 more were sympathizers, and that the Brigade, once established on the island, could expect the active support of, at the very least, a quarter of the Cuban people. They backed up such sanguine estimates by citing requests from contacts in Cuba for arms drops and assurances that a specified number of men stood ready to fight when the signal was given.

My experience in OSS during the Second World War left me with a sad skepticism about such messages. Too often the senders inflated their strength, whether out of hope or despair, or because they wanted guns, ammunition and radios to sell on the black market. Recalling disappointment and miscalculation then, one could not find the CIA assurances satisfying. But mine was a special experience; and the estimates coming, as we all supposed, with the Agency's full authority behind them, impressed most of those around the table. Again it appeared only later that the Intelligence Branch of CIA had never been officially apprised of the Cuban expedition and that CIA's elaborate national estimates procedure was never directed to the question whether an invasion would trigger other uprisings. Robert Amory, Jr., the able deputy director for intelligence, himself a veteran of amphibious landings in the Second World War, was not informed at any point about any aspect of the operation. The same men, in short, both planned the operation and judged its chances of success. Nor was anyone at State, in intelligence jargon, "witting" below Tom Mann, which meant that the men on the Cuban desk, who received the daily flow of information from the island, were not asked to comment on the feasibility of the venture. The "need-to-know" standard — i.e., that no one should be told about a project unless it becomes operationally necessary — thus had the idiotic effect of excluding much of the expertise of government at a time when every alert newspaperman knew something was afoot.

The talk with Newman strengthened misgivings about CIA's estimates. He said that, though anti-Castro sentiment had markedly increased since his last visit the year before, Castro still roused intense enthusiasm and faith, especially among the young and among those who had benefited from the social changes of the revolution. These two groups, Newman added, constituted a considerable part of the population. Even a sizable middle group, now disillusioned about Castro, would not be likely to respond with enthusiasm to an invasion backed by the United States because we were so thoroughly identified in their minds with Batista. As much as many Cubans detested the present situation, they still preferred it to a restoration of the old order. "We must understand that from the viewpoint of many Cubans, including anti-Castro Cubans, we come into the ring with exceedingly dirty hands." . . .

Dulles and Bissell, convinced that if the Cubans were ever to be sent against Castro they had to go now, sure that the Brigade could accomplish its mission and nagged by the disposal problem, now redoubled their efforts at persuasion. Dulles told Kennedy that he felt much more confident about success than he had ever been in the case of Guatemala. CIA concentrated particularly in the meetings on trying to show that, even if the expedition failed, the cost would not be excessive. Obviously no one could believe any longer that the adventure would not be attributed to the United States — news stories described the recruitment effort in Miami every day — but somehow the idea took hold around the cabinet table that this would not much matter so long as United States soldiers did not take part in the actual fighting. If the operation were truly "Cubanized," it would hopefully appear as part of the traditional ebb and flow of revolution and counterrevolution in the Caribbean.

Moreover, if worst came to worst and the invaders were beaten on the beaches, then, Dulles and Bissell said, they could easily "melt away" into the mountains. This might have been true at Trinidad, which lay near the foothills of the Escambray, and it was more true of the Bay of Pigs than of the other two alternative sites proposed in mid-March. But the CIA exposition was less than candid both in implying that the Brigade had undergone guerrilla training (which had substantially ended five months earlier, before most of the Cubans had arrived in Guatemala) and in suggesting the existence of an easy escape hatch. I don't think we fully realized that the Escambray Mountains lay eighty miles from the Bay of Pigs, across a hopeless tangle of swamps and jungles. And no one knew (until Haynes Johnson interviewed the survivors) that the CIA agents in Guatemala were saying nothing to the Cubans about this last resort of flight to the hills, apparently fearing to lower their morale. "We were never told about this," San Román said later. "What we were told was, 'If you fail *we* will go in.'" *

Our meetings were taking place in a curious atmosphere of assumed consensus. The CIA representatives dominated the discussion. The Joint

* Haynes Johnson, *The Bay of Pigs* (New York, 1964 [Dell edition]), 67.

Chiefs seemed to be going contentedly along. They met four times as a body after March 15 to review the Bay of Pigs project as it evolved; and, while their preference for Trinidad was on the record and they never formally approved the new plan, they at no time opposed it. Their collaboration with CIA in refining the scheme gave the White House the impression of their wholehearted support. Robert McNamara, who was absorbed in the endless task of trying to seize control of the Pentagon, accepted the judgment of the Chiefs on the military aspects of the plan, understood the CIA to be saying that invasion would shortly produce a revolt against Castro and supposed in any case that the new administration was following a well-established policy developed by its predecessors. Dean Rusk listened inscrutably through the discussions, confining himself to gentle warnings about possible excesses. When he went to the SEATO conference in late March and Chester Bowles as Acting Secretary sat in his place, Bowles was horrified by what he heard but reluctant to speak out in his chief's absence. On March 31 he gave Rusk a strong memorandum opposing the invasion and asked to be permitted, if Rusk disagreed, to carry the case to the President. Rusk reassured Bowles, leaving him with the impression that the project was being whittled down into a guerrilla infiltration, and filed the memorandum away. . . .

. . . the climactic meeting [came] on April 4. This meeting was held at the State Department in a small conference room beside Rusk's office. After the usual routine — persuasive expositions by the CIA, mild disclaimers by Rusk and penetrating questions by the President — Kennedy started asking people around the table what they thought. Fulbright, speaking in an emphatic and incredulous way, denounced the whole idea. The operation, he said, was wildly out of proportion to the threat. It would compromise our moral position in the world and make it impossible for us to protest treaty violations by the Communists. He gave a brave, old-fashioned American speech, honorable, sensible and strong; and he left everyone in the room, except me and perhaps the President, wholly unmoved.

Kennedy continued around the table. McNamara said that he favored the operation. Mann said that he would have opposed it at the start, but, now that it had gone so far, it should be carried through. [Special Assistant to the President for Latin American Affairs Adolph A.] Berle wanted the men to be put into Cuba but did not insist on a major production. Kennedy once again wanted to know what could be done in the way of quiet infiltration as against the beachhead assault. The meeting fell into discussion before the round of the table was completed. Soon it broke up.

. . . As we were leaving the room, the President called me back and asked for my opinion. I said that I was against the operation and tried to explain why. . . .

My opposition (expressed in this memorandum of April 5 and a second one five days later) was founded . . . on the implausibility of its two political premises: that, if only Cubans took part, the United States could dissociate itself from the consequences; and that, if the beachhead could be held for a few days and enlarged, there would be defections from the militia and uprisings behind the lines. The memorandum proposed two counter considerations as fundamental:

> (a) *No matter how "Cuban" the equipment and personnel, the U.S. will be held accountable for the operation, and our prestige will be committed to its success.*

And, because there was no convincing evidence that the invasion would touch off a mass insurrection:

> (b) *Since the Castro regime is presumably too strong to be toppled by a single landing, the operation will turn into a protracted civil conflict.*

If the military estimate was correct that the Brigade could secure its foothold in Cuba, the danger would be "that, if the rebellion appears to be failing, the rebels will call for U.S. armed help; that members of Congress will take up the cry; and that pressures will build up which will make it politically hard to resist the demand to send in the Marines."

Nor would sending in the Marines solve the problem, because the *Fidelistas* could be counted on to fight to the end, retreating, if necessary, to the Sierra Maestra. . . . A prolonged civil war in Cuba between the Castro regime and an exile army backed by the United States, the memorandum went on, would open us to damaging attack in the United Nations and elsewhere around the globe. The Russians would enlist volunteers in José Martí and probably even Abraham Lincoln Brigades and seek to convert the conflict into another Spanish Civil War.

More than that, a course of bullying intervention would destroy the new image of the United States — "the image of intelligence, reasonableness and honest firmness which has had such an extraordinary effect in changing world opinion about the U.S. and increasing world confidence in U.S. methods and purposes. . . . It is this reawakening world faith in America which is at stake in the Cuban operation." What this stately language meant was that the operation might recklessly expend one of our greatest national assets — John F. Kennedy himself. Nothing had been more depressing in the whole series of meetings than to watch a collection of officials, some of them holdovers from the previous administration, contentedly prepare to sacrifice the world's growing faith in the new American President in order to defend interests and pursue objectives of their own. Dean Rusk was almost alone in recognizing this problem; but his solution was the curious one of suggesting that someone other than the President make the final decision and do so in his absence — someone who could be sacrificed if things went wrong.   . . .

These memoranda look nice on the record, but they represented, of course, the easy way out. In the months after the Bay of Pigs I bitterly reproached myself for having kept so silent during those crucial discussions in the Cabinet Room, though my feelings of guilt were tempered by the knowledge that a course of objection would have accomplished little save to gain me a name as a nuisance. I can only explain my failure to do more than raise a few timid questions by reporting that one's impulse to blow the whistle on this nonsense was simply undone by the circumstances of the discussion.

It is one thing for a Special Assistant to talk frankly in private to a President at his request and another for a college professor, fresh to the government, to interpose his unassisted judgment in open meeting against that of such august figures as the Secretaries of State and Defense and the Joint Chiefs of Staff, each speaking with the full weight of his institution behind him. Moreover, the advocates of the adventure had a rhetorical advantage. They could strike virile poses and talk of tangible things — fire power, air strikes, landing craft and so on. To oppose the plan, one had to invoke intangibles — the moral position of the United States, the reputation of the President, the response of the United Nations, "world public opinion" and other such odious concepts. These matters were as much the institutional concern of the State Department as military hardware was of Defense. But, just as the members of the White House staff who sat in the Cabinet Room failed in their job of protecting the President, so the representatives of the State Department failed in defending the diplomatic interests of the nation. I could not help feeling that the desire to prove to the CIA and the Joint Chiefs that they were not soft-headed idealists but were really tough guys, too, influenced State's representatives at the cabinet table.   . . .

. . . By this time we were offered a sort of all-purpose operation guaranteed to work, win or lose. If it failed of its maximum hope — a mass uprising leading to the overthrow of the regime — it would at least attain its minimum objective — supply and reinforcement for the guerrillas already on the island.   . . . I arranged to see Rusk the next morning.

When I set forth my own doubts on Saturday, the Secretary listened quietly and somewhat mournfully. Finally he said he had for some time been wanting to draw a balance sheet on the project, that he planned to do it over the weekend and would try to talk with the President on Monday. He reverted to a suggestion with which he had startled the Joint Chiefs during one of the meetings. This was that the operation fan out from Guantánamo with the prospect of retreating to the base in case of failure. He remarked, "It is interesting to observe the Pentagon people.

They are perfectly willing to put the President's head on the block, but they recoil from the idea of doing anything which might risk Guantánamo."

I don't know whether Rusk ever drew his balance sheet, but probably by that Saturday morning the President had already made up his mind. . . .

Why had he decided to go ahead? So far as the operation itself was concerned, he felt, as he told me that afternoon, that he had successfully pared it down from a grandiose amphibious assault to a mass infiltration. Accepting the CIA assurances about the escape hatch, he supposed that the cost, both military and political, of failure was now reduced to a tolerable level. He added, "If we have to get rid of these 800 men, it is much better to dump them in Cuba than in the United States, especially if that is where they want to go" — a remark which suggested how much Dulles's insistence on the disposal problem had influenced the decision, as well as how greatly Kennedy was himself moved by the commitment of the Cuban patriots. He was particularly impressed by the fact that three members of the Cuban Revolutionary Council had sons in the Brigade; the exile leaders themselves obviously believed that the expedition would succeed. As the decision presented itself to him, he had to choose whether to disband a group of brave and idealistic Cubans, already trained and equipped, who wanted very much to return to Cuba on their own, or to permit them to go ahead. The President saw no obligation to protect the Castro regime from democratic Cubans and decided that, if the Cubans wished to make the try on the categorical understanding that there would be no direct United States military support, he would help them do so. If the expedition succeeded, the overthrow of Castro would greatly strengthen democratic prospects in the hemisphere; if he called it off, he would forever be haunted by the feeling that his scruples had preserved Castro in power.

More generally, the decision resulted from the fact that he had been in office only seventy-seven days. He had not had the time or opportunity to test the inherited instrumentalities of government. He could not know which of his advisers were competent and which were not. For their part, they did not know him or each other well enough to raise hard questions with force and candor. Moreover, the massed and caparisoned authority of his senior officials in the realm of foreign policy and defense was unanimous for going ahead. The director of the Central Intelligence Agency advocated the adventure; the Joint Chiefs of Staff and the Secretary of Defense approved its military aspects, the Secretary of State its political aspects. They all spoke with the sacerdotal prerogative of men vested with a unique understanding of arcane matters. "If someone comes in to tell me this or that about the minimum wage bill," Kennedy said to me later, "I have no hesitation in overruling them. But you always assume that the military and intelligence people have some secret skill not available to ordinary mortals." The only opposition came from Fulbright and myself (he knew nothing of Bowles's memorandum to Rusk, nor did he know that Edward R. Murrow, the new director of the United States Information Agency, who had learned about the operation from a *New York Times* reporter early in April, was also deeply opposed), and this did not bulk large against the united voice of institutional authority. Had one senior adviser opposed the adventure, I believe that Kennedy would have canceled it. Not one spoke against it.

Chapter Seven

PUBLIC OPINION
AND FOREIGN POLICY

The people do not actually *make* foreign policy, even in a democracy. Most Americans have neither the capacity nor the desire to deliberate on foreign policy questions. They are ill equipped to choose intelligently among the alternative courses of action available because they normally do not know what these alternatives are. Frequently, in fact, they are not even aware of the existence of important international problems.

Even Americans who *are* intensely interested in foreign affairs cannot deliberate on policy questions in town meeting fashion. The need for secrecy in international relations keeps from them critical information concerning their own and other nations' intentions and military capabilities. Because of the need to react quickly in crisis situations there may not be time for extensive public discussion of some important foreign policy decisions. Most important of all, international problems are too many and too complex for even the most intelligent and dedicated citizen to keep up with adequately in his spare time.

If the "town meeting" notion of the opinion-policy relationship is a naive illusion, what then is the actual relationship between public opinion and foreign policy? A substantial body of recent research has some relevance to this problem. Yet it is only fair to note at the start that the precise relationship between opinion and policy has not yet been defined. A review of the findings of some of this research should, however, suggest useful insights into this relationship and provide the basis for drawing a somewhat better informed — if still imperfect — picture than the "town meeting" image provides.

PUBLIC OPINION AND ITS MEASUREMENT

The words *public opinion* are merely a convenient, but not very informative, shorthand expression used to refer to an incredibly complex phenomenon. At any given time in our society, there are a large number of matters on which action is being taken — or might be taken — by public authority. In each case, a greater or lesser number of citizens will be aware that a question of policy may be involved. Of those aware of the question, a varying number will hold some articulated preference of greater or lesser consistency, intensity, and intellectual depth. Even among those unaware of the particular question, a greater or lesser number are likely to hold *latent* opinions — one or more general value preferences which they would perceive as applicable if and when they became aware of the issue. The particular configuration of opinions, latent opinions, and "non-opinions" relevant to a given public issue at any specific time might be referred to as representing public opinion on that issue at that moment.

Due to these complexities, it is not easy to measure public opinion accurately on any given issue at any specified time. Modern survey research techniques make it possible to project very accurately onto large populations findings arrived at by interviewing only a small sample of these populations. Thus interviews with a carefully selected sample of about 1,500 Americans will often make it possible to predict with only a small *sampling error* how over 100,000,000 Americans would have responded to the same questions if they had all been interviewed. Most of the research findings presented in social science journals are reliable at the 1 per cent (or occasionally at the 5 per cent) *level of significance* (or *confidence*). This means that there is only one chance in one hundred that interviews with the whole population would reverse or nullify the results obtained by interviewing just the specified sample. But sampling error is one of the *less* important hazards in measuring public opinion. The possibility of dishonesty on the part of either interviewers or respondents is another pitfall, but one which need not be gone into here.[1] More central to our concerns are the problems posed by the sheer complexity and difficulty involved in communicating and recording various shades of opinion on public issues.

On some questions these complexities can be minimized. If we ask someone during a political campaign, for instance, whom he intends to cast his presidential vote for, the likelihood is that he will have some general under-

[1] Milton Rosenberg argues that the interview situation itself is likely to yield a systematic bias in favor of responses seen by the person being interviewed as in line with the "prevailing consensus." See "Images in Relation to the Policy Process," in Herbert Kelman (ed.), *International Behavior* (New York: Holt, Rinehart and Winston, 1965), pp. 278–334, for a fuller discussion of this and other possible sources of error in survey data.

standing of the question. With few exceptions, a listing of the most prominent candidates will provide all the usable alternatives he needs to express his preference accurately.

Most questions dealing with foreign policy, on the other hand, pose much greater difficulties. For over a decade and a half, for example, the question of who should occupy China's seat in the United Nations has been a controversial issue in the United States. After the Korean War and during President Eisenhower's first term in office, two major polling organizations included questions on this issue in their opinion surveys. When asked whether Communist China "should be admitted to the United Nations," overwhelming majorities of those interviewed chose the "No" alternative. Asked whether the United States should "go along with this decision, or not," if a United Nations majority voted to "admit" Communist China, a good-sized majority thought the United States should not go along. But asked instead: "If a U.N. majority votes to admit Communist China, should the U.S. go along, or should it pull out of the U.N.?" overwhelming majorities said we *should* go along.

One survey, conducted by the National Opinion Research Center of the University of Chicago, did not restrict the alternatives offered in either of these ways, but simply asked those opposed to "admitting" Communist China what they thought the United States should do if other nations voted to seat the Peking Government in the United Nations. Their responses were then coded into a number of categories, with the following results:

1. Approve of admitting Communist China	12%
2. Disapprove	74%

If Peking admitted, U.S. should . . .

	percentage
(a) Quit the U.N.	6
(b) Use our veto	3
(c) Still oppose admission	7
(d) Keep them out	7
(e) Use force	2
(f) Don't accept admission	6
(g) Discuss with others amicably	1
(h) Go along with the majority	10
(i) Accept admission	18
(j) Miscellaneous	2
(k) Don't know; vague	12
	74

3. Depends	6%
4. Don't know	8%
	100%

If you were a public official with no other desire than to see that the "will of the people" be done on this issue, what would you interpret that will to be? Certainly, you would want to take into account not only how *many* people lined up on each side of this issue, but how *intensely* they felt about it. Were they expressing opinions on the spur of the moment and only because the interviewer called for a response? Or do they feel strongly enough to base their votes or political activities on your handling of this one issue? Would a better understanding of the question — or a different manner of posing it — cause some of the "don't know" respondents to take a stand, or induce some of those who did respond casually to change their minds? If so, fuller public discussion of the question, provoked by whatever action you might take, might activate some of their latent preferences and reveal a different alignment of opinion in the next survey taken.

In fact, public understanding of this, and many, foreign policy issues is so limited that less than one-fifth of the responses recorded above have any clear meaning at all as a guide to public policy. The United States could approve the seating of Communist China (12 per cent) or leave the United Nations if it were seated (6 per cent). It could not use the veto, because basically the question must be decided by the General Assembly, where there is no veto. To say the United States should "still oppose admission" or "keep them out" if other nations vote to seat Communist China gives no indication of *how* this is supposed to be done. Suppose it cannot. Do these respondents then want the United States to leave the United Nations or to stop short of so drastic a step? How do we "use force" to overturn a United Nations vote to seat Communist China? Do we physically invade United Nations headquarters in New York and arrest the delegates? Or do we declare war on all those who voted against us on the issue, including some of our closest allies? How do we "not accept admission" without leaving the organization? What do we do if the vote goes against us even after we have "discussed the issue with others amicably?" Even the "go along with the majority" and "accept admission" responses do not give us a clear insight into the thinking of those who made them. How hard should the United States be willing to push to keep Communist China out of the United Nations? If a majority opposes us, should we silently acquiesce in their decision? Or should we pressure those who oppose us by, say, threatening openly or tacitly to withdraw or reduce our economic aid to them?

Finally, are most of the respondents aware of the fact that the question is not actually one of *admission* at all — since China is already a member of the United Nations — but rather of which government shall *represent* China in the United Nations? And that, with the vehement opposition of both the Nationalist and Communist Chinese to any "two-China" solution, the seating of the Communists would almost certainly involve the unseating of the Nationalists? How many people might have responded differently had they known these facts? (A 1955 Gallup survey of Australian opinion on this same question showed a good-sized majority in favor of seating Communist China. But when asked whether they would still feel the same way if this meant ousting Nationalist China from the United Nations, a plurality turned out to be opposed to the idea.)[2]

In his pioneering study, *The American People and Foreign Policy*, Gabriel Almond pointed out that most Americans' foreign policy views are so lacking in intellectual structure and general knowledge that it is more appropriate to refer to them as expressions of mood rather than opinions. Most Americans care little about public policy questions. And among questions of public policy, they are far more concerned with domestic issues, which touch more closely upon their everyday lives, than they are with foreign affairs. They attend not so much to the *content* of news and speeches about foreign policy, Almond noted, as to their *tone*. Hence the urgent tones of crises are required to engage their attention to any sustained degree. Hence also the "opinions" they express are subject to broad and often sudden fluctuation between extremes of intervention and withdrawal, idealism and cynicism, optimism and pessimism, and the like.[3]

When the Gallup poll tested its respondents on terms and phrases in the news in 1950, for instance, it found that 33 per cent did not know what a tariff was, that 34 per cent could not identify Dean Acheson as Secretary of State, that 42 per cent were unfamiliar with the expression "cold war," 74 per cent with the term "bipartisan foreign policy," and 95 per cent with the words "Point Four." In October, 1951, 65 per cent did not know what the North Atlantic Treaty Organization was. During the same year, after American GI's had been fighting in Korea for thirteen months, 97 per cent of those polled could not guess even approximately the population of South Korea. The median guess was five million — just one-fourth of the actual population at the time. In 1955, less than a third could identify Karl Marx correctly. In December, 1961, 43 per cent did not know what was meant by the "fallout" from a hydrogen bomb.[4] In mid-1964, the University of Michigan's Survey Research Center found that 28 per cent of a national probability sample did not know that there was a Communist government in China. And almost two-fifths of those who *did* know this were not aware that there was another Chinese government besides the Communist one.[5]

2 See Sheldon Appleton, *The Eternal Triangle? Communist China, the United States and the United Nations* (East Lansing, Mich.: Michigan State University Press, 1961). Public opinion on this question is discussed in chap. 7 of this study.

3 (New York: Praeger, 1960.) Originally published by Harcourt, Brace in 1950. See especially chaps. 4 and 5.

4 All these figures are from Gallup poll results reported by Hazel Gaudet Erskine in "The Polls" section of *Public Opinion Quarterly*. Unless otherwise noted, subsequent survey results reported in this chapter without specific citation are from the same source, or from the files of the American Institute of Public Opinion (Gallup poll), or its monthly publication *Gallup Opinion Index*.

5 A. T. Steele, *The American People and China* (New York: McGraw-Hill, 1966), pp. 257 and 262–263. Yet between 80 and 90 per cent of similar samples have expressed either a positive or negative opinion, over the past decade, when asked whether or not Communist China should be "admitted" into the United Nations.

In March, 1966, 35 per cent could not identify Dean Rusk as Secretary of State, and more than 80 per cent failed to identify the Viet Cong correctly.[6] And no wonder, since another Gallup survey estimated that the "average" American newspaper reader squanders only two and one-third minutes of his time each day studying international news! [7]

In its study of the 1956 presidential election, the Survey Research Center tabulated thousands of open-ended responses to questions dealing with party politics and candidates. Experienced coders then classified the respondents on the basis of the level of political conceptualization observed in their replies — giving the respondents the benefit of the doubt whenever questions as to classifications arose. On this basis, the Center estimated that only 2½ per cent of the sample thought about politics in ideological or abstract terms; 9 per cent more were classed as thinking in "near-ideological" terms. Another 42 per cent perceived politics as involving group benefits or disadvantages of some sort — seeing "their" party, for example, as one which helped "working men" like themselves. Another 24 per cent perceived the election only in terms of the "nature of the times" — opposing the incumbents, for instance, because "times were bad." Finally, 22½ per cent completely "failed to comment upon any issues of political debate in their responses to the unstructured questions." [8]

The Center also tested public familiarity with six very general foreign policy issues. On virtually none of these issues did more than one-third of those interviewed have sufficient information for their policy preference rationally to influence their presidential or congressional vote. The question of whether the United States should give economic aid to foreign countries was typical of these six issues in this respect and may be used as an illustrative example. Some 17 per cent of the sample had no opinion on this issue. Another 16 per cent had an opinion (if we can call it that), but did not know what government policy on the question was — that is, whether the United States was or was not already giving economic aid to foreign nations. The lion's share, 67 per cent, had an opinion and knew what the government was doing, but saw no difference between the stands of the two major parties on the issue, thus making it irrelevant to their voting decisions. Only 23 per cent had opinions, knew what government policy was, *and* perceived partisan differences on the question. Less than one-quarter of

[6] The last figure given was computed by the writer from data presented in the "Stanford Poll" cited and reproduced in part in one of the case studies in this chapter.

[7] Reported in Bernard C. Cohen, *The Press and Foreign Policy* (Princeton, N.J.: Princeton University Press, 1963), p. 251.

[8] Angus Campbell, Philip Converse, Warren Miller, and Donald Stokes, *The American Voter* (New York: Wiley, 1960), chap. 10, and especially p. 249. As a percentage of *voters*, rather than of the total sample, the corresponding percentages are: Ideology, 3½ per cent; Near-ideology, 12 per cent; Group benefits, 45 per cent; Nature of the times, 23 per cent; No issue content, 17½ per cent.

the sample, therefore, were capable of relating their opinions on this issue to political action in any meaningful way, even if they wanted to. (For the six issues studied, the size of this last group varied from 18 to 36 per cent.) [9]

PERSONALITY AND PUBLIC OPINION

Since so many people apparently hold opinions on public issues with little or no basis in knowledge or understanding, it seems fair to ask what *are* the bases of the opinions they express. What purposes do these opinions serve for the people who hold them? There are a number of useful ways of classifying the functions served by personal opinions. We will adopt here the categories framed by Smith, Bruner, and White: *object appraisal, social adjustment,* and *externalization*.[10]

In the first place, a person's opinions help him to come to grips with reality (*object appraisal*). An aging spinster sees a television commercial hinting that the use of a particular cake of soap will make her not merely young and lovely, but perhaps even engaged. If she holds the opinion that assertions made in television commercials are usually 100 per cent accurate, she will probably soon run to the nearest supermarket to purchase a six-months' supply. In time, however, on the basis of a number of experiences with television commercials, she may decide that this opinion is not serving her well. She may therefore shift to the opinion that claims made in television commercials are best taken with a grain of salt. If this new opinion helps her appraise reality satisfactorily, by saving her money, disappointment, and repeated trips to the grocer, she will probably continue to hold it.

Second, opinions help us to relate to other people. As a rule, people prefer to be agreed with rather than disagreed with. Those who disagree with friends or business associates too often, therefore, are likely to pay a price for their opinions in loss of friendship or of business. Thus, opinions congenial to the views of friends and associates will perform an important function (*social adjustment*) for the holder. Survey research findings confirm this deduction. They indicate that the views of individuals tend to be similar to the views of those they associate with, individually or through common group memberships.[11] Those in sharp disagreement with their associates tend either to change their associates or to bring their own views

[9] *Ibid.,* chap. 8, especially pp. 174 and 182. On the foreign aid question, as for each of the other five of these vague issues, actual party differences were in emphasis, rather than in general direction. Yet this does not negate the point made by Campbell and his associates — that the connection between foreign (and, to a lesser extent, domestic) issue preferences, and actual voting behavior is ordinarily both tenuous and indirect.

[10] M. Brewster Smith, Jerome S. Bruner, and Robert W. White, *Opinions and Personality* (New York: Wiley, 1956).

[11] The similarity of views of friends and associates is undoubtedly due to the sharing by friendship groups of information, and, to a greater than average extent, of common value orientations, as well as to the effects of social adjustment described here.

closer into line with those of their friends and colleagues. Moreover, people tend to perceive their friends' opinions as being closer to their own (and vice versa) than they are, which suggests, in part, that people prefer both to agree and to *express* agreement with their friends rather than to reveal disagreement. Everyday experience suggests that a convinced socialist who did not hesitate to assert his political views would not be likely to win a popularity contest in the local Rotary club. If popularity in this club were more important to him than politics, he might well come, in time, to alter his prosocialist convictions or at least become more hesitant about advocating them publicly.

The ability of social pressures to induce opinion conformity is suggested by the results of a number of psychological experiments, including those conducted by Richard Crutchfield at the University of California. Crutchfield had subjects respond to his questions on an electrical "multiple choice" apparatus, "rigged" to record the responses of four other persons so that the subject would see them as contradicting his own perceptions or opinions. In this situation, 30 per cent of the subjects recorded themselves in agreement with the faked — and incorrect — group consensus on a series of clearcut perceptual problems which caused no errors whatever in a control group without a rigged consensus. On less clear-cut or completely ambiguous test items, the percentage adhering to the faked consensus jumped to as high as 79 per cent. Results on items involving expressions of political views were similar.[12] These striking results reflect the fact that people rely on others not only for social approval, but also for perceptual validation. That is, one of the main bases for our confidence in the capacity of our own senses to perceive reality accurately is the often noticed agreement between what *we* see and what others tell us *they* see. When this confirmation is removed, our confidence in our own perceptions — let alone our opinions — may be shaken severely.

The opinions we hold may help us to identify not only with actual face to face groups, but also with *reference groups* to which we feel some attachment — good Christians, patriotic Americans, the scholarly community, the "hip" crowd. Or they may help us to disassociate ourselves from those we dislike — bigots, "beatniks," Communists, to give a few examples. By holding (or shunning) the views such "groups" hold we make ourselves (and conceivably others as well) feel that we are like (or unlike) them.

Finally, opinions may serve unconscious emotional needs. An individual may *externalize* feelings generated by, and appropriate to, his *personal* experiences. If he feels everyone is against him, he may project this feeling by analogy to the international arena and believe that all foreign nations are

---

12 "Conformity and Character," *The American Psychologist*, X, No. 5 (May, 1955), 191–198. See also the experiments by Asch and Sherif described in Maccoby, Newcomb, and Hartley, *Readings in Social Psychology* (3rd ed.; New York: Holt, 1958), pp. 174–183 and 219–232.

out to get the country he identifies with. If, in childhood, he felt rejected or mistreated by his father, he may have a strong emotional need to hate his father. But expressions of hatred toward a stern father may bring severe punishment to a child. Even in adult life, open hatred of a parent may occasion intolerable guilt feelings in a person sensitive to social and religious precepts which call upon us to love and honor our parents. These bottled-up feelings will relentlessly seek an outlet. If it is unacceptable to hate one's father, another suitable object for hatred may be searched out. Among the safest targets for displaced hatred or hostility in our society are Communists — Communist Russia and Communist China, Fidel Castro and Mao Tse-tung — as well as many "out" groups (Negroes, Jews, "beatniks," etc.) within the society. Even the most virulent slanders are socially permissible if directed against appropriate targets.

In extreme cases, an American with strong unfulfilled needs to express both hostility and submission, say, might join the Communist party where both his impassioned denunciations of Wall Street oppressors and his slavish obedience to party authority will win approval. Or, if he has come to feel compulsively that any weakness on his part (or his country's) is intolerable, he might join the John Birch society, which will ratify his feelings that weakness and evil come from — literally — foreign sources; and may help him to rationalize his conviction that his country cannot be evil or weak by declaring that anything evil or weak found within it must come from a common *outside* source of evil — such as international communism.[13]

The extent to which any specific opinion held by an individual is based on his needs for object appraisal, social adjustment, or externalization will depend on a number of circumstances. In general, the clearer the stimulus he is responding to, and the more frequent his need to deal with it, the more likely a person is to base his opinions about a matter on object appraisals. The more ambiguous it is, and the more remote from his immediate experience, the more room will there be for social and emotional needs and influences to come into play. Since few areas of personal or public life are more unclear to Americans, or more remote from their everyday experiences, than foreign affairs, it follows that foreign policy opinions are more likely than views on most other subjects to be rooted in social or emotional needs.

This has certain implications for the possibilities of altering these opinions. Views which primarily serve object appraisal needs should be able to

13 See T. W. Adorno, Else Frenkel-Brunswik, D. J. Levinson, and R. N. Sanford, *The Authoritarian Personality* (New York: Harper, 1950); Gabriel Almond, *et al.*, *The Appeals of Communism* (Princeton, N.J.: Princeton University Press, 1954); and Eric Hoffer, *The True Believer* (New York: Harper, 1951). All examples given in the text are purely illustrative and do not imply either that all or most Communist party members or John Birchers have the psychological needs cited, or that all those with such needs join these organizations. Similar emotional needs can be expressed in a multitude of ways; and a single outlet for emotional expression may serve a multitude of needs.

be changed by providing the person who holds them with additional information or new arguments demonstrating that a different opinion would help him to cope with reality more efficiently. But we cannot expect information and rational persuasion alone to prove very successful in altering opinions primarily held, consciously or subconsciously, for social or emotional reasons. Such views are likely to be altered only if it can be shown (and not merely intellectually) that these needs can be satisfied better in other ways — if in fact they can be. (It may well be better for all, in some cases, if disturbed individuals continue to direct their hostilities at Castro or Mao rather than at their fathers, sons, or bosses.) It should be kept in mind that the categories we have described are not airtight compartments and that in many cases a single opinion serves more than one of these three functions.

The possibilities of changing a person's opinions depend also on the *intensity* with which they are held. (And emotionally based opinions tend to be more intense than others.) When confronted with inconsistencies among their opinions, people will usually try to reduce these inconsistencies by modifying the views that are least important to them, subjectively, and therefore the least "costly" for them to change. In some cases, the most acceptable way out may be simply to ignore or deny the existence of any inconsistency. When a person you admire takes a policy stand you disagree with, you can respond by modifying your own policy stand, by qualifying your admiration for him, or by declining to see any important inconsistency between your respect for him and your opposition to the views he advocates. Your choice is likely to depend on the relative intensity of your feelings about the policy and the man, respectively. "If a source with some prestige attempts to change opinions which are very different from his own and which are very strongly held, he is likely only to reduce his prestige." [14] The third alternative will most often be chosen when feelings about the man and the policy are either both weak or both strong.

MAIN CURRENTS IN OPINION
ON FOREIGN POLICY

We have discussed briefly the nature and measurement of public opinion and some of the purposes opinions serve for those who hold them. Now it is time to look at the substantive content of some of the opinions we have been examining. It would not be very useful, however, to present in detail the myriad of survey research findings concerning American views on various foreign policy issues. At best, these would merely define the popular view of particular problems at particular moments in recent history. Since both the problems and public views about them may change rather rapidly, we

14 Robert Lane and David Sears, *Public Opinion* (Englewood Cliffs, N.J.: Prentice-Hall, 1964), p. 47. This little volume provides the best short treatment available of most of the concepts treated in this chapter.

will review only findings, based on a number of nationwide surveys, which seem to reveal persistent popular approaches toward certain fundamental dimensions in foreign affairs.

Isolationism vs. Internationalism. In the first place, whatever past predilections the American people may have shown for "isolationism," it now seems unmistakably clear that since World War II a considerable majority have come to accept, at least in principle, the necessity for the United States to play an active role in world affairs. This does not mean that the masses have thought through the implications of this view and are always willing to accept the sacrifices which an active foreign policy requires. Nevertheless, large majorities have repeatedly taken what we will call the *internationalist* position on a wide range of foreign policy issues. As we use the term here, internationalism is meant to indicate support for (1) large military expenditures and a peacetime selective service system; (2) long-term treaties of alliance committing the United States to the defense of Western Europe and certain parts of Asia and the Middle East, as well as — of course — the Americas; (3) the stationing abroad, in support of these commitments, of substantial American air, naval, and ground forces; (4) the provision of sizable sums in economic and military aid to non-Communist nations throughout the world; and (5) active American participation in the United Nations. On nearly all these issues, a nationwide internationalist consensus can be said to exist, cutting across most demographic groupings within the population.

In mid-1954, Gallup interviewers asked a national sample of Americans whether they considered themselves basically isolationist or internationalist in their approach to foreign affairs. Almost four-fifths of those who replied chose the latter designation. Seven years later, a world Gallup survey found that 83 per cent of the Americans interviewed felt it "very important to make the United Nations a success," a larger percentage than that in any of the other countries polled — Norway (81 per cent); Great Britain (75 per cent); West Germany (60 per cent); and France (45 per cent). Among the six additional national capitals polled, only in the city of Manila, in the Philippines, did a larger percentage (84 per cent) take this position. These illustrations could readily be multiplied. (See Table I for additional indications of the internationalist consensus.)

Europe and Asia. Just as the pre-World War II American tradition of "isolationism" was principally concerned with keeping the United States out of Europe's affairs, so the current consensus on American internationalism applies primarily to Europe. The hard lessons of World War II and its aftermath, the absence of large ethnic groups identifying with Soviet Russia, and bipartisan political support for the Marshall Plan and NATO have made possible a truly impressive public determination to uphold American commitments to the defense of Europe. In surveys conducted in 1949, 1958, 1959, and 1961, the American people professed by overwhelming margins their

TABLE I ^a

PUBLIC RESPONSES TO SELECTED SURVEY QUESTIONS
ON FOREIGN AFFAIRS

Do you think we should keep American forces in Berlin — along with British and French forces — even at the risk of war? (Asked of 76 per cent of national sample "familiar" with Berlin situation. Gallup, Aug., 1961.)

    Yes 82%   *No* 7%   *No opinion* 11%

Do you think it would be best for this country in the long run to form even closer ties with Western Europe than we now have, or to maintain ties of about the same degree of closeness as now, or to start pulling back from our ties with these nations as soon as possible? (Roper, Sept., 1963.)

    Form closer ties 32%   *Maintain present ties* 34%
    Pull back   6%   *No opinion*   28%

In general, how do you feel about foreign aid — are you for it or against it? (Gallup, March, 1965.)

    For 57%   *Against* 33%   *No opinion* 10%

President Johnson has proposed that Congress set aside about $3.4 billion for aid to countries in other parts of the world, or about 3 per cent of the total annual budget. Would you like to see this amount increased or decreased? (Gallup, March, 1965.)

Increased 6%   *Kept same* 33%   *Decreased* 49%   *No opinion* 12%

Would you like to see the amount of money being spent on space exploration increased, decreased, or kept the same as now? (Gallup, July, 1965.)

Increased 16%   *Kept same* 42%   *Decreased* 33%   *No opinion* 9%

Do you think Communist China should or should not be admitted as a member of the United Nations? (Gallup, April, 1966.)

    Should 25%   *Should not* 55%   *No opinion* 20%

Would you favor the admission of Communist China if it would improve U.S.-Communist China relations? (Gallup, April, 1966.)

    Favor 56%   *Oppose* 28%   *No opinion* 16%

If the United Nations had not been in existence, do you think there would likely have been another war, or not? (Gallup, June, 1965.)

    Yes 59%   *No* 26%   *No opinion* 15%

It has been suggested that the United States and Russia sign a new treaty under which both countries would agree not to help other nations build atomic bombs. Such a treaty might keep the number of countries who have the atom bomb to a minimum. Would you favor or oppose such a treaty between the United States and Russia? (Harris, Oct., 1966.)

    Favor 67%   *Oppose* 14%   *Not sure* 19%

As you probably remember, in late April of this year, the U.S. sent troops into the Latin American nation of Santo Domingo [sic]. Do you think the U.S. did the right thing or the wrong thing in deciding to send troops into Santo Domingo? (Gallup, Dec., 1965.)

    Right thing 52%   *Wrong thing* 21%   *No opinion* 27%

---

^a Gallup poll questions in this table are used by permission of the American Institute of Public Opinion.

willingness to risk war in order to keep American forces in Berlin, to prevent a ground and air blockade of Berlin, or to defend the right of the people of that city to elect their own government. And this response prevailed with little variation in all regions of the country and among Republicans, Democrats, and Independents alike.

Responses to similar questions concerning American intervention in Asia, on the other hand, reveal substantial uncertainty and disagreement within the populace. In 1954–55, two National Opinion Research Center surveys showed majorities willing to defend the Chinese Nationalist bastion of Taiwan by force if necessary. In 1958, however, Gallup and Roper polls both showed majorities of those following the news on the offshore islands crisis then in progress taking a very different stand. Not only were considerable majorities opposed to risking war in defense of the offshore islands, but slim pluralities were now opposed to risking war in defense of Taiwan itself — despite the United States treaty commitment to defend that island. And United States military intervention to aid France in Indochina prior to the latter's partition in 1954 was rejected several times by sizable majorities.

A number of factors undoubtedly contribute to these divisions over United States policy in Asia in contrast to the clear consensus supporting the defense of Western Europe. Americans have fewer ethnic, cultural, and economic ties to Asia than to Europe. The nation's disillusionment at the Communist victory in China, and the unpleasant experience in Korea, may have moved many to feel that it would be well to avoid further ventures into the quicksand of Asian politics. In terms of democratic or anticolonial principle, or even from the standpoint of enlightened United States national interest, a reasonable case can be made against further United States military intervention in Asia. Most important, perhaps, Asia is so remote from the awareness of most Americans that the idea of spending American blood and treasure in defense of "far away places with strange sounding names" must appear incongruous to many citizens.

Few American schools or even colleges provide their students with even the most elementary introduction to the politics, history, and civilizations of Asia. The finding that 28 per cent of a nationwide sample in mid-1964 was not aware that China was controlled by a Communist government has already been cited.[15] At the height of the 1958 offshore islands crisis, only 14 per cent of the public knew where the islands of Quemoy and Matsu were located, and only 10 per cent knew that they were controlled by the Chinese Nationalist government on Taiwan. The amazing fact is that so many who did *not* know where they were or who controlled them, *were* willing to have the nation fight in their defense.

[15] An analysis of newspapers in a dozen American cities, covering the month of March, 1964, showed most of them devoting an average of between one-fifteenth and one-third of one column daily to news relating to China, and less relating to Japan. The only exceptions were *The New York Times* and the *Washington Post*, which averaged about one column a day on China and one-third of a column on Japan. Steele, *op. cit.*, p. 157.

Peace and War. Like all other sane peoples in the nuclear age, Americans are "for" peace, and "against" war — though there usually remains a residue of about 10 per cent who believe the United States should attack the Soviet Union at any given time. This does not mean, of course, that Americans will opt for peace under any circumstances. More than 80 per cent of those queried in 1961 by Gallup interviewers stated, for instance, that they would prefer an all-out nuclear war to life under communism. (Only 21 per cent of the Britons questioned shared this feeling. Another 48 per cent declined to answer the question.) And, as we have noted, close to 80 per cent were willing to fight to protect the Western position in Berlin.

Perhaps the American desire for peace is most evident in responses to questions about high-level negotiation on international issues. Almost always, considerable public majorities approve suggestions for negotiation with Russian or even Chinese Communist leaders. Yet follow-up questions show that many of those who approve these top-level conferences have no rosy illusions about their prospects for success. Their response seems rather a reflection of the belief that "there's no harm in trying."

Curiously, many of the same Americans who profess wholehearted devotion to the cause of peace advocate also that their country adopt a firmer (or tougher) posture in its relations with Communist nations. Survey results make it clear that national political figures perceived as being "tough" on communism usually rise in public esteem as a consequence, whereas a public image of "softness" toward communism can prove politically fatal. The public's attitude on this issue seems to favor as much "toughness" as we can get away with short of war. "Hang your clothes on a hickory limb," that is, "but don't go near the water."

In reviewing foreign policy opinion survey results at any time, then, it is well to remember that "peace" and "war," like "appeasement," "freedom," and the like are emotional words. Their inclusion in a survey item is likely to affect public response to that item regardless of its factual content.

Most people do not really think through the implications of their opinions and often will not even perceive inconsistencies in their responses which are obvious to the observer. Rather they normally seek to relate something in the question before them to a value preference they already hold. When their value preferences are potentially conflicting, as in the case of the widely shared desires for both peace and firmness against communism, their response may depend on which of these desires is most important to them. But it may also depend on which conflicting value is perceived as most relevant to the question asked — that is, on which value preference is *engaged* by the question.

Thus a question asking if the United States "should help defend the freedom of Laos against Communist aggression" would undoubtedly draw more positive replies than an item inquiring if the United States should be willing to "go to war in defense of Laos." The former question would spell out the consequences of nonintervention, but not of intervention, while engaging many respondents' attraction for freedom and their dislike of communism and aggression. The latter would spell out the cost of intervention, but not of inaction, engaging in some respondents only their opposition to war. After all, a majority have probably never heard of Laos. (This is one of the things, incidentally, which makes the nearly unanimous public willingness to "go to war" in defense of Western rights in Berlin so impressive.) [16]

Principle vs. Expediency. Americans frequently talk about foreign affairs in terms of moral precepts, and there can be little doubt that a good number are willing to subordinate self-interest to humanitarian principle in certain circumstances. Nevertheless, survey results suggest that a large majority are reluctant to hold the United States to the strict legal and moral standards which they delight in applying to its adversaries.

Immediately after the atomic bombing of Hiroshima, for example, 85 per cent of those queried approved of the use of atomic bombs against Japanese cities. Almost a quarter of those questioned four months later by *Fortune* magazine wished we had used many more atomic bombs on Japan before she had a chance to surrender. In contrast, less than 5 per cent felt we should not have used these weapons at all. Over three-quarters of those questioned by Gallup in February, 1950, approved of the United States going ahead with the development of the hydrogen bomb. Six months later, during the Korean War, approximately the same percentage approved of the United States using the atom bomb if the nation got into another world war. And in February, 1951, 66 per cent thought that in case of all-out war the United States should use atomic bombs on Russia before she used them on us.

When, in the fall of 1961, the Soviet Union violated its pledge not to conduct nuclear bomb tests, American voices rang out loud and clear in condemnation of Communist perfidy and lack of moral integrity. Yet, a few months before, a Gallup poll had revealed a greater than two-to-one majority among the American people in favor of having the United States be the first to resume nuclear tests, in violation of a similar pledge we had made. American protests against Communist violations of international law have been similarly vociferous. Yet public satisfaction with President Eisenhower's handling of the presidency did not abate significantly in the wake of the 1960 U-2 incident, which represented a clear-cut, clandestine violation of Soviet sovereignty by an American aircraft. And public approval of President Kennedy's performance of his job as President jumped *up* five percentage points immediately following the unsuccessful, United States-sponsored, exiles' invasion of Castro's Cuba in April, 1961 — again in clear violation of international law. The following month, over four-fifths of those with opinions on the matter expressed approval of Kennedy's handling of the

[16] For a comprehensive discussion of the methodological problems involved in public opinion polling — and particularly of the effects of variations in the wording of survey questions, see Hadley Cantril, *Gauging Public Opinion* (Princeton, N.J.: Princeton University Press, 1944).

Cuban problem. These figures are all the more remarkable when we consider that in both cases an issue of foreign policy effectiveness, as well as one of moral principle, was raised. A large majority also approved the United States intervention in the Dominican Republic in 1965. (For a discussion of ethics and foreign policy, see Chapter Eight.)

GROUPINGS AND FOREIGN POLICY OPINIONS

These major policy orientations prevail in all main demographic groupings in the population. But the differences among these groupings, though smaller than the differences *within* each of them, remain important. Some of these differences are summarized in Table II. The groupings listed in the left-hand column are not only more "internationalist" than those on the right, but also better informed about foreign affairs, more interested in them, more likely to vote and participate in political life, to feel that they can be politically effective, and to support long-range programs. The groupings listed in the right-hand column are more likely to be apathetic toward the political process, or alienated from it, and to favor responding to foreign affairs problems by either militant action or withdrawal — or both. The groupings listed in each column of the table are related to each other as well as to "internationalism," and are mutually reinforcing. Education is probably the most important among them, since a glance at the table will show that it is predominantly the better educated segments of the population which appear in the left-hand column, and the least educated groupings which appear on the right.[17]

TABLE II

RELATIVE "INTERNATIONALISM" OF DIFFERENT POPULATION GROUPINGS

Above average internationalism	*Below average internationalism*
College educated	Grade school educated
High income	Low income
Professionals and businessmen	Unskilled workers, farmers, small businessmen
Young and middle-aged	Old
Infrequent churchgoers	Regular churchgoers
Jews, Quakers, Unitarians, Episcopalians, Congregationalists, Presbyterians	Catholics, Southern Baptists fundamentalist Protestants
Urban residents	Country and small-town residents
	Negroes

The characteristics of some population groupings which cannot be fitted readily into the one-dimensional framework of Table II are discussed briefly below:

[17] A large quantity of survey data relevant to these differences is summarized and discussed in Alfred O. Hero, Jr., *Americans in World Affairs* (Boston: World Peace Foundation, 1959), chaps. 5 and 6.

Region. Traditionally, the Midwest has been considered a bastion of isolationism, while the Eastern seaboard states, and especially the South, have been more internationalist. As Samuel Lubell has suggested, this may have been due in large part to the fact that internationalists in both world wars called for United States intervention in support of Britain against Germany, whereas the Midwest contains sizable groups of German and Irish Americans.[18] Whatever the reasons, recent survey results show only relatively small regional differences in opinions on foreign affairs. Perhaps Midwesterners remain a trace less internationalist than those in other regions, but only a trace. And residents of the Pacific Coast states, as might be surmised, seem somewhat more interested in Asia than those in the other regions.

Southerners are more likely to support military expenditures and military approaches to foreign affairs, but less likely to support the United Nations, conciliatory and long-range programs, or economic aid to the developing (usually nonwhite and neutralist) nations. Less interested in and informed about world affairs than Northerners, Southerners tend to be more pessimistic about the prospects for peaceful resolution of the cold war. And a number of white Southerners have developed considerable sympathy for the position of white minorities in Africa.[19]

Sex. In the lower income groups especially, there seems to prevail a division of labor which assigns to women primary responsibility for the home and matters close to it, and to men primary responsibility for attending to the world beyond. Accordingly, men are on the average more interested in and informed about public affairs generally and foreign affairs in particular. Also, perhaps as a reflection of cultural expectations, women tend to be substantially less militant, more idealistic, and more internationalist than men in their responses to foreign affairs questions. The positive connotations of the words "peace" and "cooperation," for example, and the negative connotations of "war" and "force," tend to be more persuasive to members of the fair sex than to their male consorts, who sometimes see expressions of "toughness" as one means of proving their masculinity. In 1964, for the first time since the 1940's, women reported themselves as voting Democratic more often than did men, in large part, apparently, on the grounds that Lyndon Johnson was more likely to keep the peace than Barry Goldwater.

Age. Since World War II, young people have been given the opportunity to acquire more schooling than their parents and grandparents had. They have been exposed to more classes stressing the United Nations and foreign affairs — generally taught by persons who are themselves internationalists. And they have grown up in a more internationally oriented society in

18 *The Future of American Politics* (3rd ed., rev.; New York: Harper, 1965), chap. 7.
19 A comprehensive study of the nature and evolution of Southern views of United States foreign policy is Alfred O. Hero, Jr., *The Southerner and World Affairs* (Baton Rouge: Louisiana State University Press, 1965).

general. Nevertheless, *when education is held constant,* people in their twenties prove to be less interested, informed, and internationalist — and more militant — than those in their thirties and forties. This is probably because young people are often engaged in finding a place in society for themselves, a task which often pushes public affairs to the periphery of their concerns.

Race. Negroes, as an underprivileged minority group, display most of the tendencies cited as characteristic of lower status groups in general, in even more exaggerated form. Even middle-class Negroes, who might otherwise develop considerable interest in foreign affairs, often are understandably preoccupied with civil rights issues instead. During the Korean War, an unusually high proportion of Negroes were disposed toward complete American withdrawal from Korea. And of a large Negro sample polled for *Newsweek* by Louis Harris in 1963, about one-fifth were not sure that in case of another war, the United States would be worth fighting for.[20]

National Origin. So long as "internationalism" meant opposition to Germany and aid to Britain, "old stock" Americans tended to be more internationalist than those of more recent immigrant origin. Today this tendency has been very nearly reversed. More recent immigrants are more likely to be less well-educated, upwardly mobile, Catholic, and to have ties with areas in southern and eastern Europe which have fallen under Communist control. Thus they tend to be overrepresented in militant ultra-patriotic organizations. Some, like the Hungarian refugees who arrived in the wake of the abortive revolt of 1956, and the anti-Castro Cuban refugees who have concentrated in Miami, have good reason for being more hostile toward communism than most Americans. And those of German origin, who presumably were once "isolationist," may welcome the opportunity to show their patriotism without opposing the land of their historic origins.

Party. There is little difference between the adherents of the two major political parties on most major foreign policy questions. From time to time, criticisms of the foreign policy actions of incumbent presidents have yielded temporary foreign policy issues with high partisan content as, for example, during the Korean War when the Truman administration policy was much more often approved by Democrats than by Republicans. But the overall orientation of the masses of Republican and Democratic voters seem today to be basically similar.

The Democratic party national *leadership,* in contrast, is in general more internationalist in orientation than its Republican counterpart. The very lack of major differences on foreign affairs between rank and file Republicans

---

20 "The Negro in America," *Newsweek,* July 29, 1963, p. 18. Although some civil rights organizations have spoken out against American involvement in Vietnam, 1965 Gallup poll data suggested that "non-whites" were more likely than whites to approve President Johnson's handling of this conflict.

and Democrats suggests, moreover, that, all things considered, Democratic orientation tends to be an influence toward internationalism. For the Democratic party is composed disproportionately of low-income, low-education groupings which tend to favor a narrowly nationalistic approach to foreign affairs, whereas a disproportionate percentage of Republican identifiers are wealthier, better educated and therefore normally more internationalist in their foreign policy outlook. In light of these tendencies, the fact that Republicans are *not* significantly more internationalist than Democrats suggests that identification with the Democratic Party tends to encourage internationalism.

GROUPS AND FOREIGN POLICY OPINIONS

The *groupings* we have been discussing are no more than analytical categories articulated by the demographer and survey researcher. They are not, for the most part, *groups* in the sense that their members meet one another regularly or are organized in some fashion to forward what they perceive to be common interests. But it is *groups* in this sense — rather than analytical *groupings* — which play the pivotal role in molding and influencing the opinions of those who belong to them, and sometimes of those who do not. The similarities of opinion of people with common membership in one or more *groupings* is, in fact, usually due to the fact that such people are more likely to belong to one or more of the same *groups*.

The most universally influential of these primary groups is, of course, the family. It is usually within the family group that party attachments and value preferences relevant to foreign affairs are first formed. The information which supports these attachments and preferences normally is not learned until later.[21] In transmitting some image of the nation's historical experience from one generation to the next, the family probably exerts on balance, a conservative influence on the foreign policy opinions of its offspring. As the late V. O. Key has written, there are many more farmers' sons than farmers in the American population today, and the offspring of farm families show significantly more isolationist tendencies than the children of any other major occupational grouping.[22]

Parents can also influence the later foreign policy outlooks of their children indirectly, by their patterns of child rearing. Persons who score high on tests of authoritarianism, ethnocentrism, and alienation, for example, are somewhat more likely to come from lower than from upper and middleclass families. And such persons are also more likely than those with low scores on these personality tests to be nationalistic, pessimistic, and militant rather

---

21 Lane and Sears, *op. cit.*, p. 19.
22 *Public Opinion and American Democracy* (New York: Knopf, 1961), pp. 308–309.

than conciliatory in their approach to foreign affairs. (These tendencies generally remain when class status is held constant.) [23]

School and college classes comprise another set of primary groups which exercise significant influence in the formative years. The effects of education on opinion, which have already been discussed, clearly stem in part from the group pressure generated in school situations as well as from the information and analytical skills imparted in the course of the educational process. A school or college group, like any other primary group, possesses its own distinctive set of social and political norms and exacts a certain degree of conformity to these norms in return for full acceptance by the group. The more such a group involves the time and energies of its members, the greater these pressures toward conformity will be. Thus the college dormitory may be an exceptionally effective mechanism for inducing opinion change on *social adjustment* grounds, especially when the implications of material learned in the classroom point in the same — usually internationalist — direction. Friendship, work, and recreational groups also influence their members' opinions, as noted earlier.

In addition, there is in American society an abundance of organized interest groups concerned with foreign affairs. Perhaps the most important consequence of their activities on foreign policy is that *particular* interests are often so effectively represented that the task of the political leader dedicated to the service of the common *national* good is made unduly difficult and hazardous. (See Chapter Two.)

Among the main organized groups regularly taking positions on major foreign affairs issues are business organizations like the United States Chamber of Commerce and the National Association of Manufacturers; labor organizations like the AFL-CIO; farmers' organizations like the American Farm Bureau Federation, the National Grange and the Farmers' Union; Veterans' organizations like the American Legion, the Veterans of Foreign Wars, the American Veterans Committee and the AMVETS; political parties, discussed earlier; religious organizations like the Federal Council of Churches of Christ in America, the Catholic Association for International Peace, and the Friends Committee on National Legislation; civic organizations like the Foreign Policy Association, the League of Women Voters, Rotary International and the United Nations Association; ethnic group organizations such as the American Polish Association and the Zionist Organization of America; and various issue-oriented or ad hoc groups such as the American Tariff League, the Committee of One Million Against the Admission of Communist China to the United Nations, and the United World Federalists.

[23] Rosenberg, *op. cit.*, pp. 322–329; and Hero, *Americans in World Affairs*, pp. 30–36. Rosenberg also discusses briefly some of the methodological objections which have been raised against these personality scaling techniques, but concludes that they do not invalidate the gross conclusions cited here.

The influence of these groups upon the opinions of their members depends (1) on the clarity and unanimity of the positions taken by the group's leadership; (2) on the extent to which each group serves the social, economic, or emotional needs of its members — so that loss of status within the group, due to the failure to conform to group norms, would constitute a serious personal deprivation; and (3) on the perceived relevance of the group's purposes and activities to the issue in question.

When these interest groups take conflicting positions on public issues, the same factors will be important in determining the relative influence each exerts on individuals who belong to several groups, as many Americans do. Persons belonging to groups taking conflicting positions on a public issue are sometimes said to be *cross-pressured,* and they may respond by withdrawing from political participation on the issue. That is, they may hesitate to discuss it, to develop strong feelings about it, or even to form an explicit opinion about it, unless they can resolve these cross-pressures by making a clear-cut choice in favor of one group or another on the basis of the considerations cited. (This applies only to situations in which social adjustment considerations are predominant.)

In addition to influencing the opinions of their members to some extent, most interest groups try to influence public officials directly. They provide technical information and briefs supporting their point of view to Congressmen and congressional committees. Their representatives may testify at legislative hearings — where the spokesmen of business organizations, in particular, are usually well received.[24] They organize telegram and letterwriting campaigns, present their views to legislators via personal interviews, and conduct public relations and "educational" campaigns designed to influence Congressmen by persuading constituents. Sometimes they succeed in making legislators or other officials feel obliged to them by contributing handsomely to political campaign funds or performing other political or personal favors. Usually, they will claim to speak in the name of considerable segments of the electorate and imply — though rarely declare outright — that the legislator who heeds their claims will be rewarded, and the one who ignores them punished, at the polls.

Whether interest group representatives are actually capable of delivering the vote to the extent they may sometimes hint is dubious; and on many issues the competing claims of different interest groups may tend to balance one another out. Yet politicians are by nature a cautious breed when it comes to risking the loss of any substantial number of votes. Therefore, when the claims pressed by a major local or national interest group seem tolerable,

24 See Bernard C. Cohen, *The Influence of Non-Governmental Groups on Foreign Policy-Making* (Boston: World Peace Foundation, 1959). Nevertheless no satisfactory method has yet been devised which would make it possible to measure with any precision the influence of particular interest groups on specific foreign policy decisions.

and when the honoring of one group's requests seems unlikely to offend any other comparable group, the legislator's temptation to yield will be strong.

On specific occasions when a large — or even a small, but strategically located — interest group is united and vehement in its advocacy of a particular course of action, it may be capable of influencing foreign policy in some instances. To illustrate: relatively small American Zionist groups have periodically generated considerable pressure on behalf of United States recognition and support for the state of Israel. The influence of these groups depends less on the size of their membership than on the fact that large numbers of Jewish voters live in New York City and other metropolitan centers located in the big, "swing" states which decide presidential elections under the electoral college system.

Thus, when the state of Israel was formed, in the election year of 1948, following a United Nations General Assembly recommendation, the United States extended recognition almost immediately, despite strong misgivings among most State Department specialists on the Middle East. President Truman, whose policy actions were for the most part extremely favorable to Israel, has written of the period preceding this United Nations action in his memoirs: "I do not think I ever had as much pressure and propaganda aimed at the White House as I had in this instance. The persistence of a few of the extreme Zionist leaders — actuated by political motives and engaging in political threats — disturbed and annoyed me." [25] And President Eisenhower's chief assistant, Sherman Adams, has written in his memoirs, concerning the Suez crisis in the election year of 1956:

> . . . Any attempt to give aid to the Arabs always met with opposition behind the scenes in Washington, where the members of Congress were acutely aware of the strong popular sentiment in this country for Israel. Had the members of Congress either underestimated or overlooked the strength of such feeling they would have been quickly reminded of it by the alert representatives of the many well-organized pro-Israel lobbies that were always effective and influential in the Capitol. Consideration for the great body of private opinion in the United States favoring Israel was a large factor in every government decision on the Middle East issues, especially in the [Suez] crisis. . . .[26]

THE MASS MEDIA

Opinions are circulated through the citizenry principally by word of mouth and via the mass media: newspapers, magazines, radio, television, movies, public addresses — occasionally even in books.

Editorials on behalf of particular candidates for office, or in support of specific foreign policy alternatives, are among the least influential contribu-

---

[25] *Years of Trial and Hope* (Garden City, N.Y.: Doubleday, 1956), p. 158.
[26] *First-Hand Report* (New York: Harper, 1961), pp. 247–248.

tions of the mass media to public thinking on foreign policy. The interested public ordinarily looks to the media to *define* policy problems and to formulate alternative means of dealing with them. Which of the alternatives presented individual members of the public may then choose to favor is likely to depend more upon personal value preferences, group memberships, and other factors than upon the policy recommendations of the media. For an overwhelming majority of the people, the media represent their only link with the concrete realities of international affairs. The media — and the leaders they often quote — are therefore much more potent in determining what the people will think about than in dictating what they will think about it.

Even media presentations with no apparent political content may affect popular modes of thinking about foreign affairs. In the first place, the media provide convenient distractions for those disposed to avoid the burdens of giving thought to matters of public policy. The pervasive tendency of movies, television and radio melodramas, and slick fiction is to portray people in black and white and to reinforce folk notions of moral propriety. Through repeated exposure, these stock characters and stock notions undoubtedly become a part of the life experience from which many Americans draw their basic approaches to foreign affairs. The foreign policy implications, for example, of the American folk precept that virtue and effort (like true love) always triumph, is discussed — along with the effects of kindred notions — in Chapter Two.

The media devote relatively little attention to public affairs and still less to international politics. (It is an axiom of the newspaper business that a reader's interest in the news decreases as its distance from his front door increases.) But it should not be thought that this creates a hardship for most newspaper readers or television viewers. Few follow closely the scant foreign news coverage the media do provide. Those with a genuine interest in foreign affairs are always at liberty to inform themselves further by purchasing *The New York Times* or any one or more of a number of newspapers and periodicals which offer fairly extensive international news coverage. The average citizen is more likely to be influenced by newspaper *headlines* — and by the *placement* of news and accompanying photographs — than by the actual content of the news itself. (The standard radio and TV newscasts, too, provide little more than the equivalent of headlines.) Many Americans doubtless share fully the sentiments of the TV comedy fan who reacted to candidate Adlai Stevenson's pre-emption of the "I Love Lucy" show for a campaign speech by telegraphing: "I Love Lucy and I like Ike. Drop Dead."

Even those who pay above average attention to international news are susceptible to media influence through means more subtle than direct editorial suggestion. After a careful study of the three leading weekly newsmagazines, for instance, a Washington correspondent for the *Providence Journal-Bulletin* concluded:

> The outstanding characteristic of the political reporting of *Time* magazine is that without telling the reader why, the magazine surrounds personalities with an emotional aura, sometimes with adjectives, sometimes with verbs, sometimes with figures of speech.
>
> Stylistically, the result is the most dramatic, crisp and evocative language in the news profession. But politically it is a vapor of bias that seeps into the text, clouding facts and by-passing the normal political judgement of the reader. It is a highly artistic technique, but a study of *Time's* behavior in recent political campaigns shows that it is used as a partisan political weapon. . . .
>
> The bias appeared in the balance of space, in the selection of facts, and in the use of pictures and illustrations. But the chief weapon was the emotional prejudgement with which it surrounded the news. . . .
>
> . . . By using many of these methods in the presentation of news interpretation, the news magazines are influencing a generation of middle-class voters who are extremely sensitive to conventional bias in newspaper stories but almost totally unaware of the new techniques in news magazines.[27]

It would be naive, of course, to expect the media to present "just the facts," even if they wished to do so. As Bernard Cohen indicates in a detailed study,[28] foreign affairs reporters are usually deeply committed to the ideal of objective reporting. This commitment to objectivity is often reinforced, moreover, first by the fact that a large proportion of foreign affairs news originates with new agencies which must serve a large clientele with varied policy preferences; and second by the frequency with which reporters' partisan and policy preferences differ from those of their editors and publishers. But selection of *which facts* to put into news stories, the *arrangement* of these facts, and the *interpretations* of them necessary to provide the reader with the cues which give them meaning, make total objectivity impossible.

What gets printed and what does not is generally determined by reporters' and editors' conceptions of what constitutes "news." This "news sense" is usually based, in turn, on what has been considered "news" — that is, made the front pages — in the past. The top stories in yesterday's news give the reporter his first leads in search of the page one news of tomorrow. In addition, most newspapers depend heavily on news agency bulletins offering the opinions of agency editors as to what the big stories of the day are, and on the "play" given the news by *The New York Times* and other leading na-

[27] From a series of articles by Ben H. Bagdikian in the *Providence Journal and The Evening Bulletin*, October 5–17, 1958. Reprinted by permission.

[28] *The Press and Foreign Policy* (Princeton, N.J.: Princeton University Press, 1963). The next several paragraphs draw heavily on this useful study, based in part on seventy interviews with Washington correspondents and foreign news editors.

tional and regional dailies. As a result, first one, then another "continuing news story" is kept temporarily at the forefront of public attention, then consigned to relative oblivion. Since conflict and personalities are considered of particular interest to mass readership, a conflict-ridden image of the world is conveyed to the reader by sporadic and unsystematic reporting. Thus neither the mass of headline-scanners nor the relatively few interested followers of foreign affairs are provided with an accurate foundation for foreign policy judgments.

The relationship between the public and the news seems to resemble the relationship between men and women described in the old saw: it's hard to live with them — but harder still to live without them. Adequate or inadequate, the mass media serve as the principal source of information for most of those who take a serious interest in foreign affairs. It is through the media as well that influential people, including high government officials, communicate with one another. And many Congressmen view the media as important indicators of public opinion. Even the State Department depends on *The New York Times* and the wire services for much of its information on day to day events abroad. Cohen relates that "A *New York Times* reporter once asked Undersecretary of State Sumner Welles, 'Do you know anything we don't know today?' To which Welles replied, 'Of course not, where do you think we get our information?' " [29]

OPINION LEADERSHIP

The most persuasive form of political communication that can be directed at any individual is by word of mouth. Those who pay little attention to the news content of the media are especially dependent on their conversations with other people for their images of foreign affairs and for such foreign policy opinions as they may hold. The studies of personal influence conducted by Katz and Lazarsfeld and others show that there are certain individuals to whom friends and associates rather regularly turn for information and advice on different matters. These individuals they call *opinion leaders*.[30] Some individuals exercise leadership on a number of subjects. Others specialize, so to speak, in a particular area such as women's fashions, movies, or foreign affairs.

A note of caution should be sounded here, for in some respects the term "opinion leader" may be misleading. Those who are informed and concerned about particular subjects tend to discuss them most of all with *each other*, and to influence and be influenced accordingly. At the other extreme, those

29 *The Press and Foreign Policy, op. cit.*, p. 210.

30 Elihu Katz and Paul F. Lazarsfeld, *Personal Influence* (Glencoe, Ill.: The Free Press, 1955). As the following discussion suggests, there is a need for additional research in this area to clarify the process by which opinion leadership operates over a period of time and to specify with more precision the characteristics of those who exercise influence *across* — as distinguished from *within* — class, interest, and information levels.

with no interest in a particular matter — probably a considerable proportion of the citizenry in the case of most foreign affairs issues — are likely not to discuss them at all.[31] Thus the person who is a "leader" in discussing foreign affairs with a friend today is likely to be a "follower" of that same friend on another foreign affairs issue tomorrow. Who will lead and who follow on a given matter is likely to depend on the particular interests and personalities of the individuals concerned. Though most personal influence is probably exercised in this way among people who are very much alike in class status and in information and concern about foreign affairs, we must direct our attention to the exertion of influence *across* class, information, and interest levels in order to understand how opinions are spread through large segments of the citizenry. By the term "opinion leadership," we mean to signify only relationships in which the influence on foreign affairs opinions, over a period of time, is predominantly one way — from leader to follower.

There are opinion leaders, then, in virtually all social classes and demographic groupings of the population. Most of them are members of the same social, economic, and educational groupings as the people they influence — although more often than not they hold slightly higher positions within these groupings than do their followers. It is crucial to this process of influence that followers identify themselves with their leader in some basic sense — that they feel him to be "one of them." Through the process of mutual influence, therefore, the views of foreign affairs opinion leaders and their followers are kept fairly closely in line, with the leaders' views normally tending to be clearer and more in tune with the opinions of the better-educated classes generally than are the views of their followers. Leaders also typically devote more attention and energy than their followers do to informing themselves about the issues on which they exercise leadership. Thus foreign affairs leaders are somewhat more likely than their followers to pay close attention to foreign policy news presented in the media, to buy and read magazines and newspapers providing detailed information on international affairs, and to discuss foreign policy with other people. (Much of the influence which the mass media exercise is therefore exerted indirectly through opinion leaders. It follows also that a publication read by a relatively small number of opinion leaders may have more real political influence than a publication purchased by a much greater number of people less interested in public affairs.)

The opinion leader, then, gets many of his opinions and much of his information from the media, especially from "elite" media. Another key source of the views he passes on to others are *his* opinion leaders. For there

[31] Almond and Verba found 24 per cent of a national sample in the United States declaring that they never talk politics at all — compared with 29 per cent, 39 per cent, 66 per cent and 61 per cent giving the same response in Britain, West Germany, Italy, and Mexico, respectively. *The Civic Culture* (Boston: Little, Brown, 1965), p. 79. Originally published in 1963 by Princeton University Press.

appears to be a network of opinion leaders stretching from the base of the social pyramid through community, local, and regional opinion leaders, and reaching up — on subjects like foreign affairs — to the top levels of the federal government. At the apex of this pyramid, if he wants to be, is the President of the United States. Cabinet members, Congressmen, Governors, interest group leaders, reporters, and notable private citizens are in contact with him and often with each other. They, in turn, discuss foreign affairs with a large number of less exalted national and local opinion leaders — publishers, clergymen, business executives, college professors, lawyers, doctors, public school teachers, state and local government officials, and so on down to the man acting as opinion leader for his wife (or fancying he does) in disbursing tidbits of foreign affairs news picked up from his slightly more than two-and-a-third-minute excursion into the international news columns of the local daily. (Slightly more because, as an opinion leader, we can expect him to be slightly above average in his exposure to information concerning foreign affairs.)

This network of opinion leadership provides the nerve connections of the public opinion process, transmitting information and opinions laterally, from the top down, and, after a fashion, from the bottom up. Leaders are usually kept in tune with their "constituencies" of followers by the similarity of their predispositions and perhaps also by the risk that they may lose standing with their followers if they move out of line with the latter's views too fast or too far.

A recent study by James Rosenau suggests, however, that the building of an effective nationwide foreign policy consensus is hindered by certain discontinuities in the channels of communication between national opinion leaders, oriented toward the President and the federal government, and local and regional opinion leaders, oriented toward their congressional representatives and community notables.[32] If this is in fact the case, the establishment of channels to reduce these discontinuities by encouraging close contacts between these two sets of opinion leaders may be one of the critical needs of American democracy.

HOW PUBLIC OPINION AFFECTS FOREIGN POLICY

Now it is time to try to summarize and consolidate. What *is* the actual role of public opinion in the making of American foreign policy?

The first thing to acknowledge is that because of the present stage of development of the field of political science, we cannot spell out the answer

[32] *National Leadership and Foreign Policy* (Princeton, N.J.: Princeton University Press, 1963), pp. 345–360. See also the same author's *Public Opinion and Foreign Policy* (New York: Random House, 1961), for a systematic theoretical exploration of the network through which foreign policy opinions are circulated.

to this question with any precision. The phrasing of the question is decep-
tively simple. To answer this general question accurately, we would first have
to be able to answer the more specific questions of exactly what role public
opinion played in the making of foreign policy decisions A, B, and C. To
know this, in turn, would require access to incredibly detailed and reliable
documentary information of a kind seldom available to scholars of contemporary diplomacy. More difficult yet, it would require complete access to
the notes and memories of principal decisionmakers. And even with the
benefit of all these things, it would not be easy to say exactly which persons
and which elements of the situation had exactly what influence on a particular decision. The men responsible for the decision themselves can rarely
provide this kind of information, even if they want to.

Think back to the last important decision or two you yourself have
made — the decision to attend one college rather than another, the decision
which car to buy, which field to major or make a career in, when and to
whom to get married, which job to take. Precisely when did you make up
your mind on the matter in question? Can you honestly say without any
doubts just which persons and what facts exercised the determinative influence on your thinking in the matter? If you usually can answer these questions whenever you make an important decision, you are probably a more
extraordinary person than you suspect. Certainly there is no use pretending
that political scientists have come up with information of this type in
enough specific cases to support any confident attempt to formulate these
experiences into a reliable general theory describing how public opinion
influences foreign policy.

In addition, our previous discussion of the nature of public opinion
should warn us against treating the public as a unified whole. Since we must
oversimplify the innumerable gradations of popular participation in foreign
policymaking in order to discuss the subject intelligibly, we will follow the
lead of Gabriel Almond in dividing the public, for analytical purposes, into
four subgroupings.[33]

First there are the government officials who bear formal responsibility for
making foreign policy — the President and his civilian and military advisers,
the Congress, American representatives abroad, etc. Their offices and the
sources of information to which they alone have access clearly make it inevitable that they bear the lion's share of the burden of defining policy problems and of articulating alternative means of dealing with these problems.
This is particularly the case when secrecy and/or speedy decisions are required.

Few would disagree that democratic ideals make it desirable for the government to reveal to the public as much information about foreign affairs as
it can, short of jeopardizing national security. The problem is in deciding,

---

[33] *The American People and Foreign Policy, op. cit.,* chap. 7.

in practice, what information *will* endanger national security if released and what will not. To most government officials, the risks of disclosing too much information are much more apparent than the hazards of releasing too little. Almost any civil servant is at liberty to stamp "Secret" across any report he writes, but it will take the authority of a much higher official to remove this classification. Nevertheless, the inevitable price of secrecy — justified or not — is a narrowing of the opportunities for public participation in policymaking. This, in turn, shuts off important sources of values and ideas, and impedes the building of the consensus needed to sustain support for major policy decisions.[34]

Second, there is an elite grouping outside the federal government, numbered perhaps in the thousands or tens of thousands, which often plays a significant role in setting foreign policy goals and devising the means to implement them. This elite includes political and interest group leaders, top academic specialists, leading news commentators and editors, and other notables. Especially in setting long-range goals and choosing long-term policies, this grouping may play a more important role than the governmental elite itself. A book by Professor Henry A. Kissinger [35] reputedly exercised a substantial influence on American strategic thinking in the 1950's. George F. Kennan was not a government official when he made his oft-debated proposals for United States-Soviet disengagement in Europe. Former Cabinet members Dean Acheson and Robert M. Lovett were private citizens when President Kennedy called upon them for advice during the 1962 Cuban missile confrontation. Dwight D. Eisenhower, Walter Reuther, Arthur Schlesinger, Jr., and Walter Lippmann are not government officials, but any foreign policy proposals they may care to advance are assured of a hearing in Washington as well as among the interested populace as a whole.

It is this interested populace which forms the third subgrouping, the *attentive public* — perhaps two to five million Americans [36] who have some basic knowledge about and interest in foreign affairs. Lawyers, teachers, doctors, clergymen, local union officials, businessmen, or simply interested citizens, they make an effort to follow international news in the media and take their civic responsibilities seriously. It is they who are most likely to belong to interest or civic groups concerned with foreign affairs, and to

[34] In the case of the Bay of Pigs invasion in 1961 (taken up as a case study in Chapter Six), newsmen gained access to information the United States government hoped would remain secret. Some of them voluntarily kept it from publication "in the national interest." Arthur Schlesinger, Jr., then an assistant to President Kennedy, has since "wondered whether, if the press had behaved irresponsibly, it would not have spared the country a disaster." *A Thousand Days* (Boston: Houghton Mifflin, 1965), p. 261.

[35] *Nuclear Weapons and Foreign Policy* (New York: Harper, 1957).

[36] The Survey Research Center's 1956 assessment of levels of political conceptualization, cited earlier in this chapter, suggests that approximately 2½ million Americans can articulate their views within some sort of "ideological" frame of reference. Other estimates as to the size of the attentive public run as high as five to ten million.

serve as opinion leaders at (or across) various levels within the population.

The role of the attentive public in the foreign policy process is less direct than that of the elites, but still significant. The members of the attentive public constitute the audience, so to speak, which responds to the policy proposals and debates conducted — principally through the mass media — by the elites. When they are stimulated by the debate on a particular issue, they may talk to others about it — to their parishioners, their classes, their co-workers, their clients — transmitting at least a minimal level of information and interest more widely among the population, and substantially affecting the public mood on the question. They exercise some influence, too, on members of the elites. Presidents, Secretaries of State, Congressmen, and interest group leaders — like other human beings — are not insensitive to social adjustment needs. For the most part, in fact, they tend to be inordinately sensitive to them, since, in the long run, their positions depend in large part on the opinions the attentive public holds of them. Moreover, the letters, comments, and other reactions their foreign policy views elicit often serve as an important part of the external validation they need of the correctness of their own perceptions of reality. (Experienced political observers will testify that even crowd reactions to campaign addresses may sometimes subtly modify the thinking of public men on public issues.) [37]

The foreign policy role of the fourth subgrouping, the *mass public,* is much more limited. The masses know little and care less about the details of international affairs and are normally content to follow the lead of the President in such matters. Only rarely, on issues provocative of great debate among the elites and the attentive public, does the subject of foreign affairs intrude even briefly into their consciousness. This pervasive inertia itself may well be the mass public's most important contribution to the policy process, because it leaves the elites and the attentive public free — *most* of the time — to pursue whatever foreign policy alternatives they think best in specific situations.

On certain issues, however, when the attentive public communicates downward a sense of urgency, or when one or another elite group — perceiving an opportunity to gain personal or political advantage — makes extraordinary efforts to activate the masses, greater or lesser segments of those normally oblivious to foreign policy may be drawn temporarily into the attentive public. This is most readily accomplished on issues involving an immediate threat of war, tax increases, or other noticeable changes in habitual modes of day to day living. Or the size of the attentive public may be temporarily increased when the President is willing and able to make full use of his

[37] Schlesinger notes that an unexpectedly strong positive crowd response to a mention of the recently ratified nuclear test ban treaty in a speech delivered by President Kennedy in Montana led the President "to make the pursuit of peace increasingly the theme of his trip [to the West]." *Op. cit.,* p. 979.

prestige and his unparalleled access to the media to persuade the citizenry that a particular issue is relevant to their personal lives and fortunes. In such cases, a substantial proportion of the mass public may share in the influence on policy attributed above to the attentive public.

Arousing the mass public to this extent, however, usually involves great expenditures of time, energy, and money. It also entails immeasurable political risks, since the reaction of the mass public, once aroused, is both mercurial and difficult to predict accurately. Only in exceptional cases, therefore, will members of the foreign policy elites choose to run these risks. Most of the time, they will prefer to estimate as best they can beforehand how the mass public might react to their policy proposals. Unless they feel confident that the masses would support these proposals, if put to the test, they will probably choose to settle the matter through bargaining among themselves. Only when elite estimates of latent opinion on a potentially important issue differ sharply, therefore, is it likely that one or another elite group will insist on "taking its case to the people." Since the mass public ordinarily balks at conspicuous departures from traditional policies, moreover, those who are convinced that major innovations are essential to national security will usually fare better by appealing to the patriotism and sense of responsibility of national and community leaders than by seeking to bring the reserve power of the masses into play directly.

One more critical role is played by the substantial segments of the mass public which participate in national and/or interest group elections. They share in selecting the leaders who will make foreign policy in the years to follow. And at every level, public and private, the voter or rank and file group member tends to give his support to men he identifies as being "like himself" in some way — not in abilities, but in shared values and interests. Certainly there will be some error in the citizen's perceptions of the candidates. But the average American is probably a far sounder judge of people, with whom he has had some first-hand dealings, than of foreign policies, with which he has had none. As often as not he *does* influence policy very significantly by choosing leaders who *do* share his values and concerns in important ways.

Many voters, we know, cast their ballots on the basis of simple partisan attachment, or for highly trivial reasons. The Survey Research Center found, for instance, that:

> Of constituents living in Congressional districts where there was a contest between a Republican and a Democrat in 1958, less than one in five said they had read or heard something about both candidates, and well over half conceded they had read or heard nothing about either. . . . Of detailed information about policy stands not more than a chemical trace was found. Among the comments about the candidates given in response to an extended series of free-answer questions . . . only about

three comments in every hundred had to do with legislative issues of *any* description.[38]

Similarly, a November, 1965, Gallup poll found 57 per cent of a national sample unable to name their Congressman, 70 per cent not knowing when he would come up for re-election, and 81 per cent not knowing how he voted on any major bill in the past year.

Nevertheless, even among the least involved segments of the electorate, there exists some sense of what the Survey Research Center has called "the nature of the times." Voters who feel that times are bad will tend to vote against those in power; those who think times are good will more often vote for them. This provides an important check on the behavior of elected public officials. In the last of his many important contributions to the field of Political Science, the late V. O. Key examined voting patterns in Presidential elections from 1936 to 1960:

> The perverse and unorthodox argument of this little book is that voters are not fools. To be sure, many individual voters act in odd ways indeed; yet in the large the electorate behaves about as rationally and responsibly as we should expect, given the clarity of the alternatives presented to it and the character of the information available to it. In American presidential campaigns of recent decades the portrait of the American electorate that develops from the data is not one of an electorate strait-jacketed by social determinants or moved by subconscious urges triggered by devilishly skillful propagandists. It is rather one of an electorate moved by concern about central and relevant questions of public policy, of governmental performance, and of executive personality. . . .
>
> . . . Voters, or at least a large number of them, are moved by their perceptions and appraisals of policy and performance. They like or don't like the performance of the government.[39]

In foreign and domestic affairs alike, then, the masses judge the record of an administration less by its actions — of which they are often unaware — than by the results of these actions. It might be fairer to judge the wisdom of administration policies against the criterion of what alternative policies might have accomplished instead. But few voters are capable of such intricate calculations. In politics, as in football and other aspects of American life, there is much talk of the importance of how you've played the game,

[38] Warren E. Miller and Donald E. Stokes, "Constituency Influence in Congress," *The American Political Science Review* (March, 1963), pp. 45–56. The passage quoted is from pp. 53–54. Miller and Stokes found virtually no correlation (.06) between constituency views and Congressmen's roll call voting behavior on bills relating to foreign involvement. This was substantially lower than the comparable correlation for bills relating to civil rights (.39) and social welfare (.21).

[39] *The Responsible Electorate* (Cambridge, Mass.: The Belknap Press of Harvard University Press, 1966), pp. 7, 8, and 150. See also Donald E. Stokes, "Some Dynamic Elements of Contests for the Presidency," *The American Political Science Review* (March, 1966), pp. 19–28.

but the premium on winning is nevertheless very high. An American President confident that his policy actions will bear conspicuous fruit before the next election can conduct foreign relations pretty much as he pleases, despite sizable immediate elite and latent mass opposition. But he had better be right if he wants to continue to be President.

Since World War II, Democratic Presidents and presidential aspirants have probably been more vulnerable to political criticism on foreign affairs than their Republican counterparts. Because Democrats have occupied the White House each time, during the past half century, that the nation has gone to war, many voters have formed a more favorable image of the Republican than of the Democratic party's ability to keep the peace. (Republican occupancy of the White House at the start of the great depression, similarly, has left many voters more confident of the Democratic party's ability to keep the common man prosperous.) [40]

As the party in power when China and Eastern Europe came under Communist rule, the Democrats have also been particularly vulnerable to charges of "appeasement" and "softness" on communism. These simplistic images are particularly widespread among the least educated classes, which most often vote Democratic. The more domestic issues are seen to be central to an election, then, the more the Democratic candidate tends to be at an advantage — since the predispositions of working class voters on domestic issues usually correspond closely to the programs advocated by the Democratic Party. The more foreign policy issues are pushed to the forefront of the electoral stage, in contrast, the more likely is the Republican candidate to benefit — providing he does not depart from the fundamentally internationalist foreign policy consensus now accepted by the electorate.[41] (Barry Goldwater *did* threaten to depart from this consensus in significant respects and managed to convince the electorate that his party was less capable of maintaining either peace *or* prosperity than its opponent, thus consolidating an improvement in the Democratic party's image begun during the Kennedy administration.)

A Republican President, on the other hand, may run greater risks of dividing his own party if he seeks to make internationalist policy innovations, since there are more dissenters from the internationalist consensus within the Republican than within the Democratic party elite.[42]

40 See Stokes, *op. cit.*, pp. 20–22.

41 For accounts of the roles the points discussed here may have played in the elections of Harry S. Truman and Dwight Eisenhower, respectively, see Bernard Berelson, Paul Lazarsfeld and William McPhee, *Voting* (Chicago: University of Chicago Press, 1954); and Angus Campbell, Gerald Gurin, and Warren Miller, *The Voter Decides* (Evanston, Ill.: Row, Peterson, 1954). Also see V. O. Key, *Public Opinion and American Democracy, op. cit.*, chap. 17; and Stokes, *op. cit.*

42 See Herbert McClosky, Paul J. Hoffman, and Rosemary O'Hara, "Issue Conflict and Consensus Among Party Leaders and Followers," *The American Political Science Review* (June, 1960), pp. 406–427.

FOREIGN POLICY AND DEMOCRACY

Startled by the differences between the model of the opinion-policy relationship outlined here and that presented or implied as the democratic ideal in the customary folklore, some may balk at using the term "democratic" to describe the process by which American foreign policy is made. Everyone may of course define and apply the word "democratic," as he sees fit — provided that his usage is consistent. To insist that true democracy requires all adult citizens to participate nearly equally in the making of foreign policy decisions, however, is to set criteria which never have been and never will be met in the world of reality.

Whatever label we apply to the American foreign policymaking process, it is clear that there is a fundamental difference between this process and that by which foreign policy is made in dictatorial or oligarchic societies, This is the difference between a policy made by interaction among *competing* elites [43] and a policy set by a single centralized elite with a monopoly of political power; between policy conducted for the most part under public scrutiny and subject to free public criticism, and policy discussed and criticized only within the ranks of the elite itself; between policy made in a society in which individuals may gain elite status in a wide variety of ways, and policy made in a society in which unquestioning adherence to the outlook and decisions of those currently in power is the prerequisite of admission into the elite; between, in short, policy made by leaders both responsible and responsive to the values and preferences of the people, and policy made by a coercion-based elite free, to a much greater extent, to be neither responsible nor responsive to the values, opinions, and visions of the masses whose fate it decides.

The problem of the proper relationship between the masses and the makers of foreign policy is really only a special case of the problem of the relationship in modern society between the layman and the specialist in general. Take the relationship between doctor and patient. It is the patient's life which is at stake rather than the doctor's, and few would question the patient's final authority to approve the critical medical decisions made in his case. Yet we rarely hear patients berated for failing to take enough interest in matters currently in dispute within the medical profession, or told to put their fate in the hands of the physicians whose prognosis comes closest to their own. Actually, we would think it foolish of the layman — even the intelligent layman — to pit his comprehension of specific medical problems against his doctor's. We would probably counsel him instead first to choose as

[43] Surely few can entertain seriously the notion that such American influentials as Lyndon Johnson, Barry Goldwater, Robert Kennedy, Richard Nixon, J. William Fulbright, George Meany of the AFL-CIO, Roger Blough of U.S. Steel, George Wallace of Alabama, and the Rev. Martin Luther King, Jr., are all members of a single elite, conspiring to manipulate the mass public toward support for an agreed set of public policies.

his doctor a man both medically competent and in tune with the patient's own relevant value orientations. (A patient highly sensitive to pain, for instance, might hesitate to employ a physician devoted to the notion that a certain amount of pain is "good for people," regardless of his technical competence.) So long as the doctor he has chosen conducts himself so as to maintain the patient's confidence, the latter should retain him and follow his advice on medical questions. If following the doctor's advice leads to repeated disappointment, the patient would probably do best to find another qualified physician and follow *his* advice. To search instead for a doctor who would follow his *patient's* advice is certainly one of the worst things the patient could do. The same could be said of the relationship between client and lawyer, car owner and mechanic, or taxpayer and accountant.

The workings of the international political system are no less intricate or difficult to master than the workings of the human body, the law, an automobile, or even tax form 1040. Yet well-intentioned reformers frequently insist that the citizen — in contrast to the patient, client, car owner, or taxpayer — should vote on the issues instead of the candidates and otherwise participate more directly in shaping his nation's foreign policy.

It would scarcely be sensible for one writing a text on American foreign policy to undervalue the desirability of increased emphasis on education about foreign affairs. A better-educated citizenry, a larger and more farsighted attentive public, would contribute immeasurably to the nation's capacity to respond effectively to the unprecedented world challenges before it. Political leaders might then advocate new policies, subtler policies, longer-term policies, with less fear of electoral reprisal. Voters could assess more rationally the competence of candidates for public office and interest group leadership. Public willingness to make the sacrifices needed to support major foreign policy initiatives would probably increase — a very important consideration, since a broad national consensus, rather than a simple electoral majority, is essential to the unified national effort which often spells the difference between failure and success in such enterprises.

Yet it would be a great misfortune if the good sense of those who prefer to leave the day to day conduct of foreign affairs to the foreign policy elites were ever to give way to the do-it-yourself injunctions of ultrademocratic reformers. As Gabriel Almond has argued:

> In this connection perhaps the "man in the street" is sounder than some of the public opinion experts. Even if he were to meet the standards set by the polling experts, he would hardly be better off in evaluating foreign policy proposals than he is in his present state of ignorance. Some of the public opinion experts appear to operate on the theory that with each increment of knowledge there is an increment of increased capacity to understand foreign policy problems. In actual fact it takes many, many increments of knowledge plus much wisdom

before a body of factual data takes on meaningful proportions and can lead to intelligent criticism of foreign policy. So-called public apathy and indifference are at least in part an acceptance of a sound division of labor in a complex and interdependent world.[44]

In addition to the limitations on even the college educated citizen's comprehension of foreign affairs, history offers another very persuasive argument in favor of letting the people choose the men and letting the latter choose the policies. The nation's foreign policy, after all, is *managed* on the spot more often than it is *planned* in advance, *re*active as often as active. Frequently the most important foreign policy decisions Presidents have had to make were not public issues at all at the time they were elected. Woodrow Wilson and Franklin Roosevelt were first elected to office on the basis of their domestic outlooks — not on the basis of their ability to deal with world crises arising from the outbreak of war in Europe. Harry Truman was not elected Vice President in 1944 to decide whether to drop the first atomic bombs on Japan, nor President in 1948 to decide whether to resist forcibly a Communist attack on South Korea. Nor was John Kennedy elected to the presidency in 1960 to deal with a Soviet attempt to station missiles in Cuba. In light of these historical experiences, the notion of much of the public that it is the quality of the man that counts most when the chips are down seems thoroughly sound.

❦ CASE
STUDY *THE ROAD TO PEARL HARBOR*

The American people were involved at home between the world wars, basking in the joys of "normalcy" in the 1920's, and living down the morning after in the 1930's. If only the world would pack up and go home and leave us to our own troubles . . . But the world would not, and Franklin D. Roosevelt, elected to deal with the nation's worst domestic depression, soon found himself caught between his own growing awareness of the Fascist threat to American security and a public so eager to avoid involvement abroad that it declined to heed even the most urgent distress signals of the European democracies.

The events of this period have been interpreted in many different ways by political leaders, historians, journalists, and others. Some have accused President Roosevelt of deliberately misleading the American people, promising that he would keep them at peace while taking actions

---

[44] *The American People and Foreign Policy, op. cit.,* pp. 83–84. Reprinted by permission of the original publisher, Harcourt, Brace and World, Inc. See also E. E. Schattschneider, *The Semisovereign People* (New York: Holt, Rinehart and Winston, 1960.)

he well knew must ultimately plunge the nation into war. Others have complained that Roosevelt did not lead the people vigorously enough toward acceptance of their international responsibilities. Having examined the discussion in this chapter of the relationship between public opinion and foreign policy — and Chapter Three's review of presidential-congressional relations — how do *you* interpret the events leading to Pearl Harbor?

1. Was Roosevelt guilty of acting contrary to democratic practices in moving the nation toward increasing international involvement while promising in campaign speeches that the United States would not go to war? Was he too cautious in moving toward intervention? Or do you think, on balance, that he steered a judicious and effective middle course?

2. On the basis of the 1940 election and the public opinion poll results cited, can you say precisely what the American public *did* want in the months before Pearl Harbor? Did Roosevelt represent it accurately? Did the Congress?

3. What course of action would you have followed if *you* were President of the United States in the difficult years preceding Pearl Harbor? How would you have proceeded if Japan had *not* suddenly unified the nation by its attack on Pearl Harbor, but had moved into the then Dutch East Indies instead?

4. Do you believe that adherence to democratic principles requires a President to act in accordance with the views of a majority of his countrymen even if he is personally convinced that this would lead to national disaster? Defend your position.

FRANK FREIDEL

When the Roosevelt administration first took office, the threat of a second World War already darkened distant horizons. Gradually through the thirties the threat became more and more immediate, until most Americans came to feel there was little likelihood war would be avoided. At the same time, they and their President were determined that the United States should not become involved. There was no question most people wished the nation to remain a neutral bystander, but there was no certainty that the United States could avoid being pulled into the vortex of the world crisis.

Even as Roosevelt took his oath of office on March 4, 1933, the existing world order was crumbling. That was the day that the Japanese occupied the capital of the Chinese province of Jehol. The next day the last free

From *America in the Twentieth Century*, by Frank Freidel. © Copyright 1960, 1964, 1965 by Frank Freidel. Reprinted by permission of Alfred A. Knopf, Inc.

elections in Germany consolidated Hitler in power; before the end of the month, brown-shirted Nazi storm troopers were harassing Jews. Neither Roosevelt nor many other Americans harbored illusions about what lay ahead. The President was well aware of the menacing nature of Nazism, and in one of his first cabinet meetings warned that the United States might become involved in a war with Japan. But such an eventuality seemed most unlikely, because Roosevelt was ready to lead the nation in the direction it wanted to go, and for years that was toward greater isolation. . . .

As the American people struggled to extricate themselves from the disaster of depression, they abhorred war as an even worse disaster. They entered the new era of reform full of nationalistic fervor, determined to set the country right regardless of what might go on in the rest of the world. Unlike the progressives earlier, they had no predilection for police actions to bring the New Deal to less enlightened areas; above all they were determined that no matter what horrors Hitler might perpetrate, there should be no second crusade in Europe. Yet less than nine years later, they were involved in war with both Germany and Japan. . . .

The gravest of diplomatic problems continued to be relations with Japan. While Roosevelt accepted the Stimson doctrine of nonrecognition of Manchukuo, as the Japanese called Manchuria, he did not press it, and for the next several years, [Secretary of State Cordell] Hull periodically exchanged friendly assurances with the Japanese. On the surface, tensions seemed to have relaxed, but beneath it, the Japanese government continued steady pressure for a free hand in China — for a "Japanese Monroe Doctrine." . . .

In an equally unspectacular fashion, President Roosevelt kept the fleet stationed at Pearl Harbor in the Pacific, rather than in the Atlantic, and began the considerable task of modernizing and building it toward treaty strength. Pacifists and budget balancers were horrified over the enormous sum of one billion dollars necessary to bring the Navy to parity and the additional hundred million required annually for replacements. Big-navy advocates asserted the expenditure was essential, since not a single new ship had been authorized during the Hoover administration. Roosevelt quickly demonstrated where he stood by earmarking $238,000,000 of the first emergency-relief appropriation for the construction of thirty-two ships. He justified these as public works that would stimulate recovery, since 85 per cent of the money would go into wages in almost every state, but Congress stipulated in 1934 that no more public-works money should go to the navy. Under the effective pressure of the President and the congressional naval committees, Congress in March 1934 passed the Vinson-Trammell Act, which authorized both the immediate construction of four cruisers and a long-range large-scale building program to bring the navy to treaty strength by 1942.

At the London Naval Conference of 1935, the Japanese withdrew after they failed to obtain equality with the Americans and British in place of the 5:5:3 ratio, and thus opened the way for competitive naval building. So it was that in the isolationist years of the thirties, the United States built the fleet with which it was to fight the opening battles of a Pacific war.

NEUTRALITY LEGISLATION

The breakdown of the naval status quo and alarm over the threatened aggressions in both Asia and Europe convinced most Americans that at all costs they must stay out of impending wars. Many leaders of the peace movement who had been dedicated Wilsonians and advocates of the League had become disgusted with its inability to stop Japanese aggression. They reasoned that internationalism had failed, and that therefore they must fall back upon isolationism to maintain the peace. Others, taking an economic-determinist view of wars, felt that the machinations of Wall Streeters and munitions makers, combined with Wilson's legalistic insistence upon outmoded neutral rights on the high seas, had trapped the nation into the First World War. Senate investigators, under the progressive Republican Gerald P. Nye of North Dakota, revealed exorbitant wartime profits and tax evasion, and claimed that bankers sought war to rescue their loans to the Allies. President Roosevelt, himself impressed by the Nye investigation, wrote privately his regret that Bryan had left the State Department in 1915.

The Nye Committee findings and similar sensational popular writings convinced a large part of the public that entrance into the First World War had been a frightful mistake. The way to avoid its repetition seemed to be to legislate these pitfalls out of existence. As Mussolini openly prepared to conquer Ethiopia in 1935, Americans feared that a general European war might develop. They felt the way to avoid involvement was not to participate in strong deterring pressure against Italy, since Mussolini might strike back. Rather it was to isolate the nation through neutrality legislation.

President Roosevelt also favored legislation, but he and Hull wanted, as Hull had proposed in 1933, a law that would enable Roosevelt to embargo war supplies to the aggressor and allow their sale to the victim. He might thus have been able to co-operate with the League in coercing Mussolini to remain at peace. The line was this thin between collective security and isolation, but Congress did not dare risk even a mild gesture. Instead it passed a neutrality act providing a mandatory embargo against both aggressor and victim, and empowering the President to warn American citizens that they might travel on vessels of belligerents only at their own risk. This first Neutrality Act of August 1935 was temporary legislation that expired at the end of February 1936, and was then renewed, with even stronger isolationist provisions, to May 1937.

When the attack upon Ethiopia came, in October 1935, the League branded Italy an aggressor and voted sanctions against it. England and France made gestures against Italy, but showed no inclination toward stronger action even before Hitler created a new threat by militarizing the Rhineland. The German threat further restrained them from imposing an oil embargo against Italy, since they did not dare risk war in the Mediterranean for fear it would leave them vulnerable to Hitler. Also they feared alienating Russia, which supplied oil to Italy. Hull imposed a "moral embargo" upon oil which was not very effective; even had the League taken strong action, neutrality legislation would have kept him from doing more. The outcome was that Mussolini easily conquered his African empire, withdrew from the League, and in October 1936 joined with Hitler to form a new Rome-Berlin axis. Collective security had suffered a new, staggering blow and events were moving rapidly toward a European war.

The fiasco seemed to strengthen the determination of the American people to stay out of war. The new public opinion polls, based on samplings of only 1,500 to 3,500 people, with a probable error of 4 to 6 per cent, indicated top-heavy opinion against involvement. A typical poll in November 1935, after the attack on Ethiopia, queried, "If one foreign nation insists upon attacking another, should the United States join with other nations to compel it to stop?" The answer: yes, 28 per cent; no, 67 per cent; no opinion, 5 per cent. The 28 per cent answering yes were queried further as to what measures they would favor. They replied:

Economic and nonmilitary measures only	65%
Military if necessary	31%
No opinion	4%

This antiinvolvement sentiment continued to be the mood of the nation when a new danger arose in July 1936, as General Francisco Franco and the Falangists (modeled after the Fascists) revolted against the Republican government in Spain. Hitler and Mussolini sided with Franco; Russia, France, and, to a lesser extent, Great Britain favored the Loyalists. To prevent the Spanish civil war from spreading into a general European conflict, England and France agreed to send no aid to either side. Roosevelt tried to co-operate, but could impose only another "moral embargo" since the second Neutrality Act did not cover insurrections. In January 1937 Congress remedied this defect. The result was that the United States and other Western nations denied aid to Republican Spain. At first, Communists were only a trivial minority within it; there had not been a single Communist member in the Spanish Cortes (legislature). As the Republican government came to depend increasingly upon Russia for what little aid it received, gradually in the following three years Communists became more dominant. As for Franco, he received massive aid from Mussolini and Hitler, who violated their nonintervention agreement with impunity and ultimately crushed the Loyalists.

American feelings became inflamed over the invasion of Ethiopia and the Spanish civil war, but President Roosevelt voiced the majority attitude in August 1936, a month after the outbreak of the war in Spain, when he asserted, "We shun political commitments which might entangle us in foreign wars; we avoid connection with the political activities of the League of Nations. . . . We are not isolationists except in so far as we seek to isolate ourselves completely from war." He emphasized, "I hate war."

In this spirit, Congress enacted the third Neutrality Act of May 1937, which, while it increased the President's discretionary power, tightened the previous laws and relinquished American claims to freedom of the seas in wartime. Congress had legislated against the factors that had precipitated the nation into the First World War. This action had the advantage within the United States of placing questions of war and peace on issues more vital to the national interest than technicalities involving neutral rights. It had the serious disadvantage of serving notice to both totalitarian aggressors and democratic nations that in case of attack the democracies could expect no American aid. To this extent the neutrality legislation contributed to the steady deterioration of the peace. The third Neutrality Act came as Japan was about to plunge into China, and Germany was already taking aggressive steps against Austria and Czechoslovakia.

Neither President Roosevelt nor Secretary Hull wished the United States to be so uncompromisingly isolationist; consistently they had favored neutrality legislation that would give the President the discretion of favoring the victims of aggression in applying embargoes. There was some possibility that they could win public opinion to this point of view, since the nation abhorred totalitarianism. The great obstacle was a small group of powerful isolationist Senators in key positions. Previously Roosevelt had capitulated to them without serious struggle. In 1937 came a change.

The great Japanese drive into the five northern provinces of China began in the summer of 1937. At first the State Department pursued a "middle-of-the-road" policy, favoring neither country. Since Japan carefully avoided declaring war, President Roosevelt did not invoke the Neutrality Act; private American ships at their own risk could carry arms and munitions to both belligerents.

By October 1937, the administration was ready to take a firm position against Japan. The British proposed a joint arms embargo which seemed to involve no great risk. At this time and during the next four years, the consensus of the experts was that Japan was a mediocre military power. Hull persuaded Roosevelt to make a statement to counteract isolationism. The President, speaking at Chicago facing the Chicago *Tribune* tower, went beyond his advisors and declared:

> The peace-loving nations must make a concerted effort in opposition
> to those violations of treaties and those ignorings of humane instincts
> which today are creating a state of international anarchy, international

instability from which there is no escape through mere isolation or neutrality.

War, he asserted, was a contagion, which like a disease must be quarantined by the international community.

There is evidence that Roosevelt had in mind nothing more drastic than a collective breaking off of diplomatic relations, that he did not favor economic or military sanctions. Immediate press reaction and White House mail was favorable, but within a few days, as the Chicago *Tribune* and Hearst press continued to draw sinister implications from the speech, it plunged the nation, as the *Tribune* reported, into a "hurricane of war fright." Hull, dismayed, felt it set back the campaign for collective security at least six months. It also set back Roosevelt in his thinking. In November 1937 he sent to Brussels a delegate to an international conference to consider the Japanese aggression, but instructed him not to take the lead, or be a tail to the British kite.

Japan had no need to fear economic or military reprisals from the United States. On December 12, 1937, young Japanese aviators bombed and sank the United States gunboat *Panay* on the Yangtze River. At the time, and in years since, the aviators claimed they bombed it in error, but visibility was excellent and an American flag was painted on the deck. As at the time of the sinking of the *Maine* in 1898, a wave of excitement swept the country, but this time it was fear that the nation might become involved in war. The United States quickly accepted the profuse Japanese apologies and offers of indemnity.

At the end of 1938, Japan was in military and economic control of almost all of eastern China. As it supplanted the Open Door with the New Order, it was making conditions almost untenable for Americans in China. But the United States would not recognize any new status in China, and in the interior, the armies of Chiang Kai-shek continued to fight. The relations of the United States with Japan were becoming gradually more critical, but the threat of war in Europe overshadowed the Asiatic impasse. . . .

By 1938, Hitler had rebuilt such a strong German army and air force that he was ready to embark upon a course of intimidation and conquest. In March, he proclaimed union with Austria and paraded triumphantly through Vienna. This union put western Czechoslovakia into the jaws of a German vise. Hitler began tightening it with demands on behalf of the minority of 3,500,000 Germans in Czechoslovakia. In September 1938, Hitler brought Europe to the brink of war with his demands for the cession of the Sudeten area in which the minority lived. The Czechs, who had a strong army, were ready to fight rather than submit, but the people of other Western nations, appalled at the threat of another world conflict, were eager for a settlement on almost any terms. Roosevelt joined in the pleas to Hitler for a peaceful solution, but this was of minor significance. At Munich on September 29, the French and British signed a pact with Hitler granting his demands in Czechoslovakia. "This is the last territorial claim I have to make in Europe," he declared.

Within a few weeks, the once strong Czechoslovakia was whittled down to impotence. In March 1939, Hitler took over the remainder of it as German protectorates, thus demonstrating speedily the worthlessness of his Munich pledge. In April, he began harassing Poland. The British and French, seeing clearly that appeasement had failed, gave firm pledges to Poland and other threatened nations. They made half-hearted gestures toward Russia, which had been left out of the Munich settlement, but Stalin instead in August signed a nonaggression pact with Hitler. It freed Hitler to attack Poland if he could not frighten the country into submission. When Poland stood firm, Germany invaded it on September 1, 1939. Great Britain and France, true to their pledges, on September 3 declared war on Germany. The Second World War had begun. Americans wondered if they could stay out.

THE OUTBREAK OF WAR: LIMITED AID

As Hitler had moved toward war in the spring and summer of 1939, President Roosevelt tried to persuade Congress that the arms embargo would encourage Hitler, and that American security demanded that it be modified to assure arms to Great Britain and France. Senator Borah, claiming superior sources of information, asserted that there would be no war, and Congress took no action.

With the outbreak of war, Roosevelt issued a neutrality proclamation pointedly different from Wilson's 1914 plea for Americans to be neutral in thought as well as action. "This nation will remain a neutral nation," Roosevelt stated, "but I cannot ask that every American remain neutral in thought as well." The great majority of the American people did not want to become involved in the war, but also did not want the democracies to lose. This, according to every gauge of public opinion, was the American attitude from the invasion of Poland until Pearl Harbor.

Roosevelt called Congress into special session, and despite a heated debate was able to muster the votes for a revision of the Neutrality Act. The 1939 measure still prohibited American ships from entering the war zones, but it did allow belligerents to purchase arms on a "cash-and-carry" basis. Had England and France been able to restrain Hitler with this limited assistance, Roosevelt probably would have asked for nothing more. . . . During these months of the "phony war," American indignation flared hottest over the Russian invasion of Finland. The administration applied a tight "moral embargo" on shipments of munitions to Russia, but went no further.

During these months of relative quiet, President Roosevelt made only modest requests for increases in armaments. Army and navy appropriations went up only about 50 per cent in the two years ending June 30, 1940. In May 1938, after the German annexation of Austria, Roosevelt had obtained with some difficulty a 20 per cent increase in the naval program. Congressional isolationists pointed out that the navy was already the largest in history. In November 1939, Representative Carl Vinson announced another large four-year naval program to cost $1,300,000,000. In January 1940, Roosevelt asked for moderate increases in armaments expenditures, but the House Appropriations Committee cut $12,000,000 for an air base in Alaska, and slashed the 496 recommended airplanes to only 57. By the time the bill reached the Senate, events in Europe had made it obsolete.

THE FALL OF FRANCE:
ALL-OUT AID

Optimistic illusions about Hitler's weakness turned into panic in the spring of 1940 when the Nazis invaded Denmark and Norway, then swept across Holland and Belgium deep into France. On May 16, Roosevelt asked Congress for an additional billion in defense expenditures and obtained it quickly. On the premise that the United States must build great air armadas to hold off the Nazis, he set a goal of at least 50,000 airplanes a year.

On June 10, 1940, Mussolini joined the Germans by attacking France, despite an earlier strong plea from Roosevelt to "withhold your hand." Roosevelt, speaking that evening, asserted, "The hand that held the dagger has struck it into the back of its neighbor." And, with France tottering from the German onslaught, he proclaimed that the United States would "extend to the opponents of force the material resources of this nation." He was taking the United States from a status of isolation to one of nonbelligerency on the side of the democracies.

Twelve days later France fell, and in all western Europe only the shattered remnants of the British army that had been retrieved from Dunkirk opposed the Nazis. Already the new prime minister, Winston Churchill, was showering Roosevelt with requests for destroyers and arms of all kinds to help the British man their bastion. The odds against the British were heavy, but Roosevelt made the bold and dangerous decision to "scrape the bottom of the barrel" and turn over to them all available matériel of war. This plan was carried out to such an extent that, as late as 1941, some American troop units were maneuvering with pieces of telephone pole substituting for artillery that was in England. The United States also promised the British 14,375 airplanes by April 1942. Most spectacular of all, as the air softening-up for the invasion of Britain began, Roosevelt gave fifty over-age destroyers to the British in return for 99-year leases on eight bases from Newfoundland to British Guiana. It was, as Churchill later wrote, "a decidedly unneutral act."

As Roosevelt threw the resources of the United States behind the British as completely as Congress would let him, he did so with the feeling that an Axis victory would mean disaster to the nation. He believed the Germans, through either military or economic means, would encircle and destroy the United States. A large part of the public seemed suddenly to have changed its mind and to agree. In March 1940 only 43 per cent of those polled thought a German victory would be a threat to the United States; by July, 69 per cent did. In May 1940, only 35 per cent favored aid to Britain at the risk of American involvement; four months later, 60 per cent did. Yet no more people than previously wished to enter the war; as late as the month before Pearl Harbor, only 20 per cent of those polled favored a declaration of war against Germany. Roosevelt and the American public seemed to share incompatible aims. They wished to bring about the defeat of the Axis without involving the United States in a shooting war. Some time in the next eighteen months, Roosevelt probably came to feel that American entrance was desirable; the public never did.

CHART 1 — PUBLIC OPINION ABOUT INTERVENTION, 1939–1941

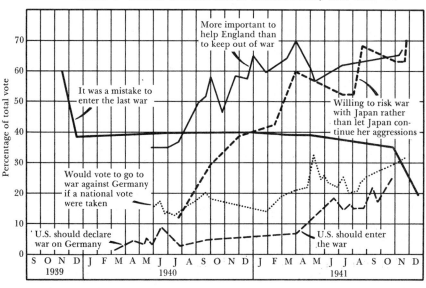

Reproduced by permission of Professor Hadley Cantril.
Source: Public Opinion Research Project of Princeton University.

All America was pulled into a great debate on the issue of war versus peace. William Allen White, the Kansas newspaper editor, headed a Committee to Defend America by Aiding the Allies, often called the White Committee. White himself (like a large percentage of Americans) favored merely aid, but a minority wanted to go further and declare war. This group, in

April 1941, founded the Fight for Freedom Committee. On the antiinvolvement side, a Yale student, R. Douglas Stuart, Jr., organized an America First Committee under the chairmanship of a leading Chicago businessman, General Robert E. Wood. It drew upon the oratorical talent of the aviation hero Charles Lindbergh, General Hugh Johnson, and Senators Nye and Wheeler. It won the editorial support of the Hearst and other large newspapers, and appealed to a considerable segment of patriotic Americans. Inevitably it also attracted a small fringe of pro-Nazi, anti-Semitic, and American fascist fanatics. The statements of its principal speaker, Lindbergh, often aroused violent controversy. In April 1941 Lindbergh asserted that Britain was defeated, and several weeks later joined with Senator Wheeler in calling for a negotiated peace. In September, he declared, "The three most important groups which have been pressing this country toward war are the British, the Jewish, and the Roosevelt Administration." Roosevelt so curtly denounced Lindbergh as an appeaser and defeatist that Lindbergh resigned his colonelcy in the Army Air Force.

It was a bitter fight, and through the summer and fall of 1940, it was complicated by a presidential election.

THE 1940 ELECTION

During the winter of the "phony war" it seemed likely that Roosevelt would retire at the end of his second term and that the Republicans would nominate either of two young men who were courting the isolationists, Senator Robert Taft of Ohio or a reforming New York City district attorney, Thomas E. Dewey. Also, a Republican victory seemed imminent. The German blitz ended these possibilities.

The Republicans met at Philadelphia in June 1940, as the sickening black shadow of the collapse of France sank over the nation. National defense was suddenly the most important issue. Roosevelt underscored this, and stole headlines from the Republican convention on June 20 by appointing to his cabinet two of the most distinguished Republicans. He made the elder statesman Henry L. Stimson Secretary of War, and appointed as Secretary of the Navy the 1936 Vice-Presidential candidate and sharp critic of the New Deal, Frank Knox.

The chagrined Republicans at Philadelphia promptly read Stimson and Knox out of the party but could not ignore the defense issue. They succumbed to the grass-roots pressure, which had been built through a careful advertising campaign, and nominated a young internationalist, Wendell Willkie. . . . He was a forerunner of the modern Republicans. On foreign policy, both the platform and Willkie pledged that the nation would be kept out of war but would aid peoples fighting for liberty.

By the time the Democrats met in mid-July, it was a foregone conclusion that they would renominate Roosevelt. . . .

. . . No matter how much Willkie and Roosevelt talked about it, the campaign did not center around the New Deal. Rather, foreign policy was paramount. On this, they both had much the same views: Willkie approved of the destroyers-bases agreement. Both made fervent antiwar statements to placate the isolationists. Willkie declared that if Roosevelt's promise to stay out of a foreign war was no better than his pledge to balance the budget, the boys were "already almost on the transports." This was an effective campaign issue which cut into Roosevelt's support. At Boston, Roosevelt (making the mental reservation that any attack upon the United States would not be a foreign war) picked up the challenge in words the isolationists were to mock incessantly:

> I have said this before, but I shall say it again and again and again: Your boys are not going to be sent into any foreign wars.

No matter what Willkie's principles and Roosevelt's protestations, a large part of the vote of those opposing aid to the Allies went to Willkie. At the same time, a considerable part of those favoring vigorous aid or even intervention (including many who fervently opposed New Deal domestic policies) voted for Roosevelt. They preferred Roosevelt's sure leadership to Willkie's inexperience. It was a relatively close vote: 27,244,000 for Roosevelt, and 22,305,000 for Willkie; 449 electoral votes to 82. The combined third-party vote was less than 200,000. Within a few weeks, Willkie was on his way to England with a letter from Roosevelt to Churchill in his pocket.

BUILDING AN ARSENAL OF DEMOCRACY

In addition to politicking, in the months after the fall of France Roosevelt had to build makeshift defense machinery. With Willkie's aid, he pushed through the Burke-Wadsworth bill, passed in September 1940, which inaugurated the first peacetime selective service in American history. This was the summer when he arranged to send destroyers to England, turned back new airplanes to the factory to be ferried across the Atlantic, and somehow ran the gauntlet of several anti-British, isolationist chairmen of Senate committees.

By mid-December, the British had so nearly exhausted their financial resources that they had practically stopped letting new contracts, yet Churchill warned Roosevelt that their needs would increase tenfold in the future. The Neutrality Act of 1939 and the Johnson Act forbade American loans; a request for repeal would have reawakened the old furore about unpaid war debts. Roosevelt, cruising in the Caribbean after the election, thought of a formula. The United States should lend goods rather than money, "to eliminate the dollar sign." If one's neighbor's house caught fire, he explained, one would lend a garden hose to prevent the fire from spreading to one's own house. Lend-Lease would create an "arsenal of democracy" as a means of protecting the American nation, he explained. The bill went into the congressional hopper at the right moment to bear a significant number: it became House Resolution 1776. The fierce debate over Lend-Lease shocked the country. Senator Wheeler charged that it was "the New Deal's triple A foreign policy; it will plow under every fourth American boy." That, Roosevelt retorted, was "the most untruthful, as well as the most dastardly, unpatriotic thing that has ever been said." The bill went through Congress by a wide margin, and in March 1941 was signed by the President. It empowered him to spend an initial seven billion dollars — a sum as large as the controversial loans of the First World War.

Lend-Lease committed the United States formally to the policy the President had been following since the fall of France, pouring aid into Great Britain to help it withstand the German onslaught. Since Lend-Lease shipments had to cross the Atlantic to be of aid, the United States acquired a vital interest in keeping the Atlantic sea lanes open against the formidable wolf packs of German submarines, which in the spring of 1941 were destroying a half-million tons of shipping a month, twice as much as shipyards could produce. The President did not dare openly convoy vessels to England as Secretary Stimson urged; isolationists in Congress were too powerful. Instead he fell back upon the device of "hemispheric defense." The American republics had proclaimed an Atlantic neutrality zone in 1939; Roosevelt in 1941 extended it far to the east, almost to Iceland, and ordered the Navy to patrol the area and give warning of aggressors. This meant radioing to the British the location of Nazi submarines. The United States occupied Greenland in April 1941 and Iceland in July, and began escorting convoys as far as Iceland.

In secret, the United States had gone even further, for in the spring of 1941 American and British officers in Washington reached agreement on the strategy to be followed if the United States entered the war. President Roosevelt demonstrated publicly in August 1941 how close he had come to carrying the United States from nonbelligerency to cobelligerency with England when he met with Prime Minister Churchill off the coast of Newfoundland. Roosevelt refused to make military commitments but did sign with Churchill a press release on war aims, the Atlantic Charter. It called for national self-determination, greater economic opportunities, freedom from fear and want, freedom of the seas, and disarmament. As Churchill later pointed out, Roosevelt, representing a nation not at war, subscribed to a document that referred to "the final destruction of the Nazi tyranny."

In June 1941, Hitler unleashed an enormous surprise attack against Russia, so powerful that American military leaders predicted that Russia would collapse in a few weeks or months. The Russians fell back before the deep Nazi incursions, but continued to fight, and in September Roosevelt, again gambling, extended Lend-Lease to them. This made it even more imperative to patrol the seas effectively.

The German answer was to strike back with submarines. In May 1941 they sank the American ship *Robin Moor* off the coast of Brazil and replied to protests by saying, "Germany will continue to sink every ship with contraband for Britain whatever its name." In September, a submarine attacked but failed to hit the destroyer *Greer,* which was radioing the submarine's position to the British. President Roosevelt, who did not know, or at least did not reveal, what the *Greer* was doing, issued orders to the navy in the future to "shoot on sight." In October, another destroyer was hit, and the *Reuben James* was sunk. Congress voted legislation to arm merchantmen and allow them to sail to belligerent ports. Naval war with the Nazis was underway.

The Chief of Naval Operations, Admiral Harold R. Stark, wrote in his diary that fall that Hitler "has every excuse in the world to declare war on us now, if he were of a mind to." But Hitler did not, and war came from the Pacific, not the Atlantic.

THE PATH TO PEARL HARBOR

In the months after the sinking of the gunboat *Panay,* the deadlock between the United States and Japan over the Open Door versus the New Order gradually deepened into an impasse. The Japanese saw in the European crisis an unparalleled opportunity to extend their empire. In the summer of 1939 they forced concessions from the British which demonstrated their intentions. The United States promptly took a most serious step and gave the requisite six months' notice to terminate its 1911 commercial treaty. Beginning in January 1940, it was free to cut off its shipments of oil, scrap iron, and other raw materials; Japan had been depending on the United States for half its supply of such commodities. Japan feared losing these supplies vital for its armed forces, but would not recede. American public opinion violently opposed war with Japan, but increasingly demanded the embargo which might bring war.

The fall of France and siege of England gave global significance to Japanese policy. Japan was eager to take advantage of the defeat or preoccupation of the colonial powers to nibble its way into Southeast Asia, beginning with northern French Indo-China. The United States was determined to restrain Japan, even at the risk of a war. More was at stake than tin, rubber, and other vital raw materials. In September 1940, Japan signed a defensive alliance with Germany and Italy (the Tripartite Pact); any further Japanese thrusts would damage the world status quo to which the State Department was committed. The administration policy toward Japan was inseparably interrelated with that toward Germany, and subordinate to it.

As the United States began to deny Japan supplies essential to her warmaking, the danger that Japan would strike back became imminent. Under the Export Control Act, by the fall of 1940 the United States had placed an embargo upon aviation gasoline and almost all raw materials with military potential, including scrap iron and steel. Already war was close. The Japanese government of Prince Konoye wished to conciliate the United States if it could do so without serious concessions. Negotiations began in the spring of 1941 and dragged on into December. At first the Japanese informally suggested rather generous proposals, but by May were making formal ones that were unacceptable: the United States should ask Chiang Kai-shek to make peace on Japan's terms, it should restore normal trade with Japan, and it should help Japan procure natural resources in Southeast Asia. Also Japan would decide for itself whether the Tripartite Pact bound it to aid Germany in a war against the United States. In return, Japan promised to expand peacefully and to respect the Philippines. The United States countered with its traditional Open Door, antiexpansionist demands. The gulf between the negotiators was broad, but the United States was gaining valuable time and hoped moderates might win control in Japan.

The contrary occurred. The German attack upon Russia relieved the Japanese of one of their greatest worries, since they no longer needed to fear interference from Siberia. They decided to move into southern Indo-China and Thailand, even though it might mean war with the United States and Great Britain. The United States had broken the Japanese code, and through intercepted messages knew this move was probably a prelude to attacks upon Singapore and the Dutch East Indies. At the end of July 1941, when the Japanese occupied southern Indo-China, the United States, acting firmly in concert with the British and the Dutch, froze Japanese assets and applied other tight economic sanctions. These put the Japanese into such a desperate plight that they would either have to abandon their aggressions or fight the United States.

Since the Japanese naval leaders wished to avoid a war they feared they might lose, the cabinet sought compromise. Prince Konoye requested a personal meeting with Roosevelt at which he was ready to make some concessions. (Simultaneously Japan prepared for war if agreement could not be reached.) Roosevelt was enthusiastic, since Konoye was ready to promise that Japan would not expand further southward and would not attack the United States in the event it fought a defensive war against Germany. Hull was discouraging because he feared Konoye could not bind the Supreme Command. On Hull's advice, Roosevelt would not meet Konoye without specific advance commitments about China, and these Konoye would not give.

Perhaps a personal meeting between Roosevelt and Konoye could have resulted in a face-saving accommodation which could have avoided war. If so, in being ruled out, the last possibility of peace evaporated. Roosevelt and Hull decidedly did not want war in the fall of 1941, but they seemed to make the foolish error of thinking Japan was bluffing when she was not. Instead of making limited concessions which would have strengthened the Japanese moderates and postponed or avoided a war which the United States was in no position to fight in 1941, they took an adamant moralistic position which played into the hands of the Japanese extremists. If there were to be a showdown over China, the time should be later, not when the United States was fighting German submarines on the Atlantic.

The Japanese made an even more grievous miscalculation by drifting into a war few of their leaders were sure they could win. On September 6, 1941, an Imperial Conference decided to attack if negotiations were not satisfactory by early October. Most leaders had misgivings, but none tried to reverse the decision. Negotiations continued through November, with the Emperor urging that a solution be found, but the Japanese timetable called for a surprise attack in early December.

Each nation refused to budge on the question of China. On November 20, 1941, Japan offered a *modus vivendi* (temporary settlement) highly favorable to herself. Hull rejected it and prepared a *modus vivendi* of his own, involving a three months' truce. It was most unlikely Japan would accept it, but anyway the Chinese objected so strongly and it was so likely to be unpopular in the United States that Hull abandoned it. Instead he replied in the basic American terms. He not only knew Japan would not accept these but knew also, through intercepted Japanese messages, that they had made their last offer and that after November 29 things automatically would happen. "I have washed my hands of the Japanese situation," Hull told Stimson on November 27, "and it is now in the hands of you and Knox, the Army and Navy."

The United States knew that Japan was on the move and that war was imminent. A large Japanese convoy was moving southward through the China Sea. The administration thought an attack upon American territory unlikely, and debated what to do if the Philippines were bypassed. The commanders in Hawaii were routinely warned, but were equally preoccupied. Negligence on their part and in Washington, not diabolical plotting, as was later charged, led to the disaster ahead. Meanwhile, on November 25, a Japanese naval task force had sailed eastward from the Kuriles.

At 7:55 on Sunday morning, December 7, 1941, the first wave of Japanese airplanes hit the United States naval base at Pearl Harbor, Hawaii; a second wave came an hour later. The attacks were successful beyond Japan's greatest expectation. Within two hours the planes destroyed or severely damaged 8 battleships, 3 light cruisers, 4 miscellaneous vessels, 188 airplanes, and important shore installations. There were 3,435 casualties. The Japanese task force withdrew without being detected, having lost 29 airplanes, 5 midget submarines, and less than 100 persons. In this first strike, the United States was almost rendered impotent in the Pacific, but the bitterly wrangling nation was suddenly unified for the global war into which it had been precipitated.

*PUBLIC OPINION AND
THE WAR IN VIETNAM*

Japan's occupation of Southeast Asia and the weakening of the European colonial powers during World War II *did* create a new order in Asia — though not the one the Japanese militarists had intended. The age of imperialism in Asia was over. Within weeks after Japan's surrender Ho Chi-minh had proclaimed the existence of a Democratic Republic of Vietnam. At first, this was recognized by France as a "free state within the French Union." But by the end of 1946 the *modus vivendi* in Indo-China had broken down, and a savage military struggle had begun.

Punished severely on the battlefield and defeated decisively at Dienbienphu in May of 1954, France agreed to a military armistice at the Geneva conference in July of that year. By this agreement, Vietnam was divided along the seventeenth parallel into northern and southern sectors, the former to be ruled by a Communist-led regime under Ho Chi-minh. Nation-wide elections leading to reunification were to be held within two years; and an International Control Commission (India, Canada, and Poland) was appointed to supervise the truce. The United States did not sign this agreement, but agreed not to use force or the threat of force to upset it. The elections provided for were not held within the period specified, however, since the new government of South Vietnam insisted that really free elections were not possible in a Communist-held area like North Vietnam.

In the years following the Geneva settlement, the United States gradually assumed increasing degrees of responsibility for preventing a Communist takeover of all Vietnam. The Southeast Asia Collective Defense Treaty (SEATO), signed within months of the Geneva agreements, pledged the United States to recognize that "aggression by means of armed attack in the treaty area," which included Vietnam, "would endanger its own peace and safety, and agrees that it will in that event act to meet the common danger in accordance with its constitutional processes." Measures taken were to be reported to the United Nations Security Council.

For about nine years, the principal alternative to communism in the South was the relatively honest, authoritarian, staunchly anti-Communist government of Ngo Dinh Diem. In its first years in power, Diem's government overcame the private armies of dissident religious castes, and appeared to be well on the way to achieving a measure of political stability. But Diem, an elitist mandarin by training, had little popular support. To spearhead the struggle against Communist infiltration and internal rivals, he depended upon members of his own family, his Catholic coreligionists — who constituted the most militantly anti-Communist segment of the populace — and landholders, generals, and bureaucrats personally loyal to him. To increase the strength and maintain the confidence of these loyal groups, he began to favor them against other groups in the population. When the latter protested vehemently and sought to oust him, Diem retaliated by suppressing opposition in an increasingly blatant fashion. Finally, open opposition by the Buddhists — including spectacular suicides-by-fire by a number of Buddhist monks and nuns — reduced the Diem regime's prestige, and the United States' appetite for continuing to support it, to the point where a group of dissident generals staged a successful coup d'état. Though Diem and his brother were killed, other casualties were few. There was wild rejoicing in the streets of the capital of Saigon and hopes were high.

Within a few months, however, another military group, headed by General Nguyen Khanh, decided that it could do a better job of prosecuting the war against communism than its predecessor, and another coup was carried out. Again the United States promised support for the new regime and sought to discourage further coups. But now Buddhist and Catholic enmities flared into open street violence; political leaders expressed their dissatisfaction with prolonged military administration; and war-wearied peasants declined to show any great enthusiasm for fighting to save a government which had done little to improve their lot — which, in fact, often had failed to provide them with basic protection against Communist guerrillas and terrorists.

General Khanh tried one constitutional arrangement, then another; he removed himself from the scene for a brief rest, then returned; he turned the government over to a group of political leaders and bureaucrats and then to a military triumvirate including both himself and his predecessor. Numerous changes followed, leading eventually to the assumption of power by a new military directorate, headed by Air Force General Nguyen Cao Ky, in June, 1965. By this time there were over 50,000 American troops in South Vietnam, and American planes were dropping thousands of tons of bombs on Vietcong (Vietnamese Communist) supply lines in *North* Vietnam.

By the fall of 1967, a presidential election had been held in South Vietnam — although the electorate was severely restricted, and a number of potential candidates were not permitted to run. A plurality of the votes cast were for General Nguyen Van Thieu. Meanwhile, the number of American GI's serving in Vietnam had risen to half a million, a wider range of targets in North Vietnam were being attacked by American bombers, and, in the United States, organized demonstrations protesting against American policy in Vietnam became fairly common.[45]

[45] To bring any biases he may have on this subject out into the open, it is hereby noted that (as of late 1967) the writer advocated cessation of the bombing of North Vietnam and other moves — short of precipitate American withdrawal — to de-escalate the Vietnam conflict. His views on some of the issues raised in this case study may be found in Sheldon Appleton, "The Public, the Polls and the War," *Vietnam Perspectives*, May, 1966, pp. 3–13.

A good starting point for further reading on the Vietnam war is Marcus G. Raskin and Bernard B. Fall (eds.), *The Vietnam Reader* (New York: Random House, 1965). (A Vintage paperback.)

1. Some journalists have accused the authors of the Stanford Poll report of "rigging" the data by the manner in which they phrased the questions put to their respondents — a charge emphatically denied by the Stanford analysts. Do you believe their questions are "rigged"? Why or why not? (If so, specify which ones and how their phrasing may have affected the results.) Do you disagree with any of the interpretations of the data offered by the Stanford authors? Explain.

2. From the data presented in this case study, what do you believe "the American people" want in Vietnam? How could the President translate these views into public policy? (Be specific.)

3. Do you believe it is patriotic for American private citizens to oppose publicly the policies of their government in situations of this kind? Why or why not? If you opposed United States policy in Vietnam, would you be willing to participate in a protest demonstration? To resist the draft? Defend your position.

4. Considering both the domestic and the international ramifications of the Vietnam problem, which broad policy alternative (withdrawal, de-escalation, continued commitment at present levels, further escalation) would you choose if you were responsible for the conduct of United States foreign policy? Why? How would you seek to persuade the public to support this policy?

THE FOREIGN POLICY ASSOCIATION

THE MORAL ISSUES

On October 1, 1954, President Eisenhower offered to President Ngo Dinh Diem a program of American aid designed to "assist the government of Vietnam in developing and maintaining a strong, viable state, capable of resisting attempted subversion or aggression through military means." Seven years later, President Kennedy went even further: "The U.S. is determined that the Republic of Vietnam [South Vietnam] shall not be lost to the Communists for lack of any support which the U.S. can render."

Do these statements, and other similar ones made by the two American presidents, morally commit us to the war in Vietnam? President Johnson thinks so. "We are there," he told a Johns Hopkins University audience on April 7, 1965, "because we have a promise to keep. Since 1954 every American President has offered support to the people of South Vietnam. . . . To dishonor that pledge, to abandon this small and brave nation to its enemies and to the terror that must follow, would be an unforgivable wrong."

United States sympathy for peoples striving to attain or maintain their freedom and independence is assuredly rooted deep in our traditions. But

Excerpted from *Vietnam: Vital Issues in the Great Debate*, prepared and published by the Foreign Policy Association, New York, Sept., 1966. Reprinted by permission. Omissions are indicated by ellipses.

there are many who deny that either our traditions or the specific nature of the White House pledges to South Vietnam adds up to a moral obligation to wage war in Vietnam. Eisenhower himself, it is pointed out, has since explained that what he had in mind in his 1954 letter to Diem was foreign aid and not a military program. And Kennedy, shortly before his assassination in 1963, told Columbia Broadcasting System correspondent Walter Cronkite: "We can help them [the South Vietnamese], we can give them equipment, we can send our men out there as advisers, but they have to win it — the people of Vietnam — against the Communists." And Hans J. Morgenthau, Chicago University political scientist, stresses that the pledges were made to a Saigon government that, he contends, we ourselves had installed — "our own agent." "I do not regard this," Mr. Morgenthau comments tartly, "as a valid foundation for our presence in South Vietnam."

But however the pledges were meant, it is incontrovertible that they were accepted by a succession of Saigon regimes as an earnest of our determination to support them against Communist aggression. Whether or not these regimes were representative, their understanding of our intent led hundreds of thousands of South Vietnamese to commit themselves to the anti-Communist cause. Many Americans feel strongly that we cannot let them down. It is noteworthy that Eisenhower, despite his careful disavowal of warlike intent in 1954, today supports the war wholeheartedly.

Moral issues are involved not only in *why* we are fighting, but *how*. We are meeting the often inhuman terror tactics of the enemy with tactics that to some seem equally inhuman: mass bombings, defoliation, the use of weapons with unprecedented killing power, the application of the torch to civilian huts.

"The real moral problem at issue in Vietnam," writes Administration critic Bernard B. Fall in *Viet-Nam Witness 1953–66,* "is that of torture and needless brutality to combatants and civilians alike," and notes that both sides are guilty of "crass and constant violations of the rules of war. . . ."

John P. Roche of Brandeis University, mindful of the murderous purges perpetrated by the Hanoi regime upon its own people, sees the moral question in another context. Other than pacifism, he writes in *The New Leader,* there would be only one ground for holding that our Vietnamese policy is immoral, namely, "that North Vietnam is a historically progressive regime confronted by a reactionary, imperialist creation in South Vietnam." It should be noted that Roche does not accept this view of the regimes in the North and South and is a vigorous supporter of Administration policy in Vietnam. . . .

THE STRATEGIC ISSUES

Some observers insist that neither morality nor legality were factors in our decision to fight in Vietnam. "Combat troops were sent," writes Richard N. Goodwin, a former special assistant to President Johnson, "because our national interest, in the judgment of our leaders, required their presence, and for no other reason." It is in our national interest, supporters of the war argue, that Southeast Asia be withheld from the Communists, and it is also argued that the key to the defense of the area lies, under present circumstances, in Vietnam.

Overt expression of this strategic concept was given by President Eisenhower in 1953 in justification of our financial support for France's war against the predecessors of the Vietcong, the Vietminh: "If Indochina goes, several things happen right away. The peninsula . . . would be scarcely defensible. The tin and tungsten that we so greatly value from that area would cease coming."

A year later — and only four days after the Geneva agreements ended France's effort to contain communism in that area — the concept was put into sharper focus by Eisenhower's Secretary of State Dulles: "The important thing from now on is not to mourn the past but to seize future opportunities to prevent the loss in North Vietnam from leading to the extension of communism throughout Southeast Asia. . . ."

In 1959 Eisenhower again pictured the results of a Communist conquest of South Vietnam: "The remaining countries of Southeast Asia would be menaced by a great flanking movement. . . . The loss of South Vietnam would set in motion a crumbling process that could, as it progressed, have grave consequences for us and for freedom."

What Eisenhower called the "crumbling process" has since been encompassed in the "domino theory," a major thesis in the pro-Administration argument. It holds that the Vietnam struggle is a test case for the "wars of liberation" upon which both Peking and Moscow have set their seals of approval; that a Communist victory in Vietnam would show us up as a "paper tiger," with the result that neighboring countries, their confidence in us shattered, would quickly fall into Communist hands; and that a Communist-dominated Indochinese peninsula would ultimately force Japan and the Philippines into a neutralist stance that would, in turn, constrict our defense line to Hawaii, Alaska and the West Coast — "too close," as U.S. News & World Report has put it, "for comfort."

Related to this concept is the conviction that there exists a confluence of interests between Hanoi and Peking; and that Communist China would exploit a Vietcong victory to further its own aggressive aims, which include not only Asian hegemony, but also leadership of a "third world" revolt against the capitalist West and a "revisionist" Soviet bloc.

This whole strategic concept is challenged by many observers. Recent history, it is said, flatly disapproves the domino theory: no country followed the Soviet Union into communism in 1917 or China in 1949; no neighbor emulated North Vietnam in 1954, or Cuba in 1960. "The 'domino theory,'" writes Professor Morgenthau, "is but a replica of vulgar Marxism which also believes in the inevitable spread of communism." The theory is held to be invalid even in reverse, *i.e.,* that by stopping communism anywhere, it is discouraged elsewhere. Communism, stopped in Greece, the Philippines and Korea, for instance, went on to succeed in Cuba and North Vietnam, and temporarily threatened Indonesia. "They little know the hydra," comments Walter Lippmann, "who think that the hydra has only one head and that it can be cut off."

From this it follows, say critics of Administration strategy, that Vietnam's importance has been vastly exaggerated; even a Communist victory there would be no catastrophe. Indeed, some American observers argue that a Communist Vietnam might prove a stronger barrier to Chinese expansionism than any Saigon regime which needed U.S. backing for survival. The centrifugal force of nationalism, they believe, plus the traditional hostility of all Indochinese peoples toward the Chinese, would make of Ho Chi Minh (or his successor) another Tito, intent on charting an independent course. It is pointed out that even North Korea, whose survival as a Communist state was unquestionably due to China's intervention in the Korean war, is now showing strong signs of independence from Peking. Jean Lacouture, French journalist and author of *Vietnam: Between Two Truces,* put the matter graphically: "Should the U.S. . . . continue to prefer dead Vietnamese to Red Vietnamese, China will have won an historic victory."

All this criticism adds up to the proposition that if we are fighting the right war, we are fighting it in the wrong place; it is, comments Lippmann, as if we were trying to stop Russia by fighting in the Balkans. He insists that China can be contained only if its Asian neighbors — Pakistan, India, Japan and the Soviet Union — are "aligned together or are at least acting on parallel lines." In a recent statement Chester Bowles, our ambassador to India, coupled a strong endorsement of the war with a plea for a similar Asian alliance against the Communists. Other observers stress India's role as a potential counterweight to Peking; they argue that we ought to concentrate our energies on strengthening New Delhi instead of wasting them — and American blood — on a war that, in the end, will decide nothing of genuine strategic value.

Some believe we are exaggerating the peril from China. Early in 1966 several university professors, specialists on Asia, expressed to the Senate Foreign Relations Committee their beliefs that (1) Peking talks more belligerently than it acts; (2) traditionally, China is not expansionist, and its recent military incursions into Tibet and India were prompted not so much by expansionism as by its own interpretation (justified or not) of certain historical facts concerning the position of its borders; and (3) it is reasonable to assume that Peking's current verbal belligerency represents a passing stage, like Stalinism in Russia.

Supporters of the Administration's policy are quick with their rebuttals.

Yugoslavia, it is pointed out, had no common frontier with Russia, a vital geographical factor which facilitated Tito's defection. Vietnam and Communist China do have common boundaries. The U.S., moreover, supported Tito's efforts to create an independent Communist state with economic and military aid. Would Communist China look kindly upon a Titoist Vietnam? Nor should it be forgotten that Tito was better able to resist Soviet pressure because of the determination of the U.S. to resist Soviet expansion in Europe. A weakening of U.S. determination to preserve South Vietnam's independence would serve to encourage the aggressive ambitions of Communist China, which has publicly stated its readiness to support revolutions throughout the underdeveloped countries of the world.

. . . both escalators and de-escalators seem to agree with the Administration's stated policy on one cardinal point: we are fighting not to conquer North Vietnam or destroy the enemy, but to weaken his will to fight sufficiently to bring him to the conference table and reach a settlement which will permit South Vietnam to determine its future in peace. It is on how best to accomplish this that the two schools differ with each other and with the Administration.

The escalators believe that the President's buildup and application of our military strength has been slow, overcautious and to a degree self-defeating, causing unnecessary American losses and prolonging the struggle. We should have attacked the oil "tank farms" around the Hanoi-Haiphong areas much sooner than we did; we ought to consider the whole area — the two Vietnams, Laos, Cambodia and Thailand — as a strategic whole for combat purposes; we ought to throttle China's seaborne flow of supplies to North Vietnam by gunfire, port blockade or other available means; we must accelerate our attacks on the Ho Chi Minh trail, particularly that part which runs through "neutralist" Laos and Cambodia.

And, privately, some of the considerable number of escalators in our armed forces argue that, on the home front, the President's refusal to mobilize the reserves, to establish priorities and controls for war production, and to delegate greater authority over the fighting to field commands has cost us both time and lives.

Many military men believe, according to military analyst Hanson W. Baldwin, that Ho Chi Minh is counting not on victory on the battlefield but on winning over American public opinion. "Some of them fear," writes Mr. Baldwin, "that the American public will not have the patience or the staying power to win the kind of war a policy of gradualism entails and that the war must be won as quickly as possible or it will be lost slowly. . . . Military power always yields the best results when it is applied in mass and as quickly as possible." And some escalators have their own version of the morality involved in fighting a restricted war. They ask: By what moral right does the President send hundreds of thousands of young

Americans to risk their lives in an alien land, and at the same time deprive them of the most effective available weapons and methods to use against the enemy?

The Administration resists escalation on the ground that it could lead to a broadened conflict, perhaps a nuclear war. "We could make this into a larger war very quickly," Secretary Rusk said in July 1966, as pressures for stepping up our war effort seemed to be increasing. "All we would have to do is turn our backs for five minutes and let events take their course." He reminded his listeners that our objective in Vietnam is "to establish a peace, not destroy somebody else." The President has forcefully declared his opposition to "mindless escalation" that would needlessly destroy lives and property and increase the risk of World War III.

Some de-escalators believe that Moscow and/or Peking will directly enter the war rather than permit the Communists to be defeated in Vietnam. If this is so, then it is likely that the present struggle will end in one of three ways: our own withdrawal (and tacit admission of defeat); World War III; or a compromise settlement. If the first two alternatives are intolerable, then the third is inevitable. And if compromise is inevitable — why not now, before more blood is spilled?

Anyway, by the Administration's own statements, our purpose in fighting is not "victory" *per se,* but to get the enemy to quit shooting and talk. How, then, is this to be accomplished? Not, say the de-escalators, by bombing North Vietnam. On the Administration's own showing, they argue, the bombing has neither decreased the flow of men and supplies southward nor has it perceptibly lessened North Vietnam's will to fight. If, as Administration spokesmen have repeatedly said in one way or another, we cannot allow the enemy to shoot their way to the conference table, neither can it be expected that they will allow us to bomb them to the table.

As for what we should do in South Vietnam, most de-escalators appear to approve some variant of the "holding strategy" advocated by Lieutenant General James M. Gavin, who served in the Korean war on the staff of General Matthew B. Ridgway. "To increase the bombing and to bomb Hanoi, or even Peking," the general told the Senate Foreign Relations Committee early in 1966, "will add to our problems rather than detract from them. . . ." Instead, he suggested that we go over to the defensive, holding what we have in South Vietnam and meanwhile seeking a political solution "through the UN or a conference in Geneva." Foremost spokesmen for the de-escalating school, including Senators J. W. Fulbright (D-Ark.) and Ernest Gruening (D-Alaska), as well as many experts outside government circles, such as Professor Morgenthau, Walter Lippmann and Arthur Schlesinger, Jr., have endorsed this suggestion in principle. But it has also been sharply attacked by supporters of the Administration, and most particularly by some of General Gavin's military colleagues. General Maxwell Taylor, former ambassador to Saigon and now one of President Johnson's military consultants, told a Senate committee: "To button up our troops in defensive positions . . . would constitute the abandonment of our allies on the battlefield. . . . It would destroy all confidence in Vietnam in ultimate success and would encourage the timid and the wavering to turn to the Vietcong for protection. . . ."

The de-escalators, while insisting that a lessening of our military pressure is a prerequisite to bringing the enemy to the negotiating table, admit that something more is needed. Some believe the additional element may be found in Hanoi's oft-repeated four-point program for peace, which calls for (1) recognition of Vietnam's independence and withdrawal of U.S. troops; (2) strict application of the military provisions of the Geneva agreements pending reunification of the country; (3) settlement of South Vietnam's "internal affairs in accordance with the program of the National Liberation Front"; and (4) reunification "without foreign interference.". . .

Many variations of this peace approach have been suggested. The UN secretary general, U Thant, has called for cessation of bombing in the North, a scaling down of the fighting in the South and discussions by all the combatants, including the Vietcong. Arthur Schlesinger, Jr., arguing that the war in Vietnam can never be won "as a war of white men against Asians," urges that we ought to encourage the rise, in Saigon, of a truly representative civilian regime — even one that would want to talk to the Vietcong and perhaps release us from our commitment to stay in Vietnam. . . .

THE ADMINISTRATION POSITION

Supporters of the Administration have mustered a wide range of rebuttals to the arguments of the de-escalators. They argue, again, that the risk of Chinese intervention remains minimal as long as we don't threaten the Chinese mainland or invade North Vietnam. While it is admitted that infiltration has increased since we started bombing North Vietnam (Secretary of Defense McNamara gave this as a principal reason for the launching of our bombing raids in the Hanoi-Haiphong area), it is asserted that our air action has inhibited the acceleration. From our military intelligence reports, moreover, it is reported that our air power has had a deleterious effect on the morale of enemy troops, who are today being captured or are deserting in larger numbers than ever before.

As for "recognizing" the Vietcong, supporters of our policy insist that the Vietcong and its political arm, the National Liberation Front, are vassals of Hanoi; and that since Hanoi is the principal instigator of the war, it has the power to end it. Moreover, aside from our own convictions on the matter, there are the feelings of others to be considered. Millions of South Vietnamese have been suffering at the hands of Communist guerrillas and

MAJOR FACTORS IN THE REAPPRAISAL OF U.S. VIETNAM POLICY

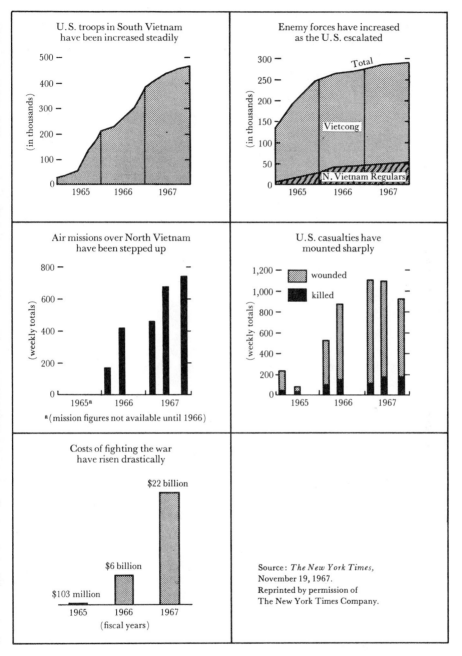

Source: *The New York Times,*
November 19, 1967.
Reprinted by permission of
The New York Times Company.

terrorists; surely they are entitled to be heard. We have had enough trouble trying to persuade Premier Ky to tone down his demands for a massive land invasion of North Vietnam; how are we going to persuade him to sit down and talk peace with the Vietcong? Would we be justified even to ask him to do so?

Finally, say Administration supporters, the fact is that we have been wanting to de-escalate the war for a long time and have been met with rebuffs by Hanoi and its allies. . . .

SIDNEY VERBA, *et al.*

Published reports from Washington in recent weeks have emphasized the extent to which policy-makers on Vietnam are concerned with the level of popular support for American commitment. Certainly no president has ever read the polls more attentively than President Johnson has on this particular issue. Thus, it becomes relevant and important to inquire about the sorts of information that the polls are communicating. So far, reports indicate that public opinion has not been explored in sufficient detail to give policy-makers a fully rounded picture of American thinking on choices in Vietnam and their possible costs.

To provide this information, a group of social scientists at Stanford University, in cooperation with the National Opinion Research Center, conducted a survey in late February and early March [1966] of a representative sample of 1,474 adults across the nation.* The questionnaire was constructed and pretested jointly by the Stanford group and NORC; sampling and nationwide field interviewing was done by the NORC organization; and data analysis and interpretation took place at Stanford.

In common with other political polls, this study shows that President Johnson has the support of the majority of the American people. Sixty-one percent of the respondents on this survey approved of the way in which the President is handling the Vietnam situation. (See Table 1.)† Unlike other studies, our more complete investigation also shows widespread support for

From Sidney Verba, Gordon Black, Richard A. Brody, Paul Ekman, Norman H. Nie, Edwin B. Parker, Nelson W. Polsby, Peter H. Rossi, and Paul Sheatsley, "Public Opinion and the War in Vietnam," privately mimeographed at Stanford University, March 15, 1966. The full text of this report is reprinted here, except that the appendices have been omitted and a number of the tables in the original have been omitted or consolidated.

* To obtain a representative sample of American adults, the National Opinion Research Center drew probability samples of blocks within each of its seventy-five sampling points throughout the country and sent its interviewers to select men and women within those blocks (or comparable areal units) to correspond to the nation in age, sex, and employment status.

† See Appendix 1 for a complete report of all data, and the exact wording of questions.

moderate de-escalation of the conflict (including negotiation with the Vietcong and inclusion of the Vietcong in a coalition government) and a reluctance to pay the increased economic and manpower costs which a substantial escalation would involve. Americans are opposed to the extreme solutions of either a massive escalation or a sudden withdrawal, leading to a Communist takeover in Vietnam.

Contrary to previous reports, a number of detailed and specific findings suggest that there is strong sentiment to de-escalate the war in Vietnam. Among these findings are clear majorities favoring policy alternatives suggested by some of the President's critics in recent debate on the topic, but which have not found favor with the administration.

Overwhelmingly, the American people favor negotiations with the Vietcong. Eighty-eight per cent say they would be willing to negotiate. Seventy per cent of the people would support a United Nations-negotiated truce in Vietnam. A 52 per cent majority would be willing to see the Vietcong assume a role in a South Vietnam coalition government, and a 54 per cent majority favored holding free elections in South Vietnam, even if the Vietcong might win. Willingness to deal with the Vietcong is not based on a misunderstanding of who they are; those who correctly identify the Vietcong are equally willing to deal with them.

Among those who approve of the President's handling of the Vietnam situation, 88 per cent would favor negotiations with the Vietcong, 51 per cent would accept a coalition government, 54 per cent favor free elections and 71 per cent would support a U.N.-negotiated truce settlement. (See Tables 4 and 5.)

Recent press reports have suggested that disagreement with the President on Vietnam policy is growing and that those opposing him think he is not pressing the war hard enough.* Contrary to these reports, the present study indicates that opposition to the President is coming from the other side. Of those who disapprove of the way President Johnson is handling the Vietnam situation, a two-to-one majority approves of having the Vietcong take part in a coalition government and of having free elections even if the Vietcong wins. They favor a U.N.-supervised truce by almost three to one. More than nine out of ten favor negotiating directly with the Vietcong.

These respondents who oppose the President's policy also would oppose stepping up the war. They are two to one against increasing troop commitment to 500,000 men, and three to two against bombing cities in North Vietnam. (See Tables 4 and 5.)

The majority of American citizens have reservations about continuing the war when they are faced with its possible costs. The study asked whether people wanted to continue the fighting in Vietnam if it meant cutting back

* *The New York Times*, March 10, 1966, p. 10. See also C. S. Sulzberger, *The New York Times*, March 7, 1966, Section IV; and *Newsweek*, March 7, 1966.

various Great Society programs, raising taxes, and imposing economic controls. On every count majorities were registered in opposition.

Seventy-nine per cent oppose cutting aid to education if necessary to continue the war. Two-thirds oppose cutting Medicare. Two-thirds oppose raising taxes. Majorities also oppose introducing economic controls or cutting back the war on poverty.* (See Table 6.)

Even those who support the President are apparently not willing to pay increased costs of continued involvement. Seventy-eight per cent of the President's supporters would oppose a cut in aid to education, and 59 per cent would oppose increased taxes if these measures were necessary to continue the war. (See Tables 4 and 5.)

Opposition to increased taxes or reduced material benefits is not an unusual finding. What is the most striking finding in this connection is that even "hawks" who are willing to escalate the war by sending half a million men to Vietnam were unwilling to bear domestic costs: 73 per cent opposed a cut in aid to education and over half opposed raising taxes, if necessary to continue the fighting. (See Tables 8 and 16.)

Those who would approve of fighting the Chinese in Vietnam also are unwilling to pay costs. Fifty-six per cent of this group oppose raising taxes, and 76 per cent would not approve of cuts in federal aid to education.

The majority of the American people would be willing to continue the war if it required calling up the National Guard, but would prefer ending the war if a full-scale mobilization was required. Sixty per cent agree to calling out the National Guard to continue the war; but only 40 per cent agree to full mobilization to continue the war. Further, only 38 per cent would approve continuing the war if it meant several hundred American casualties per week. (See Table 18.)

Both the press and Administration spokesmen have suggested that the war in Vietnam may require an increase in our commitment to 500,000 American troops. The American people are divided on this suggestion. When asked if they approved of having half a million troops in Vietnam if that were needed to continue the war, 45 per cent approved, and 46 per cent were opposed. (See Table 11.)

The respondents were asked about other possible escalation steps. On almost all escalation steps, majorities said they would rather end the war. And, the greater the escalation, the larger the majority favoring an end to the war.

* But in other times of national emergency, Americans have expressed willingness to see taxes raised. "A Gallup question in January 1958 shortly after Russia launched Sputnik showed that 63 per cent of the respondents were ready to see their income taxes raised in order '. . . to build up our military strength here and abroad. . . .' Another question which asked whether the United States would be able to keep the high standard of living it was accustomed to, or whether '. . . we will have to pull in our belts and sacrifice for stronger defense' found 61 per cent who accepted the need to sacrifice." See Gabriel A. Almond, "Public Opinion and the Development of Space Technology," Public Opinion Quarterly (Winter 1960), pp. 553–572.

When asked about bombing cities in North Vietnam, 55 per cent prefer ending the war. When asked about fighting a land war in China, 60 per cent prefer ending the war in Vietnam. When asked about an atomic war with China, 63 per cent prefer to end the war in Vietnam. On the other hand, a majority said they would support the continuation of the war even if it meant fighting the Chinese within the borders of Vietnam itself. (See Table 11.)

Americans want to focus upon reasonable rather than extreme alternatives. Public opinion favors de-escalation but opposes immediate withdrawal; opinions are divided on limited escalation, but clearly opposed to major escalation. Thus, majorities rejected extremes either up or down the scale. Public opinion is opposed to the use of nuclear weapons against the Chinese. On the other hand, although willing to negotiate, they would not favor a sudden, unilateral withdrawal of American troops followed by a Communist take-over. Eighty-one per cent rejected this alternative. Majorities also oppose other actions that denied that the United States shared responsibility for the future of Vietnam. Fifty-six per cent opposed unilateral withdrawal to let the Vietnamese work out their own difficulties and 77 per cent opposed abandoning our commitment to other countries of Asia. (When asked to choose among three unpleasant alternatives — a major war, or continuation of the present situation indefinitely or unilateral withdrawal — the largest group chose the middle course. However, when faced with the unpleasant extremes, more would take the major war than would take unilateral withdrawal.) (See Table 12.)

The majorities who favor settlement of the Vietnam conflict by negotiations with the Vietcong, or inclusion of the Vietcong in a coalition government, are not open to the charge of being "soft on communism." On the contrary, overwhelmingly these people maintain a firm anti-communist policy elsewhere in the world. Ninety-four per cent of those who want to negotiate with the Vietcong either approve our policy toward Cuba or think it should be tougher. Eighty-seven per cent of those willing to negotiate with the Vietcong think our China policy is correct or should be tougher; 93 per cent want a firm policy toward Soviet Russia. (See Table 13.)

Those who favor a South Vietnamese coalition government, including the Vietcong, or who favor free elections even though the Vietcong might win, also overwhelmingly favor firm policies elsewhere. In this respect, those who favor dealing with the Vietcong are as firm on communism elsewhere as are those who oppose dealing with the Vietcong.

If the Vietnam "dove" turns out to be a hybrid, so does the Vietnam "hawk." Large numbers of respondents who are willing to see an escalation of American involvement in Vietnam also favor de-escalation policies as well. Among those who would support increasing the American commitment to 500,000 men, 48 per cent would favor a coalition government even including the Vietcong, while only 42 per cent would oppose it. Similarly, a majority who support an increase in the number of our troops favor free Vietnamese elections even though the Vietcong might win. And 86 per cent of these "hawks" favor negotiations with the Vietcong. (See Tables 8 and 16.)

Most Americans have mixed feelings about the war in Vietnam. They are not "real hawks" or "real doves" since they do not take consistent positions on increasing or decreasing the war. Are there any "real hawks" or any "real doves"?

Only a small percentage of the American population can be characterized as "real hawks." Six per cent of the sample studied take consistent "hawk" positions in favor of escalation and opposed to de-escalation. They favor increasing our forces to 500,000 men and bombing cities in North Vietnam if necessary to win the war. And they oppose a coalition government with the Vietcong and oppose free elections if that means that the Vietcong might win.

The consistent "doves" are more than twice as numerous as the "hawks." Fourteen per cent of the American people fall into this group. They are people who oppose expansion of commitment to 500,000 troops and oppose bombing North Vietnamese cities. They favor a coalition government with the Vietcong and would favor free elections even if the Vietcong were to win.

Does President Johnson get more support from the "real hawks" or from the "real doves"? The answer is clear. He gets more from the "real hawks." Seventy-two per cent of the "real hawks" approve of the way President Johnson is handling the situation in Vietnam; 23 per cent disapprove. Of the "real doves", only 44 per cent approve of the President's actions in Vietnam, and 48 per cent disapprove.

The American public is clearly concerned about Vietnam. Sixty-one per cent say that they are worried a great deal about Vietnam; more than worry about any other public issue. But their opinions appear to be moderate and responsible. They do not want to pay the domestic costs of commitment in Vietnam, but this is consistent with their desire for a negotiated settlement. And though the settlement they prefer involves a willingness to deal with the Vietcong that goes beyond present administration policy, they reject those solutions that require irresponsible abandonment of our commitments.

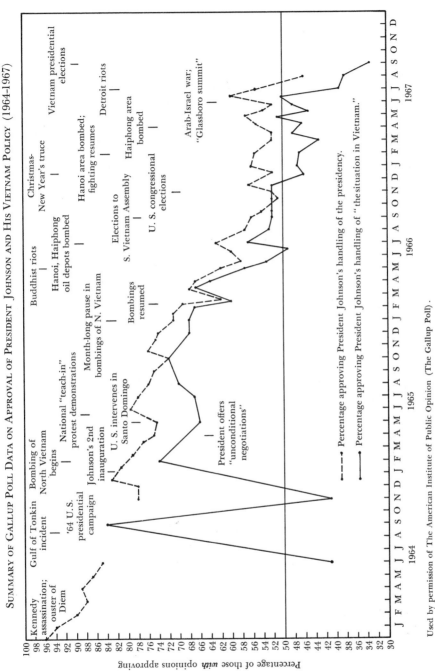

SUMMARY OF GALLUP POLL DATA ON APPROVAL OF PRESIDENT JOHNSON AND HIS VIETNAM POLICY (1964-1967)

Percentage of those *with* opinions approving

Kennedy assassination; ouster of Diem

Gulf of Tonkin incident

Bombing of North Vietnam begins

'64 U.S. presidential campaign

Johnson's 2nd inauguration

National "teach-in" protest demonstrations

U.S. intervenes in Santo Domingo

President offers "unconditional negotiations"

Month-long pause in bombings of N. Vietnam

Bombings resumed

Buddhist riots

Hanoi, Haiphong oil depots bombed

Elections to S. Vietnam Assembly

U. S. congressional elections

Christmas-New Year's truce

Hanoi area bombed; fighting resumes

Haiphong area bombed

Arab-Israel war; "Glassboro summit"

Vietnam presidential elections

Detroit riots

1964   1965   1966   1967

- - - - ● Percentage approving President Johnson's handling of the presidency.

——— ● Percentage approving President Johnson's handling of "the situation in Vietnam."

Used by permission of The American Institute of Public Opinion (The Gallup Poll).

APPENDIX 1. TABLES AND QUESTIONS

TABLE 1
ATTITUDE TOWARD JOHNSON'S HANDLING OF THE VIETNAM SITUATION

	Approve	Disapprove	DK [Don't Know]
In general, do you approve or disapprove the way the Johnson administration is handling the situation in Vietnam?	61%	29%	10%

TABLE 2
SENTIMENT TO DE-ESCALATE

	Favor or approve	Oppose or disapprove	DK
a. Would you be in favor of American negotiations with the Vietcong if they were willing to negotiate?	88%	8%	4%
Would you approve or disapprove of the following actions to end the fighting:			
b. Getting the United Nations or some neutral countries to negotiate a truce, with each side holding the territory it now holds?	70%	22%	8%
c. Forming a new government in which the Vietcong took some part?	52%	36%	12%
d. Holding free elections in South Vietnam even if the Vietcong might win?	54%	34%	12%

TABLES 4 AND 5
SENTIMENT TO DE-ESCALATE [OR ESCALATE] FOR THOSE WHO APPROVE OR DISAPPROVE THE WAY THE JOHNSON ADMINISTRATION IS HANDLING THE SITUATION IN VIETNAM [a]

[Attitude toward administration policy:]	Approve			Disapprove		
[Attitude toward proposal cited:]	Favor or approve	Oppose disapprove	DK	Favor or approve	Oppose disapprove	DK
a. Would you be in favor of American negotiations with the Vietcong if they were willing to negotiate?	88%	9%	3%	92%	7%	1%

TABLES 4 AND 5 *(Cont.)*

[Attitude toward administration policy:]	Approve			Disapprove		
[Attitude toward proposal cited:]	Favor or approve	Oppose disapprove	DK	Favor or approve	Oppose disapprove	DK
Would you approve or disapprove of the following actions to end the fighting:						
b. Forming a new government in which the Vietcong took some part?	51%	39%	10%	59%	32%	9%
c. Holding free elections in South Vietnam even if the Vietcong might win?	54%	36%	10%	57%	33%	9%
d. Getting the United Nations or some neutral countries to negotiate a truce, with each side holding the territory it now holds?	71%	23%	7%	71%	23%	6%
Would you approve or disapprove of the following in order to continue fighting:						
e. Having half a million troops in South Vietnam?	56%	36%	8%	31%	63%	6%
f. Bombing the cities of North Vietnam?	40%	54%	6%	37%	59%	4%

[a Some totals do not add to 100 per cent, apparently because of rounding.]

TABLE 6
ATTITUDE TOWARD INCREASED COSTS OF WAR

	Approve	Disapprove	DK
Approve or disapprove of doing the following in order to continue fighting?			
a. Reducing aid to education?	19%	78%	2%
b. Increasing taxes at home?	31%	67%	3%
c. Putting government controls over wages and prices?	41%	53%	6%
d. Spending less money for the War on Poverty	46%	50%	4%
e. Reducing the Medicare program?	28%	66%	6%

TABLE 7
ATTITUDE TOWARD INCREASED COSTS OF WAR OF THOSE
WHO APPROVE THE WAY THE JOHNSON ADMINISTRATION
IS HANDLING THE SITUATION IN VIETNAM

[Attitude toward administration policy:]	Approve			Disapprove		
[Attitude toward proposal cited:]	Approve	Disapprove	DK	Approve	Disapprove	DK
Approve or disapprove of doing the following in order to continue fighting:						
a. Reducing aid to education?	20%	78%	2%	16%	82%	2%
b. Increasing taxes at home?	39%	59%	2%	18%	81%	2%

TABLES 8 AND 16
ATTITUDE . . . OF THOSE WHO APPROVE HAVING HALF A MILLION
TROOPS IN SOUTH VIETNAM

[Attitude toward having half a million troops in South Vietnam:]	Approve			Disapprove		
[Attitude toward proposal cited:]	Approve	Disapprove	DK	Approve	Disapprove	DK
Approve or disapprove of doing the following in order to continue fighting:						
a. Reducing aid to education?	26%	72%	1%	13%	85%	2%
b. Increasing taxes at home?	48%	50%	2%	17%	82%	1%
Would you approve or disapprove of the following actions to end the fighting?						
a. Forming a new government in which the Vietcong took some part?	49%	42%	9%	59%	32%	9%
b. Holding free elections in South Vietnam even if the Vietcong might win?	53%	37%	10%	57%	33%	10%
c. Would you be in favor of American negotiations with the Vietcong if they were willing to negotiate?	85%	12%	3%	92%	6%	2%

TABLE 11
AMERICAN PEOPLE DIVIDED ON ENLARGING THE WAR

	Approve	Disapprove	DK
Approve or disapprove of doing the following in order to continue fighting:			
a. Having half a million troops in South Vietnam?	45%	46%	9%
b. Bombing the cities of North Vietnam?	38%	55%	7%
c. Fighting a ground war in China itself?	32%	60%	8%
d. Fighting an atomic war with China?	30%	64%	7%
e. Fighting an atomic war with Russia?	22%	71%	7%

TABLE 12
REASONABLE ALTERNATIVES

	Favor or approve	Oppose or disapprove	DK
a. If President Johnson were to announce tomorrow that we were going to withdraw from Vietnam and let the Communists take over, would you approve or disapprove?	15%	81%	4%
Would you approve or disapprove of the following action to end the fighting:			
b. Gradually withdrawing our troops and letting the South Vietnamese work out their own problems?	39%	56%	5%
c. Would you approve of ending the fighting in South Vietnam even if that meant the eventual loss of independence of other nations like Laos and Thailand?	13%	77%	10%

	Present situation	Major war	With-drawal	DK
d. Suppose you had to choose among continuing the present situation indefinitely, fighting a major war with hundreds of thousands of casualties, or a withdrawal of American troops leading to an eventual Communist takeover. Which would you choose?	49%	23%	19%	9%
e. Suppose we couldn't continue the present policy, how would you choose between a major war and a withdrawal of American troops?		60%	31%	9%

TABLE 13
THOSE WHO FAVOR NEGOTIATION

	Favor				Oppose			
	Too tough	About right	Too soft	DK	Too tough	About right	Too soft	DK
a. How about our policy toward Castro in Cuba? Have we been tough, about right, or too soft?	3%	30%	64%	3%	2%	18%	78%	2%
b. How about Communist China? (Have we been too tough, about right, or too soft?)	3%	38%	49%	10%	3%	25%	68%	4%
c. Would you say that our policy toward Russia has been too tough, just about right, or too soft?	2%	48%	46%	4%	3%	44%	51%	2%

TABLE 18
WOULD YOU APPROVE OF CONTINUING THE FIGHTING
IF IT MEANT SEVERAL HUNDRED AMERICAN SOLDIERS
WOULD BE KILLED EVERY WEEK?

Approve	Disapprove	DK
38%	54%	7%

Chapter Eight

ETHICS AND
FOREIGN POLICY

Soon after Senate ratification of the limited nuclear Test Ban Treaty signed by the Soviet Union, Great Britain, and the United States, the following letter appeared in "the Public Letter Box" columns of *The Detroit News* (Oct. 6, 1963):

> To the Editor: How coincidental, The Detroit News' article on the Munich Treaty so soon after the ratification of the Test Ban Treaty. The last 25 years have given you lots of hindsight but not much foresight.
>
> I have been taught that one should learn about the future by looking at the past. I believe they call it experience. We all know we should never make a deal with the devil, yet our allies made such a deal at Munich and we recently completed such a deal in Moscow. The main difference is that this time we have much more at stake and this time we have much more experience with the enemy — 51 broken treaties out of a possible 53.
>
> It would be nice if we conservatives could only teach you liberals to take actions based only upon moral principles; not to rely on your intellect or emotions.
>
> In regard to the Test Ban Treaty, America's intellect said that the bomb is the most dangerous weapon that has ever faced humanity, but the intellect realized that Russia has kept very few treaties. Then the emotions took over and told America that either we ban the bomb or the world would go up in smoke and that cinched it.
>
> How tragic that we never realized that moral vision sees much farther into the future. By this treaty we have neither banned the bomb nor found "peace in our time." We have dealt with the murderers of mil-

lions in the same manner normally reserved for dealing with good, respectable leaders of nations. We have become guilty of shameful appeasement. FOR A BETTER AMERICA.[1]

The inaccuracy of the figures he offers aside, the writer of this letter has fallen into a common error. He has confused the intrinsic morality of the action he condemns with the moral implications of the *consequences* of that action. Was it immoral to sign a test ban treaty with the Russians because their record of breaking treaties indicates that they will probably violate this treaty, too, with the *result* that the Soviet Union will gain a military advantage over the United States? Or was it immoral because dealing with "the murderers of millions" is unethical regardless of the results? Suppose, for the sake of argument, that there is good reason to believe that the Soviets *will* honor this treaty, and that, if kept by both sides, it will help substantially to reduce the prospect that the world will "go up in smoke." Should we still "never make a deal with the devil"? Or is it all right to deal with the devil if morally worthy results are thereby achieved? These are the questions which those who make foreign policy — and those who would understand it — must live with daily.

THE FUTILITY OF ABSOLUTES

"If wishes were horses, then beggars could ride. . . ." And if wishes were policies, then statesmen would never have to "compromise with moral principle" to achieve their foreign policy goals. Citizens reared in a Judaeo-Christian ethical tradition which teaches respect for human life and for the dignity of man would not need to participate in organized efforts to kill other human beings in time of war. A majority of the federal income taxes we pay each year would not need to be devoted to the construction and maintenance of weapons designed to murder tens of millions of people with modern technological efficiency. A society dedicated to the preservation of free institutions would not have to require its youth to submit to military discipline through a selective service system. A government which professes adherence to the principles of national sovereignty and international law would not feel called upon to violate both by sending U-2 reconnaissance planes on espionage missions over foreign soil.

But wishes are neither horses nor policies. Moral means may contribute to immoral ends and immoral means to moral goals. If we had been unwilling to compromise with the moral precept "Thou shalt not kill" in defending ourselves against the Nazi and Japanese threat in World War II, for instance, we might well have lost ultimately the freedom to lead our lives in accordance with the principles we hold to be moral. What ethical guides should we have used in deciding how to act morally in this trying situation?

An ethical system completely divorced from action is a contradiction in

---

[1] Reprinted by permission of *The Detroit News.*

terms.[2] Worse, it is an invitation to mouth pious homilies while acting with utter disregard for any moral values whatever, human or divine. The suggestion that international politics is amoral, or that we must use an ethic of total expediency in conducting foreign policy is no better. For it pretends that no moral values are at stake in decisions which may determine the physical survival and quality of life of Mankind itself. And an ethic of expediency, far from being amoral, is actually itself a moral system — and one which usually puts national self-interest, narrowly conceived, at the pinnacle of its value hierarchy.

MORAL DILEMMAS

A usable ethic must not dodge these crucial moral questions. Rather it must help us to choose, in each concrete situation, the actual course of action which will yield the most moral results in the long run. Lying, stealing, killing may not be moral acts in absolute terms — but in certain circumstances they may be the *most moral* actions possible. A meaningful ethical system is always *relative* — relative to the specific context in which choices must be made and actions taken. To be ethical in the conduct of foreign affairs, therefore, the policymaker must:

1. Study the problem before him carefully, considering all the conceivable alternatives for dealing with it;

2. Calculate as best he can the short- and long-term *consequences* of pursuing each of these alternative courses of action;

3. Evaluate each of these sets of consequences from the standpoint of his own (or his society's) moral code; and

4. Choose the action he believes will, on balance, produce the most moral — or least immoral — results.

This procedure, of course, is far from simple. The words used do not convey adequately the complexity of the operations called for. Alternatives, for example, are not always self-evident. However conscientiously we may study a policy problem, we can never be sure we have considered *all* the possible alternatives; perhaps there will remain ways of coping with the situation which have not occurred to us. The devising of additional alternatives may prove to be the key step in making a morally adequate decision. In general, the wider the range of alternatives we are able to perceive or devise, the greater the chance we will have to choose a relatively moral course of action.

Calculating the consequences of these alternatives involves incredible complexities, ambiguities, and imponderables. If the United States had not aided Britain against Hitler, what would the consequences have been? In the years to come might Germany have become so involved with consolidat-

[2] See Abraham Kaplan, "American Ethics and Public Policy," *Daedalus* (Spring, 1958), pp. 48–77.

ing its conquests in Europe that it would have decided to leave the United States alone in peace? Or would it have turned upon America with renewed strength soon after winning a victory in Europe? Might Hitler have taken care of our postwar "Communist problem" for us, if the United States had stood aside? If Germany and the United States did not go to war eventually, might the American "way of life" have been jeopardized, nevertheless, by the pressures of continued coexistence in a Fascist dominated world? What impact would an Axis victory in Europe have had on the future of the peoples of Europe's overseas colonies? Would the war have been shorter or longer if the United States had stayed out of it? Would more lives have been lost and more suffering inflicted with or without direct American participation?

Evaluating the moral desirability of each of these sets of uncertain consequences is equally difficult. It requires first of all that we have a clear and consistent moral code to guide us in making our evaluations. Are sacrifices of lives preferable to sacrifices of freedom? Are sacrifices of a limited degree of freedom in the short run preferable to sacrifices of a greater degree of freedom in the long run? Is it preferable to make certain changes in our way of life, or to invoke the destruction of war to preserve our way of life intact? If war is preferable to *some* changes in our way of life, but not to others, then just which aspects of our way of life are worth fighting for, and which are not? And on what grounds do we make the distinction?

Once these evaluations have been made, the act of choice itself may require more integrity and self-discipline than logic. But that does not make the moral burdens involved in making such choices, on inevitably uncertain bases, any easier to bear.

When a society, rather than an individual, is called upon to make such moral choices, moreover, many compromises will be required. The moral priorities of different individuals and groups may vary widely — and so may the calculations through which they translate these priorities into policy preferences. Bargaining, compromise, and political maneuvering, therefore, will probably prove unavoidable — and then the resulting *national* choice will be subjected to further modification due to the choices and actions of other states.

MORAL CHOICE AND
THE TEST BAN TREATY

It will be a useful exercise to outline how the procedure described above might be applied to the problem of the Test Ban Treaty discussed in the letter with which this chapter opened.

When the Test Ban Treaty was signed, in the fall of 1963, there were two major and two minor nuclear powers, and it was known that other nations possessed the potential to develop nuclear arsenals in the foreseeable future.

The nuclear weapons tests often conducted by the existing nuclear powers were known to have produced fallout which, in sufficient quantities, would contribute to the pollution of the earth's atmosphere. The precise effects of this atmospheric pollution were subject to controversy among scientists. Some contended that the dangers involved in testing were relatively small. Others insisted that the hazards — in genetic and bone damage, the birth of deviant offspring in future generations, and the health of existing populations — were very substantial. Whatever the true extent of these dangers, it was generally conceded that they could be significantly reduced by conducting future atomic testing underground and thereby minimizing the resultant pollution of the atmosphere. It was commonly accepted, also, that atmospheric — but *not* underground — testing by any nation could be reliably detected by other states without access to its territory. Since atmospheric tests contributed significantly to the refinement of nuclear weapons technology, it seemed clear that if either of the major nuclear powers were to continue such testing over a prolonged period while the other abstained from testing, the former might gain a significant strategic advantage over the latter. On the other hand, an effective test ban of any sort would be likely to slow down somewhat the further development of the nuclear arms race.

In the course of prolonged negotiation concerning a nuclear test ban, the Soviet Union declared its willingness to pledge that it would discontinue all nuclear tests if the United States and Great Britain did likewise. But it would not agree to the measures necessary to ensure detection of underground tests carried out in violation of this pledge. If an agreement between these three nuclear powers were reached, most — but not all — of the remaining potential nuclear powers in the world could be expected to adhere to it also, thus perhaps retarding the proliferation of nuclear weapons which might otherwise be anticipated within a decade or two.

In these circumstances, the alternatives available to the United States government were many. For purposes of illustration, however, these can be reduced to a few readily distinguishable possibilities:

1. The United States could refuse to conclude any agreements with the Soviet Union concerning nuclear tests;

2. The United States might offer to conclude an agreement only if *all* tests, atmospheric and underground, were renounced and a satisfactory inspection system for policing these treaty commitments were established;

3. The United States might agree to ban atmospheric, but not underground, weapons tests;

4. The United States might agree to ban all tests, atmospheric and underground, *without* insisting on a satisfactory inspection system for policing the underground test ban.

Alternative (1) — advocated by the letter quoted earlier — would eliminate any risk that the United States might be left at a military disadvantage if the Soviet Union should violate its pledges. But it would fail to minimize the future risks of nuclear proliferation and of air pollution due to continued testing. It would not slow down the nuclear arms race. And it would lose whatever opportunity there might be to influence future Soviet behavior in some small but desirable way through the shared experience of a mutually observed treaty agreement.

Alternative (2) might appear more flexible than (1) to other nations of the world, but given the Soviet refusal to agree to a satisfactory inspection system it would result, like alternative (1), in no agreement, with consequences similar to those outlined above.

Alternative (3) is the one chosen by the Kennedy administration and by the majority of the Senate which ratified the treaty. It risks some loss in military advantage if the Soviets should violate the agreement, since a short period would probably then elapse before the United States could plan and execute a similar series of atmospheric tests.[3] But it does minimize the risks of air pollution and nuclear proliferation referred to and gains some opportunity to limit the nuclear arms race and affect Soviet behavior as noted.

Alternative (4) would win at least the same advantages as alternative (3) — but would risk considerably greater loss of military advantage if the Soviet Union, in violation of the treaty it had signed, should successfully conduct numerous secret underground tests.

The moral consequences of each of these alternatives is impossible to weigh precisely. Given the relative strength of the two nations' nuclear arsenals, the Kennedy administration appears to have believed that the moral gains of halting atmospheric tests outweighed the relatively minimal risks of giving the Soviets a chance to resume atmospheric testing a short time before the United States. Perhaps this seems to you — as it does to me — a prudent calculation. Perhaps it does not. In any event, in order to fairly criticize this decision of the administration — and of the Senate majority which voted to ratify the treaty — as immoral, you would be obligated to argue *not* that we must not deal with the devil, but that one of the other alternatives listed — or one that you have perceived which was not listed — would have been likely to yield, on balance, more morally desirable consequences. As Arnold Wolfers has written:

> Moral condemnation, according to non-perfectionist ethics, rests not on the fact that values have been destroyed, however deplorable or downright evil such destruction may be judged. Instead it is based on

[3] Measures have been taken — at some expense — to minimize this risk by maintaining the capability to undertake further atmospheric tests at short notice in case the Soviet Union should ever violate the Test Ban Agreement.

the conviction either that the action in question rested on false ethical standards or that in terms of agreed ethical standards a less destructive choice could and should have been made.[4]

NATIONAL, SUBNATIONAL, AND SUPRANATIONAL INTERESTS

We have thus far studiously avoided the thorny question of what the point of reference for our moral assessments should be. We cannot decide that issue here, but it should be raised. Do we choose the course of action which maximizes the benefits to our own national group? Or the alternative which promises the greatest advantages to the peoples of the world as a whole? Or is our point of reference some other individual or group — ourself, our family, business, region, church, or ethnic group?

Groups or groupings which are smaller than the nation as a whole, and contained within it, may be referred to as representing *subnational* interests. General Motors Corporation, the United Auto Workers Union, the American Farm Bureau Federation, the Democratic Party, the Congress of Racial Equality, and the American South are examples of subnational groups or groupings. (Some institutions represent subnational interests in more than one country: the Catholic Church, international business cartels, international labor organizations, and certain ethnic groups, for example.) The interests of the peoples of the world as a whole, on the other hand, or of the realm of Christendom, might be referred to as *supranational* interests.

These terms are useful in distinguishing the various points of reference from which moral evaluations may be made. But the terms themselves, without further qualification, do little more than make this distinction. Even if we were to agree with those scholars who urge that the *national* interest must be the touchstone of public policy at all times, we would not thereby be provided with a foolproof guide to moral action in specific cases. What *is* the national interest? There is no magic in the phrase which protects us from the difficult questions which arose before.

Is it in the national interest to change our way of life so that the nation's people can survive? How much of a change in our way of life can be justified in the national interest? If the change required involves making the United States a totalitarian society, could it be said that the *nation* had survived along with its people? Or is it in the national interest for a majority of the people and property of the nation to be destroyed in an effort to preserve elements of our way of life? Is it in the national interest to require great sacrifices of the present citizenry now in the name of securing greater benefits for the yet unborn citizenry of the future? Or is it more in the national interest to mortgage the benefits of future generations to the pressing needs of here and now? These are among the dilemmas which those

4 "Statesmanship and Moral Choice," *World Politics,* January, 1949, p. 180.

responsible for determining the national interest must cope with as they arise, from particular case to particular case. Unfortunately for them, no neat abstract formulation can really relieve them from the burdensome responsibility for thinking through each problem on its individual merits.

No less difficult is the balancing of national against subnational and supranational interests. The existence of conflicts among these points of reference is so psychologically painful to accept, in fact, that many people try to resolve the problem through what we might call the *fallacy of identification*. This fallacy assumes that there is not and *can*not be any genuinely irreconcilable conflict of interest between the multiple points of reference involved. Among the classic statements of this fallacy are Charles E. Wilson's: "What's good for General Motors is good for the U.S.A.";[5] and Rutherford B. Hayes' dictum, putting the other foot forward: "He serves his party best who serves his country best." Other Americans — including some who laughed at Wilson's statement — would insist that there is not and cannot be any conflict of interest between the United States and the United Nations, or the Catholic Church, or the world community at large. Only when this conflict comes close to our own deepest loyalties can we begin to comprehend its cruelty.

In studying the Chinese community in the Philippines some years ago, I had an opportunity to observe personally the strength of the emotional reactions this problem can generate. Perhaps foolishly, I asked each of the Philippine Chinese I interviewed which side he would take if a conflict should happen to arise in the future between (Nationalist) China and the Philippines. Few were willing to answer. Most denied that such a confrontation could possibly materialize. Several volunteered that if it did materialize, they would probably commit suicide! One protested that he felt as though I had asked him whether he would choose first to save his father or his mother if the lives of both were in danger. Though it was not a fair question to ask, there was much to be learned from the answers. It is understandable that most Americans, and most human beings, prefer not to make such choices until it is absolutely clear that they have to.

Yet we cannot allow ourselves the luxury of refusing to face the fact that there are times when such painful choices will have to be made. This is not to say that subnational, national, and supranational interests are *never* identical or similar. To insist upon this would be to slip into a fallacy no less dangerous — and much less psychologically justifiable — than the fallacy of identification. Fortunately, when subnational or national interests are

---

[5] Wilson was responding to questions, raised by a Senate committee reviewing his appointment as Secretary of Defense, as to whether any conflict of interest might arise between his official responsibilities and his continued holding of substantial financial interests in General Motors, of which he had been President. In the end, Wilson divested himself of these holdings.

viewed in an enlightened long-term perspective, they will often be seen to coincide quite closely with one another and with the supranational interest. One of the major themes of this book, for instance, is that an attempt to build a supranational world community, in which the inevitable differences between men and nations could be resolved without resort to war, would be in *both* the national *and* the supranational interest.

Suppose, however, to return to an example used earlier, that the United States had to decide whether or not to enter World War II in circumstances somewhat different from those which actually occurred. Suppose that Pearl Harbor had not been attacked and that the Japanese threat had not been present. Assume further that there was no reason to worry that Hitler would attack America after he had conquered Europe, and that American military and economic strength were so great that the United States could readily have withstood any conceivable future Fascist attempt to undermine our way of life. If the United States had stayed out of the war, in these circumstances, many American lives would have been saved at relatively small cost to America as a nation. But hundreds of millions of Europeans presumably would have been doomed to live out their lives under Nazi tyranny. And millions more Jews and Christians might have been exterminated in Nazi concentration camps. In this hypothetical context, it might have been in the *national* interest for the United States to stay out of the war, but in the supranational interest for Americans to join in the defense of their fellow men. Which should we then have chosen? Should we feel morally obliged to sacrifice our own nation's interests completely, to a certain extent, or not at all, in the interests of the peoples of the world at large?

❧ CASE
STUDY   *THE ETHICS OF*
          USING THE ATOMIC BOMB

These perplexing moral issues are at least potentially involved in the case study which follows.[6] Factual uncertainties, tactical calculations, and moral issues were inseparably interwoven in the decision to use the atomic bomb — as they are in most major foreign policy decisions.

6 The reader is strongly urged to supplement the selection included here by reading John Hersey's graphic account of what happened when the first atomic bomb fell, killing close to 100,000 human beings and maiming many more. His book, *Hiroshima* (New York: Knopf, 1946) is widely available in a paperback edition.

1. If you, rather than Secretary of War Henry L. Stimson, had borne primary responsibility for advising the President in this matter, what would you have advised? Was the decision to use the atomic bomb on Japanese cities the most moral decision which could have been made in the circumstances? If not, what course of action do you believe would have been *more* moral? Use of the bomb against military targets only? A technical demonstration? Use of the bomb only after issuing a more specific warning of its nature and effects? Complete abstention from use of the bomb? What political and moral problems would each of these alternatives have posed?

2. Should the United States have announced its willingness to accept the retention of the Emperor as a constitutional monarch, or otherwise modified its insistence on unconditional surrender, before Hiroshima was bombed? Why or why not?

3. Was it necessary to use the second bomb so soon after the first?

4. Does it appear to you that subnational, national, or supranational considerations were uppermost in the minds of those who made the decision to use this new weapon? Do you feel this assignment of moral priorities was right? Were the short- and long-run consequences of using the bomb kept in proper political and moral perspective?

5. In retrospect, do you think the decision actually made turned out to be in the best interests — however you define them — of the United States? Of Japan? Of the world at large? Defend your positions. In case of future war, do you believe the United States might be justified, under any conceivable circumstances, in being the first participant to use large-scale nuclear weapons? Why or why not?

LOUIS MORTON

. . . The epic story of the development of the atomic bomb is by now well known. It began in 1939 when a small group of eminent scientists in this country called to the attention of the United States Government the vast potentialities of atomic energy for military purposes and warned that the Germans were already carrying on experiments in this field. The program initiated in October of that year with a very modest appropriation and later expanded into the two-billion-dollar Manhattan Project had only one purpose — to harness the energy of the atom in a chain reaction to produce a bomb that could be carried by aircraft if possible, and to produce it before the Germans could. That such a bomb, if produced, would be used, no responsible official even questioned. "At no time from 1941 to 1945," declared

Reprinted by permission from "The Decision to use the Atomic Bomb," *Foreign Affairs,* XXXV, January, 1957, pp. 334–353. Copyright © 1957 by the Council on Foreign Relations, Inc. (New York). Footnotes have been omitted. Other omissions are indicated by ellipses.

Mr. Stimson, "did I ever hear it suggested by the President, or by another responsible member of the Government, that atomic energy should not be used in the war." And Dr. J. Robert Oppenheimer recalled in 1954 that "we always assumed if they [atomic bombs] were needed, they would be used."

So long as the success of the project remained in doubt there seems to have been little or no discussion of the effects of an atomic weapon or the circumstances under which it would be used. "During the early days of the project," one scientist recalled, "we spent little time thinking about the possible effects of the bomb we were trying to make." It was a "neck-and-neck race with the Germans," the outcome of which might well determine who would be the victor in World War II. But as Germany approached defeat and as the effort to produce an atomic bomb offered increasing promise of success, those few men who knew what was being done and who appreciated the enormous implications of atomic energy became more and more concerned. Most of this concern came from the scientists in the Metallurgical Laboratory at Chicago, where by early 1945 small groups began to question the advisability of using the weapon they were trying so hard to build. It was almost as if they hoped the bomb would not work after it was completed.

On the military side, the realization that a bomb would probably be ready for testing in the summer of 1945 led to concrete planning for the use of the new weapon, on the assumption that the bomb when completed would work. By the end of 1944 a list of possible targets in Japan had been selected, and a B-29 squadron was trained for the specific job of delivering the bomb. . . .

It was not until March 1945 that it became possible to predict with certainty that the bomb would be completed in time for testing in July. On March 15, Mr. Stimson discussed the project for the last time with President Roosevelt, but their conversation dealt mainly with the effects of the use of the bomb, not with the question of whether it ought to be used. Even at this late date, there does not seem to have been any doubt at the highest levels that the bomb would be used against Japan if it would help bring the war to an early end. But on lower levels, and especially among the scientists at the Chicago laboratory, there was considerable reservation about the advisability of using the bomb.

After President Roosevelt's death, it fell to Stimson to brief the new President about the atomic weapon. At a White House meeting on April 25, he outlined the history and status of the program and predicted that "within four months we shall in all probability have completed the most terrible weapon ever known in human history." This meeting, like Stimson's last meeting with Roosevelt, dealt largely with the political and diplomatic consequences of the use of such a weapon rather than with the timing and manner of employment, the circumstances under which it would be used, or whether it would be used at all. The answers to these questions depended on factors not yet known. But Stimson recommended, and the President approved, the appointment of a special committee to consider them.

This special committee, known as the Interim Committee, played a vital rôle in the decision to use the bomb. Secretary Stimson was chairman, and George L. Harrison, President of the New York Life Insurance Company and special consultant in the Secretary's office, took the chair when he was absent. James F. Byrnes, who held no official position at the time, was President Truman's personal representative. Other members were Ralph A. Bard, Under Secretary of the Navy, William L. Clayton, Assistant Secretary of State, and Drs. Vannevar Bush, Karl T. Compton and James B. Conant. Generals Marshall and Groves attended at least one and possibly more of the meetings of the committee.

The work of the Interim Committee, in Stimson's words, "ranged over the whole field of atomic energy, in its political, military, and scientific aspects." During the first meeting the scientific members reviewed for their colleagues the development of the Manhattan Project and described vividly the destructive power of the atomic bomb. They made it clear also that there was no known defense against this kind of attack. Another day was spent with the engineers and industrialists who had designed and built the huge plants at Oak Ridge and Hanford. Of particular concern to the committee was the question of how long it would take another country, particularly the Soviet Union, to produce an atomic bomb. "Much of the discussion," recalled Dr. Oppenheimer who attended the meeting of June 1 as a member of a scientific panel, "revolved around the question raised by Secretary Stimson as to whether there was any hope at all of using this development to get less barbarous [sic] relations with the Russians."

The work of the Interim Committee was completed June 1, 1945, when it submitted its report to the President, recommending unanimously that:

1. The bomb should be used against Japan as soon as possible.

2. It should be used against a military target surrounded by other buildings.

3. It should be used without prior warning of the nature of the weapon. (One member, Ralph A. Bard, later dissented from this portion of the committee's recommendation.)

"The conclusions of the Committee," wrote Stimson, "were similar to my own, although I reached mine independently. I felt that to extract a genuine surrender from the Emperor and his military advisers, they must be administered a tremendous shock which would carry convincing proof of our power to destroy the empire. Such an effective shock would save many times the number of lives, both American and Japanese, than it would cost."

Among the scientists working on the Manhattan Project were many who did not agree. To them, the "wave of horror and repulsion" that might follow the sudden use of an atomic bomb would more than outweigh its military advantages. "It may be very difficult," they declared, "to persuade the world that a nation which was capable of secretly preparing and suddenly releasing a new weapon, as indiscriminate as the rocket bomb and a thousand times more destructive, is to be trusted in its proclaimed desire of having such weapons abolished by international agreement." The procedure these scientists recommended was, first, to demonstrate the new weapon "before the eyes of representatives of all the United Nations on the desert or a barren island," and then to issue "a preliminary ultimatum" to Japan. If this ultimatum was rejected, and "if the sanction of the United Nations (and of public opinion at home) were obtained," then and only then, said the scientists, should the United States consider using the bomb. "This may sound fantastic," they said, "but in nuclear weapons we have something entirely new in order of magnitude of destructive power, and if we want to capitalize fully on the advantage their possession gives us, we must use new and imaginative methods."

These views, which were forwarded to the Secretary of War on June 11, 1945, were strongly supported by 64 of the scientists in the Chicago Metallurgical Laboratory in a petition sent directly to the President. At about the same time, at the request of Dr. Arthur H. Compton, a poll was taken of the views of more than 150 scientists at the Chicago Laboratory. Five alternatives ranging from all-out use of the bomb to "keeping the existence of the bomb a secret" were presented. Of those polled, about two-thirds voted for a preliminary demonstration, either on a military objective or an uninhabited locality; the rest were split on all-out use and no use at all.

These views, and presumably others, were referred by Secretary Stimson to a distinguished Scientific Panel consisting of Drs. Arthur H. Compton, Enrico Fermi, E. O. Lawrence, and J. Robert Oppenheimer, all nuclear physicists of the first rank. "We didn't know beans about the military situation," Oppenheimer later said. "We didn't know whether they [the Japanese] could be caused to surrender by other means or whether the invasion [of Japan] was really inevitable. . . . We thought the two overriding considerations were the saving of lives in the war and the effect of our actions on the stability of the postwar world." On June 16 the panel reported that it had studied carefully the proposals made by the scientists but could see no practical way of ending the war by a technical demonstration. Almost regretfully, it seemed, the four members of the panel concluded that there was "no acceptable alternative to direct military use." Nothing would have been more damaging to our effort," wrote Stimson, ". . . than a warning or demonstration followed by a dud — and this was a real possibility." With this went the fear, expressed by Byrnes, that if the Japanese were warned that an atomic bomb would be exploded over a military target in Japan as a demonstration, "they might bring our boys who were prisoners of war to that area." Furthermore, only two bombs would be available by August, the number General Groves estimated would be needed to end the war; these two would have to obtain the desired effect quickly. And no one yet knew, nor would the scheduled ground test in New Mexico prove, whether a bomb dropped from an airplane would explode.

Nor, for that matter, were all those concerned certain that the bomb would work at all, on the ground or in the air. Of these doubters, the greatest was Admiral Leahy, who until the end remained unconvinced. "This is the biggest fool thing we have ever done," he told Truman after Vannevar Bush had explained to the President how the bomb worked. "The bomb will never go off, and I speak as an expert in explosives."

Thus, by mid-June 1945, there was virtual unanimity among the President's civilian advisers on the use of the bomb. The arguments of the opponents had been considered and rejected. So far as is known, the President did not solicit the views of the military or naval staffs, nor were they offered.

The military situation on June 1, 1945, when the Interim Committee submitted its recommendations on the use of the atomic bomb, was distinctly favorable to the Allied cause. Germany had surrendered in May and troops from Europe would soon be available for redeployment in the Pacific. Manila had fallen in February; Iwo Jima was in American hands; and the success of the Okinawa invasion was assured. Air and submarine attacks had virtually cut off Japan from the resources of the Indies, and B-29's from the Marianas were pulverizing Japan's cities and factories. The Pacific Fleet had virtually driven the Imperial Navy from the ocean, and planes of the fast carrier forces were striking Japanese naval bases in the Inland Sea. Clearly, Japan was a defeated nation.

Though defeated in a military sense, Japan showed no disposition to surrender unconditionally. And Japanese troops had demonstrated time and again that they could fight hard and inflict heavy casualties even when the outlook was hopeless. Allied plans in the spring of 1945 took these facts into account and proceeded on the assumption that an invasion of the home islands would be required to achieve at the earliest possible date the unconditional surrender of Japan — the announced objective of the war and the basic assumption of all strategic planning. . . .

A further difficulty was that Allied intelligence still indicated that Soviet intervention would be desirable, if not necessary, for the success of the invasion strategy. In Allied intelligence, Japan was portrayed as a defeated nation whose military leaders were blind to defeat. Though her industries had been seriously crippled by air bombardment and naval blockade and her armed forces were critically deficient in many of the resources of war, Japan was still far from surrender. She had ample reserves of weapons and ammunition and an army of 5,000,000 troops, 2,000,000 of them in the home islands. The latter could be expected to put up a strong resistance to invasion. In the opinion of the intelligence experts, neither blockade nor bombing alone would produce unconditional surrender before the date set for invasion. And the invasion itself, they believed, would be costly and possibly prolonged.

According to these intelligence reports, the Japanese leaders were fully aware of their desperate situation but would continue to fight in the hope of avoiding complete defeat by securing a better bargaining position. Allied war-weariness and disunity, or some miracle, they hoped, would offer them a way out. "The Japanese believe," declared an intelligence estimate of June 30, ". . . that unconditional surrender would be the equivalent of national extinction, and there are as yet no indications that they are ready to accept such terms." It appeared also to the intelligence experts that Japan might surrender at any time "depending upon the conditions of surrender" the Allies might offer. Clearly these conditions, to have any chance of acceptance, would have to include retention of the imperial system.

How accurate were these estimates? Judging from postwar accounts of Japan, they were very close to the truth. Since the defeat at Saipan, when Tojo had been forced to resign, the strength of the "peace party" had been increasing. In September 1944 the Swedish Minister in Tokyo had been approached unofficially, presumably in the name of Prince Konoye, to sound out the Allies on terms for peace. This overture came to naught, as did another the following March. But the Swedish Minister did learn that those who advocated peace in Japan regarded the Allied demand for unconditional surrender as their greatest obstacle.

The Suzuki Cabinet that came into power in April 1945 had an unspoken mandate from the Emperor to end the war as quickly as possible. But it was faced immediately with another problem when the Soviet Government announced it would not renew the neutrality pact after April 1946. The German surrender in May produced another crisis in the Japanese Government and led, after considerable discussion, to a decision to seek Soviet mediation. But the first approach, made on June 3 to Jacob Malik, the Soviet Ambassador, produced no results. Malik was noncommittal and merely said the problem needed further study. Another overture to Malik later in the month also came to naught.

At the end of June, the Japanese finally approached the Soviet Government directly through Ambassador Sato in Moscow, asking that it mediate with the Allies to bring the Far Eastern war to an end. In a series of messages between Tokyo and Moscow, which the Americans intercepted and decoded, the Japanese Foreign Office outlined the position of the government and instructed Ambassador Sato to make arrangements for a special envoy from the Emperor who would be empowered to make terms for Soviet mediation. Unconditional surrender, he was told, was completely unacceptable, and time was of the essence. But the Russians, on one pretext and another, delayed their answer until mid-July when Stalin and Molotov left for Potsdam. Thus, the Japanese Government had by then accepted defeat and was seeking desperately for a way out; but it was not willing even at this late date to surrender unconditionally, and would accept no terms that did not include the preservation of the imperial system.

Allied intelligence thus had estimated the situation in Japan correctly. Allied invasion strategy had been reexamined and confirmed in mid-June, and the date for the invasion fixed. The desirability of Soviet assistance had been confirmed also and plans for her entry into the war during August could now be made. No decision had been reached on the use of the atomic bomb, but the President's advisers had recommended it. The decision was the President's and he faced it squarely. But before he could make it he would want to know whether the measures already concerted would produce unconditional surrender at the earliest moment and at the lowest cost. If they could not, then he would have to decide whether circumstances warranted employment of a bomb that Stimson had already labeled as "the most terrible weapon ever known in human history."

Though responsibility for the decision to use the atomic bomb was the President's, he exercised it only after careful study of the recommendations of his senior advisers. Chief among these was the Secretary of War, under whose broad supervision the Manhattan Project had been placed. Already deeply concerned over the cost of the projected invasion, the political effects of Soviet intervention, and the potential consequences of the use of the atomic bomb, Stimson sought a course that would avoid all these evils. The difficulty, as he saw it, lay in the requirement for unconditional surrender. It was a phrase that might make the Japanese desperate and lead to a long and unnecessary campaign of attrition that would be extremely costly to both sides. But there was no way of getting around the term; it was firmly rooted in Allied war aims and its renunciation was certain to lead to charges of appeasement.

But if this difficulty could be overcome, would the Japanese respond if terms were offered? The intelligence experts thought so, and the radio intercepts from Tokyo to Moscow bore them out. So far as the Army was concerned there was much to be gained by such a course. Not only might it reduce the enormous cost of the war, but it would also make possible a settlement in the Western Pacific "before too many of our allies are committed there and have made substantial contributions towards the defeat of Japan." In the view of the War Department these aims justified "any concessions which might be attractive to the Japanese, so long as our realistic aims for peace in the Pacific are not adversely affected."

The problem was to formulate terms that would meet these conditions. There was considerable discussion of this problem in Washington in the spring of 1945 by officials in the Department of State and in the War and Navy Departments. Joseph C. Grew, Acting Secretary of State, proposed to the President late in May that he issue a proclamation urging the Japanese to surrender and assuring them that they could keep the Emperor. Though Truman did not act on the suggestion, he thought it "a sound idea" and told Grew to discuss it with his cabinet colleagues and the Joint Chiefs. On June 18, Grew was back with the report that these groups favored the idea, but that there were differences on the timing.

Grew's ideas, as well as those of others concerned, were summarized by Stimson in a long and carefully considered memorandum to the President on July 2. Representing the most informed military and political estimate of the situation at this time, this memorandum constitutes a state paper of the first importance. If any one document can be said to provide the basis for the President's warning to Japan and his final decision to use the atomic bomb, this is it.

The gist of Stimson's argument was that the most promising alternative to the long and costly struggle certain to follow invasion was to warn the Japanese "of what is to come" and to give them an opportunity to surrender. There was, he thought, enough of a chance that such a course would work to make the effort worthwhile. Japan no longer had any allies, her navy was virtually destroyed and she was increasingly vulnerable to air attack and naval blockade. Against her were arrayed the increasingly powerful forces of the Allies, with their "inexhaustible and untouched industrial resources." In these circumstances, Stimson believed the Japanese people would be susceptible to reason if properly approached. "Japan," he pointed out, "is not a nation composed of mad fanatics of an entirely different mentality from ours. On the contrary, she has within the past century shown herself to possess extremely intelligent people. . . ." But any attempt, Stimson added, "to exterminate her armies and her population by gunfire or other means will tend to produce a fusion of race solidity and antipathy. . . ."

A warning to Japan, Stimson contended, should be carefully timed. It should come before the actual invasion, before destruction had reduced the Japanese "to fanatical despair" and, if the Soviet Union had already entered the war, before the Russian attack had progressed too far. It should also emphasize, Stimson believed, the inevitability and completeness of the destruction ahead and the determination of the Allies to strip Japan of her conquests and to destroy the influence of the military clique. It should be a strong warning and should leave no doubt in Japanese minds that they would have to surrender unconditionally and submit to Allied occupation.

The warning, as Stimson envisaged it, had a double character. While promising destruction and devastation, it was also to hold out hope to the Japanese if they heeded its message. In his memorandum, therefore, Stimson stressed the positive features of the warning and recommended that it include a disavowal of any intention to destroy the Japanese nation or to occupy the country permanently. Once Japan's military clique had been removed from power and her capacity to wage war destroyed, it was Stimson's belief that the Allies should withdraw and resume normal trade relations with the new and peaceful Japanese Government. "I personally think," he declared, "that if in saying this we should add that we do not exclude a constitutional monarchy under her present dynasty, it would substantially add to the chance of acceptance."

Not once in the course of this lengthy memorandum was mention made of the atomic bomb. There was no need to do so. Everyone concerned understood clearly that the bomb was the instrument that would destroy Japan and impress on the Japanese Government the hopelessness of any course but surrender. As Stimson expressed it, the atomic bomb was "the best possible sanction," the single weapon that would convince the Japanese "of our power to destroy the empire."

Though Stimson considered a warning combined with an offer of terms and backed up by the sanction of the atomic bomb as the most promising means of inducing surrender at any early date, there were other courses that some thought might produce the same result. One was the continuation and intensification of air bombardment coupled with surface and underwater blockade. This course had already been considered and rejected as insufficient to produce surrender, though its advocates were by no means convinced that this decision was a wise one. And Stimson himself later justified the use of the bomb on the ground that by November 1 conventional bombardment would have caused greater destruction than the bomb. This apparent contradiction is explained by the fact that the atomic bomb was considered to have a psychological effect entirely apart from the damage wrought.

Nor did Stimson, in his memorandum, consider the effect of the Soviet Union's entry into the war. By itself, this action could not be counted on to force Japan to capitulate, but combined with bombardment and blockade it might do so. At least that was the view of Brigadier-General George A. Lincoln, one of the Army's top planners, who wrote in June that "probably it will take Russian entry into the war, coupled with a landing, or imminent threat of landing, on Japan proper by us, to convince them [the Japanese] of the hopelessness of their position." Why, therefore, was it not possible to issue the warning prior to a Soviet declaration of war against Japan and rely on that event, together with an intensified air bombardment, to produce the desired result? If together they could not secure Japan's surrender, would there not still be time to use the bomb before the scheduled invasion of Kyushu in November?

No final answer to this question is possible with the evidence at hand. But one cannot ignore the fact that some responsible officials feared the political consequences of Soviet intervention and hoped that ultimately it would prove unnecessary. This feeling may unconsciously have made the atom bomb solution more attractive than it might otherwise have been. Some officials may have believed, too, that the bomb could be used as a powerful deterrent to Soviet expansion in Europe, where the Red tide had successively engulfed Rumania, Bulgaria, Jugoslavia, Czechoslovakia, and Hungary. In an interview with three of the top scientists in the Manhattan Project early in June, Mr. Byrnes did not, according to Leo Szilard, argue that the bomb was needed to defeat Japan, but rather that it should be dropped to "make Russia more manageable in Europe."

It has been asserted also that the desire to justify the expenditure of the two billion dollars spent on the Manhattan Project may have disposed some favorably toward the use of the bomb. Already questions had been asked in Congress, and the end of the war would almost certainly bring on a full-scale investigation. What more striking justification of the Manhattan Project than a new weapon that had ended the war in one sudden blow and saved countless American lives? "It was my reaction," wrote Admiral Leahy, "that the scientists and others wanted to make this test because of the vast sums that had been spent on the project. Truman knew that, and so did other people involved."

This explanation hardly does credit to those involved in the Manhattan Project and not even P. M. S. Blackett, one of the severest critics of the decision to use the bomb, accepted it. "The wit of man," he declared, "could hardly devise a theory of the dropping of the bomb, both more insulting to the American people, or more likely to lead to an energetically pursued Soviet defense policy."

But even if the need to justify these huge expenditures is discounted — and certainly by itself it could not have produced the decision — the question still remains whether those who held in their hands a weapon thought capable of ending the war in one stroke could justify withholding that weapon. Would they not be open to criticism for failing to use every means at their disposal to defeat the enemy as quickly as possible, thereby saving many American lives?

And even at that time there were some who believed that the new weapon would ultimately prove the most effective deterrent to war yet produced. How better to outlaw war forever than to demonstrate the tremendous destructive power of this weapon by using it against an actual target?

By early July 1945 the stage had been set for the final decision. Stimson's memorandum had been approved in principle and on July 4 the British had given their consent to the use of the bomb against Japan. It remained only to decide on the terms and timing of the warning. This was the situation when the Potsdam Conference opened on July 17, one day after the bomb had been successfully exploded in a spectacular demonstration at Alamogordo, New Mexico. The atomic bomb was a reality and when the news reached Potsdam there was great excitement among those who were let in on the secret. Instead of the prospect of long and bitter months of fighting the Japanese, there was now a vision, "fair and bright indeed it seemed" to Churchill, "of the end of the whole war in one or two violent shocks."

President Truman's first action was to call together his chief advisers — Byrnes, Stimson, Leahy, Marshall, King, and Arnold. "I asked for their opinion whether the bomb should be used," he later wrote. The consensus was that it should. Here at last was the miracle to end the war and solve all the perplexing problems posed by the necessity for invasion. But because no one could tell what effect the bomb might have "physically or psychologically," it was decided to proceed with the military plans for the invasion.

No one at this time, or later in the conference, raised the question of whether the Japanese should be informed of the existence of the bomb. That question, it will be recalled, had been discussed by the Scientific Panel on June 16 and at the White House meeting with the JCS, the service Secretaries and Mr. McCloy on June 18. For a variety of reasons, including uncertainty as to whether the bomb would work, it had then been decided that the Japanese should not be warned of the existence of the new weapon. The successful explosion of the first bomb on July 17 did not apparently outweigh the reasons advanced earlier for keeping the bomb a secret, and evidently none of the men involved thought the question needed to be reviewed. The Japanese would learn of the atomic bomb only when it was dropped on them. . . .

All that remained now was to warn Japan and give her an opportunity to surrender. In this matter Stimson's and Grew's views, as outlined in the memorandum of July 2, were accepted, but apparently on the advice of the former Secretary of State Cordell Hull it was decided to omit any reference to the Emperor. Hull's view, solicited by Byrnes before his departure for Potsdam, was that the proposal smacked of appeasement and "seemed to guarantee continuance not only of the Emperor but also of the feudal privileges of a ruling caste." And should the Japanese reject the warning, the proposal to retain the imperial system might well encourage resistance and have "terrible political repercussions" in the United States. For these reasons he recommended that no statement about the Emperor be made until "the climax of Allied bombing and Russia's entry into the war." Thus, the final terms offered to the Japanese in the Potsdam Declaration on July 26 made no mention of the Emperor or of the imperial system. Neither did the declaration contain any reference to the atom bomb but simply warned the Japanese of the consequences of continued resistance. Only those already familiar with the weapon could have read the references to inevitable and complete destruction as a warning of atomic warfare.

The receipt of the Potsdam Declaration in Japan led to frantic meetings to decide what should be done. It was finally decided not to reject the note but to await the results of the Soviet overture. At this point, the military insisted that the government make some statement to the people, and on July 28 Premier Suzuki declared to the press that Japan would ignore the declaration, a statement that was interpreted by the Allies as a rejection.

To the Americans the rejection of the Potsdam Declaration confirmed the view that the military was still in control of Japan and that only a decisive act of violence could remove them. The instrument for such action lay at hand in the atomic bomb; events now seemed to justify its use. But in the hope that the Japanese might still change their minds, Truman held off orders on the use of the bomb for a few days. Only silence came from Tokyo, for the Japanese were waiting for a reply from the Soviet Government, which would not come until the return of Stalin and Molotov from Potsdam on August 6. Prophetically, Foreign Minister Tojo wrote Sato on August 2, the day the Potsdam Conference ended, that he could not afford to lose a single day in his efforts to conclude arrangements with the Russians "if we were to end the war before the assault on our mainland." By that time, President Truman had already decided on the use of the bomb. . . .

At General Arnold's insistence, the responsibility for selecting the particular target and fixing the exact date and hour of the attack was assigned to the field commander, General Spaatz. In orders issued on July 25 and approved by Stimson and Marshall, Spaatz was ordered to drop the "first special bomb as soon as weather will permit visual bombing after about 3 August 1945 on one of the targets: Hiroshima, Kokura, Niigata, and Nagasaki." He was instructed also to deliver a copy of this order personally to MacArthur and Nimitz. Weather was the critical factor because the bomb had to be dropped by visual means, and Spaatz delegated to his chief of staff, Major-General Curtis E. LeMay, the job of deciding when the weather was right for this most important mission. . . .

On Tinian and Guam, preparations for dropping the bomb had been completed by August 3. The original plan was to carry out the operation on August 4, but General LeMay deferred the attack because of bad weather over the target. On August 5 the forecasts were favorable and he gave the word to proceed with the mission the following day. At 0245 on August 6, the bomb-carrying plane was airborne. Six and a half hours later the bomb was released over Hiroshima, Japan's eighth largest city, to explode 50 seconds later at a height of about 2,000 feet. The age of atomic warfare had opened.

Aboard the cruiser *Augusta* on his way back to the United States, President Truman received the news by radio. That same day a previously prepared release from Washington announced to the world that an atomic bomb had been dropped on Hiroshima and warned the Japanese that if they did not surrender they could expect "a rain of ruin from the air, the like of which has never been seen on this earth."

On August 7, Ambassador Sato in Moscow received word at last that Molotov would see him the next afternoon. At the appointed hour he arrived at the Kremlin, full of hope that he would receive a favorable reply to the Japanese proposal for Soviet mediation with the Allies to end the war. Instead, he was handed the Soviet declaration of war, effective on August 9. Thus, three months to the day after Germany's surrender, Marshal Stalin had lived up to his promise to the Allies.

Meanwhile, President Truman had authorized the use of the second bomb — the last then available. The objective was Kokura, the date August 9. But the plane carrying the bomb failed to make its run over the primary target and hit the secondary target, Nagasaki, instead. The next day Japan sued for peace.

The close sequence of events between August 6 and 10, combined with the fact that the bomb was dropped almost three months before the scheduled invasion of Kyushu and while the Japanese were trying desperately to get out of the war, has suggested to some that the bombing of Hiroshima had a deeper purpose than the desire to end the war quickly. This purpose, it is claimed, was nothing less than a desire to forestall Soviet intervention into the Far Eastern war. Else why this necessity for speed? Certainly nothing in the military situation seemed to call for such hasty action. But if the purpose was to forestall Soviet intervention, then there was every reason for speed. And even if the Russians could not be kept out of the war, at least they would be prevented from making more than a token contribution to victory over Japan. In this sense it may be argued that the bomb proved a success, for the war ended with the United States in full control of Japan.

This theory leaves several matters unexplained. In the first place, the Americans did not know the exact date on which the Soviet Union would declare war but believed it would be within a week or two of August 8. If they had wished to forestall a Soviet declaration of war, then they could reasonably have been expected to act sooner than they did. Such close timing left little if any margin for error. Secondly, had the United States desired above everything else to keep the Russians out, it could have responded to one of the several unofficial Japanese overtures, or made the Potsdam Declaration more attractive to Japan. Certainly the failure to put a time limit on the declaration suggests that speed was not of the essence in American calculations. Finally, the date and time of the bombing were left to Generals Spaatz and LeMay, who certainly had no way of knowing Soviet intentions. Bad weather or any other untoward incident could have delayed the attack a week or more.

There is reason to believe that the Russians at the last moved more quickly than they had intended. In his conversations with Harry Hopkins in May 1945 and at Potsdam, Marshal Stalin had linked Soviet entry with negotiations then in progress with Chinese representatives in Moscow. When these were completed, he had said, he would act. On August 8 these negotiations were still in progress.

Did the atomic bomb accomplish its purpose? Was it, in fact, as Stimson said, "the best possible sanction" after Japan rejected the Potsdam Declaration? The sequence of events argues strongly that it was, for bombs were dropped on the 6th and 9th, and on the 10th Japan surrendered. But in the excitement over the announcement of the first use of an atomic bomb and then of Japan's surrender, many overlooked the significance of the Soviet Union's entry into the war on the 9th. The first bomb had produced consternation and confusion among the leaders of Japan, but no disposition to surrender. The Soviet declaration of war, though not entirely unexpected, was a devastating blow and, by removing all hope of Soviet mediation, gave the advocates of peace their first opportunity to come boldly out into the open. When Premier Suzuki arrived at the palace on the morning of the 9th, he was told that the Emperor believed Japan's only course now was to accept the Potsdam Declaration. The militarists could and did minimize the effects of the bomb, but they could not evade the obvious consequences of Soviet intervention, which ended all hope of dividing their enemies and securing softer peace terms.

In this atmosphere, the leaders of Japan held a series of meetings on August 9, but were unable to come to agreement. In the morning came word of the fate of Nagasaki. This additional disaster failed to resolve the issues between the military and those who advocated surrender. Finally the Emperor took the unprecedented step of calling the Imperial Conference, which lasted until 3 o'clock the next morning. When it, too, failed to produce agreement the Emperor told his ministers that he wished the war brought to an end. The constitutional significance of this action is difficult for Westerners to comprehend, but it resolved the crisis and produced in the cabinet a formal decision to accept the Potsdam Declaration, provided it did not prejudice the position of the Emperor.

What finally forced the Japanese to surrender? Was it air bombardment, naval power, the atomic bomb, or Soviet entry? The United States Strategic Bombing Survey concluded that Japan would have surrendered by the end of the year, without invasion and without the atomic bomb. Other equally informed opinion maintained that it was the atomic bomb that forced Japan to surrender. "Without its use," Dr. Karl T. Compton asserted, "the war would have continued for many months." Admiral Nimitz believed firmly that the decisive factor was "the complete impunity with which the Pacific Fleet pounded Japan," and General Arnold claimed it was air bombardment that had brought Japan to the verge of collapse. But Major-General Claire Chennault, wartime air commander in China, maintained that Soviet entry into the Far Eastern war brought about the surrender of Japan and would have done so "even if no atomic bombs had been dropped."

It would be a fruitless task to weigh accurately the relative importance of all the factors leading to the Japanese surrender. There is no doubt that Japan had been defeated by the summer of 1945, if not earlier. But defeat did not mean that the military clique had given up; the Army intended to fight on and had made elaborate preparations for the defense of the homeland. Whether air bombardment and naval blockade or the threat of invasion would have produced an early surrender and averted the heavy losses almost certain to accompany the actual landings in Japan is a moot question. Certainly they had a profound effect on the Japanese position. It is equally impossible to assert categorically that the atomic bomb alone or Soviet intervention alone was the decisive factor in bringing the war to an end. All that can be said on the available evidence is that Japan was defeated in the military sense by August 1945 and that the bombing of Hiroshima, followed by the Soviet Union's declaration of war and then the bombing of Nagasaki and the threat of still further bombing, acted as catalytic agents to produce the Japanese decision to surrender. Together they created so extreme a crisis that the Emperor himself, in an unprecedented move, took matters into his own hands and ordered his ministers to surrender. Whether any other set of circumstances would have resolved the crisis and produced the final decision to surrender is a question history cannot yet answer.

Chapter Nine

THE DEVELOPING NATIONS

Some years ago, the Bureau of Applied Social Research of Columbia University undertook a pioneering series of survey interviews in six countries of the Middle East. In carrying out this survey, an educated and well-dressed young interviewer put more than one hundred questions to a poor Syrian carpetweaver. Most of the questions asked concerned the local impact of the mass media. A few dealt with attitudes toward foreign nations. The last question asked simply: "What did you think of this interview?"

"Why should *you* go to the Universities and study," the carpetweaver responded, "while *my* children start working at ten years of age?" [1]

This question, explicit or implicit in the minds of hundreds of millions of people, is beginning to reshape the world. "Today half the people in the world are ill-fed. Half the world's children of preschool age are so undernourished that their physical and mental growth is retarded, and mortality among these children in the underdeveloped societies is sixty times as great as in more advanced societies." [2] A large majority of the world's peoples live in countries where the per capita real income is less than $300 per year (*before* taxes), as compared with almost $3,000 per year in the United States. [3]

[1] Daniel Lerner, *The Passing of Traditional Society* (Glencoe, Ill.: The Free Press, 1958), p. 294.

[2] *The New York Times,* November 6, 1966, Sec. 4, p. 4.

[3] These figures are taken from tables in Max Millikan and Donald Blackmer (eds.), *The Emerging Nations* (Boston: Little, Brown and Co., 1961), pp. 150–153. These tables, in turn, were derived from a study by P. N. Rosenstein-Rodan, "International Aid for Underdeveloped Countries," which appeared in *The Review of Economics and Statistics* (May, 1961).

If *money* estimates of Gross National Product, instead of Professor Rosenstein-Rodan's rough estimates of "real" GNP were used, the disparity between American and world living standards would appear much greater, with a majority of the world's peoples living in nations with per capita GNP's below $100.

Their poverty and hardship, in many cases, antedate recorded history. But their realization that an alternative way of life is possible is a distinctly contemporary phenomenon — so much so that in some cases it has not yet reached past the cities to the more remote rural areas. Almost every government, almost every people in the world have now set as their primary goals national independence and economic development. They are determined to accept no ideology, no way of life, no international order which seems to deny them these goals. And if repeatedly thwarted, many of them will embrace *any* ideology, *any* way of life, *any* international order which *seems* to promise to bring these goals to fruition.

To imagine that ideological considerations of any kind are foremost in the minds of the peoples of the developing nations, however, is to misunderstand completely. Most of these people have neither the education nor the relief from the day-to-day pressures of ensuring survival which might make it possible for them to think in abstract or doctrinal ways. Between 1957 and 1963, the Institute for International Social Research conducted nearly 20,000 interviews in thirteen nations with populations approaching 900 million: the United States, West Germany, India, Nigeria, Brazil, the Philippines, Israel, Egypt, Panama, the Dominican Republic, Yugoslavia, Cuba, and Poland. The people interviewed were asked openended questions concerning their personal hopes and fears and the hopes and fears they had for their native lands. In addition, they were asked to rate their own progress and their countries' — past, present, and future — according to the hopes and fears they themselves had expressed. Six hundred members of the national parliamentary bodies of six of these countries also were interviewed (one hundred in each country).

The results of this ambitious study, assembled and analyzed by Hadley Cantril, point up dramatically the high expectations held by people everywhere for improvement in their own and their nations' ways of life.[4] When those interviewed are "weighted" in proportion to the populations they represent, the personal hope mentioned most often (by nearly two-thirds of the weighted sample) was for a decent or improved standard of living. Next were the hope for welfare or opportunities for one's children, the fear of

[4] *The Pattern of Human Concerns* (New Brunswick, N.J.: Rutgers University Press, 1965), *passim*. It should be noted, however, that the rural masses in countries like India and Brazil, while looking forward to future gains for both their nations and themselves, had not yet learned even to hope for many of the things Americans take for granted. Cantril identifies five phases in the development of concerns suggested by his findings: "1. Acquiescence to circumstances. . . . 2. Awakening to potentialities. . . . 3. Awareness of means to realize goals: sensing the possibility that the new potentialities perceived can become real. . . . 4. Assurance and self-reliance: experiencing intended consequences through action. . . . 5. Satisfaction and gratification: general satisfaction with a way of life achieved which promises continued development." Much of the rural masses in India and Brazil, Cantril indicates, are in the first of these phases. Most Americans are in the fifth. *Ibid.*, chap. 15.

deterioration in living standards, and the fear of ill health, accident, or death (each mentioned by a quarter to a third). Less than 1 per cent mentioned personal hopes or fears involving freedom, political democracy, or communism.

The fear of war was the most frequently mentioned *national* concern (cited by over 40 per cent), with hopes for decent or improved living standards, for technological advances, for peace, and for employment following in that order. About 11 per cent (almost all Indians) cited fear of *Chinese* aggression, but fear of communism, or of aggression or domination by Communist power were mentioned by only about 5 per cent each. No more than 2 per cent mentioned as national concerns such matters as representative government, freedom, or law and order. And when these latter hopes (for democracy and freedom) and fears (of communism) *were* cited by respondents in the undeveloped nations, it was generally by those most satisfied with their own lots in life. Nor were these the primary concerns of the legislative elites interviewed — except that maintenance of democratic government *and* maintenance of socialist government were primary concerns of Indian legislators; and fear of communism from within was a primary concern of legislators in the Philippines, where a Communist-led (Huk) insurrection had recently been put down.

> It has often been pointed out [Cantril concludes] — by Marx and Lenin, among others — that if people are pushed down by poverty they cannot be expected to show much interest in anything except their daily bread. In other words, some conditions related to the assurance of a decent standard of living as subjectively defined seem necessary and primary for most individuals before they feel they can afford the luxury of other interests and aspirations.[5]

The structure of the world of tomorrow is being determined today by the progress of these peoples in their struggles for national development. Traditionally, Americans have balked at interfering in the affairs of other nations. We have elected to let the world of the future take care of itself, so to speak. But we have not been very happy about the upshot, and today we lament the state of the world we declined to influence. If we want a tomorrow more to our liking, most of us have learned, we will have to do what we can to help bring into being the better world we have in mind. Thus, for the first time in our history, American prestige, American arms, American wealth, and sometimes American GI's, are deeply committed to influencing the development of dozens of nations throughout the world.

UNDERDEVELOPMENT: THE "VICIOUS CIRCLE"

Unfortunately, mere willingness to undertake the effort does not ensure success, for even economically the task is formidable. Essentially, it requires the underdeveloped nations to extricate themselves from what we might call

5 *Op. cit.,* pp. 224–225.

the vicious circle of underdevelopment. (See Chart A.[6]) Since, by definition, these are nations in which per capita income is low, their ability to save is also low. For it is easier to save a given percentage of a *higher* income, than of a lower income. If your family were fortunate enough to earn $50,000 a year, for instance, it probably would not find it difficult to save 10 per cent of this, or even more. Saving 10 per cent of a $5,000 annual income might be a bit harder; and at $2,000 a year an American family would probably be so hard pressed merely to buy food and other necessities that saving even $200 (10 per cent) of this would prove an enormous hardship. Yet in the under-developed nations, most saving must come out of the subsistence expenditures of families earning only a fraction of $2,000 a year.

CHART A—THE VICIOUS CIRCLE OF UNDERDEVELOPMENT

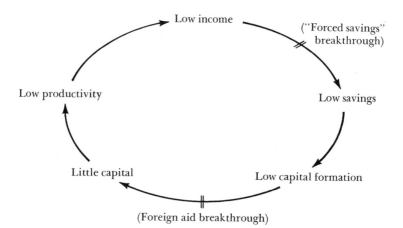

Low rates of saving, in turn, keep the rate of capital formation — and thus the quantity of available investment capital — low also. With little capital — that is, little machinery — behind each worker, productivity is bound to remain correspondingly low. And, in the long run, real income in a society cannot exceed the real wealth produced — real income cannot rise faster than productivity.[7] Thus income will remain low, and the circle is complete.

This vicious circle can be broken either (1) by importing capital or machinery from abroad, on a grant or a loan basis, and/or (2) by requiring people to save despite pitifully inadequate incomes — in many cases literally by taking the food out of the mouths of hungry and undernourished human

[6] This diagrammatic formulation was called to my attention in a lecture by Martin Bronfenbrenner.

[7] We have ignored here the possibility of such windfalls as the discovery of accessible and valuable new national resources — oil, metals, etc.

beings. Democratic nations usually have begun their development by emphasizing the first of these methods; Communist nations by emphasizing the
second, which, understandably, is likely to be unpopular with those called
upon to make the sacrifices, and may well have to be imposed on them by
force.

The vicious circle of underdevelopment is reinforced by accelerating rates
of population growth in most of the nations concerned. Breaking through
this vicious circle requires a surplus available for capital investment — a
surplus beyond what is needed to feed and clothe unproductive additions to
the population. Yet in most underdeveloped countries the rate of economic
growth barely keeps pace with the rate of population growth, which now
averages about 2 per cent a year in these areas.[8] Modern medical and sanita-
tion practices which dramatically reduce the number of deaths annually are
much easier to introduce and institutionalize than the increases in literacy
and the revolution in values which would be required to reduce the birth
rate comparably. Even so thoroughly totalitarian a regime as that in Peking
appears to have had little success in substantially cutting China's birth rate.
In nations with less centralized governments, and sometimes also with
religious inhibitions against contraception, the barriers to effective population control seem nearly insurmountable.[9] Since time immemorial, after all,
having many sons has been the only reliable form of social security in many
of these societies. Yet as declining death rates and high birth rates add to the
proportion of very old and very young in the population, the burden on the
more productive age groups increases.

Even when the government of an underdeveloped nation manages to extract from its people somewhat more output than the bare minimum needed
to meet irreducible current consumption needs and to support annual increases in population, immediate returns on the portion of this "surplus"
invested in development cannot be anticipated. Before business investments
can become profitable, for example, a basic transportation and communications network must be built. Electric and other power facilities must be
available to service future industries. Educational institutions must be built
up and staffed, and large numbers of people must be given first a basic
knowledge of the three R's and then at least some training for the industrial
jobs which will soon need filling. These tasks will require relatively massive

8 The growth in output per capita in the underdeveloped nations from 1961 to 1965
averaged only 1–2 per cent — lower than in the 1950's. Over this same period, the average
growth in output per capita in the developed nations was between 5 and 6 per cent. In
other words, the gap between living standards in the rich nations and the poor nations
has been widening, not narrowing, in recent years. Wilfred Malenbaum, "The Real
strength of Red China," *Challenge* (July–August, 1966), pp. 9–11.

9 Though successful development without population control seems most unlikely in
most of the poor nations, the attitudes toward contraception of some religious groups
within the United States deterred our government from helping the developing nations
to institute population control programs until the mid-1960's.

amounts of capital. But money invested in these so-called "social overhead" facilities will yield little profit initially. Only many years later, as industrial development and urbanization raise the demand for these facilities will large-scale operation make possible low-cost-per-unit economies and an acceptable profit margin. For a long while, too, these basic service facilities are bound to be monopolies, since the scarcity of investment capital makes the construction of duplicate facilities, in the name of free competition, highly unlikely. In these circumstances, it is only realistic to anticipate that most social overhead capital investment in the developing nations will be undertaken by governments rather than by private investors. At best, only after a minimal social overhead base has been constructed can additional investments, if efficiently administered, be expected to yield proportional increases in output, profit, and further investment capital.[10]

This does *not* mean that the economies of all or most developing nations are bound to be thoroughly socialistic. It *does* suggest that a flexible, pragmatic approach, unencumbered by excessive ideological bias, will be needed. The precise "mix" of government and private enterprise desirable will vary greatly from case to case. American rhetoric about the evils of socialism and the virtues of free enterprise will neither change these hard realities nor enhance American prestige in the developing nations. Repeated USIA polls in these countries show overwhelming endorsement of "socialism" as the economic system of the people's choice. Communism runs second, and free enterprise or capitalism a poor third.[11] If ever we should succeed in convincing the masses in the underdeveloped lands that their only choice lies between "pure" capitalism and communism, therefore, this evidence suggests we might be profoundly disappointed by their response.

[10] See Millikan and Blackmer, *op. cit.*, pp. 49–51.

[11] The difference between American and foreign reactions to these terms is in large part a result of differing perceptions of their meaning. Many Americans, for instance, use the word "socialism" with undiscriminating abandon to cover such diverse phenomena as government welfare spending, on the one hand, and communism on the other. See Chapter Thirteen, below, and Ralph K. White, " 'Socialism' and 'Capitalism': An International Misunderstanding," *Foreign Affairs,* XLIV (January, 1966), pp. 216–227.

Socialism is generally used by social scientists to mean government ownership or control of the means of producing goods and services. *Communism* is one form of (Marxian) socialism, usually combined with a totalitarian political system along the lines pioneered in the Soviet Union. (See Chapter Ten.) But there are democratic forms of socialism as well. Great Britain and the Scandinavian countries have turned over to government control many basic industries and social services, without losing their democratic freedoms. In the United States, most of our educational and highway systems are socialistic — that is, government controlled. And the Tennessee Valley Authority (TVA) is an example of socialism, in the sense we have defined, in the electric power industry. But the Medicare program, for instance, though often called "socialized medicine" by its opponents, is rather a form of compulsory national health insurance for the aged. "Socialized medicine," by our definition, would require that doctors work for the government and be paid by it for their services, as they are in Great Britain. Such a step has never been advocated seriously by American political leaders.

SOCIAL DISINTEGRATION
AND ECONOMIC DEVELOPMENT

Thus far we, like most of those interviewed for Cantril's study, have directed our attention principally to the *economic* aspects of development. Yet national development is far more than simply an economic phenomenon. Administering and maintaining public support for the Marshall Plan was child's play compared to the problems of our aid programs of today, precisely because the Marshall Plan was much more fully an *economic* proposition. The individual attitudes, social values, political structures, and basic literacy which development requires were already present in the devastated nations of postwar Europe. What was needed, principally, was investment capital, a booster to morale, and pressure toward a regional approach to the problem of reconstruction.

But encouragement and investment capital, though needed, are not enough to set most of the nations of Africa, Asia, and Latin America on the road to successful development. Fundamental changes in attitudes and values — in the everyday lives of the masses — are equally necessary. And such changes are not brought about easily and quickly anywhere, for even at best they impose severe strains on the people who must undergo them.

Industrialization, for example, inevitably requires urbanization. In underdeveloped nations, most of the population lives and works on the land. If these nations are to industrialize, a sizable proportion of these people will have to move off the farms and into the cities, where factories and necessary industrial service facilities are located. This population movement, in turn, is bound to set off a revolution in values and social organization. For in most traditional agrarian societies, the family is the key *economic* as well as the key *social* unit. Each individual spends most of his time in the company of members of his family. Their opinions of him and their relations with him are the most significant aspect of his life. The customary *social* subordination of other family members to the dominant male member of the household is, in fact, largely a reflection of their *economic* dependence upon him as owner of the family's farmland.

When the young son of one of these traditional farm families moves into the city, his whole life changes. He spends most of his time now *not* with his family in the fields, but with his co-workers at the factory. It is *their* opinion of him, and that of his foreman or supervisor, that has the greatest impact on his day-to-day life. It is upon them, rather than upon his father, that he is economically dependent. Thus, the social control exercised over him previously by his family (and by villagers whose opinion of him might affect their opinion of and relations with his family) is much more diffused. This control is centered much more fully than it used to be, moreover, on his job performance, rather than on his personal behavior during his off hours.

Similarly, the moral precepts which were relevant to — and enforced by — his family-based existence, seem much less relevant in the city. As others violate these precepts or folk norms with impunity, the norms themselves become blurred. It is no longer so clear exactly what is the right thing to do, and what is the wrong thing. Thus, one is no longer so certainly or severely punished — by loss of the esteem of others — for violations of these (now less clear-cut) norms. In circular fashion, violations become still more common and norms more blurred.[12]

It is for this reason that the farmer often views the city as a den of iniquity, in which time-honored moral and religious values are commonly flouted; while the denizens of the city may think of their country cousins as old-fashioned hicks. The strain on one who must live partly in both worlds can be enormous, as many students who live in "old-fashioned" homes while attending "modern" universities can attest. When the standards of the family group conflict with those of the peer group, it becomes indeed hard to know what is "right" and what is "wrong"; and whatever is done is bound to offend somebody and bring hardship to the person caught in the squeeze between two sets of values. The solidarity and cohesion of the society as a whole, too, based as it is upon agreed values and goals, is bound to give way, producing considerable confusion and discord.

Such changes in the peoples' ways of life are not merely *consequences* of the process of industrialization, they are essential *prerequisites* to its success. For if industrial efficiency is to be achieved, men must be able to win social as well as economic rewards on the basis of their job performance, rather than on the basis of their family background or conformity with traditional values. Traditional values would call for a plant manager or government official to provide jobs for his sons, nephews, and cousins regardless of their initial qualifications or job performance. If his venture proved profitable, traditional values would call for him to share his good fortune with his extended family, rather than to plow his profits back into his business. And when these family obligations were taken care of, he would be encouraged to invest in *land* — an investment bringing status and permanence — rather than in industrial enterprises. For land cannot easily be taken from you, while the businessman in a traditional society is forever subject to extortion at the hands of the government official whose first interest is (understandably) to fill his own family's coffers.

The social disintegration which is an unavoidable part of the development process everywhere is accentuated when *rapid* development is insisted upon — as is often the case today. The multitudes of people uprooted from their rural homes and set down in the new environment of factory and city slum are deprived of their main sources of personal security — the all-encompassing

---

[12] See George C. Homans, *The Human Group* (New York: Harcourt, Brace and World, 1950).

family and traditional religious values. The sense of disorientation and personal loss which this change occasions creates a deeply felt need for something to fill the enormous gap in their lives. A strong sense of nationalism may help. And the appeal of a persuasive doctrine which promises clear-cut answers to bewildering problems is also likely to be great. For it is precisely a new set of clear-cut answers which these people want most. A dedicated mass movement can fill this need, and, in addition, supply the sense of group solidarity, the camaraderie, the sense of belonging to something greater than oneself which these people suddenly have had stolen from them. Thus communism and other isms find in the social distintegration of the developing areas fertile ground for the spread of their own special brand of hopes and illusions. Almost any plausible set of standards for right action offers a person a better basis for living a purposeful life than no standards at all.[13]

OBSTACLES TO POLITICAL STABILITY AND DEMOCRACY

The needs and yearnings of the people add substantially to the already herculean tasks of political leadership in the underdeveloped lands. Successful development requires political unity. And political unity is hard to come by in countries often divided by language, culture, provincial or tribal loyalties, religion, geography, and immediate economic interests. The boundaries of most African nations, for instance, reflect merely the administrative convenience of colonial rulers and regularly cut across lines of economic viability, language, and tribal autonomy. Colonial rulers sometimes acerbated these divisions, for their own purposes, by playing off group against group, tribe against tribe. Nor is a sense of community and nationhood easily infused in areas where communications facilities are sparse and illiteracy is the rule.

In the period before national independence is won, opposition to the colonial power provides a serviceable negative focus of unity for native elites. But once independence has been attained latent differences in economic interest, ideological predilection, and personal ambition are likely to come to the fore. Remember that *basic constitutional questions* — questions about the framework within which public policy is to be determined — must be decided before the many important particular issues of public policy can even be considered. And on what basis shall fundamental constitutional conflicts be resolved? Can dissident political leaders be expected to acquiesce in rule by a dictator or political party committed to eliminating political dissidence in the future? Can the chief beneficiaries of the traditional social and economic power structure be expected to give their support to leaders committed to modernizing the nation by overturning the traditional power

[13] See Eric Hoffer, *The True Believer* (New York: Mentor, 1951), and the same author's *The Ordeal of Change* (New York: Harper, 1964).

structure? Can ethnic or religious minorities — such as the Turkish Cypriotes
— be expected to accept a constitution providing for democratic majority
rule, without securing what they consider to be adequate safeguards for
minority rights? Can local Communist parties be expected to refrain from
seeking to subvert any political regime which is not to their liking? Should
inhabitants of a relatively wealthy province — like the Congo's Katanga — be
expected to accept willingly the establishment of a central government strong
enough to carry out an economic leveling process which would redound to
their economic disadvantage, at least in the short run? These problems are
similar in many respects to those involved in the establishment of a world
government. (See Chapter One.)

In these difficult circumstances, the unity necessary to carry out a program of national development may only be obtainable — if at all — by the use
of force. And where the rich use their political power to avoid contributing
to their nations' progress, political revolution may prove to be an unavoidable prerequisite of economic revolution.

> In the United Kingdom and the United States . . . from 30 to 40 per
> cent of the total population pays income tax each year. In the Caribbean
> territories, on the other hand, less than 3 per cent does. In Africa and
> Asia, a country is doing relatively well if 1 per cent of its population
> pays. Whereas income subject to personal income tax amounts to some
> 75 per cent of Gross National Product in the United Kingdom, it
> amounts to only 10 per cent in the Caribbean and 5 per cent or less in
> African territories. . . . Traditional landed classes have thus far never
> accepted a progressive tax structure.[14]

These facts, and our previous discussion of the social and psychological
consequences of development, should help to indicate why political stability
in the early stages of national development is the exception rather than the
rule. Bruce Russett's figures show a sharp increase in deaths from domestic
group violence — from coups, riots, civil wars, and revolutions — as national
per capita GNP rises from $60 to about $200, followed by a continued
gradual decline in internal violence at higher levels of real income. (By the
$500 GNP per capita level deaths from these causes are lower than at $60.) [15]

If political stability is too much to expect in many of the developing nations, representative democracy in the early stages of development is even
more difficult to sustain:

> . . . The civic culture [which nourishes stable democracy] emerged
> in the West as a result of a gradual political development — relatively

14 Irving L. Horowitz, *Three Worlds of Development* (New York: Oxford University
Press, 1966), pp. 199 and 215. Horowitz concludes that expropriation of the wealth of the
landed aristocracy may be a necessary and desirable policy in these societies.

15 *Trends in World Politics* (New York: Macmillan, 1965), pp. 136–137. This is one
of the most useful short volumes available on international politics — and on the use of
quantitative approaches to this subject.

crisis-free, untroubled, and unforced. . . . This gradualness of political change characterizes British and, to a lesser extent, American political history. The problem in the new nations of the world is that such gradualness is not possible. . . . These new nations are seeking to accomplish in a brief period of time what took centuries to consummate in the West. Is it possible to find substitutes for this gradual and fusional process of political change? There is no clear answer to this question. . . .[16]

Political development involves the growth of most of the requisites for *community* discussed in another context in Chapter One: shared goals, values, symbols, and loyalties; elite agreement on "rules of the game"; overlapping group memberships, and at least the beginnings of a network of communications facilities. If a nation is to be democratic in any real sense of the word, its people must be able to make meaningful choices of leadership and policy. Free elections and secret ballots alone do not make a democracy. Are a substantial number of citizens literate enough to inform themselves of the main issues at stake in elections? Do they view the political process itself as something in which they can participate meaningfully? Is there a radio and/or press free enough and responsible enough to put the necessary information at the disposal of those who want it? Are there *functional interest groups* — beyond the traditional ones of family, tribe, and church — capable of reminding people in particular occupations or situations of their interests, and of organizing and representing their points of view? Are there political parties capable of reconciling and adjusting the positions of a large enough number of these groups to formulate coherent programs which will present significant political alternatives to potential voters? [17] Does the nation — or, at least, do its elite groups — have unifying symbols capable of transcending the conflicts and divisions inherent in the political process?

It is the answers to these questions which are likely to decide whether the country in question will develop under a democratic rather than a dictatorial regime. And merely listing a number of these requisites of political development, as we have done, should make it clear, first, that political development takes *time;* and second, that it is related to economic development. A free and responsible press will not develop until there is a substantial

[16] Gabriel Almond and Sidney Verba, *The Civic Culture* (Boston: Little, Brown, 1965), pp. 368–370. For a detailed treatment of how United States policy can contribute to democratic development, see Eugene Staley, *The Future of the Underdeveloped Countries* (rev. ed., New York: Praeger, 1961).

[17] If democracy is conceived as requiring the existence of more than one effective political party, then the cleavage between parties must not be so great as to tempt the party in power, and its supporters, to refuse to tolerate the continued existence of its opponent(s). It is also possible to consider a country dominated by a single party broadly representative of most of the nation's major interests (as in India and Mexico) to be "democratic" or at least "governed by consent." For defenses of such a conception of democracy, see John Kautsky, *Political Change in Underdeveloped Countries* (New York: Wiley, 1962), pp. 113–119; and Horowitz, *op. cit.*, pp. 225–246.

group of people literate enough to create a market for accurate reporting and interpretation of news. Literacy, in turn, will depend on the building and operation of schools. Interest groups representing specific occupations cannot be formed until substantial sectors of the economy have become specialized. Adequate interchange of views among the people and among organizations representing them will be possible only when urbanization brings a large enough number of people together to make group organization and close and frequent personal contact possible. Political parties which adjust and reconcile conflicting interest group claims are an even more sophisticated development, which *assume* a certain level of elite education, belief in unifying symbols, and working governmental institutions as a starting point. Even economically advanced Western nations — like France — have sometimes failed to develop them.[18]

Unfortunately, the growth of some of these requisites is a delicate process. The use of force, for example, tends to polarize a society, thus undermining the long-term prospects for government by consent. When one competitor for political power resorts to military force, his rivals usually must also do so if they wish to survive. In the ensuing struggle, bitter hatreds will be sown on both sides. Leaders skilled in the military, rather than the political or managerial, arts will prove most valuable to their party and will rise to key positions in its ranks. Burgeoning interest groups, newspapers, or parties which chose the "wrong" side will be suppressed. Potential sources of division will be seized upon at every opportunity and played up for all they are worth in the immediate struggle. Rival groups will develop their own symbols — dividing the nation rather than unifying it. No matter which of the competitors for power is successful in such a conflict, the prospects for government by consent probably will be diminished as a result. Political unity and understanding, no less than railroads and edifices, are far easier to tear down than to build up. This is one basic handicap under which those who advocate development by consent must always operate.

COMMUNISM VS. THE WEST
IN THE DEVELOPING AREAS

There are other handicaps. Communism, the leading competitor to government by consent in the developing nations today, identified itself with anti-colonialism as early as the 1920's. The leading exemplars of democracy, on

---

[18] This discussion of political development is based in part upon the analysis, if not the vocabulary, presented in Gabriel Almond and James Coleman, *Politics of the Developing Areas* (Princeton, N.J.: Princeton University Press, 1960). Almond's introductory essay refers to some of the requisites discussed here as the "input functions" of "political socialization and recruitment," "interest articulation," "interest aggregation," and "political communication." The requisites for government by consent cited are also consistent with the relevant data in Arthur Banks and Robert Textor (eds.), *A Cross-Polity Survey* (Cambridge, Mass.: M.I.T. Press, 1963).

the other hand, are or have been colonial powers themselves and remain identified with colonialism in the eyes of the peoples of the newly independent nations. The United States has to live down, in addition, a conspicuous record of racial discrimination in its immigration policy and in its treatment of the American Negro.

By opposing vested interests and the colonial status quo at an early date, Communist movements attracted to their ranks many of the ablest, most selfless and dedicated young people in these societies — men who have now risen to leadership positions in their national Communist parties. Communism offered, and continues to offer a unified cohesive ideology, effective organizational techniques, and the conspicuous example of rapid economic development in the Soviet Union — and to some extent in China as well. It also arms its followers with a rationale for assuming leadership roles in their own societies, in the interests of the people, and for continuing to hate Western colonialism while at the same time adopting the industrial techniques and ways of life introduced to them by the West.

In providing these local Communist movements with financial, diplomatic, and sometimes also military support, the governments of the Soviet Union and China need not concern themselves, as their democratic Western counterparts must, with rigidities in the attitudes of their constituents toward these matters. They are free to support nonaligned governments, nonsocialist governments, even democratic governments, if they choose to do so. Soviet aid to democratic India, Chinese and Soviet aid to nonaligned Egypt, and Chinese cooperation with Pakistan — formally a United States ally — against India, are instructive illustrations. In contrast, the United States Congress has criticized — and sometimes refused to approve — aid to governments whose domestic or foreign policies run counter to American public prejudices against "neutralism," socialism, or, worst of all, outright communism.

Thus, from 1951 through 1956, neutralist India, with a population (then) of 450,000,000, received much less United States *economic* aid than either of two much smaller United States military allies in Asia: South Korea, with a population of about 25,000,000, and the Republic of China on Taiwan, with a population of about 10,000,000. The defection of Communist Yugoslavia from the Soviet bloc in the 1950's created some very difficult problems for the Soviet Union and the world Communist movement. Yet Congress could never quite bring itself to support wholeheartedly a nation which continued to profess its adherence to the Communist ideology. When George Kennan resigned his position as United States Ambassador to Yugoslavia in 1963, he complained to the Senate National Security Subcommittee in no uncertain terms of the costs of this ideological rigidity:

> . . . There were times when a minor area of discretion on the part of the Ambassador would have yielded dividends from the standpoint of national interest, and when the absence of it was frustrating and em-

barrassing. This, again, was primarily a matter of congressional policy — particularly of the existence of sweeping and rigid restrictions on aid or anything that smacked of aid, toward Yugoslavia. . . .

. . . I mention with some hesitation these instances of the limitations placed by legislative action on the ability of the Ambassador to play his part effectively. I have no choice but to do so; for these were the main impediments I experienced to the full deployment of my usefulness at my post. I do not need to remind you of the restrictions placed last year, not only on the extension of anything under the heading of aid, but even on the extension of normal trading facilities to Yugoslavia. These restrictions were adopted in the face of the most solemn and formal sort of warnings and objections on my part, conveyed to congressional leaders on many occasions and in many ways. . . .

. . . If I had known, for example, when I was offered the position of Ambassador in Yugoslavia, how little value the Congress would assign to my judgment, in the light of an experience of nearly 30 years in the affairs of the Eastern European area, I would not have accepted the appointment. . . .[19]

To the extent that we continue to allow these home-grown ideological stereotypes to hamper American policymakers in their efforts to aid in the economic and political development of the developing nations, the prospects for the worldwide growth of government by consent — already none too bright — will be further diminished.

DEVELOPMENT AND FOREIGN POLICY

The foreign policies of the developing nations, too, are related to their economic and political development. Their consuming internal goal of rapid economic growth is bound to become a goal of their foreign policies as well. All other motives aside, they will naturally want to secure as much external support as they can in the form of aid and favorable trade arrangements. But all other motives can seldom be left aside. These nations are usually highly sensitive politically. Independence and xenophobia have generally provided the few unifying symbols and traditions of cooperation their elites and peoples possess. Because of the nature of the many perplexing issues which divide them — land reform; an effective system of taxation; church-state relations; central government-local government relations — anticolonialist statements or even local military adventures may seem to their harassed leaders highly useful means of promoting desperately needed national unity. They may also serve the function of diverting both the populace and the military from domestic discontents and of channeling off some of the inescapable resentments caused by the dislocations attendant upon development.

Even the most enlightened and responsible leaders of developing nations

[19] United States Congress, Senate, Subcommittee on National Security Staffing and Operations of the Committee on Government Operations (Jackson Subcommittee). *Hearings.* 88th Cong., 1st sess., Nov. 21, 1963. Part 5, p. 360.

will hesitate to add to the sources of internal political division by advocating foreign policies sure to be opposed by important political groups — such as, in many cases, the local Communist party and its front organizations. Alignment with either side in controversial international disputes may cost some sorely needed domestic political support. This is particularly true of alignment with the United States on cold war issues. The colonial rulers these people resent are usually United States allies. And news of the mistreatment of Negroes within the United States reinforces what tend to become racially oriented sensitivities. Consequently, unless the financial compensations of alignment with the West are unusually large — or unless Western protection against an obvious outside threat is greatly desired — the leaders of these nations will normally prefer to follow a policy of *nonalignment*.

Nonalignment does not mean, as has sometimes been charged, neutrality with regard to the great issues which divide the world. The governments of developing nations may prefer not to take sides on international issues of primary importance to *us*, like the threat of Communist world domination. Their material contribution to the cold war struggle would be limited in any case by their present economic and military weakness. The most important contribution they really can make is to build strong and stable economic and political institutions in their own countries — to build nations capable ultimately of defending their own independence against subversion or local Communist aggression. And that is what they are working toward, *anyway*. Would it really be in India's long-run interest — or in America's — for India to contribute substantial military forces to the anti-Communist struggle in Vietnam? Would it be worth diverting scarce resources from India's development programs? Courting a conflict with Communist China which might disrupt India's development process? Antagonizing leftist elements within India whose all-out opposition might sabotage India's efforts at economic progress? Risking the loss of aid, and diplomatic support against Peking, from the Soviet Union? Would Indian forces be likely to turn the tide against communism in Vietnam?

The nonaligned nations sometimes counter criticisms of their neutrality by asserting that it is really *we* who are neutral about the truly great issues of our day: the struggle between colonial and anticolonial forces, and between poverty and progress. Do we not often hedge or abstain in the United Nations on issues involving the rights of African colonies — like Algeria, and now Angola — against their European oppressors (our allies)? Have we not refused to support military sanctions against the white supremacist governments of South Africa and Rhodesia? Do we not often support the Europeanized Israelis against the Arab states? Do we not refuse, for fear of domestic complications, to endorse sweeping declarations of human rights (declarations which our Communist adversaries do not hesitate to accept)? Have we not declined to cooperate in setting up a large-scale United Nations fund for economic development? Or in revising the terms of international trade to the advantage of the developing nations? [20] Who is it that is really neutral, then, they ask, when the chips are down?

This is not to say that whatever the new nations do is right, or that they do not sometimes underestimate — as India did — the real meaning of the threat posed to their own interests by a Communist neighbor. Even the most charitable would find it hard to argue, for example, that Indonesia's withdrawal from the United Nations in 1965 was genuinely in its own long-term best interests. (After a military coup the new Indonesian government rejoined the organization the following year.) But if we cannot always approve the foreign policies of the developing nations, surely we should not find it so difficult to understand that many of the outbursts and epithets which they seem to be directing at us are actually intended to serve domestic functions of which we are only dimly aware. After all, we were a young nation once ourselves.

THE AMERICAN EXPERIENCE
IN NATIONAL DEVELOPMENT

A brief review of our own experience as a developing nation should broaden our comprehension of a number of the points discussed in this chapter. The United States began its drive to development under circumstances far more favorable than most of the new nations in the present era enjoy. In America, a continent full of land and rich natural resources was available; whereas in nations like China and India today the pressure of population upon scarce land and resources is a critical bottleneck in the development process. A large majority of our population — especially at first — was Protestant, and the nation has remained almost entirely Christian. The religious values and social customs of most of the European immigrants to the United States, particularly the Protestant emphasis on glorifying God through work, were far more conducive to development than the social and religious norms prevailing in many of today's underdeveloped countries. Though sectional differences were far from negligible, all areas of the United States at least spoke a common language, and the educated classes of all sections had training and substantial experience in a common — and democratic — political tradition. Neither technology nor democratic institutions were so highly developed elsewhere in the world as to whet popular aspirations and pressure the founding fathers to move too far too fast.

The America of the founding fathers, it should be recalled, was not a

[20] For an account of United States persistence in opposing the interests of the developing nations on tariff and trade issues at the 1964 United Nations Conference on Trade and Development, held in Geneva, see Horowitz, *op. cit.*, chap. 6. On several occasions, the United States was the only one of the 116 states attending to oppose statements of principle opposed to restrictive trading policies. The Soviet Union, on the other hand consistently supported the developing nations. For example, the United States cast the only vote opposed to the statement that: "Economic relations between countries, including trade relations, shall be based on respect for the principle of sovereign equality of states, self-determination of peoples, and noninterference in the internal affairs of other countries."

full-fledged democracy by contemporary standards. Its first constitutional document, the Articles of Confederation, proved unworkable and had to be scrapped after an eight-year trial. Under the federal constitution which succeeded it, only a small minority of the population was entitled to vote. The states were given the right to set voting eligibility requirements as they saw fit, and women, nonowners of property, and sometimes unpopular minority groups were long excluded from voting. Many of the founding fathers, in fact, were openly disdainful of the capacity of the "rabble" to take part in the governing process. Not until after World War I did as much as one-fifth of the population cast ballots in a presidential election. Both the President and the Senate were initially elected indirectly; and the institution of slavery was explicitly accepted by the Constitution.

In contrast, both Americans and native elites all too often expect new nations with lower literacy rates and worse communications systems than those of Thomas Jefferson's America to begin immediately to institute the most modern democratic practices and to make them work successfully.

Nor were the economic problems our forefathers faced wholly comparable to those confronting the developing nations today. The young American nation was not compelled to cope with the "population explosion" resulting from the lag — due to modern medical advances — between a greatly reduced death rate and a relatively constant birth rate. As it happens, our abundance of land and resources would have enabled us to deal with this problem far more readily than most of the already overpopulated nations which *are* faced with it today. We were not, either, a "one-crop" economy, at the mercy of fluctuations in international commodity markets, as are so many of the undeveloped nations of the 1960's.

An abundant flow of European investment capital played a major role in providing the funds required to finance American development. There were then fewer good alternative opportunities for domestic and foreign investment than there are today. Nor did inflamed popular resentment of generations of economic dominance by an alien racial minority force the new federal government to impose conditions limiting the profitability of foreign investment — as many of the governments of today's developing nations have found it necessary to do.[21] Later, the United States' lucrative role as neutral supplier to the belligerents in World War I made it possible to liquidate our foreign debt in relatively painless fashion and become the world's greatest creditor nation almost overnight. This beneficent sequence of events does not appear likely to repeat itself for the benefit of nations incurring large foreign debts today.

---

21 Despite zealous United States government efforts — including extensive investment guaranty programs — to induce private enterprises to invest in the developing nations, the flow of private capital to these nations has remained much lower than the flow of funds from government to government. And much of the private capital which *has* been invested in these countries has been in raw materials and extractive industries rather than in manufacturing.

The young United States did not have to contend, for the most part, with major threats to national survival from without, or with foreign supported conspiratorial movements seeking to overthrow its form of government from within. No possible geographic barriers today can provide the insulation from foreign intervention which the Atlantic Ocean bestowed upon the United States in its early years, while Europe was preoccupied with its own great power rivalries. The United States had scarcely any centrally controlled military establishment in its early years — and got by with it. But many of today's new nations must divert desperately needed capital resources from domestic projects to finance respectable military establishments to defend themselves against aggressive neighbors or to satisfy the nationalistic demands of their own peoples in territorial or political disputes originating in the colonial period. Thus India has been compelled to spend its meager capital resources guarding its northwestern frontiers against Chinese Communist incursions in support of age-old Chinese territorial claims. Pakistan and India spend their resources arming against one another in the Kashmir area. And the Arab nations prefer to spend scarce capital resources in an arms race with Israel rather than to accept that nation's continued existence.

Despite these advantages, America's foreign policies were not always responsible and enlightened, and its development was far from painless. In the great contest between parliamentarianism and dictatorship which shook Europe in our early years, we long pursued a policy of nonalignment. Today we often condemn other new nations for following our example. When we finally entered that contest, in 1812, it was on the side of the dictator, Napoleon; for we allowed residual anti-British sentiment from our colonial days, and violations of our rights as neutrals, to blind us to larger considerations.

More than once in the nineteenth century, the United States undertook dubious international adventures, abusing weaker neighbors, in part for the sake of promoting national unity and distracting the citizenry from domestic troubles and differences. (See Chapter Two.)

As recently as 1939–41, we sought to maintain our traditional nonalignment in a conflict between fascism and democracy surely no less suffused with moral overtones than the cold war confrontation of today. Certainly it was more important that American power be brought to bear in the struggle against Hitler in the 1930's than that Indian or Nigerian power be brought to bear in the struggle against the Soviet Union in the 1960's. Yet our internal divisions and economic problems were such that it took the direct Japanese attack on Pearl Harbor to involve us, finally, in World War II. (See Chapter Seven.)

At home, we failed to solve one of the great problems dividing our nation without a long and costly civil war which left deep scars. Discrimination against a large minority group — supposedly "freed" by that war — has continued to the present. The forces of social disintegration unleashed by our industrial development contributed to a number of disturbing problems which have persisted through all of the twentieth century — juvenile delinquency, rising crime rates, drug addiction and alcoholism, high divorce rates, unwed mothers, mental illness, and numerous less spectacular strains and stresses. The vicissitudes of our business cycle brought periodic depressions which inflicted severe privation on millions of helpless citizens, and led ultimately to "trust-busting" and anti-monopoly laws, to large-scale government welfare programs, and to extensive federal regulation of the national economy.

To offset the many harrowing barriers to their successful development, today's developing nations enjoy only two major advantages which were not available to the United States. First, they can use a far vaster store of research and technology. Atomic energy, the transistor radio, the computer, the jet airplane, chemical fertilizers, oral contraceptives, and such social inventions as Keynesian economics and the "pay-as-you-go" income tax withholding system are available for the new nations to draw upon — if they can contrive to adapt these devices successfully to their own development plans. Second, for their own reasons, the United States, the Soviet Union, and other developed nations accept now — as Europe did not accept in the nineteenth century — the responsibility for aiding developing nations through direct government-to-government grants and loans, the latter often on extremely generous terms. Under present circumstances, the prospects for successful development without such foreign assistance are dim, especially for nations seeking to develop without the short-term advantages of totalitarian administration.[22]

DILEMMAS IN ADMINISTERING FOREIGN AID

Between the end of World War II and the end of 1966, the United States appropriated close to $120 billion for aid programs of various kinds. Baldly stated, this statistic is breathtaking. Only about a third of this money, however, represents aid to the developing areas. The remaining thirds represent military aid and aid to Europe (including Greece and Turkey) and Japan. In addition, this figure includes loans as well as grants, and counts United States surplus agricultural commodities at market value. Actually, the costs of

[22] International commodity stabilization agreements, or other *trade* arrangements, may be more helpful to certain developing nations than direct aid itself. Some of the barriers to United States participation in such arrangements are reviewed in Chapter Twelve. ". . . if the underdeveloped world as a whole had paid 1958 prices for their 1962 imports, they would have benefited to the extent of $200 million; and . . . if they had received 1958 prices for their 1962 exports, they would have benefited to the extent of $1,400 million." Edward S. Mason, *Foreign Aid and Foreign Policy* (New York: Harper, 1964), p. 82.

United States economic aid have never exceeded 2 per cent — and by the mid-1960's had fallen below 1 per cent — of our Gross National Product.[23]

Nevertheless, in the generation since the inauguration of the brilliantly successful Marshall Plan, foreign aid has become a recognized and regular instrument of the foreign policy of the United States — and of most other major nations in the world as well. Western Europe and Japan, once the main recipients of American aid, themselves provided more than $40 billion worth of aid to the developing nations between 1956 and 1964. The Soviet Union provided almost $20 billion in military and economic aid to Communist and non-Communist countries between 1954 and 1965. And the United Nations, Israel, Communist *and* Nationalist China, and a number of other nations also operated modest economic or technical aid programs by the 1960's.

All of them found the administration of these aid programs far from simple. The writer is reminded, in this connection, of two cartoons which appeared in *The New Yorker* in past years. The first depicts a tribal council in a primitive hut. A medicine man has the floor and is describing his strategy to the chieftains and elders assembled: "First we invite the Americans to send an economic aid team. Then we invite the Russians to send one. Then we ask the United Nations to send one. Then we ask the Americans for technical aid, and they send more people here. Then the Russians; then the United Nations. Then we ask for military aid, and more people come here. Then, when they all get here, we eat them!"

The second shows a young executive type throwing dollar bills out an upper story window to the streets below, only to be chided by another executive type running toward him: "NO! NO! That's not the way we do things at the Ford Foundation."

The first of these cartoons suggests that the purposes of those who receive aid may be very different from the purposes of those who provide it. The second suggests the bewilderment of many well-intentioned people that there should be so many problems involved in giving money away.

Should we emphasize military aid or economic aid? Grant aid or loan aid? Bilateral or multilateral aid? Should we stress aid projects which will produce quick results or programs which will be less spectacular but have more economic impact in the long run? Should we give aid to dictatorial

[23] The figures in this paragraph, and, unless otherwise noted, all figures given in this section, were taken or computed from the 1966 Congressional Committee Hearings on United States aid programs — in particular, *Foreign Assistance, 1966*. Hearings before the Committee on Foreign Relations, U.S. Senate, 89th Cong., 2nd sess., 1966; and *Foreign Assistance and Related Agencies: Appropriations for 1967*. Hearings before a Subcommittee of the Committee on Appropriations, House of Representatives, 89th Cong., 2nd sess., 1966. To avoid damaging the United States balance of payments position (see Chapter Twelve), most United States aid funds were required, by the mid-1960's, to be spent on American goods and services. Other provisions of United States aid legislation also favor United States business and shipping interests, and, in so doing, marginally lower the value to the recipients of the funds provided.

regimes? To regimes which criticize us and follow policies opposed to our own, even while taking our aid? Should we distribute our aid widely to all who need it, or concentrate it selectively where it is most likely to yield results? Should we attach "strings" to our aid, or not?

These frequently asked questions are not easy to answer in any case. They are impossible to answer if we insist on treating "foreign aid" as a unit. Foreign aid is an omnibus term which misleads, because by saying too much it fails to say enough. Citizens, reporters, even Congressmen sometimes talk of our foreign aid as having failed, or as having succeeded. Succeeded or failed to do what, where, in what circumstances? Some claim our aid has failed to win us friends and supporters abroad. But how much of our aid was designed to win friends for us? Personally or nationally, one doesn't win friends by trying to reform people or by telling them what's good for them.

Viewed in this light, the oft-heard suggestion that we should stop giving foreign aid altogether becomes an assertion either that the goals of aid — that is, most of the goals of our foreign policy as a whole — are not worth pursuing; or that, in every case, there are better ways to achieve them. These assertions are patent nonsense. Both blanket approval for foreign aid and blanket condemnation of it are oversimplified responses, probably based more on emotional predispositions than on careful thought. The realistic questions to be asked are *how much* aid, *to whom,* for *what purposes,* and in *what circumstances?*

The dispensing of aid can be a legitimate and prudent means to a variety of foreign policy goals. It may be intended to facilitate the economic development of the recipient; to augment the military strength of an existing or potential ally, or obtain military bases on its territory. It may seek to influence a recipient government to support the donor's foreign policies in certain areas, or to maintain a favored political group in power. Or it may, conceivably, have purely humanitarian purposes.[24] The success or failure of a particular aid project or program should be judged on the basis of how well it has achieved the purpose it was intended to achieve. It may be possible to serve two or more of these purposes with one dose of aid. But this is rather to be hoped for than routinely expected, for the prerequisites for success are different in each case.

True development aid, for instance, assumes an economy capable of putting the funds made available to good use in programs which will increase the productivity of the recipient. It assumes, also, a reasonably effec-

24 See Hans Morgenthau, "A Political Theory of Foreign Aid," *The American Political Science Review* (June, 1962), pp. 301–309. Morgenthau discusses six categories of aid: humanitarian, military, development, subsistence, bribery, and "prestige" aid. The last two are collapsed into one category in the present discussion.

Each of these, except development aid, aims at essentially short-term goals. Even the goals of strengthening an ally or providing food for the hungry can best be served *in the long run* by promoting national development.

tive government, capable of administering both the aid and the economy it will go into with a minimum of corruption. It assumes that the recipient places first priority on development rather than on military adventures, for instance — otherwise the funds given will merely free the recipient to release some of its own funds for military purposes. It sometimes assumes also the existence of a certain minimum of social overhead capital needed to make the aid effective. This is assuming a good deal, and almost none of the developing nations could meet such criteria if they were not applied somewhat loosely. Nevertheless, true development aid must inevitably be selective rather than universal in scope, since the number of nations with the political and economic development needed to make good use of it at any given time are likely to be few. (By fiscal year 1967, over 90 per cent of United States economic aid was concentrated in 20 nations, and 84 per cent of development lending, in particular, was scheduled for eight countries. Economic aid programs in fifty-two additional countries were generally not much more than tokens of United States interest in their development.)

Nor should development aid normally be expected to make friends for us. Those who receive it usually know that we give it for our own sake — often because of our fear of Communist takeover of their societies from within. (Certainly our leaders tell this to our own people and their congressional representatives often enough.) If the development and continued national independence of these countries are our goals, we can afford to overlook criticisms of our current policies, and even opposition to them, within limits. Even if national development is understood to mean eventual progress toward some type of government by consent, it may be advisable to work with authoritarian or oligarchic regimes while the prerequisites of government by consent are (we hope) being created. Nevertheless, *any* aid is likely to help some segments of a society more than others, and we would be foolish if we did not try to see to it that our aid helps, as much as possible, to strengthen the groups and forces within a society most likely to promote stable democratic development in the long run.[25]

On the other hand, development aid is the only category of aid considered here which might suitably be based upon loans rather than outright grants. Loans are believed by many Americans to be more likely than grants to preserve the self-respect and financial responsibility of recipients. By the mid-1960's, close to two-thirds of United States economic aid to the developing nations — not counting the value of surplus agricultural commodities distributed under the Food for Peace Program — took the form of long-term, low-interest loans, rather than grants. But an underdeveloped nation which remains underdeveloped will be hard pressed to export enough goods to finance its current imports, let alone to withdraw additional goods from

25 See Staley, *op. cit.;* Herbert Feis, *Foreign Aid and Foreign Policy* (New York: St. Martin's Press, 1964), pp. 119 ff.; and John D. Montgomery, *The Politics of Foreign Aid: American Experience in Southeast Asia* (New York: Praeger, 1962), pp. 264 ff.

personal domestic consumption to pay off large sums borrowed previously for unproductive purposes. A nation which succeeds in industrializing its economy *may* be able to pay off debts incurred during its years of development without great hardship, but even then *only* if Americans are willing to allow it to do so. Repayment can come only as the United States imports more goods from these nations — to the value of the loans to be repaid — than we export to them; that is, only to the extent that we are willing to *buy from* them more than we *sell to* them. (See Chapter Twelve.) This certainly will not be possible if we insist on setting high tariffs on the goods these countries are able to export in the years when repayment is due. If we do, we will have been fooling only ourselves in insisting on providing loans rather than grants to the nations we aid, and a wave of disillusionment with "deadbeat" foreigners may result.

In *all* cases there will be "strings" attached, explicitly or implicitly, though the nature of the strings will vary. The proper reply to those who call for aid without strings is that "there ain't no such animal." (One envisages the medicine man in the cartoon described at the beginning of this section calling for more aid personnel to be sent — after the previous ones have been digested — with no strings attached, of course.) Nations are not accustomed to giving out aid for no reason at all; and if the purpose underlying the aid is clearly not served, why should it be continued? The common implicit string attached to all kinds of aid programs, then, is that they must seem to be fulfilling their intended purpose. Donors of development aid should be expected to require assurances or evidence that the funds provided will be used for sound developmental projects rather than to create bonanzas for the powerful few or to strengthen the position of one political faction against its rivals. Aid donors with short-term political or military goals, however, may be rightly satisfied if they succeed only in keeping a friendly government in power or picking up a vote in the General Assembly of the United Nations.

What makes it difficult for outsiders to criticize some of our aid programs intelligently, however, is that the goals of aid are not always what they seem. Aid given to induce a foreign government to support the United States on a particular issue (to encourage the recipient, for instance, to avoid fighting with a neighbor) can scarcely be advertised as such. Though it may prove eminently successful in achieving the purpose intended, it may appear to the untutored eye to be development aid gone wrong. The criticism that such adventures in polite bribery can bring down upon the whole aid program is one persuasive reason for a democratic state to employ such methods sparingly.[26]

One way of getting around the new nations' sensitivities to having "strings" attached to aid is to channel some of our aid programs through United Nations agencies, and regional international organizations. Much

26 See Feis, *op. cit.,* p. 119.

less suspect of imperialist ambitions than any single great power, these agencies are in a much better position to require that their grants and loans be utilized in accordance with sound economic planning. (On the other hand, it is much more difficult for the United Nations to distribute effectively aid designed primarily to serve immediate political purposes, because the political goals of various United Nations members are generally disparate.) However, Congress is most hesitant to channel any sizable proportion of United States aid funds through the United Nations, since this causes both the United States and Congress itself to lose control over the ultimate disposition of this aid. A United Nations decision to provide even a small amount of aid to an underdeveloped nation like Cuba could cause (and *has*) a good measure of acute political embarrassment to American supporters of channeling aid through the United Nations. The governments or legislatures of some other nations have similar reservations.

Actually, most United States development aid is already committed through multinational institutions: the International Bank for Reconstruction and Development (IBRD), which makes loans on near commercial terms; the International Development Association, which loans on more lenient terms than the IBRD, the Development Assistance Committee of the Organization for Economic Cooperation and Development, which attempts to coordinate the flow of investment to the developing nations from the United States, Western Europe, and Japan; and the Alliance for Progress and the Inter-American Development Bank, which operate on a regional basis. But these organizations are not part of the United Nations system. The Communist nations are not represented in them, and, except perhaps for the Alliance for Progress, these agencies do not afford the developing nations themselves the useful experience of helping to administer aid programs. Control of their expenditures remains firmly in the hands of the donor nations.

Not much more than 10 per cent of United States economic aid was being channeled through United Nations agencies in the mid-1960's, and, on balance, a substantial rise in that percentage seemed warranted — especially since our rivals might then feel challenged to disburse some of their aid through the United Nations also.

In addition to dilemmas of *how* to aid, there often remain even more perplexing problems of *whom* to aid. It would be delightful to have available in every recipient nation a stable, friendly, unified, competent government, firmly committed both to democratic ideals and to economic development. Even if such a government were opposed by a powerful Communist faction, our choice would be clearcut. We could serve the interest of the people concerned while serving our own interest. And we could rest assured that the resources we provided would be put to good use.

Unfortunately, such governments are rarely to be found among the undeveloped nations, for reasons already discussed. The governments in these nations are more likely to be representatives of the traditional social order in the country concerned, prepared to modernize only to the extent possible without displacing the traditional elites which support them. Or they may be military oligarchies, committed to modernization but not necessarily to government by consent.[27] There may be no leader or political group capable of maintaining a reasonable semblance of national unity by any means. Or there may be one able to maintain such unity only by devoting all of its political resources to *that* task, thus being compelled to neglect such tasks as land reform, democratization, industrialization, or even defense against a militant Communist party. Outside pressure for reform may therefore be fruitless.

If we support, or even deal with, a traditionalist regime, we will most likely be charged at home and abroad with "propping up a dictatorship." The costs of keeping it in power may increase with time, and, if it is overthrown, its successor may be understandably ill-disposed toward us. If we aid non-Communist rebels who oppose the existing government, we will be guilty of intervening in another country's internal affairs — an especially serious charge in Latin America. If we stand by and help neither, we may antagonize both; and the administration in power will be vulnerable to charges of softness on communism if our action *or* inaction leads to a Communist takeover.

Dealing with such situations requires of the United States government both a high order of political courage and a high order of political acumen. The political attractiveness of each of the alternatives open to us must be balanced carefully against the power realities of the situation. For an attractive ally who cannot win or maintain power will do us little good, and soon we will be confronted with the necessity for choice again, probably in an even more frustrating situation.

In return for accepting all of the costs and hazards recounted here, how do *we* benefit from helping the world's poor nations along the long road to development? It remains to be proven that many of these nations can succeed, even with our help. Or that, if they do succeed, they will develop into the kind of nations we will want to live with in the world of the future. Nazi Germany, we must remember, was an economically developed nation.

Clearly there are risks ahead in the course our nation has charted. But there are risks in *withholding* development aid as well. If the nations we would not help manage somehow — probably through the use of totalitarian

27 In some developing societies, the military establishment's leadership role is based not only on its command of force, but also on the relatively high level of technical training its officers may have, and even on its ability to "represent" a wider socio-economic spectrum than competing elites, due to its recruitment from among the peasantry.

methods — to squeeze enough capital out of their masses to develop a strong industrial capacity on their own, our relations with them are not likely to be any better — and may be a lot worse — than if we *had* helped them before they became powerful. If they fail to develop, if we continue to stand by unmoved year after year while most of the world's people live in poverty and want, we may somehow contrive to preserve our security — but only at the cost of destroying that which is most worthwhile within our own society and within ourselves. (This possibility is discussed further in Chapter Fourteen.)

It is impossible even to attempt any systematic assessment of what our aid efforts to date have achieved and failed to achieve. In order to make such an assessment, we would have to know what we obviously cannot know: what would have happened in various parts of the world if our aid had not been given. Since an impressionistic judgment will have to do, then, perhaps John Montgomery's will do as well as any:

> It cannot be argued . . . that American aid has converted enemies into friends or neutrals into allies; indeed, American aid probably has not changed any foreign or domestic policies in Southeast Asia that affect vital national interests of those nations. Moreover, when governments have failed to respond to their own pressing domestic or international needs, American assistance has never been able to compensate for deficiencies in national authority. Finally, the exponents of aid have not claimed for military and economic assistance the power to guarantee the survival of a nation hemmed in with vastly superior military forces or infested with guerrillas.
>
> Within these limits, much has been accomplished: decisive support has been given to governments seeking to maintain their independence; trends of international and domestic policy that will contribute toward stability and decency have been sustained; and, at times, the United States has even been able to encourage internal forces that promise greater respect for human rights and more responsible and more representative government. Foreign aid has shown a usefulness and versatility that have earned it a distinctive and permanent place in the arsenal of peace.[28]

❦ CASE STUDY   *THE COMMUNIST VICTORY IN CHINA*

United States China policy in the years following World War II has become a subject of partisan political controversy within the United States. Critics of the Roosevelt and Truman administrations charge that the United States government betrayed Chiang K'ai-shek and the

[28] Montgomery, *op. cit.*, pp. 59–60.

Chinese Nationalists by failing to provide the support they needed in their struggle against the Communists. They allege further that the United States impaired the Nationalist government's prestige by signing a secret agreement with the Russians at Yalta in February, 1945, which gave away Chinese territory to the Soviet Union without the Chinese government's consent. The more extreme of the critics go so far as to accuse supposedly disloyal elements within the State Department of consciously plotting to turn China over to International Communism. (As a result of these charges a number of career Foreign Service "China hands," who had predicted a Communist victory and urged the United States government to avoid alienating the men who would probably be the next rulers of China, were sacked as "security risks" or hounded from their jobs.)

Defenders of United States policy in China during the 1940's counter that the Yalta agreements gave the Soviet Union nothing it could not have taken for itself upon its entry into the war in Asia; and argue that a Communist victory could have been prevented, if at all, only by a large-scale commitment of American military forces in China at a time when the American people had just demobilized and were in no mood to send their boys off to China again for this dimly understood purpose.

The case study which follows was written by the author of this book, whose point of view on this question is in general closer to that of the Roosevelt-Truman administration's defenders than to that of its critics.[29]

1. What elements in China's traditional way of life interfered most in that nation's efforts to achieve military and industrial equality with the West? Was there any way in which the Manchu dynasty could have successfully resisted the incursions of the Western powers without undertaking a fundamental restructuring of the Chinese way of life? If so, how? If not, why not?

2. Why did democracy fail to take root in China in the years following the Republican revolution of 1911 or after the Nationalist victory of 1928?

3. Why did the Nationalists fail to consolidate their control over China and to industrialize it in the way that the Communists have in the years since their accession to power?

4. To what extent do you believe United States policy contributed to the Communist triumph? Might different approaches to the provision of wartime and/or postwar aid to the National government have served United States interests better? If so, explain how. Can you think of any way in which United States action could have prevented the Communist takeover? If so, explain. If not, why not?

5. What parallels do you see between the civil war in China described below and the civil war in Vietnam discussed in Chapter Seven?

[29] A sampling of American and foreign views on these matters, along with suggestions for further reading, is presented in Pichon P. Y. Loh (ed.), *The Kuomintang Debacle of 1949* (Boston: D. C. Heath, 1965).

SHELDON APPLETON

The disintegration of the traditional society of China because of Western intrusions in the second half of the nineteenth century is one of the great dramas, and one of the great tragedies, of recorded history. For during its more than three and a half millennia of continuous existence, Chinese civilization had achieved a degree of social stability, political integration, and cultural excellence rarely equalled in the annals of mankind.

The key to China's social stability was the family system. The family was the principal social *and* economic unit in the life of its members. For the peasant family, the land they tilled in common was their livelihood; marriages were arranged by the family, and the family's reputation was a matter of enormous personal concern to each individual within it. For the ruling class of scholar-administrators, family connections and support were crucial to success. One could scarcely have gained entrance to this class in the first place without being supported by the family for the prolonged period necessary to master the classical texts upon which the government's civil service examinations were based. A man's first loyalty was due, not to his nation or to himself, but to his family — past, present, and future. Filial piety was the cardinal virtue of the culture.

The base of traditional Chinese society consisted of multitudes of poor farmers tilling small plots of land to eke out the barest of livings. For a number of reasons China never developed, as Europe had, a system of capitalism and systematized technological advance. In Europe, the burgeoning capitalist class had been able to ally itself with the king against the feudal landholding nobility. In China, the status and power of the scholar-administrator class was such that merchants had to work under their patronage. The scholar-administrators, or their families, normally themselves comprised the dominant part of the landholding class and, in addition, wielded state power in alliance with the Imperial Court.

There was no system of Western style impersonal law, enforced by the state, to protect businessmen from arbitrary actions by local officials, or from the polite institutionalized extortion, known as "squeeze," customarily practiced by these officials. China's was admittedly a government of presumably virtuous men rather than presumably virtuous laws, and it was expected as a matter of course that administrative officials would apply the law with generous amounts of discretion. Those who accumulated capital, therefore, normally chose to invest it in land and in the training of their sons, which brought status and security to their families, rather than in

This article was prepared especially for this volume.

trade, which brought little of either. The rich merchant in China dreamed that his sons would become, not richer merchants, but scholar-officials. In any event, the market for quick, high-interest returns from crop loans to impoverished farmers was generally so lucrative that alternative investment opportunities paled by comparison.

Another impediment to increased production in China was the shortage of land rather than of labor. The invention of laborsaving machinery would have put many people out of work without increasing total production appreciably, since Chinese labor-intensive farming methods, developed over the centuries, produced very high yields *per acre* already — though the yields *per man* were of course very low. Consequently, as John Fairbank has noted, the way to get rich quick in China was not to produce more and profit accordingly, but to increase one's share of the profit from existing production; not to build a better mousetrap, but to secure the state mousetrap monopoly.* Thus influential personal contacts, rather than scientific expertise, were the keys to success. In traditional China, Fairbank observes, it was not so much know-*how* that counted, as know-*who*.

In this environment, there was little premium on building up an elaborate technology. Inventions were abundant: printing, gunpowder, porcelain, etc. But no system for the exchange and wide dissemination of knowledge was built up, and the cumulative possibilities of these inventions were lost. The best minds went into the humanities — via the classics — rather than into the sciences. Western industrialization in the seventeenth and eighteenth centuries consequently left China dangerously behind in technical knowledge.

The traditional Chinese state was ruled by a relatively thin layer of career scholar-administrators, most of them chosen for their proficiency in passing competitive examinations based upon the classic texts which emphasized ethics and personal virtue as the primary requisites of effective rule. At the top of the political hierarchy was an emperor reputed to be invested by Heaven (a kind of pervasive cosmic force rather than an extraworldly paradise, as in Western usage) with responsibility for governing mankind. The emperor's authority — analogous to that of the father within the traditional family — permitted wholly arbitrary despotic rule, tempered to varying degrees in different periods by the force of precedent and by the prevailing Confucian ethic's insistence on paternal benevolence.

In any event, the breadth of the empire and the limitations of its transportation and communications systems dictated a relatively loose exercise

* Fairbank's *The United States and China* (rev. ed., Cambridge, Mass.: Harvard University Press, 1959) is easily the best one-volume introduction to modern China. This case study draws heavily on it, especially chaps. 3 and 4. For a very brief introduction to Chinese history and society, it would be difficult to improve on the section on China, written by Charles O. Hucker, in Helen Matthew (ed.), *Asia in the Modern World* (New York: Mentor, 1963).

of this power, with a large degree of local autonomy. Thus did the Chinese political system blend in varying parts the teachings of each of three major schools of Chinese political thought: the Legalist emphasis on maximizing the power of the ruler and the state; the Confucian tradition of government by moral example and for the welfare of the people; and the Taoist dictum that the best government is that which governs least.

Since the emperor's mandate to rule was believed to extend beyond the confines of China alone, relations with neighboring peoples were generally handled through a "tribute system." Those who wished to trade with the Chinese simply sent tribute missions bearing gifts to the emperor. On their arrival in the Chinese capital, they performed the necessary ritual acts, such as the "kowtow," acknowledging the place of the emperor as the "Son of Heaven" and ruler of the world. In return, the Imperial Court bestowed upon them gifts of equal or greater value, formally invested their rulers, and sometimes went so far as to render aid to these rulers against domestic revolt.

This traditional equilibrium was disrupted in the nineteenth century by the coming of Western traders who did not fit into this system. They were unwilling to accept either the customary ritual acknowledgments of Chinese cultural superiority, or the limitations on their trade and conduct which the Imperial Court at Peking sought to impose. They found it difficult to understand the Emperor's persistent refusals to receive representatives of the Western powers at his Court on any regular basis. In addition, the cruelty and arbitrariness of Chinese law offended Western residents and offered them little protection from "squeeze," innumerable local taxes, and other impediments to trade. Finally, as one emperor had predicted, it proved easier to interest Westerners in buying Chinese goods than vice versa for a considerable period of time. The result was a steady drain of Western silver — an alarming development in a mercantilist era — until illegal Western exports of opium to China redressed the balance.

China's attempt to suppress the opium trade in 1840 brought war with Great Britain ("the Opium War"), and the British took advantage of their victory to establish a new basis for Sino-Western relations and trade. By the Treaty of Nanking (and subsequent treaties signed with other Western powers soon after China's defeat), five treaty ports were opened to Western trade and residence, a low fixed tariff rate was instituted — not subject to alteration by the Chinese government — and the right of Western residents in China to be tried in Western courts on the basis of Western law (extraterritoriality) was established. These treaties also included "most favored nation" clauses, providing that any concessions won from the Chinese government by *any* of the Western powers would immediately be extended to *all* of them.

By 1860, after additional hostilities between England and France, on the one hand, and China, on the other, the Western right to keep permanent representatives at Peking and to have these ministers received on a basis of formal equality — contrary to Chinese custom — had also been won. Chinese efforts to prevent the implementation of these treaties by bureaucratic delay and administrative harassment were thwarted.

Within China, these developments impaired the prestige and hastened the decline of the reigning imperial dynasty. Two centuries before, in 1644, the Manchu people, neighbors of the Chinese from Manchuria, to the northeast, had gained control of China. For two centuries they had governed in the traditional Chinese manner. But well before the Opium War the familiar process of dynastic decline had begun. Defeat at the hands of the West accelerated it. A major, peasant-based revolt, with heterodox Christian ideological overtones, began in 1850 and raged for fourteen years — coming very close at one point to overthrowing the Manchu dynasty. As a result large areas, including some of the most fertile land in China, were removed from the tax base of the dynasty. Approximately thirty million lives were lost and economic damage was widespread. In the end, this T'ai-P'ing Rebellion, and several concurrent local rebellions, were put down only with the help of specially organized regional armies, locally recruited and financed. These armies remained in existence afterward, lessening the effective authority of the central government at Peking and increasing regional autonomy.

The new "treaty system" had more direct effects also. Western trade with China expanded and the number of treaty ports increased. Within these ports, protected by Western law, there grew up a class of Chinese traders, merchants, financiers, and clerks, in addition to an increasing number of Western residents. The Occidental living standards enjoyed by these new upper classes — paved streets, modern plumbing, hospitals, schools — provided a conspicuous "demonstration effect" for Chinese laborers in the treaty ports and visitors from the surrounding countryside. In addition, Western missionaries traveled inland under extraterritorial protection to spread the gospel of Christianity and industrialization to the benighted folk of the hinterland. The implication of their message was clear: the traditional Confucian outlook was inferior to Western ways of viewing man's relationship to the universe.

This was a very serious challenge to the Manchu dynasty and to China. The whole system by which China was governed was based on the conviction that those best versed in the Confucian classics were likely to be the most moral and, therefore, the most qualified to rule. The family system which was at the inner core of Chinese society was also strongly buttressed by the traditional Confucian ethic. The very right to rule of the emperor himself was grounded in the time-honored folk idea of the "mandate of Heaven." And the inner personalities of generation upon generation of Chinese had

had these fundamental approaches to life built into them. If these hallowed beliefs were now to be discarded, what would the Chinese use in their place? Western doctrines and Western ways had evolved in a totally different cultural context and seemed utterly alien and distasteful. Were the Chinese now to throw over their family allegiances in favor of the grasping materialism, readiness to use force, and general social insensitivity which they saw the "foreign devils" display? If not, what set of organizing principles *should* Chinese society adopt?

The dynasty reacted to this quandary in the traditional manner, emphasizing vigorous and incorrupt administration. Rebellions must be put down, the power of the central government strengthened and the validity of Confucian doctrines reaffirmed by the moral example of the Imperial Court itself. The civil service examinations must be revised to include some questions relevant to the practical problems of the day. To be sure, China must adopt Western military technology in order to resist further encroachment by the Western barbarians. But the purpose of this limited imitation of the Westerners would be not to abandon the Chinese way of life, but to preserve it.

Once begun, however, the process of Westernization was not easily controlled. Improved military technology meant arsenals, factories, and improved transportation and communications systems. Masses of laborers had to be uprooted from their families in the countryside and drawn into urban centers to man these factories. To fill managerial and officer positions, thousands of Chinese had to be sent abroad to obtain Western educations to gain some understanding of Western technology and military methods. Inevitably, this involved exposing the elite of the future to Western ways and Western ideas.

Nor was this the whole of it. If Western technical efficiency were to be matched, jobs which required competent technicians or skilled workers must be filled on the basis of capability rather than family connections. Government officials must forego the opportunity to "squeeze" these new industries in order to line their own families' coffers. Allegiance to the idea of industrial efficiency — or perhaps of national strength — must take precedence over family obligations. The casualness of traditional attitudes toward time must give way to the punctuality and precision demanded by the assembly line. And not only monetary reward, but the respect of one's peers, must be achievable by first-rate job performance rather than solely through family status or personal virtue. Adapting to these requirements involved surrendering much of the way of life the Chinese were aiming to defend. They were not ready to go this far; yet when the results of the new "self-strengthening" movement were tested in 1895 in combat with rapidly modernizing Japan, the inadequacy of halfway measures became all too plain. Japan, opened to Western trade a decade later than China — and with only a fraction of China's size, population, and historic prestige — administered to its neighbor a crushing and humiliating defeat.

Now more fundamental structural and political reforms were called for by members of the scholar-administrator class themselves. A brief abortive attempt to institute such reforms, in 1898, was thwarted by a coup executed by the last-ditch supporters of the status quo. But within less than a decade, the very forces which had carried out this coup became sufficiently alarmed to begin to institute similar reforms themselves. Decrees were issued to put China on the road to becoming a constitutional monarchy, modeled after the new Japan.

It was probably too little and certainly too late. The dynasty's power and prestige had been eroding for half a century. Western intervention to put down the Boxer Rebellion in 1898 and free the legations besieged at Peking, and a Russo-Japanese war fought largely over — and often on — Chinese territory, added to the dynasty's humiliations. Since the Manchus themselves were not Chinese, moreover, their ability to appeal to Chinese nationalism in their own defense was limited. An important dispute between Peking and local leaders developed in 1911 over the issue of who should control the building of new railroad lines, financed with borrowed Western capital — and profit from the "squeeze" that would come with it. In this atmosphere, the accidental explosion of a bomb being stored for later use by an anti-Manchu conspiratorial group was enough to set off a series of local rebellions which toppled the dynasty.

Out of the 1911 revolution emerged a potential leader of the new Western-oriented classes which had come into being in the preceding half century. Born in a village near the treaty port of Canton, educated largely in an American missionary school in Hawaii and at a British mission hospital in Hong Kong, Dr. Sun Yat-sen spent much of his young adulthood in conspiratorial cliques working to overthrow the Manchu dynasty. Nearly a dozen of the revolutionary plots attempted by the group he headed failed before the accidental explosion of one of its bombs in 1911 sparked the revolution which made Dr. Sun,* for a brief historical moment, provisional president of the new Republic of China. Ironically, Sun was out of the country at the time — since there was a price on his head — and read of the successful revolt in a newspaper in Denver, Colorado.

The Republican revolutionaries lacked the military force needed to assume control of China. They were willing to compromise, therefore, with Yuan Shih-k'ai, a regional military commander with a strong army. A provisional constitution was adopted, which called for the election of a national parliament to share power with the president. In return, the Republicans agreed to accept Yuan as president.

* Chinese names customarily are written with the family name first, a reflection of the importance of the family in traditional Chinese culture.

At this point, one of Dr. Sun's colleagues, Sung Chiao-jen, organized several of the revolutionary cliques into an open political party — the first in China's history — called the Kuomintang or National People's Party (which had been the name of Sun Yat-sen's most recent revolutionary party). The Kuomintang managed to win a parliamentary majority in the elections — based on a very restricted suffrage — which followed. When Sung Chiao-jen proceeded to campaign to increase the parliament's power as against the president's, Yuan Shih-k'ai had him assassinated. The slender hopes for gradual democratic development in China were crushed, and it became clear that the new constitution was to be merely a façade for old-style strong man rule.

For a few years more, Yuan Shih-k'ai was able to hold China together. But with his death in 1916, the country disintegrated into a series of military-based local and regional warlord regimes. For the next decade there was scarcely a pretense of an effective government for China as a whole.

Yet important things happened during this warlord decade. On May 4, 1919, thousands of students rioted at Peking National University in protest against the awarding of concessions on Chinese territory to Japan by allied negotiators at Versailles. Student demonstrations, merchant boycotts, and workers' strikes followed in many parts of the country in an unprecedented demonstration of Chinese nationalism.

Some of these same students and their teachers, attracted by the recent success of the Bolshevik revolution in Russia, soon organized a new Chinese Communist party with the help of Comintern * agents dispatched to China for the purpose. The Party's first national Congress was held in Shanghai in July, 1921, and was attended by thirteen people — including a young library assistant from Peking University named Mao Tse-tung.

Sun Yat-sen meanwhile aligned himself with some local warlords in the south, but, since he was dependent upon them for military support, failed to achieve dominance even in this limited area. After his requests for Western aid repeatedly had been denied, he decided to ally his newly reorganized Kuomintang temporarily with the Chinese Communist party in return for Russian military aid and political advice. As part of the agreement between Sun and the Comintern, Sun's young military aide, Chiang K'ai-shek, was sent to Moscow for a brief period of revolutionary training, and a professional Comintern agent, Michael Borodin, was sent to China to become Sun's chief political adviser. On Chiang's return, he was assigned to head a military school at Whampoa designed to train the officer corps for a Kuomintang army. Borodin meanwhile drafted a constitution, along Leninist lines, for the Kuomintang.

---

* The "Comintern," or Communist International, was then the international arm of the world Communist movement. Through most of its history it was dominated completely by the Communist party of the Soviet Union.

Sun Yat-sen himself, at this time, sought to meet the Kuomintang's need for ideological appeal by elaborating upon his own earlier formulation of the Three Principles of the People: Nationalism, Democracy, and Livelihood. The last two of these principles, however, remained loosely defined and insufficiently thought through. "Democracy" was conceived in terms of such forms and devices as elections, initiative, referendum, and recall, rather than in terms of the institutions which might enable these forms to work. There was no provision for encouraging the formation of interest groups, which might give voice to popular aspirations, or of opposition political parties, which might coalesce and balance these interests in a national political program which could be put before the voters. Constitutional government was to be instituted only after a preparatory period of one-party "tutelage" by the Kuomintang. The Livelihood principle, though referred to by Sun as both socialistic and communistic, was in reality a vague application of the single (land)-tax concepts advocated by the nineteenth-century American economist Henry George.

These formulations crystallized the goals felt by the awakening classes of China: a place in the sun for the Chinese nation; some opportunity for the masses to feel themselves participants in deciding their own destiny; and a decent standard of living — at the least, enough rice to survive on. But they outlined no realistic means of realizing these goals, and, therefore, raised popular aspirations rather than fulfilling them. Most important, they did not serve the necessary function of inspiring the dedication required to hold the Kuomintang together. Sun's principles, after all, had been formulated as a means to bring his party to power; the party had not been called into being to serve the principles. It is not surprising, then, that throughout its history, the Kuomintang remained faction-ridden and power-oriented rather than united and ideologically oriented.

During the next few years, the Kuomintang was revitalized — due in no small part to the effective work of Borodin and its Chinese Communist members, and to Russian aid. By 1926, despite Sun Yat-sen's death the year before, it was ready to embark on a military drive to unify China. Led by Chiang K'ai-shek, this Northern Expedition was successful, though local warlords were more often absorbed into the movement and left with a great deal of local autonomy, than conquered by Kuomintang armies. By 1928, China was at least nominally united and the National (Kuomintang) government had secured general international recognition.

In its first years of power, the National government made a promising start on certain aspects of modernization. Railroads and highways were built. The postal system was improved. A number of modern schools were founded, a Westernized legal system was adopted and a sound currency established. The new government also made some gains in its relations with the West. Tariff autonomy was regained by 1929, a beginning was made toward the elimination of Western extraterritorial rights, and the number of foreign concessions on Chinese soil was reduced.

But the capacity of the National government to build China into a modern nation was limited from the start. In addition to coping with the formidable economic problems of what is now called underdevelopment, Chiang K'ai-shek's task was complicated by his political handicaps. His leadership within the faction-ridden Kuomintang was never unchallenged. He had outmaneuvered and purged the Chinese Communists within his party before the end of the Northern Expedition; but to maintain himself in power, he still had to balance the remaining factions off against one another carefully. Money to be handled, jobs to be given out, troops to be commanded, all offered opportunities for building personal or factional power. Consequently, even within the Kuomintang, Chiang was not in a position to assign tasks simply to those best qualified to perform them. Key positions had to be occupied by individuals whose personal loyalty to himself could be depended on in a showdown, and this qualification had to take priority over less critical virtues such as competence or incorruptibility.

Chiang had never really achieved administrative control over more than a small part of China. He was not in a position, therefore, to dictate policy to regional leaders with armies loyal to themselves, rather than to Chiang or China. It was one thing to legislate reforms, another thing entirely to implement them. As early as 1930, for example, a law limiting land rent to 37½ per cent of the main crop was enacted. But it was rarely implemented, since it was not in the interests of local powerholders — usually big landowners — to do so. How was Chiang to *make* them implement this law without once again plunging China into civil war and political chaos at a time when unity against foreign pressure was sorely needed?

The other side of the coin, however, was that *failure* to undertake effective land reform could also threaten national unity in the long run. For this would leave the Kuomintang serving the interests of one sector of Chinese society at the expense of another — and larger — one. Western influence on China during the preceding decades had been uneven — extensive in the coastal areas, near the treaty ports, much more limited in the interior. Thus the leaders and masses of different regions of China were subjected to sharply different sets of experiences for several generations and developed very different outlooks on China's problems. The Western-oriented classes in the coastal areas — the Kuomintang's political base — were the first to perceive the need to undertake at least the superficial aspects of modernization. But they failed to give adequate attention to the problems — many of them aggravated by the beginnings of modernization — of the rural population in the interior.

Within three years of the National government's assumption of the responsibilities of power. the Japanese army had moved into the Chinese territory of Manchuria and made it the puppet state of Manchukuo. Since Manchuria was among the areas of China most richly endowed in natural resources, this was a major blow to the Kuomintang's plans for industrial development. In addition, Chiang's inability to resist foreign aggression began to erode his government's prestige. The United States and the League of Nations condemned Japan's aggression, but did little to stop it or to help China. The Western world was undergoing the worst depression in modern history and had little energy or inclination to involve itself in major military and political action half a world away. Soon the Japanese were edging into north China as well.

There was also the Chinese Communist party to deal with. Reeling from its reverses after a brief and unsuccessful interlude in which it emphasized organizing urban insurrections, the remnants of the Chinese Communist party retreated to a rural base built up in south central China by Mao Tse-tung. There they began to fill the vacuum which the Nationalists had left in the countryside and to evolve the peasant-based strategy which eventually won them the support of the masses.

The large landowners and vested interests in the Communist-controlled areas were already committed, most of the time, to support the Kuomintang. As the government in power the Nationalists were responsible for the maintenance of law and order, and, in the absence of a systematic program of rural reform, this meant the preservation of the status quo. The renegade Communists, in contrast, had nothing to fear from a class which opposed them already and against which they were predisposed ideologically. Moreover, their survival required the support of the people among whom they were living. By enforcing the National government's own law limiting land rents, or by redistributing to the poor peasants lands abandoned by landlords fleeing the Communist revolution, Mao Tse-tung and his followers bound the grateful beneficiaries to the Communist cause. If the Nationalist armies drove the Communists out of these areas, after all, they could be expected to restore the redistributed lands to their former owners, reinstituting the ancient system of exploitation. A piece of land of his own was every Chinese peasant's personal dream. Now he had something more than an ideology to fight for.

Most of the Communist party's Red Army was recruited from among this grateful peasantry. Over the next twenty years this military force distinguished itself in guerrilla warfare against both the Nationalists and the invading Japanese. Unlike the Nationalist troops, who dealt with the populace in a time-honored and oppressive manner, the Red Army was indoctrinated in the rudiments of Communist theory and instructed to deal fairly with the peasants in the areas it occupied. Those who violated these instructions were disciplined severely. Consequently, the Communist troops understood their role to be more than merely military, and their conduct tended to build good will and win popular support wherever they travelled.

Perceiving the importance of this Communist threat, Chiang K'ai-shek devoted a large portion of his limited military strength to a series of campaigns in the early 1930's aimed at exterminating Mao and his followers. For several years, these military campaigns were unsuccessful. But in 1934, the Communist forces were compelled to retreat from their rural base and to embark upon their now legendary Long March of over 6,000 miles on foot, through some of the most difficult terrain in China. Much larger and better-equipped Nationalist armies pursued them most of the way, engaging them in skirmishes almost daily. The Communist forces were decimated en route, and it is a tribute to their heroic perseverance and dedication to their cause that even a fraction of them survived this yearlong ordeal to establish new headquarters at remote Yenan in the north.*

Desperately needing a breathing space, the Chinese Communists seized upon the United Front line then advocated by the World Communist movement due to the Soviet Union's fear of Nazi Germany. The people were receptive to the theme that Chinese should not be fighting other Chinese while Japanese forces were occupying Chinese territory. Some Manchurian troops, being used to fight far from their Japanese-occupied homeland, against the Communists, refused to obey orders. When Chiang flew to their base at Sian at the end of 1936 to take charge of the situation, they kidnapped him! The details of the negotiations which ensued among representatives of the Nationalists, Communists, and mutinous troops have never been fully revealed, so it cannot be asserted positively that Chiang accepted a United Front with the Communists as the price of his release. Whatever the reasons, however, Chiang was soon freed and a United Front agreement was concluded shortly afterward. The Japanese responded by launching an all-out invasion of China, and the National government was confronted with the necessity of prosecuting a full-scale war for eight years against an opponent with vastly superior industrial and military might.

For more than half of this period, China stood alone. While Japan occupied and set up puppet regimes in the coastal areas, the Nationalists retreated to Chungking in the interior, where they stubbornly withstood both Japanese bombings and Japanese offers of generous cooperation with Chiang if only he would surrender. This was Chiang's finest hour, and his prestige hit its zenith — while his actual power fell to its nadir — as the symbol of China's indomitable will to resist Japanese aggression.

The war exacted a heavy toll from the Kuomintang and from China. Their territorial control restricted by Japan's incursions, the Nationalists

---

* The most vivid description of this march, and of the Communist movement in the 1930's, is contained in Edgar Snow, *Red Star Over China* (New York: Random House, 1938). (Reprinted in paperback by Grove Press in 1961.) This work also includes Mao Tse-tung's autobiography, as dictated to Snow.

were unable to take in enough revenue to cover military requirements. With much of the nation's production diverted to military uses, increases in demand outraced the supply of consumer goods available, an excess of paper money was printed and skyrocketing inflation resulted. The integrity of many Nationalist officials was undermined as their fixed salaries failed to keep pace with their families' survival needs. Even near the top levels of the Kuomintang hierarchy, many officials made use of inside information and control over government expenditures to enrich themselves and their families while soldiers died at the front for lack of equipment and peasants died for want of rice to keep them alive.

After the Japanese attack at Pearl Harbor brought the United States into the war at the end of 1941, both Communists and Kuomintang confidently expected that the Americans would defeat Japan in time. They began jockeying for position against one another, therefore, rather than seeking out opportunities to engage the Japanese further. The United States, however, gave first priority to defeating Hitler in Europe and viewed the Chinese theater primarily as a means of tieing up large masses of Japanese troops while American energies concentrated on Europe. The American government and people were not interested in conducting wartime military operations in ways which would give priority to the achievement of postwar political goals. They were interested rather in winning the war in the quickest way possible. Since internal dissension between Communists and Nationalists reduced China's effectiveness in fighting the Japanese, it became a goal of United States policy to seek to eliminate friction and promote cooperation between them. The United States urged the Nationalists, for example, to make American arms available to the Chinese Communist forces, in order to increase their effectiveness against the Japanese.

Working within this frame of reference, Chiang's American advisers utilized such diplomatic leverage as the extensive wartime United States aid program afforded them to induce Chiang to undertake administrative reforms calculated to improve the efficiency of Chinese armies in the field. Most important, they pressured Chiang to turn over key military commands and government posts to men more competent and more honest than the loyal party hacks then filling them, whose only real qualifications often seemed to be their personal ties to Generalissimo Chiang. But the United States was not very successful even in gaining this relatively limited objective. President Roosevelt was too afraid that China would deal separately with the Japanese, or drop out of the war entirely, to maintain pressure on Chiang in the face of determined resistance. And Chiang could scarcely have been expected to comply readily in light of the impact such reforms might have upon his own position of primacy within China.

In the end, reforms often were promised on paper, but rarely were put into practice. American disillusionment with the Nationalists was correspondingly high. Foreign visitors to Communist-held bases — located between Japanese-occupied cities and lines of communication — were uniformly impressed, in contrast, by the dedication, élan, efficiency, and mobilization of the peasantry they saw around them.

The defeat of Japan came more suddenly than anyone had expected. On August 6, 1945, the first atomic bomb was dropped on Hiroshima. On August 8, the Soviet Union declared war on Japan. A second atomic bomb hit Nagasaki the following day, and within a week Japan had surrendered. Communist forces were in a better geographic position to take advantage of this surprising turn of events than were the Nationalists. Against American advice, Chiang chose to race the Communists for control over north China and Manchuria instead of first consolidating his hold on territories closer to his wartime bases. It was over Manchuria, after all, that the war with Japan had begun.

The morale of Chiang's war-weary armies was low, while that of the Communists was high. Chiang's troops, disdainful of "collaborationists" who had lived under Japanese domination rather than withdrawing westward with the Nationalists, treated the areas they reoccupied as conquered territories rather than as liberated ones, alienating the local populations. Inflation and famine spread as the Japanese armies — which often had at least kept the people employed and eating — withdrew.

The United States provided the Nationalists with more than $2 billion in economic and military aid over the next four years, and transported over 400,000 Nationalist troops and 50,000 United States Marines to Shanghai and north China to accept the Japanese surrender. Nevertheless, the Nationalist position deteriorated steadily. Much of the military equipment provided by the United States found its way into Communist hands when Nationalist generals surrendered their armies en masse. The Communists also picked up large stores of surrendered Japanese arms left behind for them by withdrawing Soviet Russian armies.

Fearful of growing Communist strength and eager to promote a unified China capable of serving as a counterweight to Japan in postwar Asia, the United States accelerated its efforts to get the Nationalists and Communists together in a coalition government. Promises of American aid, and threats to withhold it, were employed toward this end. To United States policymakers, a coalition government appeared more attractive than what seemed to be the alternatives: (1) withdrawing American support for the Nationalists — thus, in effect acquiescing in a Communist victory; or (2) making the major commitment of American troops and resources which it was believed would be necessary in order to keep Chiang K'ai-shek's corrupt, incompetent, and unpopular regime in power. President Truman, therefore, sent to China as his personal representative General George C. Marshall — a man of ability, patience, high reputation, and unimpeachable integrity — to try to arrange a truce.

That Marshall was able to do so, even briefly, is a tribute to his personal qualities. The Kuomintang and Communist leaders had known each other for more than a generation. Each understood, as most Americans did not, the depth of the other's commitment to ultimately winning total victory and annihilating its enemies. For twenty years, they had fought one another, collaborated for tactical reasons, and renewed the struggle at opportune moments. Mao Tse-tung, the Chinese Communist leader, had participated in the Long March, and his brother, sister, and wife had been killed on his account by the Kuomintang. Other leaders on both sides could recall similar experiences. Neither group trusted the other — and with good reason. Each would enter into a coalition with the other — once again — only to the extent that the agreement promised to advance the cause of *its* eventual victory. The two parties differed, moreover, in their estimates of their relative strength. That no permanent truce or coalition government was possible in these circumstances is scarcely astonishing. General Marshall's hope was that liberal "third force" elements in Chinese politics would bridge the gap and keep Kuomintang and Communists together in a coalition by wielding the balance of power between them. But these meager third-force elements had no power base they could make use of to perform this function. They had no armies, no extensive party organization — just a few handfuls of intellectuals with good intentions.

The truce arranged by General Marshall collapsed soon after it was concluded and the climactic chapter of the Chinese civil war began. The Communists' grassroots strength and organizational competence began to tell. As the cold war dawned in Europe and American attitudes toward Communism changed, the United States turned against the idea of a Kuomintang-Communist coalition government. Now it sought to use whatever influence its aid program provided to persuade the Nationalists to introduce political and economic reforms which might have helped broaden their base of popular support — but still to no avail.

Between September, 1948 and February, 1949, the number of Nationalist men under arms fell from 2.7 million to about 1.5 million, despite continued American aid. By October of 1949, the Communists had captured the ancient capital of Peking and from it announced the formation of the Central People's Government of the People's Republic of China. Three months later the Kuomintang forces had been driven from the mainland entirely, in disorganized and demoralized retreat to their last refuge on the island of Taiwan (Formosa), one hundred miles southeast of the mainland. A quarter of mankind had come under Communist rule.

❧ CASE
STUDY   *UNITED STATES AID TO BRAZIL*

In both area and population, Brazil is the largest nation in Latin America. It is also one of the poorest. Brazil's infant mortality rate is the highest, and the percentage of its population in school the lowest, in South America. Only Bolivia, among South American states, has a lower per capita income. In the 1967 fiscal year, Brazil was one of the twenty nations in which over 90 per cent of United States economic aid was concentrated.

The administration witness quoted in this case study is Lincoln Gordon, then Assistant Secretary of State for Inter-American Affairs and United States Coordinator of the Alliance for Progress, and now President of Johns Hopkins University. The questioners are Representatives Otto E. Passman (D., La.), chairman of the subcommittee, and Silvio O. Conte (R., Mass.).

In the months following these hearings, President Humberto Castelo Branco made use of the emergency powers granted him to deprive a number of opposition deputies of their seats in Brazil's legislature. But the direct popular elections promised for November, 1966, were held on schedule, income tax collections continued to increase, and the government's budget deficits continued to be reduced. In March, 1967, having been chosen in an election in which he was the only authorized candidate, Arthur Costa e Silva succeeded Castelo Branco as President.[30]

In the United States, meanwhile, President Johnson's request for about $3.4 billion in military and economic aid was cut by the Congress to $2.9 billion, the lowest aid appropriation in ten years. In addition, the distribution of surplus foods to countries trading with North Vietnam or Cuba was prohibited.

1. Are you convinced, from Assistant Secretary Gordon's testimony, that American aid to Brazil has been worthwhile? Why or why not? If you were a member of Congressman Passman's subcommittee, would you vote to continue aid to Brazil, or to reduce or eliminate it? Defend your position.

2. Secretary Gordon and Congressman Passman agree that stable and democratic government for Brazil should be among the principal aims of United States policy toward that country. But what if these goals prove incompatible? If the United States must choose *between* democracy and stability, which of these should receive first priority? Why?

3. If you were the State Department official assigned to explain to Congressman Passman's subcommittee why United States aid to Brazil

---

[30] For background on Brazil, see Celso Furtado, "Brazil: What Kind of Revolution?" *Foreign Affairs* (April, 1963), pp. 526–536; and Hilgard O'Reilly Sternberg, "Brazil: Complex Giant," *ibid.* (January, 1965), pp. 291–311.

should be continued, how would you present your case. Outline briefly the main arguments you would make. In what ways, if any, would your presentation differ from Secretary Gordon's? Why?

FOREIGN OPERATIONS SUBCOMMITTEE OF THE HOUSE COMMITTEE ON APPROPRIATIONS

MR. PASSMAN. One of the goals of the Alliance for Progress, and a noble one if I recall correctly, was democratic and stable governments in Latin America. Is that correct?

MR. GORDON. Yes.

MR. PASSMAN. How can you reconcile that goal with President Branco's assumption of dictatorial policies in that he abolished all existing political parties, declared unto himself the power to declare a state of siege for up to 180 days, gave the federal government power to intervene in the states, gave himself power to oust federal and local legislators, and authority to suspend political rights of any citizen for 10 years, and also abolished direct election of the President by the people?

If that is democratic, I am a monkey up a tree.

MR. GORDON. That is a situation I know about intimately, having served in Brazil as Ambassador during the revolution in 1964 and during the period up to the end of February of this year.

Unfortunately, in the last year or so of the Goulart administration the President himself appeared to be determined on a course of subversion of the country's institutions with Communist support.

On March 31 a revolution broke out against him. It turned out to be a bloodless revolution. It deposed him from power in 48 hours.

This revolution was led by the army officer corps, but also had the support of 20 out of the 22 governors in the states of the country and the great mass of the civilian public opinion. This is why it was bloodless.

The congress then elected a few days later Gen. Castelo Branco to serve out the remainder of the term which originally had been the term of Janio L. Quadros, elected in 1960 and who resigned after 8 months in office, leading to a very difficult situation, a political crisis which lasted until that revolution.

The revolutionary government did assume certain arbitrary powers at the very beginning. They were not fully arbitrary powers. They did include

Foreign Assistance and Related Agencies: Appropriations for 1967, Hearings before the Committee on Appropriations, House of Representatives, 89th Cong., 2nd sess., 1966, pp. 655–664. Omissions are indicated by ellipses, security deletions by dashes. Footnotes, in brackets, have been added.

the power to deprive individuals of their political rights for up to 10 years, and that was in fact applied to some 375 individuals.

The President and the leaders of the new government then undertook an extremely difficult program for economic stabilization, development, and reform which they have been working at very hard in the subsequent 2 years.

In October of last year there were direct elections for the governors of the 11 States. Two of the major states of the 11 had opposition candidates elected and a so-called hard line group, partly military and partly civilian, sought to prevent those elected governors from being installed.

This led to another major political crisis in October, and at that point the President did assume the extra arbitrary powers summarized in the question you asked me.

Those powers, however, everybody exercised with very great moderation, and the purpose of the regime has been to return to full constitutional government as soon as possible. . . .

The abolition of the old political parties had been foreseen in legislation passed by the congress there last July because it was felt that a system with 15 political parties is too many. In fact the old political parties are being replaced by two new parties, really coalitions of the old forces, so that while certain quite arbitrary and exceptional powers were assumed and used with moderation, nonetheless dictatorial powers have not been assumed, congress has not been abolished, criticism in the press remains free.

There is a strong opposition political party, and political life remains very lively. There is no single party system as exists in dictatorships and there is no purpose on the part of the president to keep himself in office, which is typical of dictators.

This is a mixed situation in which, because of the chaotic years which preceded the revolution, arbitrary and exceptional powers have been assumed and, as I say, exercised up to a certain point, but with a purpose of restoring the system to constitutional democracy.

MR. PASSMAN. In effect, you are saying, "I will not shoot you but I have a loaded pistol. I want you to give me the right to, just in case I want to."

I just want to be factual about this. I have been sitting in this chair 14 years. It has been my honor to chair this committee for 12 years.

In reality there is nothing ever wrong with a program from your side of the table. Anything that happens, Mr. Ambassador, always has a good reason.

All I want to know is whether this is true.

I believe we established as one of our goals for the Alliance for Progress in Brazil and in Latin America as a whole, democratic and stable government. We hoped for and worked for that goal. However, it is true that today the President is President Branco?

MR. GORDON. Castelo Branco; yes.

MR. PASSMAN. Under his declaration, if carried through to the ultimate, it would be a complete dictatorship.

MR. GORDON. If the powers were used to the full extent, that is true.

MR. PASSMAN. Of course, that is what we are interested in, if they are used.

He has a right to use them under this proclamation, and we are supporting his government.

Now the question would be, and I think this is being completely fair, how long has there been a Brazil?

MR. GORDON. Brazil became an independent government on September 7, 1822.

MR. PASSMAN. We became an independent country in terms of the Constitution in 1789.

MR. GORDON. 1776.

MR. PASSMAN. Or 1789 when the Constitution was adopted.

MR. GORDON. The Constitution in 1789 but independence in 1776.

MR. PASSMAN. I am talking about the Constitution. That was the kickoff for the great progress we made.

What did they have in Brazil before they became an independent nation?

MR. GORDON. It was a colony of Portugal before it became independent.

MR. PASSMAN. You had a civilization there?

MR. GORDON. For several hundred years.

MR. PASSMAN. So you were dealing with a civilization which has been up and down for thousands of years, we might say.

MR. GORDON. I would say Brazil was —

MR. PASSMAN. For many centuries.

MR. GORDON. Brazil was discovered in 1500 by a Portuguese sailor.

MR. PASSMAN. 1500. Let us use that date. What did he find?

MR. GORDON. A handful of not very civilized Indians.

MR. PASSMAN. But it has been there for centuries.

MR. GORDON. Certainly.

MR. PASSMAN. They have had these problems for hundreds of years and they will have them long after we are dust.

What have we given to Brazil since the inception of this program from all spigots? . . .

MR. GORDON. Economic and military?

MR. PASSMAN. Yes; all spigots of foreign aid.

MR. GORDON. Since 1946, $2,788,300,000, including AID loans and grants, Export-Import Bank loans, Public Law 480 and military aid.

MR. PASSMAN. Let me repeat that figure for emphasis — $2,788,300,000?

MR. GORDON. That is right.

MR. PASSMAN. Is the Government any more stable now than before we started giving them this almost $3 billion in aid?

MR. GORDON. Indeed they are.

MR. PASSMAN. They have a complete dictatorship now, if the President wants to exercise his powers, and you have filled the till and he has something to maintain the dictatorship on. Is that a fair statement?

MR. GORDON. I respectfully must disagree entirely with that statement.

MR. PASSMAN. Certainly I expect you to, but you cannot change the facts.

MR. GORDON. Sir, that is not an accurate characterization of the present situation.

MR. PASSMAN. According to your interpretation. One man, Branco, has the authority under his declaration to be a dictator if he wants to, has he not?

MR. GORDON. He does not want to.

MR. PASSMAN. How do you know he does not want to?

MR. GORDON. I know from the record of his actions.

MR. PASSMAN. Does he have the right under his declaration of power to do the things that I read into the record?

MR. GORDON. Yes.

MR. PASSMAN. Is that not just as close to a dictatorship as you can get, if he carried it out, if he used his authority?

MR. GORDON. If he used the authority —

MR. PASSMAN. He asked for the right.

MR. GORDON. I have not finished my answer.

MR. PASSMAN. I know you have not. You are trying to muddle the record —

MR. GORDON. No, sir.

MR. PASSMAN (continuing). So we will not show that this fellow is a dictator. He has the right to be a dictator. I am thinking about the almost $3 billion we have given those people, and still they have turmoil and confusion.

MR. GORDON. They do not have turmoil and confusion, sir.

MR. PASSMAN. If this is not turmoil and confusion, I wonder what would make it.

MR. GORDON. They were threatened slightly over 2 years ago with extreme turmoil and confusion and, indeed, even the danger of a Communist capture of power, which would have been a very serious thing for the United States. The revolution, fortunately, put an end to that danger.

MR. PASSMAN. Why did the man want to take unto himself such extreme powers?

MR. GORDON. He asserted the extreme powers for the extremely nondictatorial purpose of insuring the inauguration into power of two opposition governors-elect.

MR. PASSMAN. My point is, what impression are we making upon the people if they react that way to a friendly government?

MR. GORDON. Which people?

MR. PASSMAN. The people of Brazil.

MR. GORDON. If they react how to a friendly government?

MR. PASSMAN. If they react to what you have indicated for the record about the governments they have had, and they still have Communists there, if they still have that attitude, what do you see bright about the future?

MR. GORDON. Mr. Chairman, I think the bright thing about this record of the last few years is that they reacted against an effort of the previous President and previous regime to turn Brazil into a leftwing, totalitarian dictatorship. They did not want that. They supported the revolution which prevented that from happening. Now they are trying to work themselves out of both a very severe economic and very severe political crisis. Working their way out of that, in both economic and political terms, is exactly what we have been supporting.

MR. PASSMAN. This is an awful lot of money, is it not — $2.788 billion?

MR. GORDON. Yes, it is a large amount of money.

MR. PASSMAN. You would have thought those people would be tremendously impressed with their leaders as well as with our generous nature. It just looks as if we are trying to make dollars do everything. If we are not very careful, it creates turmoil and confusion. I can only hope that someday I can share your optimism, if only briefly. I just do not believe that giving people our wealth away is accomplishing what we had hoped it would.

MR. GORDON. I would hope so, too, Mr. Chairman. I would strongly urge a firsthand visit to Brazil to see what sort of nation is there. I think you might change your view.

MR. PASSMAN. I want this program to work as well as you do, but being optimistic about these things will not accomplish for us these noble objectives, because we have given away an awful lot of money.

If you include the interest, we have given away over $150 billion of our wealth since the end of World War II, and I am still looking for our friends and I cannot find them.

MR. CONTE. Will the chairman yield?

Would you say, Mr. Ambassador, this is somewhat analogous to the situation that happened in Spain with Franco?

MR. GORDON. (Off the record.)

MR. CONTE. But he has eased up and has built up a government underneath him to take over.

MR. GORDON. ———

I think the enlightening thing about Brazil is while the so-called hardliners in the revolutionary movement thought there ought to be a period of absolute dictatorship to purge the country of these unfortunate elements that had existed in the past, it was President Castelo Branco and his supporters who resisted that because they really are democrats by instinct. They were not able, unfortunately — and they are just as unhappy about this as the chairman or anybody here — they were not able to return at once to full democratic institutions. They are maintaining the whole basis of democratic institutions and a Congress in being. It is true 40 or 50 members were expelled, but they did maintain a Congress in being.

They maintained free criticism of the government and anything else in the press. This is a very free press, indeed. I received a fair amount of criticism in it myself from time to time.

They did maintain an electoral process. It is true that they shifted the presidential election for this year from direct elections to indirect elections by the Congress, but they did not establish a dictatorship or one-party system or a controlled press or censorship or all of the other things which right after the Spanish Civil War Franco did. I think this is partly because they were fortunate enough not to have a civil war. This bloodless revolution of 48 hours on March 31 and April 1, 1964, I think really is one of the great miracles of this century.

It is a very large country in which the previous regime had been encouraging Communist infiltration and subversion in trade unions and governmental agencies, in strategic points all over the country, and trying also to get them in the noncommissioned officer ranks and even the enlisted ranks of the armed forces. In spite of that effort — and it was a systematic effort over most of the year — the structure of the nation was sufficiently solid that they rejected this and, in 48 hours, this nightmare came to an end.

In Spain, as all of us recall, in the 3 years of civil war there was frightful loss of life. It was a civil war comparable to the Mexican Civil War of 1910–14. I think Brazil is very lucky.

The arbitrary powers were assumed in October, as the chairman has mentioned, ——. The President did not like assuming them himself. ——.

He is opposed to an outright military dictatorship. This is a transitional transformation. The point I make is, the transition is headed in the right direction.

On the side of the economic program, they have been working very hard. Their self-help record is indeed one of the best in the whole hemisphere. They are doing this against an extraordinary chaotic situation, a situation in which just before the revolution there was 140 per cent per year inflation. We talk about inflation in this country. We have no idea what inflation is by standards of that kind.

MR. CONTE. It is down to about 45 per cent now?

MR. GORDON. Last year they got it down to 45 per cent. Their hope this year is to get it down further, and sometime during the course of next year to get it completely under control. This is a very difficult exercise.*

* [In the first months of 1967, Brazil's rate of inflation remained close to 40 per cent per year.]

MR. PASSMAN. Brazil had a duly and legally elected President who served for 8 months and quit.

MR. GORDON. Right.

MR. PASSMAN. On account of the difficulties in the country. You do not agree or disagree?

MR. GORDON. No; I am sorry. I do disagree on that.

MR. PASSMAN. Anyway, the Vice President, duly and legally elected under the constitution, moved up to the Presidency, did he not?

MR. GORDON. Yes.

MR. PASSMAN. Were we supporting the original President?

MR. GORDON. Yes.

MR. PASSMAN. We were supporting the Vice President?

MR. GORDON. Yes.

MR. PASSMAN. Then they had a coup and threw the Vice President out.

MR. GORDON. Yes.

MR. PASSMAN. This man came in on the basis of being selected by the legislature.

MR. GORDON. That is right, in accordance with the constitution.

MR. PASSMAN. In accordance with the constitution. I hastily add that.

That is a clear indication that the people themselves are not satisfied with what they have, our wealth being poured in notwithstanding.

MR. GORDON. No, sir.

MR. PASSMAN. Those are my observations. I have been sitting over here seeing these things pop up. Sometimes we have four or five governments in a country over a period of a year or two. We support each one. We do not fail to support any of them.

I am thinking about stability, a democratic government whereby the things that we so much desire can be brought to fruition. It does not appear that those things are happening. Glossing over these facts and being an optimist and making it look good does not add up, because in Brazil the Vice President, for what reasons, I do not know, moved up, but was overthrown by a coup, and now you have another man serving as President.

What is the possibility of a good, free election in Brazil at this time?

MR. GORDON. The President is to be elected by the Congress. That is an indirect election. Then the Congress is to be elected by the people.

MR. PASSMAN. Previously, all Presidents were elected by the Congress?

MR. GORDON. No.

MR. PASSMAN. How many members are there in the Congress?

MR. GORDON. At the present time, there are 409 members of the lower house, and 66 senators, 3 each from 22 States.

MR. PASSMAN. There is no such thing as a lower House. You ought to know that, being a constitutionalist.

MR. GORDON. A chamber of deputies.

MR. PASSMAN. There is no such thing as a lower House. That term had only to do with the Congress when they were meeting in Philadelphia. The House Members being the elected Members, and the Senators being appointed, in effect, by the Governors, the Senators had to walk up the steps and meet in the attic, while the elected Members took the lower chamber. It was their location in the building which resulted in their becoming the lower and upper chambers.

Some of our great constitutional experts confuse themselves and do not recognize that under the Constitution, the House of Representatives is actually the superior body, and that the upper and lower bodies terms has [sic] only to do with where they met when the Congress was meeting in Philadelphia.

MR. GORDON. I beg your pardon, Mr. Chairman.

MR. PASSMAN. Do not beg my pardon.

MR. GORDON. I was only translating from the Portuguese.

MR. PASSMAN. And also from what the press picks up in this country. I am a great defender of the House of Representatives.

MR. GORDON. I think I have said all that need be said about the Brazilian situation. I will be glad to answer your questions.

MR. PASSMAN. Then I will ask some questions.

MR. GORDON. Let me make a comment in general. There is no subject which is of more concern to us in the executive branch or to me in my particular job than political stability in Latin America.

MR. PASSMAN. We all hope for it.

MR. GORDON. I do not think I am just an ignorant optimist.

MR. PASSMAN. I did not say you were an ignorant optimist. I said you were an optimist. If you want to add to that, that is your privilege. I had not observed you as being that way. I do not think you ought to assign yourself that title.

MR. GORDON. All right. I was not planning to. I do not think that I have an unfounded optimism on this particular subject. It is a subject of great concern. Before I went before the Senate Foreign Relations Committee for confirmation hearings, I asked for the record, and the record shows that in the last 36 years there have been 106 unconstitutional changes of regime in Latin America. This is an average of three a year. That is a very, very high figure, indeed. Certainly it is one of the purposes of the Alliance for Progress to help bring about conditions of political stability as well as economic developments and social progress. That is a continuing process.

The record in the last couple of years has been better. Indeed, the record in the last few months has been unusually good, because in two or three countries where there was great concern about political stability, elections have come off peacefully and it looks as if the elected government will successfully be installed in office.

I cite the cases of Guatemala and Colombia specifically. This is a trend we hope to encourage.

In Brazil, the record over the 140 years since independence has in fact been one of greater stability than in most of Latin America.

Mr. Passman. They have had more turmoil in recent years than in previous history.

Mr. Gordon. They have had much more in the last 20 years.

Mr. Passman. That is since the aid program started — coincidentally, of course.

Mr. Gordon. It certainly has absolutely nothing to do whatever ——

Mr. Passman. According to your interpretation.

Mr. Gordon. According to my interpretation. I think this is one situation I know fairly intimately.

Mr. Passman. I am sure you do, but I am not completely unfamiliar about it myself, either.

Mr. Gordon. No, I am not suggesting that you are. I am only saying that having just come back from 4½ years of full-time work in Brazil and having known the country for some years before that, and knowing its political history very well, I think I understand the elements which have led to the relative political instability of this postwar period.

What happened in the last 4 years was partly a historical tragedy. You were commenting on the resignation of President Quadros. ——. The Vice President had been elected by a very small majority in a three-cornered race. He had a background which was considered suspicious by many people in both civilian and military life. He was at that time just finishing a visit to Communist China and he was out in Asia at the time the President quit.

Indeed, the then military ministers in Brazil wanted to keep him from coming back. There was a 2-week political crisis in the fall of 1961 about his installation. It was not a simple accession of an elected Vice President to replace a President who had resigned. It was much more complex than that.

Indeed, they altered the Constitution to institute a parliamentary system. The Vice President was allowed back. For a year or so, there was moderate government. He visited the United States, where he spoke before this Congress in April 1962, and spoke in quite moderate terms. He then began to give signs of dictatorial ambitions of his own, based in this case on an extreme leftwing power base, including Communists and certain strategically placed trade unionists. This led to an increasingly critical situation.

The forces that sought to oppose him in the first instance did not want to depose him. They wanted to constrain him. They wanted to keep him on the constitutional rails. By March of 1964, that proved impossible in their view — and they moved at the end of that month actually to remove him by force.

The problem of picking up the pieces from this economic and political crisis and period of chaos has been an extraordinarily difficult one. I do not think we should ever forget that this is a country of 85 million people today, with a very rapid population increase, which represents 35 per cent of the area and population and resources of Latin America, and its fate, therefore, is of the very greatest interest to us, to this hemisphere as a whole, and to the world as a whole. We certainly have a great interest in the political stability in Brazil.

The Brazilian economy has developed a great deal during the post-war period, and it has been helped a great deal in that by the $2.8 billion worth of assistance received from us. The expansion of the steel industry, the automotive industry, the electrical equipment industry, shipbuilding industry, roads, powerplants, agricultural development — all of these things have in one way or another benefited from our assistance.

These are the things which I believe made it possible for Brazil to assert itself against President Goulart's dictatorial ambitions in 1964. So, far from contributing to the instability, I would say that we have contributed to such stability as Brazil enjoys, and I am optimistic about the future.

MR. PASSMAN. Thank you, Mr. Ambassador. We now have a record full of nice statements and pretty words. I know you feel that way.

The record follows, nevertheless, that Brazil had a President who served 8 months of a duly elected term and stepped down for reasons none of us know. A Vice President, duly elected, moved up under the Constitution, and he went out with a coup.

Now a President is serving, elected by the Congress. Whoever his successor may be, in all probability he likewise will be elected by the Congress and not by the people.

MR. GORDON. That is right.

MR. PASSMAN. I only hope that we can succeed in our objectives, because we are sincere about what we are trying to do. That I will concede. It follows, nevertheless, whether there is any relationship or not — you have a right to your opinion and I have a right to my opinion — we had a more stable Brazil before we started pouring vast sums into the country.

It may have been worse if we had not given them these sums, but I have always argued that we are trying to make dollars do things that dollars were never intended to do. I have said this before and I will say again that we are check grabbers in America. We all seem to have that in our system. We go out with a friend and if we are not very careful, if we have had one too many, we create a scene trying to grab the check.

I guess it is because we are trying to impress people who may be observing. We grab the check. We just think if we give people our wealth and spend our money, we can correct all evils and make a tremendous impression.

I just do not subscribe to that philosophy.

MR. GORDON. Mr. Chairman, could I add one figure for the record. During the same 20-year period, 1946 to 1965, to which the $2.788-billion figure referred, Brazil has repaid to the United States in repayments and interest $929 million.

MR. PASSMAN. That is good. I had a brother one time who dropped a nickel through a big crack in the floor of the old hog house. They claimed that rattlesnakes were around the house, so he was afraid to go under. We wanted something to make it worthwhile, so he borrowed a quarter from my sister and dropped that through the crack. Thirty cents was worth going after, but not the nickel.

I guess Brazil does not mind paying something back if they are going to get more. The net result is to bring it down to slightly under $2 billion. I hope we succeed in our objectives. . . .

Chapter Ten

THE CHALLENGE
OF COMMUNISM

In 1955 — thirty-eight years after the Communist victory in Russia, six years after the Communist victory in China, and less than two years after some 25,000 Americans were killed in combat against Communist forces in the Korean War — less than one-third of a national sample of adult Americans could identify correctly the name Karl Marx.[1] We have repeated in an earlier chapter the story of an American swearing his readiness to die for the Monroe Doctrine while confessing humbly that he does not know what it is. The attitude of many Americans today toward communism is quite literally the same: they are ready to die, if need be, to defend their country against it. But they have not been moved, apparently, to find out what communism is and what impact it has on the international environment with which their country's leaders must deal.

Two of the world's most powerful national states, and well over a billion of its people, are governed today by regimes which profess their adherence to Communist ideology. Communist parties, moreover, constitute potent political forces in many other countries where they have not won governmental power. Communism is a significant force in the contemporary world both as a potential *shaper* and as an *instrument* of the policies of these Communist nations and parties.

Communism also provides a *language* of discourse which the leaders of Communist governments and parties customarily use in communicating with one another and with non-Communist governments and peoples. For this reason, in the summary of major Communist concepts which follows, we will pay special attention to terminology. An effort will be made, in particular, to clarify words and phrases used by Communists to convey mean-

[1] This was noted — and footnoted — in Chapter Seven.

424

ings very different from those commonly assigned them in the West. And, in the case study in this chapter, the reader will be asked to try his hand at unraveling the meaning of Soviet and Chinese policy statements couched in this terminology. Anyone who cannot "translate" even the most elementary terms in the Communist vocabulary is wholly at the mercy of those who would interpret them for him and is thus in a poor position to form independent judgments on many of the great foreign policy issues of the day.

We can gain a deeper insight into Communist ways of viewing the world if we suspend our critical faculties for a while and try our best to see things as Communists see them. It would not be very hard to turn this chapter into an impassioned refutation of Communist theory, challenging each Communist formulation as it is explained, pointing out weaknesses and inconsistencies in Communist theory and emphasizing the disparities between theory and practice.[2] Such an approach, however, would be likely to strengthen our prejudices more than our understanding. Instead, let us examine some of the most serious weaknesses of Communist theory at the start, and then proceed to view this theory mainly through Communist eyes in the pages that follow.

First, communism lays false claim to being scientific. Marxism is grounded in historical observation. But when events have failed to confirm — have even seemed to contradict — Marxist hypotheses, Communists have not, as scientific method requires, acknowledged the contradiction and modified their theory accordingly. They have rather adopted the counterscientific methods of interpreting events to fit their theory, or of revising their theory by interpretation while insisting it to have been right all along. To claim both immutable conclusions and scientific method is already a contradiction — because the essence of scientific method as understood in the West is that conclusions must remain open to change in the light of additional evidence.

Although Marx envisaged Communist revolutions first in the most advanced industrial nations, they have in fact taken place only in the least developed nations of the world (with the exception of a few Eastern European neighbors of the Soviet Union where communism was imposed largely by external pressure rather than by internal revolt). Though Marx postulated that the development of capitalism would lead to a reduction in the size of the middle class, that class has grown rather than dwindled in the most advanced industrial nations. And, unforeseen by Marx, new forms of property ownership have developed — corporate shareholding most prominent among them — which greatly reduce the utility of employing property

[2] An excellent capsule summary and rebuttal of the main tenets of communism can be found in W. W. Rostow, *The Stages of Economic Growth: A Non-Communist Manifesto* (New York: Cambridge University Press, 1960), chap. 10. A useful summary of Communist doctrine and Soviet practice is Alfred G. Meyer, *Communism* (New York: Random House, 1960). And a good short selection of the basic writings of communism is contained in Carl Cohen (ed.), *Communism, Fascism, and Democracy* (New York: Random House, 1962).

ownership as a key index of wealth and status. If communism were genuinely scientific, accounting for these unanticipated developments would have
occasioned major efforts to rethink and revise Marx's hypotheses. Instead
they produced, in Lenin's theory of imperialism, a shallow (though brilliant) rationalization designed to prove that the theories which had failed so
signally to predict accurately the trend of events were nevertheless eternally
true and valid. Thus, though Communist leaders have been willing to revise
their theories in important respects in response to practical needs, they have
refused to consider the possibility that the entire Marxist frame of reference
may itself be at fault.

The fundamentals of Marxism, then, may be interpreted — but not questioned. For authoritative interpretations all Communist movements have
relied, in the end, on a self-appointed elite to discriminate between truth
and falsehood, right and wrong. It is a situation most disconcerting to an
outsider in search of a way to learn the truth. If leading Communists like
Lenin and Plekhanov, Stalin and Trotsky, Khrushchev and Mao could disagree sharply as to the meaning of the doctrine they espoused, how is a poor
outsider to know which is the true prophet of the true way? If men of such
power, importance, and political acumen can fail to understand communism
correctly, what assurance can *we* have that our interpretation of the doctrine
— or our choice of interpreters to guide us — will turn out to be correct?
And how can we be sure that it is not, say, the Fascists — who make similar
claims to holding a monopoly on truth — rather than the Communists, who
really have found the true way?

It is vital that our interpretation *be* correct, moreover, for on the basis of
it communism asks us to be willing to sacrifice our own lives and those of
others — even of whole generations of humanity. To its purposes, also, we
are required to subordinate any other values we may have been taught to
cherish — family life, patriotism, honor, religion, and more. For communism
— like laissez faire capitalism — accepts human suffering in the short run as
the necessary price of benefits in the long run. It operates on the dual pre-
sumption that the end justifies the means and that good ends can be
brought into being by whatever means prove expedient. Its ultimate goal —
a society in which human beings can realize their full potential — suggests
that it begins by assuming human welfare and self-realization as its criteria
of value. But, somewhere along the way, the revolution needed to bring this
society into being appears to become the predominant goal, for no consideration seems to be given to the human costs this revolution entails. In
most of the Communist classics, curiously enough (and particularly in the
works of Lenin), *tactical* goals and considerations receive much more attention than descriptions or explanations of the ultimate goal.[3]

[3] Thus, a content analysis of Stalin's *History of the Communist Party of the Soviet
Union (Bolshevik)* by Howard Wriggins showed that "Only 6 per cent of a total of more

In addition, Marxism — again like the theory of laissez faire capitalism — overemphasizes the importance of economic goals and of economic influences on human behavior. Initially, this emphasis was a useful corrective to the general tendency to fail to perceive the full impact of economic forms on political and social life. However, important as material goals and motivations are, they are not the be-all and end-all of man's existence. We have all seen for ourselves many conspicuous examples of individuals and groups subordinating their economic interests to other goals which were more important to them — conceptions of honor, religious beliefs, impulses to power, irrational personality needs, public service, opportunities for self-realization.

At the lowest levels of subsistence, of course, material goals — of necessity — assume a greater importance. But once men have achieved a modicum of material comfort — let alone affluence — they may prove quite ready to sacrifice additional material gains for the sake of nonmaterial purposes — like the actor who turns down a million dollar part in a movie to work in an off-Broadway play at Equity minimum wages, the girl who chooses to marry the less economically promising of her suitors because she loves him, or the corporation lawyer who accepts one-tenth of what he is capable of earning in private practice in order to serve his government. Perhaps this is why communism has been so much more successful in the world's poorest countries than in the industrially advanced countries where Marx expected it to take hold first.

Marx compounded this overemphasis on economics by dividing men into analytical categories (classes) for the sake of analysis, and then treating these categories as though they described the whole range of the human beings they represented. Analytical constructs are extremely useful, but they can lead to dangerous conclusions in the hands of those who forget their limitations. A simple dichotomy of mankind into two classes based on each man's relationship to the means of production is a construct with serious limitations indeed.

FUNDAMENTALS OF MARXISM

Karl Marx (1818–1883) lived at a time when the appalling human costs of the industrial revolution in Britain and parts of Europe had become apparent. Men, women, and children worked in the factories each day, performing monotonous repetitive tasks to the point of utter exhaustion, only to return each night to overcrowded, vermin-infested homes in the city slums. These were the lucky ones, for others were not working and not eating. Free pub-

than 2,000 references to the party and its activities describe it as achieving non-power goals." The comparable percentage of goal-oriented references in Lenin's *Left-Wing Communism* and *What Is to Be Done?* is even lower. Gabriel Almond, *The Appeals of Communism* (Princeton, N.J.: Princeton University Press, 1954), pp. 22 and 27–28.

lic education was not provided for these hapless people, living always at the brink of starvation, and a normal family life was nearly impossible.[4]

What had brought humanity to such a state? Soon Social Darwinists, particularly in the United States, would argue that, in one sense at least, men got what they deserved and deserved what they got; that this unfortunate human suffering was an indispensable part of a regrettable but necessary process of natural selection which enabled the competent to flourish and left the inept to their fate as the price of the progress of the race. The system itself may have been unfair, but it was efficient. The sufferings it produced reflected not its own weakness, but the inferiority of the sufferers.

Marx came up with a more incisive analysis. It was not human inadequacy that produced impoverishment, but impoverishment that produced human inadequacy. Under the industrial system, the whole organization of society contrived to keep the poor worker in his unhappy place. All items of value were produced by his labors — yet he received little of value in return. The capitalist system required him to sell his labor for money, as though human labor were a mere commodity. The capitalist factory owner did not return to him the full fruit of his labors, but only so much, in wages, as the market for the commodity of human labor required. Usually, this was not much more — and sometimes it was less — than the worker needed merely to remain alive in order to return to work the next day. The difference between the real value of the worker's labors and the meager wages paid him — this surplus value — was, to put it bluntly, stolen from him by his employer and usually reinvested in more machinery which could be used for exploiting additional surplus value from more workers.[5]

What determined who did the exploiting and who the suffering was not the virtue of the men concerned but their *relationship to the means of production*. Men could be divided into two *classes* on the basis of this relationship. Those who *owned* the means of production were *bourgeois* capitalists — exploiters by definition, since the exploitation of human labor was the very essence of the capitalist system. Those who did not own the means of production and who sold their labor to others for wages constituted *the proletariat* — the exploited. Clearly, the interests of these two classes were diametrically opposed.

---

[4] For an absorbing and enlightening account of the evolution of the basic ideas of communism, and for accounts of the lives of Marx, Engels, Lenin, Trotsky, and other Communist leaders, see Edmund Wilson, *To the Finland Station* (Garden City, N.Y.: Doubleday, 1940).

[5] Marx thus adopted a *labor theory of value*, maintaining that the value of an article was determined by the value of the labor which produced it, not, as laissez faire theory maintains, by the result of the market forces of supply and demand. Such a theory of value does not consider capital investment and entrepreneurship — apart from the labor that goes into *these* — as making a real contribution to the value of a product. Profits, then, are not a legitimate return on investment and entrepreneurship, but, by definition, the result of exploitation of the worker.

In order to perpetuate this system which enabled them to flourish and enjoy unheard of luxury while the masses starved, the bourgeoisie required a special instrument of oppression, known as the *state*. Far from being an impartial arbiter of the class struggle, the state was nothing other than the instrument by which the capitalist exploiters kept their victims in their place. The fundamental duty of the police was to defend the property rights of the rich. But what rights had the poor workers besides the right to continue to be exploited? In some capitalist countries, like England, politics might be ostensibly democratic. But with child labor, and without free public education, there was obviously no opportunity for the children of the workers to advance themselves. Property holding was generally a prerequisite to the "right" to vote. Discrimination of every kind against the lower classes was common. The laws were drawn to protect the propertied and administered toward the same end.

The principal political question in such a society clearly centered upon the antagonism between the two classes. The true nature of any political party then, would be known only by the position it took on this great question. Did it represent the interests of the capitalists or of the workers, of the oppressors or of the oppressed? A *political party* was nothing but the political instrument of an economic class. In a capitalist system, it must serve either the proletariat or the bourgeoisie. Differences between bourgeois parties reflecting merely the personal interests of various sections of the bourgeoisie were insignificant and diversionary from the point of view of the proletariat.[6] So too, bourgeois religion, bourgeois ideologies, and bourgeois morality were merely diversions — opiates designed to distract the attention of the workers from the real and burning issue of class antagonisms and to reconcile them to their awful fate.

Fortunately, however, this system could not endure. From the great German philosopher Georg Hegel, Marx had absorbed and adapted a world view of some profundity, which saw history as developing through a *dialectic* process. Each idea, or *thesis,* believed Hegel as an idealist, creates its own opposite, or *antithesis.* Through conflict between these opposites, the *contradiction* is resolved in a new *synthesis* combining elements of both. This synthesis becomes the starting point (thesis) of a repetition of this process. In this way, historical development takes place.

[6] The 1961 Program of the Communist Party of the Soviet Union dealt with the question of "bourgeois democracy" in this way: "The bourgeoisie gives extensive publicity to the allegedly democratic nature of its election laws, singing special praise to its multiparty system and the possibility of nominating many candidates. In reality, however, the monopolists deprive the masses of the opportunity to express their will and elect genuine champions of their interests. Being in control of such potent means as capital, the press, radio, cinema, television, and using their henchmen in the trade unions and other mass organizations, they mislead the masses and impose their own candidates on the electorate. The different bourgeois parties are usually no more than different factions of the ruling bourgeoisie."

Marx, however, was not an idealist, but a materialist. He believed that theory must be grounded not in a vague conception of idea-essences, like Hegel's, but in observable historic realities. He therefore applied the dialectic process to the recorded events of human history. (Thus Marx's philosophy is often referred to as *dialectical materialism*.)

The key to understanding any given period of history, Marx noted, was to observe its *mode of production,* that is, its organization for the production of material wealth. For political, legal, religious, philosophical, and social institutions are merely a superstructure designed to complement and support that mode of production. Classes can then be distinguished on the basis of the relationship of men to this mode of production. And the dialectic process operates through the conflict between these classes. Thus Marx wrote in the Communist Manifesto, in collaboration with his friend and cotheorist, Friedrich Engels:

> The history of all hitherto existing society is the history of class struggles.
>
> Freeman and slave, patrician and plebeian, lord and serf, guildmaster and journeyman, in a word, oppressor and oppressed, stood in constant opposition to one another, carried on an uninterrupted, now hidden, now open fight, a fight that each time ended, either in a revolutionary reconstitution of society at large, or in the common ruin of the contending classes. . . .
>
> The modern bourgeoisie is itself the product of a long course of development, of a series of revolutions in the modes of production and exchange. . . .
>
> But not only has the bourgeoisie forged the weapons that bring death to itself; it has also called into existence the men who are to wield those weapons — the modern working class — the proletarians. . . .
>
> The lower strata of the middle class — the small tradespeople, shopkeepers, and retired tradesmen generally, the handicraftsmen and peasants — all these sink gradually into the proletariat, partly because their diminutive capital does not suffice for the scale on which modern industry is carried on, and is swamped in the competition with the large capitalists, partly because their specialized skill is rendered worthless by new methods of production. Thus the proletariat is recruited from all classes of the population. . . .
>
> But with the development of industry the proletariat not only increases in number; it becomes concentrated in greater masses, its strength grows, and it feels that strength more. . . . The growing competition among the bourgeois, and the resulting commercial crises, make the wages of the workers ever more fluctuating. The unceasing improvement of machinery, ever more rapidly developing, makes their livelihood more and more precarious; the collisions between individual workmen and individual bourgeois take more and more the character of collisions between two classes. Thereupon the workers begin to form combinations

(trade unions) against the bourgeoisie; they club together in order to keep up the rate of wages; they found permanent associations in order to make provision beforehand for these occasional revolts. Here and there the contest breaks out into riots. . . .

Altogether, collisions between the classes of the old society further the course of the development of the proletariat in many ways. The bourgeoisie finds itself involved in a constant battle. At first with the aristocracy; later on, with those portions of the bourgeoisie itself whose interests have become antagonistic to the progress of industry; at all times with the bourgeoisie of foreign countries. In all these battles it sees itself compelled to appeal to the proletariat, to ask for its help, and thus, to drag it into the political arena. The bourgeoisie itself, therefore, supplies the proletariat with its own elements of political and general education, in other words, it furnishes the proletariat with weapons for fighting the bourgeoisie. . . .

Finally, in times when the class struggle nears the decisive hour, the process of dissolution going on within the ruling class, in fact within the whole range of the old society, assumes such a violent, glaring character, that a small section of the ruling class cuts itself adrift and joins the revolutionary class, the class that holds the future in its hands. . . . in particular, a portion of the bourgeois ideologists, who have raised themselves to the level of comprehending theoretically the historical movement as a whole. . . .

The Communists . . . are on the one hand, practically, the most advanced and resolute section of the working class parties of every country, that section which pushes forward all others; on the other hand, theoretically, they have over the great mass of the proletariat the advantage of clearly understanding the line of march, the conditions, and the ultimate general results of the proletarian movement. . . .

The Communists disdain to conceal their views and aims. They openly declare that their ends can be attained only by the forcible overthrow of all existing social conditions. Let the ruling classes tremble at a Communist revolution. The proletarians have nothing to lose but their chains. They have a world to win.

Workingmen of all countries, unite!

The proletarian revolution would have to be carried out by force of arms, not because the Communists wanted it that way, but because they felt certain that their opponents, the bourgeoisie, would not surrender their privileged position without a fight. Since the proletariat so outnumbered the capitalists, the latter would have no chance to maintain their position without the use of force — wielded, presumably, by their usual agent of oppression, the bourgeois state. But the capitalists' effort to stop the progress of history itself was obviously foredoomed. In the end, the proletariat would triumph. It would seize control of the means of production in the name of the workers and inaugurate a new epoch. By changing the relationship of men to the means of production, it would abolish classes and the conflicts between them. In the new Communist society, for the first time in history — at least since primitive times — the relationship of all men to the means of production would be the same. A classless society would be created — and with it a society free from the major historical sources of conflicts among men. The alienation of men from the products of their labors, the exploitation, oppression, and suffering characteristic of the capitalist system, would be ended, and a new age of abundance and self-realization for all men would be attained.

This new age could not be expected to come into being, however, immediately upon the triumph of the proletariat. The residual effects of capitalism — particularly the habits of bourgeois thought and morality ingrained in those raised in bourgeois society — made necessary first a period of transition of uncertain duration. During this period, the working class would be required to create a state, or repressive instrument, of its own, to hold down its class enemies and begin the process of building the new Communist society.

(This transitional society is usually referred to by the Communists as *Socialist,* and should not be confused with the democratic socialism advocated by many individuals and groups — such as the British Labor party — in the West. To the Communists, democratic socialism is not true socialism at all, but a brand of opportunist *reformism,* which has "sold out" the true interests of the working class to gain acceptance by the bourgeoisie. The nations we refer to now as "Communist" ordinarily speak of themselves as "Socialist" societies, since none claims yet to have emerged from this transitional stage. The 1961 Communist Party Program, however, held out to the people of the Soviet Union the prospect that the stage of true communism will be realized "in the main," by 1980.)

Politically, the transitional stage is characterized by the rule of a *people's democratic dictatorship.* That is, the masses of the people themselves enjoy democracy, but maintain a dictatorship over their class enemies. Joseph Stalin, in *The Foundations of Leninism,* described it precisely:

> The state is a machine in the hands of the ruling class for suppressing the resistance of its enemies. *In this respect* the dictatorship of the proletariat does not differ essentially from the dictatorship of any other class, for the proletarian state is a machine for the suppression of the bourgeoisie. But there is one *substantial* difference. This difference consists in the fact that all hitherto existing class states have been dictatorships of an exploiting minority over the exploited majority, whereas the dictatorship of the proletariat is the dictatorship of the exploited majority over the exploiting minority.
>
> Briefly: *the dictatorship of the proletariat is the rule — unrestricted by law and based on force — of the proletariat over the bourgeoisie, a*

rule enjoying the sympathy and support of the laboring and exploited masses. [Stalin's italics.]

Once the habits of thought and action remaining from bourgeois society have been eliminated, the final stage — the new Communist society — will be realized. There will then be no need for a special instrument of repression — a state. Having no function, the state will wither away. Lenin wrote, in *State and Revolution:*

> Only in Communist society, when the resistance of the capitalists has been completely broken, when the capitalists have disappeared, when there are no classes (i.e., there is no difference between the members of society in their relation to the social means of production), *only then* "the state ceases to exist," and *"it becomes possible to speak of freedom."* Only then a really full democracy, a democracy without any exceptions, will be possible and will be realized. . . . [Lenin's italics.]

In their later years, Marx and Engels came to feel that in certain countries in the West conditions had been altered to the point where it might be possible for the goals of communism to be achieved by peaceful means. Great Britain and the United States were mentioned by Marx as illustrations.

But the first Communist revolution did not come in the United States or Great Britain or Germany or France, as the Communists themselves had expected. It came in the least industrially advanced of the great powers of Europe — Tsarist Russia — under conditions which left an ineradicable stamp upon the future development of communism.

LENIN'S CONTRIBUTIONS

The leader of the Russian Communist revolution was Nikolai Lenin (a name assumed by Vladimir Ilyich Ulyanov in connection with his revolutionary activities). Lenin was the heir to a long and varied revolutionary tradition, for Russian society at the turn of the century was a society in ferment, ruled by an uncompromising autocrat, the Tsar, who claimed to be the agent of God. In response principally to the ideas and examples of the more industrialized nations of Western Europe, a number of movements for social reform had sprung up in Russia in the late nineteenth century. Some important gains were achieved during this period, including an edict emancipating the serfs in 1861 and the establishment of local elective assemblies in 1864. Nevertheless, the fundamentals of autocracy and arbitrary rule remained, along with the vast inequalities in Russian society which they supported. These who sought significant, revolutionary change were increasingly frustrated and dissatisfied with the results of moderate peaceful approaches.

Some Russian intellectuals then initiated a movement aimed at activating the peasant masses. Their effort to go "back to the villages," however, brought little success with the peasantry and much persecution by the Tsar's police. With the failure of this movement, a number of intellectuals turned in desperation to sheer terrorism in an effort to erode governmental authority and move the peasantry to revolution. In 1881, the terrorists won a pyrrhic victory when Tsar Alexander II was assassinated. The result was not reform, but greatly intensified repression.

It was within this milieu that Lenin operated. Neither moderate constitutional action nor blind terrorism, he understood full well, would win the day for communism in Russia. Carrying on revolutionary activities against the opposition of the ruthless Tsarist police was no job for amateurs — as Lenin had learned in his youth when his older brother, Alexander, was executed by the police for his part in an attempt to assassinate a public official. And the price of loose discipline in such a revolutionary struggle was exposure and death. Lenin was convinced that *a revolution could be carried out only by a dedicated group of full-time "professional" revolutionaries, acting under strict centralized discipline.*

It followed that this revolutionary movement could not be led simply by the working class as a whole. The class *consciousness* (understanding of their historic mission) of the masses was not adequate to such a task without guidance. The responsibility for providing this guidance, for directing the revolution, must therefore be assumed by the *vanguard* of the working class, the Communist party, a disciplined organization of professional revolutionaries whose consciousness was equal to this mandate. To quote again from Stalin's *The Foundations of Leninism:*

> The Party must be, first of all, the *vanguard* of the working class. . . . But in order that it may really be the vanguard, the Party must be armed with revolutionary theory. . . . The Party cannot be a real party if it limits itself to registering what the masses of the working class feel and think . . . if it is unable to rise above the momentary interests of the proletariat. . . . The Party must stand at the head of the working class; it must see farther than the working class; it must lead the proletariat, and not follow in the tail of the spontaneous movement.

In order to attain a disciplined centralized party organization, while making at least a gesture to demands for democratic procedures within the Party, Lenin devised the principle of *democratic centralism.* There was to be free and full discussion within the Party of issues which arose in the course of conducting its activities. But once a decision had been reached, discussion was to stop, and the Party's directives were to be carried out without further question. Party members were not permitted to continue to press their personal viewpoints once a decision had been made, or to organize a group (faction) for the purpose of overturning this decision subsequently.

Such action — *factionalism* — would be punished by expulsion from the Party.

Lenin's writings were concerned predominantly with the tactics necessary to bring about the Communist revolution. The world they describe is a world of bitter and incessant struggle — Lenin's phrases are studded with military imagery — in which militancy and calculating rationality are the primary qualifications of the successful Party worker.[7] Bourgeois conceptions of honor and sentimentality, and other sources of tactical rigidity, must be done away with absolutely: they are luxuries which cannot be afforded. There should be no hesitation, for example, about retreating when the situation in which the Party finds itself appears to call for retreat. The existence of the Party — in the last analysis, the agent of history and therefore inevitably victorious — must not be risked unnecessarily in speculative ventures (*adventurism*). *Temporary* compromises with ultimate Communist principles are to be accepted readily when rational calculation makes it plain that this will quicken the winning of long-range goals. To take one step backward today in order to make possible two steps forward tomorrow is commendable and wise. To fail to make such compromises when the situation demands them is to be guilty of the left-wing deviation of *dogmatism*. On the other hand, under no circumstances may any Communist objectives be *permanently* compromised in order to gain tactical advantages, however great. This would constitute *reformism, opportunism,* or *revisionism* — the right-wing deviations of which most Western trade unions and social democratic parties are guilty.[8]

Lenin made brilliant use of the principle of tactical flexibility in his own conduct of the Bolshevik revolution in 1917 and in the years in which he ruled the new Soviet Union. When the Tsarist regime was overturned by rioting workers and mutinous soldiers in March, 1917, the Bolsheviks were less than 25,000 strong and Lenin was in exile in Switzerland.[9] World War I was raging and creating within Russia increasing chaos and disintegration. The key Bolshevik leaders within Russia were preparing to cooperate to some extent with the newly formed republican government — but Lenin, on his return, persuaded the Party that a unique revolutionary situation existed and that they must strike now. Agitation, parliamentary tactics, and insurrection were all employed. Other parties and factions refused to accept the surrender of Russian honor and interests involved in getting out of the

---

[7] See the content analysis, referred to above, in chap. 2 ("The Power-Oriented Tactician") of Almond's *The Appeals of Communism.*

[8] In general, *right*-wing deviations consist in moving *closer to* the bourgeoisie's position than a "correct" interpretation of the situation demands, while *left*-wing deviations consist in holding a position even further from the bourgeoisie's position than a "correct" interpretation demands.

[9] Merle Fainsod, *How Russia Is Ruled* (Cambridge, Mass.: Harvard University Press, 1953), p. 60. The following paragraphs owe much to this standard work.

war on whatever terms could be obtained. Lenin, however, did not hesitate to capitalize on the war-weariness of a people engaged in a fierce conflict for reasons they did not comprehend. "Peace" became one of the Bolsheviks' slogans. "Land" to the peasants became another — though the establishment of a class of individual peasant proprietors was far from Marxist theory and from the Bolsheviks' goal of large-scale collectivization. "Worker's control" and "Bread" were other slogans, though Lenin intended that actual control should be exercised by the Communist party and knew that consumer goods soon would be sacrificed to industrial development.

In power, Lenin was no less flexible and resourceful. When Germany insisted on harsh terms as the price of peace, Lenin ordered that this price be paid at Brest-Litovsk so that the Party could consolidate its control over Russia. When opposition by Russian "Whites" and foreign expeditionary forces (European, Japanese, and American) required the provision of large supplies of grain to the Red Army, the peasants were subjected to forcible requisitions. When these struggles had ended, and strong peasant opposition to requisitions helped to create a food shortage, the requisition policy was abandoned. Tsarist officers and technicians were readily made use of to meet the need for men with specialized military and industrial skills. When increased industrial production was needed to still mass unrest and provide the peasant with consumer goods as an incentive to increased agricultural production, the New Economic Policy was adopted, promising freedom from nationalization to small businesses, restoring private commercial trade, and attempting to attract foreign capital by offering special concessions to Western businessmen. Inaugurated in 1921, this New Economic Policy remained in force until well after Lenin's death in 1924, at the age of 53.

One more of Lenin's important contributions to the Communist movement should be discussed here. Although it had little to do with the success of the Bolshevik revolution in Russia in the fall of 1917, it has had much to do with the appeal of communism in China, and in the rest of Asia, Africa, and Latin America, in more recent times. This is *the Leninist theory of imperialism.*

By the first decade of the twentieth century, some disparity between actual events and certain Marxist expectations had become evident. The prospects for revolution in the most developed nations of Europe, far from advancing, appeared to have declined. The living standards of the workers in these countries had been raised appreciably; and the socialist parties and trade unions of Europe were working increasingly toward reforming existing economic and political institutions rather than toward overturning them. Mass reactions to the outbreak of World War I indicated, in addition, that national loyalties took precedence over class loyalty among the workers of Europe.

The explanation for these events, according to Lenin, was to be found in the extension of capitalist markets and investments to the underdeveloped nations of Asia, Africa, and Latin America. The need of the capitalists to obtain the highest possible rates of interest on their capital eventually drove them to seek high-return investments abroad. The extension of political control over these undeveloped areas — that is, the division of Asia, Africa, and Latin America into colonies — was merely the political counterpart of this movement of capital. The bourgeois state, as the political agent of the capitalists, moved to assume administrative control — or establish spheres of influence — in these continents in order to secure raw materials for its capitalists, and to cultivate markets and investment opportunities for them. Toward these ends, bourgeois colonial administrators often acted to create a legal framework and a technological base — railroads, communications facilities, etc. — conducive to profitable investment in these areas.

Since these developments represented an inevitable consequence of the nature of capitalism — in its advanced or monopoly stage — *imperialism should be rightly understood to be simply an inherent manifestation of capitalism itself.* Stalin wrote in *The Foundations of Leninism:*

> Formerly, it was the accepted thing to speak of the existence or absence of objective conditions for the proletarian revolution in individual countries, or, to be more precise, in one or another developed country. Now this point of view is no longer adequate. Now we must speak of the existence of objective conditions for the revolution in the entire system of world imperialist economy as an integral unit. . . .
>
> Where will the revolution begin? . . .
>
> Where industry is more developed, where the proletariat constitutes the majority, where there is more culture, where there is more democracy — that was the reply given formerly.
>
> No, objects the Leninist theory of revolution [imperialism]; *not necessarily where industry is more developed,* and so forth. The front of capital will be pierced where the chain of imperialism is weakest. . . .

Thus, there are in the modern world, not only oppressing and oppressed *classes,* but oppressing and oppressed *nations* and peoples. And though imperialism may make it possible for capitalists in the industrially advanced countries to stave off proletarian revolution temporarily by using their ill-gotten colonial profits to buy-off elements of the working class in their own countries, in the end the destruction of capitalism remains inevitable. For imperialism strengthens the hold of monopolies at home,[10] and may actually accelerate the disintegration of capitalism in some cases by promoting wars among rival capitalist nations for markets, raw materials, and colonies. World War I was an excellent illustration of this tendency.

---

10 Industry comes under the control of monopolists in the later stages of capitalism because all but the biggest capitalists have been thrust back into the proletariat by their failure to compete successfully in the laissez faire marketplace.

Here, as elsewhere, however, Communists are careful to distinguish between the *peoples* of the imperialist countries and their governments. The latter represent only the bourgeois ruling classes of these countries, whereas the working masses are considered to be the natural class allies of the Communists. Whatever positions their governments may take, the "peace-loving peoples of the world" are — virtually by definition — assumed to be in sympathy with the policies of the Communist nations. In specific instances, dissident views expressed by Western Communist parties — or even by non-Communist opponents of the government of the day — are prominently reported in the Communist press as evidence that "the people" support the Communist line. This insistence on separating the interests of foreign governments from that of their peoples has much in common with the traditional American view (noted in Chapter Two) that United States policy, being synonymous with the cause of democracy, is bound to be supported by other peoples, even when it is opposed by the undemocratic governments which rule them. Thus, throughout the cold war, the United States, on one side, and Russia and China on the other, have proclaimed repeatedly their friendship with and high regard for each other's *peoples* — while building up massive military establishments to protect themselves against the aggressive policies of each other's *governments*.

SINCE LENIN

The theory of imperialism was not the last important elaboration of Marxist theory to originate in an effort to reconcile that theory with unexpected events. When it became clear that the Bolshevik success in Russia was *not* merely the prelude to a series of revolutions in the more developed countries of Europe, as Communist theory had suggested it would be, Stalin explained (once again, in *The Foundations of Leninism*):

> . . . Formerly, the victory of revolution in one country was considered impossible, on the assumption that it would require the combined action of the proletarians of all or at least a majority of the advanced countries to achieve victory over the bourgeoisie. Now [1924] this point of view no longer accords with the facts. Now we must proceed from the possibility of such a victory, for the uneven and spasmodic character of the development of the various capitalist countries under the conditions of imperialism, the development, within imperialism, of catastrophic conditions leading to inevitable wars, the growth of the revolutionary movements in all countries of the world — all this leads, not only to the possibility, but also to the necessity of the victory of the proletariat in individual countries. The history of the Russian revolution is direct proof of this.

A dispute between Stalin and Trotsky on this point — the former asserting the tenability of building *socialism in one country*, the latter insisting on the necessity for a *permanent* (that is, worldwide) *revolution* — was resolved by Stalin's triumph over Trotsky in the struggle for succession to Lenin.[11]

Stalin's formula rationalized the need to concentrate first on building up the strength of the Soviet Union, while postponing major efforts to foment further Communist revolution to a more propitious moment. Nevertheless, the dangers to communism as a result of *capitalist encirclement* of the Soviet Union were stressed. Not until the working class had triumphed in several more countries could its hold on Soviet Russia be deemed secure. In the meantime, extensive armament and strict suppression of internal opposition were obviously warranted. Only after Stalin's death in 1953 was the period of capitalist encirclement declared to be ended.

In the course of the rise to power of communism in China, Mao Tsetung worked out a number of adaptations of Marxist-Leninist doctrine to the special conditions of China, as we have seen in a case study in the preceding chapter. Using a *peasant base* for the revolution in a predominantly agricultural country, forming a *Red Army* to carry on a prolonged military struggle, envisaging a *two-stage revolution* — (the bourgeois-democratic revolution being carried out under the leadership of the proletariat — that is, the Communist party — which then proceeds to bring about, through industrialization, the conditions necessary for the true socialist revolution) — all of these theoretical adaptations involve somewhat unorthodox interpretations of the letter of Marxism. But all are very much in consonance with the spirit of Leninism.

More recently, the rise of the Soviet Union to great power status and the emerging nuclear stalemate between it and the United States moved Nikita Khrushchev to an extremely important reinterpretation of Communist doctrine — one clearly foreshadowed, however, in Stalin's later writings.[12] World war between the forces of capitalism and those of communism, Khrushchev declared, was no longer inevitable — although the ultimate triumph of communism, of course, remained assured. Communist theory, it should be recalled, expects wars to be initiated *not* by the Communists themselves, but by the bourgeoisie-dominated governments of the capitalist countries. Now, Khrushchev asserted, the growing strength of the Communist nations — and the obvious destructiveness of nuclear warfare — raised the possibility

---

11 Lev Davydovich Bronstein, who took the revolutionary name Leon Trotsky, was Lenin's key lieutenant in the struggle to establish the Bolsheviks in power. He lived in exile from 1929 until his assassination, by Stalin's agents, in 1940.

12 For a persuasive argument that the foreign policies of Stalin's heirs evolved without sharp discontinuities from those followed by Stalin himself, see Marshall Shulman, *Stalin's Foreign Policy Reappraised* (Cambridge, Mass.: Harvard University Press, 1963). For a viewpoint which puts more emphasis on the cruel idiosyncrasies of Stalin's personality, see George F. Kennan, *Russia and the West Under Lenin and Stalin* (Boston: Atlantic-Little, Brown, 1961). This book also provides a fascinating introduction to Soviet-Western relations from 1917 through World War II.

that the bourgeoisie might in time be persuaded to let history run its course (that is, to accept communism's inevitable triumph) without resorting to what plainly would be a desperate suicidal attempt to prevent this by launching a nuclear war. Three years after Stalin's death, Khrushchev told the Twentieth Congress of the Soviet Communist party (in the same speech in which he attacked Stalin as "brutal," "capricious" and "despotic"):

> There is, of course, a Marxist-Leninist precept that wars are inevitable as long as imperialism [that is, capitalism] exists. This precept was evolved at a time when (i) imperialism was an all-embracing world system, and (ii) the social and political forces which did not want war were weak, poorly organized, and hence unable to compel the imperialists to renounce war. . . .
>
> . . . But war is not fatalistically inevitable. Today there are mighty social and political forces possessing formidable means to prevent the imperialists from unleashing war, and if they actually do try to start it, to give a smashing rebuff to the aggressors and frustrate their adventurist plans. . . .
>
> . . . Our enemies like to depict us Leninists as advocates of violence always and everywhere. True, we recognize the need for the revolutionary transformation of capitalist society into socialist society. It is this that distinguishes the revolutionary Marxists from the reformists, the opportunists. There is no doubt that in a number of capitalist countries the violent overthrow of the dictatorship of the bourgeoisie and the sharp aggravation of class struggle connected with this are inevitable. But the forms of social revolution vary. It is not true that we regard violence and civil war as the only way to remake society. . . .
>
> Leninism teaches us that the ruling classes will not surrender their power voluntarily. . . . The use or non-use of violence in the transition to socialism depends on the resistance of the exploiters, on whether the exploiting class itself resorts to violence, rather than on the proletariat.
>
> In this connection the question arises of whether it is possible to go over to socialism by using parliamentary means. No such course was open to the Russian Bolsheviks. . . .
>
> Since then, however, the historical situation has undergone radical changes which make possible a new approach to the question. The forces of socialism and democracy [13] have grown immeasurably throughout the world, and capitalism has become much weaker. The mighty camp of socialism with its population of over 900 million is growing and gaining in strength. Its gigantic internal forces, its decisive advantages over capitalism, are being increasingly revealed from day to day. Socialism has a great power of attraction for the workers, peasants and intellectuals of all countries. The ideas of socialism are indeed coming to dominate the minds of all working mankind.

[13] [Note that the terms "socialism" and "democracy" are used here in the particular sense indicated above, rather than as they are commonly used in the West.]

At the same time the present situation offers the working class in a number of capitalist countries a real opportunity . . . to capture a stable majority in parliament, and transform the latter from an organ of bourgeois democracy into a genuine instrument of the people's will. In such an event this institution, traditional in many highly developed capitalist countries, may become an organ of genuine democracy — democracy for the working people.

PEKING'S DISSENT

These views of Khrushchev and his successors have in fact become the core of a bitter division within the world Communist movement. For the Chinese Communist party does not accept them, and has railed incessantly against the evils of "Khrushchevian revisionism." (The Soviets reply that the Chinese are *dogmatists,* who do not know when it is necessary to adapt Marxism-Leninism creatively to new situations, but prefer to elevate the letter of Communist doctrine over its spirit.)

For all the acrimony it has caused, this dispute mostly involves matters of emphasis rather than of basic doctrine. Both the Russians and the Chinese believe that conflict between capitalism and communism, and ultimate Communist victory, are inevitable. Both believe that if war is started it will be by the capitalists, not by the Communists themselves. Both favor *peaceful coexistence* — that is, both would rather see world communism triumph through peaceful competition rather than by force of arms — especially in the nuclear age. Yet neither would balk at using force to attain this end, should it prove necessary.

Where they differ is in their respective assessments of the *likelihood* of a peaceful Communist victory — the Russians apparently think it more likely than do the Chinese — and consequently in their willingness to risk war in the course of their struggle to bring a Communist world into being. This is a difference of emphasis, as we have noted, yet when we consider its effect on actual policy, it is one which may be important enough to spell the difference between life and death for hundreds of millions of human beings.

How this difference in theoretical emphasis affects actual Soviet and Chinese foreign policy orientations is illustrated by the attitudes of each toward support of *wars of national liberation.* In colonies or nations under the political or economic domination of the West, according to Communist theory, the first step toward eventual Communist revolution is a struggle for national liberation from the Western imperialists and their local adherents (often called "running dogs"). This struggle is carried on by an alliance of all patriotic classes opposing imperialist domination — the working class, the peasantry, and often, also, substantial sections of the local bourgeoisie. If this alliance is already led by the working class (that is, by the Communist party) in the nation concerned, so much the better. In any

case, a further — Communist — revolution is expected to take place at some
point subsequent to the victory of the "progressive" forces in their struggle
for national liberation.

But the historic course of these anti-imperialistic struggles may be altered by the intervention of outside capitalist powers, seeking to protect
their investments and their native "running dogs." In order to prevent such
external interference from blocking the otherwise inevitable victory of the
progressive forces, it is incumbent upon the major Communist nations to
provide aid to the latter at appropriate points.

Thus far, Russians and Chinese are agreed. Their differences in approach
come to this: (1) Whether a particular government in a former colony or
economic dependency of the West should be cooperated with or subverted
depends, as we have seen, on whether it is classified as genuinely nationalist
or as a "tool of the imperialists." In general, the Chinese have been more
inclined to adopt the latter, more revolutionary, of these strategies and
classifications than have the Russians. For the Soviets have felt that, in the
long run, cooperation with nationalist governments in the developing nations may make possible a peaceful transition to socialism, in some cases at
least. (2) Once a liberation war is in progress, moreover, the Chinese are
more likely than the Russians to advocate direct intervention in support of
the "local patriotic forces." [14] The Soviets seem to see their role as that of
"holding the ring" by deterring Western intervention rather than that of
leaping into the fray themselves. Direct intervention on their part, they fear,
might lead to increased intervention by the United States and other imperialist powers. This, in turn, would mean running substantial risks that a
limited war might escalate into a world war, to the benefit of no one.

The Chinese profess to be less concerned about the likelihood of escalation. The United States, they say, is a *paper tiger*. Its war potential is
admittedly great, but in a real sense it is weaker than its Communist adversaries because its staying power and determination are not equal to theirs.
Handled properly — militantly, but carefully and cautiously — the United
States can be defeated in the long run. An excellent way to accomplish this
is to make use of the tactics of sublimited and guerrilla warfare pioneered
by Mao Tse-tung in leading the Communists to victory in China. This is a
carefully worked out and tested system for dealing with an adversary possessing superior immediate tactical strength but strategically vulnerable to a
long war of attrition.

---

14 It is important to distinguish here between advocacy and action. The Chinese have
spoken very militantly about intervention against the imperialist forces led by the United
States, but put to the test (for instance, in Vietnam), they have acted with a caution which
suggests a healthy respect for American military power. Perhaps they feel it is principally
the Russians who should act more boldly. The Chinese have also warned those who would
make revolutions that they must be prepared to do so on their own, without outside
support, if necessary.

When the Russians reply that this is a dangerous game because, in Khrushchev's words, this "paper tiger has nuclear teeth," the Chinese counter that revolutions cannot be made by quailing in fear of nuclear blackmail. In the last analysis, men, rather than nuclear weapons, are decisive in war. Besides, how will the use of nuclear weapons bring the United States any closer to its goals? It is the United States which must fear a nuclear conflict, more than the Communist nations, for, even should worst come to worst: "On the debris of a dead imperialism, the victorious people would create very swiftly a civilization thousands of times higher than the capitalist system and a truly beautiful future for themselves." [15] The Soviet view, in contrast, is that:

> . . . Modern nuclear war of itself could in no way be a factor which would hasten revolution or bring nearer the victory of socialism. On the contrary, it would throw back humanity, the world revolutionary workers' movement and the cause of building socialism and communism for many dozens of years. . . .[16]

The Soviet Union's willingness to rely on economic and ideological competition — and on its appeal as a model of rapid national economic development — to advance the cause of communism is also reflected in its readiness, at least for the record, to conclude an arms control or disarmament treaty with the West, if satisfactory terms can be agreed on. The Chinese, for their part, believe that disarmament is inconceivable so long as imperialism continues to exist and that it is an illusion to imagine the imperialists would ever accept a genuine disarmament agreement. Thus the Chinese opposed the limited nuclear test ban treaty signed by the Soviet Union, the United States, and other powers, and have since exploded their first nuclear bombs in the atmosphere.

These differences between the Soviet Union and China have led not only to name calling and mutual recrimination but to state action. There is considerable evidence suggesting that Mao and Khrushchev, through internal political maneuvering,[17] lent their support to efforts to unseat each other. Most Soviet technicians and aid to China — including assistance in nuclear power development — were withdrawn in 1960 or soon afterward. Border conflicts

[15] "Long Live Leninism," an editorial in *Hung Chi (Red Flag)*, the official theoretical journal of the Chinese Communist Party, reprinted in translation in the *Peking Review* (April 26, 1960).

[16] "Lenin's Theory of the Socialist Revolution and Present Day Conditions," *Kommunist*, No. 13 (September, 1960).

[17] Harold Hinton has advanced the hypothesis that Khrushchev may well have been removed from office by his colleagues in 1964 primarily to keep him from carrying out a plan "to knock out" Communist China's "nuclear weapons installations with a missile strike" as soon as China's first nuclear test was carried out. *Communist China in World Politics*, chap. 17 ("The Chinese Nuclear Test and the Fall of Khrushchev") (Boston: Houghton Mifflin, 1966).

have arisen between the two nations, which share 4,000 miles of common frontiers. And the volume of trade between the quarreling Communist nations has fallen sharply in recent years.

Encouraged by the possibility of playing China off against Russia and vice versa — as well as by Titoist Yugoslavia's earlier success in defying Stalin — other Communist nations have begun to exercise growing independence of Moscow. Albania has become a firm supporter of Peking — partly due to their common hatred of Yugoslav "revisionism." Rumania has rejected the economic role urged upon it by the Soviet-dominated COMECON (Council for Mutual Economic Aid) and, along with Poland and even Hungary, has moved to establish some trade and cultural ties with the West. The United States has made a beginning at adjusting its trade and other policies to encourage this development. But the "myth of the Communist monolith" dies hard, and a number of specialists on Communist affairs feel that we have not gone far enough fast enough in revising our policies to fit the new phenomenon of "polycentric communism."

BEHIND THE IDEOLOGICAL DIFFERENCES

It would be naive to attribute the Sino-Soviet dispute solely, or even primarily, to ideological differences. We are not in a position to know certainly all the factors which underlie it, but a study of recent history, and informed speculation, suggest a number of hypotheses which may be helpful starting points.[18]

First, China's willingness to take greater risks than the Soviet Union to change the international status quo may very simply be related to the fact that China has less reason to be satisfied with that status quo. The Soviet Union is universally recognized as one of the two great powers of the world. It has achieved more fully than ever in its history the traditional Russian goals of having a cordon of friendly states on its western frontiers and gaining access to warm water ports. It has few unfulfilled territorial ambitions. China, in contrast, has not even been allowed to complete its victory over its civil war opponent. The latter, in fact, is entrenched, with the aid of

---

[18] On the Sino-Soviet dispute, its origins and its underlying motivations, see — among the many works available — G. F. Hudson, Richard Lowenthal, and Roderick Mac-Farquhar, *The Sino-Soviet Dispute* (New York: Praeger, 1961). (This includes translations of key statements of the Chinese and Soviet positions); Donald S. Zagoria, *The Sino-Soviet Conflict, 1956–1961* (Princeton, N.J.: Princeton University Press, 1962); *Sino-Soviet Conflict, Report on Sino-Soviet Conflict and Its Implications, by the Subcommittee on the Far East and the Pacific of the Committee on Foreign Affairs, House of Representatives, together with Hearings held by Subcommittee on the Far East and the Pacific, March 10, 11, 15, 16, 17, 18, 23 and 31, 1965* (Washington, D.C.: Government Printing Office, May 14, 1965); and William E. Griffith, *Sino-Soviet Relations, 1964–65* (Cambridge, Mass.: M.I.T. Press, 1966).

The most useful volume on this subject for the general reader is Klaus Mehnert, *Peking and Moscow* (New York: New American Library, 1964). (Originally published in 1962.)

United States military and economic support, on what both Peking and the Chinese Nationalists agree is the Chinese province of Taiwan. Even a number of islands immediately off the China coast are occupied by United States protected Nationalist forces. These forces periodically conduct raids against the mainland and U-2 espionage flights over it and promise to renew the civil war against the Communists at the first opportunity. As Donald Zagoria has said: "The situation might be more understandable to Americans if we imagined an American government-in-exile set up in Havana, supported by the Soviet Union, periodically raiding the Florida coast and proclaiming its intention to conquer the entire country." [19] The Soviet Union, meanwhile, has been quite reluctant to go all out in support of Chinese Communist efforts to change this rankling situation.

The Nationalists represent China in the United Nations and in half — or more — of the capitals of the world. American forces are based in Japan, China's archenemy in this century, in South Korea, and in Southeast Asia — areas traditionally subject to strong Chinese influence. Thus far, moreover, these American forces have thwarted the efforts of Communist governments in North Korea and North Vietnam to unify their countries under Communist auspices.

The extreme hostility between the United States and Communist China which these issues, and popular feeling in the United States, have helped to create, rule out the possibility of Sino-American rapprochement in the near future. This, in turn, means that any improvement in relations between the United States and the Soviet Union, the other major military powers in the Pacific area, is bound to put Peking at a disadvantage. The more tension between Washington and Moscow, the more the Soviet Union will need Peking's support; and the more the Russians need China's support, the more the Chinese will be able to press the Russians to back Peking's efforts to advance *its* national goals. Given China's need for a Soviet nuclear shield in order to press vigorously its claims against the United States, it seems perfectly understandable that the Chinese should try to convince the Soviets to take a very militant line against the United States.

In internal development, similarly, the Russians have a lot more to be satisfied with than do the Chinese. The former are of course in a much more advanced stage of industrial growth. Western estimates which put the "real" Gross National Product of the Soviet Union, per capita, at $986 show a comparable figure of $167 for Communist China.[20] With radios and television sets — and thinking about washing machines, automobiles, and apart-

19 *Sino-Soviet Conflict*, House Far East Subcommittee Hearings, *op. cit.*, p. 113.
20 Figures compiled by Professor P. N. Rodenstein-Rodan for "International Aid for Underdeveloped Countries," *The Review of Economics and Statistics* (May, 1961), and reprinted in Millikan and Blackmer (eds.), *The Emerging Nations* (Boston: Little, Brown, 1961), p. 150.

ments of their own — the Soviet Communists have much more to lose today than simply their chains; the Chinese still not so very much more. And the Russians have been through the worst stage of capital accumulation in the industrialization process, with its need to keep production high and consumption low. The Chinese, on the other hand, have much of this stage and its hardships ahead of them. It may be that in this stage a threatening foreign enemy is a useful thing for the Chinese government to have available, since it provides a legitimate target for resentments caused by constant personal sacrifice — resentments which might otherwise be channeled against the Chinese Communist regime itself. Perhaps, then, this too has something to do with Peking's insistence on maintaining an atmosphere of militant class struggle in international affairs.

Again, some of Peking's confidence that limited wars can be prosecuted militantly and yet contained seems to stem from differing estimates of the balance of military power between the Communist camp and the West. Paradoxically, the Chinese appear to have been more impressed than the Russians themselves by the impact of Soviet space and missile advances on the balance of power. The doctrine that "The East wind prevails over the West wind" was enunciated by Mao, not by Khrushchev or Brezhnev. The Soviet leadership has been most scrupulous about claiming military equality with — but not superiority over — the West. Perhaps the Russians have more relevant information on this point. Perhaps they are sobered by the thought that, in the event of all-out nuclear war, their very strength ensures that they, rather than the Chinese, will have to be the prime initial target for United States nuclear strength. (If so, their concern about having an ally declare "my big brother can lick any man in the house" is understandable.) In any case, their higher level of industrial development leaves the Soviets more strategically vulnerable than their Chinese comrades to a nuclear attack.

It would not be surprising, either, if the Chinese leadership's assessments of Western power, Western intentions, and probable Western behavior were colored by their own relative lack of first-hand experience in dealing with the West. Donald Klein has written that "the Chinese Communist leaders are easily the most isolated in the world." As of 1961, a third of the members of the Central Committee of the Chinese Communist party had never been outside their own country at all. Less than a third had ever traveled to *any* non-Communist nation, and only a sixth had traveled to any "advanced" nation since the Communist victory in China.[21]

The absence of diplomatic relations between Peking and many Western nations, including the United States, may add to this isolation. There have been numerous points of contact between China and the West in recent

[21] Donald W. Klein, "Peking's Leaders: A Study of Isolation," pp. 40–41. *The China Quarterly*, No. 7 (July–September, 1961), pp. 35–43.

years, to be sure — including periodic conversations between Chinese Communist and American government representatives at Geneva and Warsaw since 1955. Nevertheless, on-the-spot observation and residence sometimes give a sense of realism and an understanding of other nations and their leaders which no amount of reading and indirect contacts can provide.

Communist China's leaders, too, belong to a revolutionary generation different from that of their counterparts in the Soviet Union. Most of them joined the Chinese Communist party when it was a small revolutionary group fleeing from Chiang K'ai-shek. They spent as much as twenty-five years of their lives as underdogs, carrying on guerrilla warfare activities against Chiang and the Japanese, before carrying out the revolution to which they had dedicated their lives. Many saw their families and comrades killed and tortured by their enemies before their eyes. Their determined participation in such a revolutionary movement is testimony to their fierce dissatisfaction with the status quo. Their revolutionary experience left them familiar with, and perhaps even comfortable in, a hostile environment, carrying on a long-range war of attrition against a foe with superior military strength. Certainly, it left them confident of their ability to succeed in this kind of situation by the use of this kind of strategy.

Most of the present Soviet leaders, on the other hand, joined the Soviet Communist party when it was already in control of the Russian state. They came into the party, in most cases, not to revolt against the established order but to rise within it. Throughout their careers, they have been rewarded for their skills in party organization, administration, and industrial management, rather than for their effectiveness in revolutionary enterprises. Not having lived so long and so intimately with adversity and hardship as their Chinese comrades, they are perhaps less confident of their ability to deal with it successfully. It is understandable — and not entirely unwarranted — that the Chinese should think of them as "powder puff" revolutionaries, without real experience in revolution-making, and afraid to risk their positions and comforts to bring about cherished revolutionary goals. (Recent events in China suggest that even most of his own colleagues are not sufficiently dedicated to realizing revolutionary goals, whatever the cost, to suit Mao Tse-tung.)

In the contest for leadership of the Communist camp, it is largely the allegiance of the out-of-power parties which is "up for grabs," so to speak. Most of the in-power parties are in Eastern European nations tied by geography and history to the Soviet Union. Peking's advocacy that greater risks should be taken in support of the out-of-power movements, therefore, is a great aid to China in appealing to these parties to back its bid for international Communist leadership. The Chinese cannot compete with the Russians in economic aid, international prestige, or nuclear power, but their bolder strategy provides them with at least one significant advantage.

China's humiliations at the hands of the West and the fact that the Russians have white skins, while the Chinese do not, are further sources of Peking's appeal in certain instances. In many of the Communist parties of the developing nations — and in some developed countries as well — pro-Chinese and pro-Russian factions compete with each other actively for influence and power. In a few, the break has been complete, and separate parties have been formed.

Specific irritants have also played a part in the development of the dispute. In particular, the Chinese have objected to Russia's refusal to provide them with nuclear weapons or the know-how needed to build them. Also, they appear to have resented the fact that the Soviet Union provided relatively little economic aid for China's development efforts at a time when it seemed to have plenty to spend courting India's "neutralist" government. Thus we can understand the Chinese emphasis on helping real Communists rather than cooperating with and courting non-Communist governments in the developing nations in the hope of encouraging "peaceful transitions to socialism." (But the Chinese, too, have proved willing to collaborate with non-Communist nationalist regimes — like Pakistan's — when it suited their purposes.) The Chinese leaders have plainly been displeased, also, by the Soviet leaders' disinclination to use Russian strength in behalf of Chinese efforts to obtain their national policy goals in Asia — especially with respect to Taiwan.

There is no provision in Communist theory for resolving conflicts among Communist parties ruling different nations. (Marxism, of course, envisions communism as a movement cutting across national lines, rather than as based on national power.) If and when one or another contender for leadership of the world Communist movement wins the day, its interpretations will be deemed to have been the correct ones all along. A prolonged stalemate, on the other hand — which seems more likely — would leave world communism with competing sets of "true" interpretations, casting doubt in some quarters on Marxism's claims to scientific validity.

Since a key part of the Sino-Soviet dispute turns on the most effective way of dealing with the United States, American actions over the years may have an important effect on its progress. Although no simple formula for promoting American interests in this complex situation is readily apparent, careful forethought about the likely effect of our own actions on this dispute is obviously called for. Our task is complicated, moreover, by the need to be constantly alert to the possibility of changes in the position of one or both of the Communist great powers. Their progress in industrial development, certainly, will change with time. And China's original revolutionary leaders cannot live forever: already four-fifths of the membership of the Chinese Communist party are men (and women) who joined after the Party's victory in 1949. And before, or after, Mao's death, power may gravitate to the hands of those who have become his opponents. None of this guarantees that the Chinese position will become less militant with the passage of time. But it should warn us against building our policy on the gratuitous assumption that there will be *no* change. No precept emerges more clearly from the brief review of Communist theory and tactics we have undertaken than that tactical flexibility is a primary requisite for dealing with practitioners of Leninism, of whatever nationality.

COMMUNIST IDEOLOGY AND NATIONAL FOREIGN POLICIES

Precisely what influence does Communist ideology have on the foreign policy actions of Communist states? The attention paid to Communist theory in this chapter obviously suggests that the author believes it to be an influence of some significance. Yet the answer to this question must be that we cannot specify precisely how ideology affects a given policy decision at a given time. Even if we had access — as we do not — to minutes of the meetings of the Soviet and Chinese politburos and other top foreign policy-making organs, we could not pin down the influence of ideology on specific policy decisions — any more than we can pin down the influence of American ideas and value patterns on specific American policy decisions. (See Chapter Two.)

Almost any action that can be attributed to ideological influence can also be explained in other ways. Was Soviet eagerness to expand its influence into Eastern Europe at the end of World War II due to its leaders' ideological zeal for spreading world communism? Or was it rather an expression of traditional Russian expansionism, rooted in Russia's habitual use of geographical vastness as a mode of defense against aggression (Napoleon; Hitler) from the west? Is the Soviet Union's conception of itself as the leader of a messianic movement with universal aspirations based on the Marxist future or on the Russian past? Does it originate in Russia's role as the first Communist state, or in its earlier role as the "third Rome," repository of the "true" orthodox Christian tradition? Do the Chinese contend against the Russians for leadership of the Communist movement because they feel they must defend true Leninist orthodoxy? Because a century of Chinese humiliation at the hands of the West makes them supersensitive to white domination? Or because they are heirs to a culture which was the center of its part of the world for millennia — whose very name, in Chinese, means "middle kingdom"?

There are no demonstrable answers to these rhetorical questions beyond the suggestion that the alternative explanations they pose are not necessarily mutually exclusive. A few general observations may nevertheless be useful.[22] First, to whatever extent communism may influence the foreign policies of Communist states, it unquestionably provides them with a potent *instrument* of foreign policy. It offers an ideological banner and a set of organizational techniques around which dissident groups in foreign countries can rally. In the process, communism can transform an aggregation of discontented men into an institution with a mission — a much more difficult phenomenon to deal with, and one almost impossible to destroy entirely, given its external sources of financial and diplomatic support. These foreign Communist parties then often can be used to serve the interests of Communist parties in power — as Western Communists were used to help the Soviet Union penetrate American and British atomic secrets in the early postwar years.

When the occasion seems to demand it, Communist parties in power will not hesitate to subordinate ruthlessly the interests of their comrades in other countries to their own national needs — as the Soviet Union compromised the positions of the Communist parties of the United States and Western Europe, in 1939, by signing a nonaggression pact with Hitler's Germany. But merely to preserve the usefulness of these foreign parties, the Communist great powers must take into account the positions of other members of the world Communist movement — at least to some extent — in formulating their own foreign policies.

Second, it is a mistake to think of ideology and national interest as polar opposites competing for influence over national policy. "National interests" have no objective existence independent of policymakers who define them in light of their own values, attitudes, and ways of looking at the world. And it is in the process of formulating such definitions that ideology can be most influential. For ideology *is* a way of looking at the world, a lens which mediates between the wearer and reality — giving him a more or less distorted view of events, depending on the nature of the situation being observed and on the content of the ideology itself. Ideology rarely dictates particular policy choices directly. But it may affect them indirectly by influencing policymakers' perceptions; by structuring their definitions of the situations they face; and by suggesting to them certain standard tactics or techniques, which they then may or may not choose to employ, but which they can scarcely help considering.

Some points covered in our discussion in Chapter Seven of the underlying bases of men's opinions are applicable here. To review briefly the most relevant: leaders tend to internalize — more than most of their followers — the essential values and attitudes of their societies; all other things being

[22] An excellent discussion of the importance of ideology and national interest in Soviet and Chinese foreign policy may be found in Vernon V. Aspaturian, "Soviet Foreign Policy" and Allen S. Whiting, "Foreign Policy of Communist China," pp. 141–152 and 275–286, respectively, in Roy C. Macridis (ed.), *Foreign Policy in World Politics* (2nd ed.; Englewood Cliffs, N.J.: Prentice-Hall, 1962).

equal (which they seldom are), there is a general tendency toward consistency between men's professed and their actual beliefs; the more concrete information an individual can bring to bear on a given subject (again, all other things being equal), the less room there will be for him to be influenced in forming opinions on that subject by emotional or ideological predispositions.

To the extent that these hypotheses — generated largely by research with Western subjects — can be generalized to apply also to non-Western elites, it follows that Russian and Chinese leaders are likely to be influenced significantly by the ideology which dominates their societies. Mastery of Communist doctrine has been a contributing factor in the rise to power of many of them. In addition, during their revolutionary and Party careers, many of them have found it necessary to act in ways which would be judged harshly by other value systems, but which communism condones — thus adding to the psychological benefits to them of a genuine belief in that doctrine. And though any expedient action they may wish to take can no doubt be rationalized ideologically, the construction of a tortured ideological rationalization involves both going to some trouble intellectually and risking the opposition or defection of some "true believers" whose inclinations may be more orthodox.

The hypotheses cited suggest further that ideology will be more influential in choosing goals than means, more influential in determining long-run than short-run policies — more influential, that is, when relevant factual information is sparse and when considerations of immediate expediency are least pressing. Thus, as we noted above, the Chinese leaders' lesser contact with the nations of the West and with the nature of nuclear weapons may leave them with fewer concrete reasons than their Soviet comrades for modifying orthodox Communist doctrine — on war, coexistence, and the possibilities of peaceful transitions to socialism — in the light of new developments.

It is possibly in their overall orientation toward history as struggle that both Soviet and Chinese leaders have been most significantly — and most unfortunately — biased by their ideological outlook. For the interests of the various nations and classes in the contemporary world are far from diametrically opposed or, as the Communists themselves would put it, antagonistic. We have, all of us, a common interest in living to see tomorrow. And we have begun to discover that this fundamental common interest has profound ramifications — that it creates a common interest, too, in the conditions under which other peoples live. Their continued suffering, in the long run, threatens our continued existence.

We in America have a quasi-ideological orientation of our own — in favor of single-minded pursuit of private interest even at the expense of community interest — to surmount in adjusting to these new facts of life in the nuclear age. The Communists, with their emphasis on struggle and on re-making the world by force have an even more dangerous ideological cast of mind to overcome. Americans and other Westerners are generally satisfied with their political and economic institutions. They are not likely to opt for communism voluntarily and are too powerful and determined to allow others to force it upon them — just as the Communist nations are unlikely to be converted to democracy by force.

If there is to be a tomorrow, then, the adherents of communism must adjust their ways of thought and their doctrine to encompass these fundamental facts. It is not impossible. Islam and Christianity were once believed to be unable to coexist with one another, but have managed to do so rather well for several centuries. In certain respects, some contemporary Communist theoreticians have made a promising start — but only a start — in the necessary direction. We, on our part, must do what we can to help convince them — by words and deeds — that our ultimate aspirations and theirs are not so very far apart; that a world in which they are free to go their way and we are free to go ours does not conflict with Marx's ultimate vision of abundance and self-realization for the masses of mankind.

❧ CASE
STUDY   *ORIGINS OF THE SINO-SOVIET SPLIT*

The case study for this chapter consists of statements by the Soviet and Chinese Communist parties concerning the origins and the nature of the differences between them. These statements are couched in the jargon introduced in this chapter and can be understood fully only by keeping in mind the special meanings Communists assign to such terms as "socialist," "democratic," "imperialist," "proletarian," "bourgeois," "the people," "national liberation struggles," "adventurism," and many others.

1. When did the Sino-Soviet split originate, according to each of the participants? What critical issues were involved? Who was responsible for inaugurating the split in the first place? For bringing it out into the open? Which of the contestants appears to have won more support within the international Communist movement? Where the Russian and Chinese versions of these developments differ, does one or the other seem clearly more persuasive to you? Why? Does either party make accusations against the other which are patently false or insincere? If so, specify and explain.

2. Which of the parties to this dispute do you believe to be more faithful to the letter and the spirit of Marxist-Leninist doctrine itself?

Is either one guilty (as charged) of right- or left-wing deviations from basic Communist beliefs? Explain.

3. What Chinese *ideological* positions does the Soviet letter take exception to? What specific Chinese *policy actions* does it find objectionable? What Soviet ideological interpretations and specific policy actions do the Chinese statements condemn? (List them separately.) Does it seem to you that the ideological or the concrete policy differences have been more decisive in creating and maintaining the Sino-Soviet dispute? Explain.

4. What do you think are the prospects that this split will be healed over the next five to ten years?

5. What future United States policies, in Vietnam and elsewhere, do you think would be most likely to affect Sino-Soviet relations in ways advantageous to the United States? Defend your position.

CENTRAL COMMITTEE OF THE COMMUNIST PARTY
OF THE SOVIET UNION (CPSU)

For nearly half a century the Soviet country under the leadership of the Communist Party is leading a struggle for the triumph of the ideas of Marxism-Leninism, in the name of the freedom and happiness of the working people in the whole world. World history knew no example when one country would render such extensive aid to other countries in developing their economy, science and technology. And only a short time ago Chinese leaders spoke much and justly about the friendship of the peoples of China and the Soviet Union, about the unity of the CPSU and the CPC [Communist Party of China], highly appreciated Soviet aid, and urged people to learn on the experience of the Soviet Union.

This was how matters stood until the Chinese leaders began retreating from the general line of the world communist movement. In April 1960 the Chinese comrades openly revealed their differences with the world communist movement by publishing a collection of articles called "Long Live Leninism!" This collection, based on distortions, truncated and incorrectly interpreted theses of the well-known works of Lenin. . . .

At the meeting of representatives of 81 Communist and Workers' Parties,

From an "Open Letter of the Central Committee of the Communist Party of the Soviet Union to Its Members and Sub-Units," July 14, 1963. These paragraphs are excerpted from the much longer document named, which appeared in *Pravda,* the official newspaper of the Soviet Communist Party, on July 14, 1963. This text has been checked against the translation that appears in *Current Digest of the Soviet Press,* vol. XV, No. 28 (August 7, 1963). The wording of these translations differs, of course. But there are no important substantive differences between the two versions in the passages quoted. As in the excerpts from official Chinese Communist press statements that follow, ellipses have been used only to indicate omission of parts of sentences.

which took place in November 1960, the absolute majority of the fraternal Parties rejected the incorrect views and concepts of the CPC leadership. The Chinese delegation at this meeting stubbornly upheld its own particular views and signed the Statement only when the danger arose of its full isolation.

Today it has become absolutely obvious that the CPC leaders were only maneuvering when they affixed their signatures to the Statement of 1960. Shortly after the meeting they resumed the propaganda of their course, using as the mouthpiece the leadership of the Albanian Party of Labor. Behind the back of our Party they launched a campaign against the CPSU Central Committee and the Soviet Government.

Deepening their ideological differences with the fraternal Parties, the leaders of the CPC began carrying them over to international relations. The Chinese organs began curtailing economic and trade relations of the PRC [People's Republic of China] with the Soviet Union and other socialist countries. On the initiative of the PRC Government the volume of China's trade with the Soviet Union was cut almost 67 per cent in the past three years; deliveries of industrial plant dropped forty times. This reduction took place on the initiative of the Chinese leaders. We regret that the PRC leadership has embarked on such a road. We have always believed and believe now that it is necessary to go on developing Soviet-Chinese relations, to develop co-operation. This would have been mutually beneficial for both sides, and above all to People's China, which had received great assistance from the Soviet Union and other socialist countries.

Since the end of 1961 the Chinese representatives at international democratic organizations began openly imposing their erroneous views. They came out against the participation of representatives of the Afro-Asian Solidarity Committees of the European socialist countries in the Third Solidarity Conference of the Peoples of Asian and African Countries in Moshi. The leader of the Chinese delegation told the Soviet representatives that "the white have nothing to do here." At the Journalists' Conference in Djakarta the Chinese representatives followed a line towards preventing Soviet journalists from participating as full-fledged delegates on the plea that the Soviet Union . . . is not an Asian country.

What is the gist of differences between the CPC on the one hand and . . . the international communist movement on the other hand? . . . the questions which bear on vital interests of the peoples are in the center of the dispute. These are the questions of war and peace, the question of the role and development of the world socialist system, these are the questions of the struggle against the ideology and practice of the "personality cult," these are the questions of strategy and tactics of the world labor movement and the national-liberation struggle.

The nuclear rocket weapons that were created in the middle of our century changed the old notions about war. These weapons possess an un-heard-of devastating force. Suffice it to say that the explosion of only one powerful thermonuclear bomb surpasses the explosive force of all ammuni-tion used during all previous wars, including the First and the Second World Wars. And many thousands [of] such bombs have been accumulated!

The 20th Congress of our Party made the extremely important conclu-sion that in our times there is no fatal inevitability of war between the states.

The Chinese comrades obviously underestimate all the danger of thermo-nuclear war. "The atomic bomb is a paper tiger," it "is not terrible at all," they contend.

The main thing, don't you see, is to put an end to imperialism as quickly as possible, but how, with what losses will this be achieved seems to be a secondary question. To whom, it is right to ask, is it secondary? To the hundreds of millions of people who are doomed to death in the event of the unleashing of a thermonuclear war? To the states that will be erased from the face of the earth in the very first hours of such a war? No one, including also big states, has the right to play with the destinies of millions of people.

We would like to ask the Chinese comrades, who suggest to build a bright future on the ruins of the old world destroyed by a thermonuclear war, if they consulted the working class of the countries where imperialism dominates? The working class of the capitalist countries would be sure to tell them: Do we ask you to trigger off a war and destroy our countries while annihilating imperialists? Is it not a fact that the monopolists, the imperialists are only a comparatively small group while the bulk of the population of the capitalist countries consists of the working class, working peasantry, working intelligentsia. The atomic bomb does not distinguish between the imperialists and working people, it hits big areas and therefore millions of workers would be destroyed per one monopolist. The working class, the working people will ask such "revolutionaries": What right do you have to settle for us the questions of our existence and our class strug-gle? We are also in favor of socialism but we want to gain it through the class struggle and not by unleashing a world war.

Such posing of the question by the Chinese comrades may engender well justified suspicion that this is no longer a class approach in the struggle for the abolition of capitalism but some entirely different aims. If both the exploiters and the exploited are buried under the ruins of the old world, who will build the "bright future"?

In this connection it is impossible not to note the fact that instead of the class internationalist approach expressed in the call "workers of the world, unite" the Chinese comrades stubbornly propagate the slogan de-prived of any class meaning: "The wind from the East prevails over the wind from the West."

The deep difference in the views of the CPSU, other Marxist-Leninist parties on the one hand and the CPC leaders on the other hand on the questions of war, peace and peaceful coexistence was manifested with particular clarity during the 1962 crisis in the Caribbean Sea. It was a sharp international crisis: never before did mankind come so close to the brink of a thermonuclear war as it did in October last year. The Chinese comrades allege that in the period of the Caribbean crisis we made an "adventurist" mistake by introducing rockets in Cuba and then, "capitulated" to the American imperialism when we removed the rockets from Cuba.

What was the actual state of affairs? The CPSU Central Committee and the Soviet Government possessed trustworthy information that an armed aggression of United States imperialism against Cuba was about to start. We realized with sufficient clarity that the most resolute steps were needed to rebuff aggression, to defend the Cuban revolution effectively.

Proceeding from the need of defending the Cuban revolution, the Soviet Government and the Government of Cuba reached agreement on the delivery of missiles to Cuba, because this was the only effective way of preventing aggression on the part of American imperialism. The delivery of missiles to Cuba signified that an attack on her would meet resolute rebuff with the employment of rocket weapons against the organizers of aggression.

A real danger of world thermonuclear war arose. There was one alternative in the prevailing situation: either to follow in the wake of the "madmen" (that is how the most aggressive and reactionary representatives of American imperialism were called) and embark upon the road of unleashing a world thermonuclear war, or, using the opportunities offered by the delivery of missiles, to take all measures to reach agreement on the peaceful solution of the crisis and to prevent aggression against the Cuban Republic. We have chosen, as is known, the second road and are convinced that we have done the right thing.

Agreement on the removal of missile weapons in reply to the United States Government's commitment not to invade Cuba and to keep its allies from doing this, the heroic struggle of the Cuban people, the support rendered to them by the peace-loving nations, have made possible the frustration of the plans of extreme adventuristic circles of American imperialism, which were ready to go the whole hog. As a result it was possible to defend revolutionary Cuba and save peace.

The Chinese comrades argue that the imperialists cannot be trusted in anything, that they are bound to cheat. But this is not a case of faith, but rather a case of sober calculation. Eight months have passed since the liquidation of the crisis in the Caribbean Sea area, and the United States Government is keeping its word — there is no invasion of Cuba. We have also assumed a commitment to remove our missiles from Cuba and we have fulfilled it.

The CPC leadership . . . assumed the stand of a critic, not of a militant ally and comrade at the most responsible moment. Nobody has heard from the Chinese leaders in those days statements about their practical actions in defense of the Cuban revolution. Instead of this the Chinese leaders obviously endeavoured to aggravate the situation in the Caribbean Sea area, which was tense even without this, added fuel to the smouldering fire of the conflict.

The CPC leaders have such weak arguments in the struggle against the CPSU and other fraternal Parties that they have to resort to all sorts of ruses. They begin by ascribing to us absolutely groundless positions of their own invention and then accuse us and fight against us by exposing these positions. Such precisely is the case with their absurd allegation that the CPSU and other fraternal Parties renounce revolution and substitute peaceful coexistence for class struggle. It is well known in any political study group in our country that when we speak of peaceful coexistence we mean the interstate relations of the socialist countries with the countries of capitalism. The principle of peaceful coexistence, naturally, can in no way be extended to the relations between the antagonistic classes in the capitalist states; it is impermissible to extend it to the struggle of the working class against the bourgeoisie for its class interests, to the struggle of the oppressed peoples against the colonialists. The CPSU resolutely comes out against peaceful coexistence in ideology. This is a simple truth which all who regard themselves as Marxist-Leninists should have mastered.

EDITORIAL DEPARTMENTS OF "RENMIN RIBAO" (THE PEKING "PEOPLES' DAILY") AND "HUNG CHI" ("RED FLAG")

How have the differences in the international communist movement and between the leadership of the CPSU and ourselves arisen? And how have they grown to their present serious dimensions?

The open letter of the Central Committee of the CPSU spreads the notion that the differences in the international communist movement were started by the three articles which we published in April 1960 under the title of *Long Live Leninism!* This is a big lie.

What is the truth? The truth is that the whole series of differences of

From "The Origin and Development of the Differences Between the Leadership of the CPSU and Ourselves" (A commentary on the "Open Letter of the Central Committee of the CPSU") September 6, 1963. This and the following document quoted from were written by the editorial departments of *Renmin Ribao* (the Peking *Peoples' Daily*) and *Hung Chi (Red Flag)*, the official newspaper and theoretical journal, respectively, of the Communist Party of China. The English language text appeared in the *Peking Review*, September 13, 1963.

principle in the international communist movement began more than seven years ago. To be specific, it began with the 20th Congress of the CPSU in 1956.

Khrushchev viciously and demagogically told a host of lies in his secret report, and threw around charges that Stalin had a "persecution mania," indulged in "brutal arbitrariness," took the path of "mass repressions and terror," "knew the country and agriculture only from films" and "planned operations on a globe," that Stalin's leadership "became a serious obstacle in the path of Soviet social development," and so on and so forth. He completely obliterated the meritorious deeds of . . . Stalin. . . .

In his report to the 20th Congress, under the pretext that "radical changes" had taken place in the world situation, Khrushchev put forward the thesis of "peaceful transition." He said that the road of the October Revolution * was "the only correct road in those historical conditions," but that as the situation had changed, it had become possible to effect the transition from capitalism to socialism "through the parliamentary road." In essence, the erroneous thesis is a clear revision of the Marxist-Leninist teachings on the state and revolution and a clear denial of the universal significance of the road of the October Revolution.

Khrushchev pictured the U.S. Government and its head as people resisting the forces of war, and not as representatives of the imperialist forces of war. It was as much as saying that it was possible for the U.S. Government and its head not to represent the interests of U.S. monopoly capital and for them to abandon their policies of war and aggression and that they had become forces defending peace.

The questions raised by the leadership of the CPSU at the 20th Congress, and especially the questions of Stalin and of "peaceful transition," are by no means simply internal affairs of the CPSU; they are vital issues of common interest for all fraternal Parties. Without any prior consultation with the fraternal Parties, the leadership of the CPSU drew arbitrary conclusions; it forced the fraternal Parties to accept a fait accompli and, on the pretext of "combatting the personality cult," crudely interfered in the internal affairs of fraternal Parties and countries and subverted their leaderships, thus pushing its policy of sectarianism and splittism in the international communist movement.

On many occasions in internal discussions after the 20th Congress of the CPSU, leading comrades of the Central Committee of the CPC solemnly criticized the errors of the CPSU leadership.

> In April 1956, less than two months after the 20th Congress, in conversations both with Comrade Mikoyan, Member of the Presidium of the Central Committee of the CPSU, and with the Soviet Ambassador

* [The 1917 Communist revolution in Russia.]

to China, Comrade Mao Tse-tung expressed our views on the question of Stalin. He emphasized that Stalin's "merits outweighed his faults" and that it was necessary to "make a concrete analysis" and "an all-round evaluation" of Stalin.

The fact is that at no time and in no place did the Chinese Communist Party completely affirm the 20th Congress of the CPSU, agree with the complete negation of Stalin or endorse the view of peaceful transition to socialism through the "parliamentary road.". . . For the sake of unity against the enemy and out of consideration for the difficult position the leaders of the CPSU were then in, we refrained in those days from open criticism of the errors of the 20th Congress. . . .

The errors of the 20th Congress brought great ideological confusion in the international communist movement and caused it to be deluged with revisionist ideas. Most striking among the events which took place during this period were the incident in Soviet-Polish relations and the counter-revolutionary rebellion in Hungary. The two events were different in character. But the leadership of the CPSU made grave errors in both. By moving up troops in an attempt to subdue the Polish comrades by armed force it committed the error of great-power chauvinism. And at the critical moment when the Hungarian counter-revolutionaries had occupied Budapest, for a time it intended to adopt a policy of capitulation and abandon socialist Hungary to counter-revolution. We insisted on the taking of all necessary measures to smash the counter-revolutionary rebellion in Hungary and firmly opposed the abandonment of socialist Hungary. We insisted that in the handling of problems between fraternal Parties and countries correct principles should be followed so as to strengthen the unity of the socialist camp, and we firmly opposed the erroneous methods of great-power chauvinism. . . .

The 1957 Meeting of Representatives of the Communist and Workers' Parties took place in Moscow. . . . The delegation of the CPC, which was headed by Comrade Mao Tse-tung, did a great deal of work during the meeting. The original draft said not a word about non-peaceful transition, mentioning only peaceful transition; moreover, it described peaceful transition as "securing a majority in parliament and transforming parliament from an instrument of the bourgeois dictatorship into an instrument of a genuine people's state power."

As a result of the common efforts of the delegations of the CPC and the other fraternal Parties, the meeting finally adopted the present version of the Declaration, which contains two major changes on the question of the transition from capitalism to socialism compared with the first draft put forward by the leadership of the CPSU. First, while indicating the possibility of peaceful transition, the Declaration also points to the road of non-peaceful transition and stresses that "Leninism teaches, and experience confirms, that the ruling classes never relinquish power voluntarily." Secondly, while speaking of securing "a firm majority in parliament" the Declaration emphasizes the need to "launch an extra-parliamentary mass struggle, smash the resistance of the reactionary forces and create the necessary conditions for peaceful realization of the socialist revolution."

Despite these changes, the formulation in the Declaration on the question of the transition from capitalism to socialism was still unsatisfactory. We finally conceded the point only out of consideration for the repeatedly expressed wish of the leaders of the CPSU that the formulation should show some connection with that of the 20th Congress of the CPSU.

We have pointed out long ago, and deem it necessary to reiterate now, that in accordance with the principle that all fraternal Parties are independent and equal, no one is entitled to demand of fraternal Parties that they accept the resolutions of the congress of one Party or for that matter anything else; and the resolutions of a Party congress, whatever the Party, cannot be regarded as the common line of the international communist movement and have no binding force on other fraternal Parties. Only Marxism-Leninism and the documents unanimously agreed upon constitute the common code binding us and all fraternal Parties.

After the Moscow Meeting of 1957. . . . In complete disregard of the common conclusion of the 1957 Declaration that U.S. imperialism is the enemy of all the people of the world, the leadership of the CPSU passionately sought collaboration with U.S. imperialism and the settlement of world problems by the heads of the Soviet Union and the United States. Particularly around the time of the Camp David Talks in September 1959, Khrushchev lauded Eisenhower to the skies.

In 1958 the leadership of the CPSU put forward unreasonable demands designed to bring China under Soviet military control. These unreasonable demands were rightly and firmly rejected by the Chinese government. Not long afterwards, in June 1959, the Soviet Government unilaterally tore up the agreement on new technology for national defence concluded between China and the Soviet Union in October 1957, and refused to provide China with a sample of an atomic bomb and technical data concerning its manufacture.

Then, on the eve of Khrushchev's visit to the United States, ignoring China's repeated objections the leadership of the CPSU rushed out the TASS * statement of September 9 on the Sino-Indian border incident, siding with the Indian reactionaries. In this way, the leadership of the CPSU brought the differences between China and the Soviet Union right into the open before the world.

The leaders of the CPSU and Soviet publications also levelled many virulent attacks on the domestic and foreign policies of the Chinese Com-

* [TASS is the Soviet Union's official news agency.]

munist Party. These attacks were almost invariably led by Khrushchev in person. He insinuated that China's socialist construction was "skipping over a stage" and was "equalitarian communism" and that China's people's communes were "in essence reactionary." By innuendo he maligned China as warlike, guilty of "adventurism," and so on and so forth. Back from the Camp David Talks, he went so far as to try to sell China the U.S. plot of "two Chinas" and, at the state banquet celebrating the Tenth Anniversary of the founding of the People's Republic of China, he read China a lecture against "testing by force the stability of the capitalist system."

In the circumstances, in order to defend Marxism-Leninism and the 1957 Declaration and clear up the ideological confusion in the international communist movement, the Communist Party of China published "Long Live Leninism!" and two other articles in April 1960.

A week after the publication of "Long Live Leninism!" and our two other articles, an American U-2 plane intruded into Soviet air space and the United States aborted the four-power summit conference. The "spirit of Camp David" completely vanished. Thus events entirely confirmed our views. But . . . In the summer of 1960 . . . the leadership of the CPSU extended the ideological differences between the Chinese and Soviet Parties to the sphere of state relations.

In July the Soviet Government suddenly unilaterally decided to recall all the Soviet experts in China within one month, thereby tearing up hundreds of agreements and contracts. . . . It took the unwarranted step of demanding the recall by the Chinese Government of a staff member of the Chinese Embassy in the Soviet Union; and it provoked troubles on the Sino-Soviet border.

. . . The open letter of the Central Committee of the CPSU falsely charges China with extending the ideological differences to the sphere of state relations and with reducing trade between the two countries, while deliberately concealing the fact that the Soviet Government withdrew all its experts from China and unilaterally tore up hundreds of agreements and contracts, and that it was these unilateral Soviet actions which made Sino-Soviet trade shrink.

The Meeting of the Representatives of the 81 Fraternal Parties was held in Moscow in November 1960. . . . After the leaders of the CPSU agreed to drop their erroneous propositions and accepted the correct propositions of other Parties, the delegations of the CPC and some other fraternal Parties also made certain concessions. For instance, we differed on the questions of the 20th Congress of the CPSU and of the forms of transition from capitalism to socialism, but out of consideration for the needs of the CPSU and certain other fraternal Parties we agreed to the inclusion of the same wording on these two questions as that used in the 1957 Declaration. But we made it plain at the time to the leaders of the CPSU that this would be the last time we accommodated ourselves to such a formulation about the 20th Congress; we would never do so again.

. . . The main political content of the wrong line they were attempting to impose on the fraternal Parties consisted of the erroneous theories of "peaceful coexistence," "peaceful competition" and "peaceful transition.". . .

The ink was scarcely dry on their signature to the 1960 Statement before they began wrecking it. . . . They took as their friend U.S. imperialism which the Statement declares to be the enemy of the people of the world, advocating "U.S.-Soviet co-operation" and expressing the desire to work together with Kennedy to "set about building durable bridges of confidence, mutual understanding and friendship."

. . . The Programme adopted at the 22nd Congress . . . crudely revises the essence of Marxism-Leninism, namely, its teachings on proletarian revolution, on the dictatorship of the proletariat and on the party of the proletariat, declaring that the dictatorship of the proletariat is no longer needed in the Soviet Union and that the nature of the CPSU as the vanguard of the proletariat has changed, and advancing preposterous theories of a "state of the whole people" and a "party of the entire people."

It is a programme which opposes revolution on the part of the people still living under the imperialist and capitalist system, who comprise two-thirds of the world's population, and opposes the carrying of revolution through to completion on the part of the people already on the socialist road, who comprise one-third of the world's population. It is a revisionist programme for the preservation or restoration of capitalism.

In April and May 1962 the leaders of the CPSU used their organs and personnel in Sinkiang, China, to carry out large-scale subversive activities in the Ili region and enticed and coerced several tens of thousands of Chinese citizens into going to the Soviet Union.

In August 1962 the Soviet Government formally notified China that the Soviet Union would conclude an agreement with the United States on the prevention of nuclear proliferation. This was a joint Soviet-U.S. plot to monopolize nuclear weapons and an attempt to deprive China of the right to possess nuclear weapons to resist the U.S. nuclear threat. The Chinese Government lodged repeated protests against this.

The leadership of the CPSU has become increasingly anxious to strike political bargains with U.S. imperialism and has been bent on forming a reactionary alliance with Kennedy, even at the expense of the interests of the socialist camp and the international communist movement. An outstanding example was the fact that, during the Caribbean crisis, the leadership of the CPSU committed the error of capitulationism by submitting to the nuclear blackmail of the U.S. imperialists and accepting the U.S. Government's demand for "international inspection" in violation of Cuban sovereignty.

The leadership of the CPSU has become increasingly anxious to collude with the Indian reactionaries and has been bent on forming a reactionary alliance with Nehru against socialist China. The leadership of the CPSU and its press openly sided with Indian reaction, condemned China for its just stand on the Sino-Indian border conflict and defended the Nehru government. Two-thirds of Soviet economic aid to India have been given since the Indian reactionaries provoked the Sino-Indian border conflict. Even after large-scale armed conflict on the Sino-Indian border began in the autumn of 1962, the leadership of the CPSU has continued to extend military aid to the Indian reactionaries.

The leadership of the CPSU has become increasingly anxious to collude with the Tito clique of Yugoslavia and has been bent on forming a reactionary alliance with the renegade Tito to oppose all Marxist-Leninist parties.

In these grave circumstances, the Chinese Communist Party had no alternative but to make open replies to the attacks of some fraternal Parties.

The leaders of the CPSU have a bad habit: they undiscriminatingly stick labels on anyone who criticizes them.

They say, "You are anti-Soviet!" No, friends! The label "anti-Soviet" cannot be stuck on us. Our criticism of your errors is precisely for the sake of defending the great CPSU and the great Soviet Union and preventing their prestige from being badly damaged by you. To put it plainly, it is you, and not we, who are really anti-Soviet and who are defaming and discrediting the CPSU and the Soviet Union. Ever since the complete negation of Stalin at the 20th Congress of the CPSU, you have committed innumerable foul deeds. Not all the water in the Volga can wash away the great shame you have brought upon the CPSU and upon the Soviet Union.

They say, "You are trying to seize the leadership!" No, friends! It is not at all clever of you to make this slander. The way you put it, it would seem that some people are contending with you for some such thing as "the leadership." Is this not tantamount to shamelessly claiming that some sort of "leadership" exists in the international communist movement and that you have this "leadership"? It is a very, very bad habit of yours thus to put on the airs of a patriarchal party. It is entirely illegitimate. The 1957 Declaration and the 1960 Statement clearly state that all Communist Parties are independent and equal. According to this principle, the relations among fraternal Parties should under no circumstances be like the relations between a leading Party and the led, and much less like the relations between a patriarchal father and his son. We have always opposed any one Party commanding other fraternal Parties, and it has never occurred to us that we ourselves should command other fraternal Parties, and so the question of contending for leadership simply does not arise.

The international communist movement is going through an important period. The present debate has a vital bearing on the future of the proletarian world revolution and the destiny of mankind. As history will prove, after this great debate Marxism-Leninism will shine forth still more brilliantly and the revolutionary cause of the international proletariat and the people of the world will win still greater victories.

EDITORIAL DEPARTMENTS OF "RENMIN RIBAO" (THE PEKING "PEOPLES' DAILY") AND "HUNG CHI" ("RED FLAG")

The new leaders of the CPSU have faithfully taken over the mantle of Khrushchev. Immediately after taking office, the new leaders of the CPSU extolled Johnson as "sensible" and "moderate." They have continued to proclaim that the Soviet Union and the United States are two superpowers on which the fate of the world depends, that "there are sufficiently broad areas for co-operation" between them, and that "there are still many unutilized potentialities."

Catering to U.S. imperialism, Khrushchev used the United Nations as a stock exchange for the domination of the world by two great powers, the Soviet Union and the United States. The new leaders of the CPSU have continued this reactionary policy. They have again brought up Khrushchev's proposal for a standing U.N. armed force. They voted in the United Nations for a "ceasefire" and for the realization of "national reconciliation" in the Congo (L),* and they also voted for the "ceasefire" in the Dominican Republic. Wherever the people rise up in armed struggle against U.S. imperialism or win victories in such struggle, and wherever U.S. imperialism suffers defeats and finds itself in a predicament, the new leaders of the CPSU hurriedly come forward to help it out.

The situation in Viet Nam developed directly contrary to the wishes of the Khrushchev revisionists. The new leaders of the CPSU have been busy running errands for the U.S. aggressors, who are anxious to find a way out of their predicament in Viet Nam. Johnson wanted to play his fraudulent game of "unconditional discussions." So the new leaders of the CPSU put forward the idea of "unconditional negotiations." On February 16 this year, the day after Kosygin's return to Moscow, the Soviet Government officially put before Viet Nam and China a proposal to convene a new international conference on Indo-China without prior conditions, which in fact was the advocacy of "unconditional negotiations" on the Viet Nam ques-

From "Refutation of the New Leaders of the CPSU on 'United Action'" (November, 1965). The English language text of this article appeared in the *Peking Review,* November 12, 1965.

* [Leopoldville — that is, the former Belgian Congo, as distinguished from the Congo (Brazzaville), a former French colony.]

tion. In a nutshell, their purpose is to help the United States to bring about "peace talks" by deception, "peace talks" which could go on indefinitely and also allow the United States to hang on in South Viet Nam indefinitely.

Because they are the political representatives of the privileged bourgeois stratum in the Soviet Union, just as Khrushchev was, the new leaders of the CPSU pursue domestic and foreign policies which are not proletarian but bourgeois, not socialist but capitalist. Like Khrushchev, they are in a position of antagonism to the Soviet people, who constitute more than 90 per cent of the Soviet population, and they are encountering even stronger dissatisfaction and opposition on the part of the Soviet people.

In the final analysis, in all parts of the world including the Soviet Union, the masses of the people, who constitute the overwhelming majority of Communists and cadres want revolution and are upholding or will uphold Marxism-Leninism. As Lenin told the old-line revisionists, the proletariat will sooner or later unite and eventually win on a world scale, "only it is moving and will move, is proceeding and will proceed, against you, it will be a victory over you."

Chapter Eleven

THE INSTRUMENTS OF POLICY: THE NEW WEAPONRY AND THE NEW DIPLOMACY

In one of the case studies in this book we reviewed the decision to drop the first atomic bomb on the city of Hiroshima at the close of World War II. That bomb, the one that ushered in the atomic age, had a destructive power equivalent to that of approximately 20,000 tons (20 *kilo*tons) of TNT. Today, both the United States and the Soviet Union possess hundreds upon hundreds of thermonuclear (hydrogen) weapons, each many times more powerful than the Hiroshima bomb. Some of these bombs have, individually, a destructive capacity of at least 50 *mega*tons — that is, the equivalent of the destructive power of 50 *million* tons of TNT — 2,500 times that of the Hiroshima bomb, and 20 times as great as that of all the bombs dropped on Germany during World War II.[1] And existing technology can permit the production of bombs several times as powerful. Great Britain, France, and Communist China already have exploded bombs much more

[1] All told, it was estimated that by 1966 the United States had close to a thousand land-based intercontinental ballistic missiles (ICBM's) and between 400 and 600 submarine-based missiles in a total nuclear weapons stockpile approaching 25,000 megatons of destructive capacity, while the Soviet Union had about 400–450 ICBM's, 120–150 submarine-based missiles and 750 medium and intermediate range ballistic missiles in a nuclear weapons stockpile approaching 12,000 megatons. William Beecher in *The New York Times,* November 13, 1966, p. 84; and Hanson Baldwin, *ibid.,* July 14, 1966, reprinted in *Department of Defense Appropriations for Fiscal Year 1967,* Part 2, pp. 715–717. Hearings Before the Subcommittee on Department of Defense of the Committee on Appropriations and the Committee on Armed Services, United States Senate, 89th Cong., 2nd sess., February–August, 1966. Hereafter: *1967 Senate Defense Appropriations Hearings.*

In addition, the two great powers possess literally thousands of "tactical" nuclear weapons, some of them as much as five times more powerful than the Hiroshima bomb.

466

powerful than the Hiroshima bomb, and there can be little doubt that other nations will soon join this select company.

It has been estimated that a twenty megaton bomb could almost totally devastate an area of 48 square miles, spreading radioactive fallout over many thousands of square miles — an area as large as a middle-sized state. President Kennedy once noted that a full-scale nuclear exchange with the weapons then in existence could kill more than 300 million Americans, Russians, and Europeans in less than one hour! More recently, Secretary of Defense McNamara estimated — by projecting existing United States and Soviet offensive and defensive capabilities — that a Soviet first strike against the United States in 1970 could be expected to kill between 130 and 135 million Americans, close to two-thirds of our population. He added that no conceivable defensive measures, regardless of cost, could be expected to reduce American fatalities in case of an all-out Soviet attack "below some tens of millions." [2] These estimates, it should be noted, refer to deaths only, and do not include other casualties, property damage, etc.

The truly revolutionary destructive capacity of these new weapons has posed new problems for mankind, and created new patterns of diplomacy and strategic thought. In this chapter, we will try to introduce some of the new terminology created to describe these problems, and to hint at a few of the considerations which scholars and policymakers dealing with these problems must take into account.[3]

DETERRENCE

The very destructiveness of the new weaponry has made how to avoid their use the fundamental concern in any overall strategy. Since it seems perfectly clear that any full-scale nuclear war could benefit *none* of the participants, every nation's strategic policy must put primary emphasis not on "winning" such a war once it has begun, but on preventing it from occurring in the first place. This might be achieved simply by yielding to those who threaten to use these weapons — an alternative rejected out of hand by most Americans. It might be achieved by negotiating a reliable disarmament agreement with the Soviet Union and other nuclear powers. But for reasons discussed in Chapter One two decades of sporadic negotiation have failed to realize this objective, which now, since Communist China's entry into the

---

2 *1967 Senate Defense Appropriations Hearings*, Part 1, pp. 51 and 58.

3 A good starting point for those wishing to study these problems in more detail would be Henry A. Kissinger, *Nuclear Weapons and Foreign Policy* (New York: Harper and Row, 1957); Herman Kahn, *On Thermonuclear War* (Princeton, N.J.: Princeton University Press, 1960); Herman Kahn, *Thinking About the Unthinkable* (New York: Avon Books, 1962); and a collection of readings, edited by Kissinger, *Problems of National Strategy* (New York: Praeger, 1965). In this collection, deserving of particular attention is the article by Albert Wohlstetter, "The Delicate Balance of Terror," which appeared originally in *Foreign Affairs* (January, 1959).

nuclear "club," seems further away than ever. Finally, a nuclear war might conceivably be avoided by *deterring* the nations which possess nuclear weapons from using them — by convincing them that they would lose more by launching a nuclear attack than they could possibly gain from it.

The concept of deterrence, of course, is not applicable to nuclear weapons alone. Its basic principle is well understood by the preschooler warning his big brother: "If you hit me, I'll tell mommy." In our context, deterrence — in its most general form — means something like: "If you do X, I will see to it that you get hurt more than doing X can possibly be worth to you." For such a threat to be effective, the party making it (1) must *appear to* possess the *means* to carry it out, (2) must *appear* to have the *will* to employ these means,[4] and (3) must be able to *communicate* this threat to those to be deterred. In addition, (4) the threatened party must behave rationally enough to consider and weigh the likely consequences of his actions. It is clear immediately, then, that deterrence is not a "thing," but a *relationship* between individuals or groups of people, and that it cannot be effective unless both parties meet the requisites cited.

Whether a deterrent threat will prove effective, however, depends not only on the characteristics of the parties, but also on the nature of the action to be deterred. Though the children involved may be the same, it is one thing to say: "If you hit me, I'll tell mommy, and she'll spank you," and quite another to say: "If you don't give me that new toy, I'll tell mommy you hit me, and she'll spank you." Herman Kahn, for instance, has referred to at least three types of deterrence relevant to the relationship between the United States and the Soviet Union.[5] The first type involves deterrence of a major attack upon the United States itself. The second involves deterrence of extreme provocations *short of* a major attack on the United States — a large-scale attack on Western Europe, for example. The third involves deterrence of other undesirable Soviet actions short of those covered in the preceding categories. The requirements for successful deterrence in each of these types of situations — in power, credibility, etc. — will often differ. (Other typologies than Kahn's are of course possible.)

DETERRENCE IN ACTION: BERLIN

Perhaps the most useful way to approach the complexities of deterrence is to outline and analyze the evolving deterrent relationship between East and West in a critical zone of cold war confrontation.

Since World War II, the city of Berlin, like the German nation of which

---

[4] Actually, it is only necessary that the party to be deterred be convinced that there is *some significant likelihood* that the threatener *can* and *will* make good his threat. The less likely that the threat will be carried out, however, the more the threatened party may discount it. But this complication will be ignored here.

[5] See the works by this author cited in footnote 3 above.

it was once the capital, has been divided. By 1948, the United States, Britain, and France had consolidated their sectors of occupation, both in Germany and in Berlin, into unified Western zones, while the Soviet Union continued to occupy East Germany and East Berlin. Since the city of Berlin is located wholly within Soviet-dominated East Germany, and since there are no clear written guarantees of the West's freedom of access to West Berlin across East German territory, the Western military garrisons there have always been in a vulnerable position.

In the two world wars in this century, Germany had given convincing evidence of its industrial and military potential. As the short-lived Soviet-American alliance during World War II rapidly deteriorated into the rivalry of the cold war, both the Russians and the Western allies were very much aware that the addition of a united Germany to either the Western or the Communist camp could create a major change in the postwar balance of power.

The West, hampered by the rapid American demobilization, soon sought to make use of the manpower and resources of West Germany to help redress the imbalance of conventional forces in Europe. Thus, a West German government was chosen by free elections in 1949 and five years later the Federal Republic of (West) Germany was restored to full sovereignty and brought into the North Atlantic Treaty Organization (NATO). The German people, however, were not reconciled to remaining divided permanently, and West Germany's elected political leaders were careful never to say anything which might be interpreted as an abandonment of the goal of someday reuniting the German nation.

Meanwhile, the Western presence in Berlin, in the heart of the (East) German Democratic Republic, became a symbol to the people of West Germany of their aspirations for reunification; and the Western commitment to defend West Berlin became a symbol of the Western commitment to support these aspirations.

In 1948, the Russians had tried to prevent the consolidation of the Western sectors of Germany by closing off the ground access routes to West Berlin. The primary Western response was the famous "airlift," which flew supplies into the blockaded city for almost a year, at great expense, until the blockade was ended. A Western counterblockade against trade with East Germany was also instituted.

In later years, West Berlin became a thriving island of prosperity and democracy in a bleak sea of austerity and hated foreign domination. In addition, it provided an escape hatch through which close to 3½ million persons — a disproportionate share of them young people, skilled workers, and professionals — made their way out of East Germany. Aside from the propaganda implications of this "voting with the feet," the labor supply and productivity of East Germany were seriously impaired by the exodus.

The Russians also claimed that the Western outpost in Berlin was a major espionage center. In Premier Khrushchev's words, West Berlin had become, for the Soviet Union, "a bone in the throat."

These circumstances set the stage for a series of dramatic Soviet-American confrontations over Berlin. Throughout the 1950's and the early 1960's, Soviet pressure against the Western position in Berlin was constant. On more than one occasion actual ultimatums were issued by the Soviets, warning that they would take action unilaterally if the West did not make significant concessions. But though the concessions demanded were not made, the Russian threats were not carried out.

Finally, in August, 1961, a wall was built across the middle of the city, sealing off East from West Berlin and stopping the flow of refugees. The West protested that this action was illegal, but did not try to knock the wall down. Since then, the Berlin situation appears to have stabilized somewhat, though it remains a very dangerous area of tension between East and West. From time to time, concerned Westerners' emotions are rekindled by spectacular incidents in which East German citizens attempting dramatic escapes into West Berlin are shot and killed by East German border guards.

This is the situation in briefest outline.[6] Now let us address ourselves to the question: Why has the Soviet Union not made use of its geographic advantages and local military superiority to force the West to abandon Berlin?

Though it is always dangerous to speculate about peoples' motives, it seems fair to say, in general, that the Soviets have been *deterred* from using military force in Berlin by the rational calculation that the Western response to such a use of force would cause them to lose more than they could hope to gain by such a move.

Suppose, for instance, that the Soviet Union had decided in 1949 to extend its blockade of Berlin to the air corridors above East Germany as well as to the ground access routes to West Berlin. This would probably have made it impossible for the allied airlift to operate successfully, but only at the cost of precipitating a shooting war in the air between Soviet and allied forces. In turn, this might have led, either directly — or, more likely, via a sequence of Soviet and American responses at successively higher levels of violence (that is, via *escalation*) — to the United States making use of its then small atomic arsenal against the Soviet Union. (Another consideration may well have been that, at first, there was real reason to doubt that the "airlift" would work as well and as long as it did. Thus, Soviet policymakers may have believed that waiting would prove as effective as military action — and a good deal safer. By the time the viability of

6 A fuller account of the evolution of the problem of Germany and Berlin may be found in Frederick H. Hartmann, *Germany Between East and West* (Englewood Cliffs, N.J.: Prentice-Hall, 1965).

the airlift had been demonstrated, the Western commitment to maintain it was much greater than when it was first instituted.)

Notice, first, that a relatively small United States nuclear capacity seems to have served satisfactorily as an effective deterrent at this time when the Soviet Union had no nuclear capacity of its own. The implicit United States threat [7] to punish the Soviet Union if it insisted on attacking American planes to force the West out of Berlin seems to have been *credible*. The United States had made use of its atomic capacity once already — against Japan — just three years earlier. Why should it fail to make use of it again, if, in the last resort, it saw no other means of preserving its position in Western Europe? The cost to the United States of using its nuclear weapons was by no means clearly greater than the cost of failing to use them in such a situation. American willingness to bear the costs and take the risks of the airlift — including the risk that American lives might be lost in direct encounters with Soviet forces — provided an impressive boost to the credibility of this threat.

Second, although in political terms it can be argued that the American strategy here was essentially defensive, in *military* terms it was clearly offensive. It was, in fact, what would now be called a *first-strike strategy*. It called for the United States, not the Soviet Union, to initiate both a direct attack on its opponent's homeland and the use of atomic weapons.

Third, the doctrine operating here — at least implicitly — later became known as the strategy of *massive retaliation*. The Soviets were to be deterred from using force in Berlin, *not* because the West was militarily capable of preventing that force from being effective in Berlin, or even in Germany as a whole, but because the West could not be expected to allow the German question to be settled locally. The effective threat was that the United States might counter by means and at places of its own choice — with, for instance, an atomic first strike against the Soviet Union itself.

The next major confrontation over Berlin came during the years 1958–1961, in the post-Sputnik era. By this time, the Soviet Union had demonstrated its ability to produce and deliver on a large scale not merely atomic, but thermonuclear weapons. Though superficially the outcome of this crisis was somewhat similar to that of the 1948 crisis — the Soviets retreated from enforcing their major demands and contented themselves with building the Berlin wall — the dynamics of the deterrence involved are very different.

In 1958, the Soviet Union's geographic advantage and local superiority in military forces remained. So did the possibility of American *massive retaliation* — most likely following a step-by-step *escalation* — in response to a

[7] Actually, this threat did not remain wholly implicit throughout the crisis. In April, 1949, President Truman stated publicly that he would not hesitate to use the atomic bomb again if it were necessary to protect the United States and the Western democracies. See Marshall D. Shulman, *Stalin's Foreign Policy Reappraised* (Cambridge, Mass.: Harvard University Press, 1963), pp. 64–73.

Soviet move to force the West out of Berlin. But the *credibility* of this threat was jeopardized by the fact that the Soviet Union now possessed a *counterdeterrent*. An American nuclear attack on the Soviet Union could expect to be met by a Soviet nuclear counterattack on the United States.

Was it credible that the United States would risk nuclear attacks on its own cities in order to maintain its presence in West Berlin? This was the crucial question dealt with in the prolonged diplomatic sparring which followed. Certain features added to the situation since 1948 seemed to offset to some extent the Soviet Union's new nuclear might. A formal treaty of alliance — NATO — had been concluded by the Western powers. An independent sovereign West Germany was a member of this alliance, and the West was formally committed to the defense of West German territory. Extensive congressional and public discussion within the United States appeared to have developed a solid and overwhelming consensus on the desirability of defending Berlin. The political costs, both foreign and domestic, of retreating from this commitment would therefore be very high.

If the United States could be frightened away from defending Berlin, what nation — in Europe or elsewhere — could depend on an American commitment to defend *it,* however solemnly taken? Would it not be best for nations, within the range of Russian conventional military power at least, to make the best terms they could to accommodate themselves to the Soviet Union? Or in Asia, to Communist China, so long as it was backed by Soviet nuclear power? Would not the Soviet Union itself be encouraged to engage in a series of further provocations and ultimatums? If so, and if we chose *not* to give way the next time, might the result not be the nuclear war we wished so much to avoid rather than the peace we had sacrificed so much to preserve? Domestically, would not the President or his party be susceptible to charges of appeasement or worse in the next election campaign? (Yet the foreign and domestic costs of nuclear war would surely be no less.)

A series of complex political maneuvers followed, with United States officials reaffirming their commitment to the defense of Berlin in the strongest terms — yet indicating also some willingness to make minor concessions. Soviet leaders, in turn, alternately offered assurances that their demands [8] should not be taken as an ultimatum and insisted that a failure to meet them within the time specified would bring grave consequences. Foreign Ministers' meetings, an Eisenhower-Khrushchev conference at Camp David, and the scheduled 1960 summit meeting — aborted by the U-2 fiasco — put off the day of reckoning to the Kennedy administration.

After another unsatisfactory summit meeting between Kennedy and

---

[8] The crux of the Soviet demands was that the West must give up its political and military control over West Berlin. A number of arrangements which would have achieved that goal were put forward, including proposals that West (but not East) Berlin should be declared a "free city" or be administered by the United Nations.

Khrushchev in Vienna in June, 1961, the new administration proposed an immediate increase in defense spending, put a large proportion of Strategic Air Command bombers on "ready airborne alert" (see below), reactivated a number of military reserve units, and dispatched additional ground and air forces to Europe. Perhaps these moves helped to increase American credibility over Berlin. In any event the end of the immediate crisis came soon — with the building of the Berlin wall in August.[9] The Kennedy administration's experience in this crisis reinforced its determination to abandon the strategy of "massive retaliation" and make major changes in American strategic doctrine.

Underlying the 1958–61 Berlin crisis was the likelihood that both sides — and certainly the United States — possessed a reliable *second-strike capacity:* that is, that each possessed the ability to launch a highly destructive attack on its adversary even after it had itself suffered a surprise first strike. The reverse of this coin was that neither opponent — certainly not the Soviet Union — was in a position to know that it could launch a successful *preemptive strike* — an attack which would destroy its rival's ability to retaliate effectively against it. Had the Soviet Union, but not the United States, been in a position to launch such an attack, the American quandary in Berlin would have been nearly complete. A United States first strike against the Soviet Union would have meant the destruction of the United States. Unwillingness to initiate such a strike would have ensured that Soviet local conventional military superiority would prevail. And a strong American response at any point in the development of the crisis would have involved a substantial risk of preemptive Soviet attack.

"THE BALANCE OF TERROR"

Today there can be little doubt that both the United States and the Soviet Union have secure second-strike capacities.[10] The key to a second-

---

[9] Differing views of the outcome of this crisis are presented in Hartmann, *op. cit.*, chaps. 6–8, and in John Spanier, *American Foreign Policy Since World War II* (2nd rev. ed.; New York: Praeger, 1965), chap. 16. Hartmann emphasizes the Soviet retreat, Spanier the Western concessions spawned by the weakness of the massive retaliation strategy.

[10] Secretary McNamara has described the second-strike capacity called for by American strategic policy as "a highly reliable ability to inflict an unacceptable degree of damage" on any potential aggressor(s) "even after absorbing a surprise first strike." *1967 Senate Defense Appropriations Hearings,* Part 1, p. 50. In this sense, the Soviet Union probably did not have an adequate second-strike capacity by 1961 — though how much damage is "unacceptable" in any given case is far from clear. The Soviets probably did have, by 1961, the capacity to deliver *some* nuclear weapons against European and American cities — a fact in itself sufficient to limit the willingness of American policymakers to respond with nuclear weapons to a conventional attack in Europe.

According to Secretary McNamara, it was believed that by 1970 the effective delivery by the United States, following an all-out first strike against it, "of even one-fifth of the surviving weapons on Soviet cities would destroy about one-third of the total population and one-half of the industrial capacity of the Soviet Union. . . . A considerably smaller strike capacity is not simply the possession of a large number of nuclear bombs or ballistic missiles, but the possession of the means to keep a substantial number of these weapons safe from a surprise attack. There are a number of ways of doing this. Missile sites may be "hardened" — by being placed underground, or dispersed so that a maximum number of enemy "hits" will be required to destroy them. Or missiles may be made mobile and moved from place to place periodically. A proportion of a nation's manned bombers may be kept in the air at all times on "ready airborne alert," so that if ever an attack comes a good number will remain away from their bases, ready to retaliate against the attacker if so ordered. Nuclear submarines, such as the American Polaris fleet, provide an ideal component of a second-strike force since they are "hardened," mobile, dispersed, and always on "ready alert."

It cannot be assumed that this "balance of terror" will continue indefinitely. All forms of deterrence describe *relationships,* rather than simple states of being. What constitutes an adequate second-strike force with respect to one nation at one time may not be adequate with respect to the same nation at other times, or to other nations at the same time. If the Soviet Union, for example, should develop a highly efficient antimissile system and a greatly strengthened civil defense program, it is conceivable that the United States might no longer be certain of its ability to devastate the Soviet Union following a successful surprise attack.

For the present, however, offensive capabilities have far outpaced defensive capabilities. In order to obtain a preemptive first-strike capacity vis-à-vis its opponent, therefore, either the United States or the Soviet Union probably would have to increase its armaments budget enormously — *without* stimulating its adversary to do likewise. This suggests that the balance of terror is likely to be with us for a while. It seems useful, therefore, to explore some of the most important strategic implications of this variety of deterrent relationship.

First, although the words "balance of terror" scarcely have a comfortable ring, the state of affairs they describe is far from the worst of all possible nuclear worlds. The balance of terror tends to induce caution rather than recklessness in the policies of the great powers; to maximize the freedom of action of small nations; and to reduce the possibilities of war by accident or miscalculation, and the opportunities for simple nuclear blackmail.

Some of these implications of the balance of terror emerge most clearly if we contrast this situation in which both major powers possess reliable second-strike capacities, with a hypothetical world in which two major

---

number of weapons detonated over 50 Chinese urban centers would destroy half of the urban population (more than 50 million people) and destroy more than half of their industry." *Ibid.,* Part 1, pp. 53–54.

powers possess effective first-strike, but *not* second-strike capacities. In this hypothetical world, whoever struck first would be sure to win. He who hesitated would indeed be lost. Whenever a tense situation arose, there would be a high premium on striking first. And since both parties would know this, the slightest suspicion that one might be preparing to strike would be likely to lead its adversary to initiate a preemptive strike of its own. In these unhappy circumstances, even an accident — a flock of geese or a meteor producing a blip on an early warning system radar screen; a commercial or weather reconnaissance plane straying off course over the territory of a potential enemy (as a U-2 plane did during the 1962 Cuban missile crisis); a single mad pilot striking out on his own — might cause an understandably nervous great power to initiate a preemptive attack and risk wiping a rival out, rather than waiting and risking its own annihilation.[11] Deliberate adoption of a policy of preventive war on the part of either side would be a real possibility and for many people a very tempting one.

A nation with a secure second-strike capacity, on the other hand, can afford to wait to investigate the cause of blips on a radar screen, or of rivals' planes straying from their courses. Should these actions prove deliberate, plenty of time will remain to retaliate against the offender. Since the defender knows that its opponent knows this, it is, in fact, bound to feel that such actions probably are *not* deliberate. After all, if they *were* deliberate, they would be suicidal and not a rational way to start a major war.

Again, since both sides must realize that launching an all-out attack means bringing about their own destruction, each is likely to tolerate a fairly wide range of political and even military maneuvers — shows of strength and determination, etc. — before making the ultimate move. Wariness of its opponent's destructive power is likely to make a potential aggressor reluctant to attempt nuclear blackmail even against small nations lest its great power opponent feel constrained to extend its "nuclear umbrella" over them. For the same reason, a nuclear power is even likely to exercise a good deal of restraint in responding to fairly provocative actions by smaller states. These observations do not merely follow from the theoretical nature of the balance of terror situation; they are reasonably accurate descriptions of the ways in which the United States and the Soviet Union *have* behaved, in practice, since the balance of terror became a reality.

However, the conclusion that we will all be saved from the horrors of war by the blessed balance of terror is obviously premature. International problems, disputes, and conflicts still exist. The balance of terror does not banish them, but simply makes it irrational to attempt to resolve them by recourse

---

11 The relationship between technology and international stability touched upon here is discussed in detail in Oskar Morgenstern, *The Question of National Defense* (New York: Random House, 1960).

to all-out war. The result has been, not an end to war, but more frequent recourse to violence short of all-out war — in addition to the political-eco-nomic-ideological competition we know as the cold war.[12]

Thus, in Korea from 1950 to 1953 — even before the advent of the balance of terror — the United States found itself engaged in a war unlike any in its history. The nation we saw as our principal opponent (the Soviet Union) was not directly engaged in the struggle at all, although it has a common border with North Korea. (The Soviet Union did provide North Korea with extensive military aid and advice, however.) Massive Chinese Communist forces were directly engaged after the early stages of the war — but on the pretext of being merely "volunteers" aiding their North Korean comrades. The Communist forces involved refrained not only from bomb-ing United States bases in Japan, but, for the most part, from bombing anywhere in South Korea — including the port of Pusan — as well. The United States, on its side, refrained from bombing Communist forces and supply lines in Manchuria, from attempting a naval blockade of the Chi-nese mainland or helping Chiang K'ai-shek's forces on Taiwan to launch an invasion of it, and from using atomic weapons — despite strong pressure from General MacArthur and his influential civilian supporters to resort to several of these expedients. (See the first case study in Chapter Five.) And none of the participants in this conflict issued a formal declaration of war at any time.

Thus, in Vietnam — a very different kind of conflict in many ways — during the Johnson administration, certain restraints again were observed by both sides. To mention only a few: virtually no Chinese Communist forces and only relatively limited North Vietnamese regular forces took part in the fighting; no attempt was made by the Communists to bomb Saigon or other key ports in South Vietnam, or to inflict the level of damage on Saigon by sabotage which Vietcong agents were probably capable of inflicting. The United States, in turn — again despite substantial political pressure to "escalate" — refrained from using even tactical nuclear weapons, from saturation bombing of population centers in North Vietnam — like the capital city, Hanoi; from blockading the port of Haiphong; and from strik-ing directly at the Vietcong's supporters in Communist China.

With these revisions in the practice of international violence came com-parable revisions in American strategic thought. The doctrine of massive retaliation was clearly outdated very soon after — if not actually before — Secretary of State John Foster Dulles enunciated it as a means of trimming

---

[12] Secretary McNamara declared in 1966 that there had been 164 "internationally sig-nificant outbreaks of violence," involving 82 governments, between 1958 and 1966. Only 15 of these involved more than one state, and none involved a formal declaration of war. Moreover, the number of such outbreaks per year had increased each year during this period. See the text of his remarkable address to the American Society of Newspaper Editors in Montreal in *The New York Times,* May 19, 1966, p. 11.

American strategic doctrine to proportions acceptable to a budget-minded administration and Congress. The simple fact was that no United States government was prepared to launch a massive nuclear attack on Moscow — and therefore on New York and Washington — in response to Soviet exports of arms to the Middle East, to Communist guerrilla attacks in Vietnam or Laos, to the movement of Russian tanks into Hungary, or even to Soviet threats to Western rights of access to Berlin.

"GRADUATED DETERRENCE"
OR "FLEXIBLE RESPONSE"

A very different strategic doctrine was advocated by critics of massive retaliation and later adopted and put into effect to a considerable extent in the Kennedy administration: the doctrine of *graduated deterrence* or *flexible response*. As President Kennedy himself told the nation in reporting on the Berlin crisis within months of his inauguration:

> . . . We need the capability of placing in any critical area at the appropriate time a force which, combined with our allies, is large enough . . . to meet all levels of aggressor pressure with whatever force levels are required. . . . We need to have a wider choice than humiliation or all-out nuclear action.[13]

Graduated deterrence calls for the United States to be able to tailor its responses to fit the challenges presented to it. We should be capable of meeting a conventional attack, therefore, with our conventional forces, a nuclear attack with our own nuclear capacity, a guerrilla attack with counterinsurgency warfare. A totally effective graduated deterrent would always place on our opponents the burden of choosing between escalating to a higher level of violence or accepting the thwarting of their aggressive designs. The logic of deterrence then would work against our adversaries as it had worked against us under the massive retaliation strategy. The development of a wide range of military capabilities would maximize the flexibility of response open to American policymakers in future crises.

The trouble with graduated deterrence, however, is that it must be effective at *every* level of violence from sublimited guerrilla warfare to all-out thermonuclear war. Otherwise, an opponent who holds the initiative would be likely to challenge us at precisely the level of violence — and in precisely the locale — where we are weakest. It is very expensive to be able to match potential opponents at places and at levels of violence of their choosing. Moreover, at particular levels of violence, the very nature of our society imposes such critical handicaps that we may find it nearly impossible to contain our opponents' thrusts effectively.

[13] Quoted in David W. Tarr, *American Strategy in the Nuclear Age* (New York: Macmillan, 1966), p. 102. This volume provides a good historical account and analysis of the evolution of American strategic doctrine since World War II.

The United States involvement in Vietnam provides a vivid illustration. American forces cannot merge into the peasantry as their Vietcong opponents can. The very color of their skin identifies them as outsiders. Nor, for the most part, do we feel able to send Americans to live overseas at the stark level of poverty at which most Vietcong live as a matter of course. The relative wealth of American G.I.'s, their P.X.'s, the inflation brought by the influx of American money they spend, and their conspicuousness when they associate with Vietnamese girls, inevitably create resentments which make their military and political tasks that much harder. Most important, the political costs to an administration of fighting a long, inconclusive, and confused limited war — while criticism and politics remain as usual back home — may be prohibitively high. How many Vietnams can Lyndon Johnson, the Democratic party, and the American body politic stand?

Chinese Communist theoreticians contend that sublimited war is the weak link in the American graduated deterrent, that the United States can be beaten by guerrilla-type "national liberation wars." It was precisely to disprove this contention that the Kennedy administration put so much emphasis on counterinsurgency doctrine and the Johnson administration committed so much of its prestige and the nation's resources to the struggle in Vietnam.

In fact, we and our allies have been unwilling to pay the full cost of a "pure" graduated deterrent strategy. The United States reply to Vietcong guerrilla warfare has been, in part, large-scale conventional bombing in both North and South Vietnam. Similarly, NATO still does not depend solely on its conventional forces to deter a Soviet attack on Europe. Rather, it depends on these forces to cope with *less* than massive Soviet military initiatives, and to help make credible our threat that a massive *conventional* attack will draw a nuclear response if it cannot be stopped in any other way. The sheer numbers of American and allied troops and European civilians the Soviets would have to run over and kill in the course of such an attack help to make our threat of nuclear retaliation more credible than it would be if fewer American and European lives were at stake.

Actually, the European members of NATO have little incentive to strain their economies to build up conventional forces capable of withstanding by themselves a major Soviet thrust, and they have not done so. For the principal virtue of such a conventional forces capability would be to reduce the possibility that a Soviet attack on Western Europe would escalate into all-out nuclear war; but the cost would be to increase the possibility that Europe would once again be the primary battleground of a major conventional conflict. That such a "conventional" struggle might conceivably involve the use of "tactical" nuclear weapons more powerful than the Hiroshima bomb can hardly add to the comfort European observers derive from this prospect. In any event, France's withdrawal from NATO probably has pushed into the realm of wishful thinking any hope that a full-scale Communist military initiative in Western Europe could be contained wholly by conventional means.

This does not mean that a blatant and massive Soviet attack in an area as essential to American security as Western Europe must immediately escalate into all-out nuclear war. A conventional defense by the United States and NATO would probably be attempted initially, at least until the magnitude of the Soviet offensive was clearly established. If this failed, a number of intermediate steps short of an all-out nuclear response would still remain. Local defense with tactical nuclear weapons might be attempted, for example — a dangerous step, since the line between "tactical" and "strategic" nuclear weapons is not nearly as clear as the line between nuclear weapons and conventional ones. (Nevertheless NATO's military plans contemplate the use of tactical nuclear weapons in response to a Soviet conventional assault, if necessary.)

If this proved unsuccessful, the next step might be a "controlled reprisal," or show of force. The United States might explode a nuclear weapon high in the air above Siberia, for example, where it would be expected to do little or no real damage, as a manifest of its determination and willingness to take further risks in the defense of Europe. If this, too, failed to deter further Soviet advances, nuclear attacks might be made, say, on a limited number of Soviet military bases away from major population centers. In like manner, a number of possible steps toward escalation can be conceived of between this point and an all-out attack intended to destroy as much as possible of Soviet society and population.[14] And following any of these steps, bargaining — including exchanges of threats — might conceivably take place.

It is important that while a long series of neat and readily distinguishable stages of escalation is readily imaginable in theory, such meticulously rational responses might be wholly impractical in a real situation. It is impossible to predict the effect upon national decisionmakers of the tensions, emotions, and uncertainties bound to be generated in nations approaching the threshold between survival and annihilation. (Conceivably, the top leadership of one or both of these nations might itself be wiped out — or prevented from communicating its decisions effectively — in the early stages of a nuclear war.)

On the other hand, the thinking through in advance of esoteric theories of escalation might just possibly prove of real help in limiting any nuclear conflict which might break out, or in minimizing the damage inflicted, in such a conflict, on the nations and peoples concerned. We simply do not know — and must pray that we do not find out.

To some extent, at least, such theorizing has already affected United

14 See the works by Herman Kahn cited above and the same author's *On Escalation: Metaphors and Scenarios* (New York: Praeger, 1965).

States government policy. Secretary of Defense McNamara announced in a commencement address at Ann Arbor, Michigan on June 16, 1962:

> The United States has come to the conclusion that, to the extent feasible, basic military strategy in a possible general nuclear war should be approached in much the same way that more conventional military operations have been regarded in the past. That is to say, principal military objectives, in the event of a nuclear war stemming from a major attack on the Atlantic alliance, should be the destruction of the enemy's military forces, not of his civilian population.
>
> The very strength and nature of the [Western] alliance forces make is possible for us to retain, even in the face of a massive surprise attack, sufficient reserve striking power to destroy an enemy society if driven to it. In other words, we are giving a possible opponent the strongest imaginable incentive to refrain from striking our own cities.

McNamara was here announcing United States adherence to what strategic theorists call a *counterforce* strategy, aimed at the destruction of an opponent's military forces, rather than to a *counter-city* (or counter-value) strategy aimed at destruction of its urban centers and civilian population. Underlying this approach, of course, is the assumption that it might in some circumstances be possible for the United States and the Soviet Union to engage in counterforce nuclear exchanges while continuing to exercise sufficient restraint to avoid mutually suicidal counter-city exchanges. Presumably a clear demonstration of military superiority by one side in a counterforce exchange would be expected to induce the disadvantaged party to accept a negotiated settlement on more reasonable terms than those it insisted upon initially. Its sole alternative, after all, would be to follow through with counter-city attacks which could only result in the devastation of its own society.

For just this reason, though, it would not be to the strategic advantage of the Soviet Union, which is believed to have a smaller quantity of nuclear weapons, to be drawn into a strictly counterforce exchange. And, whether for this reason or another, the writings of top Soviet military strategists suggest that Soviet strategic doctrine excludes the possibility of a strictly counterforce war.[15] By 1965, Secretary McNamara himself conceded in the course of congressional testimony that it was unlikely that the Russians would confine themselves to counterforce strikes in case of war with the United States.

The "no-cities" strategy disturbed some thoughtful Europeans already wondering whether the United States, despite its commitments, really would treat an attack on Europe as an attack on itself. If worst came to worst, would an American President be willing to repay an attack on Paris

15 On Soviet strategic doctrine, see Raymond Garthoff, *Soviet Military Policy* (New York: Praeger, 1966).

or Bonn in a way that would ensure the destruction of New York and Washington? If the Russians had some reason to doubt that he would, at least some of the deterrent effect of the American commitment to Europe would be lost. Yet the "no-cities" doctrine suggested that, under certain conditions, the Soviets might be allowed to overrun Europe without necessarily suffering direct retaliation against Moscow and Leningrad. If this were the case, would it not be advisable for Europeans to develop a nuclear deterrent of their own?

To borrow a Madison Avenue metaphor, when Secretary McNamara ran the "no-cities" strategy up the flagpole, it drew more Bronx cheers than salutes. Its colors have rarely been since in the vicinity of the Pentagon. Counterforce doctrine is discussed these days as part of a "damage-limiting strategy," designed to minimize the damage to American society, in case of nuclear attack, by striking directly at our opponent's strategic forces.

NUCLEAR PROLIFERATION

All that has been written above is predicated on the assumption that only two powers have significant nuclear capabilities. Both the hazards and the complications multiply in a multinuclear world. Already Britain, France, and Communist China have some nuclear weapons, and Secretary McNamara has estimated that the Chinese can be expected to have the capability to launch a limited nuclear attack on the United States by the mid-1970's. Many other nations, too, will be able to develop some nuclear weapons systems in the next ten or fifteen years, if they want to — and it appears that the pressures of international competition and national prestige will make most of them want to. The strategic and political implications of these facts are enormous. They have just begun to be thought and written about by nuclear strategists and can only be touched upon here.

Aside from the prestige involved, some nuclear weapons capability might be of value to small or middle-sized nations, first, in helping to deter attack by a great power, and second, in support of their own policies vis-a-vis other small or middle-sized nations. The fact that France has some nuclear weapons of its own, for example, might convince the Soviet Union that a conventional attack on France is impractical since France might retaliate by striking Soviet cities. A nuclear pre-emptive strike against France, on the other hand, might involve more danger of eliciting United States nuclear retaliation than a conventional attack would. Thus, in certain situations, France's relatively small nuclear force might help to deter an attack against it — but at the price of increasing the possibility that such an attack, if undertaken anyway, would be a nuclear one. Even if an attack elsewhere in Europe is contemplated, France's nuclear force is one more thing the Soviet Union might have to worry about.

Similarly, if, say, India should develop some nuclear force, its position —

over an issue such as the status of Kashmir — might be greatly improved relative to a Pakistan which didn't possess a nuclear capacity; in any future military action over Kashmir, Pakistan would have to worry about the possibility of sudden nuclear strikes at Dacca and Karachi.

However much individual nations might benefit, particularly in the short run, from developing nuclear capabilities of their own, there is little doubt that the world as a whole has much more to lose than to gain from *nuclear proliferation* — the acquisition of nuclear forces by a large number of nations.

In the first place, the more powers possess nuclear weapons, test them, keep missiles ready on launching pads, and bombers on airborne alerts, the more danger there is of an accident taking place. And the greater the possible number of sources of an actual nuclear attack, the more difficult for a nation struck accidentally to ascertain the true nature of what has happened in the period of time available before it feels a response is called for.

The more nations control nuclear weapons, the more sets of leaders able to initiate nuclear actions, the greater the possibility that men who are un-reasonable, irresponsible, or merely fanatically opposed to the status quo will gain access to them.

Even if all nuclear powers are blessed continuously with responsible — or at least rational [16] — leaders, the mechanics and technology of the situation seem likely to work against stability. A number of simultaneous nuclear arms races might be taking place: Egypt vs. Israel; India vs. Pakistan; Communist China vs. India; Nationalist China vs. Communist China; Greece vs. Turkey; North Korea vs. South Korea; North Vietnam vs. South Vietnam; Communist China vs. the United States; Communist China vs. the Soviet Union; Guinea vs. Ghana; Zambia vs. Rhodesia — to name relatively few of the multitude of possibilities. Not all of these will progress symmetrically — let alone begin immediately with both sides having secure second-strike capacities.

Suppose Israel should develop a preemptive strike capacity relative to Egypt — with the latter some six months to a year away from developing

[16] Thomas Schelling writes on the concept of "rationality": "Decision-makers are not simply distributed along a one-dimensional scale that stretches from complete rationality at one end to complete irrationality at the other. Rationality is a collection of attributes, and departures from complete rationality may be in many different directions. Irrationality can imply a disorderly and inconsistent value system, faulty calculation, an inability to receive messages or to communicate efficiently; it can imply random or haphazard influences in the reaching of decisions or the transmission of them, or in the receipt or conveyance of information; and it sometimes merely reflects the collective nature of a decision among individuals who do not have identical value systems and whose organizational arrange-ments and communication systems do not cause them to act like a single entity." *The Strategy of Conflict* (New York: Oxford University Press, 1963), p. 16. Reprinted by per-mission of the publisher of the original clothbound edition, Harvard University Press.

a preemptive strike capacity vis-à-vis Israel. This possibility is not unlikely, since second-strike capacities are more expensive than first-strike capacities. Thus if both Egypt and Israel should each build their own small but vulnerable nuclear force, each might achieve a pre-emptive strike capacity relative to the other. Since Egypt is pledged to destroy Israel, who could blame Israel if it decided to make use of a temporary advantage to ward off the possibility of a nuclear Pearl Harbor at Egypt's hands a year later? How would the great powers respond to such a nuclear Suez? Would the Soviet Union feel able to ignore this "unprovoked" attack on its associate in the Middle East? If not, could the United States allow Soviet — or Chinese Communist — retaliation against Israel to go unpunished? What if Britain and France declared that they would attack Israel's attacker if we did not? Could we fail to respond to a counterattack against them also?

Since supporting even small nuclear forces would strain the finances of many nations, might not at least some of them elect to maximize firepower at the cost of cutting corners on some safeguards against war by accident or miscalculation? A vulnerable counter-city capacity is relatively cheap to acquire, but it has to be set in motion very rapidly once evidence of a possible attack is detected.

A desperate small power might be tempted in certain circumstances to try to ignite what Herman Kahn calls a "catalytic war" between a great power ally and a great power opponent. Suppose Nationalist China, for instance, should come to feel that its only hope of return to the mainland lay in provoking a war between Communist China and the United States. There would be many possibilities. Chinese Nationalist nuclear submarines could launch an attack on the mainland and pretend innocence. If the United States denied involvement, would the Chinese Communists believe us? How might they respond? Or suppose the Chinese Nationalists "simulated" a small-scale Chinese Communist attack on the United States, at a moment of extreme tension between these two nations. Would the United States be able to discover the real source of the attack in time?

What if a bomb dropped by one country on another caused fallout and resulting deaths in a third (say, an Indian attack on Dacca, in a dispute over Kashmir, caused a substantial number of deaths due to fallout in Communist China)?

These possibilities are, of course, all very remote. But then it would not have sounded very likely to suggest in 1914 that war would start over the assassination of the Austrian Archduke by a conspiratorial Serbian organization. (And recall the rumors that floated about parts of the United States in the first hours following President Kennedy's assassination.)

In addition, proliferation probably would make it more difficult to secure general agreement on any arms control formula, would divert to military purposes of a staggering quantity of financial resources which would better serve world stability if invested in national development programs, and would raise the possibility, ultimately, that some nongovernmental insurgent or even private conspiratorial groups might gain access to one or more nuclear weapons at some point.[17]

Proliferation is also bound to affect the arms race between the great powers. Weapons systems actually directed at a minor nuclear power may nevertheless cause a great power opponent to respond. For some time, for instance, both the United States and the Soviet Union appeared to be avoiding the construction of antimissile missile systems. Strategists reasoned that this was because the cost of developing such systems was much greater than the cost of adding sufficient offensive firepower and decoy systems to overcome them. Since an antimissile missile system must be very efficient to be really effective — even one or a few nuclear missiles getting through unscathed could do a terrible amount of damage — neither great power could expect to alter fundamentally its strategic position relative to the other by developing such a system. If such a system were developed, though, both would be saddled with great additional financial burdens. Moreover, both — but especially the United States — would be faced with important political problems: the need to undertake major fallout shelter programs — since even incoming missiles caught in the air by antimissiles create lethal fallout; and the need to decide which cities (and bases) should, and which should not, be protected by antimissile systems (New York, but not Los Angeles? Los Angeles, but not Cleveland? Cleveland, but not Cincinnati? Cincinnati, but not Fort Worth, Honolulu, Des Moines?).[18]

But an antimissile system of minimal value against a possible Soviet or United States attack might be perfectly capable of neutralizing any attempted assault by a minor nuclear power. And this consideration could affect a great power's decision as to whether or not to develop an antiballistic missile (ABM) system.

[17] The possible consequences of nuclear proliferation are discussed in Kahn, *Thinking About the Unthinkable, op. cit.,* chap. 7, and in Albert Wohlstetter, "Nuclear Sharing: NATO and the N + 1 Country," in Kissinger (ed.), *op. cit.* The Wohlstetter article appeared originally in *Foreign Affairs* (April, 1961).

[18] Early in 1967, Secretary McNamara released a list of cities which "might" be included in an antimissile defense *if* the United States decided to build one. A $12 billion ABM system, he indicated, would cover the following cities: New York, Los Angeles, Chicago, Philadelphia, Detroit, San Francisco, Washington, Boston, Cleveland, St. Louis, Baltimore, Houston, Pittsburgh, Minneapolis, Miami, Denver, Atlanta, Seattle, New Orleans, Buffalo, Portland (Ore.), Albany, El Paso. A $22 billion system might include in addition: Paterson (N.J.), San Jose, Dallas, Milwaukee, Kansas City, Cincinnati, San Diego, San Antonio, Indianapolis, Columbus, Memphis, Louisville, Providence, Norfolk, Rochester, Springfield (Mass.), Dayton, San Bernardino, Toledo, Bridgeport (Conn.), New Haven, Flint, Allentown (Pa.), Tacoma, and Trenton. A $40 billion system, according to Secretary McNamara, could include another 130 cities with populations of 100,000 or over. As might have been anticipated, there were sharp outcries from Congressmen and other devotees of cities omitted from these lists. *The New York Times,* February 16, 1967, p. 1.

For whatever reasons, it seemed clear by 1966 that the Soviet Union had decided to go ahead with the deployment of an ABM system, and the Joint Chiefs of Staff were recommending that the United States respond in kind. Secretary McNamara continued to emphasize that a full-scale ABM system would cost at least $30 billion to develop over a ten-year period, that it would cost the Soviets only about one-tenth as much to offset it with additional offensive capabilities, and that "Even so, against a massive and sophisticated Soviet surprise attack on civil targets, there would be little hope of reducing fatalities below 50 or more millions.[19] His critics countered that a full-scale antimissile system (including a fallout shelter program) might save between 50 million and 80 million American lives in case of an all-out war, and that the United States could certainly afford such a program as well as the Russians can.

The desirability of undertaking a "thin" antimissile defense, based on the use of long-range interceptor missiles, appeared much less controversial. Such a defense could provide excellent protection against the kind of nuclear attack Communist China might be capable of launching in the next decade or two, at a cost of "only" $8 billion to $10½ billion. Secretary McNamara announced in 1967 that the United States would undertake to develop this kind of ABM system.

By 1967, a technique had been developed for dividing a large missile warhead into several smaller ones, which could be directed to different targets when the big warhead containing them exploded; and the Soviet Union had tested a rocket which could be placed in orbit around the earth at a distance of about 100 miles. By approaching the United States from the south, such a weapon could avoid detection by our early warning missile system. (The first of these developments is often referred to as MIRV (Multiple, Independently Targetable Re-entry Vehicles); the second as FOBS (Fractional Orbital Bombardment System).)

All of this should emphasize the value of reaching reliable arms control arrangements before the era of nuclear proliferation is upon us. Arms control requires some systematic *limitation* of armaments rather than actual *dis*armament and might as readily be brought about by informal tacit agreement as by treaty commitment. But mutual distrust, sharply differing ideological orientations, and the many traditional obstacles to disarmament

---

[19] *1967 Senate Defense Appropriations Hearings*, Part 1, p. 60. The estimates cited in this and the preceding and following paragraphs are from *ibid.*, Part 1, pp. 56–63, 74–76, and 253–254. It was generally agreed, in the words of Chairman of the Joint Chiefs of Staff Earle G. Wheeler, that "a fallout shelter program would be more effective in terms of lives saved than any other program we could buy," saving some 15–20 million lives, in case of war, at a cost of about $3.4 billion. *Ibid.*, p. 253. Yet, apparently for political reasons, no appropriation for a full-scale shelter program was requested. According to one analyst quoted anonymously by *The New York Times:* " 'The American people have never been properly prepared to accept the need for shelters. Congressmen say they don't dare discuss the issue.' " December 25, 1966, Sec. 3, p. 1.

discussed elsewhere in this book stand in the way and have so far prevented any but the most minimal steps toward arms control, in spite of the urgency of the problem.

Treaties have been signed excluding military uses of Antarctica (1959); outlawing nuclear weapons tests in the atmosphere (1963) — an agreement which France, Communist China, and a few others, significantly, failed to sign; and prohibiting the use of the moon and other celestial bodies as military bases (1967). A "hot-line" telephone communication link has been installed between Washington and Moscow. And serious negotiations toward a nonproliferation treaty were underway by 1967, although these negotiations were threatening to founder in view of the attitudes of West Germany and other nonnuclear nations toward such a treaty. In many other ways that we take for granted, also, restraint has been exercised [20] and useful precedents have been set. Above all, no nuclear weapon of any kind has been fired in anger since Nagasaki. Perhaps this is the supreme accomplishment of the first two decades of the nuclear age.

But the future clearly will demand more of us. For the fundamental paradox of the nuclear epoch is that we who live in it depend for our survival on the continued effectiveness after repeated use of a threat which, by its very nature, cannot be carried out except at the cost of mutual suicide.[21] How long will our omnipotent but unusable deterrents continue to deter?

NEGOTIATION AND DIPLOMACY

A world in which survival depends on deterrence requires new kinds of diplomacy and new techniques of negotiation. If credibility cannot be confirmed by *military* means — that is, by the carrying out of threats — then *diplomatic* means of establishing credibility must be devised. But before we can understand these new modes of diplomacy, we must review some of the fundamentals of the traditional diplomacy in which they are grounded.

The terrifying prospect of a nuclear war has, understandably, led to an increased emphasis on the importance of resolving disputes among nations by diplomacy or negotiation. Often no distinction at all is made between these two words — negotiation and recourse to violence are assumed to be the two antithetical and mutually exclusive ways in which a foreign policy crisis can be dealt with. Those who view matters in this light are consequently always urging their governments to pursue a policy of negotiation —

[20] No major power, for example, seems to have pushed as hard as it might have to develop chemical, bacteriological, and radiological warfare, although the potential power of such weapons is every bit as frightening as that of nuclear weapons, and there is no effective defense against them.

[21] See Hans J. Morgenthau, "The Four Paradoxes of Nuclear Strategy," *The American Political Science Review* (March, 1964), pp. 23–35.

presumably in preference to its one alternative, a policy of force, ultimately leading to war. Thus, during the early stages of the Johnson administration's involvement in Vietnam, protesters against United States policy in Vietnam frequently carried placards reading simply "negotiate." A similar course had been urged on President Kennedy during the Cuban missile crisis.

"Diplomacy" is commonly used in so many different senses that any definition adopted here is bound to be arbitrary. Let us use the word, then, in its broadest sense, to denote the conduct of relations between and among national governments. "Negotiation," on the other hand, refers to the process of communication (usually verbal) among governments engaged in an effort (or at least an apparent effort) to reach agreement on certain points. Note that by these definitions negotiation is one form of diplomacy. Others include not only the use of military force but economic pressures and incentives, propaganda and persuasion, attempted subversion, and the formation of alliances and coalitions. Nor are these various subcategories of diplomacy necessarily mutually exclusive. It is perfectly possible — in fact, usual — for one nation to employ several of these instruments of policy simultaneously in its relations with other states. The United States and Communist China, for instance, both fought and negotiated during much of the Korean War, while the United States implemented a trade embargo against Peking, and each launched propaganda campaigns against the other.

The old saw that so long as nations are talking they're not fighting has a grain of truth in it — but not much more than a grain. Nations can both fight and negotiate or do neither. In the Korean War, as we have seen, Washington and Peking did both. From 1917 to 1933, Washington and Moscow, for the most part, did neither.

Negotiation is not a policy, then, but *a means of implementing policy.* Any state but one desiring war for its own sake should be willing to negotiate if there is a good likelihood of obtaining through negotiation the terms of settlement it wants. But a state which will consider no alternative but negotiation, no matter what terms its adversary insists upon, is following a policy of pacifism. This is a perfectly respectable policy to advocate. But it is not the policy that many of those accustomed to the indiscriminate use of the term "negotiate" *mean* to advocate.

What is involved here is what we might call "slippage" — the failure to distinguish between the different and inconsistent meanings of a single word, resulting in a frequent slipping from one meaning of the word to another. Slippage is involved when we use the word "free" sometimes to describe democratic nations, sometimes to describe non-Communist ones, without distinguishing carefully between the two meanings. Thus we may be led to believe, if only momentarily, that all nations allied with the

United States — though they may be dictatorships, like Portugal — must be in some sense "free" since they are part of what we commonly refer to as the "free world."

Similarly, advocates of a policy of pacifism, or of withdrawal from a particular region of the world, call for "negotiation" because this implies that they are merely asking for a "reasonable" willingness to sit down and talk things over. That this sort of appeal can be effective, to a certain extent, is shown by the fact that public opinion surveys regularly show as willing to "negotiate" about almost *anything* large numbers of people (often majorities) who applaud "toughness" and decry "softness" in international affairs, and who often oppose even "concessions" which their government has already indicated its willingness to make.

THE SIGNIFICANCE OF THE TRIVIAL

If a government can be made to look bad for seeming to be reluctant to negotiate, it can sometimes be made to look ridiculous for dickering over what appear to be trivial details concerning the conditions under which negotiations should take place. Partly in response to those urging his administration to negotiate in Vietnam, President Johnson announced in May, 1965, that the United States was prepared for "unconditional negotiations" concerning the Vietnam conflict. Later, one of the slogans of those protesting his policy became "negotiate directly with the Vietcong." The Government of the Republic of (South) Vietnam took the position that *it* was the legally sovereign power in South Vietnam and that it would not be appropriate for an ally, the United States, to discuss the future of Vietnam with a renegade force seeking to usurp the legitimate government's authority.

The Johnson administration, hesitant to offend its ally when the Vietcong seemed unlikely to agree to negotiations anyway, countered that there would be no problem in bringing the Vietcong into negotiations if they and the North Vietnamese were in fact ready to negotiate. (The implication was that the Vietcong might be dealt with as part of the North Vietnamese delegation.) For their part, the Vietcong insisted that they would negotiate only with those who recognized them as the *sole* representatives of the Vietnamese people. Meanwhile, close to 90 per cent of the American public — including almost 95 per cent of the large majority which could not identify the Vietcong correctly — were reported to favor "negotiation with the Vietcong to end the war in Vietnam." [22]

Though it could be claimed that negotiations were being prevented — while men died in combat — because of a small-minded preoccupation on

[22] Sidney Verba, *et al.*, "Public Opinion and the War in Vietnam," privately mimeographed at Stanford University, March 15, 1966. (Reprinted as part of the second case study in Chapter Seven.) By 1967, the Johnson administration had indicated that it was now willing to deal with the Vietcong directly.

both sides with trivialities, the fact of the matter was that it was *substantive* differences that stood in the way of negotiations. In fact, by the definition we have been using, negotiations were actually taking place through published statements and informal diplomatic channels. And these negotiations revealed that each side insisted on terms unacceptable to the other. The failure to begin formal negotiations did not create this impasse, but reflected and symbolized it.

One of the critical functions of negotiations is the obtaining and conveying of information. What parts of an adversary's formal position does he regard as vital, what parts not so vital? Which parts of your own position does your rival see as essentially reasonable, which parts as especially offensive? Is it possible to avoid or postpone some issues with intentionally ambiguous phrasing, or to gloss over them entirely? What is your adversary likely to do if no agreement is reached?

In the nature of the negotiating process, it is difficult to obtain this kind of information directly. A negotiator cannot very well walk in and say: "Though my formal position calls for this piece of territory to go to my country, it is not really very important to us, and if you will give us something else for it, we will let you have it." Why should his opponent then take seriously a demand already admitted to be unimportant? After all, anyone can stake out wild claims prior to negotiations and then offer to trade them off against someone else's more reasonable demands. Such trades of concessions may be made, but they normally may not be admitted. In addition, "face" is often involved. A nation threatened crudely, or insulted, may feel compelled to react hostilely even if it would prefer not to — especially when the negotiations are or may be made public.

For these reasons, nations prefer to deal with one another with a certain amount of indirection and formal politeness. We often do this ourselves in our personal relations whenever matters of delicacy and personal sensitivity are involved. People in other cultures — such as traditional China's — do it even more.

When a man asks for a date a lady who is not interested in dating him, she does not usually tell him this, but rather pleads a previous commitment. If it is understood by both parties that such a response may really indicate a lack of interest, how does a lady who *is* interested in a date, but *does* have a prior engagement, make this known? By the *way* she says it. She may specifically say: "How about another time?" But even if she does not, usually the more specific her response, the more likely it is that she wants to be asked again. Different things are communicated by: "I'm sorry, but I already have a date for Saturday" and "Oh gosh! The whole family is going out to Aunt Carolyn's this Saturday for our big once-a-year family reunion, and I've *got* to go along."

Conventions, too, have symbolic meanings. It is conventional that the man asks for the date, calls for the lady, pays for the evening. The girl who phones to say she has bought tickets for a show Saturday and will drive over and pick her date up if he is willing has given him a message — intentionally or not — beyond the factual information conveyed. The message is that she is inordinately anxious to see him — and he may be forgiven for inferring more.

A girl determined to test her "steady's" devotion to her, similarly, is as likely as not to make an issue of something at the symbolic rather than at the direct level. Thus the terribly serious lovers' quarrels over "little things." And when the time has come to "make up," symbols or intentionally inadvertent meetings may come again into play.

Nations, too, use codes and symbols to secure and convey information. It is not entirely accidental that the negotiations leading up to the Nazi occupation of the Czech Sudetenland in 1938 began with an offer by British Prime Minister Chamberlain to meet with Hitler at a time and place of the latter's choosing, nor that the final conference disposing of this "problem" took place at Munich, Germany, with one of Czechoslovakia's main allies (the Soviet Union) not represented. Within the year, when Hitler became convinced that an agreement between Germany and the Soviet Union was essential to his plan to advance into Poland, he did not hesitate to send his Foreign Minister to Moscow to sign the Nazi-Soviet nonaggression pact. The terms upon which negotiations begin usually influence their outcome — in fact deciding upon these terms forms a critical *part* of the negotiations themselves.

This is not to say that differences concerning procedure *always* reflect substantive differences, nor that nations are to be commended for arguing over fine points of procedure while men die on the battlefield. It is merely to point out that *when* procedural squabbles become major obstacles to negotiation, more may be involved than meets the eye. Readiness to accede to the other side's procedural terms, therefore, may not always be advisable.

Not only procedural but substantive agreements can be made more difficult when one or more of the parties concerned views the issues involved in symbolic terms. Thus, one of the stumbling blocks to a peaceful resolution of the Vietnam conflict is the fact that key officials in both Washington and Peking appear to view it as a "test case" of whether "national liberation wars" are an effective technique for inflicting defeats on the American "paper tiger." If this war *is* such a test case — and the firm conviction that it is of the main parties concerned may make it so! — then each side must consider the costs of any concessions it might make in terms of their effect on allies', adversaries', and observers' future expectations, as well as in terms of their inherent value in Vietnam itself.

Thus, if a United States retreat in Vietnam would encourage further guerrilla wars in Southeast Asia — and perhaps in Africa and Latin America, too; if it would cause United States allies to doubt the value of American commitments to defend them, and suggest to neutrals that they would do better to seek Soviet or Chinese Communist rather than American support when the chips are down — then clearly the costs of such a withdrawal would far exceed the direct costs of the loss of South Vietnam itself. (Of course, it is advisable not to allow an adversary to develop into a symbolic test a situation in which he holds most of the advantages. To avoid this, however, requires that we see the disadvantages of our position at an early point. As our predicament in Vietnam suggests, this is not always possible.)

Though procedural arguments may sometimes merely reflect substantive differences, at other times inability to get together on procedural points actually may prevent or delay the reaching of a substantive agreement. In the Korean War, more than a month elapsed between the first Soviet indication of interest in negotiating a cease-fire and the actual start of formal discussions on the first agenda items. Later, formal negotiations were suspended for more than two months while attempts were made to agree on the relocation of the site of the negotiations. The United Nations Command felt itself disadvantaged by negotiating on a site within Communist-held territory and held out, successfully, for a new site in neutral territory.[23] Though no one can say for certain, it is quite possible that this procedural wrangling delayed somewhat the conclusion of an armistice.

The loss of time in such cases due to procedural arguments indicates the value of pre-existing agreements among nations on diplomatic procedures and conventions. The availability of regular channels for contact and negotiations among nations is literally of life and death importance. Even the diplomatic cocktail party may have the redeeming virtue of enabling governments to communicate with each other routinely on an informal and unpublicized basis. The representatives of governments at odds with each other are likely to meet at diplomatic functions of this sort in some capital city of the world virtually every day without the need for any of them to take any special initiative. One of the most useful aspects of the United Nations is its constant availability as a forum for negotiations in a previously agreed upon place and in a procedural setting where a multitude of third parties — including the Secretary General — is on hand to perform mediatory functions if desired.

Thus it has been argued — by Prime Minister Nehru of India, Prime Minister Attlee of Great Britain, and United Nations Secretary General

---

[23] See William H. Vatcher, Jr., *Panmunjom* (New York: Praeger, 1958); and (Admiral) C. Turner Joy, *How Communists Negotiate* (New York: Macmillan, 1955). The authors, adviser to and member of the American negotiating team at the Korean armistice negotiations, respectively, both emphasize the frequency with which their Communist counterparts sought to make use of procedural decisions — such as adoption of an agenda — to gain symbolic and important substantive advantages.

Trygve Lie, among others — that the confrontation between American and Chinese Communist forces in Korea might never have taken place if Communist China had been represented in the United Nations in 1950, or if Washington and Peking had exchanged ambassadors before that time. Allen Whiting, in his study of Peking's intervention in Korea, concluded that: "Inadequate communication or the failure to convey accurately one's probable responses, played a pivotal role between August and November 1950 in precipitating war" between Chinese Communist and United Nations Command forces:

> In retrospect, both sides ran afoul of the political hazards inherent in public communication. In open diplomacy, political prestige limits the choice of action to what seems popularly acceptable. It was impossible for [Soviet representative to the U.N.] Jacob Malik to formulate his statements more explicitly in the world forum of the Security Council. It was only slightly more possible for U.S. policy to reverse course in response to publicly delivered threats of Chinese Communist intervention. This is simply to say that the success of the Malik proposal and of the Chinese threat to intervene was in part dependent upon international communications that, in fact, failed to work because of the constraints of publicity.
>
> Korean developments were affected in other ways by the absence of direct relations between Peking and Washington. On the one side, Chinese Communist calculations depended primarily upon Soviet interpretations of American and U.N. intentions. This introduced a Soviet bias into the information available to decisionmakers in Peking. On the other side, American knowledge of Chinese Communist views came, to a considerable degree, through Indian channels. For a number of reasons, this made such information difficult and, for some officials, impossible to evaluate. Hence Chinese calculations exaggerated the threat posed by American policy, while American calculations downgraded the seriousness of Chinese concern. An "entirely new war" resulted.[24]

And President Truman, who has indicated that he would not have ordered American troops to cross the thirty-eighth parallel if he had believed Chinese forces would intervene in response, has written:

> Chou En-lai . . . had called in the Indian Ambassador to Peiping, K. M. Panikkar, and had told him that if United Nations forces crossed the 38th parallel China would send troops in to help the North Koreans. . . . However, the problem that arose in connection with these reports was that Mr. Panikkar had in the past played the game of the Chinese Communists fairly regularly, so that his statement could not be taken as that of an impartial observer. It might very well be no

[24] *China Crosses the Yalu: The Decision to Enter the Korean War* (New York: Macmillan, 1960), pp. 168 and 171–172. Reprinted by permission.

more than a relay of Communist propaganda . . . a bald attempt to blackmail the United Nations by threats of intervention in Korea.[25]

THE CONDITIONS OF NEGOTIATION

In addition to pointing up the hazards of inadequate communication among nations, Whiting's analysis indicates the importance which the external setting for negotiations may have on their outcome. Negotiations may be held publicly or secretly, bilaterally or multilaterally, formally or informally, and with low- or high-level officials — or heads of government — participating. None of these conditions is necessarily good or bad in itself. Different settings are conducive to successful negotiations in different circumstances.

After World War I, there was a reaction against the secret treaties which were blamed for plunging Europe into war. One of Wilson's fourteen points was "Open covenants, openly arrived at" — a rule Wilson himself readily violated at the Paris Peace Conference concluding the war. Others have tried to amend this to "open covenants, secretly arrived at," distinguishing between the agreements themselves, which admittedly ought to be made public, and the process by which they are reached.

Clearly, publicity often makes agreement more difficult. A negotiator, for instance, who put forward a demand publicly, emphasized its importance, and then yielded in return for some anticipated but unspecified concessions from the other side probably would be roundly criticized by his own countrymen. Yet such tactics are often essential to the success of negotiations.

Useful proposals which might offend third nations — or domestic interest groups within the negotiating countries — may never be made in public forums, because merely making them, in an effort to feel out the other side, would entail serious political consequences. A government may be willing to endure some criticism from those adversely affected once an agreement is concluded and published, but it can scarcely afford to risk offense every time it puts forward a tentative proposal.

On the other hand, when the possibility of applying public pressure or of making propaganda gains is very important to one or both parties, public negotiations may seem preferable. The very publicity involved may help push one or more of the parties toward agreement (with results that may or may not prove fortunate). And in public negotiations, the temptation to reach agreement at the expense of absent third parties is likely to be reduced.

Bilateral and multilateral negotiations, correspondingly, each have their

25 *Years of Trial and Hope* (Garden City, N.Y.: Doubleday, 1956), p. 362. The "Peking" in Whiting's statement and the "Peiping" in Truman's refer, of course, to the same capital. "Peking" in Chinese means "northern capital." "Peiping" means "northern peace," and is often used by those who wish to indicate that they do not recognize the Chinese Communist capital as the capital of China.

virtues and liabilities. In the case of multilateral negotiations, the presence of a large number of nations will, in some cases, discourage frankness and lead to "playing to the gallery." The need to get more nations to agree may make agreement more difficult. And the way may be opened for attempts to divide friendly nations and promote interallied bickering. Yet, at the same time, a multilateral setting may encourage mediation, efforts at "good behavior" to maintain the goodwill of the many nations represented, and a spirit of cooperation in general. Thus Western delegates, who were hesitant to include the representatives of neutral states in East-West disarmament negotiations before the Eighteen-Nation Disarmament Conference of 1962, came to feel that the presence of these neutrals caused the Soviet negotiators to use more reasonable arguments than had been their custom in past negotiations of this sort.[26]

Informal negotiations allow a great deal more flexibility than formal ones in making and withdrawing proposals, testing an adversary's position, and in discussing items in whatever order seems most profitable. But at other times the discipline of formal negotiations — the greater attention to precision they may call for, the reluctance the parties to them may feel to terminate them without agreement — may prove more helpful. In any event, negotiations must be formalized at *some* point, if an explicit agreement is to be reached.

The higher the level of the officials who participate in the negotiating process, the greater their ability to be flexible. High officials can do more than their subordinates to change policy if necessary in the process of the negotiations. The higher the officials, also, the greater the range of the issues that may be brought into the negotiations, if this seems advisable. But, conversely, the higher the official involved, the less time he is likely to have to attend to the concrete detail which can sometimes be all-important.

At the very top level, the summit, when heads of government meet, there are special hazards. Such meetings may give key policymakers a chance to get to know personally, to some extent, the men they perennially deal with at a distance and may provide the flexibility to surmount minor problems that created impasses at lower levels. But summit meetings also attract enormous publicity which may create public pressures for "agreements" to be reached even when there is no agreement. Chiefs of state seldom have the time to attend to divisive issues with the precision and detail required for sound agreements. And the possibility of an *apparent* agreement masking a *real* difference — and leading later to feelings of disillusionment and betrayal — is always present. (Recall the salutary "Spirit of Camp David" arising from one Eisenhower-Khrushchev summit leading into the very different "spirit of the U-2 incident" the next time the two men met. The fact that the two may not have understood each other completely at their first meet-

26 Fred Charles Iklé, *How Nations Negotiate* (New York: Harper and Row, 1964), p. 205.

ing may have had as much to do with the unpleasantness of their second as the U-2 incident itself.)

Moreover, a president's or a prime minister's proposals cannot be as readily disavowed as a subordinate's, if this should later prove advisable; nor can much be done about it if it turns out that the summit negotiators rub each other the wrong way. If the negotiations are prolonged, who will take care of running the nation back home and of keeping in tune with congressional (or parliamentary) and public opinion on the home front? (Remember Wilson at Versailles.) Thus, Dean Rusk wrote, prior to becoming Secretary of State:

> . . . Summit diplomacy is to be approached with the wariness with which a prudent physician prescribes a habit-forming drug – a technique to be employed rarely and under the most exceptional circumstances. . . . Negotiation needs time, patience and precision, three resources which are not found in abundance at the highest political level. . . . The costs of error or misunderstanding are multiplied by the seriousness of the issues and the power of those present.[27]

Finally, Fred Charles Iklé's *How Nations Negotiate* (cited), a useful general introduction to the subject under discussion, emphasizes that in all negotiations the parties concerned are faced constantly with three basic alternatives: (1) to accept agreement at the terms the adversary has indicated he will accept; (2) to break off negotiations and accept the consequences of failing to reach an agreement; or (3) to continue negotiations in an effort to secure better terms by further bargaining – or to put the onus for failure to agree on the other party.

BARGAINING: THE SEARCH FOR CREDIBILITY

The process of bargaining itself is incredibly complex. It involves more than negotiations, as we have defined them, because it includes actions as well as words. Indeed, as Thomas Schelling has pointed out, tacit bargains can be worked out without any verbal communication at all.[28] Such tacit bargaining was behind the successful effort to keep the Korean War limited by having each side accept certain restrictions on its freedom of action. Even when verbal communication takes place, troop movements, military maneuvers and "ready alerts," shows of force, etc., may play a critical supplementary role.

Before the twentieth century, the consolidation or shifting of alignments among the great powers of Europe played a key role in bargaining and in

27 "The President," *Foreign Affairs* (April, 1960), p. 361.

28 *The Strategy of Conflict, op. cit., passim.* Much of the contents of the next several pages is drawn from the analysis and illustrations presented in this superb and imaginative series of essays on bargaining and game theory.

tests of strength. Today, shows of allied solidarity and of the changing orientations of uncommitted nations — in and out of the United Nations — are of much less importance in great power confrontations. For one thing, both the United States and the Soviet Union have enough power to "go it alone," if they are determined to. For another, shifts in diplomatic alignments are much more difficult in an age, like our own, of ideologically based alliances. Instead, the key to successful bargaining in the missile age is often the capacity to communicate *credibility* — that is, to make others believe you can and will carry out both your threats and your promises.[29]

Two cars approach an unmarked intersection simultaneously. It is clear that they will crash if one does not swerve, reduce speed, or otherwise give way. Both drivers presumably want, above all, to avoid a collision, but each also wants to go first — that is, they have both a *common* and a *conflicting* interest. How will it be decided whether a collision will be averted, and, if so, which car will go through the intersection first?

Since both drivers are determined to avoid a crash, the first one to be convinced that the choice of whether there is a crash or not is up to *him,* is likely to give way. Thus if one of the drivers is patently drunk, the burden of the pressure to yield will be on the sober driver. If neither is obviously drunk, the "winner" is likely to be the first one to make it clear by his *actions* that he will not — because he cannot — yield. The *last clear chance* to avoid the collision that both wish to avoid will then lie with his opponent. A driver determined to prevail might thus press on his accelerator full force while honking his horn loudly. Once this is seen by his opponent, the last clear chance to avert an accident will appear to rest with the latter.

A much safer and more gentlemanly procedure might be for the drivers to refer to the convention that the car on the right has the "right of way." But this will work only if this convention is recognized and honored — partly to his own disadvantage — by the driver of the car on the left. Or other considerations or conventions might operate. The driver of the smaller car, or the newer one, might feel constrained to yield first. If one driver is a man and the other a woman, the man might feel that he should yield as a matter of courtesy — or that the woman must yield so as not to threaten his masculinity. In each of these cases, whether a collision will be averted may be determined by whether both drivers follow the *same* rule or different ones. Thus, if there is time for such calculations, each driver might be well

---

[29] In some cases, the bargaining reputation built up over the years by individual negotiators may provide a valuable *marginal* supplement to credibility — by putting the individual's reputation (and future utility) at stake, as well as his country's. Thus Arthur Schlesinger, Jr., reports that when Averell Harriman was named to conduct negotiations in Moscow for the nuclear test-ban treaty, someone from the Soviet Embassy remarked to Schlesinger: "As soon as I heard that Harriman was going, I knew you were serious." And Premier Khrushchev himself later added: "Harriman is a responsible man." *A Thousand Days* (Boston: Houghton Mifflin, 1965), p. 903.

advised to take into account what rule his opposite number is likely to consider relevant in the circumstances.

Such a confrontation is similar in certain respects to a confrontation on the international level between major powers with reliable second-strike deterrent capacities. To use the continuing Soviet-American crisis over Berlin, described earlier, as an illustration: both in this crisis and in the hypothetical encounter between automobiles, the principals had a cooperative interest in avoiding mutual disaster as well as a competitive interest in prevailing. In both cases, *commitments* (of bargaining reputation and future credibility) and actions (Kennedy accepting the domestic political costs of reactivating military reserve units, for example) seemed more effective than mere words; and it was important to try to demonstrate to an opponent that the *last clear chance* to avoid unpleasant consequences was really *his*. Both cases involved the actual or potential use of explicit or implicit threats which would have done more harm than good to the threatening party if he had actually had to carry them out. Thus, in order to make the threatened party believe that they *would* be carried out, even though it might not then be strictly rational to do so, the parties concerned sometimes sought to limit or restrict their own future freedom of action.

Premier Khrushchev, for example, threatened to force his own hand by turning over control of the access routes to Berlin to the Government of East Germany.[30] If this maneuver had been carried out successfully, the burden of the last clear chance would have rested with the United States and its allies, since East Germany itself would be expected to be inflexible on a matter so vital to its own survival. The Western powers countered by making clear their belief that the Soviets could control the East Germans if they wanted to, and by stressing that Khrushchev would be held responsible for East Germany's actions in any case. Similarly we noted that if the driver of one of the cars concerned could have indicated that he was drunk — that is, presumably incapable of rational decision — his sober rival would have been put at a disadvantage because of the "drunken" driver's presumed irrationality. And this would remain true whether the drunkenness was genuine or merely convincingly feigned.

Finally, though perhaps not so obviously, both cases suggest that the role of *conventions, or psychological focal points,* may be decisive. Both drivers may respect conventional rules of the road or of masculine chivalry. Both East and West were willing in 1948 to accept the distinction between *ground*

---

[30] This move would also have changed the *legal* context of the Berlin issue, since the West's right to be in Berlin rests on agreements negotiated at the close of World War II with the Soviet Union as the sovereign power in the Eastern zone of Germany. A treaty in which the Soviets sought to transfer legal sovereignty in this area to the East German regime (not recognized as a government by the Western allies) would open the way for these rights to be challenged. (Khrushchev's actual threat was that he would conclude such a treaty without allied consent, with the effect — among others — of transferring control over the access routes to Berlin to the East German regime.)

access routes from *air* access routes. In the later Berlin crisis, both sides acquiesced in interpreting American U-2 flights over Soviet soil and Soviet destruction of an American plane as less than acts of war. The United States allowed the construction of the Berlin Wall in part because it was recognized as being located within the Soviet zone of occupation — though a legal case against the Soviet right to build it, and in favor of the Western right to knock it down, could readily have been made had the United States had no need to worry about Soviet counteraction to such a forceful move. (Recall also the United States unwillingness to intervene in Hungary in 1956, partly because Hungary was defined as being within a Soviet "sphere of influence.") [31]

Among the important *differences* between these two confrontations is the fact that for the automobile drivers their encounter was one of a kind, whereas the participants in the Berlin crisis viewed it as one of a series of past, present, and future confrontations, major and minor. For this reason, perhaps uppermost in the minds of Western statesmen during this crisis was the effect which an allied retreat in Berlin might have had on the expectations and actions of their allies, of nonaligned observers, and — not least — of their adversaries in subsequent encounters. Similar considerations were clearly operative in the Cuban missile crisis of 1962. One reason for President Kennedy's strong stand during that crisis was undoubtedly his desire to avoid encouraging Soviet leaders to believe that the United States was too afraid of the risk of war to defend its interests forcefully.

❦CASE
STUDY   *THE CUBAN MISSILE CRISIS*

Probably the closest the world has ever come to a nuclear war was the Cuban missile crisis of 1962. Beginning near the climax of a hard-fought United States congressional election campaign, the Soviet Union's attempt to place intermediate range ballistic missiles (IRBM's) in Cuba left the Kennedy administration with a series of delicate and dangerous choices to make. United States (and presumably also Soviet) strategic retaliatory forces were kept on ready alert through much of the crisis.

[31] A critical convention, mentioned earlier in this chapter, is the distinction between nuclear and nonnuclear weapons. If conflicts among nuclear powers are to be kept limited, it is vital that this distinction be maintained, despite the fact that some tactical nuclear weapons are less destructive than some conventional weapons. For there is no other psychological milestone along the escalator to doomsday nearly so compelling or useful in "drawing a line" as the qualitative distinction between nuclear and conventional weapons. If the "line" is not drawn here now, how will the parties to a conflict in progress be able to come to (explicit or tacit) agreement *then* as to where a mutually acceptable line should be drawn?

Missiles were on their launching pads ready to be fired. President Kennedy later told his aide and confidante, Theodore Sorenson, that during the crisis he believed the odds on its escalation into a Soviet-American war were "somewhere between one out of three and even." [32] Most Americans will retain for a long time vivid memories of their own activities during this tensest week of the cold war.

Most of the case study which follows consists of two remarkably accurate reports which appeared in *The New York Times* during the crisis itself, enabling us to view the Soviet-American confrontation over Cuba through the eyes of informed observers at the time it took place. A statement by President Kennedy at the end of the crisis, and a subsequent account of some of the not quite official negotiations which led to its resolution, are also included.

Since the outcome of this episode led most observers to define it as a signal success for President Kennedy and the United States, it is very difficult to be persuasively critical of the wisdom of the President's choices during the crisis. Nevertheless, there are many insights to be gained by a careful analysis of the Kennedy administration's management of this confrontation.

1. How did the administration seek to induce Premier Khrushchev to back down in Cuba? What means did it employ to buttress the credibility of its threats, explicit and implied? How did it seek to avoid encouraging an escalatory Soviet response?

2. What "messages" did Soviet actions and words early in the crisis communicate to the President and his advisers? (Be specific.)

3. Which of the strategic concepts discussed in this chapter are illustrated in this case? On the basis of information available subsequent to the crisis, it appears unlikely that the Soviets could have attained a reliable pre-emptive first-strike capacity, relative to the United States, even if it had been allowed to retain missile bases in Cuba. If the estimates of some analysts at the time of the crisis had been correct, however — that is, if the Cuban bases *had* afforded Russia a pre-emptive strike capability — what would have been the implications of this fact for the United States? For the prospects for international peace and stability in the years ahead? In such a case, do you feel a United States surprise attack on these missile sites would have been ethical? Why or why not?

4. What types and techniques of negotiation were employed in bringing about a settlement of this dispute? What were the advantages, if any, of having negotiations conducted between Scali and Fomin, instead of, say, between Andrei Gromyko and Dean Rusk in Washington, between

32 The chapters dealing with the Cuban missile crisis in Sorenson's *Kennedy* (New York: Harper and Row, 1965) offer one of the fullest and most valuable pictures of top-level foreign policy decisionmaking during a major crisis that the present author has encountered. Though this account is too lengthy to include here, it is highly recommended as supplementary reading.

Zorin and Stevenson in New York (who, in the end, negotiated the specifics of the final settlement), or — as Khrushchev himself suggested at one point — between Kennedy and Khrushchev personally? Why do you think there was so relatively little difficulty in arranging to start negotiations and in avoiding procedural arguments?

5. What contribution, if any, did the United Nations and its Secretary General make toward the resolution of the crisis?

6. United Nations inspection of the missile sites was never arranged because of the Castro government's refusal to allow it. The United States had to content itself instead with continued aerial surveillance by U-2's and similar aircraft. Do you think the United States acted wisely in accepting this outcome rather than pushing harder for full adherence to the Soviet-American agreement? If not, what steps would you have taken to ensure Cuban acceptance of on-site inspection? What risks, if any, do you think these steps would have incurred?

7. In what ways might the progress and outcome of the crisis have been altered if the Cuban government had been given full title to, and control of, a number of already operational IRBM's with nuclear warheads?

THE NEW YORK TIMES

There were signs in Washington the week before last — elusive but persistent — that something unusual was afoot. The atmosphere of crisis reached a climax on Sunday — a day that was to set the mood and tempo for the feverish week that was to follow.

Key Presidential aides came in a stream to the White House Sunday, usually by the side doors. At the State and Defense Departments and the Central Intelligence Agency there were urgent meetings. Messages went out to Congressional leaders to return to Washington.

The air of crisis grew despite the fact that, so far as was known, a meeting between President Kennedy and Soviet Foreign Minister [Andrei] Gromyko on Thursday had produced no new developments in Soviet-American relations. The two men had met for two hours and fifteen minutes. There was no official word on what had been discussed.

At the very moment of the Kennedy-Gromyko meeting, however, and all during that week, the U.S. was conducting intense aerial surveillance of Cuba. Photographs were being taken that were to play a key role in the dramatic events of the following week.

Secrecy was the rule, but the tension that precedes momentous developments spread throughout the capital. As the tension mounted last Sunday night, the cause of concern and the White House decision remained one of the best kept secrets of the Administration. Then the drama began to unfold, in Washington, in Moscow, in the U.N. and at sea.

MONDAY

In Washington at mid-afternoon the White House announced the President would go on national radio and television in the evening with a message of great "national urgency." Anxious questions were asked: Was the crisis about Berlin? Cuba? Did it mean war?

U.S. embassies were being alerted, and Dean Acheson, former Secretary of State and close adviser to President Kennedy, was on his way to Paris with urgent information for the NATO allies.

At 7 o'clock the secrecy was lifted. Speaking to a tensely waiting nation, Mr. Kennedy said the crisis was about Cuba. In an 18-minute address he made three major points.

First, on the cause of the crisis, Mr. Kennedy said:

> Within the past week, unmistakable evidence has established the fact that a series of offensive missile sites is now in preparation on that imprisoned island.

Second, on the U.S. response, Mr. Kennedy said:

> . . . to halt this offensive build-up a strict quarantine of all offensive military equipment under shipment to Cuba is being initiated. . . .

The U.S., he emphasized, would also call for "prompt dismantling and withdrawal" of the offensive bases in emergency action before the Security Council of the U.N. The removal of the bases would be a condition for any consideration to lift the quarantine.

Third, on the broad problems of the cold war, Mr. Kennedy said:

> . . . It shall be the policy of this nation to regard any nuclear missile launched from Cuba against any nation in the Western Hemisphere as an attack by the Soviet Union on the United States requiring a full retaliatory response on the Soviet Union. . . .
>
> Any hostile move anywhere in the world against the safety and freedom of peoples to whom we are committed, including in particular the brave people of West Berlin, will be met with whatever action is needed. . . .

The line was thus clearly drawn — with Russia, not its puppet, Cuba. It was drawn also across the entire frontier of the cold war, not merely in the Caribbean. The choice of peace or war was clearly placed on Russia.

As for the immediate crisis and the response to it, these considerations were involved.

The missile site, as Mr. Kennedy pointed out, included medium-range missiles capable of carrying nuclear warheads 1,000 nautical miles. Others, still under construction, appeared capable of launching intermediate-range nuclear missiles "more than twice that far . . . capable of striking most of the major cities in the Western Hemisphere ranging as far north as Hudson's Bay and as far south as Lima, Peru."

Missiles of that range in Cuba held an ominous threat. Although Russia admittedly had nuclear intercontinental missiles that could strike anywhere in the U.S. from Soviet soil, the accuracy and added firepower in intermediate-range missiles in Cuba could, in the view of military analysts, give Russia "first strike" power possibly capable of neutralizing U.S. power to retaliate.

The missile installations — of which reconnaissance photographs were released by the Pentagon — clearly belied Russian protestations that the Soviet arms build-up of Cuba was "defensive."

Mr. Kennedy said sharply that Mr. Gromyko the week before had given him "false" assurances to that effect.

The offensive build-up was a clear test of the Administration's stand on Cuba. A month ago, Mr. Kennedy said direct action against the Cuban arms build-up was unwarranted as long as the build-up remained "defensive" in character. The position was criticized by some who thought it too soft, and there were calls for blockade and invasion, regardless of the consequences.

The President avoided the word "blockade." Under international law, a blockade is an act of war, since it is enforced by arms. The "quarantine," nevertheless was a selective blockade; ships carrying offensive arms would be ordered back at gunpoint or face sinking, but ships carrying nonoffensive material would be allowed through.

The President further announced he had ordered stepped-up surveillance of Cuba and had directed the armed forces "to prepare for any eventualities."

TUESDAY

This was a day of wide repercussions from the U.S. moves.

In Moscow, the Soviet news agency Tass issued a Government statement, 13 hours after the Kennedy speech, excoriating the blockade as "piracy." The armed forces of the Soviet and other Warsaw Pact nations were alerted. The Kremlin, however, made no threat to fight, and observers detected uncertainty and indecision in the immediate Soviet response.

In Washington, the Council of the Organization of American States recommended that member nations "take all measures . . . including the use of armed force" to block the flow of offensive weapons to Cuba and "to prevent the missiles . . . from ever becoming a threat to the peace and security of the continent." The vote was 19 to 0 for the resolution (Uruguay, which abstained for lack of instructions from its Government, later registered approval).

The crisis over Cuba thus produced the clearest show of hemispheric unity since World War II. O.A.S., while not able to impose its will on member states, carries broad influence. It has world recognition as bearing a special responsibility for hemispheric peace and security, and its decision on Cuba was expected to carry considerable weight in the U.N.

In the U.N. Ambassador Adlai Stevenson lodged the U.S. demand for withdrawal of the missile bases. The Russian delegate, Valerian Zorin, countered with a resolution to condemn the U.S. and call for an end to the blockade. He proposed negotiation between Russia, Cuba and the U.S. toward "removing the threat of war."

The exchange was the opening gun of a continuing debate after which the U.S. resolution appeared certain to die on a Russian veto. The next move would be to the General Assembly, where the outcome was uncertain; many of the Afro-Asian neutrals were clearly alarmed at the U.S. move, and began pressure for summit negotiation.

WEDNESDAY

At sea, the "quarantine" zero-hour, 10 A.M., Eastern daylight time, passed without incident. Some Russian ships known to be approaching changed course. Aerial reconnaissance showed they carried jet aircraft and other "quarantine" weapons. Their diversion from the Cuban route indicated Russian unwillingness to precipitate an immediate showdown.

In Moscow, Premier Khrushchev, responding to a letter from British pacifist Lord Bertrand Russell, assailed the U.S. but suggested a summit meeting to avert war. It was apparent he welcomed a chance to pose as a "peacemaker" by associating himself with the pacifist movement.

In the U.N., Secretary General U Thant made "urgent" appeals to President Kennedy and Premier Khrushchev to suspend the build-up and the blockade and enter negotiations. The appeals were his response to pressures from neutral nations for U.N. intervention.

THURSDAY

At sea, the Navy had its first encounter. A Russian tanker stopped and was allowed to pass after it was "ascertained" by observation — not by a boarding party — that she carried petroleum, not on the "quarantine" list. The encounter clearly indicated that Russia, for the moment at least, was not going to test the U.S. will at sea.

In Moscow, Mr. Khrushchev said he was in accord with Mr. Thant's proposal for "suspension" of the Caribbean confrontation and moving it to the conference table.

In Washington, President Kennedy politely declined Mr. Thant's proposal as it stood, but left the way open to discussion on acceptable ground rules. Any U.S. agreement to "suspend" the blockade would hinge on removal of the Russian missile bases from Cuba and international inspection to assure the offensive arms build-up had stopped.

In the U.N., Ambassador Stevenson and Ambassador Zorin engaged in a bitter exchange of charges of deceit. When Mr. Stevenson displayed enlargements of the photographs of the missile bases in Cuba, Mr. Zorin said they were "falsified evidence." Mr. Stevenson retorted by demanding a "yes or no" answer on whether the Soviets had installed offensive missiles in Cuba. This dialogue took place:

> ZORIN: I do not wish to answer a question that is put to me in the fashion in which a prosecutor puts questions. In due course, sir, you will have your reply.
>
> STEVENSON: I am prepared to wait for my answer until hell freezes over, if that's your decision.

By this time, however, attention was turning from the question of the outcome of debate in the U.N. to the question of the outcome of U Thant's intervention.

FRIDAY

At sea, a Navy party, for the first time, boarded a Soviet supply vessel, a Lebanese freighter under Soviet charter. The ship submitted to inspection. Its cargo included no "quarantine" contraband, and it was allowed to pass.

At the U.N., Mr. Thant got from both sides promises of efforts to avoid incidents at sea. Premier Khrushchev agreed to keep Russian vessels away from the blockade area; President Kennedy pledged that U.S. ships would try to avoid direct confrontation for "the next few days." Thus there was something of a respite for discussion of the Cuban issues.

In Washington, the White House took pains to emphasize that the core of the crisis was the missile bases already in Cuba. It released intelligence reports showing that construction of the bases was going ahead at a pace intended to achieve "full operational capability as soon as possible."

SATURDAY

In Moscow, Tass said Mr. Khrushchev had sent messages to Mr. Kennedy and Mr. Thant proposing a deal — Russia would move from Cuba weapons that "the U.S. President considers to be offensive ones" if the U.S. moved similar weapons from Turkey.

In Washington it was learned from a responsible source that an earlier personal message from Mr. Khrushchev to the President represented in fact a major retreat by the Soviet Union on the question of maintaining missile bases in Cuba and did not suggest the quid pro quo mentioned by Tass of a NATO withdrawal from Turkey.

President Kennedy last night answered this in a personal message to the

Soviet Premier in which he indicated that the first offer from Mr. Khrushchev might be acceptable to the U.S. as a basis for further negotiation. But he rejected the swap of Cuba's bases for NATO's in Turkey.

The conciliatory tone of the East-West exchange was in sharp contrast with events in Cuba where the Castro regime announced that it had fired upon U.S. reconnaissance aircraft and driven them off. Last night the Defense Department announced that one of its reconnaissance planes was missing and presumed lost. Other sources said it was a U-2, which supported earlier reports that among the weapons delivered to Cuba by the Soviet Union were high-altitude ground-to-air anti-aircraft rockets.

In Havana, Premier Castro came through with a proposal of his own, offering, in a message to Secretary General U Thant, to stop work on missile bases provided the U.S. lifts its quarantine of Cuban ports. The offer was regarded in Washington as likely to be rejected by the U.S. as not meeting its requirement that the bases be made inoperable.

While the focus of the week's events was the Caribbean, a much greater test was involved than missile sites in Cuba. At stake was no less than a fundamental confrontation of the U.S. and the Soviet Union in their world struggle.

Cuba is a comparative late-comer as a cold-war issue. Large-scale Soviet technical and material aid has been going to Cuba only for about a year: large-scale military aid only for a few months. Since Premier Khrushchev must have known that the close U.S. surveillance of Cuba assured that the missile bases would be detected, the question arises: Why did he choose to make a test in Cuba — an area where Russia is at an obvious strategic disadvantage?

The answer, most Western observers believe, is that the Soviet leader was seeking a reading on the U.S. determination to resist, not simply or even mainly in Cuba, but in Berlin and possibly other areas as well. And, as he has now made clear, he undoubtedly was planning to use the Cuban bases as a bargaining counter in negotiations with the U.S.

The Soviet leader has intimated several times in recent months that he was skeptical of the proclaimed Western determination to fight if necessary to maintain access to Berlin. Yet a test in Berlin itself could quickly lead to an escalating military commitment that neither side might be able to reverse. A test in Cuba, on the other hand, might not run comparable risks and could still provide a gauge as to whether the U.S. was really prepared to fight in defense of vital interests.

There may have been other considerations. Premier Khrushchev may have believed that U.S. preoccupation with Cuba would provide a cover for a Soviet take-over in Berlin, as the Suez invasion in 1956 provided a cover for Soviet suppression of the Hungarian revolt. Or he may even have felt that he could "trade" a cessation of the Soviet build-up in Cuba for major concessions on Berlin. Or perhaps, at a minimum, trade abandonment of the Soviet base in Cuba for withdrawal of the U.S. bases in Turkey, as he proposed last week.

From Washington's point of view, the establishment of Soviet missiles in Cuba was — as the President emphasized — an attempt to alter the status quo. The United States has viewed with distaste and antagonism the creation of a communist state in Cuba. It has been concerned over the flow of propaganda, funds and agents from Cuba to other areas of Latin America. But with its overwhelming military power, the United States had not regarded Cuba as any direct and immediate threat to its security.

The presence of Soviet medium- and intermediate-range missiles in Cuba — 90 miles from the United States' shores — has changed that view. Nor does Washington accept the argument that a Soviet base in Cuba can be equated with the U.S. base in Turkey. The Turkish base, U.S. officials argue, was established many years ago in response to Soviet pressures against the Middle East. It has long been accepted as part of the Western defense system and does not represent, as does the Cuba base, a new attempt to alter drastically the world power balance.

Apart from military considerations, the U.S. believes that a failure to respond to the Soviet challenge in Cuba — precisely because it apparently was a calculated test — might have marked a major turning point in the East-West struggle. For the elements of prestige, propaganda and influence on the unaligned nations are all vital factors in that struggle — as vital, many observers, believe, as the number of missile bases or the size of the nuclear arsenal each side possesses.

The possibility of a military showdown between the U.S. and Russia sent a shiver through most of the world. Apart from that general concern, there were varied reactions to the week's fast-breaking developments in the U.S., among the Allies, in Latin America and among the uncommitted nations.

In the U.S., the dominant reaction was rallying behind the President and a feeling of satisfaction that "something," at last was being done about Cuba. The Cuban problem had produced a national sense of frustration. Thus while there was apprehension about the course on which the U.S. had embarked — manifested mainly in a renewed interest in civil defense and in some scare buying of food, bottled water, medicines, etc. — there were widespread expressions of support that crossed party lines.

Insofar as there was serious criticism of the President's initial course, it came mainly from two sources:

First, there were those who raised questions about why the President had waited so long before acting. This group argued that the Soviet missile bases could not have been constructed overnight. They pointed out that Cuban refugee groups and some Republicans, including Senator [Kenneth] Keating of New York, had claimed as long as a month ago that there was evidence of Soviet offensive missiles in Cuba. Unofficially Administration sources answered these charges with the argument that it was necessary to gather irrefutable evidence before acting.

Second, there were those who argued that the Administration action did not go far enough. They questioned whether a blockade would be effective and said that, in any case, it would not solve the problem of the missile bases already in Cuba. This group — among them Senator Richard B. Russell of Georgia, who argued the case in the White House briefing Monday — favored stronger measures. The Administration argument was that stronger measures — an air strike or an invasion, for example — with their grave risk of war could always be taken later if the initial measures did not prove adequate.

Among the *Allies,* the reaction on official levels was support for the U.S., although there were some qualifications and in some countries — notably Britain — there were vociferous demonstrations against the U.S. by minority groups. Prime Minister [Harold] Macmillan took the position that the Soviet move in Cuba could be regarded "only as a deliberate adventure designed to test the ability and determination of the United States."

In France, President [Charles] de Gaulle was said to have been annoyed at not having been consulted in advance about the U.S. action. Nevertheless, the French Government expressed support for the U.S. position in the face of "recent and growing installations of Soviet offensive armament in Cuba." The reaction in West Germany, Italy and the other NATO countries was also generally favorable.

One question raised in Allied circles was whether the U.S. should not have given an advance private warning to the Russians — perhaps during President Kennedy's meeting with Soviet Foreign Minister Gromyko — to halt the Cuban missile build-up or face U.S. counter-action. The argument was that this might have given the Russians an opportunity to back down without the public loss of face now involved. The Administration answer was that such a warning probably would have, first, involved new delays without proving effective; and second, might have enabled the Russians to capture the initiative with moves in the U.N. or elsewhere.

In *Latin America,* where Cuba has been a highly controversial issue, the widespread official support for the U.S. was reflected in the unanimous vote in the O.A.S. Nevertheless, some of the Latin American countries — notably Brazil, Bolivia and Mexico — had reservations about a clause in the O.A.S. [resolution] that seemed to endorse invasion of Cuba if the U.S. deemed it necessary.

These nations, along with some of the Latin countries, strongly urged a negotiated settlement of the crisis.

Among the uncommitted nations — the United Arab Republic, for example — there was a tendency to blame both sides for the Cuban crisis. A prevalent reaction was that the United States should have taken its case to the U.N. before ordering a blockade. Thus pressure was strong from the un-committed nations for unqualified acceptance now by both sides of the U Thant offer of mediation.

The week's critical developments raised, among others, three urgent questions: (1) Will there be war? (2) What will the Russians do? (3) What will the U.S. do?

Basic to a consideration of these questions were two fundamental problems:

First, there was the problem of Soviet shipments of offensive missiles to Cuba and what was to be done about them — the issue of the blockade.

Second, there was the problem of whether and how the missile sites already in Cuba were to be dismantled — the primary objective cited by the U.S. in taking action on Cuba.

As for the question of war, the actions by both sides last week strongly suggested that they wanted to avoid a military showdown. They both were proceeding warily and slamming no doors that might offer a way out of the crisis.

Moscow's willingness to divert its ships, even temporarily, and Premier Khrushchev's bid for negotiations, up to and including a summit, indicated that the Russians were not eager for a test of arms. While President Kennedy's replies to Mr. Thant were qualified by reiteration that construction of missile bases in Cuba was proceeding uninterruptedly, the President, too, seemed to be delaying any new move in order to provide an opportunity for negotiations.

The caution was prompted by the stark facts of nuclear power. When all was said and done about which side possessed the nuclear edge, the fact was that each had the power to do enormous damage to the other, and each knew it. Nor could either guarantee that once a showdown was forced in Cuba — even an armed encounter between two ships at sea — it would be able to reverse the process of escalation that might begin.

Premier Khrushchev had made plain that he is not eager to risk the empire he has built in a nuclear holocaust. The United States, since World War II, has been working to avoid nuclear disaster.

As for what the Russians will do, they appeared to be pursuing a two-fold course. On the one hand, they were working hard to gain U.N. intercession to stop the blockade. Premier Khrushchev's quick acceptance of U Thant's suggestion for a suspension of the blockade, coupled with a suspension of Soviet shipments to Cuba, indicated he wanted to bring the U.N. squarely into the crisis.

His purpose appeared to be the opening of negotiations to return matters to his own version of the "status quo" — namely, the situation that existed before the U.S. imposed the blockade.

On the other hand, Premier Khrushchev was maneuvering for broader negotiations on his proposal to swap the Cuban base for the U.S. base in Turkey. On the surface, it seemed like a simple quid pro quo proposal. Yet there were many puzzling aspects.

Why was the Soviet leader prepared to abandon Cuba? The proposed swap, if accepted, might mean the fatal undermining of the Castro regime. One answer might be that Premier Khrushchev believed U.S. agreement to abandon its Turkish base might seriously weaken NATO morale.

Another explanation might be that Premier Khrushchev is looking for a face-saving way out of the Cuba box. There is reason to believe that he was taken by surprise by the sternness and vigor of the U.S. response to his placing of missiles in Cuba. Thus he may now be retreating to his minimum fall-back position and possibly trying to achieve one of the objectives that lay behind the construction of the Cuban base in the first place.

Finally, Premier Khrushchev may believe that he can obtain widespread support for a proposal to swap the Cuban and Turkish bases, and even appear to be championing "disarmament." It has been evident that many people see little difference between the presence of Soviet missiles in Cuba and the presence of U.S. missiles in Turkey. The comparison was frequently cited last week by the neutrals in criticizing the U.S. blockade.

As for what the U.S. will do, various arguments, pro and con, were advanced last week on the desirability of accepting the proposed Soviet exchange.

One argument in favor was that the Turkish base was no longer vital to the Western defense system and that its loss, from the U.S. point of view, could not be equated with the advantage of keeping long-range missiles out of Cuba. The U.S. has already begun to dismantle some of its overseas missile sites — in Britain, for example. Thus, it was argued, abandonment of the Turkish base would not even involve any drastic new policy.

Another argument in favor was that Premier Khrushchev should be offered a line of retreat from the Cuban dilemma. Soviet prestige was too heavily engaged, it was argued, to expect Moscow to agree to dismantle the Cuban bases without some quid pro quo.

Whether the President's reply last night represented the kind of inflexible U.S. position that might either impel the Russians to bring pressure on a more critical area such as Berlin, or even force the military showdown neither side wanted, remained to be seen.

If the U.S. flatly rejects negotiations along the lines suggested by Premier Khrushchev, it appears faced with fairly grim alternatives to achieve the objective of dismantling the Cuban bases. The main conceivable measures in inverse order of severity are: (1) a total blockade of Cuba which would quickly bring the island's economy to a standstill; (2) air attacks to destroy

the missile bases — a step that probably would involve killing Soviet personnel now in Cuba; or (3) an invasion of the island which would probably
involve three to five divisions and supporting forces — about 150,000 men.

In sum, the Caribbean confrontation remains loaded with danger and,
although the consensus was that neither side wanted war, no one last week
was prepared categorically to rule out that possibility.

MAX FRANKEL

President Kennedy and his advisers gave long and serious thought to ordering a surprise air attack on Soviet missile bases in Cuba before deciding that
a limited blockade could achieve their objectives.

Administration officials, looking back today on the fateful choice, recalled
that the final decision was made for moral as well as tactical reasons. Grave
questions were raised in the President's inner circle about the blot that an
assault on Cuba would place on the United States record and the repercussions it would have around the world.

The discovery of Soviet missile installations two weeks ago led to the immediate study of various responses — from doing nothing to protests to the
United Nations and the Organization of American States, blockade, surprise
air strike and invasion.

Inaction was quickly rejected as intolerable and humiliating. Invasion
was soon recognized as an excessive response — the immediate objective was
elimination of Soviet bases, not of the Castro Government.

Protests for action by international organizations, the President and his
staff agreed, would be ineffective. So the choice narrowed to blockade or
air attack.

Before the 10 or 12 men making the decision was an estimate that the
mobile medium-range missile sites were appearing almost daily, with some
assumed to be already operational. The first of the longer-range intermediate missile installations found to be under construction was expected to be
completed November 1, the second November 15 and a third December 1.

The proposal to bomb the Soviet installations raised a number of tactical
questions. Officials thought it probably would have involved killing some
of the Russian officers and technicians who controlled the bases. This, in
turn, would have greatly raised the chances of violent Soviet counter-action,
they believed.

What is more, the planners here developed what they came to call the

From "Air Attack on Missile Sites Was Seriously Weighed," *The New York Times,* October
30, 1962, p. 1. Copyright © 1962 by The New York Times Company. Reprinted by permission.

"bounce-back" theory. This assumed a surprise Soviet attack in Berlin or against some other allied base in a strategically weak position and an immediate clamor around the world for both sides to cease all military action.

In such a situation, the feeling was that the United States would have been faced with a choice of all-out nuclear war or an immediate truce that would have left the bases in Cuba damaged but not removed.

But overriding these concerns, officials report, was the general feeling that a surprise attack would be contrary to the country's tradition, history and aspiration, that it would be a response not commensurate with the provocation and that it would permanently damage the President's ability to promote responsible conduct in international relations.

As the President's speech a week ago made plain, he decided to retain his freedom of action throughout the power confrontation with the Soviet Union and, as last week's events demonstrated, he used the threat of further action effectively.

But the consensus among his most trusted associates was that the selective blockade, vigorous diplomatic activity and an impressive military build-up would force the Russians back.

Although the combination of these moves spread the impression toward the end of last week that an air strike or invasion was imminent, informed sources said today that the President was still far from such a decision. They did not deny, however, that officials here freely let the impression stand.

Privately, too, the President sought to impress upon Premier Khrushchev the need for a prompt settlement. His letters to the Soviet leader, including one or more that are still secret, were full of time references like "promptly," "matter of days" and "urgency." At no time, however, did Mr. Kennedy commit himself to a deadline for further action.

The next step, if the first efforts had failed, probably would have been a total blockade of Cuba, denying the island fuel and food as well as weapons. Had Mr. Khrushchev not ordered the dismantling of the missiles, a decision for further action probably would have been made today.

The only factor that might have upset the schedule was counter-action by the Russians or the Cubans. For weeks, the close air and sea surveillance of the island had met with no resistance and Premier Fidel Castro seemed determined to avoid any brush with American forces that might have provoked a full-scale attack.

The Russians were presumed to have known of this restraint, or perhaps even to have ordered it. That is why the announcement Saturday that the Cubans had decided to fire on the reconnaissance planes brought the situation to its most dangerous point.

A U-2 of the Strategic Air Command was missed Saturday and presumed lost over Cuba. Another reconnaissance aircraft drew Cuban anti-aircraft fire. On the chance that Premier Castro was taking independent action,

Mr. Kennedy arranged to leave time for the Russians to call a halt on these attacks.

There was no intention here of ending the surveillance. In fact, to obtain clear close-up photographs of the Soviet sites for diplomatic and propaganda purposes, American planes flew over the installations repeatedly and at extremely low altitudes.

Fearing an "escalation" of the situation, the Defense Department warned that the reconnaissance planes would be protected. It also used the occasion to announce the call-up of more than 14,000 air reservists.

Had the firing continued, the intention was to strike back at the anti-aircraft emplacements, though not at the long-range missile sites. Most of the anti-aircraft weapons were in Cuban hands, although Cubans are only beginning to learn from Russian crews the operation of SA-2 batteries, a Nike-like anti-aircraft missile that is the most elaborate defensive weapon on the island.

But whatever political difficulties may have existed between Moscow and Havana in the rapidly moving situation, there were no further attacks on the American planes, which are still flying over Cuba.

Officials are pleased, therefore, that they chose the blockade as their most dramatic maneuver, for it was a retrievable action that could be undone once the Russians acceded to the President's demands. It will not be lifted, however, they stressed, until ground inspectors of the United Nations certify Soviet compliance with the agreement.

ARTHUR SCHLESINGER, JR.

At one-thirty on Friday John Scali, the State Department correspondent for the American Broadcasting Company, received a call from Aleksander Fomin, a counselor at the Soviet Embassy, insisting on an immediate meeting. Scali, who had lunched occasionally with Fomin in the past, joined him at once at the Occidental Restaurant. The usually phlegmatic Russian, now haggard and alarmed, said, "War seems about to break out. Something must be done to save the situation." Scali replied that they should have thought of that before they put the missiles in Cuba. The Russian sat in silence for a moment. Then he said, "There might be a way out. What would you think of a proposition whereby we would promise to remove our missiles under United Nations inspection, where Mr. Khrushchev would promise never to introduce such offensive weapons into Cuba again? Would the President of the United States be willing to promise publicly not to invade Cuba?" When Scali said he did not know, Fomin begged him to find out immediately from his State Department friends. Then, reaching for a pencil, he wrote down his home telephone number: "If I'm not at the Embassy, call me here. This is of vital importance."

Scali carried the proposal to Roger Hilsman at State, and Hilsman carried it to Rusk. After discussion with the Executive Committee, Rusk asked Scali to tell the Russian that we saw "real possibilities" for a negotiation but they must understand that time was short — no more than forty-eight hours. At seven-thirty Friday evening Scali passed this word along. They met this time in the coffee shop of the Statler Hilton. Fomin, once he had satisfied himself about the authenticity of Scali's message and after a brief attempt to introduce the idea of UN inspection of Florida as well as Cuba, rose and, in his haste to get the word back, tossed down a five-dollar bill for a thirty-cent check and speeded off without waiting for the change.

Two hours later a long letter from Khrushchev to the President began to come in by cable. The Soviet leader started by insisting that the weapons shipments were complete and that their purpose was defensive. Then he declared his profound longing for peace; let us, he said with evident emotion, not permit this situation to get out of hand. The enforcement of the quarantine would only drive the Soviet Union to take necessary measures of its own. But if the United States would give assurances that it would not invade Cuba nor permit others to do so and if it would recall its fleet from the quarantine, this would immediately change everything. Then the necessity for a Soviet presence in Cuba would disappear. The crisis, Khrushchev said, was like a rope with a knot in the middle: the more each side pulled, the more the knot would tighten, until finally it could be severed only by a sword. But if each side slackened the rope, the knot could be untied.

The letter was not, as subsequently described, hysterical. Though it pulsated with a passion to avoid nuclear war and gave the impression of having been written in deep emotion, why not? In general, it displayed an entirely rational understanding of the implications of the crisis. Together with the Scali proposal, it promised light at the end of the cave. And in New York on Friday we heard that Zorin had advanced the same proposal to U Thant, and that the Cubans at the UN were beginning to hint to unaligned delegates that the bases might be dismantled and removed if the United States would guarantee the territorial integrity of Cuba. The President probably had his first good night's sleep for ten days; certainly the rest of us did.

But when the Executive Committee assembled on Saturday morning, prospects suddenly darkened. The Moscow radio began to broadcast a new Khrushchev letter containing, to everyone's consternation, an entirely different proposition from the one transmitted through Scali and embodied in Khrushchev's letter of the night before. The Soviet Union now said it would remove its missiles from Cuba and offer a non-aggression pledge to Turkey if the United States would remove its missiles from Turkey and offer a non-aggression pledge to Cuba. The notion of trading the Cuban and Turkish bases had been much discussed in England; Walter Lippmann and others had urged it in the United States. But Kennedy regarded the idea as unacceptable, and the swap was promptly rejected. . . .

. . . There remained the Khrushchev letters, and the Executive Committee turned to them again with bafflement and something close to despair. It was noted that Defense Minister Rodion Malinovsky had mentioned Cuba and Turkey together as early as Tuesday, and the *Red Star,* the army paper, had coupled them again on Friday. Could the military have taken over in Moscow? Rusk called in Scali and asked him to find out anything he could from his Soviet contact. Scali, fearful that he had been used to deceive his own country, up-braided Fomin, accusing him of a double cross. The Russian said miserably that there must have been a cable delay, that the Embassy was waiting word from Khrushchev at any moment. Scali brought this report immediately to the President and the Executive Committee at the White House (where Pierre Salinger nearly had heart failure when, in the midst of the rigorous security precautions of the week, he suddenly saw the ABC reporter sitting at the door of the President's inner office) . . . .

. . . When Kennedy received Khrushchev's reply that golden October morning, he showed profound relief. Later he said, "This is the night to go to the theater, like Abraham Lincoln."

STATEMENT OF PRESIDENT KENNEDY AT
HIS PRESS CONFERENCE, NOVEMBER 20, 1962

I have today been informed by Chairman Khrushchev that all of the IL-28 bombers now in Cuba will be withdrawn in 30 days. He also agrees that these planes can be observed and counted as they leave. Inasmuch as this goes a long way toward reducing the danger which faced this hemisphere four weeks ago, I have this afternoon instructed the Secretary of Defense to lift our naval quarantine.

In view of this action, I want to take this opportunity to bring the American people up to date on the Cuban crisis and to review the progress made thus far in fulfilling the understandings between Soviet Chairman Khrushchev and myself as set forth in our letters of October 27 and 28.

Chairman Khrushchev, it will be recalled, agreed to remove from Cuba all weapons systems capable of offensive use, to halt the further introduction of such weapons into Cuba, and to permit appropriate United Nations observation and supervision to insure the carrying out and continuation of these commitments. We on our part agreed that, once these adequate arrangements for verification had been established, we would remove our naval quarantine and give assurances against invasion of Cuba.

The evidence to date indicates that all known offensive-missile sites in Cuba have been dismantled. The missiles and their associated equipment have been loaded on Soviet ships. And our inspection at sea of these departing ships has confirmed that the number of missiles reported by the Soviet Union as having been brought into Cuba, which closely corresponded to our own information, has now been removed.

In addition, the Soviet Government has stated that all nuclear weapons have been withdrawn from Cuba and no offensive weapons will be reintroduced.

Nevertheless, important parts of the understanding of October 27 and 28 remain to be carried out. The Cuban Government has not yet permitted the United Nations to verify whether all offensive weapons have been removed, and no lasting safeguards have yet been established against the future introduction of offensive weapons back into Cuba.

Consequently, if the Western Hemisphere is to continue to be protected against offensive weapons, this Government has no choice but to pursue its own means of checking on military activities in Cuba. The importance of our continued vigilance is underlined by our identification in recent days of a number of Soviet ground combat units in Cuba, although we are informed that these and other Soviet units were associated with the protection of offensive-weapons systems, and will also be withdrawn in due course. . . .

May I add this final thought: In this week of Thanksgiving, there is much for which we can be grateful as we look back to where we stood only four weeks ago — the unity of this hemisphere, the support of our allies, and the calm determination of the American people. These qualities may be tested many more times in this decade, but we have increased reason to be confident that those qualities will continue to serve the cause of freedom with distinction in the years to come.

❦ CASE
STUDY   *NUCLEAR WEAPONS AND NATO*

The second case study in this chapter is taken from Henry A. Kissinger's *The Troubled Partnership.* It deals primarily with the effect on the Atlantic alliance of the revolution in nuclear technology. In addition, Kissinger makes a number of incisive comments on the nature of alliances in general. A basic thesis of Kissinger's book is that the needs for coordination and centralization imposed by the new technology are not fully compatible with existing notions of national sovereignty. How can a nation be sovereign if it cannot decide for itself when it will or will not risk its very existence as a nation by going to war? But if each member of an alliance is to decide this ultimate question independently, how can joint strategic plans — depending on the participation of all the allies — be drawn up?

One of the most pressing problems of NATO has been who shall control the West's nuclear deterrent. The United States, Britain, and France have nuclear forces of their own — a fact which makes some Western observers nervous. Why should France need its own nuclear force, they argue, unless it is thinking of making use of it in situations in which the United States would not want to allow American nuclear forces to be used? If France should use its nuclear forces on the Soviet Union, might not the Russians feel they had no choice but to respond against the United States as well as against France, in anticipation of a United States nuclear response to an attack on its errant ally?

Besides, if Britain and France are to have nuclear weapons of their own, how long will West Germany be willing to forego following suit, its formal pledges not to produce nuclear weapons notwithstanding? And if West Germany develops a nuclear deterrent, is there not a danger that someday it will seek to use threats of nuclear force to achieve reunification? Even if this seems too remote a possibility for *us* to worry about, there is no doubt that *the Russians do* worry about it. They almost certainly would refuse to consider any nonproliferation agreement which did not prohibit West Germany from acquiring nuclear weapons, and might feel it necessary to take forceful steps to avert such a development.

In an effort to avoid nuclear proliferation and anticipated German demands for nuclear equality,[33] various sorts of multinationally controlled nuclear forces have been proposed. One possibility would be a European nuclear force. Another, pushed by the United States in 1963 and 1964, was the multilateral force (MLF), to be controlled jointly by the United States and those of its NATO allies which elected to participate. After some discussion among the allies, this force was envisaged as containing a number of surface ships, carrying Polaris missiles with nuclear warheads, manned by crews including nationals of at least three participating NATO countries. Ultimately, however, European reluctance caused the Johnson administration to stop pressing for the MLF. And the issue of how such a force would be controlled was never really settled. Albert Wohlstetter has commented:

> . . . If those who jointly control the NATO force are principally interested in the power to say "No," then the response of the joint

[33] Kissinger, Arthur Schlesinger, Jr., and others have suggested that this anticipation of West German demands for nuclear equality may have been premature, and may, in fact, have helped to create, rather than head off, such demands. Surveys of the opinions of West German elite groups conducted by Karl Deutsch "tend to disconfirm the notion of a supposedly strong German desire for national nuclear weapons. . . . So far as our evidence goes there is no such German desire for national nuclear weapons at this time." "Integration and Arms Control in the European Political Environment: A Summary Report," *The American Political Science Review* (June, 1966), p. 363.

force is less credible than the U.S. guarantee. For one thing, as a member of NATO, the United States has a vote, and if a strike is not in our interest, we would presumably exercise our veto. . . . On the other hand, if the purpose of joint control is to say "Yes," then what is its meaning? No one to my knowledge has suggested that the NATO strike force be at the disposal of any member of NATO who desires to use it, regardless of what the others think. This of course would be the extreme short cut to the nuclear decentralization which the NATO strike force is supposed to avoid.[34]

Even the making of decisions by majority vote would still fail to give individual nations the power to decide questions involving their own survival.

More recently it has been suggested that the European members of NATO might be satisfied without any physical control of the alliance's nuclear deterrent if they were accorded a significant role in the formulation of NATO's strategic policy. Consequently, a joint committee for alliance nuclear planning, composed of representatives of the key NATO countries, was established late in 1966. But NATO's nuclear control problem remained far from solved as the alliance approached its twentieth anniversary (1969).

Soon after Kissinger's analysis was published, President de Gaulle announced the formal termination of France's participation in the North Atlantic Treaty *Organization*. France would no longer take part in NATO's military planning, nor put its territory and military forces at NATO's disposal. Yet, De Gaulle declared, France would continue to consider itself bound by the provision of the North Atlantic *Treaty* pledging its signatories to treat an attack on one as an attack on all. American troops were later withdrawn from France, at the French Government's request, and NATO's political headquarters were moved from Paris to Brussels.

1. According to Kissinger, what are the traditional purposes of alliance systems? How has the advent of nuclear weapons technology modified these purposes? To what extent have the changes in the nature of the Sino-Soviet relationship, discussed in Chapter Ten, been due to the impact of nuclear weapons on the nature of alliances in general?

2. What are the principal causes of the divisions within the Atlantic alliance? To what extent are they a function of difficulties inherent in alliances per se? To what extent are they due to historical factors? To the nature of nuclear technology itself? To the diplomacy pursued by President de Gaulle and by the United States?

3. In your opinion, what would be the most satisfactory way of handling the nuclear control problem? (Or would it be best to disband NATO — as an organization — now that France has withdrawn?)

[34] "Nuclear Sharing: NATO and the N + 1 Country," *Foreign Affairs* (April, 1961), pp. 372–373. Reprinted by permission.

HENRY A. KISSINGER

The most constructive American foreign policy since the end of World War II has been the development of Atlantic relationships. Through a series of far-sighted and bold measures starting with the Greek-Turkish aid program and the Marshall Plan, the United States helped Europe recover from the economic dislocations of six years of war. When the Communist coup in Czechoslovakia and the Berlin blockade raised fears about Soviet aggressiveness, the United States organized the Atlantic Alliance to insure the security of Europe. Every administration since then has promoted European recovery, Atlantic cooperation and joint defense. As a result, Europe has become more prosperous than ever and it feels safe from invasion. Significant steps toward European integration have been taken, such as the Coal and Steel Community, EURATOM (an agency for the joint development of the peaceful uses of atomic energy) and, above all, the Common Market. Until President de Gaulle's veto of Britain's entry into the Common Market on January 14, 1963, a form of European political union seemed the logical next step. According to the expectation of most American leaders, an ever more intimate Atlantic association would have followed. This was expressed in President Kennedy's Grand Design for a partnership between a united Europe and the United States.

In recent years this promise has been flawed by increasingly sharp disputes among the Allies. The absence of agreement on major policies is striking. On the Continent, the fear of a bilateral United States-Soviet arrangement is pervasive. The United States-British view with respect to disarmament is rejected by France and greeted with distrust and fear by the [German] Federal Republic. The United States finds little support in Europe for its Asian or Latin American policies. The attempt to establish a common trade policy with the Communist world has been generally ineffective. For over a decade, the Western Allies have been unable to agree on a common attitude toward the former colonial areas. Progress toward European political unity has been slowed. Britain has been excluded from the Common Market. Basic issues of strategic doctrine have gone unresolved. The issue of nuclear control threatens to divide the Alliance.

Of course, in an alliance of sovereign states, a measure of disagreement is to be expected. What makes current disputes so complex is that they really involve basic assumptions about the nature of Atlantic relationships, the future of Europe and the relative influence of the various partners. For the first time since the war there exists an open challenge not just to the technical implementation of American plans but to the validity of American conceptions. Our strategic conceptions no longer go unquestioned; our preferences concerning the organization of Europe and the most efficient Atlantic relationship are being contested.

Many blame this on the somewhat out-of-scale figure of President de Gaulle. There is no question that the intransigent tactics of the French President have severely strained the pattern of Allied relationships which emerged after the war. But no one man could have disrupted the Alliance by himself. Fundamental changes have been taking place in the relative weights of Europe and the United States, in the nature of alliances and in the character of strategy. Allied relationships would have had to be adapted to new conditions, no matter who governed in Paris — or in Washington, for that matter.

The Atlantic Alliance has been brought face to face with two questions not unlike those with which each Western society has had to deal in its domestic affairs: How much unity do we want? How much pluralism can we stand? Too formalistic a conception of unity risks destroying the sense of responsibility of our Allies. Too absolute an insistence on national particularity must lead to a fragmentation of any common effort.

THE CHANGED NATURE OF ATLANTIC RELATIONSHIPS

The impact of particular statesmen aside, the Atlantic Alliance is beset by two kinds of problems: those produced by structural conditions, with which policymakers must learn to live, and those caused by acts of policy. This chapter will deal with the structural problems of the Atlantic Alliance.

Perhaps the deepest danger we face is that, as with all great achievements, nostalgia for the patterns of action that were appropriate when America was predominant and Europe impotent may become an obstacle to the creativity needed to deal with an entirely new situation. Those Americans who deserve the greatest credit for promoting the recovery of Europe and forging existing Atlantic ties are finding it most difficult to adjust to conditions in which American leadership is no longer unquestioned. The fact of a challenge to American pre-eminence is almost as irritating to them as its content. They suffer from the distortion of perspective produced when, in the late forties, the end of America's isolation coincided with the temporary loss of Europe's ability to play an effective international role or to protect itself against foreign danger. They remember a Europe torn by World War II. Every European country — with the exception of Great Britain — had known defeat at one time or another during that conflict. Every country — again with the exception of Great Britain — had been the victim of foreign occupation. Societies were shattered. Europe was dependent on the United

States for its material well-being, domestic cohesion and safety from invasion.

United States-European relationships took on their present cast during this period. Faced with a ravaged Europe, the United States came to deal with its Allies paternalistically. This has involved a certain self-righteousness and impatience with criticism. American policymakers often act as if disagreement with their views is due to ignorance which must be overcome by extensive briefings and insistent reiteration. They are less inclined to inquire whether there may be some merit in an opposing view than in overwhelming it with floods of emissaries, official and semi-official. As a result, the United States and Europe have too often conducted their dialogue over the technical implementation of a blueprint manufactured in America.

In part, this American attitude was both the cause and the product of some bad habits developed by Europe during the period of unchallengeable American dominance. Throughout much of the postwar period, the policy of our European Allies has consisted essentially in influencing American decisions rather than developing conceptions of their own. This, in turn, produced querulousness and insecurity. At times, our Allies have seemed more eager to extract American reassurance than to encourage a consistent United States policy. Excessive suspicion has been coupled with formal pliancy. For a decade, European statesmen showed their disagreement by stalling on agreed measures rather than by developing alternatives. This has led to a negativism characterized by a greater awareness of risks than of opportunities and by a general fear of any departure from the status quo.

The period of American hegemony came to an end in the late fifties and early sixties under the impact of four events in which United States policy had played a major role: European economic recovery; European integration; decolonization; and the Cuban missile crisis and its aftermath. Each of these events illustrates that results cannot always be judged by the intentions of those whose policies start a historical process, even less by their pronouncements.

The United States promoted European recovery in a constructive and farsighted spirit. We saw Europe as a potential partner eventually sharing with us the burdens and responsibilities of world leadership. Most pronouncements of American purposes reflected our expectation that after its recovery Europe would no longer require American economic assistance but would continue to pursue parallel, if not identical policies.

This was, however, always unlikely. With the growth of European economic vigor, Europe's traditional political dynamism was bound to return. The trend was given impetus by the existence of an intact younger generation — the first since the carnage of World War I — eager to assert its own view of the world.

The process of European economic integration magnified Europe's new-found assertiveness. The orthodox American view was that the Common Market should be "outward-looking," by which we meant that its economic strength would buttress all free peoples without discrimination. However, it is the essence of a common market that it will maintain *some* tariff barriers against the outside world, and, as internal barriers are lower than external ones, a measure of discrimination will be unavoidable. Moreover, these external barriers can be reduced only as the result of governmental negotiations. And, obviously, the stronger the economic unit, the more formidable its bargaining power.

The increasing economic strength of the European Common Market was bound to complicate economic negotiations with Europe — a fact not to be eliminated by epithets like "inward-looking," which American policymakers tend to use to oppose policies they consider unfavorable to American interests. The internal logic of the Common Market produces its own necessities. It is no accident that in most economic negotiations — whether they concerned Britain's entry into the Common Market or the so-called Kennedy Round of negotiations designed to adjust tariffs between the Common Market and the United States — the position of the Common Market Commission has been close to that of France despite profound differences about the political organization of Europe. The economic interests of the Common Market often coincide with the political goal of France to assert a more independent role for Europe.

The process of decolonization has also contributed to Europe's new vigor. Freed from overseas commitments, many European countries for the first time in a generation are able to develop a specifically European role for themselves. Ironically, the end of Europe's colonial empires has led to a reversal of the traditional postwar attitudes of the United States and Europe toward many underdeveloped countries. Some European leaders are now repeating the American argument of the fifties: that the larger interests of the free world are sometimes served by allowing for differing, occasionally even competing, Western approaches to the emerging nations.

This attitude, too, was inevitable, even though it bears the marks of de Gaulle's high-handed tactics. Having shed their colonial possessions, often under American pressure, our European Allies have a psychological block against running major risks on behalf of areas from which they have been so recently ejected. As a result of decolonization, our European Allies have ceased to think of themselves as world powers. They possess neither the resources nor the domestic framework for distant enterprises. No European government, with the possible exception of the United Kingdom, is likely to be convinced that its security is jeopardized by events in another part of the globe.

United States spokesmen often exhort our Allies to play a more active global role with the argument that their resources are now adequate for such a task.* But the problem is more complicated. The availability of resources does not guarantee an interest in assuming world-wide responsibilities as is demonstrated by United States policy prior to World War II.

The same is true today for almost all our European Allies. Each of them has an interest in preserving the peace. But this general concern will not produce meaningful support for such United States policies as the defense of Southeast Asia. If our Allies give assistance, it will be token in nature, and the motive will be to obtain a veto over United States actions. The thrust of their recommendations will be to avoid a direct showdown and even the semblance of risk. In other words, we are now the only member of NATO with world-wide interests, and this produces unavoidable differences in perspective.

Finally, relations with the Communist world have changed dramatically since the Cuban missile crisis. Most of our European Allies have reached the conclusion that the two main nuclear powers will avoid a direct military confrontation for an indefinite period. This conviction has been strengthened by the hope of some, and the suspicion of others, that bilateral United States-Soviet dealings are underway. Such an atmosphere of detente removes the previous urgency for Allied cohesion. As the Soviet threat appears to recede, the scope for largely national action widens proportionately. As the impression grows that bilateral Soviet-United States negotiations are proceeding, Third Force tendencies in Europe are stimulated. The issue is not whether the United States would make a "deal" contrary to the interests of its Allies. It is rather that in an alliance of sovereign states each country will think that it is a better judge of its own requirements than any partner, however close. No ally will be prepared to let another negotiate about what it considers its vital interests.

As the detente develops, the need to transform the Alliance from its present defensive concept into a political arrangement defining itself by some positive goals will grow ever more urgent. Defense against a military threat will soon lose its force as a political bond. Negotiations with the East will prove corrosive unless they go hand in hand with the creation of common political purposes and the institutions to embody them. The need, in short, is to go from alliance to community.

Thus major changes have occurred in U.S.-European relations that have not been caused by any individual, though they may have been exploited by willful men. On both sides of the Atlantic the persistence of old attitudes in new circumstances has contributed to the impasse. Adjusting to a loss of preeminence is always a difficult process. Grown accustomed to finding its views unchallenged, the dominant ally tends to identify its policies with the general interest. This conviction is reinforced by a network of connections

* See, for example, George W. Ball, "NATO and World Responsibility," *The Atlantic Community Quarterly*, Vol. 2, No. 2 (Summer 1964), p. 215.

with individuals who have helped develop the existing pattern and who consider it natural. The desire of the erstwhile protégés for autonomy appears as distrust; the quest for independence seems indistinguishable from self-will. Why should a country want freedom of action when, by definition, its interests cannot diverge from those of the dominant partner?

By the same token, countries striving to alter a relationship of tutelage will be tempted to emphasize the burdensome aspects of the existing relationship and to neglect its benefits. They will not credit the motives of the senior partner and look for hegemonial designs in sincere efforts to achieve a consensus.

In the process, both sides emphasize form over substance. On one side, the method of integration becomes a good in itself; on the other, a posture of autonomy is sought for its own sake. Wisdom and restraint would be severely tested in the best of circumstances. But the circumstances have not been fortuitous. The change in relationships within the Atlantic area has had to be carried out at a moment when the whole concept of alliances is in a state of transition, and it has been overshadowed by the dread specter of nuclear warfare.

THE CHANGE IN
THE NATURE OF ALLIANCES

During the last decade, an important change has taken place in the nature of alliances. In the past, alliances have been created for three basic reasons: (1) To provide an accretion of power. With conventional weapons, overwhelming power could generally be assembled only by way of coalition. The wider the alliance, the greater its power to resist aggression. (2) To leave no doubt about the alignment of forces. It has often been argued that had Germany known at the beginning of both world wars that the United States — or even England — would join the war, aggression would have been averted. (3) To transform a tacit interest in mutual assistance into a formal obligation.

To be sure, even before the advent of nuclear weapons, there was some inconsistency among these requirements: The attempt to combine the maximum number of states for joint action occasionally conflicted with the desire to leave no doubt about the collective motivation. The wider the alliance, the more various were the motives animating it and the more intense and direct had to be a threat to produce a united response.

This difficulty has been compounded in the nuclear age. Nuclear war requires tight command of all weapons, which is to some degree inconsistent with a coalition of sovereign states. Moreover, the enormous risks of nuclear warfare affect the credibility of traditional pledges of mutual assistance. In the past, alliances held together because it was believed that the *immediate* risk of conflict was less than the *ultimate* danger of facing a preponderant enemy alone. But when nuclear war hazards the lives of tens of millions, some allies may consider the outbreak of a war the worst contingency and, in times of crisis, act accordingly.

As a result, many of the theories of nuclear control now current within the Western Alliance have a tendency either to turn NATO into a unilateral United States guarantee or to call into question the utility of the Alliance altogether. American strategic thought verges on the first extreme; some French theorists have hinted at the second.

As for the United States, official spokesmen have consistently emphasized that the European contribution to the over-all nuclear strength of the Alliance is negligible. European nuclear forces have been described as "provocative," "prone to obsolescence" and "weak." * For a time during the Kennedy Administration, some high officials held the view that the Allies might be induced to ask the President to serve as the Executive Agent of the Alliance on nuclear matters. Since then, the United States has made various proposals for nuclear sharing; the common feature of these has been the retention of the United States veto over the use of nuclear weapons.

However sensible such schemes may appear from the point of view of division of labor, they would perpetuate American hegemony in nuclear matters. Allies seem to be considered necessary not so much to increase over-all strength as to provide the ability to apply power discriminately. Allies are useful because they permit resistance to aggression by means less cataclysmic than all-out war. In such a structure, American decisions must continue to be paramount. The nuclear weapons of the Alliance have to remain under central control, which in effect means American control. The predominant United States theory is a sophisticated elaboration of the situation of the late forties and early fifties. It is designed to make our hegemony more bearable, not to alter it.

According to the opposing view, alliances have lost their significance altogether. A French theorist, General Gallois, has argued, for example, that nuclear weapons have made alliances obsolete.† Faced with the risk of total destruction, no nation will jeopardize its survival for another. Hence, he maintains, each country must have its own nuclear arsenal to defend itself against direct attack, while leaving all other countries to their fate.

This formula would mark the end of collective security [35] and would likely lead to international chaos. In the face of the growing nuclear arsenals of the major protagonists, it would be idle to deny that the threat of nuclear

---

* For the classic indictment of Europe's national nuclear forces, see Secretary McNamara's speech at Ann Arbor, Michigan, June 16, 1962, *Department of State Bulletin* (hereafter referred to as *DOSB*), Vol. XLVII, No. 1202 (July 9, 1962), pp. 64–69.

† Pierre M. Gallois, "U.S. Strategy and the Defense of Europe," *Orbis*, Vol. VII, No. 2 (Summer 1963), pp. 226–249.

[35] [This term is used here to mean collective *defense, not* "collective security" in the strict sense in which it is defined in Chapter One of this book.]

retaliation has lost some of its credibility. The Gallois theory would, however, transform a degree of uncertainty into a guarantee that the United
States would *not* come to the assistance of its Allies, thus greatly simplifying
an aggressor's calculation.

Moreover, in order to protect itself in this new situation, each country
would need to develop not only a nuclear arsenal of its own but also foolproof procedures for assuring the Soviets that a given nuclear blow did not
originate from its territory. If Gallois is right, and no ally is willing to risk
nuclear devastation for another, it will also want to avoid being forced into
nuclear war by its partners. Thus it will have a high incentive to devise
methods to protect itself against attacks based on misinformation. The
Gallois theory would lead to a multiplication of national nuclear forces
side by side with the development of methods of surrender or guarantees of
non-involvement.

When views such as these carry influence on both sides of the Atlantic, it is
no accident that much of the debate on nuclear matters within NATO turns
on the issue of confidence. The United States tends to ask those of its allies
possessing nuclear arsenals: If you trust us, why do you need nuclear weapons of your own? The allies reply: If you trust us, why are you so concerned
about our possession of nuclear weapons? Since the answer must inevitably
emphasize contingencies in which either the goals of the Allies or their
strategy would be incompatible, the debate on nuclear control within
NATO has been inherently divisive.

The preponderance of nuclear power in the hands of the United States
poses one set of problems; the range of modern weapons raises another. In
the past, a threatened country had the choice either of resisting or of surrendering. If it resisted, it had to be prepared to accept the consequences in
terms of physical damage and loss of life. A distant ally could generally be
helpful only if it was able to bring its strength to bear in the area of conflict.

Modern weapons have changed this. What each member country wants
from the Atlantic Alliance is the assurance that an attack on it will be considered a *casus belli*. It strives for deterrence by adding the strength of a distant ally to its power. But, equally, each state has an incentive to reduce
damage to itself to a minimum should deterrence fail. For the first time
the range of modern weapons provides the technical possibility of combining these objectives. In 1914 Belgium could not base its defense on a strategy
that transferred to Britain the primary risks of devastation. In the age of
intercontinental rockets this is technically feasible.

Part of the strategic dispute within the Alliance, therefore, involves
jockeying to determine which geographic area will be the theater of war if
deterrence fails (though this obviously cannot be made explicit). A conventional war confined to Europe must appear in a different light to Americans than to Europeans, on whose territory such a war would be fought. A

nuclear exchange which spares their territory may seem to Europeans a more attractive strategy and the threat of nuclear retaliation a more effective deterrent. Although the interests of the Alliance may be indivisible in an ultimate sense, this does not guarantee that there will not be sharply clashing perceptions about methods to reach common objectives.

Thus the deepest problem before the Alliance is that the pressures of the new technology run counter to traditional notions of national sovereignty. The risks of nuclear warfare may be too great to be combined reliably with what has heretofore been considered a key attribute of sovereignty: the unilateral right of a sovereign state to alter its strategic or political views. The destructiveness and range of modern weapons have a tendency to produce both extreme nationalism and neutralism. A wise alliance policy must take care that in dealing with one of these dangers it does not produce the other.

The nature of alliances has changed in yet another way. In the past, one of the reasons for joining an alliance was to impose an additional obligation for assistance in time of need. Were each country's national interests completely unambiguous, it would know precisely on whose assistance it could count; a formal commitment would be unnecessary. Both the aggressor and the defender would understand what they would confront and could act accordingly. Wars would not be caused by a misunderstanding of intentions. They would occur only if the protagonists calculated the existing power relationships differently.

Traditionally, however, the national interest has not been unambiguous. Often the aggressor did not know which countries would ultimately be lined up against it; Germany in 1914 was genuinely surprised by the British reaction to the invasion of Belgium. Occasionally the defenders could not be certain of their potential support — for example, Great Britain and France had no assurance of U.S. assistance at the beginning of both world wars. A formal understanding, tacit or explicit, has often been the determining factor in the decision to go to war. In the decade prior to World War I, the staff talks between Britain and France which led to the transfer of the French fleet to the Mediterranean were one of the key factors in Britain's decision to enter the conflict in August 1914. (Thus the talks achieved one objective of traditional alliances: to commit Britain to the defense of France. They failed in another: to make the opposing alignment clear to the potential aggressor.)

In the contemporary period, ideology and technology have combined to produce a global confrontation. This, in turn, has rendered the national interest of the major antagonists less ambiguous. Neither the United States nor the Soviet Union can permit a major advance by its opponent whether the area in which it occurs is formally protected by an alliance or not. Neutral India was no less assured of American assistance when Communist China attacked than allied Pakistan would have been in similar circumstances. In these conditions, the distinction between allies and neutrals is likely to diminish. A country gains little from being allied and risks little by being neutral.

This inevitably results in the weakening of allied cohesion, producing what some have described as polycentrism. But polycentrism does not reflect so much the emergence of new centers of physical power as the attempt by allies to establish new centers of decision.

The gap in military strength between the United States and its European Allies has in fact widened, not narrowed, in the past decade. What *has* changed is the use to which the power can be put. On the one hand, the enormous risks of nuclear warfare call into question traditional pledges of formal assistance. On the other hand, those issues with respect to which nuclear threats *are* credible are so clear-cut as not to seem to require formal reinforcement. Polycentrism is on the rise not because the world has ceased to be bipolar, but because with respect to nuclear weapons it essentially remains so. President de Gaulle is convinced that those circumstances in which the United States might be prepared to resort to its nuclear weapons cannot be fundamentally affected by his actions. In other words, the United States commitment need not be purchased by being conciliatory and cannot be jeopardized by intransigence — within very wide limits at least.

Thus President de Gaulle sees little risk and considerable potential gain in political independence. In a curious way, it is possible for him to add American power to his own. Measures contradictory to those of the United States are thus in a sense supported by the American nuclear umbrella — a fact that adds to the irony of the situation and to the annoyance of some American policymakers. Although traditionally a state's diplomatic influence corresponded roughly to its military strength, this is no longer inevitably the case. Influence can now be achieved by using another country's protection even for policies not in accord with the ally's preferences.

The frequent insistence of United States officials and commentators that in the nuclear age an isolated strategy is no longer possible misses the central point: Precisely because an isolated strategy is indeed impossible, allies have unprecedented scope for the pursuit of their own objectives. And the more the detente — real or imaginary — proceeds, the more momentum these tendencies will gather. We live in a curious world where neutrals enjoy most of the protection of allies and allies aspire to have the same freedom of action as do neutrals.

THE NATURE OF
THE STRATEGIC DEBATE

The nature of power has never been easy to assess. But in the nuclear age this problem is complicated by the enormous destructiveness of weapons and the rapid change of technology. A basic discontinuity has developed when a statesman is compelled to risk millions of lives instead of thousands, when his decision no longer involves the loss of a province but the survival of society itself. Even if the classic principles of strategy are not entirely outmoded, the statesman will inevitably be reluctant to put them to the test.

This situation reflects the basic paradox of the nuclear age: Power has never been greater; it has also never been less useful. In the past, the major problem for strategists was to assemble superior strength; in the contemporary period the problem more frequently is how to make the available power relevant to objectives likely to be in dispute. Yet no matter what spectrum of power the major contenders may have at their disposal, the fear of escalation is inescapable. Though states have an unprecedented capacity to devastate their opponent, their threats to do so have only a limited credibility. This is because the ability to destroy is not related to the ability to disarm — so that using one's nuclear arsenal indiscriminately against a major opponent guarantees only self-destruction.

This dilemma creates potent pressures against the very concept of strategy. War, it is said, has become unthinkable, and diplomacy is therefore asked to take over. But if nuclear war has become the last resort of desperate men, this has not made the conduct of diplomacy any easier. In the past, unsuccessful negotiations never returned matters to their starting point; they called other pressures into play. But many of these pressures are no longer available, and thus diplomacy, too, has become less flexible. Where no penalty for noncompliance exists — no *ultima ratio* — there is no incentive to reach agreement. As statesmen have become increasingly reluctant to resort to war, negotiations have become more and more ritualistic. Even when tension persists, the Alliance may well remain uncertain and divided about the conclusions to be drawn from this situation. Though pacifism is not a novel attitude, the pressures within the Alliance against the need for any effective military policy are likely to mount.

This problem is made more acute because the primary purpose of modern weapons is deterrence. But deterrence is as much a psychological as a military problem. It depends on the aggressor's assessment of risks, not the defender's. A threat meant as a bluff but taken seriously is more useful for purposes of deterrence than a "genuine" threat interpreted as a bluff.

Moreover, if deterrence is successful, aggression does *not* take place. It is impossible, however, to demonstrate why something has *not* occurred. It can never be proved, for example, whether peace has been maintained because NATO pursues an optimum strategy or a marginally effective one. Finally, the more effective deterrence is, the more credible becomes the argument that perhaps the Communists never intended to attack in the first place. An effective NATO deterrent strategy may thus have built-in pressures to strengthen the arguments of the quasi-neutralists.

Even when the necessity for a military policy is not challenged, serious disputes are produced by the novelty of modern weapons. Never before in history has so much depended on weapons so new, so untested, so "abstract." Nuclear weapons have been used in wartime only against Japan, which did not possess means of retaliation. No one knows how governments or peoples will react to a nuclear explosion under conditions where both sides possess vast arsenals.

Then, too, modern weapons systems are relatively untested. During the debate over the Nuclear Test Ban Treaty, a great deal of attention was focused on the adequacy of nuclear warheads. In fact, the other components of modern weapons systems contain many more factors of uncertainty. The estimated "hardness" of Minuteman [ICBM] silos depends entirely on theoretical studies. Of the thousands of missiles in our arsenal, relatively few of each category have been tested under operational conditions. There is little experience with salvo firing. Air-defense systems are designed without any definite knowledge of the nature of the offense. A high proportion of the phenomena discovered in nuclear testing has been unexpected.

The novelty of modern weapons is compounded by the difficulty of forming a plausible conception for their use. How does one threaten with solid-fuel missiles? As these are always in an extreme state of readiness, how does one demonstrate an increase in preparedness which has historically served as a warning? From a technical point of view, it is highly probable that missiles can perform most of the functions heretofore assigned to airplanes. The shift from airplanes to missiles described by former Deputy Secretary of Defense Roswell Gilpatric makes a great deal of sense technically.* But has adequate attention been given to the kind of diplomacy which results — particularly in crisis situations — when the retaliatory threat depends entirely on solid-fuel missiles in underground silos? During the Cuban missile crisis, dispersing SAC planes to civilian airports proved an effective warning. What will be an equivalent move when our strategic forces are composed entirely of missiles? [36]

The intricacy of these problems has had a demoralizing effect on Allied relationships. An ever-widening gap has appeared between the sophistication of United States technical studies and the capacity of Allied leaders to absorb them — a gap that makes meaningful consultation increasingly difficult. It is unlikely that even the most conscientious Allied leader can devote as many hours to a given problem as the American experts have had months to study it. And few of our Allies have the technical possibility to develop expertise of their own. Thus, side by side with the restoration of European economic and political vigor, the military predominance of the

---

* Roswell Gilpatric, "Our Defense Needs: The Long View," *Foreign Affairs*, Vol. 42, No. 3 (April 1964), p. 373.

[36] [Secretary McNamara announced in 1966 that the U.S. planned to maintain at least a small manned bomber force — in addition to our large missile forces — indefinitely. *1967 Senate Defense Appropriations Hearings, op. cit.*, part 1, pp. 55–56.]

United States continues. Differences in perspective are unavoidable when one partner possesses not only an effective monopoly of power but also a monopoly of expertise. The American tendency to treat psychological and political problems as if they were primarily technical compounds the difficulty. As leader of the Alliance, the United States cannot rest on the theoretical adequacy of its views. It is also responsible for the answer to [such] questions as these: Do the Allies understand American strategic doctrine? Do they believe it? Does it encourage confidence or a sense of impotence? A too complicated strategy can lead to the paralysis of will of those who may ultimately have to implement it.

Moreover, the United States has been slow to admit to itself that real differences of interest between us and our Allies are possible. Our penchant for treating the Atlantic area as if it were a single unit runs counter to the fact that the Alliance is still composed of sovereign states. If NATO were, in fact, one political entity, it could concentrate on the most efficient form of over-all defense. In that case, exposing a part of the Alliance's territory to the fluctuations of a local conflict could seem a small price to avoid the devastation of general war.

But as long as the Alliance is based on sovereign states, they will not acquiesce in a strategy which appears to them to spell the end of their national existence. If NATO forces withdraw as little as 100 miles on the central front, the Federal Republic would have lost the greater part of its territory. What might be tolerable for a single state becomes unacceptable to a coalition. It is therefore not enough to say that the United States will take the defense of Europe as seriously as that of Alaska. Precisely because Alaska is not sovereign, it can be defended by a strategy which might prove unacceptable to our European Allies.

The reluctance to face this conflict of interests has produced what the French call a "dialogue among the deaf." The United States is concerned primarily with the most efficient organization of the common resources for defense against attack from the East. For many Europeans, assembling an adequate defensive force is not enough if, in the process, their historical position is destroyed. American proposals tend toward a rationalization of efforts for an objective so much taken for granted that it requires no debate. Many Europeans opposing American conceptions are not content with acting simply as advisors in an American decision-making process; instead, they strive for a structure in which they have autonomous responsibility. They want their agreement to represent an act of will, not an organizational necessity.

This is why in many countries the leaders and groups traditionally most committed to national defense have developed views on strategy that challenge American concepts, while some of those most ready to accept U.S. strategic hegemony have in the past been the least interested in making a serious defense effort. Acquiescence in American strategic hegemony can have two meanings: It can either represent a sincere commitment to Atlantic partnership or disguise a neutralist wish to abdicate responsibility. Many who applaud our views may do so for reasons that will not prove very comforting in the long run. The American nuclear umbrella, now sometimes exploited by President de Gaulle for his own purposes, can also be used — and more dangerously for the West — to support policies amounting to neutralism.

The United States may, therefore, have to make a choice between the technical and the political side of Atlantic policy, between the requirements of conducting a nuclear war and the imperatives of a vital Alliance diplomacy. From a technical point of view, there is undoubtedly great merit to the American insistence on central command and control of military operations. But, from a psychological point of view, unless centralization of strategy is coupled with an effective sharing of political decisions — far beyond anything so far envisaged — the practical consequence could be a growing sense of irresponsibility among our Allies.

DIFFERENCES IN HISTORICAL
PERSPECTIVE AND ACTUAL STRENGTH

Some of the strains on Atlantic relationships have resulted from factors outside anybody's control. Many reflect the growth in Europe of the very strength and self-confidence which American policy has attempted to promote since the end of World War II. Others have been caused by the nature of modern weapons whose destructiveness is not really compatible with insistence on undiluted sovereignty.

But perhaps the deepest cause of misunderstandings — and the reason that structural problems have proved so intense — is a difference in historical perspective. Americans live in an environment uniquely suited to a technological approach to policymaking. As a result, our society has been characterized by a conviction that any problem will yield if subjected to a sufficient dose of expertise. With such an approach, problems tend to appear as discrete issues without any inner relationship. It is thought that they can be solved "on their merits" as they arise. It is rarely understood that a "solution" to a problem may mortgage the future — especially as there is sufficient optimism to assume that, even should this prove to be the case, it will still be possible to overcome the new problem when it materializes.

When applied to foreign policy, such an approach tends to treat division of labor as its own justification. Allies are considered factors in a security arrangement. Their utility is measured in terms of their contribution to a common effort. Criteria are often determined abstractly with each nation assigned a specific role with little regard to its history or domestic structure. There is a great proclivity toward abstract models. Means sometimes become exalted as ends.

But Europeans live on a continent covered with ruins testifying to the fallibility of human foresight. In European history, the recognition of a problem has often defined a dilemma rather than pointed to a solution. The margin of survival of European countries has been more precarious than that of the United States. Each country — with the possible exception of Great Britain — has known national catastrophe as America has not. European reasoning is thus likely to be more complicated and less confident than ours. Our European Allies think of themselves not simply as components of security schemes but as expressions of a historical experience. Policies that neglect their sense of identity may destroy the psychological basis of any common effort.

This difference in perspective is crucial to understanding some of the strains in Atlantic relationships. Americans tend to be impatient with what seems to them Europe's almost morbid obsession with the past, while Europeans sometimes complain about a lack of sensitivity and compassion on the part of Americans. In the fall of 1963, our newspapers were filled with derisive comments about French maneuvers then taking place. These maneuvers were based on the assumption that an aggressor was attacking through Germany. France's allies had surrendered. As the aggressor's armies were approaching her borders, France resorted to her nuclear weapons.

It is, of course, easy to ridicule this scenario by contrasting the small size of the French bomber force with the magnitude of the disaster envisaged. But the crucial issue is not technical. It arises from the fact that France has undergone shattering historical experiences with which Americans find it difficult to identify. The French maneuvers recalled importantly — though perhaps too rigidly — France's traumatic experience of 1940, when foreign armies attacked all along the Western front and France's Allies collapsed. The British Fighter Command remained in England. The fact that this critical decision was wise does not affect the basic psychological point.

Moreover, the French disaster came at the end of two decades in which France almost single-handedly shouldered the responsibility for the defense of Europe while her erstwhile Allies withdrew into isolation or offered strictures about France's obsession with security. The nightmare that some day France might again stand alone goes far deeper than the obstinate ill-will of a single individual.

A comparable problem exists in Germany. Washington has at times shown signs of impatience toward the German leaders and their frequent need for reassurance. Secretary Rusk has been reported more than once to be restless with what he has called the "pledging sessions" which the Germans seem so often to demand. However, insecurity is endemic in the German situation. A divided country with frontiers that correspond to no historical experience, a society that has lived through two disastrous defeats and four domestic upheavals in forty years cannot know inward security. The need to belong to something, to rescue some predictability out of chaos, is overwhelming. To subject such a country to constant changes of policy —

as we have done — is to undermine its stability. The memories of our Allies should be factors as real in the discussions of our policymakers as the analysis of weapons systems.

The importance of this difference in historical perspective is compounded by the continuing disparity in strength between the two sides of the Atlantic. While Europe has recovered remarkably, it is important not to draw too sweeping conclusions from its new-found vigor. Europe *has* gained in economic strength over the past decade and a half. It can and should play an increasingly responsible role. But for the foreseeable future we are likely to be by far the stronger partner.

It is important to be clear about this because it requires that the United States show unusual tact and steadiness. Many of our Allies have been guilty of unilateral actions far more flagrant than ours. But when we act unilaterally, disarray in the Alliance is almost inevitable. Sudden, drastic and, above all, unilateral changes in United States strategic doctrine — whatever their merit — create a sense of impotence and are resisted as much for symbolic as for substantive reasons. Actions without adequate consultation, either in diplomacy or in troop deployment, increase European pressures for more autonomy. Bilateral dealings with the Soviets, from which our Allies are excluded or about which they are informed only at the last moment, are bound to magnify Third Force tendencies. When our Allies oppose such practices, it is not necessarily because they disagree with our view but because they are afraid of creating a precedent for unilateral changes in other policies. (Even statements of substantive disagreement may be a smoke screen for deeper concerns.) Moreover, many Allied leaders who have staked their prestige on United States policies can suffer serious domestic setbacks if we change them unilaterally.

All of this causes the voice of Europe to reach us in extremely distorted form. President de Gaulle sharpens all disputes and even creates them in pursuit of his policy of independence. But some other leaders do not give full expression to their disquiet because they do not want to undermine further the solidarity on which their security is thought to depend. Whereas France exaggerates her disagreements, some other countries obscure theirs. Thus the dialogue with Europe is often conducted on false issues, while real issues — such as the future of Germany, or arms control, or the role of tactical nuclear weapons — are swept under the rug in order not to magnify the existing discord.

American policy toward Europe must therefore take account of two contradictory trends: Europe's economic and psychological recovery and the tenuousness of this assertiveness. Many United States policies are geared only to the first of these tendencies. The assumption seems to be that European vitality will be permanent and that the only obstacle to Atlantic cohesion is an excessive estimate by the Europeans of their power.

However, de Gaulle's policy may have produced an illusion of European strength and self-confidence which is more a reflection of his personality than of underlying factors. If one moves from Europe in the abstract to an examination of the individual European countries, it becomes apparent how precarious Europe's stability really is. On the Iberian peninsula, stability may not survive two aged dictators. Italy's center-left coalition is tenuous; its capacity for major policy initiatives is limited. A post-de Gaulle France may be rent by internal schisms. Germany suffers from the absence of traditions and the pressures produced by a divided country. The vigor so noticeable in Europe today is very close in time to nihilism; European self-confidence is still shaky. Little would be gained by replacing a nationalism of insufficient strength by a neutralism which exalts impotence. To avoid both dangers and to create a new and more vital structure is the challenge before the Atlantic Alliance.

In the redefinition of Allied relationships a great deal depends on America's sense of proportion. Any new act of construction involves stress. The danger is that an attempt may be made to solve new problems by applying outmoded concepts. There is a great deal of talk about "unity," "community" or "indivisible interests." But the issue before the West is precisely to give these terms concrete meaning. Invoking the need for unity will not change the fact that American and European interests outside of Europe are not identical. Disparagement of national sovereignty emphasizes a contradiction in United States policy which exalts nationalism as the most reliable bulwark against Communist domination everywhere except in Western Europe, where the concept originated. Proclaiming indivisible interests does not explain how Allied cohesion can be maintained in negotiations with a suddenly multifaceted Communism. Slogans about integration do not answer the question of how national sovereignty can be related to the need for community in the era of nuclear weapons. In moving from alliance to community the United States will not long be able to evade the issue of how much of its own freedom of action it is prepared to give up.

All the realities of human aspirations and of a technology of global impact require a close association of the nations bordering the North Atlantic. But Western history is full of tragedies, where a basic community of interests has been submerged by subsidiary rivalries or insufficient understanding. Ancient Greece foundered on this dilemma. Western Europe nearly tore itself apart before it discovered its underlying unity. And now the nations bordering the North Atlantic face the perennial problem of the West: Whether they can generate sufficient purpose to achieve community without first experiencing disaster.

Chapter Twelve

THE INSTRUMENTS
OF POLICY: ECONOMICS

Economics can provide both the *goals* of a nation's foreign policy and the *means* by which political and other goals may be pursued. Every nation includes among its foreign policy aims the promotion of its own economic strength and the prosperity of its citizens. One of communism's fundamental themes, as we have seen, is that most of the political acts of capitalist nations are economically motivated. Thus ruthless competition among capitalist powers for the alleged economic advantages of colonial exploitation is advanced by Communist theoreticians as a major explanation for the frequency of war in the modern age. In the United States, too, especially in the wake of the Nye Committee's investigations into the causes of American entry into World War I, it has sometimes been asserted that wars are rooted in the desire of munitions makers for wartime profits.

Those who have carefully studied, rather than merely theorized about, the causes of modern wars, have generally rejected the hypothesis that economic motivations have been predominant. Even investigations into the more limited hypothesis that private American overseas investors have often dominated American foreign policymaking have concluded that economic investments were more often the *result* than the *cause* of American political involvements abroad. Today, the primary threat to American security *and* material well-being is military, political, and ideological, rather than narrowly economic. As a result, our economic strength is more often the servant than the master of our overall strategic and political goals. Consequently, this section is largely concerned with the ways in which American economic resources are — and can be — used to promote national security, rather than with the ways in which our political power can be used to support our financial and commercial interests abroad.

Though we cannot take up here the problems involved in managing our domestic economy, we must not overlook the close relationship between the health of our domestic economy and the effectiveness of United States foreign policy. With only about one-sixteenth of the world's total population, the United States, in the 1960's, produces approximately one-third of the world's total economic output. Our Gross National Product (GNP) — over $700 billion in 1966 — is more than twice that of our closest national rival, the Soviet Union, and considerably greater than the total GNP of all the world's Communist nations combined. It is this industrial strength which makes possible our military strength, our aid programs, and our leading role in international affairs. It should be clear, then, that the first essential of a sound foreign economic policy is a sound domestic economic policy, designed to preserve and enlarge the industrial power of the American nation.

Actually, international economics is far too intricate a subject to be introduced adequately in the few pages available to us. A fundamental grasp of the economic and statistical concepts used in analyzing our *national* economy is a basic prerequisite to understanding the complexities of international trade and finance. Those who have had no previous background in economics are therefore referred to one of the many fine introductory works in that field — such as the classic text by Paul Samuelson.[1] Here we can merely discuss in inevitably oversimplified fashion the essential nature of international trade, and review briefly a few of the international economic policies pursued and problems encountered by the United States in recent years. (One important economic instrument of policy — foreign aid — was treated in detail in Chapter Nine.)

INTERNATIONAL TRADE
VS. ECONOMIC NATIONALISM

One instrument of economic foreign policy that can often be made to serve both political and economic goals simultaneously is the promotion of international trade. In economic terms, the value of international trade is based on the principle of *comparative advantage*. According to this principle, trade between two nations will prove mutually beneficial whenever each can produce some desired items *relatively* more efficiently (although not necessarily less expensively) than the other can. Thus trade between two

---

[1] *Economics: An Introductory Analysis* (6th ed.; New York: McGraw-Hill, 1964). See especially Part 5: International Trade and Finance.

Among the useful volumes dealing with recent United States economic foreign policies and problems are Peter B. Kenen, *Giant Among Nations* (2nd ed.; New York: Rand Mc-Nally, 1963); and Paul H. Douglas, *America in the Marketplace* (New York: Holt, Rinehart and Winston, 1966). (Once a University of Chicago Professor of Economics, Mr. Douglas served as United States Senator from Illinois from 1948 until his defeat in 1966.) A good very short introductory treatment is Elliot Zupnick, "Primer of U.S. Foreign Economic Policy," Foreign Policy Association, *Headline Series* No. 169, February, 1965.

nations may be profitable even if one can produce *everything* more efficiently, in absolute terms, than the other. After all, we know that it is profitable for a doctor to hire a nurse to do things — administer blood tests, injections, etc. — which he might himself be able to do quicker or better because this frees him to diagnose and treat more patients — the field in which his comparative advantage is greatest.

Similarly, it might pay the United States to import much of the sugar it needs from Latin America even if we could produce it more cheaply, in absolute terms, ourselves. It would pay us to do this *if* the labor and resources used to produce this domestic sugar could be more profitably employed in manufacturing, say, automobiles, which could then be traded to Latin America for the sugar we need *plus* some additional desired commodities. To the extent that the economies of large-scale production are applicable, moreover, the benefits gained from this specialization and trade will be increased.

The principle of comparative advantage notes the *economic* advantages of trade. There may be important noneconomic advantages, too. The aesthetic advantage of having a wider variety of products to choose from is one. Significant political advantages may also be gained because extensive trade among nations helps, in the most literal sense, to build a degree of community of interest among these nations. (See Chapter One.) The European Common Market is a good example. Scholars have observed remarkably close connections between the volume of trade between pairs of nations and their propensity to vote in agreement on certain issues in the United Nations and other international organizations. Undoubtedly this is as much due to the fact that good political relations facilitate trade as to the converse: trade alone does not make a community. Nevertheless, the relationship remains. Since it works both ways, the political advantages of trade should not be overlooked.

Substantial trade with friendly nations is also desirable, from the American standpoint, because it contributes to the industrial power, military potential and, sometimes, to the political stability of these nations. Marxist doctrine to the contrary, history has shown communism's greatest appeal to be to nations in dire economic straits searching for a way to increase their national power and wealth. (See Chapters Nine and Ten.) Largely for this reason, American policy since World War II has sought to build up the economic strength and political viability of non-Communist nations. Trade as well as — and sometimes better than — aid can serve these twin goals.

All of the economic and political benefits cited are sacrificed when the United States government interferes with the free flow of international trade by imposing tariffs, import quotas, or other restrictions on the importation of goods into this country. Nevertheless, the United States — and most other nations — do impose tariffs and enact trade restrictions.

Why? Tariff advocates offer a number of reasons. Tariffs can help to protect "infant industries" until they grow large and efficient enough to compete successfully in world markets. If there is a great deal of slack in our economy, it might serve our interests in the short run to use unemployed resources at home to produce goods which normally could be produced more cheaply abroad. (It is more efficient to produce *something*, however inefficiently, than to produce *nothing* with the same resources.) It may be advisable to ensure that a supply of certain commodities essential to national defense will be available to us in the event of war or national emergency. Thus, although these commodities may normally be produced most cheaply abroad, it may be wise for us to provide sufficient tariff protection for domestic producers of these strategic goods to make it profitable for them to keep their productive plants active in peacetime. Finally, tariffs could conceivably be used primarily as a source of government revenue.

More often than not, however, these "good" reasons are simply rationalizations. The real reasons are the political pressure applied by special interest groups, and an appalling public ignorance of the basic principles of international economics. Most of the industries protected by American tariffs, for example, are neither infant industries nor essential to national defense — by any reasonable definition of those terms. Most economists agree that tariffs are a relatively unfair and regressive form of taxation, and neither in the United States nor in any other modern industrial nation today are they used primarily as a source of government revenue. And whatever may be gained by using in inefficient tariff-protected industries resources which might otherwise remain idle is more than offset in the long run by the loss of existing or potential export markets which high tariffs entail. For failing export industries, too, lead to unemployment and idle resources.

Why should tariff protection against foreign imports cut down on American exports? Because in the long run international trade is just that — *trade*. When an American businessman sells goods abroad, he must get dollars for them. He will not normally accept pounds or francs or rupees or cruzeiros unless he knows that he can convert these readily into dollars. After all, he can only buy the things he wants at home with dollars. Where will England or France or India or Brazil get the dollars to pay him for his goods? Obviously, (American) dollars can only be obtained from the United States (or from some third country which has acquired them from the United States). And unless the United States or its citizens lend, give away, or invest dollars abroad, the only way foreign nations can get them is by *selling* goods to the United States in return (or by selling them to some third nation which has obtained dollars by selling to the United States).

Or, look at it another way. When we import goods into the United States, what do we give the exporting nations for them? American dollars. And what can these countries do with these dollars? They can be saved for a while, but ultimately they are of use primarily in purchasing goods from the United States (or from a third nation which wants to purchase an equivalent quantity of goods from the United States). In international trade terms, all these dollars are, in effect, are promises to deliver desired American goods in the future. *The fewer dollars other nations have, the fewer American goods they can buy in the long run.* In the short run, of course, they can spend more dollars than they take in and *owe* us the difference. But this cannot continue indefinitely since the only way they can repay us is to *earn* more dollars at some later date by selling more to us than they buy from us. In the long run, then, *the volume of our exports depends in large part on the volume of our imports.*[2]

It is completely irrelevant, incidentally, whether the goods we buy are produced with "cheap foreign labor" or not. From the standpoint of narrow economic self-interest, the more cheaply the goods we want can be produced, the more likely we are to get them at a relatively low cost to ourselves. The high wages paid to American labor are based primarily on the actual productivity of American industry. With complex machinery at their disposal, American workers receiving three dollars an hour can produce an automobile at a lower total cost than the same number of Japanese workers with less efficient machinery at their disposal. If low wages make it possible for the Japanese to produce cotton textiles at a lower total cost, the answer is not to impose a protective tariff on imported cotton textiles, but to buy our cotton textiles from Japan, shift workers and resources within the United States from textile to automobile production, and sell more cars to the Japanese in return for the dollars they have earned by selling us textiles. (This illustration is of course a gross oversimplification of the workings of international markets involving many countries and many goods, but the simplification serves to clarify the basic principle involved.)

An important qualification is in order. It is a lot easier to announce that it pays, in theory, to shift workers and capital from one domestic industry to another — instead of imposing protective tariffs — than it is to carry this plan out in practice. *In the long run,* all that we have said is true. But what about the short run? Within the domestic economy, "shifting" resources means that many American textile plants will be forced by falling

---

[2] The generalizations in this and the preceding paragraph need qualification. Since the American dollar is a reserve currency (see below), the nations which hold dollars can use them in place of gold as reserve backing for their own currencies, without ever using them to buy goods from the United States. Second, in fact the United States *can* sell abroad more than it buys — and *has* done so regularly since World War II. But this has been possible only because United States military expenditures abroad, aid programs, and private and governmental investments and loans overseas have made available to our foreign customers more dollars than they have earned strictly by the export of goods and services to the United States (or to Americans abroad). These qualifications do not invalidate the main point of these paragraphs, which is that how much we can expect to *sell* abroad is in large part dependent on how much we are willing to *buy* abroad.

profits to go out of business and many textile workers will be put out of jobs. Later, to be sure, *other* American businessmen and workers will find more profitable employment in more efficient export industries — but this may not be very comforting to the men put out of work or out of business in the textile industry. Even if they were to accept all of the arguments we have presented here, and agree that this shift of resources was in the long-run national interest, they might be forgiven for asking why the national interest must be served at *their* particular expense. If the whole nation will reap the benefits, they might fairly ask, why doesn't the whole nation pay the costs?

Actually, we could absorb these costs if we wanted to by making special arrangements to compensate the investors and workers individually hurt by the shifts of resources called for. Special tax arrangements could compensate the investors affected, and government financed job-retraining programs and special temporary unemployment benefits could minimize the losses to the workers involved.[3] For the most part, however, Americans resist the degree of government intervention in the economy which this would involve. Even the workers receiving the benefits would probably feel unhappy at being on what seemed to them a public dole and, given the choice, would prefer to continue in their old jobs. Thus, the nation as a whole chooses — though probably few see the real nature of the choice clearly — to forego the lower prices and personal and national advantages of increased trade. We prefer to minimize individually painful shifts of resources — or large-scale government intervention in our economy — by maintaining protective tariffs on a large number of items which could be produced more cheaply abroad than at home.

This problem, incidentally, is basically similar to the problem of adjusting to large-scale automation — or to large-scale disarmament, if an effective arms limitation agreement should by some unexpected turn of good fortune materialize in the near future. In both cases, the nation's *real wealth* — the actual quantity of goods and services available for personal consumption and productive investment — would be greatly increased. The problem of adjustment would be primarily a political and psychological rather than an economic problem. *If* Congress and the public were *willing* to take the measures necessary to maintain demand and reallocate productive resources during a transitional period, the nation's economy could not merely survive — it could move into a period of unprecedented material prosperity. (Even

---

[3] The Trade Expansion Act of 1962 authorized the provision of government loans, tax benefits, or technical assistance to United States firms hurt by tariff reductions negotiated under this Act, and the provision of readjustment and retraining allowances to workers in the industries affected. However, according to Senator Douglas, "the final result of this provision was highly unsatisfactory. As of March 7, 1966, not a single American worker had ever received any compensation for damages suffered by reductions in the tariff." *Op. cit.*, p. 127.

if all those engaged in designing and manufacturing military hardware were kept on full salary for doing absolutely nothing, to take an extreme example, the real wealth of the nation would not be diminished!) On the other hand, if carefully planned and vigorous governmental initiatives were blocked by popular attitudes toward government intervention, either rapid large-scale automation or rapid large-scale disarmament could lead to a major depression and national disaster.

THE BALANCE OF PAYMENTS

The most pressing economic foreign policy problem facing the United States in the late 1960's is the recurring deficit in its balance of payments. To understand this problem, or even the meaning of the term "balance of payments," requires us to outline briefly how the international monetary system operates.

When the United States and its citizens buy foreign goods or services, or give, lend, or invest money abroad, they make American dollars available to foreign governments and their citizens. When foreigners buy American goods or services, or give, lend, or invest money in the United States, they make their currencies available to us. To a certain extent, these transactions will cancel each other out. But unless our imports and exports of these items balance perfectly, there will be a residue on one side or the other: either we will be left with some foreign currencies which we have not used, or others will be left with dollars they have not used. This residue will remain as a claim upon the resources of the nation(s) concerned. Dollars held by other countries represent a claim on *our* resources, to be settled at some future date. Foreign currencies held by Americans represent claims on *their* resources, to be paid at some future date.

So long as these residual claims do not accumulate over the years, there will be no serious problem. Residual dollar claims against us one year will be cancelled by our residual currency claims against others the next year. But if this *balance of payments* [4] runs against a country consistently, year after year, and the steadily mounting claims of other nations against it remain unsettled, a point will be reached at which these nations will hesitate to accept the currency of the chronic deficit country in return for their goods, services, etc.

At some point, then, these balances must be redressed. One way this can be done is by exporting gold — traditionally accepted as of value by all nations — to meet these claims. But no nation can continue to export gold indefinitely. Therefore, in addition to settling the claims already outstand-

[4] The balance of payments should be distinguished from the balance of *trade*. In addition to trade, balance of payments calculations include tourist expenditures, travel on foreign ships and planes, private investments and loans abroad, and military and economic aid. This point is discussed further below.

ing against it, the deficit country must alter the trade, investment, and other transaction patterns which produce its recurring deficits.

If the international market were a free market, *price* adjustments — expressed in changes in the value of one nation's currency relative to another's — would automatically bring about an equilibrium and prevent these deficits from accumulating year after year. By regularly giving out more of its currency than it redeemed in goods, services, etc., a deficit country would increase the *supply* of this currency on the world market. If the demand for it — for the products of the deficit country — did not increase comparably, the "price" of the deficit currency would fall. The international money market, however, is not free, but regulated. Currency exchange rates usually are fixed by government policies rather than by the workings of supply and demand. As a result, it is quite likely that some nations will develop "balance of payments" problems.

An example should help us understand how a change in currency exchange rates would alter international trade patterns so as to keep payments deficits within bounds: When the price of American dollars rises relative to British pounds,[5] the price of American goods to Englishmen will rise, while the price of British goods to Americans falls. If the dollar value of the pound changes so that it now takes only $3 to buy £1 instead of $4, an English-made sweater valued at £3 can now be sold on the American market at about $9 (£3 at the new rate) instead of at $12 (£3 at the old rate).

The lower price can be expected to encourage Americans to buy more English-made sweaters. Meanwhile Englishmen will have to pay £40 instead of £30 for a $120 American typewriter and can be expected to buy less of these at the higher price than they did at the lower. In this way, the demand for dollars on the world market will be reduced, and the demand for pounds increased, until an equilibrium is reached at a given exchange rate. (This would represent a *devaluation* of the pound relative to the dollar.)

The adjustment described, however, might cause considerable hardship to the British consumer. His real income would be cut since he could now buy less with the same number of pounds than he could formerly. There might be a certain amount of temporary dislocation in the United States, too, as a result of reduced sales to Britain by American export industries, perhaps causing some American firms to lay off workers or go out of business. And if fluctuations in the dollar-pound exchange rate were frequent and sizable, the risks of doing business would be increased to both British and American importers and exporters, and trade between the two nations would be dis-

---

[5] This would happen, under a free market international exchange system, whenever British imports from the United States (that is, British demand for United States dollars) regularly exceeded United States imports from Britain (demand for British pounds). For the sake of simplicity, we are ignoring here transactions involving any countries beyond the two used in our example. Here, as elsewhere in this section, moreover, "import" and "export" are used to refer to *all* of the transactions involved in the balance of payments (loans, grants, investments, etc.) and *not* merely to exchanges of goods and services.

couraged somewhat. Moreover, this instability in the exchange rate would probably be multiplied by the activities of speculators out to make a killing on the market by buying and selling dollars and pounds rapidly in accordance with the fluctuations they anticipate in rates of exchange.[6]

For these and other reasons, the nations of the world today usually prefer not to allow rates of currency exchange to be regulated by the market forces of supply and demand, over which they have no control. They prefer instead to utilize various devices to keep exchange rates relatively stable.

This can be achieved by exporting or importing gold, which is then used to purchase currencies in demand and make up shortages; by imposing import or exchange controls to force exports to balance imports — usually at substantial economic cost both at home and abroad; or by maintaining exchange rates at a legally established "official rate" through governmental open-market operations. Under this last method, if there were too many pounds on the international market relative to the demand for them, the British government might offset this deficit by using its own gold or currency reserves to buy pounds, thereby increasing the demand for them and stabilizing their value.

No nation can deal with a trade imbalance by these means indefinitely, however. Ultimately, its capacity to offset its international deficits will be limited by the extent of its gold and foreign currency reserves. When these are exhausted, it may turn to outside sources for help. The International Monetary Fund (IMF) was established by the Bretton Woods Agreement of 1944 to meet just this need. The Fund holds about $21 billion in gold and currency reserves, provided by member nations in relation to their international financial position, and loans them to members faced with monetary crises. In addition, other nations may sometimes be induced to help a country with a chronic payments deficit through a crisis — as the United States and ten other nations did for Great Britain in 1964.[7] But these expedients can only help a deficit nation stave off disaster and gain time; they cannot enable it to continue to run deficits with impunity. Thus, after a series of severe measures — including "freezes" of domestic wage and price levels — had failed to improve Britain's competitive trade position and eliminate its chronic payments deficits, Prime Minister Harold Wilson's Labor Government, in November, 1967, resorted to devaluing the pound — the second time Britain had done so since World War II. In addition to reducing the value of the pound from $2.80 to $2.40, Britain sought to obtain another $3 billion from the IMF and other sources to tide it over its financial crisis.

[6] Changes in transaction flows can also be brought about by changes in the interest rate paid by borrowers in the countries concerned, again at the cost of affecting domestic production and employment in these countries. But this method of adjustment to payments imbalances will not be discussed here.

[7] The eleven leading industrial nations provided Britain — which had already borrowed $1 billion from the International Monetary Fund — with another $2 billion in short-term credits. But in time Britain must pay back both of these loans.

(Ireland, Denmark, and a number of other states felt compelled to respond by devaluing their own currencies almost immediately. But the United States and the Common Market countries, appreciating Britain's plight, announced that they would not devalue their currencies.)

The United States has not been driven to such drastic action. But it has run a balance of payments deficit in every year but one between 1950 and 1966. (See Chart A.) In the first five postwar years we had a payments *surplus,* despite our Marshall Plan aid programs. With the beginning of the Korean War, we began to run a deficit averaging somewhat over $1 billion a year through 1956. The aftermath of the Suez crisis left us with a small surplus in 1957. But our payments deficit jumped to $3.5 billion in 1958, $3.7 billion in 1959 and $3.9 billion in 1960. Measures taken by the Kennedy administration helped reduce this deficit to $2.4 billion in 1961, $2.2 billion in 1962, $2.7 billion in 1963, and $2.8 billion in 1964. Further steps taken by the Johnson administration cut it to $1.3 billion in 1965 and $1.4 billion in 1966. But then the overseas armaments and other costs of the American involvement in Vietnam interrupted this promising improvement, and the deficit for 1967 was expected to run close to $4 billion.[8]

CHART A — THE US BALANCE OF PAYMENTS: 1950–1966

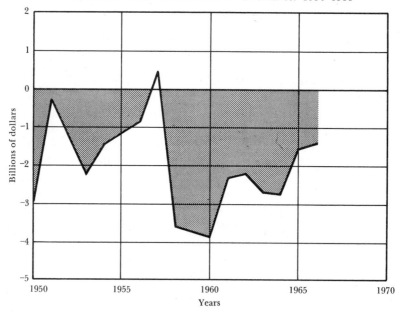

Source: US Department of Commerce figures.

[8] These figures are computed according to the United States government's official definition of a deficit, which tends to exaggerate its size somewhat. Other definitions have been offered by economists, and the merits of differing definitions are sometimes debated in the literature of the field, but we cannot concern ourselves with these debates.

As a result of these deficits, United States gold holdings were reduced from a peak of almost $25 billion in 1959 to below $14 billion in 1966. And over the same period foreign short-term claims on the dollar more than tripled — to over $28 billion. The United States still has the world's largest gold reserves, and there was no immediate prospect in the late 1960's that other nations' confidence in the soundness of the dollar would soon be impaired. But it was also clear that steps must be taken to prevent the United States from continuing to run sizable payments deficits year after year.

One way to deal with this balance of payments problem would be to devalue the dollar relative to gold and other currencies, with results similar to those outlined earlier in this chapter when the workings of a (hypothetical) free international money market were discussed. In this case, however, it would be the dollar whose value would be lowered relative to the pound (and other currencies). Thus American goods would sell at lower prices abroad, encouraging the purchase of more American exports; and foreign goods would cost Americans more — discouraging imports (and also reducing the real income of American consumers). But since today's international market is a regulated market rather than a free one, other governments would be at liberty to respond to a devaluation of the dollar by devaluing their own currencies also. To the extent that they did so, our trading position would not be improved.

More important, the dollar is the world's principal *reserve currency*. Dollar holdings as well as actual gold stocks of other nations are used as reserves to back their currencies for both domestic and international purposes. (The British pound is also a reserve currency, though a less important one.) This situation developed largely because the world's stores of gold cannot keep pace with the expanding credit and currency needs of the international financial community. Thus there has been a need for an additional source of *liquidity* — assets readily convertible into gold and therefore generally acceptable in conducting financial transactions. Since the United States government has guaranteed that it will freely convert foreign dollar holdings into gold, on request, at the fixed price of $35 an ounce, other countries have adopted the practice of keeping considerable portions of their currency reserves in dollars instead of gold. (Dollar reserves, moreover, can be invested in American securities, where they will earn interest or dividends. Gold reserves cannot.)

If the dollar were devalued, these countries that hold dollars would be able to get less gold than they can at present (for the dollars they have been holding). They would therefore suffer financial losses — in some cases very severe ones. The most badly hurt would be the underdeveloped nations, most of which hold a majority of their reserves in dollars or in pounds (which are convertible only into dollars — not directly into gold). The domestic backing of the currencies of these nations would be reduced accordingly, and their economies might be seriously disrupted. The main beneficiaries would be the Soviet Union and the Union of South Africa, whose large gold stocks would now be worth more dollars than before; and the Western European countries which hold a large proportion of their reserves in gold.[9]

In addition, since other countries might now hesitate to use dollars as part of their currency reserves, an important source of international liquidity would be removed, and the volume of international trade might fall sharply.

Another way to attack our payments deficits would be to try to improve our trade position *without* resorting to devaluation — by selling more goods and services abroad and buying less. We could, for instance, attempt to do this by raising our tariffs. But such a policy would probably prompt many other countries to retaliate in kind, to the disadvantage of both our consumers and theirs, and would yield only a very limited improvement in our payments position. And a reversion to high tariffs by the United States would probably damage our political relations with friendly nations whose domestic economies are much more dependent on international trade than is our own.

More constructively, we could improve our trade position by increasing productivity within the United States, and thus better our competitive position in world markets. But increases in productivity cannot simply be arranged by government fiat. And the government is already trying (with only limited success) to encourage United States exports and foreign tourism in the United States.

It is important to point out here that it is not the inability of American products to compete in world markets that has caused our payments deficits. To the contrary, we have been consistently selling more goods and services abroad than we have bought from other nations. Over the past decade, in fact, we have averaged a trade *surplus* of close to $5 billion a year. The trouble is that these surpluses have been more than offset by our military expenditures abroad, by United States government grants and loans to other nations, and by private American investments, gifts, and loans abroad.

The net adverse balance for military spending was reduced substantially by the Defense Department between 1961 and 1965, but has jumped again since the United States undertook its large-scale military involvement in Vietnam. United States economic aid programs abroad have also been cut back in recent years, and by 1966–67 close to 90 per cent of expenditures for these programs was "tied" directly to the purchase of American services and goods. In addition, we have tried — with very limited success — to induce our NATO allies to bear a greater share of the costs of our common defense and aid burdens. In 1966, a group of influential Congressmen, including

9 See Douglas, *op. cit.*, chap. 17.

Senate majority leader Mike Mansfield, began to press for a reduction in the number of American troops stationed in Germany — partly for political, partly for balance of payments reasons.[10] Aside from implementing this proposal, it would probably be difficult to reduce our deficits in the defense and aid categories much further, at present, without seriously impairing programs and activities defined by our government as critical to United States national security.

A special "interest equalization tax" imposed by the Kennedy administration in 1963 cut down on the flow of United States investment abroad, for a while, by increasing the cost to foreigners of borrowing American dollars. And when the effectiveness of this measure waned, the Johnson administration extended the application of this tax and made a major effort to persuade American bankers and businessmen to reduce their loans and investments abroad. But the initial results of this effort were not encouraging, and the government remained reluctant to take compulsory action which would antagonize the American business community. (At some point in the future American investments abroad can be expected to bring returns — in interest and profits — which would *aid* our nation's balance of payments position.) Britain's devaluation of the pound, however, increased the pressure on the dollar and raised the possibility that additional restrictions on the investment of American capital abroad might soon have to be imposed.

By the end of 1967, the Johnson administration, while determined to keep the nation's payments deficits to a minimum, seemed resigned to living with its inability to eliminate these deficits entirely so long as the United States remained heavily engaged in military action in Southeast Asia.[11]

The success of the United States in eliminating its balance of payments deficit by any method might have adverse effects on international liquidity — and thus on the expansion of world trade. (The United States "deficit" means that foreigners hold more dollars than they are prepared to spend, and it is precisely these deficit dollars which have been meeting the liquidity needs of the international financial community until now.) For this reason ten of the world's leading trading nations agreed in 1967 to establish a new

10 From 1961 to 1966, West Germany offset the dollar costs of maintaining American troops on its territory by purchasing military equipment from the United States. When the Germans balked at continuing this arrangement, it was agreed instead, in March, 1967, that they would subsequently offset a large part — but not all — of the costs of maintaining these United States forces by purchasing medium term United States Treasury bonds.

11 On the United States balance of payments problem, see, in addition to the works already cited, Henry G. Aubrey, *The Dollar in World Affairs* (New York: Harper and Row, 1964); and Sidney E. Rolfe, *Gold and World Power* (New York: Harper and Row, 1966). Rolfe suggests that allowing the rate of exchange among national currencies to fluctuate a little more than it does at present would help to moderate the adjustment problems caused by persistent payments imbalances. Like the suggestions made by some leading United States bankers in 1967 that the United States could stop tying the value of the dollar to that of gold, if necessary, Rolfe's recommendation would have effects very similar to that of a relatively slight devaluation of the dollar, with the consequences discussed above.

source of international liquidity in the form of *Special Drawing Rights* (SDR's) for members of the IMF. Under this plan, to be put into operation perhaps in 1969 or 1970, the Director of the IMF would first have to decide that a need for additional liquidity existed and propose that a certain amount of SDR's be created to meet this need. His proposal would then have to be approved by nations holding 85 per cent of the voting rights in the Fund. (These votes are weighted in accordance with members' quotas in the Fund — that is, roughly, with their importance in world trade.) The SDR's thus created would add to the world's supply of currency reserves and increase international liquidity, relieving some of the pressure on countries with payments deficits. Each IMF member could then use in settling its international accounts a percentage of these new SDR's proportionate to its quota in the Fund. The SDR plan therefore represents a first step toward transforming the IMF into a world central bank with power to manage the international money supply as the Federal Reserve System manages the domestic money supply of the United States.

ECONOMICS OF COOPERATION

Since World War II, the economic foreign policy of the United States has been less narrowly nationalistic than that of most nations. Probably the most successful American foreign policy initiative of the postwar period was the Marshall Plan, under which the United States government channeled more than $12 billion into war-devastated Europe between 1948 and 1951. The Plan was implemented, moreover, in a manner calculated to encourage trade and economic cooperation among the countries of Western Europe as well as between them and the United States. Given Europe's technical know-how, trained labor forces, and social and political institutions, the influx of United States capital and goods was sufficient to do the job required. Western Europe, which was in danger of economic bankruptcy — and even of Communist takeover — at the start of the Marshall Plan, is today politically stable and more prosperous than it has ever been before. The restrictive trade barriers of prewar years have given way to the substantial economic and limited political integration of the European Common Market, with a prospect of almost total elimination of trade barriers within the market area in the near future. The acute dollar shortage which led to devaluation of the pound and other European currencies in the late 1940's has been eliminated to the point where, as we have noted, the United States, rather than Europe, is now faced with a balance of payments problem. And the ability of a resurgent Europe (and Japan) to buy American exports has, in turn, been an important contributing factor to the continuing postwar prosperity of the United States.

In its trade and policies the United States has moved far from the narrow protectionism of the interwar period. The 1930 Hawley-Smoot tariff rates —

the highest in American history — have been modified greatly as a result of the reciprocal trade agreements program inaugurated by Cordell Hull and Franklin Roosevelt in 1934, which have been renewed and extended periodically since. The first Reciprocal Trade Agreements Act authorized the President to negotiate bilateral trade agreements with other nations under which the Hawley-Smoot tariff levels could be reduced by up to 50 per cent in return for equivalent tariff concessions on American exports. In accordance with the "most favored nation" principle embodied in the act, these bilateral concessions would then be extended on a nondiscriminatory basis to all other nations importing or exporting the goods affected, so long as these countries did not discriminate against American goods.

CHART B — U.S. TRADE: LOWERING THE BARRIERS

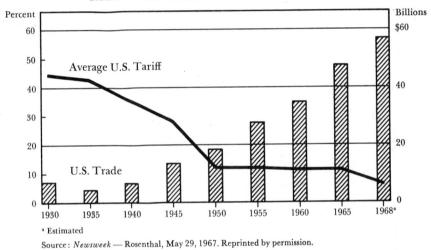

ª Estimated

Source: *Newsweek* — Rosenthal, May 29, 1967. Reprinted by permission.

A renewal of the reciprocal trade agreements program in 1945 permitted the further reduction of tariffs by 50 per cent below the rates prevailing in that year. And in 1962, the Kennedy administration secured congressional approval of a Trade Expansion Act authorizing an additional 50 per cent reduction in tariffs on most manufactured goods, the complete removal of a number of tariffs already below 5 per cent, and, through negotiations with the Common Market countries, the reciprocal elimination of all tariffs on goods where 80 per cent of the world's total trade was conducted by these nations and the United States.[12] It was not until 1967, however, when the authority extended by the Trade Expansion Act was about to expire, that United States and Common Market negotiators were able to reach an agree-

12 At the time this Act was passed, it was thought that the scope of this last authorization might soon be enlarged by the admission of Great Britain to the Common Market. Due to General de Gaulle's opposition to British membership, however, the five-year period in which the Act remained in force expired before this hope materialized.

ment lowering by about 30 per cent the tariffs applied to goods traded among fifty nations accounting for four-fifths of all international trade. (The negotiators also agreed that their governments would supply about $4\frac{1}{2}$ million metric tons of grain each year to the developing nations.)

A number of escape clauses and exceptions have been part of the price of congressional passage of these acts. A Tariff Commission has been set up to hear appeals from domestic producers and to recommend upward revision of tariff rates when it is convinced that these producers have been "injured" by increased imports after tariff reductions have been put into effect. A National Defense Amendment calls for exceptions in the cases of industries which produce goods or nourish skills which might conceivably be related to present or future national security requirements.

In both domestic injury and National Defense Amendment cases, the President is not required to follow recommendations that tariff levels be increased (though the Congress, in turn, can overrule him if it chooses). But the recommendations are made public, and the interests concerned are afforded an opportunity to apply such political pressure as they can muster in their own behalf. Thus far, Presidents of both parties have more often rejected than honored recommendations for tariff increases on these grounds. Finally, "Buy American" legislation continues to require the United States government to favor American firms over lower foreign bidders in making purchases for defense, foreign aid, or other governmental programs. (This legislation protects our balance of payments position in some respects.)

The United States has also participated in a number of international arrangements designed to promote freer trade among non-Communist nations. Probably the most important of these at present is the General Agreement on Tariffs and Trade (GATT). This agreement provides an institutional framework within which member countries can negotiate reciprocal trade agreements. Its members are pledged to try to reduce barriers to international trade, including tariffs, quotas, and other restrictive practices. Under GATT's rules, trade concessions made by any one of its members to another normally are extended to all members. But GATT has no administrative machinery or coercive power beyond the capacity to authorize members to suspend tariff concessions to nations violating their obligations under the agreement. And, in accordance with American legislative requirements, GATT includes escape clauses permitting its members to raise established tariffs if they believe domestic industries have been injured by tariff concessions.

GATT's membership includes all the principal trading nations of the West — and, as associate members, some Eastern European Communist states. Most of the world's underdeveloped nations also participate, except for a number of new African states. But these nations have not felt that GATT serves their needs adequately. GATT, after all, is designed to preserve and build upon the *existing* international economic system which favors modern industrial nations in important respects. If the developing nations are to be aided substantially, significant *changes* in the international economic status quo will have to be made.

Many of the developing nations are resentful, for instance, of their economic dependence upon single crops or other natural resources, especially since the *terms of trade* have turned sharply against such primary commodities over the past decade (that is, the price of these commodities in the international marketplace has fallen relative to the price of the manufactured goods produced by the industrial nations). Spokesmen for the developing states, therefore, have called for a system of preferential tariffs favoring their own countries' exports until their export industries have grown large enough to reap the benefits of mass production and strong enough to compete effectively in world markets. These spokesmen also advocate the establishment of commodity stabilization agreements to lessen the dependence of one-crop or one-commodity economies on the fluctuations of the international marketplace.[13]

There has been some opposition to both of these proposals among the nations of the West on grounds of economic self-interest and economic principle. Preferential tariff treatment, one economist has written,

> . . . can make only a marginal contribution. . . . To derive any benefit from it, the developing countries must be able to offer their goods for sale at prices not substantially higher than those prevailing in industrial countries. Reducing costs and gaining access to markets thus should remain fundamentally more important objectives for the developing economies than tariff preferences.[14]

Nevertheless, by the end of 1967, the Johnson administration had declared its willingness to give preferential tariff treatment to the developing nations if other industrial nations would do so also — and if the United States Congress could be persuaded to go along.

Commodity stabilization arrangements for wheat, tin, sugar, and coffee *have* been instituted in recent years, but, for various reasons, have not been conspicuously successful. Since they generally depend on restricting production, such arrangements create economic inefficiencies and "almost inevitably lead to a misallocation of resources. The increase in prices which these agreements bring about tends to attract resources from other sectors of the

---

[13] These demands, among others, were put forward forcefully by representatives of underdeveloped nations at the United Nations Conference on Trade and Development, held at Geneva in 1964, but were received unenthusiastically by the United States and some other industrial nations. See Irving L. Horowitz, *Three Worlds of Development* (New York: Oxford University Press, 1966), chap. 6.

[14] Zupnick, *op. cit.*, p. 37.

economy into producing unsalable surpluses and may thus ultimately impede development." [15]

Thus it has been suggested that the needs of the developing nations might better be met by the establishment of an "international stabilization fund" which would make up the difference between the actual foreign exchange earnings of the developing nations each year and a figure previously agreed upon — on the basis of past sales — as their "normal" earnings.[16] Of course, this fund would have to be paid for by the United States and other economically advanced nations, and the difficulties involved in gaining legislative approval for such "giveaways" can well be imagined.

The relative economic and domestic political feasibility of the various suggestions proposed for aiding the developing nations are legitimately debatable. But the importance of taking *some* measures toward this end, before it is too late, are not. Mere injunctions to these nations to increase their productive efficiency will not suffice.

COLD WAR ECONOMICS

Though economic and political advantages frequently seem to go hand in hand in America's dealings with friendly nations, the United States is often forced to choose, in formulating its policies toward the Communist camp, *between* economic and political advantages. In these circumstances, successive administrations have chosen unhesitatingly to subordinate possible economic gains to political and strategic considerations.

In the early days of the cold war, the Soviet Union and its East European satellites were invited to take part in the European Recovery Program made possible by the Marshall Plan. Whether the Congress would have been willing to accept Soviet participation if Stalin had taken up the American offer is problematical. (See Chapter Three.) Soviet refusal to take part in the program saved us the trouble — and possibly the embarrassment — of finding out. In the absence of United States aid, East-West trade was bound to be meager, since the war-devastated Communist nations of Europe had no other means of securing the dollars which extensive purchases of American goods would have required.

In 1949, the United States banned exports of strategic goods to Communist nations. Then, after the outbreak of the Korean War, it attempted to influence its friends and allies to do likewise. The Battle Act of 1951 (named after the Congressman sponsoring it) embargoed United States trade in arms or other strategic materials with the Soviet Union

> . . . and all countries under its domination, in order to (1) increase the
> national strength of the United States and of the cooperating nations;
> (2) impede the ability of nations threatening the security of the United

15 *Ibid.*, p. 39.
16 *Ibid.*, pp. 28–41.

> States to conduct military operations; and (3) assist the people of the
> nations under the domination of foreign aggressors to reestablish their
> freedom. It is further declared to be the policy of the United States that
> no military, economic, or financial assistance shall be supplied to any
> nation unless it [too] applies [such] an embargo. . . .

The President was permitted to make exceptions to this last provision, however, when he deemed it essential to American security to do so.

This policy, of course, had the incidental effect of denying the United
States the economic benefits it might have gained through trade with
the Communist nations. But it was reasoned that, in view of our relatively
greater industrial strength, the United States could more easily bear to lose
the advantages of this trade than the Communist nations could.

It was also argued that there are inherent dangers in large-scale trading
with nations like the Soviet Union, which have totally centralized economies. The Soviet *government* was bound to be at an advantage in dealing
with *private* businessmen from non-Communist countries. It could manipulate its domestic price and wage levels almost at will. It could export some
Russian-made products at prices below cost, if it chose to do so. It could —
and did — import foreign machines principally for the purpose of copying
their designs (since it did not participate in international patent agreements). It could — and did — withhold or manipulate information concerning its internal economy — the kind of information upon which business
dealings among traders in non-Communist nations are usually based. It
could rapidly and massively shift purchase orders from one nation or firm to
another for political purposes, thus imposing serious economic dislocations
upon trading partners who dared to thwart its foreign policy objectives. And
it could arrange, by means of its centrally determined trade practices, to
deny Soviet strategic materials to the West without passing legislation toward that end. Under the circumstances, it could be persuasively argued that
it was advantageous for the United States to curtail sharply its trade with
the Communist countries.

Some of America's allies were less easily persuaded of the wisdom of
this policy. The nations of Western Europe and Japan, in particular, are
much more dependent on world trade for their domestic prosperity than is
the United States. As their economic dependence upon the United States
declined, therefore, they secured our acquiescence in a progressive narrowing of the definition of goods deemed "strategic" for purposes of the embargo. In the late 1950's and the early 1960's, then, trade between Western
and Eastern Europe expanded substantially, though it remained low compared with trade levels among the major Western powers themselves.[17]

[17] In 1966, for instance, the Fiat Company of Italy agreed to provide an automobile
factory to the Soviet Union which could use Western machinery to produce cars of the
Fiat type.

In support of their policy of engaging in nonstrategic trade with Eastern Europe, America's allies argued that a tighter embargo would detract from their own economic strength and prosperity at least as much as it would from that of the Communist nations. They pointed out further that whatever fulcrum for political pressure might be provided by threatening to discontinue this East-West trade was bound to work *both* ways. Finally, they noted the possible political gains from the establishment of areas of shared East-West economic advantage, which might help in a limited way to relax international tensions.

By the 1960's, the United States itself was beginning to see some merit in these arguments. Even before the Korean War, American willingness to aid and trade with Communist Yugoslavia had been instrumental in enabling that nation to maintain its independence from Moscow after the Tito-Stalin break of 1948. When, in the wake of this precedent, Khrushchev's de-Stalinization campaign, and the Sino-Soviet split, other Eastern European Communist states showed signs of restiveness with domination from Moscow, the Kennedy and Johnson administrations moved to liberalize commercial relations between them and the United States in the hope of encouraging this emergent trend toward the decentralization of power in the Communist bloc. Thus, in a dedication address at the opening of the George C. Marshall Research Library at the Virginia Military Institute in May, 1964, President Johnson called for the United States "to build bridges across the gulf which has divided us from Eastern Europe . . . bridges of increased trade, of ideas, of visitors and of humanitarian aid." Soon afterward, the President asked Congress to eliminate tariff discrimination on some categories of imports from Eastern Europe; but this request had not been approved by the middle of 1967. (Many Congressmen were reluctant to approve a measure which would increase United States trade with nations supplying military equipment to our adversaries in Vietnam.)

Even with respect to the Soviet Union itself, United States policy seemed gradually to be mellowing in response to changes in the international situation. The conclusion of the 1963 limited nuclear test ban treaty, and other small steps toward Soviet-American detente, led the Kennedy administration to approve the sale of United States surplus wheat to a Russia then in the throes of agricultural crisis. There was a good deal of domestic criticism of this action — as there had been in the past of United States willingness to aid Yugoslavia and to grant most-favored-nation treatment both to that nation and to Poland — on the ground that anything that aided Communists hurt the United States. But the Kennedy administration's position seemed to be that the risks of bolstering Communist strength by trading American wheat to Russia were less significant than the risks of losing even a minor opportunity to work toward the gradual lessening of Soviet-American tensions.[18] Perhaps this position was influenced by the realization of how close the two nations had come to mutual annihilation during the Cuban missile crisis the previous year.

Yet formidable barriers to the expansion of Soviet-American nonstrategic trade remain. The 1934 Johnson Debt Default Act (see the case study in this chapter) prevents us from extending credits to the Soviet Union to finance its purchases from us because they have never paid their World War II "lend-lease" debts to the United States. And anti-Communist feeling in this country is still sufficient to make any administration hesitate to be caught advocating trade with the Soviet Union without very good reason. Thus the United States continues to embargo items traded freely to the Soviet Union by our allies.

Even the 1963 wheat deal referred to above never did work out quite as originally planned because the United States required that half of this wheat be transported in American ships, whose rates substantially exceed those of other nations' shipping lines. The Soviets therefore elected to buy only 63 million bushels of American wheat, instead of the 150 million initially envisaged. In 1965, another Soviet-American wheat deal was blocked by this same requirement and by the threat of the Longshoremen's Union to boycott any wheat shipments destined for the Soviet Union. In both cases, the Russians simply increased their wheat purchases from Canada and Australia instead.[19]

RUSSIA, SÍ; CHINA AND CUBA, NO!

Communist China, North Korea, North Vietnam, and Castro's Cuba have been singled out for even more unfavorable treatment by the United States than has the Soviet Union. United States trade with these countries has been almost completely proscribed, not only in strategic materials but in all other goods as well. (In the case of Cuba, trade in food and medicines is permitted.)

The all-out embargo on trade with China and North Korea originated during the Korean War when these countries' military forces were fighting American G.I.'s. United States allies and many other United Nations members cooperated in the embargo throughout the conflict. By 1957, however, the United States was no longer able to induce even its principal allies to

[18] The trade offered economic benefits, too, and, according to Theodore Sorenson, the President "preferred to base his approval *publicly*" on these. (My italics.) The sale "would bring added income and employment to American agriculture and business, benefit our balance of payments and reduce Federal storage costs. *Kennedy* (Bantam ed.; New York: Harper and Row, 1965), p. 835.

[19] Douglas, *op. cit.*, pp. 157–159. Senator Douglas opposed the wheat deal. Lyndon Johnson, then Vice President, is also reported as believing it to be a mistake. Arthur Schlesinger, Jr., *A Thousand Days* (Boston: Houghton Mifflin, 1965), pp. 920 and 1019.

withhold from Communist China nonstrategic materials which were shipped freely to the Soviet Union. The American position was scarcely tenable on rational grounds since there was nothing to prevent the Soviet Union from buying nonstrategic goods from the West and then reselling them to Peking. The additional transportation costs, to be sure, would increase the price to Communist China slightly, but this scarcely seemed to justify the interallied frictions occasioned by American efforts to maintain a total embargo.

After the defection of our main allies in 1957, the economic significance of the American embargo declined further, since Peking was now able to secure the prohibited goods directly from our allies. The food shortage caused by Communist Chinese agricultural failures after 1959, for example, was relieved in part by sizable purchases of wheat from Canada and Australia.

Ironically, the emergence of sharp Sino-Soviet differences in the 1960's might have re-established a tenable rationale for the American position, *if* our allies had still been fully supporting the China embargo at that time. For it then might at least have assisted the Soviet Union to apply pressure for the moderation of Peking's militancy as the price for relaying to China goods denied it by the allied embargo. In the absence of this interallied co-operation, however, American insistence on maintaining the "China differential" seems to reflect not a reasoned calculation of the national interest, but a fear of emotionally rooted, domestic political opposition to making any "concessions" to Peking.

Since large numbers of American troops were dispatched to South Vietnam in 1965, the willingness of some United States allies to continue trading with North Vietnam has produced a good deal of American indignation. A number of proposals have been made that the United States apply coercive measures, if necessary, to halt this trade; and some Congressmen have advocated blockading (or bombing) the North Vietnamese harbor of Haiphong despite the confrontation this might entail of American military forces and allied (and Soviet) shipping. The costs of using force against our allies (or the Soviets), however, seemed likely to be much greater than any strategic gains which the further limitation of this trade might bring. Thus, at least until late 1967, the Johnson administration resisted these suggestions.

Many of the considerations noted above as applicable to the total American embargo against Communist China are also relevant to our insistence on maintaining a similar ban on trade with Cuba — a ban which the Kennedy and Johnson administrations have sought, with only partial success, to persuade our European and Latin American allies to adopt also. But there is an important difference. China is a nation of about 700 million people more than 6,000 miles from American shores; Cuba is a nation of about 7 million people 90 miles from American shores. Though a few Americans may still believe that an all-out allied economic embargo could overthrow the Communist government of China, it should be clear by now that this is wishful thinking — or unthinkful wishing. But it is by no means inconceivable — even if it is not *probable* — that an allied and inter-American embargo might contribute significantly to the downfall of the Communist government of Cuba at some time not too far in the future. At the least, by requiring the Soviet Union to spend over $350 million each year subsidizing the Castro regime to keep it economically viable, this trade ban may help to limit the Russians' enthusiasm for obtaining further expensive dependencies in the Americas. In addition, it helps to restrict Cuba's ability to subsidize revolutionary activities in other Latin American states, and remains a sign to Latin American peoples of the austerity that may be imposed on those who venture to follow in Cuba's footsteps.

In the cases of both China *and* Cuba there is a price to be paid for a total trade embargo, in political, and human terms, as well as economic. In the first place, assuming that the present pro-Communist governments remain in power, this policy precludes any major initiative aimed at abating Sino-American or Cuban-American mutual hostility. Second, it creates troublesome minor frictions between the United States and our European, Asian, and Latin American allies. Finally, a policy of all-out embargo could succeed in overthrowing the governments we think of as our enemies only by first imposing hardships on hundreds of millions of impoverished peoples whom we like to think of as our friends. This should not be a negligible consideration to a nation which believes its highest purpose to be the upholding of the dignity and welfare of the human individual.[20]

20 As a result of United Nations action, the United States was engaged by the close of 1966 in one additional venture in the use of trade restrictions for political purposes. The Security Council adopted mandatory economic sanctions, for the first time in United Nations history, in an effort to topple the "white supremacy" government of Rhodesia — a British colony which declared its independence unilaterally in order to maintain the dominance of its 220,000 whites over its 4 million "blacks." President Johnson implemented the Security Council's resolution by issuing an executive order which was expected to prohibit about 80 per cent of the United States' approximately $10 million in annual purchases from Rhodesia.

These sanctions hurt Rhodesia, cutting its exports by at least 40 per cent. But a series of austerity measures imposed by Premier Ian Smith's government enabled the country to record a surplus in its balance of payments, nevertheless. The morale of white Rhodesians remained high, the Smith government remained popular, and a year after the sanctions were instituted, it seemed highly unlikely that they would force the Rhodesian government to accept a settlement which would bring majority representation in parliament for Rhodesia's "blacks." See Anthony Astrachan, "Sanctions Fail to Bow Rhodesia," *The Washington Post*, November 19, 1967, p. 22.

If the Smith government had been brought to terms by this embargo it would have been the first time in the modern era that economic sanctions ordered by an international organization had succeeded to this extent.

*WAR DEBTS AND REPARATIONS
AFTER WORLD WAR I*

The case study for this chapter deals with United States economic
foreign policy during the years between the two world wars — when
economic nationalism and short-term profits were given priority over
the broader requirements of national security and international peace.
The victorious allies of World War I insisted at Versailles upon saddling
Germany with an unrealistically high reparations burden — without considering how these debts were to be repaid. American insistence that its
allies must repay in full, and with interest, debts incurred to us during
the war was similarly unrealistic and shortsighted.

The general decline in international trade which these policies promoted contributed to the severity of the world-wide depression of the
1930's. The depression, in turn, was an important factor in the rise of
an aggressive militarism in Japan, which sought to alleviate the misery
of impoverished Japanese farmers by creating a "Greater East Asia Co-
Prosperity Sphere." In Europe, meanwhile, the Weimar Republic of
Germany had intentionally inflated its currency by nearly 1,000 per cent
as early as 1921 to 1923, partly in an effort to escape the staggering
reparations burden imposed upon it. Millions of Germans saw their
savings, pensions, or businesses wiped out; the discontent of these dis-
possessed classes helped to provide the political base upon which the
Nazis climbed to power. (See the case study in Chapter Four.) At home,
during this period, Americans bought the relief from responsibilities
called "normalcy" now — and paid, with compound interest, later.

1. Why did our former allies default on debts they had voluntarily
contracted during the war? What effect would rapid repayment of the
war debts have had on the private citizens of the European countries
involved? On the American domestic economy?

2. What effect would a devaluation of the dollar during the 1920's
have had on the war debts problem? Why?

3. Was President Hoover right in warning that a general tariff reduction "would fill our streets with idle workers"? Why or why not?

4. Outline the essentials of the economic foreign policy *you* think the
United States should have followed during the interwar years. Explain
why you believe the policy you have outlined is the best one the United
States could have pursued during this period.

ALEXANDER DeConde

Of all the major belligerents in the First World War, only the United States emerged unscathed and stronger than at the start of the war. In urging support of the League covenant, Wilson had said: "The financial leadership will be ours. The industrial primacy will be ours. The commercial advantage will be ours. The other countries of the world are looking to us for leadership and direction." His prediction proved accurate.

In four years the war had transformed America's industrial and financial relations abroad, making the United States the new international economic leader. New York instead of London ruled as the financial center of the world. Most other nations, in some form, became economically dependent on the United States.

The war had reduced Europe's industrial production to a low level, but American production had risen and continued to rise after the war. According to the estimates of economists, by 1929 American industrial production amounted to 46 per cent of the world's total, and American national income equaled the combined incomes of twenty-three of the world's important countries, including Britain and France.

The war had accelerated American industrialization, resulting in an expansion in industrial output of 15 per cent and an establishment of industries producing goods formerly imported from Europe. Before the war Europe had supplied about 50 per cent of America's imports; after the war she provided only about 30 per cent. The European countries never regained their prewar position as sources of finished goods for the United States.

Since the war had also hastened industrialization in other countries, as in Japan, Canada, and parts of Latin America, the older industrial nations of Europe could not easily compensate for the losses in the American market. This trend away from dependence on European manufacturers continued all through the 1920's and 1930's.

In those years the United States also became the world's most important market for raw materials and semi-finished goods. This shift in the nature of American imports might not have caused immediate difficulty in Europe if the United States had remained in debt to European nations, but from a debtor owing 3.7 billion dollars in 1914, the United States in 1919 had become a creditor nation who was owed 12.5 billion dollars. Some 10 billion dollars of this money represented debts connected with the war that European nations had incurred. Since the Allied nations had liquidated their investments in the United States to help finance the war, they found themselves suddenly faced with fewer opportunities to earn dollars and with new obligations to the United States to be paid in dollars.

The United States, moreover, had captured another source of Europe's income. It replaced Europe as a supplier of capital, particularly to "under-developed" countries, or those countries producing essentially raw materials.

As was the case with its enhanced political power, the United States did not use its strategic position in the world's economy with a sense of responsibility. In 1918, for example, Congress passed the Webb-Pomerene Act, which provided that the Sherman Antitrust Act would not apply to combinations of industrialists engaged solely in the export trade if those combinations did not restrain trade within the United States or injure domestic competitors. The Webb-Pomerene Act, endorsed by President Wilson and by business leaders, emphasized the drive of manufacturers for expanded exports and buttressed the economic nationalism that characterized American foreign relations in the 1920's and 1930's.

Internally, the United States followed an antimonopoly and antitrust policy. Yet its leaders saw nothing inconsistent in giving government support to combinations of manufacturers to engage in monopolistic marketing practices abroad. A number of trade associations became members of international combinations engaged in dividing up markets and fixing prices. In 1939, there were 179 international cartels, or organizations designed to control prices and production; 109 of them included American firms. Not until that year did the Department of Justice begin action against American firms participating in international cartels controlling such vital products as optical instruments, petroleum, explosives, and synthetic rubber. Throughout the 1920's and 1930's the American people, imbued with economic nationalism, also insisted on a high tariff and on payment of war debts by European nations.

THE WAR DEBTS

During the First World War, when the United States had suddenly found itself transformed from a debtor to a creditor nation, it had loaned its allies 7.7 billion dollars. The American government had charged 5 per cent interest, a rate related to the cost of borrowing from its own people through the sale of "liberty bonds." Most of the money, since the Allies spent nine-tenths of their loans on American supplies and war materials, never left the United States.

After the war, until May, 1922, the American government had continued to loan money to its former Allies and to other European governments as well. Those loans were for relief and reconstruction in areas struck hard by the war. The United States also contributed billions of dollars in direct relief to the countries devastated by the war and its aftermath. Americans referred to all those loans, those made during the war and those made afterward for peaceful purposes, as the foreign war debts. All the loans amounted to 10.3 billion dollars, exclusive of interest.

In actual war debts at the end of 1918, Britain owed the American government 4.1 billion dollars, France 2.9 billion, Italy 1.6 billion, and the lesser European countries owed smaller amounts. The American people and their Congress assumed that the debtor countries would pay their obligations in full, though some congressmen had voted the wartime loans without expecting repayment. "I am perfectly willing to give to any of the allied nations the money which they need to carry on our war," one senator told his colleagues, "for it is now our war."

Some of the European statesmen had believed that the United States would consider the debts as part of its general contribution to the defeat of Germany and hence would cancel them. Britain, France, and Italy were all creditors as well as debtors. Britain, for instance, had loaned her allies 10 billion dollars. She offered to cancel her claims against her debtors if the United States would cancel its claims against her, but President Wilson and his advisers at the Paris Peace Conference had refused to discuss the debts. Later Wilson told Prime Minister Lloyd George that it was "highly improbable that either the Congress or popular opinion in this country will ever permit a cancellation of any part of the debt of the British government to the United States," or of the debts of any of the Allied governments, as a practical settlement of all claims.

Several years later Secretary of the Treasury Andrew W. Mellon wrote that "these were loans and not contributions and though not in form in actual effect loans from individual American citizens rather than contributions from the Treasury of the United States." This was the view that prevailed in the United States throughout the 1920's and 1930's. "What we allowed our associates to do, in effect," Mellon explained, "was to borrow money in our investment market, but since their credit was not as good as ours, to borrow on the credit of the United States rather than on their own."

To facilitate collection of the war debts, President Harding asked Congress in June, 1921, to authorize negotiations with the debtor governments over terms of payment. In the following February, Congress created the World War Foreign Debt Commission with the Secretary of the Treasury as chairman. Under the terms of the act, the commission could not accept an interest rate lower than 4.25 per cent and a maturity date beyond 1947, or of twenty-five years. It could not cancel any of the principal or accept any transfer of Allied obligations to former enemy countries to be paid as reparations. The Act of 1922, therefore, recognized no connection between debts and reparations, ignored the capacity of the debtors to pay, and did not take into account the difficulty of what economists call the transfer problem, the means of transferring money across international boundaries.

To most Americans, repayment of the debts was a matter of integrity and of national honor. "Well," President Coolidge said in speaking for his countrymen, "they hired the money, didn't they?" The Europeans, regarding the war as a common cause in which they had borne the brunt of the fighting, insisted that the United States had benefited from the victory as much as had any belligerent. Moreover, since the United States had not claimed reparations from Germany, they thought that they could repay the American loans from the reparations they expected to receive from Germany.

When the Debt Commission attempted to negotiate settlements with the debtors, it found that none were willing to accept the terms imposed by Congress. The commission, therefore, went ahead and negotiated thirteen funding agreements on the best terms obtainable. It began its negotiations with Britain in January, 1923, and continued with the other debtors until 1926. During that time the United States gradually came to recognize the principle of capacity to pay.

Although the terms of the British debt settlement, as did the others, called for full repayment of the principal, the commission accepted a low interest rate averaging 3.3 per cent and extended the maturity date to sixty-two years. This amounted to a cancellation of 19.3 per cent of the British debt. In the other settlements the United States retained the payment period of sixty-two years and was more generous in reducing the interest rate, cancelling from 50 to 80 per cent of the debts, as in the case of Italy.

As the debt settlements did not adhere to the terms of the Act of 1922, the commission sought congressional approval for each case. In urging approval of the Italian agreement in January, 1926, Secretary of the Treasury Mellon told a congressional committee that "the settlements are made in the real interests of those American producers who must have a foreign market able to pay. The American producer needs these debt settlements. The entire foreign debt is not worth as much to the American people in dollars and cents as a prosperous Europe as a customer." The settlements, considered fair and even generous by Americans, involved a large part of the income in dollars the rest of the world received from the goods and services it sold to the United States.

Meanwhile, the question of reparations became more entangled in power politics and added complications to the repayment of the war debts. In April, 1921, a special Allied Reparations Commission had set the amount Germany was to pay in reparations at about 33 billion dollars. This was a figure lower than most Frenchmen considered adequate but higher than some other financial experts, particularly the British, regarded as fair. Substantial annual payments were to begin at once. Later payments were to be adjusted according to capacity to pay and to an evaluation of payments in kind that the Germans had already made.

Within fifteen months, whether wilfully or through inability to pay, a resentful Germany defaulted. The Reparations Commission, as allowed under the Treaty of Versailles, therefore, voted for strong measures against Germany. In January, 1923, French and Belgian troops began marching into the industrial Ruhr Valley and occupied it until September, 1924. The British deducted 26 per cent from their payments for German imports and applied that money to their reparations account. The Germans attempted to defeat the occupation with a policy of inflation that reduced the value of their currency, the mark, by more than 99.9 per cent. Reparations payments stopped completely.

Two weeks before the occupation of the Ruhr began, Secretary of State [Charles Evans] Hughes had suggested that an independent commission of financial experts study Germany's capacity to pay and devise a plan to facilitate reparations deliveries. In autumn, 1923, Germany abandoned passive resistance, and all governments concerned accepted Hughes' suggestion. In November, the Reparations Commission appointed two committees to study the German problem. The United States did not participate in the investigations, but Charles G. Dawes, a banker from Chicago who acted solely as a private citizen, headed the committee that submitted the plan which the Reparations Commission adopted.

Accepted by all concerned as a temporary expedient, the Dawes Plan, as it came to be known, went into effect in September, 1924. Under it, Germany received an international loan of 200 million dollars, most of it from American bankers, to replenish her working capital. She agreed to make reparations payments on a rising scale, ostensibly to be parallel with the growth of her economic life.

For five years, from 1924 to 1928, the Dawes Plan worked well. Germany's creditors, therefore, decided to attempt a final settlement. In September, 1928, a new committee of financial experts headed by Owen D. Young, a financier from New York also acting as a private citizen, proposed a plan that Germany and her creditors finally accepted in modified form in January, 1930. The Young Plan, calling for fifty-nine annual payments, reduced Germany's reparations debt by about 9 billion dollars.

That plan also recognized a connection between reparations and the war debts owed to the United States. Through a "concurrent memorandum," the Europeans agreed that if the United States scaled down the war debts they would reduce the reparations. Instead of being linked to Germany's capacity to pay, the obligations under the Young Plan were fixed so as to cover the payment of Allied debts to the United States.

Germany had been able, in part, to meet her obligations under the Dawes Plan because inflation had wiped out her domestic debts, and because she did not need to divert huge sums to armaments that were forbidden her under the Treaty of Versailles. During the prosperous 1920's when Germany met her reparations obligations, the Allies paid their debts to the United States. The debtors might have continued to pay with funds obtained from Germany under the Young Plan if the great depression had not intervened.

Private American loans complicated the payment of reparations and war debts. In the 1920's Americans had invested in the bonds of German state governments, in German industries ranging from steel mills to chain stores, and had loaned money to other European nations. The heavy flow of American capital into Germany had helped make possible the payment of her reparations. The result was a chain of private and public international payments. "Reparations and Interallied Debts," John Maynard Keynes, the British economist, explained in 1926, "are being mainly settled in paper not in goods. The United States lends money to Germany, Germany transfers its equivalent to the Allies, the Allies pay it back to the United States Government."

THE RELATIONSHIP OF PRIVATE LOANS AND WAR DEBTS
AFTER THE FIRST WORLD WAR

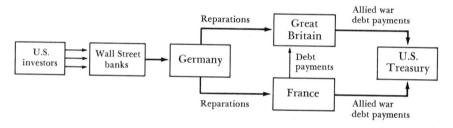

From 1919 to 1930 total private American capital, in loans and investments abroad, amounted to 11.4 billion dollars, or a flow of long-range loans of about a billion dollars a year. By 1929, the rest of the world owed the American government and private investors some twenty billion dollars.

Many of the private loans to Germany and other countries did not meet the tests of sound international lending by providing adequate means of repayment. Most of them were for reconstruction, restocking, and for stabilizing currencies. They did not go into projects that could be expected to earn foreign funds necessary to repay the lenders. With the onset of the depression, moreover, private American international loans to Germany were suspended and the chain of payments broken. A large number of defaults, therefore, should have been expected.

TARIFF POLICY

American tariff policy also made repayment of foreign loans, public and private, difficult. Foreigners said they could not pay their debts unless the United States allowed them to earn dollars by selling their goods and services in the American market, but a high protective tariff kept foreigners from obtaining the dollars they needed.

Since its birth the Republican party had been committed to the principle of a protective tariff and had supported that principle whenever it held power. In 1913, the Democrats had reversed the trend toward increasingly higher tariffs by passing the Underwood-Simmons Act, the lowest tariff since the Civil War.

After the First World War, Harding's victory and an economic slump seemed to give urgency to Republican demands for the restoration of higher tariff walls. Congress passed an emergency tariff act that Wilson vetoed the day before he left office. Congress re-enacted it and Harding signed it in May, 1921, thus placing higher duties on certain farm products and on industrial goods. A year later, in September, 1922, despite the protests of European financial leaders who warned that Europe could not pay her debts if the bill became law, Harding approved the Fordney-McCumber Tariff Act that established the highest average duties up to that time.

During the boom years of the 1920's, Americans thus insisted that the Europeans pay their debts, sought high returns from investments abroad, tried to expand their exports, and raised tariff barriers against imports. This was a paradoxical economic foreign policy. It lasted until the creditors caught up with the borrowers. When the stock market crashed in October, 1929, and world-wide depression followed, that policy collapsed.

When the flow of dollars for foreign investment stopped, foreigners were unable to buy American goods and to pay their American debts. A lower tariff might have helped in easing the plight of the debtors by allowing them to sell some of their products in the United States, but Herbert Hoover, before he became President, had warned against tampering with the tariff. "A general reduction of the tariff," he said, "would fill our streets with idle workers." When Congress passed the Hawley-Smoot Act in June, 1930, raising tariff rates to their highest point in history, Hoover signed it.

Over a thousand economists had pleaded with the President not to sign the bill, pointing out that higher rates would hamper foreign exports, block collection of the war debts, invite foreign retaliation, and embitter foreign relations. The predictions proved true. Other countries viewed the Hawley-Smoot Tariff as the unfriendly act of a powerful creditor country and as a symbol of American isolationism and economic nationalism. Since many countries raised their own tariffs against the United States and placed quotas on imports, international trade dwindled.

THE HOOVER MORATORIUM

As the great depression spread to Europe, it struck Austria with particular severity. In March, 1931, the Germans attempted to form a customs union with Austria. The French opposed the move, fearing it would lead to a permanent political union, or *Anschluss,* prohibited by Austria's peace treaty, and withdrew their funds from Austrian banks. In June, the *Kreditanstalt,* Austria's largest private bank and one of the most important in Europe, almost collapsed. The financial crisis also affected Germany, where bankruptcy seemed imminent.

Alarmed by the crisis, President Hoover thought that a temporary suspension of reparations and debt payments might help ease the strain on Germany by giving her time to strengthen her credit and thus avert world-wide economic chaos. On June 20, therefore, he announced that the United States would waive all intergovernmental payments for one year beginning July 1 if other governments would do the same. "This is," Hoover told his press secretary, "perhaps the most daring statement I ever thought of issuing."

Other countries, except France who hesitated for over two weeks before agreeing, promptly accepted the proposed moratorium. In December, Congress approved the moratorium but refused the President's request to revive the World War Foreign Debt Commission and gave it authority to re-examine the problem of the war debts. Congress said it would not allow any of the debts to be "in any manner canceled or reduced."

Although the Hoover Moratorium brought temporary relief, it was no substitute for international discussion of the entire problem of intergovernmental debts. Germany and her creditors, therefore, met in Lausanne, Switzerland, in June and July, 1932, to discuss the status of reparations after the expiration of the Hoover Moratorium. Although invited, the United States refused to participate.

At Lausanne, Germany's creditors agreed to forgive her about 90 per cent of her reparations bill due under the Young Plan if, according to a "gentlemen's agreement" between them, they could obtain corresponding relief from their creditors. This meant that the debtors had shifted the burden of cancelling the reparations to the United States.

This shift appeared logical to the Europeans. When France's Premier, Pierre Laval, had visited Hoover in October, 1931, the two leaders had issued a vague statement saying that during the depression further adjustments of intergovernmental debts might be necessary. Europeans had assumed that the United States had at last become ready to recognize the connection between reparations and war debts, but they were wrong. Americans regarded the Lausanne agreement as an anti-American conspiracy, and Hoover announced publicly that the United States would not cancel the war debts.

After his defeat in November, 1932, Hoover met twice with President-elect Franklin D. Roosevelt in vain efforts to try to reach some agreement on meeting the immediate crisis of war debt payments. Hoover wanted Roosevelt's support in urging Congress to reconstitute the old War Debts Commission with the purpose of renegotiating the debt settlements. Roosevelt refused to bind his administration to any policy on the debts before taking power.

Some European debtors, notably Britain and Italy, paid the first installment after the end of the Hoover Moratorium. France, Poland, and others defaulted. On the next installment, due in June, 1933, Britain and Italy among the great powers made token payments acknowledging at least the validity of the debt. France and others continued to default. The token payments continued until December but ceased after the Attorney General ruled that they did not save debtor governments from being held in default. After that only Finland among the European debtors, who had a small post-war loan and a favorable balance in dollars, continued to meet her payments. Thus, payments on reparations and debts ceased. No formal settlement of the debts has ever been made. . . .

Within a year, on April 13, 1934, Congress passed the Johnson Debt Default Act . . . prohibiting both private and public loans to governments of nations in default to the United States. This act failed to stimulate payment of the debts and increased foreign ill will against the United States.

Chapter Thirteen

THE INSTRUMENTS
OF POLICY: PROPAGANDA

Of the major instruments available to the makers of United States foreign policy, propaganda is probably the least understood: last in war, last in peace, last in the hearts of our countrymen. Despite occasional rhetoric about the cold war being a war for the minds of men, Congress has kept appropriations for the United States Information Agency (USIA) well below $200 million a year through the mid-1960's. This amounts to about one-fortieth of one per cent of our Gross National Product, one-third of one per cent of our military budget, less than 3 per cent of our space budget, and about 7 per cent of our foreign aid expenditures. There have been years, in the past, when the Russians spent more in jamming Voice of America broadcasts aimed at their citizens than the United States spent on all its global "information" programs combined.[1]

It is difficult even to find a name to describe this instrument of policy without evoking stereotyped reactions that confuse more than they clarify. "Propaganda" and "psychological warfare" are dirty words in peacetime. Certainly they do not sound like the kind of policy instrument a democracy should be eager to use extensively. "Information programs" and "truth campaigns," on the other hand, are patent euphemisms. Were this not the case, the dissemination of information would be a *goal* rather than an *instrument* of national policy. In 1954, the Central Intelligence Agency assisted in the overthrow of a leftist government in Guatemala. If a USIA correspondent in the area at the time had learned of the CIA's role through unofficial sources, should he have made this known to the world

---

[1] Even college textbooks on United States foreign policy more often than not ignore propaganda as an instrument of policy, or dismiss it in a few pages.

because it was the truth? If the success of the operation appeared to depend on his emphasizing instead the role of Guatemalans themselves in the anti-government coup, should he nevertheless have avoided this emphasis in order to report the facts objectively? Even the correspondent of a private American news agency would be likely to think twice before responding affirmatively to questions like these. To an official of a United States government agency, it should be clear that negative answers are called for.

It is very difficult to influence those who do not believe you, and it is usually necessary to be truthful at least a good part of the time in order to be believed. But the main goal of any government's "information" programs is not the furtherance of human knowledge, but the furtherance of national policy objectives.

THE MISSION OF USIA

Thus a 1963 memorandum from President Johnson redefining USIA's role in making and executing United States foreign policy stated:

> The mission of the United States Information Agency is to help achieve United States foreign policy objectives by (a) influencing public attitudes in other nations, and (b) advising the President, his representatives abroad, and the various departments and agencies on the implications of foreign opinion for present and contemplated United States policies, programs and official statements. . . .
>
> Agency activities should (a) encourage constructive public support abroad for the goal of a "peaceful world community of free and independent states, free to choose their own future and their own system so long as it does not threaten the freedom of others"; (b) identify the United States as a strong, democratic, dynamic nation qualified for its leadership of world efforts toward this goal; and (c) unmask and counter hostile attempts to distort or frustrate the objectives and policies of the United States. These activities should emphasize the ways in which United States policies harmonize with those of other peoples and governments, and those aspects of American life and culture which facilitate sympathetic understanding of United States policies.[2]

Despite its undesirable negative connotations, the term "propaganda" will be used here because of its familiarity and the inapplicability or awkwardness of the alternatives. The reader is asked to keep in mind that no implication of disapproval is intended. On the contrary, *propaganda* is viewed in this section as a legitimate and necessary instrument of national policy. It refers to efforts to influence the policies of other states, or the actions of their citizens, by means of *communications* directed primarily to

2 United States Information Agency, "The Agency in Brief" (Washington, D.C., February, 1965), p. C-2. (Mimeographed.)

private citizens in these countries. The communications involved will often
— but not invariably — be verbal or pictorial. Actions, substantive and
symbolic, are sometimes the most effective possible communications — especially when attention is called to them verbally as well.

The content of these communications is as likely to be informative as
persuasive:

> . . . Information or propaganda programs . . . [can] tell people how
> to do things they want to do already, or . . . provide them with am-
> munition to support existing opinions. . . . They frequently make it
> possible for organizations to form by rallying people to a flag or to a
> cause, or by enabling widely separated individuals to join in a common
> effort; or they provide existing organizations with information that en-
> ables them to function more efficiently. . . . The political implications
> of following advice regarding crop productivity or personal hygiene in
> underdeveloped countries, or even in industrialized societies, are clear.
> . . . In short, factual knowledge in the minds of those who want to use
> it can be a powerful force in inducing and shaping action.[3]

Notice that this conception of propaganda as an instrument of policy
envisages as its ultimate goal influencing the *actions* of foreign states or
their citizens. Efforts to influence the opinions of peoples about the United
States are only one means toward this goal. (In fact, the results of a major
study sponsored by UNESCO suggest that popular attitudes toward foreign
states and peoples are more often determined *by* intergovernmental relations than vice versa.) [4] In specific situations in particular areas of the world,
the immediate aims of United States propaganda programs might range
from building support for an existing government to promoting its overthrow or urging its citizens to defect; from encouraging a climate of opinion
which will enable a friendly government to contribute military forces to
the war in Vietnam to encouraging an Eastern European Communist country to assert increasing independence from the Soviet Union; from promoting attitudes conducive to economic development in a new African state
to minimizing support for Castroism in parts of Latin America.

Normally, several instruments of policy, rather than merely propaganda
alone, will be utilized in support of such objectives. And success will be
determined not only by the extent and quality of the military, economic,
diplomatic, and propaganda programs undertaken in behalf of these goals,
but by the effectiveness with which these instruments are coordinated. Thus
an effective information program may be a prerequisite to a successful aid

---

[3] W. Phillips Davison, *International Political Communication* (New York: Praeger,
1965), pp. 6 and 40. This is the most useful introduction to the field dealt with in this
chapter.

[4] Hadley Cantril and William Buchanan, *How Nations See Each Other* (Urbana, Ill.:
University of Illinois Press, 1953).

program in an area where mass attitudes, rather than lack of capital, constitute the key obstacle to material progress. And the impact of Peace Corps Volunteers on the attitudes of host peoples and governments is often more important than the direct economic effects of the projects undertaken by these Volunteers.

If the psychological impact of American military, diplomatic, and economic policies is to be taken adequately into account, the men responsible for assessing foreign opinion toward the United States must be consulted whenever important policy decisions are made in any of these fields. In practice, this means that the Director of the USIA or his representative(s) should take part in the formulation of virtually all top-level foreign policy decisions.[5]

When the Soviet Union, in August, 1961, announced its intention to resume nuclear testing in violation of the informal moratorium then in force, Edward R. Murrow, as Director of USIA, participated directly in the top-level meetings called to determine how the United States should respond. According to Theodore Sorenson, the USIA Director was influential in persuading President Kennedy to delay any immediate announcement that the United States too would resume atmospheric testing.[6] Instead, by waiting until the Soviet test series was completed and by proposing meanwhile a formal ban on atmospheric testing, the United States left the Russians to bear the full responsibility, in the eyes of large numbers of people in most of the non-Communist nations of the world, for their violation of the test moratorium. Not until eight months later, after the Soviets had turned down another major allied initiative toward a test ban treaty, did the United States resume atmospheric testing.

But this kind of USIA participation in high-level policymaking seems to have been the exception, rather than the rule, during the cold war decades. The USIA apparently learned of both the U-2 and the Bay of Pigs operations only after the fact.[7] And one wonders to what extent USIA

[5] In the Soviet Union "information and cultural policy originates along with other forms of policy at the very highest level." Davison, *op. cit.*, p. 168.

[6] *Kennedy* (Bantam ed., New York: Harper and Row, 1965), pp. 695–704.

[7] The Acting Director of USIA told a House Subcommittee that the USIA was not informed of the Bay of Pigs invasion until after it was under way, and that it was initially dependent on the private news services for the information on which to base its broadcasts. U.S. Congress, Subcommittee on International Organizations and Movements of the Committee on Foreign Affairs of the House of Representatives, *Hearings: Winning the Cold War: The U.S. Ideological Offensive*, 88th Cong., 2nd sess., 1964, Part 6, 784–785. See also "The Bay of Pigs" case study in Chapter Six.

In the case of the U-2 flights, according to W. Phillips Davison, USIA personnel learned of them only after Francis Powers' plane was shot down. "As a result, a number of conflicting statements were made and the U.S. damaged its own credibility." *Op. cit.*, p. 167.

New York Times correspondent Tad Szulc reports that USIA specialists still had not arrived in Santo Domingo four days after the beginning of the United States intervention there in April, 1965. "Therefore the explanation of what the United States was doing in Santo Domingo and the psychological aspects of its operation were left entirely in military hands." *Dominican Diary* (New York: Dell, 1965), p. 115.

officials were consulted, more recently, when the decisions were made to intervene in the Dominican Republic, and to use nonlethal poison gases in combat operations in Vietnam.

Making the Director of USIA a regular and full participant in the deliberations of the National Security Council, and appointing men of considerable personal and political stature to head this agency, would help to make more common the kind of consultation which is desirable. But even more fundamental is the need for the President and his key foreign policy advisers to accept propaganda as an instrument of policy equal in stature and potential to the military, economic, and diplomatic instruments. The Johnson administration's proposal to integrate USIA officers into the Foreign Service Officer corps, whatever its other liabilities, should aid substantially, if adopted, in bringing to high level career posts in the Department of State men well versed in the techniques, uses and limitations of propaganda.[8]

SELECTING AND REACHING
MASS AUDIENCES ABROAD

Once the action objectives of our propaganda programs in a particular place at a particular time have been defined, the problem of how best to attain these objectives remains. This problem may be divided for purposes of analysis into three parts: *what* must be communicated to *whom* and *how* in order to help bring about the action desired. Each of these components — the message, the audience, and the means of communication — depends in part on the nature of the other two in the specific case at hand. A message suitable for Bolivian peasants is unlikely to be suitable for Parisian intellectuals. Skilled workers may be easier to reach by newspapers, farmers by radio or mobile motion picture units. Reviews of American progress in race relations may be handled best in books or magazines, while American space achievements may be brought home most graphically by motion pictures, television, or other photographic media.

Whom we want to influence, in a given case, will depend also on what we want done. If we want to encourage increased European investment in India or Brazil, we will do well to focus our efforts upon European businessmen and financiers. These men may be reached by American government officials directly, through personal contact with their American counterparts, and through books, newspapers, and business and financial publications in their own countries. (One-minute spot announcements on daytime television or airdrops of leaflets over rural areas, on the other hand, would not seem very appropriate means of reaching this audience.)

Some audiences will prove extremely difficult to reach by any means. Government control over the means of communications in Communist na-

8 See Chapter Four.

tions, and the willingness of some Communist governments to jam or otherwise interfere with American efforts to reach their populations, severely limit our ability to send messages across or through the Iron Curtain.[9]

In the hinterlands of underdeveloped countries, primitive communications networks, illiteracy, and the momentum of tradition may constitute equally formidable barriers. Surveying urban and rural Brazilians soon after the 1960 Brazilian presidential elections, Lloyd Free found that a majority of his rural sample could not identify either the incoming (Quadros) or outgoing (Kubitschek) presidents; that 65 per cent of the urban and 95 per cent of the rural sample could not identify the man who had been President of the United States for the past eight years (Eisenhower); and that only 6 per cent of those in the rural areas could name Fidel Castro as "prime minister and top leader" of Cuba.[10] The writer of this book has conversed with a fisherman on Taiwan who believed, thirteen years after the event, that Franklin Roosevelt was still President of the United States, and that the Japanese still ruled the island on which he lived and worked. Obviously, it is unrealistic to expect USIA to reach most of these people with *any* sort of political message.

Holt and van der Velde propose two criteria for the selection of audiences to which propaganda messages may be addressed: *cruciality* and *susceptibility*.[11] The first of these is concerned with the ability of the audience addressed to help bring about the specific results desired — that is, usually, their ability to influence national policy in specified ways. The second criterion, susceptibility, is concerned with the likelihood that the audience addressed *can* be influenced in the desired manner by means available to us.

Often the most susceptible potential audience is not the most crucial, and vice versa. If we want to encourage land reform in an underdeveloped country, for instance, the peasantry may be most sympathetic to our appeals;

---

9 Soviet jamming of broadcasts by the USIA's Voice of America terminated in 1963. But Communist China, Cuba, Bulgaria, and East Germany were still attempting to jam these broadcasts in 1966.

10 *Some International Implications of the Political Psychology of Brazilians* (Princeton, N.J.: Institute for International Social Research, 1961), pp. 3 and 50. Free notes that one rural illiterate said he wasn't sure who the president of his country was, but thought it was God. See also the same author's *The Attitudes, Hopes and Fears of Nigerians* (Princeton, N.J.: Institute for International Social Research, 1964).

Our discussion of public opinion in the United States should warn us against expecting any great political attentiveness even in urban areas, or in Western Europe. Thus USIA surveys taken soon after the Cuban missile crisis found barely half of a sample of residents of four leading Latin American cities aware that there had been a recent crisis over Cuba. "Worldwide Public Reaction to the Cuban Crisis" (USIA Survey Research Studies, World Opinion Series, September, 1963). And in the same year 47 per cent of the Italians interviewed, 32 per cent of the French, 26 per cent of the British, and 17 per cent of the Germans, had never heard of NATO. "Public Opinion About NATO and Nuclear Issues in Western Europe" (USIA Research and Reference Service, July, 1963).

11 *Strategic Psychological Operations and American Foreign Policy* (Chicago: University of Chicago Press, 1960). The next several paragraphs draw on this work.

but landowners, bureaucrats; or military officers, *if* they could be convinced, might be better able to put such reforms into effect. Conversely, a Western- ized urban elite might be more readily persuaded that birth control is an essential prerequisite to economic development in their country, while, in this instance, it might be more effective if the peasantry could be convinced of this fact.

Regardless of whom we may be trying to reach, it is essential that we keep our audiences' purposes in mind as well as our own. People will attend only to messages they have some use for. "Will [our messages] . . . help people to satisfy a need or attain a goal? If not, they are likely to be disregarded or forgotten." [12]

The conception held by some American citizens and Congressmen that USIA's principal role should be to convert pro-Communist "heathens" to the democratic faith can be another obstacle to successful propaganda.[13] Few things are harder to achieve than inducing large numbers of people to change their whole outlook on life. And few people are less susceptible to pro-American appeals than those firmly committed to a militant rival ideol- ogy. Our specific foreign policy goals will most often be advanced far more effectively by attempts to reinforce the opinions and activate the efforts of those already disposed to be sympathetic to our goals than by attempts to convert those most hostile to us. An American political campaign manager who attempted to win an election for the Republicans by spending most of his efforts trying to persuade staunch Democrats to change their party affiliation would be completely out of his mind. Odds are, he would help his opponent more than his own candidate by increasing the likelihood that the staunch Democrats he contacted would vote — in most cases, for the same party they usually vote for. Surely it is no less difficult to convert pro- Communists into democrats than to convert Democrats into Republicans.[14]

Once an appropriate audience has been selected and a message tailored to its susceptibilities, the message must be delivered to this audience in a

---

[12] Davison, *op. cit.,* p. 55.

[13] See W. Phillips Davison, "Political Communication as an Instrument of Foreign Policy," *The Public Opinion Quarterly* (Spring, 1963), pp. 28–36. "The most rewarding target for propaganda is ordinarily not the individual with differing opinions, but rather the person who shares at least partly the views of the propagandist or whose attitudes have not yet become firmly established." *Ibid.,* p. 33.

[14] In 1956, Hadley Cantril tested the reactions of Communist protest voters (*not* Com- munist party members) in France and Italy to several different types of pro-American ap- peals, printed as though they were excerpts from American newspapers. One of these appeals, in each case, was a relatively straightforward statement of American reasons for opposing communism and preferring democracy, based on recent United States government policy statements. In France, this approach had a negative effect on the respondents' atti- tudes toward the United States and was the least effective of the five appeals tested. In Italy, none of the appeals tested had any significant effect on attitudes toward the United States, and the straightforward anti-Communist approach was rated least "believable" of the four appeals tested. *The Politics of Despair* (New York: Basic Books, 1958), chap. 8 and Ap- pendix 3.

credible (that is, believable) form. Among the means which may be available will be printed media (books, magazines, newspapers, pamphlets, letters, leaflets); visual media (movies, television, photographs, exhibits, slides, filmstrips); auditory media (radio, records); face-to-face personal communications (speeches, conversations, exchange of persons, rumor campaigns); and observable actions. (Chart A summarizes USIA use of some of these media during the first half of 1966.) The messages conveyed may be substantially accurate or sheer fabrication, and they may be spread openly (that is, through sources admittedly sponsored or supported by the United States government) or covertly (through anonymous sources or sources not admittedly sponsored or supported by the United States government).

Covert (or "black") operations may vary from the allied radio stations which masqueraded as German stations during World War II in order to give misleading information to the enemy at critical moments, to intellectual journals in friendly nations which are enabled to flourish through indirect

CHART A — THE UNITED STATES INFORMATION AGENCY
DURING THE FIRST HALF OF 1966.

we broadcast 845 hours weekly in 38 languages to a worldwide audience of 25,000,000 daily	we exhibited our motion pictures to 350,000,000 people in 120 countries	we placed our television programs and series on 2,082 TV stations for telecasting in 94 countries
we compiled and transmitted by radio-teletype 12,000 words a day to USIS posts abroad for placement in newspapers and periodicals	we produced over 400,000 leaflets and pamphlets a week in 47 languages for use in 115 countries	we published more than 1,300,000 copies per month of 24 magazines in 29 languages for distribution in 90 countries
we assisted foreign publishers to produce 6,000,000 copies of 799 books, including translations	we operated 223 libraries and reading rooms, which were visited by over 12,000,000 people	we received nearly 700,000 visitors in Budapest and approximately 400,000 in Poznan at our *Hand Tools, U.S.A.* exhibit

Source: *USIA 26th Review of Operations, January-June, 1966,* p. 3.

subsidies from front organizations of the Central Intelligence Agency. (In 1966, *The New York Times* reported that the well-known British monthly *Encounter* "with editions in Spanish and German, as well as English, was for a long time — though it is not now — one of the indirect beneficiaries of CIA funds." [15]

EVALUATING OUR PROPAGANDA'S EFFECTIVENESS

Both to improve our selection of messages, audiences, and media, and to help convince Congress and the Executive branch of the value of our "information" programs, accurate means of evaluating the actual impact of these programs are essential. It is particularly unfortunate, therefore, that reliable evaluations in this field are almost impossible to obtain. Useful clues may be gleaned by analyzing the news and editorial content of important foreign newspapers and journals, by interviewing expatriates, or by studying the results of surveys of foreign public opinion sponsored periodically by USIA [16] or conducted by independent scholars. But it is very seldom possible to obtain evidence demonstrating that a particular action taken by a foreign government is directly or indirectly attributable to the effects of United States propaganda programs in the nation concerned. If a shift in responses to successive public opinion surveys is detected, how can we be sure that this is due to USIA programs or United States government actions rather than to domestic or international events in general? And if we could be sure that our "information" efforts had caused a shift in *opinion,* how could we establish that it was this shift which led to a change in government *policy* or personal *action?*

Any political scientist who can establish a clear connection between political propaganda and specific changes in public policy in the United States is likely to be justifiably pleased with himself. To establish such a connection in a developing nation is much more difficult. In a closed society, it is close to impossible. We are left with no choice, then, but to muddle through as best we can with the meager "feedback" that public opinion surveys, content analysis of foreign media, and the impressions of American officials stationed abroad can provide.[17]

[15] April 27, 1966, p. 28. USIA has also subsidized some books published commercially in the United States which it wished to make use of abroad. But, due to public criticism of this activity, no book subsidies have been authorized since 1965.

[16] These surveys are normally made available to the public about two years after their issuance and are on file at USIA headquarters in Washington and in a number of major libraries across the United States. They have been most helpful in the preparation of this section. In the opinion of the writer of this book they have not received the attention they deserve from scholars in the field of survey research.

[17] As USIA officials are themselves aware, however, there is room for considerable improvement in evaluation methods, beginning with a more precise statement of goals by United States policymakers. In the course of an October, 1966, "Seminar on Effectiveness," Agency officials expressed the views that "there is a basic lack of research data," that ". . .

PRESTIGE: LIKING AND RESPECT

Implicit — and at times explicit — in what has been said above is the conviction that making other peoples like us is not and should not be the principal objective of either our "information" programs or our foreign policy. Nevertheless, it is certainly true that our specific policy goals will sometimes be advanced by having other peoples favorably rather than unfavorably disposed toward us. Our annual allocation of close to $7 billion for space exploration has been justified in large part on the ground that reaching the moon before the Soviet Union does is crucial to the maintenance of our international prestige.[18] And apart from the actual utility of maintaining a favorable image of America abroad — a utility difficult to estimate accurately, for reasons already discussed — there remains the fact that many Americans are puzzled and concerned by the gap between their own image of America and that apparently held by many foreign peoples. It seems worth our while, then, to inquire into this matter in some detail.

Our first need in this inquiry is a modicum of precision. "Prestige" is a nebulous concept, with more than one component. Being respected and being liked are not the same thing. Respect generally comes to those who show that they have both the power and the will to do what they say they are going to do — or more. This holds regardless of the popularity of the action concerned. The quarantine President Kennedy imposed against Cuba in the 1962 missile crisis ultimately increased American "prestige" — but not because others "liked" this action. Rather our prestige went up because we coordinated our words and deeds in the crisis in a way which convinced others that we meant what we said.

The Soviet "sputnik" damaged American prestige, not because people dis-

---

reporting requirements tend to emphasize deeds and statistics and not attitude, opinion and behavior change," and that "too much evaluation is now being done by operators themselves . . . and is therefore subjective." "Proceedings of the Seminar on Effectiveness Held at Airlie House, Warrenton, Virginia, October 6–8, 1966." (USIA Office of Policy and Research, November 7, 1966).

Nor is this aspect of USIA operations immune from political pressures. There were indications in 1966 that the Johnson administration was hesitant to undertake a major world opinion survey prior to the 1968 elections, perhaps for fear that its results might be "leaked" and used as a campaign issue if, as expected, United States "prestige" appeared to have fallen due to our involvement in Vietnam. It may be recalled that Senator John F. Kennedy made a presidential campaign issue in 1960 of alleged drops in United States "prestige" in the closing months of the Eisenhower administration.

18 USIA studies suggest that foreign citizens' views of the United States standing vis à vis the Soviet Union in the "space race" *do* seem to have a far-reaching effect on these people's view of the relative *general* scientific competence of the United States and the Soviet Union, on their identification of their own nation's interests with those of the United States, and on their willingness to see their country side with the United States "in the present world situation." See "The Image of United States Versus Soviet Science in West European Public Opinion" (USIA Research and Reference Service, Survey Research Studies, Attitude and Opinion Series, October, 1961).

liked us for not putting one up first, but because it seemed to puncture our frequent claims to overwhelming scientific and military superiority. Future space successes may help to restore world belief in United States scientific primacy — but the reassessment of Soviet technological competence occasioned by the "sputniks" is not likely to be reversed.

The thwarting of the Hungarian revolution of 1956 hurt Russian prestige in the sense that it made people *like* the Soviet Union less — for a while, at least; but it also hurt American prestige to the extent that we failed to back up our talk about support for the "liberation of captive peoples." The Bay of Pigs invasion of 1961 hurt the United States on both counts — it put in doubt at one and the same time *both* our devotion to international law and nonintervention *and* our capacity to execute a covert military action successfully once we had begun it.

Sometimes respect can only be obtained at the price of risking a loss in others' affection for us. In 1948, for example, the United States made a concerted effort to prevent a Communist victory in the important Italian elections of that year. Stepped-up Voice of America broadcasts, pamphlets, hundreds of thousands of letters and postcards written by Italian Americans, and carefully timed grants of aid and goodwill gestures were all utilized toward this end. One of the main themes of this barrage of activities was that United States aid to Italy would be cut off if the Communist-backed parties won the elections. Messages pressing this theme could scarcely be expected to make Italians like Americans more. Rather, the decision to emphasize this point was based on the underlying assumption that the Italians addressed were more likely to vote for pro-American parties if they felt they had an economic stake in voting for them than if they simply felt more favorably disposed toward the United States. Whatever the specific effects of this United States propaganda campaign may have been, the Communist-supported parties were defeated decisively at the polls.[19]

THE AMERICAN IMAGE

Undoubtedly, millions of Americans first heard of USIA libraries abroad when newspaper headlines reported the stoning, burning, or picketing of these libraries by angry mobs in protest against this or that American policy. Most Americans find this and other indications of foreign resentment of the United States very hard to accept and understand. Why should others hate us? At home, we enjoy the American Way of Life — an unprecedented level of material prosperity combined with an intense devotion to the principles of Democracy, Freedom, and Equal Opportunity. Abroad, we seek no dominion: just the right to go our own way in peace. For the past two decades we have reluctantly undertaken the burden of protecting the right of most of the non-Communist nations of the world to do the same. In so doing, we have probably saved some of them from Communist domination.

[19] Holt and van der Velde, *op. cit.*, chap. 6.

To preserve their freedom, as well as our own, hundreds of thousands of Americans have fought — and tens of thousands died — far from our shores, in the remote hills of Korea and jungles of Vietnam. In addition, we have spent close to $120 billion to aid other nations to defend themselves against communism and to help them build strong, self-sufficient economies of their own.

If the peoples we have helped and protected respond to our generosity by condemning us, stoning our embassies, and burning the libraries we built to serve them, then, say many Americans, let us be done with them. Perhaps there is something to be said for "isolationism" after all. In any event the whole business does not speak well for those responsible for interpreting American policies abroad. If they cannot succeed in selling so splendid — and historically popular — a product as the American Way of Life, there must be something wrong somewhere.[20]

Indeed there is. In part, it is our willingness to put so much stock in isolated — and sometimes manufactured — incidents. More representative evidence suggests that the United States is *not* widely disliked in the non-Communist world, except when specific United States policies occasion strong negative reactions. USIA has conducted three major "world" opinion surveys. (The results of the most recent of these, conducted in 1965, was still classified when this book was written.) Though foreign esteem for the United States has probably fallen considerably, due to our Vietnam policy, since the second of these surveys was taken, it may be helpful to review here a summary of some of that (1964) survey's principal findings (see also Chart B): [21]

USIA's second world opinion survey conducted in early 1964 in some

---

[20] A 1966 Gallup survey showed only 21 per cent of a United States national sample "extremely satisfied" or "considerably satisfied" with America's success in the "war of ideas," compared to about 60 per cent who were "somewhat" or "not at all" satisfied. In contrast, 58 per cent were "extremely" or "considerably" satisfied with United States military strength, compared to only 32 per cent "somewhat" or "not at all" satisfied. *The Washington Post,* June 11, 1966, p. 2.

[21] This summary is reprinted from "A Balance Sheet on U.S. vs. Soviet Standing in World Opinion" (USIA Research and Reference Service, World Survey Series, August, 1964), p. i. The countries and cities surveyed were West Germany, Italy, Austria, Great Britain, France, Japan, India, Morocco, Mexico City, Buenos Aires (Argentina), Caracas (Venezuela), Rio de Janeiro (Brazil), Manila (the Philippines), Kuala Lumpur (Malaysia), Singapore, Teheran (Iran), Ankara (Turkey), Dacca and Karachi (Pakistan), and Lagos (Nigeria).

This report also showed that the persons interviewed in a majority of these countries and cities judged the United States to be ahead of the Soviet Union (in 1964) in total military strength, total economic strength, fair distribution of wealth, education, and individual freedom. The Soviet Union was judged to be ahead of the United States in strength in nuclear weapons, space developments and scientific development, and opinion was almost evenly divided as to which of the two superpowers would be stronger in the future. *Ibid.,* p. ii.

Chart B, showing trends in Western European attitudes toward United States, Soviet,

21 countries and major cities indicates, first, on the score of general esteem:

> The U.S. as a country is widely liked throughout the non-Communist world, with expressions of good opinion strongly predominating in all but one (Karachi) of the countries and cities surveyed.
>
> America's recent foreign policies everywhere surveyed receive a predominant vote of confidence among those with opinions, except in two places — Karachi and Ankara.
>
> That America is dedicated to peace is the viewpoint that prevails by large margins in all but one of the areas surveyed (Karachi), and wherever trend information is available U.S. peace standing is at a record high.

In contrast, though many applaud what they perceive to be a friendlier attitude on the part of the Soviet Union:

> Unfavorable feelings about the USSR continue to prevail in most of the countries and cities surveyed.
>
> Reactions to recent Soviet policies are no better than mixed, with approval predominating in some areas and disapproval in others.
>
> And despite whatever gains are associated with greater recent friendliness, the Soviet Union continues in most instances to be judged far behind the U.S. in dedication to peace.

> Generally high esteem for the U.S. is coupled with the strongly predominant judgment among most of the peoples surveyed that their basic interests and those of the U.S. are "fairly well" to "very much" in accord. The opposite view prevails for the most part in regard to Soviet interests.
>
> The widespread liking for the U.S. and perception of shared interests does not mean, however, that similar proportions are willing to align their countries with the U.S. in the present world situation. Many appear to feel that such alignment, as they variously express it, means a sacrifice of independence, freedom of action, or self-reliance.

Yet whatever the percentages, there is no denying that many tens of millions of individuals, in Western Europe as well as in the developing nations, feel genuine hostility toward the United States. We will have less difficulty in understanding *why* they do, if we try, for a moment, to see ourselves as these people may see us.

No doubt we *are* the richest nation of all time — rightfully a matter of some satisfaction to us. But why should we expect others, including millions of people starving or living at bare subsistence level, to be overjoyed at our good fortune? *We* feel that our example should suggest that they can live this way too if they will but follow the time-honored principles of hard

---

and Chinese Communist efforts to avoid war, is taken from "West European Attitudes Toward U.S.-Soviet Relations and Recent Disarmament Developments" (USIA Research and Reference Service, World Survey Series, September, 1964), p. 10.

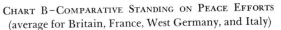

CHART B–COMPARATIVE STANDING ON PEACE EFFORTS
(average for Britain, France, West Germany, and Italy)

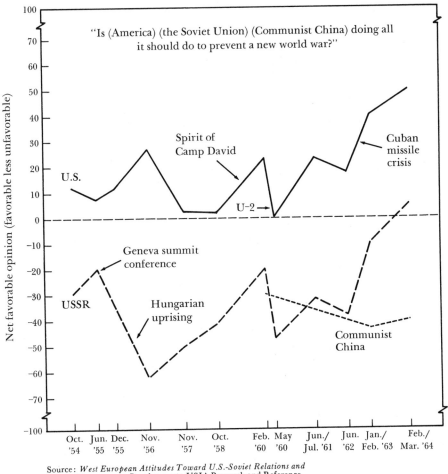

Source: *West European Attitudes Toward U.S.-Soviet Relations and Recent Disarmament Developments*, USIA Research and Reference Service, May, 1964, p. 10.

work and thrift we have followed. The chapter on the developing nations in this book indicates that this is a highly oversimplified analysis. The Communists offer one equally oversimplified, and about equally accurate: the Americans are rich and you are poor because the imperialistic West has organized the world so that they can exploit the sweat of *your* brow for *their* benefit.

With *our* simple theory comes the implication that *our* way of life is better — not just materially, but somehow morally — than that of the people we are addressing. With the Communists' explanation comes the more satisfying conviction that the listeners' plight is not due to *their* moral inferiority, but to the West's. Even the thumbnail review of the principles of opinion formation and change included in Chapter Seven should make it clear which of these fundamental appeals has the better chance of acceptance. Yet for years a fairly crude emphasis on American wealth and American power formed one of the basic themes of our propaganda efforts abroad.

Why should others be happy, for that matter, to learn that we are mighty and that we usually win? Appeals for voluntary contributions to help finance the United States Olympic team have sometimes been made on the basis that American victories in the Olympics add to American prestige abroad. If "prestige" here means *respect*, this may be true. If it means *liking*, the assumption is rather dubious. For a good while, some years ago, the New York Yankees won baseball championships with almost monotonous regularity. But, somehow, this did not make them popular and well-liked outside of New York. To the contrary, Chicago fans and Boston fans, Cleveland fans and Detroit fans all united, when their own teams' hopes faded, in hoping that the Yankees would get their comeuppance. May there not be something of this apparently elemental desire to see the fellow at the top of the heap "get his" in the reaction of some foreign peoples to American power and American wealth?

Why, in particular, should we expect the European peoples who for so long occupied the position of political and economic primacy which we now hold, to be elated that we have displaced them? In the eyes of some of them, we are still a young and upstart nation with a highly derivative culture. And we have overtaken them partly because we stood by while they bore the brunt of the Axis assault which threatened all our freedoms in the early years of World War II. Since the war, we have pressed them to support us — whatever their own predilections in the matter — whenever we have felt our interests threatened: in the Cuban missile crisis, in Vietnam, in the Dominican Republic, in blocking the seating of Communist China at the United Nations, and in applying tight embargoes against trade with Communist China, Cuba, and North Vietnam. But we have been most reluctant to return the favor by supporting them when they have felt their interests threatened in quarrels involving their colonies and ex-colonies, as our actions in the Suez crisis proved. How would we feel if the tables were turned?

Our professed devotion to Democracy, Freedom, and Equal Opportunity is also unquestionably great. But we tend to overlook — while others sometimes tend to magnify — our frequent departures from these lofty principles.

America's record of racial discrimination, for instance, casts justifiable doubt on the depth of our society's commitment to its professed ideals. A 1964 USIA survey found that ". . . West European judgments of the treatment of the Negro in America are negative among large majorities of the population," although "other evidence from the survey suggests that this reaction is not a controlling element in arriving at general judgments of the U.S. as a nation." [22] In some of the (nonwhite) developing nations, of course, adverse reactions on this point are even stronger — especially when buttressed by personal experience. (Davison cites a study indicating that *every* African visitor to the United States during 1962 had at least one bad personal experience, and witnessed or was told of many more.) [23]

When American Negroes are locked out of the public schools in Little Rock, Arkansas; when they are intimidated with billy clubs, cattle prods, and water hoses in Birmingham and Selma, Alabama; when African diplomats are discriminated against at hotels and restaurants in Washington, D.C., and near United Nations headquarters in New York; when our Congress refuses to pass laws outlawing discrimination in the sale and rental of private homes; when United States immigration legislation excludes many Orientals and sets up discriminatory quotas on a national origins basis (as it did until 1965) — when these things happen nothing the USIA can say is capable of wholly glossing over the hypocrisy evident in the loud verbal commitments of many Americans to democratic ideals.

If USIA tries to ignore these happenings when they are emblazoned in the headlines of most of the world's newspapers, the Agency's credibility is severely damaged. Why should people believe a source which is so patently unwilling to discuss real events frankly? [24] Equally important, USIA's silence simply makes it more likely that the world's peoples will get this news in a form more damaging to American prestige than a candid but carefully balanced USIA account would be. That foreign reactions to accounts of racial incidents may depend heavily on the manner in which these events are presented is shown by a USIA study in New Delhi, India, where the incidents surrounding James Meredith's admission to the University of Mississippi more often than not were seen as a sign of improving — rather than of deteriorating — race relations in the United States. The study concludes that the episode certainly did not lower — and may have raised — United States standing among Indians.[25]

Nor do others view our *foreign* policies in quite the way we do. If we are so peace-loving, why do we boast so much of our military power and

[22] "European Opinions of Race Relations in America" (USIA Research and Reference Service, World Survey Series, June, 1964), p. 12.

[23] *International Political Communication*, p. 301.

[24] Despite the increased emphasis on honest and credible USIA presentations during the Kennedy administration, some Voice of America officials continued to complain of political interference with their radio scripts. One official asserted, for instance, that "Voice" officials were reprimanded for broadcasting to Africa accounts of the funeral of "black nationalist" leader Malcolm X and were ordered to delete from a roundup of United States editorial opinion on Vietnam a highly critical editorial from *The New York Times*. USIA Director Carl Rowan, however, denied that there had been any interference with the content of news programs, or that editorial control of news commentaries had been tightened. *The New York Times*, June 6, 1965, p. 1.

[25] "New Delhi Reactions to the Mississippi Segregation Crisis" (USIA Research and Reference Service, November 29, 1962).

spend over $70 billion a year on armaments? Why were we the first nation in history to use nuclear weapons — and on a nonwhite people at that? Why do we object to Communist proposals for general and complete disarmament? If we are so devoted to international law, why have we violated Soviet, Chinese, and Cuban airspace with our U-2s and other "spy planes"? Why did we sponsor an exiles' invasion of Cuba in 1961 in violation of international law? Why did we intervene unilaterally in the Dominican Republic in 1965 in violation of the charters of the United Nations and the Organization of American States? And why do we use noxious gases in Vietnam?

If we are as interested as we claim in other people's independence, why have we allied ourselves with the European colonial powers, including those, like Portugal, which ruthlessly suppress national independence movements in their colonies? Why are we so much more hesitant than are the Communists to support anticolonial resolutions in the United Nations? Why do we drop napalm bombs on Vietnamese who believe they are seeking independence from Western domination? Why did we support men like Moise Tshombe in the Congo — a man who employed white mercenaries to kill his own people and made his public reputation as a last-ditch defender of Belgian colonial interests?

There are good answers to some (though, alas, not all) of these questions. But, good or bad, they are much more complicated than the questions. Why should these answers be apparent to, or easily accepted by black- or yellow- or brown-skinned foreigners barely able to read but well able to remember the humiliations of white colonial overlordship?

Why should these foreigners believe that we are arming ourselves to protect *them,* that we fought in Korea and fight now in Vietnam to protect *them,* that we dispense aid abroad to help *them,* when they see that our own leaders justify these sacrifices to our Congress and to the American people on the ground that they are necessary in our own self-interest — to protect *our* security, *our* prosperity, *our* way of life?

DEMOCRATIC VS. COMMUNIST PROPAGANDA: A BALANCE SHEET

There are a number of respects, clearly, in which the Communist nations — or any totalitarian societies — have distinct advantages over "open" societies in the propaganda field. Their ideology and centralized organization provides them with a coherent orientation and a clear policy line. They do not have to justify their propaganda operations to their own people; we must often make our policies look more selfish than they are in order to secure broad political support at home. They can exercise nearly complete control over their media and over their citizens abroad; we must tolerate a sometimes painful diversity of voices as the price of maintaining our openness. An American Senator or Congressman can make racist speeches — not only at home, but in the heart of Africa — and nothing can be done about it. He can even help the Communists by attributing most civil rights activities in the United States to them.[26] American newspapers, magazines, and books can criticize foreigners and portray them in offensive stereotypes as much as their editors — or their readers — please. American film companies can send movies abroad for commercial gain which highlight crime, sadism, and sex deviation in American life — and the United States government usually can do no more than plead with them to keep their country's interests in mind. Certainly USIA's information budget does not allow it to compete with Hollywood in the production of motion pictures for showing abroad.[27]

The Communist nations are free to pitch their propaganda appeals to the beliefs and prejudices of their potential foreign audiences. They can play communism down and nationalism, land reform — even "democracy" — up, without worrying about offending members of the Supreme Soviet back home. But USIA had better think twice before saying openly anything that might offend Americans devoted to Christianity or free enterprise — even in countries where Buddhism and socialism are much more acceptable to the people it addresses.

This can be a formidable handicap. USIA-sponsored surveys show that to the people of most non-Communist nations, including Europeans, "capitalism" means *not* just private ownership of industry, but a high concentration of power in the hands of rich "capitalists" and a lack of government welfare programs to aid the poor. "Socialism" on the other hand, means to them *not* just government ownership of industrial enterprises, but the assumption by government of the responsibility for aiding those in need through welfare programs. Given these perceptions, it is not surprising that they prefer socialism to capitalism for themselves (see Chart C), although, given the choice, they prefer even more a mixed system leaning slightly to the "socialist" side. By their definitions of these words, the United States, in fact, departs only slightly from their own ideal. But, much to our own detriment, we have convinced a large majority that we are completely or almost completely "capitalistic." [28]

Congressional sensitivities can also limit USIA's ability to maintain its credibility by presenting a fundamentally honest picture of American society to its foreign audiences. Thus in a recent congressional hearing, USIA was criticized for reporting demonstrations in the United States protesting

26 See Davison, *International Political Communication*, p. 224.

27 "The American commercial motion picture plays to about 75 million admissions *each week* outside the United States." Howland H. Sargeant, "Information and Cultural Representation Abroad," in Vincent Barnett, Jr. (ed.), *The Representation of the United States Abroad* (rev ed.; New York: Praeger, 1965), p. 108.

28 For a detailed discussion of this phenomenon, see Ralph K. White, " 'Socialism' and 'Capitalism': An International Misunderstanding," *Foreign Affairs* (January, 1966), pp. 216–227; and the study, drafted by the same author, from which Chart C is taken.

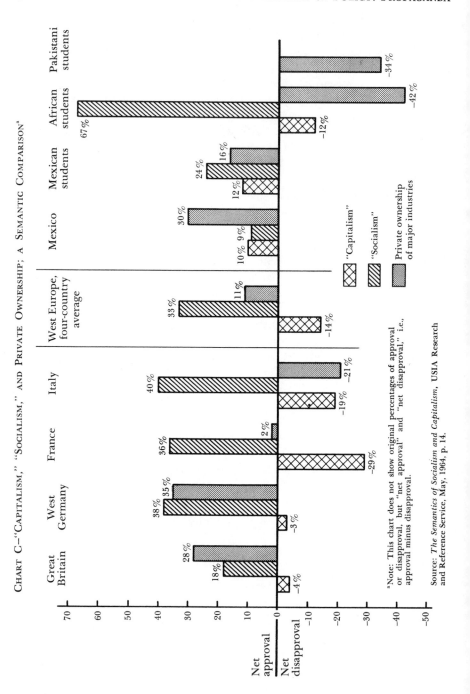

CHART C—"CAPITALISM," "SOCIALISM," AND PRIVATE OWNERSHIP; A SEMANTIC COMPARISON[a]

[a]Note: This chart does not show original percentages of approval or disapproval, but "net approval" and "net disapproval," i.e., approval minus disapproval.

Source: *The Semantics of Socialism and Capitalism*, USIA Research and Reference Service, May, 1964, p. 14.

American policy in the Dominican Republic and Vietnam. (Senator Frank Lausche: ". . . it serves our country in telling the people of the world that the right of free speech is unlimited in the United States. But should there not be some self-imposed restriction when it may be and probably is that you are reporting what is the view of an irresponsible minority?") A few moments later USIA was challenged by another Senator concerning its coverage of civil rights demonstrations in the United States:

> Senator [Bourke] Hickenlooper. Do you also carry with it an equal amount of emphasis on the fact that in almost all the States of the Union the Negro has no trouble whatsoever to vote? . . . Do you point out the number of Negro millionaires in the United States? Do you point out the number of automobiles owned by Negroes? . . . I get rumors to the effect that the progress of the Negro in the United States is just given a lick and a promise and not much emphasis.[29]

The Communist countries are often at an advantage in cultural exchanges, too, because their governments do not have to compete with private interests — as ours must — for the services of the artists or performers most likely to enhance their country's artistic standing abroad. And their system encourages state subsidies to outstanding artists who might not be able to afford to devote themselves to their crafts if they had to depend, as some of their American counterparts do, on the vicissitudes of the "box office."

Yet, as the USIA survey results quoted earlier suggest, not all the advantages in the propaganda field rest with the Communist nations. Much of the propaganda output of these bureaucratized states is humorless and — to put it bluntly — dull. The sharp reversals of policy line sometimes forced on their centrally coordinated propaganda apparatus — as in the case of the Nazi-Soviet pact of 1939 and the de-Stalinization campaign of 1956 — tend to reduce their long-run credibility.[30] And from time to time the lack of individual freedom in the Soviet Union leads to such embarrassments as having a Soviet writer (Boris Pasternak) win the Nobel Prize, in part for a novel (*Doctor Zhivago*) he could not publish in his own country; to the jailing of writers Andrei Sinyavsky and Yuli Daniel, in 1965, for publishing "anti-Soviet" writings abroad; and to the defection to the United States, in 1967 of Joseph Stalin's daughter, partly in reaction to the imprisonment of Sinyavsky and Daniel. None of these incidents can have helped to improve the world's image of the Soviet Union.

---

29 U.S. Congress, Senate, Committee on Foreign Relations, *Hearings on the Nomination of U.S. Information Agency Officers to be Foreign Service Officers; United States Information Agency Nominations*, 89th Cong., 1st sess., April 27 and May 18, 1965, pp. 86 and 98–101.
  USIA duly denied the rumors and emphasized that the Agency seeks to make "balanced" presentations of American life.

30 Davison, *International Political Communication*, pp. 223–227.

American movies, publications, and radio and TV broadcasts may mis-represent American life in certain respects and offend some foreigners. But for all of this, a number of USIA studies show that more often than not they exercise a net *favorable* influence on the impressions of America held by their viewers, listeners, and readers abroad — due largely to the high standards of living they depict.

Even our babel of conflicting voices can at times be an asset. For those who understand the meaning of democracy know that vigorous dissent is one of the most reliable indications of real freedom known to man:

> . . . One of our major aims is to convey a clear picture of American pluralism, and completely consistent communications could never do this. Self-critical statements, and a moderate quota of foolish ones, are a characteristic of our society. No one can claim to understand this country until he is able to take these in stride.[31]

What others think of us, therefore, is not merely a result of how well USIA does its job. It is not merely what we *say,* but what we *do* that counts; and not merely what we *do;* but what we *are.* This does *not* mean that we should change what we do and what we are in order to win popularity abroad. The potential impact of our actions on governments and peoples abroad deserves to be taken carefully into account before we act — and officials of the USIA are specially qualified to advise the President and the State Department what that impact is likely to be. But obviously we can rarely please everybody, and there are many things more truly important to us than our image overseas. We would indeed be worthy of contempt and pity — as a nation or as individuals — if we tailored our lives mainly to influ-ence our neighbors' opinions of us.[32] When we want to do things in our own way despite what others may think, however, we should not blame USIA or some other convenient scapegoat for its inability to make others like us for doing what *we* believe is right.

♥CASE
STUDY   *AMERICA THROUGH BRITISH EYES*

> The case study in this chapter is taken from a USIA research report — one of the most comprehensive and clearly focused of the unclassified studies undertaken by that Agency. Since it was conducted in 1959, it cannot be assumed to be an accurate representation of British attitudes

31 *Ibid.,* p. 302.

32 Thus the fact that our free market system may put us at a disadvantage vis-à-vis the Soviet Union in cultural exchange programs does not mean that we should adopt state socialism in order to overcome this disadvantage. Nor should fear of an unfavorable Ameri-can image in Africa be our principal reason for letting American Negroes vote in Mississippi and live next door to whites in Levittown.

toward the United States today. Nevertheless, some aspects of the image of America held by Britons in 1959 undoubtedly persist. And this study offers important insights into the sources of the attitudes it reports and into the connections among them. The special values of concentrating attention upon our nation's closest ally are noted in the study itself.

1. What are the most salient aspects of the British image of America and Americans? Which aspects of this image are most favorable, and which least favorable, to the United States?

2. Are there any facets of this image which you believe are fundamentally inaccurate or grossly distorted? If so, specify. Can you find any clues as to what the sources of these misconceptions might be?

3. From the references to French opinion made in this case study, how much can you reconstruct of the image of America held by educated Frenchmen? How does this differ from that held by the Britons surveyed?

4. Is the theme of "progress and high living standards" — most commonly noted by Britons exposed to USIA materials — the most useful message the United States government could transmit to the British public? Why or why not? If not, what theme(s) do you believe should be substituted? Why?

5. What facets of its image of the United States seem to affect most significantly the British public's willingness to support basic American policy objectives? If you were put in charge of United States government propaganda activities in Britain, and were granted a budget of about $1 million to build support there for United States policy objectives, how would you divide this appropriation among the various alternative propaganda activities open to the United States? Defend your choices.

USIA RESEARCH AND REFERENCE SERVICE

Some might wonder why Britain was chosen for this intensive study of the U.S. image rather than a country that would seem to pose a greater problem in this respect. It was chosen precisely because it is America's closest ally. There is presumably a greater understanding of one another among the two peoples than there is among other nations. The British people presumably have the greatest knowledge about the United States. Thus the results from Britain ought to give an idea of the best situation that can be found. Any deficiencies in U.S. information and understanding in that country are apt to be found in even more serious form elsewhere. The study, therefore, will give an idea of the problems and difficulties to be found

From "Some Aspects of the U.S. Image in Great Britain and the Influence of the Mass Media." USIA Research and Reference Service, Survey Research Studies, Program and Media Series, Special Report, October, 1959. (Mimeographed. Declassified in June, 1963.) This case study was excerpted, from the 78-page report cited, by the writer of this book, who bears the responsibility for selecting portions reasonably representative of the study as a whole.

even with a "best friend," and thus indicate to what extent it is safe to take one's friends for granted.

The fieldwork for the present study was conducted by Social Surveys (Gallup Poll) Limited during the period 12–20 January, 1959. The sample consisted of 1,000 persons drawn by random methods from the jury lists of Great Britain. At any given time, jurors represent about 4 per cent of the electorate. They are not the top 4 per cent of the population since they are distributed through all social classes. However, within each class the juror, because of property qualifications involved, represents a substantial person within that class. In the words of Social Surveys, Ltd., they "represent a very small group 'creamed off the top' of the electorate." A comparison of the sample to the total population indicates that the jurors are nearly all men; mainly over thirty; they tend to be better-educated than average and to represent the prestige occupations. If not precisely an elite, the group can be classified as "quasi-elite." Further indication of elite characteristics is the fact that in terms of an opinion-leader score based on voluntary membership in groups and in office-holding, two thirds were classified as "active" or "very active."

The reasons for using this specialized group were twofold: first, it was desired to check the influence of various media of small circulation on audiences, and a sample based on the total population would turn up too few examples to be of value; secondly, it was desirable to have a group somewhat better-informed about the U.S. than average on the principle that distortion and misinformation here should be at a minimum, compared to what would be found among the general population.

. . . comparisons in the cultural section are made with results stemming from an earlier study conducted among Frenchmen with secondary or college education. In comparing the British and French results, it should be remembered that only the better-educated Britons can be compared to their French counterparts, and then with some caution since the sampling methods differ somewhat.

With a sample of 1,000 persons, the results are highly unlikely to vary more than the order of 3 per cent plus or minus from the results which would have been obtained from interviewing the entire elite population sampled. All conclusions drawn in the text of this report have taken statistical considerations into account.

I. THE EXTENT OF PERSONAL CONTACT
WITH AMERICANS AND AMERICA

[About] half of the elite sample of jurors in the present study report having known Americans at some time, as often as not as closely as friends rather than as mere acquaintances. However the extent of present association is considerably less with only 7 per cent reporting personal contact and an additional 10 per cent by letter.

Those who have known any Americans — whether they were friends or mere acquaintances — are considerably better informed about the U.S. than those who have never known an American, and, more important, they are more likely to be in accord with American policy objectives.

An interesting point is that it appears to make little difference how close the relationship was: apparently, mere acquaintance with Americans is just as much associated with favorable attitudes as actual friendship. The implications here seem to be that techniques of achieving widespread surface contacts (e.g., mass invitation to visit military bases) might well be useful even where they do not lead to individual friendships.

Another form of contact with America and one of particular importance is that arising from friends and relatives who have emigrated to the U.S. One third of the sample report such connections, and half of this group say they have kept up contacts with one or more persons in the U.S.

Nearly all of those who are in touch with friends and relatives who have emigrated to the U.S. appear to receive favorable — almost glowing — reports of America from these sources.

Only one in twenty, even of this special sample, have been to America — as often as not more than once. The length of time in the U.S. is evenly divided between a short trip, a stay of some months, and a stay of a year and more. The time in America tends to have been spent during World War II.

II. THE FEELING OF "CLOSENESS" TO AMERICANS

Perhaps the greatest single asset of the U.S. in Britain turned up in the present study is the feeling among a plurality of the sample that Americans are really basically British. Even among those who do not go this far, a large group — a fourth of the sample — volunteer the feeling that Americans fall somewhere between being British and being foreigners. All told, only the order of one in four specifically state that Americans to them are foreigners. The sample is admittedly not representative of all British opinion and it is among those less elite elements of the population which are underrepresented that the tendency is smallest to consider Americans as actually British. But even among these groups a plurality still see Americans as basically British — indication that the findings probably hold for Britain as a whole.

In assessing other results of the survey, this basic feeling should always be kept in mind and perhaps allowed to mitigate unfavorable findings. So long as this often-maligned "blood is thicker than water" psychological milieu continues to be real to the greater part of the English people, criticisms and unfavorable reactions can be viewed in a somewhat different light than they would be viewed in other nations.

For as many as a fifth — rather evenly distributed among all social classes

— Americans of their own class are felt to be closer to them than Britons of another social class. To some degree, of course, this may represent a by-product of the traditionally rather rigid British class system, and is felt throughout all strata of society; but it also represents a definite affinity to Americans of similar status: such a question asked about French or Germans, for example, would probably draw a considerably lower level of identification. However, the predominant feeling is that of having more in common with British compatriots even when they are of a different class.

Over the course of recent years about a fifth of the respondents say they have felt a decline in their feelings toward America; but this loss is equalled by another fifth who report an improvement. In general, there is little variation between sub-groups in the sample in this respect.

Even among the one in five who report a cooling of regard for America, few actually indicate unfriendly feelings. In response to a direct question, only the order of one in twenty actually report unfavorable reaction to the U.S. The results also indicate that while in some respects the juror sample may be atypical, it is very close to representing national reaction when it comes to general esteem of the U.S.

"Please use this card to tell me your feelings about the U.S.A."

	Special sample	National sample (Oct. '58)
Number of cases	(1,000)	(611)
Very good opinion	12%	15%
Good opinion	42	46
Neither good nor bad opinion	33	19
Bad opinion	4	8
Very bad opinion	1	1
No opinion	8	11
	100%	100%
Net Favorable	49	52

For those who report improved opinions of America, three reasons for the change stand out: getting to know America and Americans better; a similar better understanding on the part of Americans; and American friendship and generosity.

If "feelings have grown warmer":
"Why have your feelings toward the U.S.A. grown warmer?"

Number of cases   (1,000)

I have come to know them better through personal contact, through going to the U.S.A. Servicemen and tourists have spread good-will. We understand them better. I have got to know them better through other sources; I have been more interested, thought more about them.   6%

They have come to understand us better. They listen to us more. They have shared their knowledge with us.	4
They are friendly, generous, kind people. They have helped a lot. Helped us during and after the war, they have lent everyone money.	4
We stand for the same things, are allies.	2
They are our only hope, we need them. They are more advanced, we have started to decline. Their advanced technology.	1
Their great peace effort.	1
They are consistent, determined, have made a firm stand (on Formosa etc.).	1
Other comments	1
No opinion	1
	21%

Those who report a cooling of regard for America tend to stress Suez, a general series of alleged rebuffs and American foreign policy as a whole as reasons for this shift of opinion.

> If *"Feelings have grown cooler"*:
> "Why have your feelings toward the U.S.A. grown cooler?"

Suez	5%
They have not supported Britain/under-rate Britain/resist British imports/ignore our advice/have not co-operated over atomic energy	2
Poor foreign policy, making a botch of things	2
Interference with other peoples' affairs	1
Aftermath of the war, recent revelations of American war activities (Montgomery, etc.)	1
Are not always sincere/are selfish/not sincere over H-bomb tests or peace talks	1
Bad social attitudes; Negroes, Little Rock, minorities	1
McCarthyism; treatment of Chaplin, Robeson	1
Other	3
No opinion	1
	18%

III. BRITISH ASSESSMENTS OF AREAS OF AMERICAN LIFE

A. *The Primary Image.* American material prowess — factories and production, the standard of living — appear to be most salient to respondents when they characterize the U.S. Another subject also determined largely by material power — America's role in world affairs — is in third place. In contrast, the American temperament and character, American mass culture and group relations in America are most often deemed least important.

This concentration on the materialistic aspects of American life should not necessarily be assessed as unfavorable. In an earlier study it was found that a large proportion of the British people believed that the adjective "materialistic" particularly applied to Americans, but that on balance this was something they liked about Americans. Thus, in Britain at least, there is evidence that this close association of America with materialism and material prowess may in some instances actually be a psychological asset.

Additional confirmation of this primary image of American life is provided by another type of question of the open-end variety in which respondents, rather than being shown a list, were asked to say what came into their minds first when they thought of the way Americans live.

"What about life in America in general?
When you think of the way Americans live,
what comes into your mind first?"

No. of cases

Probably favorable:		96%
High standard of living, prosperity	31%	
Luxury, easy living, comfort	11	
Cars	9	
Push, drive, progress	8	
Efficiency, hard work	8	
Gadgets, household appliances	8	
Social, enjoy life	8	
Hospitable	6	
Democracy	2	
Food	2	
Other favorable	3	
Probably unfavorable:		79
Live fast, fast pace, high pressure	26	
Living above their means	18	
Selfish, boastful, self-centered	7	
Superficial, insincere, exaggerate	6	
Too much money	5	
Class differences	4	
Hysterical, unstable	3	
Materialism	3	
Bad social services	3	
Other unfavorable	4	
Neutral comments:		10
No opinion		7
		192%[a]

[a] Some respondents mentioned more than one impression so the total exceeds 100 per cent.

B. *Some Aspects of the Political Image of America.* Only the order of half the sample feel that the American government really carries out the wishes of the ordinary citizens, and one in four actually deny this. In assessing the degree of specific negativity to the American government on the part of those who felt that it did not carry out the wishes of ordinary citizens, it should be noted that for an undetermined number of the respondents this might be considered a virtue. Others might feel that no governments really carry out the wishes of the ordinary citizens and that the American government was neither better nor worse. But even with such extenuations, the results can hardly be considered satisfactory.

Again, only half feel that an ordinary citizen in America can count on a fair trial in court, and again one in four disagree. In a nation which prides itself on its system of justice such a reaction deserves serious attention. Evidence that these results can be considered particularly adverse is available in a comparison with opinions of a sample of better-educated French respondents surveyed in 1955. Even among this group, which exhibited considerable and consistent hostility toward the U.S., reactions to American justice were no more unfavorable than they were among those Britons of comparable education level.

Several studies in the past have documented a generally negative reaction in Western Europe to the status of Negroes in the U.S. In earlier surveys such negative feelings have often been offset by the belief that despite interracial friction progress was being made. The most recent West European survey, however, revealed a definite decline in this point of view. And among the British elite group sampled in the present study the weight of opinion on this score is distinctly adverse.

Judgments about the three aspects of American political democracy that have been discussed in this section appear to be of no little significance in terms of their relationship to general support for America's basic foreign policy objectives. Apparent from this summary comparison below is the indication that persons who most support U.S. foreign policy (as evidenced by their scores on a test in this respect) have a much more favorable political image of the U.S. in the three respects tested, than do those who have the least support for American policy.

Net agreement among those expressing: (Number of cases)	Greatest support of U.S. objectives (149)	Least support of U.S. objectives (84)
"The American Government really carries out the wishes of the ordinary citizens."	51	−7
"If an ordinary citizen in the U.S. is accused of a crime he can count on a fair trial."	38	−11
"The U.S. is making substantial progress in its treatment of the Negro and other minority groups."	−10	−53

Correlations of this kind never point unequivocally to cause and effect. But the pattern definitely adds to the probability that a favorable political image of America tends to pay dividends in increased support for basic U.S. foreign policy objectives.

C. *Some Aspects of the Economic Image of America.* Two aspects of the American economy — opportunity for advancement and a high material standard of living — are widely acknowledged. But again the British sample is somewhat less likely to accept these favorable statements than the French sample cited earlier — at least as far as the standard of living is concerned.

Majority opinion, with few denials, accepts the view that employers and workers get along well in America. Though trade union members in the sample are apt to be a little more skeptical of the proposition, even among this group the statement enjoys clearly predominant acceptance.

Along with this feeling that capital and labor get along well goes the clearly predominant belief that American unions are very powerful and exert a strong influence on the government. Trade union members and non-members react almost identically to the statement. But here again, well-educated French respondents are more likely than their British equivalents to accept the high status of labor unions in the U.S.

Along with this favorable view of the status of labor unions goes the prevailing belief that a few families and large corporations run the economic life of America. The two views, often shared by the same persons, suggest the possibility of a prevalent conception of a relatively helpless individual caught between big business and big labor. The picture of American business domination by a few families and corporations is more frequently held by educated Britons than by the general public, but it is even more widespread among the educated French.

Although there is general agreement that the American worker is materially well-off, gets along with his boss well, and is represented by powerful unions, there is also the feeling on the part of a large proportion that the price paid for this by the American factory worker is that of becoming a mere machine without individuality. As many disagree as agree with the proposition; but a mere even division on this unfavorable stereotype can hardly be considered a favorable state of opinion. With the increase of automation, it is possible that this view might be strengthened. At present it is particularly widespread among union members.

The better-educated elements of the sample display a somewhat greater tendency to deny the statement — in particularly sharp contrast to their educational equivalents in France, where the "dehumanization" of the American factory worker appears to be almost an article of faith for the great majority.

For a majority, ranging from half to three-fourths of the various subgroups in the sample, the concept of a "classless society" in America is lacking in credibility.

D. *Some Aspects of the Cultural Image of America.* That the average American is ignorant of the most basic facts about Britain is a belief shared by a majority of the respondents, though not quite to the same extent that a belief in a similar ignorance on the part of Americans about Europe appears to be endemic among the better-educated French.

When it comes to a comparative rating of Britain and America in "some of the important fields of learning and accomplishment," respondents are generally willing, in the net, to concede equality (but not superiority) to the United States in the physical sciences and in material accomplishments. But in the case of the fine arts and the humanities, the American level is considered to be definitely below that of Britain. The question, it should be noted, compares the U.S. with "present-day" Britain. Thus, for example, it is not a matter of respondents having to compare the whole body of English literature with its American equivalent.

The question is obviously susceptible to nationalistic distortions — certainly for example in the case of the favored British health and welfare system. Yet a comparison of the results on many of the items with the results deriving from a sample of better-educated French indicates a significant difference in reaction between the two peoples: the better-educated British respondents conceded no more than equality to America; the supposedly chauvinistic French, while equally or more likely to claim preeminence in the fine arts and humanities, were willing to grant America a large measure of superiority in the physical sciences and in engineering.* It is possible that the French are so thoroughly convinced of their "cultural" superiority that they are willing to concede U.S. superiority in noncultural activities, whereas the British may be considerably less sure of preeminence in specific areas and thus less able to concede U.S. superiority anywhere.

Comparative ratings of various fields of learning and accomplishment in America are of importance in themselves. They take on added importance when it can be noted that such ratings often appear to be associated with support for America's basic objectives. . . . [The] group in the sample which shows greatest support for America's basic objectives tends to give consistently higher ratings to various aspects of American culture. The findings do not indicate that one fact "causes" the other, but they do indicate an association and inter-relationship of attitudes. Why the group differences are so pronounced in the group ratings of the physical sciences and architecture, for example, and low or non-existent in other areas of accomplishment is a problem for future investigation, but there is indication that the connection between ratings of various aspects of American culture and support

* The wording of the earlier question used in France was biased toward granting America superiority, so results are not completely comparable. However, the bias does not appear to have been very important, since in practice this did not seem to affect heavy negative responses in many fields.

for American basic objectives tends to be greatest in the sciences and relatively low in the fine arts.*

Further evidence of the primacy of the material in British stereotypes of America can be noted in open-end responses to a question concerning the most important things which could be learned from the Americans. Methods of production, general enterprise, business methods, engineering, science, gadgets — these account for the bulk of the responses. Indeed, almost every response can be classified as something dealing with the manipulation of nonhuman objects. In contrast, the social and intellectual spheres are barely cited, except for a few respondents who admire the status of women in America. As many as one in five simply said there was nothing to be learned from Americans.

When it comes to what Americans could learn from Britons, the situation is reversed. Nearly every response is in the social and intellectual sphere or deals with a personal quality. Thus, Americans are not merely seen as deficient in social services, but also in tolerance, tact, coolness, manners, modesty, and similar self-attributed qualities. Part of this may represent no more than a nationalistic pride on the part of respondents in the human qualities of their fellow citizens, but the feeling should still not be underestimated.

The evidence is rather persuasive that this British sample sees Americans as often superior in a functional sense (as machine tenders and organizers and arrangers and developers) but definitely deficient as human beings. Earlier studies have indicated a similar pattern of reaction on the part of the people of other West European nations. Thus there is a tendency often to admit American equality or superiority in measurable material qualities whose existence is hard to deny, while stressing their inferiority in the intangible area of human qualities.

IV. AMERICA AND THE AMERICANS — CHILDHOOD MEMORIES AND CURRENT REACTIONS

Since early impressions are likely to have a lasting influence on one's attitudes, the childhood picture of America is apt to be a particularly important one. For most it is on the surface relatively innocuous — the Wild West, cowboys, wide open spaces; but within that context also lurks the underlying theme of an undeveloped civilization, of frontier mores, of crudeness and violence. (It is a stereotype which among a large proportion of the respondents is being reinforced many times a year.)

The childhood pictures of America as reported by respondents may have had an underlying mood of violence and lawlessness beneath the apparently harmless concentration on the Wild West. Nevertheless, it appears to be considerably more favorable than the present surface picture of America,

* The assumption is made here that, consistent with the pattern found elsewhere, favorable reactions to American architecture were in terms of its modernity and practicality rather than in its capacity as a fine art.

with the chief stereotypes adding up to a rather jaundiced picture of a wealthy nation inhabited by fast-living, boastful but essentially worried and confused people. This frame of reference conceivably lurks behind the more neutral answers which simply stress America's size, power, and industrial capacity. The childhood images appear to have become more sharply focussed and more adverse.

In order to ascertain the most common immediate stereotypes — both favorable and unfavorable — held of ordinary Americans, a projective technique was used. Respondents were shown a picture-card containing two neutral-appearing, undifferentiated individuals. They were then told that this represented a picture of an ordinary American talking to an ordinary Briton about the U.S.A. and were asked what they thought the American was saying.

The results indicate a widespread and primary stereotype of Americans as boastful. All told, the order of four in ten give such responses — a remarkable clustering of responses for this type of question. And as a second result, the bulk of the responses are unfavorable, by a margin of more than three to one, over favorable responses.

The results here indicate at least a widespread surface irritability concentrated on a particular American trait. How intense and fundamental this feeling may be is another matter. In a preceding portion of this report it was noted that the respondents tended to give Americans special status — more as fellow-Britons than as foreigners. Viewed in this light, the reaction to American boastfulness may perhaps be considered more as a family quarrel than as actual hostility. However, in an earlier study a near majority of the total British population said that boastfulness was something they disliked very much in Americans. The subject is one for further research.

V. REACTIONS TO AMERICAN FOREIGN POLICIES

"Now I am going to ask you a question about the foreign policies the American government has followed over the last two or three years. Please take this card and tell me your considered opinion of the foreign policies the American government has followed in general over the past few years?" (CARD)

Number of cases	(1,000)
Very good opinion	3%
Good opinion	16
Neither good nor bad opinion	33
Bad opinion	29
Very bad opinion	5
No opinion	14
	100%
Net favorable	−15

Although unfavorable reaction predominates among all the major sub-groups of the sample, it tends to be most widespread among the upper socio-economic groups, the better-educated, the young. It does not appear to be a matter of party politics, since Tories and Laborites display identical results.

For a sizable proportion of those who react negatively to American policies, the stated reason for the reaction is the Suez "let-down" or a general belief in an anti-British orientation. Others find American policies dictatorial, vacillating, or inexperienced.

American help and support for other nations, its work for peace and against communism, and a general liking for America appear to be the main reasons for a favorable view of U.S. foreign policies.

Closer cooperation with Britain, more "reasonableness" with Russia, a willingness to learn and outgrow dogmatism are the chief suggestions for improving the conduct of American foreign policy. The results indicate a considerable desire for improvement even among many of those already neutral or favorable to U.S. policies.

Unless "no opinion" of American foreign policies:

"Well, whatever your present opinion, can you tell me some of the things the American government should do in its foreign policies in order to improve your opinion of it?"

Consult more, keep in line with Britain, Commonwealth, appreciate our position; cooperate with Europe, NATO, allies	15%
Try to be friendly with Russia, meet Russia halfway; be more willing to talk	10
Try to learn from other nations; be less dogmatic, excitable, impetuous	9
Be firmer, more definite in policies	5
Recognize Red China, drop Chiang	5
Help other nations more economically	4
Interfere less with other countries	4
Get rid of present leaders	3
Suspend H-bomb tests; make more effort for peace	2
Stop worrying about dollar interests	2
Other	4
Nothing: it's all right as it is	4
No opinion	24
	91%[a]

[a] Some respondents gave more than one suggestion so total exceeds 86 per cent with opinions on American foreign policies.

VI. THE IMAGE OF AMERICA IN THE MASS MEDIA

Behind the various attitudes toward the United States and the various concepts of America and American life noted in this report are certain broad pictures of America. Some are inculcated in childhood, almost without conscious awareness; others are introduced later in life; but both are reinforced day by day by exposure to the various media of communications, British and American, with their varying stereotypes of American life.

A. *Television — American and British.* Indication of the importance of television as a medium of communication for the respondents can be noted in the finding that three out of four can be classified as TV viewers — with half of this group watching TV anywhere from an hour to several hours daily. The level of viewing can be considered as rather high in view of the fact that the bulk of the respondents are thirty years of age or older.

Nearly all report seeing American-made programs, and this viewing is apt to be "quite often" or even "regularly." All told, four out of ten of the total sample report quite frequent exposure to American-made programs.

The impressions of America which viewers feel derive from the programs they watch appear to divide rather evenly between favorable and unfavorable, with a considerable proportion unable to report any particular impressions. Most frequent favorable impressions concern the personal characteristics of Americans as helpful, happy, friendly, easygoing; or the visible evidences of a high standard of living. Negative impressions cover such items as: high pressure; restless way of life; selfishness and slick superficiality; crime and low morality.

The impressions given by American TV shows must be modified by the evaluations of the audience as to their probable truth or falsity. Thus, while only one in four of those who cite favorable or neutral impressions feel that these impressions are untrue, nearly half of those who mention unfavorable impressions question their accuracy. It is to be remembered that the sample is well above the national average in education and information; but even with a national cross-section, the factor of disbelief would tend to apply in a similar way if to a somewhat lesser degree. From British-made TV programs, the sample believes it gets an impression of America very similar to that it receives from American TV sources.

As a final step, the data can be recombined so as to take into account two factors simultaneously: the favorable or unfavorable tone of the impressions received; and whether or not the respondent believes this impression to be true.

When this is done the results make it seem probable that in the net the gains exceed the losses, though slightly more for British than American TV programs. The results, of course, are limited to the third of the sample who could cite fairly specific impressions received from TV; in the case of the others who received impressions without being able to recall them, the results may be somewhat different.

B. *British Radio.* Only the order of one in ten report having heard any radio programs about America during the past week; and what is mentioned is almost entirely Alistair Cooke. The bulk of the few impressions of America reported as stemming from this source are generally favorable or neutral. Apparently, very little in the way of hostile stereotypes are being derived from this single source.

C. *American Motion Pictures.* In contrast to American-made TV programs, American films can count on frequent attendance on the part of only the order of one in ten. Another fourth say they see American films "occasionally"; but for nearly two out of three, it is "rarely" or never.

Respondents divide evenly among favorable, unfavorable, and neutral specific impressions of America deriving from American films. The high standard of living, for example, is offset by an impression of lawlessness and corruption.

Unlike the case of American and British TV, where "gains" clearly outweighed "losses" among those citing specific impressions received from these sources, among a similar group citing impressions from American movies, the gains appear to be only slightly more frequent than the losses.

D. *American Periodicals.* A third of the respondents report reading American periodicals in the course of the last few months. A single publication, *Reader's Digest,* is cited by one in four, and accounts for the bulk of the readers. When *Life* and *Time* are included (each mentioned by one in ten) most of the exposure to American magazines is accounted for. Whatever the impressions derived, they are apt to come from one of these three publications.

Unlike the situation with the other American-made media mentioned earlier, the usual impressions reported of America by the readers of the periodicals are favorable ones, with the ideas of efficiency and a high standard of living predominating.

Whatever the type of impression received from American magazines, their credibility appears to be high among those citing specific impressions. Unfavorable impressions, however, appear to have less net acceptance as true.

Under the same type of cross-analysis described earlier in the cases of impressions received from TV and movies, the direction of the impressions received from American magazines appears to be well over to the "gain" side — considerably more so than with the other two media.

E. *U.S. Information Service [USIS].* The proportion of one in ten report some contact with USIS material. In general, exposure to USIS material is particularly common among the more elite elements of the sample, the better educated and the wealthier.

There is little evidence of other than favorable effects on those who have had contact with USIS material. Although the number of responses is too small to be percentaged, the broad direction is, not surprisingly, clearly favorable, with the theme of progress and high living standards most commonly mentioned.*

F. *Books.* Fiction accounts for the larger part of contact with America through books during the preceding year. All told, the order of one in five report reading one or more books about life in the U.S. in the course of the year.

Those who mention books about America are just as likely to report an unfavorable as a favorable impression of America deriving from this source.

Of the unfavorable impressions of the U.S. received from books, the bulk appear to stem from fiction rather than non-fiction. For fiction, the net impression given appears to be unfavorable — in sharp contrast to the non-fiction books.

For two out of three of those who cite impressions of America received from books, these impressions are considered to present a true picture of the United States. By use of the same analysis described earlier, it can be seen that among those citing specific impressions of America received from books, the "gains" exceed the losses, though the small number of cases precludes any firm conclusion in this report.

A recapitulation of the "gains" and "losses" from the impressions of America received from the various media covered in the survey suggests an appreciable net gain in nearly every instance, particularly so in the case of American magazines. Only in a single medium — American motion pictures — do gains appear to be largely offset by losses.

The most balanced and complete picture of America is attributed to the British press — daily and weekly — followed by British-made TV. [The] most distorted and untrue picture is attributed to motion pictures and American-made TV. Of the American sources, American friends and USIS rank higher in the net than any of the commercial mass media.

* Too few cases were involved to ascertain whether or not respondents believed the impressions they got from USIS material, and this remains a matter for future research. However, in a count of individual cases rather than percentages, the results indicate that the impressions (nearly all favorable) were accepted as true or partly true in most cases.

Chapter Fourteen

A CHOICE OF
TOMORROWS

This chapter begins rather than ends with a case study, and this time the reader is left to formulate the questions about it. On March 27, 1964, *The New York Times* printed on page one the following story concerning the death, two weeks earlier, of Catharine Genovese, of Kew Gardens, Queens, New York.

MARTIN GANSBERG

For more than half an hour thirty-eight respectable, law-abiding citizens in Queens watched a killer stalk and stab a woman in three separate attacks in Kew Gardens.

Twice the sound of their voices and the sudden glow of their bedroom lights interrupted him and frightened him off. Each time he returned, sought her out and stabbed her again. Not one person telephoned the police during the assault; one witness called after the woman was dead.

That was two weeks ago today. But Assistant Chief Inspector Frederick M. Lussen, in charge of the borough's detectives and a veteran of twenty-five years of homicide investigations, is still shocked.

He can give a matter-of-fact recitation of many murders. But the Kew Gardens slaying baffles him — not because it is a murder, but because the "good people" failed to call the police.

"As we have reconstructed the crime," he said, "the assailant had three chances to kill this woman during a thirty-five-minute period. He returned twice to complete the job. If we had been called when he first attacked, the woman might not be dead now."

This is what the police say happened beginning at 3:20 A.M. in the staid, middle-class, tree-lined Austin Street area:

Twenty-eight-year-old Catharine Genovese, who was called Kitty by almost everyone in the neighborhood, was returning home from her job as manager of a bar in Hollis. She parked her red Fiat in a lot adjacent to the Kew Gardens Long Island Rail Road Station, facing Mowbray Place. Like many residents of the neighborhood, she had parked there day after day since her arrival from Connecticut a year ago, although the railroad frowns on the practice.

She turned off the lights of her car, locked the door and started to walk the 100 feet to the entrance of her apartment at 82-70 Austin Street, which is in a Tudor building, with stores on the first floor and apartments on the second.

The entrance to the apartment is in the rear of the building because the front is rented to retail stores. At night the quiet neighborhood is shrouded in the slumbering darkness that marks most residential areas.

Miss Genovese noticed a man at the far end of the lot, near a seven-story apartment house at 82-40 Austin Street. She halted. Then, nervously, she headed up Austin Street toward Lefferts Boulevard, where there is a call box to the 102d Police Precinct in nearby Richmond Hill.

She got as far as a street light in front of a bookstore before the man grabbed her. She screamed. Lights went on in the ten-story apartment house at 82-67 Austin Street, which faces the bookstore. Windows slid open and voices punctured the early morning stillness.

Miss Genovese screamed: "Oh, my God, he stabbed me! Please help me! Please help me!"

From one of the upper windows in the apartment house, a man called down: "Let that girl alone!"

The assailant looked up at him, shrugged and walked down Austin Street toward a white sedan parked a short distance away. Miss Genovese struggled to her feet.

Lights went out. The killer returned to Miss Genovese, now trying to make her way around the side of the building by the parking lot to get to her apartment. The assailant stabbed her again.

"I'm dying!" she shrieked. "I'm dying!"

Windows were opened again, and lights went on in many apartments. The assailant got into his car and drove away. Miss Genovese staggered to her feet. A city bus, Q-10, the Lefferts Boulevard line to Kennedy International Airport, passed. It was 3:35 A.M.

The assailant returned. By then, Miss Genovese had crawled to the back of the building, where the freshly painted brown doors to the apartment house held out hope of safety. The killer tried the first door; she wasn't there. At the second door, 82-62 Austin Street, he saw her slumped on the floor at the foot of the stairs. He stabbed her a third time — fatally.

It was 3:50 by the time the police received their first call from a man who was a neighbor of Miss Genovese. In two minutes they were at the scene. The neighbor, a seventy-year-old woman and another woman were the only persons on the street. Nobody else came forward.

The man explained that he had called the police after much deliberation. He had phoned a friend in Nassau County for advice and then he had crossed the roof of the building to the apartment of the elderly woman to get her to make the call.

"I didn't want to get involved," he sheepishly told the police.

Six days later, the police arrested Winston Moseley, a twenty-nine-year-old business-machine operator, and charged him with the homicide. Moseley had no previous record. He is married, has two children and owns a home at 133-19 Sutter Avenue, South Ozone Park, Queens. On Wednesday, a court committed him to Kings County Hospital for psychiatric observation. . . .

The police stressed how simple it would have been to have gotten in touch with them. "A phone call," said one of the detectives, "would have done it." . . .

The question of whether the witnesses can be held legally responsible in any way for failure to report the crime was put to the Police Department's legal bureau. There, a spokesman said:

"There is no legal responsibility, with few exceptions, for any citizen to report a crime." . . .

Today witnesses from the neighborhood, which is made up of one-family homes in the $35,000 to $60,000 range with the exception of the two apartment houses near the railroad station, find it difficult to explain why they didn't call the police.

Lieut. Bernard Jacobs, who handled the investigation by the detectives, said:

"It is one of the better neighborhoods. There are few reports of crimes. You only get the usual complaints about boys playing or garbage cans being turned over."

The police said most persons had told them they had been afraid to call, but had given meaningless answers when asked what they had feared.

"We can understand the reticence of people to become involved in an area of violence," Lieutenant Jacobs said, "but where they are in their homes, near phones, why should they be afraid to call the police?"

He said his men were able to piece together what happened — and capture the suspect — because the residents furnished all the information when detectives rang doorbells during the days following the slaying.

"But why didn't someone call us that night?" he asked unbelievingly.

Witnesses — some of them unable to believe what they had allowed to happen — told a reporter why.

A housewife, knowingly if quite casually, said, "We thought it was a lover's quarrel." A husband and wife both said, "Frankly, we were afraid." They seemed aware of the fact that events might have been different. A distraught woman, wiping her hands in her apron, said, "I didn't want my husband to get involved."

One couple, now willing to talk about that night, said they heard the first screams. The husband looked thoughtfully at the bookstore where the killer first stabbed Miss Genovese.

"We went to the window to see what was happening," he said, "but the light from our bedroom made it difficult to see in the street." The wife, still apprehensive, added: "I put out the light and we were able to see better."

Asked why they hadn't called the police, she shrugged and replied: "I don't know."

A man peeked out from a slight opening in the doorway to his apartment and rattled off an account of the killer's second attack. Why hadn't he called the police at the time? "I was tired," he said without emotion. "I went back to bed."

It was 4:25 A.M. when the ambulance arrived for the body of Miss Genovese. It drove off. "Then," a solemn police detective said, "the people came out."

* * * * *

Unfortunately, Catharine Genovese's fate is not an isolated incident. This case and others like it reflect a tendency very deep in human nature and an important and longstanding emphasis in American life. This emphasis, which we might call *privatization,* is the other side of the individualism on which we pride ourselves. It calls for individuals to make their own way in the world by self-reliance and resourcefulness.

At its best, this orientation has helped to produce self-reliant and resourceful people, aggressive enough to exploit the resources of the North American continent and to help provide the American people with the highest standard of living in the world. At its worst, it has permitted the successful to shrug off all too readily the sufferings of the less fortunate, at home and abroad. And with the growth of large depersonalized cities, businesses, and institutions, this attitude has evolved so far that many cases like Catharine Genovese's can be gleaned without great effort from the pages of our nation's metropolitan dailies.

A 1966 symposium held by the American Psychological Association on "The Unconcerned Bystander: Studies in Social Responsibility" suggests insights into the reasons underlying the behavior of Catharine Genovese's neighbors on Austin Street. The authors of one of the papers presented during this symposium conclude that a single witness might have been more likely to help Miss Genovese than a group of thirty-eight. For the presence of a group helps to relieve the individual from some of the responsibility for inaction, to provide him with comforting models of nonresponsive behavior, and to help him define the situation he is witnessing as one in which no action on his part is called for.[1]

Unfortunately, the fate of many persons within and without our national boundaries depend on the actions of Americans *as members of a national group*. When the group which must act expands from one to 38 to 200 million, how much easier it becomes to melt into the mass — to stand by while others suffer injury and privation.

Philip Jacob's study of the attitudes and values of American college students is revealing in this connection:

> Students' self-centeredness is striking. . . . Generally an aspiration for power . . . or practical, material satisfactions . . . predominate over the "social" value (love and concern for people) or religious values.
>
> The overriding aspiration of the self-seeking American student is a "rich, full life" filled with variety, interest and perhaps excitement. . . .
>
> On the other hand, most American students have little time or concern for the welfare of others and their interest in social problems is extremely low.
>
> Only one in five anticipates that a socially-oriented activity (community, national, international or religious) will be one of his three main sources of satisfaction in life, or considers helpfulness to others a highly important requirement for an ideal job.
>
> Even fewer would choose to devote a "windfall" or any part of one to alleviate human misery or in some way better the lot of others. . . . Most would rather invest, save or spend the money for their own or their family's security or enjoyment.[2]

Nor did Jacob find most of the American colleges studied successful in altering these student value orientations by the time of their graduation.

If privatization was once a functional outlook for Americans, it is no longer. We have reviewed at length in this book some of the critical problems which face America in its new role of world leadership, and some of the instruments of policy available to us in dealing with them. But this is not meant to signify that skillful manipulation of these instruments of policy is enough to preserve peace and security indefinitely. Quite the contrary. The dangers of thermonuclear war are real and constant. How

[1] Bibb Latane and John Darley, "The Unresponsive Bystander: Is He Indifferent or Ambivalent?" Prepublication draft (mimeographed). November 1, 1966. Some of the conclusions of this paper were reported in London Wainwright, "Challenge to Unconcerned Bystanders," *Life*, September 23, 1966, p. 32. I am indebted to Keith Gerritz for calling this study to my attention.

[2] *Changing Values in College* (New York: Harper, 1957), pp. 15–18. Reprinted by permission.

many Berlin crises and Cuban crises can we expect to get through safely? A world in which the recurrence of such crises from year to year is assured is a world in which our doom, in time, is sealed. We must be skillful, we must be steady, we must be wise, to minimize the number of such crises and to survive them when they come. But we must do more. We must use the time we gain in this way to move gradually toward a world in which crises are much less frequent, toward a world community which regularly employs means other than armed force for resolving the disputes which inevitably arise among nations and men.

The prerequisites for building such a world community were reviewed in Chapter One. There it was noted that greater efforts to work through the United Nations, expanded economic aid programs, and the freer and more frequent movement of men, capital, and goods across national frontiers could help, over the years, to make the gradual growth of such a world community possible.

But these and other necessary steps toward a world community will not be taken in great enough measure to make a difference if we cannot overcome the trend toward privatization as well. Our institutions are too democratic to permit our leaders to do what is necessary without our ultimate consent.

If we are to take the lead in building a safer and better world, moreover — and if we do not take the lead, who will? — others must be willing to follow. But, as our review of public opinion in Chapter Seven indicates, others will make us their leader and identify their fortunes with ours only when we have *shown* (not *proclaimed*) that we care about them and identify our fortunes with theirs.

We have food in abundance, while others go hungry.[3] Our children go to universities and study, while other people's start working in the fields at ten years of age. We are moving toward the 35-hour week and the $2-an-hour minimum wage, while others work from dawn till dusk for fifty cents a day. Though these people may be illiterate, no words of ours — however cunning — will convince them that men who are satisfied with the world as it is are on *their* side. We talk to them of "peace and freedom," but they will not concern themselves with our peace until we concern ourselves with their freedom — and in more than the formal political sense.

Nor is the United States alone subject to this implacable truth. The Soviets, too, have proved more dedicated in Marxist word than in Stalinist deed to the cause of the downtrodden. Behind all the dialectics, behind

---

3 "Each day about 10,000 people in the underdeveloped countries die as a result of illness caused by malnutrition. Of every 20 children born in these countries, 10 are likely to perish in infancy from hunger or from the effects of an improper diet. Another 7 may suffer physical or mental retardation.

"Half the world's people experience chronic hunger or serious dietary deficiency." "War on Hunger," *Intercom* (November–December, 1966), p. 24.

the direct clashes of national interest, this fact is close to the heart of the Chinese disenchantment with Moscow. The great fraternal Soviet nation turned out to be more concerned with increasing its own substantial standard of living, international prestige, and military power, than with helping its Chinese comrades to begin the long pull toward the better things in life. One can almost hear the whisper between the phrases of the doctrinal polemics "— Revisionists. Traitors to the revolution. Betrayers of the dream for which we fought a quarter of a century in the remote mountain outposts of China. False revolutionaries. Betrayers of the dream!"

No nation has a monopoly on indifference, on cruelty, on a lack of concern for fellow men. A. M. Rosenthal, long a foreign correspondent for *The New York Times*, commented on the Catharine Genovese incident:

> The self-protective shells in which we live are determined not only by the difference between big cities and small. They are determined by economics and social class, by caste and by color, and by religion, and by politics.
>
> If I were to see a beggar starving to death in rags in the streets of Paris or New York or London I would be moved to take some kind of action. But many times I have seen starving men lying like broken dolls in the streets of Calcutta or Madras and have done nothing.
>
> I think I would have called the police to save Miss Genovese but I know that I did not save a beggar in Calcutta. Was my failing really so much smaller than that of the people who watched from their windows on Austin Street? And what was the apathy of the people of Austin Street compared, let's say, with the apathy of non-Nazi Germans toward Jews?
>
> Geography is a factor of apathy. Indians reacted to Portuguese imprisoning Goans, but not to Russians killing Hungarians.
>
> Color is a factor, Ghanaians reacted toward Frenchmen killing Algerians, not toward Congolese killing white missionaries.
>
> Strangeness is a factor. Americans react to the extermination of Jews but not to the extermination of Watusis.
>
> There are national as well as individual apathies, all inhibiting the ability to react. The "mind-your-own-business" attitude is despised among individuals, and clucked at by sociologists, but glorified as pragmatic national policy among nations.
>
> Only in scattered moments, and then in halting embarrassment, does the United States, the most involved nation in the world, get down to hard cases about the nature of the governments with which it deals and how they treat their subject citizens. People who believe that a free government should react to oppression of people in the mass by other governments are regarded as fanatics or romantics by the same diplomats who would react in horror to the oppression of one single individual in Washington. Between apathy, regarded as a moral disease, and national policy, the line is often hard to find.
>
> There are, it seems to me, only two logical ways to look at the story of the murder of Catharine Genovese. One is the way of the neighbor on Austin Street — "Let's forget the whole thing."

The other is to recognize that the bell tolls even on each man's individual island, to recognize that every man must fear the witness in himself who whispers to close the window.[4]

As we have been impelled to follow the Russians' example in the arms race and the space race, it is likely that they would feel impelled to follow ours if we should take the lead in trying to build a world of opportunity for the masses of mankind.

Yet we have shown ourselves more willing to spend tens of billions of dollars each year to build weapons of destruction to protect our own lives and wealth, even to send men into space, than to help to build better lives for the people of the poor nations on our own planet. As a junior official in the public information office of a forerunner of AID, the writer of this book learned that aid requests are better defended before Congress and the American people by emphasizing the military rather than the humanitarian purposes they serve. Thus for many years, to help in securing congressional approval, the major part of American economic aid was officially categorized as "defense support" aid. In like fashion, we are willing to draft our young men to serve their country by killing others, but we are unwilling to draft them to serve their country by helping those in need both abroad and at home.[5]

For it is not foreigners only who fall outside our circle of concern. At home, too, we have stood by for more than a hundred years since the civil war without worrying ourselves excessively about the fate of the twenty million Negroes in our midst. We have allowed them to be clubbed, hosed, cattle-prodded, disfranchised, and legally segregated in the South, and to be snubbed, confined to slum ghettos, unemployed twice as often as whites, deprived of a decent education, and informally segregated in the North. The improvement in their status in the past decade has been noteworthy, but fundamentally it has been the result of the actions of the few — many of them Negroes — rather than of the concern of the many. And the civil rights movement has mobilized, in the hearts of too many Americans, not understanding and concern, but fearful resistance and hatred.

The aged, the unemployable, dependent children — born, poor sinners!, out of wedlock — the infirm, the disadvantaged in America have also felt the cutting edge of our privatization. We devote less of our gross national product to social security programs than any other major developed nation. And our exclusion of millions of Americans from real participation in our national life hurts not only those we neglect, but our country as a whole. The human and intellectual achievements of which some of these millions

4 "Study of the Sickness called Apathy," *The New York Times Magazine*, May 3, 1964, Sec. 6, pp. 24 ff. Reprinted by permission of A. M. Rosenthal. © 1964 by The New York Times Company.

5 See footnote 8, below.

might have been capable — with proper nourishment — are irreplaceably lost, to us and to the world. Moreover, our ability as a nation to pursue intelligent foreign policies is limited by the lack of education and the emotional immaturity which our unconcern has helped to impose upon too many among these disadvantaged minorities.

An old woman lives on my street, near an elegant suburb of Detroit. Her sole sources of income are a small federal old-age pension and a smaller residual pension her deceased husband earned by being disabled during World War I.[6] Physically and mentally she is not what she once was. She is eager to pick up occasional baby-sitting jobs to augment her inadequate income, but it is hard to get them because she is now only minimally competent, because there is no public transportation in our neighborhood, and because, of course, she cannot afford a car. Old friends and some neighbors help her with gifts of food from time to time. But our society as a whole is officially unconcerned with her and millions in far worse circumstances. (Though the Gallup polls show majorities believing poverty to be due more often to lack of effort than to circumstances, United States Census Bureau figures show that of families with annual incomes below $3,000 in 1963, 35 per cent were headed by persons over 65, 26 per cent by women, 23 per cent by nonwhites, and 59 per cent by persons with no more than an eighth grade education.) [7]

By our example of not caring, we teach our children, too, not to care, but to get what they can for themselves. But because our words, especially on Sundays, pay lip service to the ideal of loving others, we feel astonished when these children show they have learned from our example. We are shocked to find that some of our young people put their own pleasures first and are reluctant to serve their nation in the armed forces if they can possibly avoid it. We are shocked even more by those who perceive the gap between our words and our actions and rebel against it — and against us. Whatever the truth about Vietnam, many young Americans who protest against United States policy there do so because our whole way of life has led them to suspect that we would rather see our leaders use napalm against innocent children than risk the growth of social revolution among the masses of the Orient. Before we dismiss their protests too readily from our minds, we must ask ourselves how many of us would really be willing to make substantial *personal* sacrifices to stop the killing. How many of us, in the end, look far enough ahead to be willing to see American resources used today to help build better lives for those who might in time become

---

[6] United States government figures show the average monthly old-age benefit in 1963 for residents of Michigan (which is well above average in this respect) to be $92.81. The average monthly pension for widows of World War I veterans is about $56. The two together make a total of under $150 a month, $1800 a year.

[7] The totals add to over 100 per cent because many poor families are headed by persons who fall into more than one of these categories.

our friends, instead of using them to snuff out tomorrow the lives of those we have failed to prevent from becoming our enemies?

When riots come in the Watts district of Los Angeles, or in Harlem or Detroit, New Haven, Newark, or Birmingham, how many of us react by condemning the rioters' disrespect for the law and order which has kept them down, and calling for more police with more clubs to suppress more "crime in the streets"? [8] Others, more enlightened, hope to keep things under control by distributing a relatively small amount of government funds for reconstruction or slum clearance programs. But the rioters know that our principal concern is simply to get them to leave us alone — that our fears are more readily appealed to than our consciences. And they will not stop.

So, in the world at large, we can seek to keep down the rising tides of nationalism and revolution with more soldiers and more missiles. And so wealthy and militarily strong are we that it is just barely possible that we can hold back the tide indefinitely and continue to enjoy "the American way of life" while others seek as best they can to get through another day. But this comfortable course has its disadvantages also. It will require us to turn the other way while our bombs beat the poor, mobilized against us, into submission. It will require a greater and greater use of euphemisms and rationalizations to enable us to avoid facing the realities of what our government is doing in our name. And it will require measures to punish those of our countrymen, afflicted with compassion, who "defect" and turn their energies and skills to helping the underprivileged to revolt. Among these defectors may be our own children. (The Union of South Africa has made a good start toward showing us the way to exist as a rich and powerful but embattled white enclave in a sea of oppressed colored peoples.)

If we are to avoid this fate — or a nuclear disaster — we must begin now to identify ourselves with the aspirations of the masses of mankind. We must, first of all, learn to care about what happens to other human beings. In our homes as in our schools, from kindergarten up, we must teach this by deed as well as by word. Without it, our literacy and scientific knowledge are ominous playthings in the hands of moral savages. Compassion alone will not enable us to survive. But neither will we get anywhere worth going by building a society devoid of compassion.

For if we care for none but ourselves, who will care for *us*? And what will we do with all of our abundance in a society where each individual

8 Recent surveys by Louis Harris and Associates show that in general the public prefers a crime prevention approach to a repressive enforcement approach to crime. Whether this support would extend to approval of the specific project costs and expenditures necessary to reduce crime and violence substantially, however, is another matter — a matter highly relevant to the subject of this chapter. Similarly, a recent Gallup poll shows a large majority of the public willing to see all American young men required to give two years of either military or nonmilitary national service. But it is difficult to imagine the public supporting the expenditures and specific programs required to implement this general approval. Some of the reasons behind this apparent paradox are suggested in Chapter Seven.

is an alienated, depersonalized object, cut off from his fellow men and from his own capacity to feel?

There is an old parable concerning a family among whom lived an aged invalid grandfather. Since he was troublesome to care for, the family took him, in his wheelchair, to the edge of a cliff far from home, and the head of the family made ready to push him over the precipice, chair and all. The small children in the family, however, stopped the proceedings. "Wait, daddy!" they shouted. "Why throw away a perfectly good chair? We can save it for you."

Truly, though all of the roads before us are hazardous and complex, a chance at least worth taking remains that our fate may depend on our own skills and choices, on our own maturity and compassion. Our time of testing, in a world not entirely of our own making, is *now*. Just beyond our windows, as we go about our business, continents full of hungry children and helpless parents are crying out, unheeded, into the night.

INDEX

(Italicized page references denote definitions)